Immigrants in the Far West

Historical Identities and Experiences

EDITED BY
Jessie L. Embry and Brian Q. Cannon

A PROJECT OF THE CHARLES REDD CENTER
FOR WESTERN STUDIES

THE UNIVERSITY OF UTAH PRESS
Salt Lake City

Immigrants in the Far West is a project of the Charles Redd Center for Western Studies. The publisher gratefully acknowledges their support.

The Defiance House Man colophon is a registered trademark of the University of Utah Press. It is based on a four-foot-tall Ancient Puebloan pictograph (late PIII) near Glen Canyon, Utah.

19 18 17 16 15 1 2 3 4 5

LIBRARY OF CONGRESS CATALOGING-IN-PUBLICATION DATA

Immigrants in the far West : historical identities and experiences / edited by Jessie L. Embry and Brian Q. Cannon.
pages cm
"A Project of the Charles Redd Center for Western Studies."
Includes bibliographical references and index.
ISBN 978-1-60781-380-4 (paperback) ISBN 978-1-60781-381-1 (ebook)
1. Immigrants--West (U.S.)--History. 2. West (U.S.)--Emigration and immigration--History. 3. Acculturation--West (U.S.)--History. 4. Cultural pluralism--West (U.S.)--History. I. Embry, Jessie L., editor of compilation. II. Cannon, Brian Q., editor of compilation. III. Charles Redd Center for Western Studies, sponsoring body.
F596.2.I66 2014
305.9'06912078--dc23

2014036317

Please consider page 459 an extension of this copyright page.

Printed and bound by Sheridan Books, Inc., Ann Arbor, Michigan

Immigrants in the Far West

Contents

Part II

Figures

Tables

Acknowledgments

When we identified immigration as the topic for our triennial Charles Redd Center summer seminar in 2011, the United States was embroiled in controversy over immigration policy. An interdisciplinary examination of immigration in the West seemed timely even though our limited training in immigration studies would heighten our challenge in editing a volume on the topic. Participants in the seminar came from multiple disciplines in the social sciences and humanities, which enriched the seminar discussions but steepened the learning curve for us as historians. As editors we are especially grateful to those who attended the seminar and shared their insights at the meetings and their expertise throughout the editing process. Nearly all of those who participated in the seminar have their work represented in this volume. We acknowledge the significant contributions to our seminar of three scholars whose work is not published here: Katy Fry, Phylis Martinelli, and Alicia Ratterree.

The Redd Center staff was especially helpful in putting together the seminar and in creating this volume. Mary Nelson, the Redd Center office specialist, graciously made all the travel arrangements for the seminar participants and in the process made friends and helped the visitors feel appreciated and valued. Mary left the Redd Center before the volume was complete, and Amy Carlin, now the office specialist, brought her excellent editing skills to the project. John Alley of the University of Utah Press enthusiastically shared his expertise, carefully read and critiqued each essay, and suggested the book's organization. His insights made our work easier. Brigham Young University student Kristen Kitchen enhanced the accuracy of our work through careful source checking.

The College of Family, Home, and Social Sciences at BYU and the Charles and Annaley Naegle Redd family make it possible for the Redd Center to sponsor seminars, promote dialogue, and share knowledge in volumes like this.

Introduction

Jessie L. Embry and Brian Q. Cannon

In 1847, members of the Church of Jesus Christ of Latter-day Saints, also known as Mormons or LDS, arrived in the Great Basin seeking refuge from the persecution they felt they had endured in the United States. Brigham Young and his followers were settling Mexican territory, so they were technically immigrants to that country. From the perspective of the Utes and Shoshones, whose lands they occupied, the Mormons could also be viewed as aliens and immigrants. But the signing of the Treaty of Guadalupe Hidalgo in February 1848 brought the religious group back into the United States. Over the rest of the nineteenth century, Mormon missionaries to England and northern Europe encouraged converts to gather in the American West. Between 1847 and 1887, close to 85,000 Mormon immigrants from Europe arrived.[1] Others came from the Pacific Islands, Asia, and Africa. Although the Mormons were often seen as "others" by Americans, the LDS Church encouraged the newcomers to learn English and adapt to the dominant, largely Anglo-American culture.

The Mormons sought admission to the Union as a single, large state they called Deseret. Instead, Congress created the much smaller territory of Utah. Mormons moved across Utah's territorial borders, sometimes accidentally, to create settlements, and sometimes on purpose, to escape U.S. marshals enforcing antipolygamy laws. Beginning in the 1880s, thousands of Mormons became immigrants again as they crossed international borders and established communities in Mexico and Canada to avoid antipolygamy laws. These LDS enclaves still exist. They differ little from other towns in southern Alberta, but contrast sharply with most communities in northern Chihuahua.

Almost a century later, in the 1980s, Olga de la Rosa began working as a secretary at the Charles Redd Center. De la Rosa had immigrated to Utah from Guatemala because her sister and other family members lived in the area. Like many other immigrants she and her family moved in response to economic and political unrest that "pushed" them from their home country. Guatemala was experiencing a civil war, which created not only political but economic concerns. At the same time, a combination of better work, greater educational opportunities, and religious beliefs "pulled" the family to Utah.

The family settled in southwest Provo because housing there was relatively inexpensive and because other Spanish-speakers lived in the area. As Latter-day Saints, they attended a Spanish-speaking ward, or congregation. They felt at home in the new ward despite some cultural differences from the predominately Mexican congregation. Many of the church socials reminded them of home. It was harder to feel at home with some of their Anglo neighbors because of language barriers and a feeling among some that they should learn English and assimilate. Other neighbors, however, no longer saw the United States as a melting pot or insisted on cultural uniformity. Instead, they appreciated cultural diversity.

Olga de la Rosa's sister spoke fluent English, had excellent office skills, and worked as a secretary. De la Rosa was working on those same skills and taking classes in English and accounting at Utah Valley Community College when she applied for the job at the Redd Center. She worked at the center for about a year, then eventually married and continued to live in the United States. Despite some setbacks, she achieved much of the American dream of becoming educated and economically independent.

The foregoing examples incorporate many themes related to immigration that are addressed in this volume. Those themes include the complexity of immigrant status and identity in a region of shifting geopolitical boundaries and border crossings; the intricate combination of push and pull factors that have galvanized immigration; and the interplay between immigrant agency, cultural capital, societal attitudes, and institutional realities that has shaped immigrant experiences in the West.

This introductory essay provides historical background and context for the chapters that follow. First, it explores various definitions of the term *immigrant*. Then it briefly outlines major laws that have regulated immigration to the United States. It next surveys ways that scholars have studied immigration. Finally, it explores how immigration to the Far West was unique, shaped the region's development, and fulfilled immigrants' expectations.[2]

Definition of Immigration/Immigrant

On the surface, identifying someone as an immigrant seems easy. According to historian Frank Thistlethwaite, Samuel Morse coined the term in 1789 as "an Americanism essential to describe someone whom language had hitherto universally described as an emigrant."[3] In modern usage, emigrant has come to mean someone who leaves a country; that person becomes an immigrant after they arrive in a new country. By contrast, the term migrant often refers to people moving within the same country, although it is increasingly employed today in reference to international movement; after all, people who move share similar experiences whether or not they cross or recross international borders. The U.S. census uses the term *foreign born* to refer to different types of immigrants. "This includes naturalized US citizens, lawful permanent residents (immigrants), temporary migrants (such as foreign students), humanitarian migrants (such as refugees), and people illegally present in the United States."[4] Some distinguish between sojourners, who only come temporarily for education or seasonal work, and immigrants. Although many migrants themselves have made this distinction, it obscures the fact that few migrants initially planned on staying. Technically, all who stayed became "immigrants," but white Euro-Americans continued to regard nonwhites as sojourners even if the nonwhites had more permanent settlement plans. As Lawrence Fuchs observed, "Nonwhites did not so much choose to be sojourners as they were constrained to remain as such by the dominant society."[5]

Immigration Laws

Since its dedication in 1886, the Statue of Liberty in New York Harbor has represented a dream for a new world to Americans and newcomers alike. "Give me your tired, your poor, / Your huddled masses yearning to breathe free, / The wretched refuse of your teeming shore. / Send these, the homeless, tempest-tossed to me, / I lift my lamp beside the golden door!"[6] But the doorway to the United States has not always been open. The U.S. government has changed laws (or opened and closed the door) based on four major factors: economics, race, nationalism, and foreign policy. Significant economic downturns usually preceded major changes in immigration policy. Immigration policy also changed to reflect some Americans' fears of people with different cultural and religious beliefs or complexions. Catering to those fears, political parties made immigration restriction an important part of their platforms, and laws were passed which effectively barred specific groups from coming to the United States. Relationships between the United States and other nations also affected migration policy. In order to preserve good relationships, the United States sometimes permitted free immigration from specific nations.[7]

In 1790, the U.S. Congress passed the first law restricting citizenship for immigrants to "free white persons" who had been in the United States for at least two years.[8] Other laws followed which prevented certain immigrants from coming to America. The Page Act (1875) restricted Chinese, Japanese, and other Asian workers from entering the nation against their will. It primarily targeted Chinese women and reflected westerners' fears of the growing Chinese presence in the West. (Only 3 percent of the Chinese in the nation lived east of Denver at the time.) The sentiment behind that law was strengthened with the 1882 Chinese Exclusion Act, which prohibited the immigration of all Chinese laborers.

The first general immigration law was passed three months after the Chinese Exclusion Act. It prohibited "any convict, lunatic, idiot, or any person unable to take care of himself or herself without becoming a public charge" from entering the country. To enforce such rules, Congress created a Bureau of Immigration in 1891.

New laws were tweaked during the Progressive Era, but larger changes came in 1917 with the enactment of a literacy test for immigrants and in the 1920s in response to the Dillingham Commission. This commission was created in 1907 to examine the impact of immigration partly in response to concerns regarding the Japanese in San Francisco. The commission's findings influenced lawmakers in drafting and passing the Emergency Quota Act in 1921 and the Immigration Act of 1924, which set national quotas for nations outside of the Western Hemisphere. Mexico was exempted largely because American Westerners relied upon Mexican workers for cheap agricultural labor.

Congress passed other immigration laws over the next decades, but the next major change was the 1965 Immigration Act, which set annual hemispheric limits to replace the national quotas. The law gave priority status to applications from relatives of U.S. citizens for family reunification purposes, which stimulated immigration to a degree Congress had not anticipated. The heightened visibility of illegal immigration and economic problems incited more anti-immigration views in the late 1970s and early 1980s and contributed to the passage of the Immigration Reform and Control Act (IRCA) in 1986. The law permitted those who had been living in the United States illegally since 1982 to apply for residential status, or amnesty. As a concession to southwestern senators and representatives, the law also provided for amnesty to migrant agricultural workers who had worked in the country for at least ninety days in the previous year.

But more newcomers were coming into the United States illegally, especially from and through Mexico. Western states feared that the federal government was not enforcing the law, so state legislatures passed laws and voters approved propositions to limit the rights of newcomers. These included California's Proposition 187 in 1994 and Arizona's 2010 immigration law. In 2012, the U.S. Supreme Court struck down part of the Arizona law. In 2013, Congress was once again debating immigration law.

The Far West has played an important role in the development of policies toward newcomers to the United States. The Chinese presence in California led to the passage of the Chinese Exclusion Act. Controversies surrounding segregated schools for Japanese students in San Francisco helped spur the U.S. Congress to form the Dillingham Commission to examine the impact of immigrants. The commission's report in turn influenced the quota system adopted in the 1920s. Quotas were not applied to immigrants from the Western Hemisphere because westerners insisted that they needed cheap labor, especially from Mexico, to be able to compete economically. The laws enacted by California voters in 1994 and Arizona lawmakers in 2010 show how western states have led out in attempts to control illegal crossings from the south. In other words, immigration law has repeatedly been influenced by the Far West.

Immigration Studies

Just as immigration laws have evolved, so have scholarly approaches to the study of newcomers to the United States. Since the 1920s, scholars in the social sciences, history, and the humanities have developed models for interpreting the experiences of immigrants. Theories or approaches developed in one discipline were often adapted and augmented by scholars in other disciplines. In part, these theories and approaches reflected the political and cultural concerns and currents of the era in which they developed. In this essay, we highlight theoretical developments that have shaped the approaches taken in this volume.[9]

During the 1920s, Robert Park and his colleagues at the University of Chicago pioneered an influential model known today as classical assimilation theory. According to their views, European newcomers passed through four sequential stages: contact, conflict, accommodation, and assimilation. This four-step progression remained the dominant model for studying immigration until the 1960s and influenced scholars in many fields. For instance, geographers building upon classical assimilation theory linked immigrants' assimilation to their migration outward from urban enclaves into more heterogeneous suburbs, a process they called spatial assimilation.

The end point of Park's model, assimilation into the American middle class, matched Americans' expectations for newcomers to the United States in the 1920s. They expected immigrants to learn English and embrace American traditions. When immigrants failed to do so, politicians and well-meaning social workers devised Americanization programs to acculturate the immigrants. They believed the American dream that it was possible for an immigrant to start with nothing in the United States and for a descendant to become president of a large company in two or three generations.[10]

In the 1960s, ethnic and racial minorities celebrated their distinctiveness. In this multicultural arena, social scientists pointed out that immigrants did not move in lock-step fashion along the pathway to assimilation. Sociologist Milton Gordon argued that an immigrant may assimilate culturally (acculturation) without achieving structural assimilation, including equal access to social institutions, marriage partners, or the privileges of citizenship. Historians showed how many immigrants returned to their homelands while others maintained facets of their traditional culture in their new homes. In the 1970s, Virginia Yans-McLaughlin and Kathleen Conzen emphasized the pliability of immigrant cultures and the resourcefulness of immigrants in retaining some features of traditional culture, adapting others to fit changed circumstances, and discarding others to fashion a hybrid ethnic identity and culture. John Bodnar argued in an influential 1985 book that immigrants and many of their lifeways were "transplanted."[11]

Scholars continued to refine their understanding of immigrants' relationship to the dominant culture. In the 1990s, Alejandro Portes and Min Zhou characterized the assimilation of modern immigrants as a "segmented" process: some immigrants enter and are acculturated within the white middle class, others assimilate "downward" into the underclass, and others prosper economically but continue to socialize primarily with their immigrant group.[12] Beginning in the 1970s, geographers observed that new immigrants were increasingly clustering in suburban "ethnoburbs" rather than in urban ethnic enclaves. They also hypothesized that geographical concentration was becoming less crucial to maintaining ethnic identity. Wilbur Zelinsky and Barrett Lee's theory of heterolocalism posited that in an era of rapid transit, electronics, and telecommunications, ethnic groups maintain identity without living in ethnic neighborhoods.[13]

In their studies of immigrants' assimilation and cultural retention, scholars also identified two related factors as important variables: social networks and social capital. Social networks are linkages between individuals and groups that facilitate the sharing of information and resources. Scholars mapped those networks and traced their impact upon immigrants' decisions to move and their ability to adjust in new settings. Social capital, a concept promoted by sociologists James Coleman and Pierre Bourdieu, refers to the advantages and resources available to individuals as a result of their social networks.[14]

Scholarship in biology and anthropology from the 1920s onward highlighted the subjectivity of racial categories.[15] The civil rights movements of African Americans and other minorities also pushed Americans to rethink race and racial exclusion. Increasingly, scholars wrote about race as a cultural construct that had influenced how Americans had treated people of color rather than as a biological given.[16] Beginning in the 1990s, scholars applied this view in studies of immigration, including David Roediger's pathbreaking *The Wages of Whiteness* (1991), a study of Irish immigrants.[17]

For many past immigrants, leaving their homeland meant that they had almost moved to another planet. Communication was slow through letters; transportation was also difficult and expensive. Some immigrants never saw their families and friends in the old country again. But modern communication and transportation changed that. Telegraphs, telephones, railroads, airplanes, and eventually computers, to name a few, enabled immigrants to maintain contact. Newcomers could be part of both their homeland and their new countries. These advancements also changed social scientists' views of immigration.

In the 1990s, cultural anthropologists Nina Glick Schiller, Linda Basch, and Cristina Blanc-Szanton made a key theoretical contribution to the study of migration as they developed and applied the term "transmigrant" with reference to the movement of modern migrants. They argued that many immigrants in the 1990s nurtured a "transnational" identity in the sense that their "networks, activities and patterns of life encompass both their host and home societies." Three factors that promote these transnational identities are economic insecurity in both the sending and receiving countries that leave immigrants in a state of economic limbo, racism in the receiving countries, and the attempts by both the sending and receiving countries to cultivate political and national loyalties among the migrants.[18]

The concepts of transmigrants and transnationalism have influenced scholars studying immigration in many disciplines including geography, literary criticism, and history.[19] Among geographers, some transnational theorists have argued that political borders have lost some of their salience in recent decades, becoming "permeable sites of flexible and hybrid migrant identities." Literary and linguistic scholars have investigated the hybrid identities and linguistic adaptations of transnational migrant communities following the lead of Homi Bhabha, whose work on vernacular cosmopolitanism explores the ways in which colonized peoples negotiate the values, symbols, and language of their occupiers. For instance, Ana Patricia Rodriguez has examined the impact of transnationalism upon the language patterns of Salvadorans residing in the United States. Literary scholars including Claudia Sadowski-Smith have examined the ways that national borders and border-crossers are treated in fiction.[20] In 1997 historian Dirk Hoerder proposed the term "transregional" for immigrants because many migrants "act out their life-projects in more than one location," often based upon local or regional affinities rather than national ones. Applying transnational perspectives to immigration, historians showed that many immigrants nurtured rich, multilayered ties to their homelands through letters, print media, electronic media, and travel.[21] However, in a trenchant critique of transnationalism, historian Elliott Barkan pointed out that the model does not fit all immigrants' experiences: Many immigrants' ties to their homelands were "moderate and periodic, somewhat casual and uneven and not routine," a phenomenon he labels "translocalism." Moreover, some immigrants firmly turned their backs on their native lands.[22]

When studying immigration, some scholars focus so intently on the individual stories that it is impossible to find common trends. In a sense, they cannot see the forest for the trees. Others tend to notice general, overarching theories so much that they miss the individual story. As a result, these scholars sometimes "resort . . . to stock phrases and buzzwords" such as "assimilate," "acculturate," "diasporic," and "transnational." To avoid either of these views, Hasia Diner suggested that scholars "precisely chart with the concrete material we have collected . . . what immigrants and their children in actuality said and did."[23] The chapters in this book attempt from a variety of disciplinary perspectives to chart a middle course between these extremes. The chapters evaluate the experiences of immigrants in light of theoretical insights regarding spatial assimilation, social networks, the state, transnationalism, and whiteness.

Western United States and Historical Studies

Historians largely neglected the history of immigration to the West until late in the twentieth century. In 2007, Elliott Barkan pointed out that most historians neglected the West's immigration history from the beginning, leaving "the remarkable array of immigrants in the West . . . figuratively speaking in the wings."[24] Richard White explains, "Old Western Historians . . . eliminated from their history as so much human garbage the diverse people of the West—Indians, Hispanics, Asians, and other ethnic Europeans—whose very presence endangered their regional homogeneity."[25]

One of the first historians to study the experiences of multiple immigrant groups in the West was Frederick Luebke, who edited a pioneering collection of essays, *Ethnicity on the Great Plains*, in 1980. Nevertheless, as late as 1998, Luebke complained, "European immigrants are the forgotten people of the American West." They had been ignored or minimized by historians of the frontier and in general surveys of western history ranging from Robert Hine's *The American West* to the *Oxford History of the American West* to revisionist works in the New Western History.[26] Similarly, Roger W. Lotchin observed that European immigrants to the West were often collapsed into the categories "Anglo,"

"Caucasian," and "white." "In the interest of multiculturalism itself, these groups deserve their own studies."[27]

While immigration in the West at large was understudied, excellent histories of individual immigrant groups, often in specific cities or states, were published. These include George J. Sanchez's prizewinning 1993 book, *Becoming Mexican American: Ethnicity, Culture and Identity in Chicano Los Angeles*, and Judy Yung's acclaimed *Unbound Feet: A Social History of Chinese Women in San Francisco*.[28]

Beyond the state and local level, scholars pooled their research to provide composite portraits of specific immigrant groups in the West at large. These studies include essays in Moses Rischin and John Livingston's edited volume *Jews of the American West* (1991) and Richard Etulain and Jeronima Echeverria's *Portraits of Basques in the New World* (1999). Other monographs surveyed and narrated the experiences of specific ethnoracial groups in the West more fully, such as Ferenc Szasz's *Scots in the North American West, 1790–1917* (2000); Donald Warrin and Geoffrey L. Gomes's *Land, As Far as the Eye Can See: Portuguese in the Old West* (2001); Jorge Iber and Arnoldo de Léon's *Hispanics in the American West* (2006); and David Emmons's *Beyond the American Pale: The Irish in the West* (2010).[29]

Near the turn of the century, individual stories of western immigrants were interpreted within a larger context in two ambitious general studies. In 1999 Walter Nugent published his award-winning book *Into the West: The Story of Its People*. His "continuing plot line" was *e pluribus unum*. As he explained, "The peopling of the West is complex. Yet it is one story, just as western Americans are one people, sharing magnificent space and promise."[30] Nugent approached the history of migrants chronologically, focusing on internal migration as well as immigrants. Elliott Barkan's ambitious study *From All Points: America's Immigrant West, 1870s–1952* sought to tell the story of immigrants to the West broadly by "capturing the multiplicity of peoples and multiple locations." He embedded individual stories within a chronological narrative to explain immigrants' "varied social, cultural, political, and economic roles—their human capital." Barkan referred briefly to race theory and showed that whiteness was "freighted with various meanings and shadings depending on time, place, and situational circumstances," but his work was more narrative than theoretical. He developed four interpretive themes: changes over time in who came and their prospects, the ways that the West's economic development affected the migrants, the impact of government and law upon the migrants, and the relationships between immigrants and Americans including adaptation and accommodation.[31]

Why Study Immigration to the West

We argue that there are still advantages to studying migration from around the world to a specific, distinctive region—the West—despite the focus of some current immigration research on globalism. The West deserves attention in studies of immigration for several reasons, including the fact that the region has been an important immigrant destination. The West was always the major gateway for immigrants from Asia and Mexico, and it gained even more prominence as a destination for immigrants over the twentieth century. While less than 10 percent of the foreign-born in the country lived in the Far West in 1900, 24 percent did so in 1970, and nearly 40 percent lived there by 1990.[32]

Immigration also deserves attention from scholars who study the West, partly because the foreign-born and their children have comprised a significant portion of the West's population. From 1860 to 1900, over one quarter of those residing in the Far West were born outside the United States. Although the percentage of immigrants in the U.S. white population fell to 20.7 in 1900, white immigrants and their children constituted 46.7 percent of the white population in the Pacific states in 1900 and 43.3 percent of the white residents of the Mountain States. Immigrants and their children comprised 41.3 percent of the entire Far West's population in 1920.[33]

First- and second-generation immigrants in the West comprised a critical mass without which economic development and resource extraction would have been slowed considerably. The Dillingham Commission found that nearly 60 percent of the West's railroad workers in 1908 were immigrants. Over 56 percent of the workers in salmon fisheries were foreign-born, and they also dominated the workforce of salmon canneries. In western mines and smelters, two-thirds of the workers were immigrants, and another one-sixth were second-generation immigrants. Sixty percent of the workers in western lumber and shingle mills studied by the commission were immigrants. The numbers were even more dramatic in the coal and coke industries, where 80 percent of the workers in 1908 were immigrants. As Elliott Barkan has observed, the three volumes of the Dillingham Report make it clear that the West's industries could not have functioned "without the continued inflows of foreign workers, men and women, and the second-generation children." At the same time, farming was also "an immigrant labor economy."[34]

The overwhelming immigrant presence in the region isn't the only justification for the study of immigration in the West. As Barkan explains, the West deserves our attention "because so many have used the West to define the American character, because so many have looked to it for inspiration, for role models, and even for cultural icons, because so many have emulated aspects of it, even people in other countries, because so many fiction and nonfiction authors have written about it."[35] In national mythology, the West more than any other region was a land of opportunity and liberty that validated the American Dream and Americans' faith in progress. Therefore, as Patricia Nelson Limerick argued, the West at large is an ideal laboratory for testing those myths: "As a depositary of enormous hopes for progress, the American West may well be the best place in which to observe the complex and contradictory outcome of that fruit."[36] The western immigrant experience is particularly well suited to that test because it contrasts opportunity abroad and opportunity in America.

Immigration to the West also merits a regional focus because of its distinctive elements; immigration to the West was not purely a smaller reflection of national trends. Limerick argues that part of the West's "regional significance" for the nation at large arose from its "proximity to Mexico [and] ports open to the Pacific Basin and Asia."[37] This gave the West high populations of Mexicans, Chinese, Japanese, and Filipinos. In tandem with its substantial American Indian population, this made the West a distinctive "meeting ground of Europe, Asia, and Latin America" that "made no peace with the problems of pluralism."[38]

The unique combination of ethnicities and races in the West gave a distinctive cast to national themes. For example, what Barkan calls the "desirable passkey of whiteness" was defined differently in the West than elsewhere.[39] As Linda Gordon has explained, "the chance to become white" was greater in the West than it was in other regions for some groups. In the East, Irish and Italians were seen as the "other" and could not become "white" until they were Americanized, although their skin color was already white.[40] By contrast, in southwestern states like Arizona and New Mexico with small African American populations, there were two race categories: Anglos and Mexicans. "At that time 'Mexican American' would have seemed an oxymoron to the Anglos. No matter that many of the Mexicans had lived on this soil far longer than the Anglo immigrants, . . . the whole category [was] one of outsiders, aliens."[41]

Owing to the Mexican presence, those who were not Mexican were considered whites. That was true of Irish Catholic "orphans" who were gathered up by church leaders in 1904 in New York and shipped across the country to new homes in Arizona. Gordon concludes that the children's trip to Arizona "was to offer them not only parents but also upward mobility. . . . The same train ride had transformed them from Irish to white." Because that transformation could only take place in an Anglo home, the community removed the children from the Catholic Hispanic homes where they were initially placed.[42]

The aforementioned example shows a biracial classification of identity. But with the wide variety of immigrants to the West, there were not always such clear distinctions. Groups were considered white or nonwhite based on which other groups were in the area. For example, Tomas Almaguer argues that in California, the Native Americans "were singled out as the most complete antithesis of white Californians and were summarily relegated to the very bottom of the racial hierarchy." Other cultural groups were rated based on that comparison. Therefore, Mexicans were seen as closer to European-American immigrants when compared to Native Americans, and Asian immigrants were seen as almost, but not quite, as different as the Native Americans. While these differences were usually expressed as racial, Almaguer explains they also represented class division and separated owners from laborers.[43]

These classifications varied over time. For example, Almaguer explains that there was a closer relationship between the Euro-Americans and the Mexican ranchero elite who were considered white as part of the Treaty of Guadalupe Hidalgo of 1848.[44] Religion, language, and, most importantly, work assignments and competition led Euro-Americans to view the rancheros and the working class Mexicans differently, often with a negative view of the new Mexican immigrants.[45] Similar changes took place when Euro-Americans opposed Chinese immigrants. They were replaced by Japanese immigrants, who were first welcomed but were later prevented from coming when they threatened the white working class.[46]

The Western immigrant experience was also distinctive because it included large numbers of religiously motivated Mormon migrants, whose experience is often neglected. Jan Shipps has referred to this neglect as the "donut hole" phenomenon; she argues that historians of the West have skipped Utah, "circling all around the Great Basin, taking into account and telling nearly every western story except the Mormon one."[47] Richard White described common perceptions of Utah as "a beautiful, dramatic, but odd place where people hold certain social views that are now regarded as somewhat archaic." As a result, "New Western Historians have decided, so to speak, to skip Utah."[48] Yet the Mormon story provides a rich opportunity to look at the experiences of immigrants from several countries who came West primarily for religious reasons.

A common religious belief tempered ethnic divisions and facilitated assimilation within Mormon communities. An interior wall of the Logan LDS Temple expresses that view. Immigrants worked on the temple as a public works project in the 1870s and 1880s. One worker wrote in the wet cement, "We are all here several nations, and the best of feelings among all men." The words are spelled phonetically, since English was not the worker's native tongue.[49] Many of the immigrants worked together, learned English, and adapted to American customs. They attended church with other Mormons and grew together as they worshipped and served each other. They were assimilated into the larger society within two generations as they intermarried and became part of new communities. But historians have shown that the journey had bumps. In the nineteenth century, some groups attended two religious services: one in English in a congregation based on geography, and one in their native language. Swiss settlers in Midway, Utah, had disagreements over who had the right to baptize and what language should be spoken in irrigation meetings. In Midway, the problems were resolved.[50] Other Mormon immigrants could not find work in their trades in the Mormon settlements, so they had to leave in search of work. Some who moved on looking for work stayed active spiritually, while others left both spiritually and physically. In all instances, religion conditioned their experiences and perspectives.[51]

While the Mormon immigrant experience is unique to the West, so is the California immigrant experience and legacy. California is one of the most diverse states in the nation. From 1980 onward, immigrants have comprised a higher percentage of the population of California than that of any other state. By 2000, over one in four residents in California was an immigrant.[52] The sunny weather, long coastline with numerous ports, and rich resources have long attracted immigrants from throughout the world. First came the Spanish explorers and missionaries, who established missions to convert and subdue American Indians. The 1847 gold rush expanded the population as North Americans, Asians, Europeans, and South Americans flocked to find their fortune by mining or providing services.

According to Roger Daniels and Spencer C. Olin Jr., some have argued that Californians are more prejudiced than other Americans. They point out, however, "In California there have always been greater numbers and varieties of people against whom to discriminate, or against whom to be prejudiced" based on color. "Had Swedes been red, yellow, brown, or black, Minnesota might also have been a racial battleground."[53] Understanding some of California's immigration history helps explain the shifting racial tensions in the state.

California became a state almost immediately after Mexico ceded it to the United States. Immigrant identity became unclear with that transfer. Were the Mexicans who had lived in the area for generations now the immigrants, or were the Americans? And how did the native people fit into that process? In many cases, though, the dominant newcomers from the eastern United States saw themselves as being in charge and saw the Mexicans as newcomers.

The California immigrant story does not end with the initial Americans and Mexicans. Asians arrived through Angel Island and the San Francisco Port. Chinese and Japanese also came to work in agriculture, sometimes coming via Hawaii, until they were restricted by immigration laws. Roger Daniels points out that Asian immigrants became a "special category" because they were "the first ethnic group against whom our immigration laws discriminated and the only group ever totally barred."[54] Once the Asians were banned, the focus of prejudice shifted increasingly to a new wave of Mexicans who arrived as laborers in California.[55]

While immigration to California slowed during the Great Depression and World War II, it picked up again following passage of the 1965 immigration law that allowed families to reunite. After the Korean and Vietnam wars, refugees from those countries came to California and established ethnic enclaves. But California also attracted groups who were not in distress. The exploding technology world attracted engineers and other technology experts, and the U.S. government and companies encouraged these newcomers. Immigrant entrepreneurs also started new businesses in the state. A quarter of the nation's legal immigrants settled in California, and the Los Angeles Airport was the main gateway to America from 1965 onward.[56]

Geographer William A. V. Clark (University of California, Los Angeles) pointed out in 1998 that "about one-third of all immigrants who come to the United States choose to live in California."[57] Their experiences differed widely; Asians who were recruited to come to America for business had education and fit into society faster, as measured by home ownership, economic conditions, political participation, and acceptance. Over time, Hispanic immigrants also improved their economic conditions and even fulfilled the American dream of owning a home, although their homes were often shared and more crowded. But as the number of immigrants soared, Clark found that the pace of economic progress and rate of social acceptance for recent Hispanic immigrants was slowing.[58] "The pace of immigration must be slowed [in Southern California] if social integration is to occur," he argued.[59]

The longstanding presence and influence of immigrants from Mexico and other Latin American countries in the Southwest also makes immigration to the West unique. While Spanish-speaking immigrants can be found throughout the United States in the twenty-first century, most enter the United States through Texas, New Mexico, Arizona, and California. Historically, the Southwest was also the first region to experience and negotiate the questions and opportunities raised by heavy immigration from Latin America. Some western Americans feared Latinos because they had a different language, culture, and religion. Yet these immigrants were willing to do work that Americans avoided, such as field labor and work in canneries. Because farmers saw the Mexican labor as essential, they prevented laws from being passed that would restrict Latino immigration. In the twentieth century, immigrants' work was so valuable that the United States and the Mexican government developed the Bracero Program to bring workers to the United States.

Mexicans and other Latin Americans, however, were often seen as sojourners who only came to the United States to work. Some Americans expected them to stay only as temporary workers and then return to their homeland. As more workers arrived, these Americans were concerned about providing services and education for a growing immigrant population. As discussed earlier, federal immigration laws did not control the flow of newcomers. Therefore, state governments passed laws to control the numbers and the expense of these newcomers. While immigrants continue to come to all parts of the United States, much of the current debate about immigration is focused on the American Southwest and on arrivals from countries south of the U.S. border.

Immigrants to the Far West and the American Dream

Frederick Jackson Turner's frontier thesis dominated western studies into the 1980s. Turner's thesis resonated with Americans because it articulated widespread myths about American exceptionalism and the American Dream. Although Turner did not focus on immigrants, the westward migration and occupation of frontier regions were central to his thesis, and immigrants played key roles in those processes. As Malcolm Rohrbaugh has observed, the West was a fabled land of opportunity that fueled immigrant hopes. Turner claimed that the abundance of free land on the frontier provided genuine economic opportunity and therefore exerted a leveling influence upon western migrants. On the frontier, industry and resourcefulness were supposedly more valuable than nobility of birth. Consequently, frontier conditions nurtured socioeconomic egalitarianism and political democracy.[60]

To what degree did immigrants realize the American Dream, as Turner posited, in the West? Immigrants who possessed valuable skills, financial resources, and social networks were more likely to thrive than those who lacked these assets, as was the case elsewhere in the nation. Moreover, their adjustment was easier nationwide if they already spoke English and if their culture resembled the dominant Anglo-American outlook. Within those parameters, though, the West did offer unique opportunities to immigrants.

Class divisions existed in the region, but the socioeconomic order in the West was relatively fluid in the late nineteenth century. As Elliott

Barkan concluded, "racial and ethnic barriers were not insurmountable" for immigrants, and "opportunities abounded for those of modest means but with ambition and drive." Work was plentiful when products from the West's extractive industries were in high demand. Recruiters scoured foreign and domestic labor markets, seeking workers for the West's mines, smelters, farms, and railroads, and workers poured in from China, Mexico, Europe, and eastern American cities. Low population density helped to keep wages relatively high in the West when compared to those of other regions of the nation, even after accounting for the high cost of living in places like mining towns. In 1890, the average real daily wage for workers in the West was $3.14; elsewhere in the nation average daily wages ranged from $2.06 in the South Atlantic states to $2.78 in the West South Central region. Both skilled workers and common laborers commanded higher wages in the West than elsewhere. Seasonal periods of unemployment offset the high wages somewhat in extractive industries that were vulnerable to boom-and-bust cycles. Working conditions were often dangerous, and living conditions were primitive. Unskilled workers on farms and ranches and in logging camps labored long hours—often from five in the morning until eight in the evening.[61]

In addition to offering higher wages, the West offered more opportunities to own real property, due in part to grants of free land under the Homestead Act. The 1890 census showed that a higher percentage of white immigrant farmers owned their land in the Far West than in any other section of the country (83.96 percent), although nearly as many owned land in the North Central states, which included the homestead lands of the Dakotas and Minnesota (83.49 percent). Home ownership among white immigrants was also highest in the North Central states (49.37 percent) and the West (44.27 percent).[62]

The relatively fluid social environment and nascent institutions in the West also facilitated social mobility for many "white" immigrants. Scandinavian and German immigrants "melted" into the American mainstream with relative ease. As Linda Gordon observed, immigrants from southern and eastern Europe—Jews, Slavs, Italians, and Greeks—often faced less discrimination in Western cities and towns with large Mexican or Chinese immigrant populations than they did elsewhere in the nation because "non-white" Asians and Mexicans there attracted the brunt of racial and ethnic prejudice. Thus "the western version of whiteness expanded to take in many of these other races even more quickly."[63]

Those who were classified as nonwhites constituted a second class of immigrants; even for them, opportunities were good compared to what they had enjoyed in their home countries. Mexican immigrants in the American

Southwest often earned three times what they could earn in Mexico. The Dillingham Commission reported that wages in Japan were a "mere fraction" of what immigrants managed to set aside after paying for their living expenses in the United States. But their wages paled in comparison to those of Euro-Americans. In the early twentieth century, Mexican workers in California earned 20 to 50 percent less than other workers in similar positions, and they enjoyed fewer opportunities for advancement. Mexicans and their children also experienced greater difficulty in acquiring farmland.[64]

Asian immigrants also encountered intense economic discrimination in the West. The Chinese Exclusion Act of 1882 prohibited the immigration of Chinese laborers and prevented Chinese nationals from becoming citizens. Early in the twentieth century, Japanese workers could obtain jobs in canneries and logging camps of the Northwest, but were generally barred from employment in sawmills. Their wages were generally lower than those of "white" workers. Opportunities for land ownership were also limited. In 1890, only 6 percent of the Chinese and Japanese farmers in the West owned land—the lowest percentage of any region in the country. By the 1920s, nine of the far western states, including California, had enacted alien land laws that prohibited Asian immigrants, who were ineligible for citizenship, from purchasing land. Some immigrants coped with such statutes by purchasing land in their children's names.[65]

The liberties of nonwhite immigrants were also curbed in the West. Mexican workers were subject to repatriation campaigns as the agricultural economy worsened and jobs became scarce in the late 1920s and early 1930s. An estimated one million Mexicans, primarily in Texas and California, were either deported forcibly or pressured to leave as welfare benefits were denied. During World War II, Japanese and Japanese Americans were forcibly relocated from the West Coast and incarcerated in prison camps behind barbed wire. Mobs attacked Japanese, Chinese, and Asian Indian workers and terrorized Greeks who dated "white" women.[66]

The essays in this volume explore the experiences of some of the West's immigrant groups, including their quest for liberty and economic opportunity. They address significant questions and illuminate key facets of the immigrant experience but do not offer a complete overview of western immigration. A comprehensive discussion of immigrant groups would be nearly impossible; at some point every group of people has immigrated to the West. Archaeologists suggest that even the ancestors of present-day Native Americans in the region migrated from elsewhere.

Earlier versions of the chapters in this volume were presented as papers at a Charles Redd Center seminar in 2011. They are divided into two sections: (1) Who We Were and Who They Said We Should Be, and (2) What We Came For and What We Made of It. As case studies, the chapters explore significant facets of immigration to the Far West (Arizona, California, Colorado, Idaho, Montana, Nevada, New Mexico, Oregon, Utah, Washington, and Wyoming) and demonstrate a variety of contemporary scholarly approaches to immigration.

Notes

1. Leonard J. Arrington and Davis Bitton, *The Mormon Experience: A History of the Latter-day Saints* (New York: Knopf, 1979), 136. The authors explain, "Through 1855 the 21,911 emigrants included 19,535 Britons, 2,000 Scandinavians, a few French, Italians, and Germans. In the late period the non-British nationalities made up a larger portion of the total. The number of Scandinavians eventually reached over 30,000 before the end of the nineteenth century."
2. The Far West comprises roughly the western third of the contiguous United States: Arizona, California, Colorado, Idaho, Montana, Nevada, New Mexico, Oregon, Utah, Washington, and Wyoming.
3. Frank Thistlethwaite, "Migration from Europe Overseas in the Nineteenth and Twentieth Centuries," *A Century of European Migrations, 1830–1930,* ed. Rudolph J. Vecoli and Suzanne M. Sinke (Urbana: University of Illinois Press, 1991), 19. Thistlethwaite's article was first written in 1960 and reprinted as part of the volume on immigration for the Statue of Liberty's centennial.
4. "The Foreign-Born Population in the United States: 2010, American Community Survey Reports," issued May 2012, http://www.census.gov/prod/2012pubs/acs-19.pdf, accessed August 1, 2012.
5. Jason McDonald, *American Ethnic History: Themes and Perspectives* (New Brunswick, NJ: Rutgers University Press, 2007), 37–38; Gunther Barth, *Bitter Strength: A History of the Chinese in the United States, 1850–1870* (Cambridge, MA: Harvard University Press, 1964); Suchen Chan, "European and Asian Immigration into the United States in Comparative Perspective, 1820s to 1920s," in *Immigration Reconsidered: History, Sociology, and Politics*, ed. Virginia Yans-McLaughlin (New York: Oxford University Press, 1990), 38; Matt S. Meier and Feliciano Ribera, *Mexican Americans/American Mexicans: From Conquistadors to Chicanos* (New York: Hill and Wang, 1993), 4; John Bodnar, *The Transplanted: A History of Immigrants in Urban America* (Bloomington: Indiana University Press, 1985), 53; Lawrence Fuchs, *The American Kaleidoscope: Race, Ethnicity and the Civic Culture* (Hanover, NH: University Press of New England, 1990), 37.
6. Emma Lazarus, "The New Colossus," http://www.statueoflibertynow.com statue-of-liberty-poem.html, accessed on August 2, 2012.
7. This introduction briefly summarizes immigration laws. For more information, see Roger Daniels, *Guarding the Golden Door: American Immigration Policy and Immigrants since 1882* (New York: Hill and Wang, 2004); Michael C. LeMay, *From Open Door to Dutch Door: An Analysis of U.S. Immigration Policy since 1820* (New York: Praeger, 1987); and Aristide R. Zolberg, *A Nation by Design: Immigrant Policy in the Fashioning of America* (New York: Russell Sage Foundation, 2006). For information on how the laws impacted the American Far West, see Elliott

Robert Barkan, *From All Points: America's Immigrant West, 1870s–1952* (Bloomington: Indiana University Press, 2007).

8. Erika Lee, "Immigrants and Immigration Law: A State of the Field Assessment," *Journal of American Ethnic History* 18, no. 4 (Summer 1999): 87.
9. Excellent studies such as Caroline B. Brettell and James F. Hollifield, *Migration Theory: Talking Across Disciplines* (New York: Routledge, 2008) outline how many of the social sciences developed and adapted these theories.
10. Frank Van Nuys, *Americanizing the West: Race, Immigrants, and Citizenship, 1890–1930* (Lawrence: University Press of Kansas, 2002).
11. Bodnar, *The Transplanted*; Kathleen Conzen, "Immigrants, Immigrant Neighborhoods, and Ethnic Identity: Historical Issues," *Journal of American History* 66, no. 3 (December 1979): 603–15; Virginia Yans-McLaughlin, *Family and Community: Italian Immigrants in Buffalo, 1880–1930* (Ithaca, NY: Cornell University Press, 1977). In 2002, Lon Kurashige's *Japanese American Celebration and Conflict: A History of Ethnic Identity and Festival, 1934–1990* (Berkeley: University of California Press, 2002) demonstrated how Japanese Americans' group identity developed through shared experiences at the celebrations rather than because of a pre-existing shared understanding of what it meant to be Japanese.
12. Min Zhou, "Segmented Assimilation: Issues, Controversies and Recent Research on the New Second Generation," *International Migration Review* 31, no. 4 (Winter 1997): 976–77; Alejandro Portes and Min Zou, "The New Second Generation: Segmented Assimilation and Its Variants among Post-1965 Immigrant Youth," *Annals of the American Academy of Political and Social Science* 530 (November 1993): 74–98.
13. J. Logan, R. Alba, and W. Zhang, "Immigrant Enclaves and Ethnic Communities in New York and Los Angeles," *American Sociological Review* 67, no. 2 (April 2002): 299–322; Douglas S. Massey and Nancy A. Denton, "Spatial Assimilation as a Socioeconomic Outcome," *American Sociological Review* 50, no. 1 (February 1985): 94–106; Susan W. Hardwick, "Place, Space and Pattern: Geographical Theories in International Migration," in Brettell and Hollifield, *Migration Theory*, 161–69.
14. Chris Lee, "Sociological Theories of Immigration: Pathways to Integration for U.S. Immigrants," *Journal of Human Behavior in the Social Environment* 19, no. 6 (2009): 730–44. See also Barbara Schmitter Heisler, "The Sociology of Immigration: From Assimilation to Segmented Assimilation, from the American Experience to the Global Arena," in Brettell and Hollifield, *Migration Theory*, 83–112.
15. Elazar Barkan, *The Retreat of Scientific Racism: Changing Concepts of Race in Britain and the United States between the World Wars* (New York: Cambridge University Press, 1992).
16. Barbara J. Fields, "Ideology and Race in American History," in *Region, Race and Reconstruction: Essays in Honor of C. Vann Woodward*, ed. J. Morgan Kousser and James M. McPherson (New York: Oxford University Press, 1982), 143–77; Michael Omi and Howard Winant, *Racial Formation in the United States: From the 1960s to the 1980s* (New York: Routledge, 1986).
17. David R. Roediger, *The Wages of Whiteness: Race and the Making of the American Working Class* (London: Verso, 1991). Scholarship that was inspired by the whiteness paradigm includes Michael Rogin, *Blackface, White Noise: Jewish Immigrants*

in the Hollywood Melting Pot (Berkeley: University of California Press, 1996); Gary K. Okihiro, "Is Yellow Black or White?" in *Margins and Mainstreams: Asians in American History and Culture* (Seattle: University of Washington Press, 1994), 31–63; Linda Gordon, *The Great Arizona Orphan Abduction* (Cambridge, MA: Harvard University Press, 1999); and Thomas A. Guglielmo, *White on Arrival: Italians, Race, Color and Power in Chicago, 1890–1945* (New York: Oxford University Press, 2003). See also George J. Sanchez, "Race, Nation, and Culture in Recent Immigration Studies," *Journal of American Ethnic History* 18, no. 4 (Summer 1999): 69.

18. Nina Glick Schiller, Linda Basch, and Cristina Blanc-Szanton, "Transnationalism: A New Analytic Framework for Understanding Migration," in *Towards a Transnational Perspective on Migration: Race, Class, Ethnicity and Nationalism Reconsidered*, ed. Nina Glick Schiller, Linda Basch, and Cristina Blanc-Szanton (New York: New York Academy of Sciences, 1992), 1.
19. Nina Glick Schiller, Linda Basch, and Cristina Szanton Blanc, "From Immigrant to Transmigrant: Theorizing Transnational Migration," *Anthropological Quarterly* 68, no. 1 (January 1995): 48–50; Roger Rouse, "Mexican Migration to the United States: Family Relations in the Development of a Transnational Migrant Circuit" (PhD diss., Stanford University, 1989), 45.
20. Homi K. Bhabha, "Unsatisfied: Notes on Vernacular Cosmopolitanism," in *Text and Nation*, ed. Laura Garcia-Morena and Peter C. Pfeifer (London: Camden House, 1996), 191–207; Kevin Concannon, Francisco A. Lomelí, and Marc Priewe, eds., *Imagined Transnationalism: U.S. Latino/a Literature, Culture, and Identity* (New York: Palgrave Macmillan, 2009), 1–12; Ana Patricia Rodriguez, "¿Dónde estás vos/z?: Performing Salvadoreñidades in Washington DC," in ibid., 201–20; Claudia Sadowski-Smith, "Imagining Transnational Chicano/a Activism against Gender-Based Violence at the U.S.-Mexican Border," in ibid., 75–94.
21. Jon Gjerde, "New Growth on Old Vines: The State of the Field: The Social History of Immigration to and Ethnicity in the United States," *Journal of American Ethnic History* 18, no. 4 (Summer 1999): 51–52; Dirk Hoerder, "Historians and Their Data: The Complex Shift from Nation-State Approaches to the Study of People's Transcultural Lives," *Journal of American Ethnic History* 25, no. 4 (Summer 2006): 86–87, 90, 91–92.
22. Elliott R. Barkan, "America in the Hand, Homeland in the Heart: Transnational and Translocal Immigrant Experiences in the American West," *Western Historical Quarterly* 35, no. 3 (Autumn 2004): 340–41.
23. Hasia Diner, "American Immigration and Ethnic History: Moving the Field Forward, Staying the Course," *Journal of American Ethnic History* 25, no. 4 (Summer 2006): 137.
24. Barkan, *From All Points*, xi.
25. Richard White, "Trashing the Trails," in *Trails: Toward a New Western History*, ed. Patricia Nelson Limerick, Clyde A. Milner II, Charles E. Rankin (Lawrence: University Press of Kansas, 1991), 36.
26. Frederick C. Luebke, ed., *European Immigrants in the American West: Community Histories* (Albuquerque: University of New Mexico Press, 1998), vii.
27. Roger W. Lotchin, "The Impending Urban Past," in *Researching Western History: Topics in the Twentieth Century*, ed. Gerald D. Nash and Richard W. Etulain (Albuquerque: University of New Mexico Press, 1997), 61.

28. George J. Sanchez, *Becoming Mexican American: Ethnicity, Culture and Identity in Chicano Los Angeles, 1900–1945* (New York: Oxford University Press, 1993); Judy Yung, *Unbound Feet: A Social History of Chinese Women in San Francisco* (Berkeley: University of California Press, 1995). Utah provides a representative example of state-based approaches to immigration. In 1957 William Mulder, a University of Utah professor, published *Homeward to Zion: The Mormon Migration from Scandinavia* (Minneapolis: University of Minnesota Press, 1957). Then beginning in the 1960s, the *Utah Historical Quarterly* frequently printed articles about specific immigrant groups and their experiences in Utah. The journal's editor, Stanford J. Layton, reported that there were so many possible immigration articles that in 1976, as part of the U.S. bicentennial, the Utah State Historical Society decided to publish *The Peoples of Utah*, edited by Helen Papanikolas, a daughter of Greek immigrants. The book included articles by scholars, connected to their subjects by blood and training, who examined the experiences of several immigrant groups that came to Utah. The articles were descriptive rather than theory-based, but they showed the wide variety of people who settled in what some Americans saw as a uniform Mormon culture region. Helen Papanikolas, ed., *The Peoples of Utah* (Salt Lake City: Utah State Historical Society, 1976). Interest in documenting immigrant groups in Utah continued. In 1982 Leslie G. Kelen and Eileen Hallett received a grant from the Utah Humanities Council to interview the state's minority populations. The project resulted in an edited collection of interviews entitled *Missing Stories: An Oral History of Ethnic and Minority Groups in Utah* (Salt Lake City: University of Utah Press, 1997). See also Stanford Layton, *Being Different: Stories of Utah's Minorities* (Salt Lake City: Signature Books, 2001).
29. Moses Rischin and John Livingston, eds., *Jews of the American West* (Detroit: Wayne State University Press, 1991); Richard W. Etulain and Jeronima Echeverria, eds., *Portraits of Basques in the New World* (Reno: University of Nevada Press, 1999); Ferenc Morton Szasz, *Scots in the North American West, 1790–1917* (Norman: University of Oklahoma Press, 2000); Donald Warrin and Geoffrey L. Gomes, *Land, As Far as the Eye Can See: Portuguese in the Old West* (Spokane, WA: Arthur H. Clark Co., 2001); Jorge Iber and Arnoldo de Léon, *Hispanics in the American West* (Santa Barbara: ABC Clio, 2006); David Emmons, *Beyond the American Pale: The Irish in the West, 1845–1910* (Norman: University of Oklahoma Press, 2010).
30. Walter Nugent, *Into the West: The Story of Its People* (New York: A. A. Knopf, 1999), xix.
31. Barkan, *From All Points*, xv, 8–15.
32. Campbell Gibson and Kay Jung, *Historical Census Statistics on the Foreign-Born Population of the United States: 1850 to 2000*, Population Division Working Paper No. 81 (Washington, DC: US Census Bureau, 2006), [60–69], http://www.census.gov/population/www/documentation/twps0081/twps0081.html, accessed July 16, 2013.
33. Niles Carpenter, *Immigrants and Their Children, 1920*, Census Monographs VII (Washington, DC: GPO, 1927), 15, 306–7; Gibson and Jung, *Historical Census Statistics*, 60–69. Late in the twentieth century, the percentage of immigrants in the West's population again rose, from 10.6 percent in 1980 to 18.6 percent in 2000.
34. Barkan, *From All Points*, 119–23. In its studies of mining, the commission relied upon sample data drawn from Colorado, Arizona, Montana, and California

for mines and smelters and from California, Washington, Utah, Wyoming, and New Mexico for the coal and coke industries.

35. Barkan, *From All Points*, xv.
36. Patricia Nelson Limerick, *The Legacy of Conquest: The Unbroken Past of the American West* (New York: W. W. Norton, 1987), 29–30.
37. Ibid., 30.
38. Ibid., 269.
39. Barkan, *From All Points*, xiii.
40. Gordon, *The Great Arizona Orphan Abduction*, 1–19 (quote from p. 19), 76–77.
41. Ibid., 105.
42. Ibid, 76–77, 104–5.
43. Tomas Almaguer, *Racial Fault Lines: The Historical Origins of White Supremacy in California* (Berkeley: University of California Press, 1994), 7–8, 12.
44. Ibid., 54.
45. Ibid., 62–63, 103–4.
46. Ibid., 180–81, 183–204.
47. Jan Shipps, "Gentiles, Mormons, and the History of the American West," in *Sojourner in the Promised Land: Forty Years among the Mormons* (Urbana: University of Illinois Press, 2000), 21.
48. White, "Trashing the Trails," 29.
49. Jessie L. Embry, *History of Wasatch County* (Salt Lake City: Utah State Historical Society, 1996), 40.
50. Ibid., 40–46.
51. See Mindi Sitterud-McCluskey's article in this volume.
52. Gibson and Jung, *Historical Census Statistics*, 60–61; U.S. Census Bureau, *Statistical Abstract of the United States: 2012*, 43, http://www.census.gov/compendia/statab/2012edition.html, accessed July 17, 2013.
53. Roger Daniels and Spencer C. Olin Jr., eds., *Racism in California: A Reader in the History of Oppression* (New York: Macmillan, 1972), v.
54. Roger Daniels, "Westerners from the East: Oriental Immigrants Reappraised," in Daniels and Olin, *Racism in California*, 59.
55. Daniels and Olin, *Racism in California*, 181–82.
56. Sarah Deutsch, George J. Sanchez, and Gary Y. Okihiro, "Contemporary People/Contested Places," in *The Oxford History of the American West*, ed. Clyde A. Milner II, Carol A. O'Connor, and Martha A. Sandweiss (New York: Oxford University Press, 1994), 639, 647.
57. William A. V. Clark, *The California Cauldron: Immigration and the Fortunes of Local Communities* (New York: Guilford Press, 1998), 193.
58. Ibid. This is a summary of Clark's ideas that are found throughout the book. Roger Daniels and Spencer C. Olin Jr. also describe how "the Orientals" were seen as "an achieving minority" in the 1970s. Daniels and Olin, *Racism in California*, 334–45. Robert M. Jiobu, *Ethnicity & Assimilation: Blacks, Chinese, Filipinos, Japanese, Koreans, Mexicans, Vietnamese, and Whites* (Albany: State University of New York Press, 1988) also looks at how these groups interacted in California in the latter twentieth century.
59. Clark, *The California Cauldron*, 201. As immigrants spread out from the West

Coast to adjoining states, California may be the forerunner of what happens in those places.

60. Frederick Jackson Turner, *Frontier and Section: Selected Essays of Frederick Jackson Turner* (Englewood Cliffs, NJ: Prentice-Hall, 1961); Malcolm Rohrbaugh, "Preface," in *Encyclopedia of Immigration and Migration in the American West,* ed. Gordon Morris Bakken (Thousand Oaks, CA: Sage Publications, 2006), xxvi.
61. Barkan, *From All Points*, 39, 238; Richard White, *"It's Your Misfortune and None of My Own": A New History of the American West* (Norman: University of Oklahoma Press, 1991), 278–79; Carlos A. Schwantes, "Wage Earners and Wealth Makers," in Milner, O'Connor, and Sandweisss, *The Oxford History of the American West*, 439.
62. Bureau of the Census, *Report on Farms and Homes: Proprietorship and Indebtedness in the United States at the Eleventh Census: 1890* (Washington, DC: GPO, 1896), 190–94. Immigrant farmers fared worst in the South Central states, where 65.69 percent owned land. Home ownership for immigrants was lowest in the densely populated North Atlantic region (26.61 percent). Census takers also found that a higher percentage of second-generation immigrants owned property in the West than elsewhere. Eighty percent of white farmers in the region whose parent[s] had immigrated to the United States owned their land, compared to 70 percent in the nation at large. Forty percent of second-generation immigrants owned their homes in both the West and the North Central states, contrasted with 33.8 percent nationwide. Ibid., 201.
63. Barkan, *From All Points*, 172–80; Gordon, *The Great Arizona Orphan Abduction*, 104.
64. Barkan, *From All Points*, 119, 197; Harry A. Millis, *Japanese and Other Immigrant Races in the Pacific Coast and Rocky Mountain States* (Washington, DC: GPO, 1911), 11; E. P. Hutchinson, *Immigrants and Their Children, 1850–1950* (New York: John Wiley & Sons, 1956), 266. In 1950 in the nation at large, the children of immigrants from Poland, Hungary, Czechoslovakia, Yugoslavia, Greece, and French Canada also differed significantly from the national norms.
65. Despite their second-class status, some Japanese immigrants managed to farm. In 1909, an estimated three thousand Japanese farmers worked 153,683 acres, 10 percent of which were owned. In California by 1920 they farmed 458,000 acres, most of it under leasing arrangements. In the Seattle area, Japanese farmers grew three-quarters of the Seattle area's vegetables and supplied half of the area's milk in the 1920s. Barkan, *From All Points*, 117, 166, 175–76, 259; Cherstin M. Lyon, "Alien Land Laws," Densho Encyclopedia, http://encyclopedia.densho.org/Alien_land_laws/, accessed July 9, 2013; Millis, *Japanese and Other Immigrant Races*, 58, 76.
66. Barkan, *From All Points*, 165, 329–30.

PART
I

Who We Were and Who They Thought We Should Be

Jessie L. Embry and Brian Q. Cannon

Identity is complicated, and it is bound up in the two interrelated questions posed in the title of this section: who were the immigrants, and what did American society expect them to be? Although we often distinguish immigrants on the basis of nationality, those broad categories gloss over many differences. If immigrants were asked, "Who are you?" they would probably identify themselves individually by name. Then they might discuss their relationship to their families, their communities, and geopolitical or cultural parts of their homelands, as well as their countries of origin. They might identify themselves in terms of their religion, occupation, membership in voluntary associations, race, or language.

Most first-generation adult immigrants remained enmeshed in the language and culture of their homelands, but they did not necessarily identify with nation-states. Some were alienated from hostile regimes in their homelands, others came from occupied lands or loose confederations of semiautonomous provinces, and some had been persona non grata in their homelands. But, in America, they reacted to the conditions they found, including the presence of other immigrants who spoke the same language and the ways in which Americans defined or discriminated against them on the basis of supposed national traits. In the process, their country of origin often became "the primary basis of group solidarity, overwhelming other competing identifications," Alejandro Portes and Rubén Rumbaut explain.[1] Thus, broad national groupings are not merely convenient analytical categories; nationality has been and remains a significant identity marker and factor in social relations.

The articles in this section focus on immigrants who came to areas that are part of the American West, illuminating immigrant identity and societal efforts to shape or recast that identity. Many came directly to the West from their home country; others first landed elsewhere in the United States or abroad and later moved to the Far West. This introduction provides an overview of immigration to the region, highlighting the largest immigrant nationalities in the West over the twentieth and into the twenty-first century. It also describes Americans' expectations of the newcomers, setting a context for the chapters that follow.

Who We Were

In 1900 the ten largest immigrant nationalities in the Far West were (1) Germans, (2) English, (3) Canadians, (4) Irish, (5) Swedes, (6) Chinese, (7) Italians, (8) Danes, (9) Mexicans, and (10) Scots. In the first decade heavy immigration from Japan, Norway, and the Austrian Empire (including what would become Czechoslovakia and Yugoslavia after World War I) pushed those nationalities into the top groups by 1910. Russian peasants, including Jewish refugees, many of whom had initially settled in the East, came west in sufficient numbers during the 1910s to make Russians the ninth largest group in 1920. Although their rankings changed, the top countries in 1920 remained the leading immigrant nationalities in 1930 and 1940. By midcentury, the top groups were (1) Mexicans, (2) Canadians, (3) Italians, (4) English, (5) Germans, (6) Russians, (7) Swedes, (8) Norwegians, (9) Irish, and (10) Scots.[2]

TABLE 0.1. TOP 10 NATIONALITIES OF FOREIGN-BORN RESIDENTS; 1860–1900

1860	1870	1880	1890	1900
Ireland 38,010	Ireland 69,418	China 100,404	Germany 120,367	Germany 136,459
China 35,363	China 62,363	Ireland 90,212	England 114,393	England 111,085
Germany[1] 25,053	England 46,334	England 74,094	Ireland 105,473	Canada 89,800
England[2] 23,522	Germany 39,661	Germany 64,969	China 95,477	Ireland 83,532
Mexico 14,129	Mexico 18,108	Canada 29,041	Canada 75,484	Sweden 68,518
France 9,014	Canada 13,412	Mexico 23,751	Sweden 47,897	China 60,615
Canada 8,123	France 9,762	Scotland 15,136	Scotland 27,593	Italy 40,210
Scotland 5,574	Scotland 9,533	Denmark 14,195	Denmark 25,702	Denmark 29,657
Denmark 3,262	Denmark 7,521	Sweden 13,076	Italy 24,914	Mexico 29,579
Italy 3,121	Italy 5,095	France 12,463	Mexico 24,181	Scotland 28,129

[1] Includes German-speaking Austrians [2] Includes Wales

Table 0.2. Top 10 Nationalities of Foreign-Born Residents in the Far West; 1910–1950

1910	1920	1930	1940	1950
Germany 166,551	Mexico 184,115	Mexico 290,541	Mexico 173,011	Mexico 308,581
Canada 146,422	Canada 149,991	Canada 195,405	Canada 165,842	Canada 200,111
England 141,619	England 142,801	England 156,325	Italy 124,410	Italy 131,218
Italy 116,707	Germany 136,887	Italy 146,030	England 119,323	England 121,192
Sweden 103,995	Italy 132,136	Germany 144,026	Germany 111,312	Germany 110,068
Ireland 94,526	Sweden 109,462	Sweden 112,689	Sweden8 2,602	USSR 97,493
Mexico 79,861	Japan (90–100,000?)	Russia 80,420	Russia 75,068	Sweden 71,669
Austria 67,479	Ireland 78,072	Norway 71,833	Norway 61,642	Norway 53,696
Japan 63,904	Russia 72,017	Ireland 69,747	Japan 43,141	Ireland 42,428
Norway 55,292	Norway 66,119	Japan 65,917	Scotland 39,232	Scotland 39,618

Immigrants gravitated toward some far western states more than others. California was consistently the prime destination. With over one million immigrants by 1930, California was a cornucopia of ethnic diversity, far more diverse than any other far western state. The 1930 census identified over one thousand immigrants from each of twenty-seven European nations residing in the Golden State. Immigrants there comprised nearly 19 percent of the population.[3] Washington, with about one-fourth as many immigrants as California, had the second largest immigrant population in the West (255,268). Among the Mountain States in 1930, the leading copper producers had the largest immigrant populations because the industry relied heavily upon immigrant labor. Meanwhile, New Mexico's 24,052 immigrants comprised less than 1 percent of its population.[4]

Over time, the immigrant presence in various western states shifted. Montana had been a prime immigrant destination because of its mines, smelters, and homestead lands early in the twentieth century, but by 2009, it was home to only around 19,000 immigrants. Meanwhile, Nevada, which had been home to the smallest number of immigrants of any western state in 1930, had over 500,000 immigrant residents in 2009.[5]

Starting in the 1970s, the ethnic composition of the West's population changed dramatically, as the Immigration and Nationality Act of 1965 and U.S. refugee policies facilitated waves of immigration from Asia and Latin America. By 1990 the largest immigrant groups in the West were (1) Mexicans, (2) Filipinos, (3) Vietnamese, (4) Salvadorans, (5) Canadians, (6) Koreans, (7) mainland Chinese (excluding Hong Kong), (8) Germans, (9) Guatemalans, and (10) Japanese. By 2010, immigrants from India and Iran had replaced Germans and Japanese within the top ten groups.[6]

Table 0.3. Top 10 Nationalities of Foreign-Born Residents; 1970–2010

1970	1980	1990	2000	2010
Mexico 470,910	Mexico 1,436,880	Mexico 2,840,574	Mexico 5,175,325	Mexico 5,974,033
Canada 228,400	Canada 272,072	Philippines 532,943	Philippines 775,871	Philippines 1,000,482
Germany 153,288	Philippines 264,468	Vietnam 311,608	Vietnam 511,136	China 696,530
England 127,768	Germany 184,645	El Salvador 288,932	El Salvador 393,016	Vietnam 618,161
Philippines 90,830	England 135,005	Canada 259,219	China 381,939	El Salvador 477,594
Italy 96,959	China 131,132	Korea 245,033	Korea 350,286	Korea 454,367
China 76,013	Central and South America 112,013	China 236,219	Canada 277,720	India 425,716
Japan 55,482	Korea 110,321	Germany 173,534	India 244,298	Guatemala 396,403 [1]
USSR 73,167	Vietnam 06,127	Guatemala 140,985	Guatemala 238,252	Canada 273,288
Central and South America 61,565	Japan 102,160	Japan 126,515	Germany 182,178	Iran 218,813

[1] Includes Second-Generation

In the following discussion of leading immigrant nationalities, immigrants are grouped based on geographical area as well as similar immigration and assimilation patterns. For instance, we have divided Europe because Northern Europeans often seemed to face less prejudice than Southern Europeans. This organization allows us to compare and contrast immigration experiences based on geographical location.

North America: Mexico and Canada

Citizens of the United States' two neighboring countries, Mexico and Canada, had to cross only one international border to come to the

United States. They traversed fewer miles than other immigrants to reach their destination.

Mexico was the leading native country of immigrants in the West from the 1910s onward. This was logical given the ease of border crossings, the economic incentives for migration, and the fact that much of what is now the American West was part of Mexico until 1848. During the Mexican revolution in the 1910s, many refugees from Mexico entered the United States. In 1920, census takers enumerated 184,621 Mexican immigrants in the West, nearly 80 percent of whom lived in Arizona and California. Mexicans poured across the border during the 1920s—by 1930 there were 291,041 Mexicans in the West. Most settled in California, but significant numbers settled elsewhere, finding work in sugar beet fields, on railroad crews, and in mines: for instance, over three thousand lived in Wyoming by 1930. Many returned to Mexico during the Great Depression. The need for laborers in the West during World War II led the United States and Mexico to develop the Bracero Program whereby Mexican guest workers were brought to work on American farms. But it was not only that program that brought Mexicans northward. Mexicans often lost economic ground in the international flow of capital and resources. In order to escape poor conditions, Mexicans moved northward seeking more opportunities.[7]

By the late twentieth century, Mexicans and other Latin American immigrants found employment not only in the Far West but throughout the United States. Still, the initial point of entry and often the final stopping place was the American West. Mexicans were often attracted to urban areas: in 2011, close to 1.4 million Mexican immigrants resided in the Los Angeles metropolitan area. But Mexicans also settled elsewhere in the region, from small towns in Idaho to the metropolitan areas of Washington State.[8]

While the Mexicans have dominated immigration to the West, Canadians were the second largest immigrant group residing in the West from 1920 to 1980.[9] In 1920 they were most numerous in California, Washington, Oregon, and Montana. Even in 2009, after massive influxes of immigrants from Asia and Latin America, Canadians remained the largest immigrant group in Montana; the second largest group in Arizona, Idaho, Utah, and Wyoming; and the fifth largest group in the West at large.[10] In many ways it was much easier for Canadians to immigrate to the United States than for Mexicans because most of them shared the same language and many of the same cultural traditions. And the immigration historically was a two-way movement: Americans also moved north for economic and religious purposes. In the 2006 Canadian census, over 10 percent of Canadians identified their ethnic background as American. The Mormons provide just one example of that movement. The first Mormons to emigrate to the Canadian West went to escape U.S. antipolygamy laws in the late nineteenth century. A second wave of Mormon migrants moved there in response to invitations from the government and companies to build canals and railroads. For these groups and others who often crossed the border, it was not immediately obvious that they were in a different country. Despite cultural and economic similarities, it became harder to cross the border because of the American government's attempts to control its borders after September 11, 2001.[11]

Western Europe and Scandinavia: Germany, England, Sweden, Denmark, and Scotland

Immigrants from western Europe and Scandinavia comprised over half of the West's immigrant population in 1900. In that year, Germans (first), English (second), Swedes (fifth), Danes (eighth), and Scots (tenth) were among the top ten foreign-born groups in the region. Although their relative rankings shifted, immigrants from these nations continued to figure prominently in the West's immigrant profile at midcentury.[12] Some of these groups spoke English as their native language, so they could be understood easily. Even those who did not speak English often shared other cultural traits with the American majority, including Protestantism, and this eased their adjustment to their new home. As Roger Lotchin has observed, many of these groups have been understudied in their western setting because they blended so readily.[13]

Most German immigrants came to the United States between 1840 and 1914, with the largest number coming in the early 1880s. The majority settled in the Upper Midwest and the Central Atlantic states; nevertheless, by 1920 over 130,000 (about 8 percent of the nation's total) lived in the Far West. In the early twentieth century, over 75 percent of the region's Germans lived in California, Washington, and Oregon. The San Francisco Bay area particularly attracted German immigrants: in 1900, over 41,000 lived in San Francisco and Alameda Counties. Large concentrations were also found in Oregon's Willamette River Valley and in the Seattle, Tacoma, and Spokane areas of Washington. In the Rocky Mountain states, Germans were most numerous in Colorado. They were concentrated in the Denver area, but hundreds inhabited mining towns near Pikes Peak or homesteads on the plains in the southeastern corner of the state. Most Germans came to the United States seeking economic opportunities. They initially experienced language differences, but often shared other cultural traits that enabled them to fit into the areas they settled. They often established German-speaking religious organizations, mutual-aid societies, and newspapers, but it appeared that they had almost seamlessly assimilated into the mainstream until the 1910s. Then, anti-German prejudice during World War I fueled persecution and government restrictions. After World War I, some German refugees moved to the western United States. Germans experienced continued discrimination during World War II, but it was less pronounced in most areas of the West than it had been during World War I. The end of the war brought more displaced Germans to the Far West. In 1990, Germans still ranked among the ten largest immigrant populations in the West.[14]

Thousands of English immigrants settled in the West along with others from Wales and Scotland. Many were Mormon converts who made their way to Utah; in 1860 over seven thousand immigrants from England lived in Utah—over half of the territory's immigrant population. Other English immigrants came west to work in the region's mines. By 1880 many lived in silver- and gold-mining districts in the Sierra Nevadas and the Colorado Rockies. Others who had been lower-middle-class farmers, tenants, and farm laborers in England were pushed out by crop failures, mechanization, and falling commodity prices and came west looking for land. A real estate and ranching boom that climaxed in 1877 also drew wealthy English investors to the Colorado plains. Some American companies also recruited English workers. They attracted little notice because of their language and culture, but they were the fifth largest immigrant population in the country in 1950.[15]

The peak decades of immigration from Scotland to the United States were the 1880s, the 1900s, and the 1920s. Scots played significant roles in the development of sheepherding and in the range cattle industry in the West. They settled in largest numbers in California, Colorado, and Washington.[16]

Elliott Barkan explains, "Scandinavians are in particular written off as 'melted.'" That is an oversimplification, he notes, because "they did seek a balance between their ethnicity and their Americanism rather than entirely giving up one for the other." Nevertheless, they did "blend . . . rather easily into the mainstream of American culture." About 10 percent of the Scandinavians who came to America between 1899 and 1910 were bound for the Pacific Northwest, especially Washington. Others later moved to the region. They came to the Northwest seeking jobs in industries that they knew, such as fishing, logging, mining, and farming; others hoped to escape the moral and social strictures of immigrant towns in the rural Midwest. Most who moved west joined English-speaking churches rather than native-language congregations.[17]

Swedes and Norwegians flocked to the United States between 1885 and 1915. They found agricultural lands and employment in industry. Most settled in the Midwest, but some moved in step-migration format from the Midwest to the Northwest. For instance, in 1881 several Norwegian Lutheran families from Minnesota, discouraged by crop failure there, decided to purchase land in Sweet Grass County, Montana; by 1900, some 291 Norwegians lived in the county. In 1920, over sixty thousand Swedes and Norwegians resided in Washington—more than one-fourth of the state's immigrant population. Swedes also moved into the Mountain West, especially Colorado, Montana, and Utah, where they found land to farm and work in mines and smelters. Norwegians were present in every state in the Mountain West, but by 1920 more lived in Montana than in the all the other mountain states combined. Assimilation sometimes came slowly for these largely Lutheran people, but by 1920 most Swedish communities spoke English, and by the 1930s assimilation was complete. After 1940, there were few Swedish enclaves in the United States.[18]

Denmark, a much smaller nation, had fewer immigrants than Norway and Sweden; the peak immigration period for Danes was during the 1880s. In the nineteenth century, Mormon missionaries converted thousands of Danes who came to America for religious reasons. By 1900, over 9,100 Danes lived in Utah—more than in any other western state; they concentrated disproportionately in rural Box Elder, Sanpete, and Sevier Counties. In 1990, Sanpete and Sevier Counties ranked second and fifth in the United States in terms of the percentage of residents claiming Danish ancestry. Danes also gravitated toward California and Washington, especially after 1900. The Danish Folk Society helped establish agricultural colonies in the Pacific states in the twentieth century. One of the most famous is Solvang, California, founded in 1911 by Danes who had formerly lived in the Midwest. Danish immigration had largely ended by 1930; by that date, economic and political reform in Denmark and the gradual closing of the American farming frontier had limited the appeal of immigration. In the 1950s and 1960s some Danish professionals settled in far western cities, mainly Los Angeles and San Francisco.[19]

Ireland

Ireland has a divided identity. While part of the island is culturally, religiously, and linguistically connected to England, the rest is very Catholic and was often at odds with the United Kingdom. The Irish are considered separately here from other western Europeans because of their large numbers and the hostile reception they received in America. Irish immigration was particularly pronounced in the nineteenth century. The largest migration to America occurred prior to the Civil War, when many flocked to the mining towns of California and Nevada's Comstock Lode. By 1860, Irish were the largest immigrant group in the West, comprising one-fifth of all immigrants to the region. Only in New Mexico and Utah were they heavily outnumbered by other nationalities (English and Welsh in Utah and Mexicans in New Mexico). Immigration continued after the Civil War. Irish immigrants played key roles in the mining industries in Colorado and Montana and in the construction of the transcontinental railroad. Some settled in the Northwest, where they secured work in industries. Others moved west to escape poor conditions and prejudice in eastern factories and cities. Few farmed; they lacked both capital to buy land and large-scale farming expertise. As late as 1890, the Irish were the second largest immigrant group in the Far West, tallied in the census at 113,647.

As with all immigrant groups, the Irish were not distributed equally across the West. They concentrated in states with mining and industry—especially California, Montana, and Colorado. They wielded particular political power in San Francisco, where nearly sixteen thousand lived in 1900, and in the copper mining and smelting centers of Butte and Anaconda, where they comprised over one-fourth of the immigrants. In Storey County, Nevada, in 1880, when the Virginia City mines were at their peak, 27 percent of the immigrants were Irish. In the nineteenth century, most of the Irish in the West were single men. Few Irish women chose to go to the western states and those who did lived in the cities rather than in the mining camps.[20]

The Irish did not escape all discrimination by coming west. Many westerners opposed them, especially because the Irish were Catholic. Emmons refers to the California Organizations of Vigilance as the Know-Nothing Party of the Pacific. Many westerners believed the Irish were not their equals; they had to be made "white" by adopting Protestant American ideals and reducing their connections to Catholicism. The Irish shared prejudiced American views of Native Americans and Chinese, but at least some of their contempt of the Chinese arose from labor issues rather than ethnoracial biases.[21]

Southern and Eastern Europe: Italy, Russia, and Austria-Hungary

To an even greater degree than Irish Catholics, immigrants from Russia, Italy, Greece, and Slavic-speaking regions of Austria-Hungary were spurned because of their religious beliefs, complexions, poverty, and labor practices. While Europeans from many countries in southern and eastern Europe settled in the West, the Italians were most numerous. In 1900, Italians were the seventh largest immigrant group in the Far West. The arrival of more Italians during the Progressive Era pushed their ranking to fourth by 1910 and second by 1920. Italians were the largest immigrant group in Nevada, Colorado, and California in 1920. They secured work in the West's mines, smelters, lumber mills, railroads, and fisheries; some became truck farmers and others developed successful wineries, fruit-packing sheds, and canneries. They settled in large numbers in San Francisco and were disproportionately represented in the coal-mining districts of Trinidad and Ludlow in Colorado and the copper mines of Ely, Nevada. Regional origins and culture affected the Italian immigrant experience: northern Italians often assimilated faster because they had lighter skins and some were Protestants. Southern Italians were sometimes employed as strikebreakers, and that, along with their peasant backgrounds, Catholicism, and dark complexions, led to negative stereotyping.[22]

German-speaking Russians from the Volga River valley settled on the high plains of Colorado and Montana and in eastern Washington beginning in the 1870s. But the great decades of migration from Russia were from 1900 to 1917. By 1920, some 1.4 million Russian immigrants, most of them Jews who had fled anti-Semitic pogroms, lived in the United States. A small minority but a fairly large number of Russian migrants to America (72,000) had settled in the West by 1920. They included thousands of members of a persecuted Christian sect, the Molokans, who settled in the Los Angeles and San Francisco areas. The Molokans also established agricultural settlements in the rural interior West, such as Grouse Creek in Utah. After the Communist Revolution, few Russians were able to emigrate, but Russian immigrants who had initially settled in the eastern United States continued to move westward; thus Russians remained among the top ten immigrant nationalities in the region for decades.[23]

Thousands of Slavic-speaking immigrants from the Austro-Hungarian Empire came to the United States in the years prior to World War I. Many found work in the coal mines of northern New Mexico, Washington, southern Colorado, southeastern Wyoming, and central Utah and in the copper mining and smelting towns of Arizona, Nevada, Montana, and Utah. In 1920, they were more highly concentrated relative to the general population in Nevada, Montana, and Wyoming than in any other states in the country.[24]

Asia: Japan, China, Korea, Philippines, Vietnam, and Iran

The Chinese were the first substantial group of Asian immigrants to the West. Between the California Gold Rush and 1882, over three hundred thousand entered the United States, concentrating primarily in the Far West. Most of the emigrants were male laborers, half of whom left wives and children behind in China. They hailed primarily from the Pearl River Delta along the Chinese coast in Guangdong Province. Close to twelve thousand helped construct the Central Pacific railroad, and perhaps one in ten lost their lives to accidents or disease in the process. Thousands more worked in mines, fisheries, salmon canneries, or service establishments like laundries and restaurants. In 1880, Chinese comprised 38 percent of the population in Boise County, Idaho, a gold-mining region. In contrast, one in three residents of Clatsop County, Oregon, was Chinese in the 1880s because of the salmon-canning industry. In the 1870s and early 1880s, Chinese were the primary source of agricultural labor in California. They dug irrigation ditches, cleared and leveled land, and planted and harvested crops. Faced with mounting racism and violence, they clustered in Chinatowns. After Congress passed the Chinese Exclusion Act in 1882, which barred Chinese laborers from entering the country, the number of Chinese in the United States dwindled, although some new workers managed to come anyway.

A second infusion of Chinese immigrants came as refugees around the time of the Communist Revolution in China. This elite group included many professionals, academics, and business owners. After the Communist takeover, nearly all Chinese-speakers who entered the United States in the 1950s and 1960s came from Taiwan and Hong Kong. However, after the United States normalized relations with China in the 1970s, limited emigration was permitted. Some came from Guangdong Province to join their relatives in America and settled primarily in Chinatowns. Beginning in the 1980s, many more came illegally, paying a "snakehead" to smuggle them into the country. After the Tiananmen Square uprising, about sixty thousand Chinese intellectuals studying in the United States were allowed to remain permanently. By 1990, close to 236,000 immigrants from China lived in the West.[25]

Japanese ranked among the top ten immigrant groups in the West in the first half of the twentieth century. Many came first to Hawaii as contract laborers and then to California. The 1882 Chinese Exclusion Act indirectly created a demand for more Japanese immigrants by opening job opportunities that the Chinese had formerly filled. After the United States annexed Hawaii, Japanese residents there could move freely to the mainland. They were often perceived by Americans as "the other" because of their different culture, language, and physiognomy. A Gentleman's Agreement between the U.S. and Japanese governments in 1907–1908 reduced Japanese immigration. But with increased labor needs, more Japanese from Hawaii moved to the West Coast. By 1924, close to a quarter million Japanese immigrants had settled in the West.

The Japanese came as farm workers, but they were anxious to purchase their own land as well. By 1909 many Japanese had their own farms, but they still dominated the farm labor force in California. In many places they comprised more than two-thirds of the farm workers. Many who had their own land were truck farmers. In Washington, Japanese immigrants worked in fisheries. Japanese men frequently immigrated alone and later married picture brides from their homelands.[26]

Many Americans feared the Japanese. In 1919, for example, California senator James Phelan called Japanese farmers "the rats in the granary" and said they threatened "the white race in California."[27] With those attitudes, states passed laws against Japanese immigration. In addition, the U.S. Supreme Court ruled in 1922 that Japanese immigrants could not become naturalized U.S. citizens because of race, a ruling that was not reversed until 1952. The Japanese experienced their greatest discrimination when those residing on the West Coast were interned in relocation camps during World War II. Japanese immigration accelerated after the liberalization of immigration laws in the 1960s. In 1990, Japanese were the tenth largest immigrant group in the Far West.

Several thousand Koreans immigrated to the United States before the early twentieth century. Like the Japanese, some came to Hawaii and later moved to the mainland. The 1907 Gentleman's Agreement with Japan, which controlled Korea at the time, permitted Korean picture brides to emigrate, but not workers. Over the decades, a few political refugees and students came, such as Syngman Rhee, the future leader of South Korea. The McCarran-Walter Act of 1952 permitted one hundred Koreans to immigrate each year. However, thousands of Koreans who had married American GIs during and after the Korean War were exempt from the quota: close to 17,000 had followed their husbands to the United States by 1965, and many more came over the next decade. The Immigration Act of 1965 opened the door to other Koreans, mainly upper-middle-class professionals, students, and family members. Once in the United States, immigrants were able to sponsor the immigration of parents and siblings. The number of Korean immigrants soared in the 1970s and 1980s. By 1990, with over 261,000, they were the sixth largest immigrant group in the West. Nearly all had settled in California, where many operated fruit and vegetable stores and restaurants; Los Angeles boasted the largest Koreatown in the nation.[28]

Filipinos had unique opportunities to immigrate because of the United States' occupation of the Philippines for much of the first half of the twentieth century. Although they were not considered citizens, Filipinos could immigrate in that era as American nationals. By 1930, nearly thirty-five thousand Filipinos resided in the Far West. Some westerners voiced concerns in the late 1920s and 1930s that they drove down wages and did not assimilate well. Attempts to ship them back home during the Depression failed, but immigration stalled. Before World War II, most lived in "Little

Manilas" on the West Coast in Seattle, San Francisco, and Stockton. They worked in canneries, service industries, or agriculture. In the 1940s, Filipinos were encouraged to enlist in the U.S. Navy and then allowed to immigrate. After 1965, they came as family members of others who had previously immigrated and as medical and other professionals. While many settled on the East Coast, they also clustered in the large cities of California.[29]

Vietnamese are among the more recent immigrants, dating back to the United States' involvement in the Vietnam War. Among the first immigrants were the wives of American servicemen, eight thousand of whom had immigrated by the end of 1975. As the Communist forces took control of Saigon in 1975, the U.S. government airlifted those who had worked for the government, their families, and other refugees. About 130,000 were admitted. Hundreds of thousands more Vietnamese and other Southeast Asians—as many as 14,000 a month in some years—came as boat people in the 1980s. By 1990, over 316,000 Vietnamese immigrants resided in the Far West. The vast majority settled in California, with many others in Washington and Oregon, but they were scattered throughout the Far West: in 2010, there were nearly 19,000 in Colorado, over 17,000 in Arizona, and nearly 15,000 in Utah. Because they had higher education, the first wave of Vietnamese refugees coming in 1975 assimilated more rapidly than others who came in subsequent years. Even so, because of language and professional requirements, many took lower-paying jobs than their educational background warranted.[30]

In 2010, Asian Indians were the fourth largest immigrant nationality in the United States and the seventh largest group in the Far West. While many had settled in the East, they were the seventh largest immigrant group in California, Oregon, and Washington and the fourth largest group in Arizona. The East Indians are latecomers; few immigrated to the United States until after 1950. After 1965, more came as doctors and worked in hospitals. They also came as other professionals such as scientists and engineers. In 1989, Indians owned 40 percent of the smaller motels in the United States.[31]

Iranians came to the United States in modest numbers between 1950 and 1977. Most who came were students studying at American universities who secured employment in Iran following their graduation. Only about 34,000 permanently immigrated in that era. The Islamic Revolution of 1978–1979 which toppled Iran's American-backed ruler, Mohammad Reza Shah, induced thousands of western-educated, elite Iranians, along with religious and ethnic minorities, to seek asylum in the United States. Although the largest number (154,857) came between 1981 and 1990, nearly as many (153,808) came between 1991 and 2004. The continued influx made Iranians the tenth largest immigrant group in the Far West in 2010. Nearly half of all Iranians who came to America chose to live in California, where they were particularly concentrated in the Los Angeles–Riverside–Orange County area. College-educated and relatively affluent, Iranian Americans generally dispersed in suburban neighborhoods. As anthropologist Diane Hoffman observed in 1989, "Their great religious, political, and ethnic heterogeneity, and their lack of well-defined geographic communities and internal cohesiveness . . . make their status as a minority community somewhat problematic."[32]

Central America: El Salvador and Guatemala

The Salvadoran presence in the West was small until the late 1970s and 1980s when political instability and a ten-year civil war pushed refugees from that nation. In 1989 alone, over 57,000 entered the United States seeking asylum. Because the United States was assisting the Salvadoran government in its civil war, it insisted that most Salvadorans seeking entry were economic opportunists rather than genuine political refugees and refused to grant them asylum, making them illegal aliens. Church groups mobilized to assist the refugees economically and prevent their deportation. In the West, many Salvadorans labored at or below minimum wage in menial jobs but still managed to send substantial remittances to relatives back home. They clustered especially in California; in 2010, over 88 percent of the Salvadorans in the Far West lived in the Golden State. Nevada, with 17,562 Salvadoran residents, ranked second in the region.[33]

Guatemalans came to the Far West in much smaller numbers than the Salvadorans. In 1990 there were around 141,000 Guatemalans in the region compared to almost 290,000 Salvadorans. Guatemalans were the tenth largest immigrant nationality in the region. In the 1970s, migrants left Guatemala because of inflation, political turmoil, land shortages, and a population explosion especially among native groups. A massive earthquake in 1976 also led to some immigration. Most Guatemalan immigrants came after 1980 because of continued political unrest that made life difficult for peasants and landowners alike. Many entered America illegally, so it is impossible to establish an exact count. In 1984, some studies estimated that one million Guatemalan refugees had fled their country and traveled to Mexico, other Central American countries, and the United States. By 1990, roughly 59 percent of the Guatemalan immigrant population in the United States lived in the Los Angeles area. And as with most immigrant nationalities, Guatemalans are diverse. In their native country, there are twenty-three separate ethnic groups that have different languages and traditions.[34]

Who They Thought We Should Be

As these newcomers arrived, they met long-time residents who had their own ideas of what the immigrants should be. The interaction could produce a range of possible outcomes, some of which are described here. One possibility was assimilation. Some argue that in the United States assimilation has generally meant that an ethnic minority abandons its own culture and embraces the dominant Anglo-American culture. This kind of assimilation is sometimes referred to as Anglo-Conformity. Another outcome, fusion, describes two cultures that have completely blended together, but this rarely happens. Another possible response, cultural pluralism, entails all groups having a voice without fusing together. Severe conflict between groups who are unable to identify common interests can lead to extermination, expulsion, or secession. Segregation is a less drastic negative response.[35] These terms can be understood using food as a metaphor. Segregation is having meat and potatoes in separate spots on a plate, cultural pluralism is stew, and fusion is a puree where meat and potatoes have been blended until they become indistinguishable from each other. Anglo-Conformity would be a cultural stew that features meat and no potatoes.

Many scholars and Americans have described the United States as a melting pot, an idea that can be traced back to the late eighteenth century when Frenchman J. Hector St. John de Crèvecoeur wrote in *Letters from an American Farmer*, "Individuals of all nations are melted into a new race of men." The use of the term continued in the nineteenth century but received more attention when Israel Zangwill, a Jewish immigrant, wrote a play in 1908 entitled *The Melting Pot*.[36]

This "melting pot" worked for some groups. As Roger W. Lotchin points out, "The group currently labeled *Caucasian*, *white*, or *Anglo* initially came to the West as Jews, midwesterners, Germans, English, Canadians, Irish, Cornish, . . . Serbs, and so forth." Because "these groups are no longer Jewish, Midwestern, German, English, Canadian, Irish, Cornish, Basque . . . , Scots, and southerners, then the melting pot must have largely succeeded."[37]

By the 1890s, many old-stock Americans worried that the melting pot was not working for new immigrants, who were failing to conform to Anglo norms. While they celebrated their own immigrant ancestors they decried the corrosive impact of contemporary immigration.[38] When immigrants failed to learn English and embrace American traditions readily, politicians and social workers devised Americanization programs to assimilate them. In 1913, for example, the California state government created the California Commission of Immigration and Housing to encourage immigrants to learn English. Progressive reformers across the West promoted Americanization through programs such as home visits, evening English classes for adults, and school programs that involved both children and their parents. Americanization and English-speaking were linked to patriotism during World War I. In the 1920s, the federal government offered classes through its Bureau of Naturalization to encourage immigrants to conform linguistically and culturally.[39]

Even with these programs, many Americans in the nineteenth and early twentieth centuries feared that some groups, including Slavs, Greeks, Asians, and Mexicans, could not assimilate because of their cultural differences and supposed racial inferiority. And race was not necessarily based on skin color. At the turn of the twentieth century, the U.S. Immigration Commission hired anthropologist Daniel Folkman to prepare a dictionary of races which incorporated many stereotypes. As Charles E. Orser Jr. points out, "With every new wave of immigrants, American nativists racialized the newcomers by slotting them" in a lower echelon in the racial hierarchy.[40]

Alongside racial stereotypes, some Americans associated certain immigrant groups with political radicalism and therefore sought to exclude them.[41] Some immigrant laborers did bring a class consciousness and heritage of labor activism with them to the United States. In addition, immigrant groups were often attracted to what many mainstream Americans saw as radical organizations such as the Industrial Workers of the World (Wobblies). While the IWW was often associated with immigrants, and many of its leaders were newcomers to the United States, it appealed broadly to members of the working class who were underrepresented by the mainstream unions, such as hard rock miners and unskilled workers.

Reacting to stereotypes and the fear of immigrants that they fed, some Americans formed organizations that opposed newcomers or tried to alter the immigrant profile. Sometimes these groups succeeded in stirring up even more concerns about newcomers. The Know-Nothing party, formed in 1849 as the Order of the Star Spangled Banner, was an anti-immigrant, anti-Catholic party. In the 1880s some Americans embraced nativism in response to labor strife and radicalism. Competition with immigrants for scarce jobs during the depressions of the 1890s and 1930s made many Americans in those eras hostile to newcomers. The Red Scare of 1919 also fanned anti-immigrant hysteria.

After World War I, the United States chose to isolate itself from other countries. The Ku Klux Klan, which originally opposed Reconstruction in the post-Civil War South, became popular again partly because of its opposition to immigrants who were not white, Anglo-Saxon Protestants.[42] While most historians trace the beginnings of the twentieth-century Klan to Georgia, some evidence shows that there was an earlier, short-lived organization in San Francisco.[43] In some western cities like Denver the Klan promoted progressive political reforms more than it attacked ethnic minorities. But its agenda included underlying anti-immigrant messages. For example, the Klan women collected funds for a Protestant boarding school for orphans, but the school was also designed to keep children out of Catholic orphanages.[44] The Klan in Utah was comprised primarily of white Protestants who disagreed with Mormons but also persecuted Greek and Italian immigrants.[45]

The melting pot conviction and nativist anti-immigrant concerns became less common in the 1960s as minority groups demanded more rights and civil rights movements swept the nation. After those changes, fewer Americans demanded that all immigrants conform to a single standard. For example, in the late twentieth and early twenty-first centuries, there has been greater emphasis on allowing people to speak their native language and having society adjust to their culture. Some Americans began to describe the United States not as a melting pot but as a multicultural salad bowl, closer to cultural pluralism, where cultures were bound only by a salad dressing of laws and markets.

One quotidian food-related manifestation of Americans' greater affinity for multiculturalism is their use of salsa as a condiment. What was once considered Mexican is now a mainstay in the American diet. Sometimes the change in cultural behavior is so thorough that a second generation does not even recognize the cultural origins of the behavior. Economists Barry Chiswick and Paul Miller describe "a Korean immigrant teenager [who] indicated that she wanted to be just like other American teenagers. . . . [S]he wanted to eat pizza and bagels. When this story was told to a class, the students did not see the humor. They too were unaware of the immigrant origins of pizza and bagels."[46]

But the multicultural salad bowl approach, entailing acceptance of other cultures, did not catch on with all Americans or eliminate fear of immigrants. As Charles C. Alexander observed in 1966, "The Klan of the twenties has disappeared. But its spirit and its goals remain sustenance for new crusades for 100 percent Americanism and moral conformity."[47] In the 1980s and 1990s nativists fretted that many Latino and Asian immigrants were clinging too tightly to their native languages and cultures.[48] Through the rest of the twentieth century and into the twenty-first, some Americans feared that immigrants—especially the illegal ones—were taking American jobs, particularly when there were downturns in the economy.

Summary

Each chapter in this section extends and enriches the context for discussion of immigrant identity and Americans' expectations. The chapters demonstrate the importance of local context, immigrant agency, legislation, and activism in shaping and contesting identity. They focus upon a rich variety of western places and the people who lived there: California under Mexican rule, Utah during the construction of the transcontinental railroad, the West Coast during the Progressive Era, the Mexican-American border during the 1910s and 1920s, polyglot Los Angeles in the early twentieth century, and Montana copper mining and smelting districts from the 1880s to the 1930s.

Notes

1. Alejandro Portes and Rubén G. Rumbaut, *Immigrant America: A Portrait*, 3rd ed. (Berkeley: University of California Press, 2006), 120, 126–27; Jason McDonald, *American Ethnic History: Themes and Perspectives* (New Brunswick, NJ: Rutgers University Press, 2007), 171–76. See also Caroline B. Brettell, "Theorizing Migration in Anthropology: The Social Construction of Networks, Identities, Communities and Globalscapes," *Migration Theory: Talking Across Disciplines*, ed. Caroline B. Brettell and James F. Hollifield (New York: Routledge, 2008), 132.
2. Bureau of the Census, *Census of Population, 1950*, vol. 2, *Population: United States Summary* (Washington, DC: GPO, 1952), 122–23; Bureau of the Census, *Twelfth Census of the United States Taken in the Year 1900*, vol. 1, *Population*, part 1 (Washington, DC: United States Census Office, 1901), 732–33; Bureau of the Census, *Thirteenth Census of the United States Taken in the Year 1910*, vol. 1, *Population: General Report and Analysis* (Washington, DC: GPO, 1913), 794–96, 820–21, 847–49. Compare tabulations in Elliott Robert Barkan, *From All Points: America's Immigrant West, 1870s–1952* (Bloomington: Indiana University Press, 2007), 463, 486. Barkan's tabulations include Texas, Alaska, and Hawaii, states and territories excluded from our calculations.
3. The top European nationalities in California in 1930 were Italians (107,254), English (86,074), and Germans (81,840). Nearly 200,000 Mexican immigrants were living in California as well as 101,677 Canadians. Close to 21,000 Chinese immigrants, 48,642 Japanese, 12,700 immigrants from the Azores Islands, 6,112 Armenians, 5,119 Australians, and nearly 5,000 Turks resided there.
4. Bureau of the Census, *Fifteenth Census of the United States 1930: Population*, vol. 2, *General Report Statistics by Subjects* (Washington, DC: GPO, 1933), 234–36, 524–26; Campbell Gibson and Kay Jung, *Historical Census Statistics on the Foreign-Born Population of the United States: 1850 to 2000*, Population Division Working Paper No. 81 (Washington, DC: Census Bureau, 2006), [60–69], http://www.census.gov/population/www/documentation/twps0081/twps0081.html, accessed July 16, 2013.
5. *Fifteenth Census of the United States*, 234–36; Migration Policy Institute, Data Hub, "2009 American Community Survey and Census Data on the Foreign-born

by State," http://www.migrationinformation.org/datahub/acscensus.cfm#, accessed August 8, 2012, printed copy in authors' possession.

6. Susan J. Lapham, *The Foreign-Born Population in the United States: 1990* (Washington, DC: Ethnic and Hispanic Branch, Bureau of the Census, n.d.), http://www.pacificweb.org/DOCS/PopRaceAncestry/Ancestry/1990%20Foreign%20Born%20in%20the%20US.pdf, accessed July 17, 2013; Migration Policy Institute, Data Hub, "2010 American Community Survey and Census Data."
7. Bureau of the Census, *Fourteenth Census of the United States Taken in the Year 1920: Population*, vol. 3, *Composition and Characteristics of the Population by States* (Washington, DC: GPO, 1922), 49; *Fifteenth Census of the United States*, 236.
8. Ana Gonzalez-Barrera and Mark Hugo Lopez, "A Demographic Portrait of Mexican-Origin Hispanics in the United States," Pew Research Hispanic Trends Project (2013), http://www.pewhispanic.org/2013/05/01/appendix-a-geographic-distribution-of-mexican-immigrants-in-the-u-s/, accessed September 4, 2013.
9. Due to the large number of Italian and German immigrants in the East, in the nation at large Canadians were the third largest group from 1960 to 1980. See William A. Kandel, *The U.S. Foreign-Born Population: Trends and Selected Characteristics* (Washington, DC: Congressional Research Service, 2001), 6, http://www.fas.org/sgp/crs/misc/R41592.pdf, accessed July 31, 2012.
10. Migration Policy Institute, Data Hub, "2010 American Community Survey and Census Data."
11. Marianne Fedunkiw, "Canadian Americans," *Gale Encyclopedia of Multicultural America*, ed. Rudolph J. Vecoli (New York: Gale Research Inc., 1995), 1:238–51; Statistics Canada, "Ethnic Origins, 2006 Counts, for Canada," http://www12.statcan.ca/census-recensement/2006/dp-pd/hlt/97-562/pages/page.cfm?Lang=E&Geo=PR&Code=01&Data=Count&Table=2&StartRec=1&Sort=3&Display=All&CSDFilter=5000#Notes, accessed July 17, 2013.
12. Barkan, *From All Points,* 463, 486; Bureau of the Census, *Census of Population, 1950*, vol. 2, *Population: United States Summary*, 122–23; *Twelfth Census of the United States*, 732–33.
13. Roger W. Lotchin, "The Impending Urban Past," *Researching Western History: Topics in the Twentieth Century*, ed. Gerald D. Nash and Richard W. Etulain (Albuquerque: University of New Mexico Press, 1997), 61.
14. *Twelfth Census of the United States*, 738–40, 778–79, 792; *Fourteenth Census of the United States*, 48; *Fifteenth Census of the United States*, 234; Portes and Rumbaut, *Immigrant America*, 128–29. For more information on German Americans, see La Vern J. Rippley, "German Americans," *Gale Encyclopedia of Multicultural America*, 1:565–77, and Barkan, *From All Points*, 75–80. The German immigrant population illustrates the complex layering of immigrant identity. Many Jews who came west hailed from German-speaking states that became the German nation. In 1870 San Francisco had America's second largest Jewish community. By 1920 Los Angeles boasted the largest Jewish community in the West. Other German Jews moved to the Pacific Northwest, but they were present in many states. Their identity was influenced not only by their geographical origins and language but also their ethno-religious culture, their occupations and economic class, and the social organizations they joined in America. German Jews comprised 20 percent of San

Francisco's elite in 1880 and 8 percent of the elite in Portland in 1891. William Toll, *The Making of an Ethnic Middle Class: Portland Jewry Over Four Generations* (Albany: State University of New York Press, 1982), 5–6, 8–106, 107, 134.

15. Oscar O. Winther, "English Migration to the American West, 1865–1900," *Huntington Library Quarterly* 27, no. 2 (February 1964): 159–73; Sheldon Hanft, "English Americans," *Gale Encyclopedia of Multicultural America* 1:471–85; *Population of the United States in 1860; Compiled from the Original Returns of the Eighth Census* (Washington, DC: GPO, 1864), 578; Census Office, *Compendium of the Tenth Census (June 1, 1880)* (Washington, DC: GPO, 1883), 491–92.
16. Ferenc Morton Szasz, *Scots in the North American West, 1790–1917* (Norman: University of Oklahoma Press, 2000), xii, 11.
17. Barkan, *From All Points*, 173–84.
18. Lucille Anderson, "Melville Lutheran Church Complete History," (1976), http://www.peaksofglory.org/Websites/peaksofglory/Images/MLC%20Complete%20History.pdf, accessed July 18, 2013; Bureau of the Census, *Twelfth Census of the United States*, 768; Bureau of the Census, *Fourteenth Census of the United States Taken in the Year 1920*, 47; Jennifer Eastman Attebery, *Up in the Rocky Mountains: Writing the Swedish Immigrant Experience* (Minneapolis: University of Minnesota Press, 2007); Mark A. Granquist, "Swedish Americans," *Gale Encyclopedia of Multicultural America*, 2:1284–97. Granquist's entry offers limited information about the West.
19. Barkan, *From All Points*, 72–73, 173; John Mark Nielson and Peter L. Peterson, "Danish Americans," *Gale Encyclopedia of Multicultural America*, 1:410–24; information on the West on 414.
20. David M. Emmons, *Beyond the American Pale: The Irish in the West, 1845–1910* (Norman: University of Oklahoma Press, 2010), 216–19; Brendan A. Rapple, "Irish Americans," *Gale Encyclopedia of Multicultural America*, 2:731–49, esp. 734. *Population of the United States in 1860*, 405, 549, 565, 573, 578, 584; Census Office, *Compendium of the Tenth Census*, 520; *Twelfth Census of the United States*, 734, 738–41, 768.
21. Emmons, *Beyond the American Pale*, 85, 88, 89, 178, 225, 318–19.
22. Barkan, *From All Points*, 185–87; *Twelfth Census of the United States*, 732–33; *Fourteenth Census of the United States*, 47.
23. Barkan, *From All Points*, 17, 78, 79; Erika Lee and Judy Yung, *Angel Island: Immigrant Gateway to America* (New York: Oxford University Press, 2010), 211–46.
24. Joseph Stipanovich, *The South Slavs in Utah: A Social History* (San Francisco: R and E Research Associates, 1975); E. P. Hutchinson, *Immigrants and Their Children, 1850–1950* (New York: John Wiley & Sons, 1956), 51.
25. Judy Yung, Gordon H. Chang, and Him Mark Lai, eds., *Chinese American Voices: From the Gold Rush to the Present* (Berkeley: University of California Press, 2006), 1–6, 225–32; Barkan, *From All Points*, 60–68; Census Bureau, *Compendium of the Tenth Census* (Washington, DC: GPO, 1883), 344, 367.
26. Barkan, *From All Points*, 164.
27. Ibid., 163–64.
28. David M. Reimers, *Still the Golden Door: The Third World Comes to America* (New York: Columbia University Press, 1992), 3, 5, 29–30, 110–14; Lee and Yung, *Angel Island*, 177–210.

29. Reimers, *Still the Golden Door*, 6–7, 27–29, 108–10.
30. Ibid., 23, 93, 117, 175–88; http://www.migrationinformation.org/datahub/acscensus.cfm#, accessed August 2, 2012.
31. Reimers, *Still the Golden Door*, 114–16; http://www.census.gov/prod/2010pubs/acsbr09-15.pdf, accessed August 2, 2012.
32. Mary Gillis, "Iranian Americans," *Gale Encyclopedia of Multicultural America*, 1:719–23; Shirin Hakimzadeh and David Dixon, "Spotlight on Iranian Foreign Born" (Migration Policy Institute, 2005), http://www.migrationinformation.org/usfocus/print.cfm?ID=404, accessed August 10, 2012.
33. Portes and Rumbaut, *Immigrant America*, 132–34; Reimers, *Still the Golden Door*, 203–5.
34. Maria Hong, "Guatemalan Americans," *Gale Encyclopedia of Multicultural America*, 1:596–616; Nora Hamilton and Norma Stolz Chincilla, *Seeking Community in a Global City: Guatemalans and Salvadorans in Los Angeles* (Philadelphia: Temple University Press, 2001), 2. Bertis L. Embry, the father of Jessie L. Embry, one of the editors of this volume, worked for USAID designing irrigation projects for small farmers. Jessie was in Guatemala immediately after the earthquake in 1976 and saw the destruction. Her parents left Guatemala in the 1980s at the time of the new political and economic unrest. One friend, a woman from New Mexico married to a Guatemalan landowner, told of the repression of political dissenters during that time. For that reason, they spent much of their time in New Mexico.
35. Richard T. Schaefer, *Racial and Ethnic Groups* (Boston: Little, Brown, and Co., 1979), 33–35; McDonald, *American Ethnic History*, 53.
36. McDonald, *American Ethnic History*, 50–51.
37. Lotchin, "The Impending Urban Past," 61.
38. Roger Daniels, *Guarding the Golden Door: American Immigration Policy and Immigrants since 1882* (New York: Hill and Wang, 2004), 6.
39. Frank Van Nuys, *Americanizing the West: Race, Immigrants, and Citizenship, 1890–1930* (Lawrence: University Press of Kansas, 2002), 39–41, 57, 165.
40. Charles E. Orser Jr., *Archaeology of Race and Racialization in Historic America* (Gainesville: University Press of Florida, 2007), 1–2, 9, 40, 124, 181.
41. Herbert J. Gans, "Symbolic Ethnicity: The Future of Ethnic Groups and Cultures in America," *Ethnic and Racial Studies* 2, no. 1 (1979): 3–5.
42. Michael C. LeMay, *From Open Door to Dutch Door: An Analysis of U.S. Immigration Policy since 1820* (New York: Praeger, 1987), 31–32, 56–57, 77–80, 109.
43. Shawn Lay, "Introduction: The Second Invisible Empire," *The Invisible Empire in the West: Toward a New Historical Appraisal of the Ku Klux Klan of the 1920s*, ed. Shawn Lay (Urbana: University of Illinois Press, 1992), 4–5.
44. Betty Jo Brenner, "The Colorado Women of the Ku Klux Klan," *Denver Inside & Out*, ed. Jeanne Abrams et al. (Boulder: University Press of Colorado, 2011), 63–65, quote from 65. For more on the KKK in Denver, see Robert Alan Goldberg, *Hooded Empire: The Ku Klux Klan in Colorado* (Urbana: University of Illinois Press, 1981); and Robert A. Goldberg, "Denver: Queen City of the Colorado Realm," in *The Invisible Empire in the West*, 39–66.
45. Leonard J. Moore, "Historical Interpretations of the 1920 Klan: The Traditional View and Recent Revisions," in *The Invisible Empire in the West*, 30–33. Moore summarizes Goldberg's and Gerlach's arguments in his article. For Utah, see

Larry R. Gerlach, *Blazing Crosses in Zion: The Ku Klux Klan in Utah* (Logan: Utah State University Press, 1982); and Gerlach, "A Battle of Empires: The Klan in Salt Lake City," in *The Invisible Empire in the West*, 121–52.

46. Barry R. Chiswick and Paul W. Miller, "Immigrant Enclaves, Ethnic Goods, and the Adjustment Process," in *From Arrival to Incorporation: Migrants to the U.S. in a Global Era,* ed. Elliot R. Barkan, Hasia Diner, and Alan M. Kraut (New York: New York University Press, 2008), 84.
47. Charles C. Alexander, *The Ku Klux Klan in the Southwest* (Lexington: University Press of Kentucky, 1966), 256.
48. Rudolph J. Vecoli, "Return to the Melting Pot: Ethnicity in the United States in the Eighties," *Journal of American Ethnic History* 5, no. 1 (Fall 1985): 8–9.

1

Immigrants and Colonists
Three Accounts of Mexican California

Brett Garcia Myhren

Brett Garcia Myhren's article provides an excellent example of how difficult it is to define terms such as immigration and assimilation. First, he asks who an immigrant is. Technically, Americans who went to California before 1850 moved to Mexico. The first wave, those who came by sea prior to 1841, tried to fit into the Mexican society; the second, overland wave arrived after 1841 and refused to adapt to the predominant culture. Myhren's research shows that Oscar Handlin's "uprooted" and John Bodnar's "transplanted" are oversimplified metaphors for the immigrant experience. He argues instead for Dirk Hoerder's more complex views of migration and adjustment as multidirectional processes. Myhren makes this point through a careful reading of three texts written by immigrants to California before 1841: Alfred Robinson, a Euro-American; José Bandini, a Spaniard; and Hugo Reid, a Scot, wrote about their experiences with the politics and cultures of those already living in California. His examples show that assimilation takes place on several levels and is never the same. It sometimes takes place between the dominant culture and the newcomers, but it can also exist between minority groups. In addition, those attitudes are not static; they change as individuals and communities change. Myhren's comparisons are possible because he approaches these historical documents as literary texts; examines their writing styles, images, and tropes; and situates the texts within a broad literary and cultural context.

If asked to imagine an immigrant in California prior to its statehood, many individuals would picture a ragged, bearded man with a bottle of whiskey in his back pocket, a rusted rifle in one hand, and a homemade "Bear Flag" in the other. Someone with a little more knowledge of California history might imagine another potential immigrant, this one as lean as a New England winter, contemplative rather than boisterous, and modest but distinctive in his dress. If the two men stood in the same room, one might also imagine the second immigrant whispering in Spanish to his Mexican wife about the first immigrant's bad manners. Of course, both images are caricatures. Like most enduring images, however, they contain elements of truth, and they highlight a dichotomy that appears in scholarship.

What scholars know of early immigration in California, at least in its general outlines, is fairly easy to summarize.[1] It began roughly two decades before the gold rush with a small set of maritime merchants, mostly from the United States, who blended into the existing Californio culture, and whose arrival was partly due to a change in trading policy. During the Spanish period, the government in California outlawed trade with foreign vessels, a closed-port policy that was rescinded in 1821 when control of California shifted from Spain to Mexico. The more liberal policies regarding trade encouraged more foreign activity, which in turn attracted more foreign visitors, a number of whom elected to stay in California.[2] Because of their commercial interests, they were motivated to assimilate into local society, making use of its resources and social networks. They integrated using some conventional and powerful social tools: marriage with local women, conversion to Catholicism, and citizenship, which allowed them to own land.[3]

In the 1840s, these maritime immigrants were followed by overland immigrants who were not merchants, who were not eager to integrate, and who clamored for conquest. They typically did not marry into local families, did not convert to Catholicism, and, perhaps most importantly, did not change their citizenship. Indeed, these later immigrants are known for their refusal to adopt the customs of the new country. The most famous (or infamous) of them, the organizers of the Bear Flag Revolt, made separation from Californio culture into one of their primary markers of individuality.[4] Scholars typically designate 1841 as the beginning of this second immigration stage. This was the year that the Bidwell-Bartleson party entered California by wagon and precipitated a major shift toward land routes from the east, a shift that was accompanied by a rapid increase in the number of arrivals in California. Prior to this date, most immigrants to California came by ship, usually via an arduous voyage around the tip of South America.[5]

According to the conventional definition of the term, both those arriving before and those arriving after 1841 are immigrants. *Immigrant,* in this sense, simply designates "a migrant whose move has involved crossing at least one international frontier," regardless of the distance traveled.[6] Yet, as suggested by the brief description above, the first stage of immigrants to California appears to be qualitatively different from the second stage, a distinction that goes beyond means of arrival and considers degree of assimilation into California's culture.[7] It is worth asking, however, whether the first group was as inclined to assimilation as they seem to have been and whether the term *immigrant* sufficiently describes their complex behavior. These kinds of questions require an examination of immigration historiography and its vexed relationship with ideas of assimilation. A brief synopsis of that conversation may be helpful.

In the past, scholars imagined immigration as a linear progression from unassimilated outsider to assimilated insider, including a painful but necessary jettisoning of old cultural habits and attachments in order to acquire new ones, taking their cue from Oscar Handlin's *The Uprooted* (1951). Later scholars theorized, however, that immigrants did not completely cast off their former selves. John Bodnar's *The Transplanted* (1985) reconfigured Handlin's metaphor and heralded a shift in the way immigrants were understood, shifting the focus away from what was left behind to what was maintained.[8] During the 1990s, scholars continued to eschew debates about whether or not immigrants assimilated and embraced "the possibility of multiple identities and contradictory positions" existing simultaneously.[9] In the latest iterations, scholars have even begun to abandon terms like "immigrant" or "emigrant" in favor of the term "migrant," choosing to view the movement of people in terms of "migration systems" rather than linear movements across national boundaries.[10] Dirk Hoerder, one of the main advocates of the shift away from the linear, nation-state approach, describes the realignment this way: "A first reconceptualization thus involved the integration of the binary perspectives into *migration* history as well as recognition that people's moves, rather than being one-way routes, were multi-directional, could involve return, might be seasonal, multi-annual, or permanent, might be circular, in stages, or other."[11]

Three migrants who arrived in California in the years before 1841—Alfred Robinson, José Bandini, and Hugo Reid—wrote texts that complicate these old paradigms of immigration, especially in regard to California. All three of these writers are considered "immigrants" because they crossed a national boundary in their journey to California and arrived in a society with its own customs and culture, where they needed to adapt to survive. A careful reading of their texts, however, demonstrates how national and cultural allegiance fractured in the years before California statehood, often in surprising ways. Given the expectations for early immigrants in California and the contemporaneous literature by nonimmigrants, these three authors show that "assimilation," at least as represented in their texts, was a very complex process, one that frequently involved abrupt, even bewildering, shifts in allegiance.

These accounts suggest, first, that migrants who arrived before 1841 were not necessarily more assimilated than those who arrived later. Despite the appearance of acculturation into Californio society, their allegiance was often tenuous, compartmental, and opportunistic. Second, this fractured and ad hoc assimilation was not unique to migrants from the United States or even Europe. In fact, some of the migrants who were most closely connected to the culture of California and Latin America advocated almost as fervently for conquest as did U.S. migrants. Finally, not all migrants assimilated exclusively with the "dominant" culture. Some of the migrants who would appear most inclined to align themselves with the elite also adapted to and advocated for Native Californians, typically the least powerful members in local politics. The existence of these narratives does not mean that prior categories or descriptions of immigration to California are without merit, nor does it mean that these specific actors represent entirely new paradigms or patterns. Instead, these narratives suggest that scholars may want to re-examine the ways that some migrants to California are labeled or understood, especially earlier migrants, who occasionally appear to behave in ways quite different from stereotypical descriptions of immigrant behavior.

One of the best ways to see these complexities in individual immigrants is to examine their texts and treat them deliberately as writers, placing them within a broader literary and cultural context. While mostly ignored by literary scholars, a large body of literature was written about California before the gold rush and the Mexican-American War.[12] This literature was composed predominately by Spanish colonists and visiting foreigners and read by a global audience that included heads of state as well as common sailors, and it profoundly shaped the imagining of California in the years before it became part of the United States. Beginning in the early sixteenth century with the publication of Garcí Rodríguez de Montalvo's *Las Sergas de Esplandián*, writers fashioned an image of California suited to their imperial goals and continually reincorporated these tropes into later texts due to traditions of authorship. Primarily, they imagined California in polarizing terms as a vulnerable paradise or an empty wasteland, creating narratives that advocated intervention by their own governments. Early maritime writers like William Shaler and George Vancouver, for example, fixated on California's supposed penchant for indolence and squandered profit, while simultaneously highlighting its weak defenses, and inadvertently revealed the racial, economic, and political forces shaping their observations. Fur trappers, much like their ocean-based counterparts, continued to envision California as a contradictory place, both debased and alluring, in need of containment and rescue. Ultimately, whether they saw it as beautiful or awful, visiting writers agreed that California needed a fresh start and used this rhetoric, under the guise of "liberation," to promote a future under foreign rule.

This tradition of California writing offers a baseline by which to compare these narratives and to ask whether or not immigrants tended to see California differently. Did they, because of their status as immigrants, display an allegiance to the local culture that other travelers did not? Immigrant texts, in other words, should be read as part of a conversation that was over three hundred years old by the time they were written. If scholars look at the writing of immigrants against the backdrop of the writing of travelers, they can broaden their understanding of California literature and immigration.

A Euro-American Conversion: Alfred Robinson

According to the narrative of the early maritime immigrant, Alfred Robinson, a merchant and U.S. citizen from New England, was exactly the sort of person who should have best assimilated into Mexican California. He first arrived in California via a merchant ship out of Boston, but he decided to stay, unlike most traders working the California coast. He married Anita de la Guerra, the daughter of a wealthy Californio from Santa Barbara, and set himself up as a merchant, using the property he acquired through marriage to start a thriving business in hides and tallow. He also converted to Catholicism, learned to speak Spanish, and became a Mexican citizen.[13] Indeed, simply because Robinson *lived* in California, he offers a significant alteration from the usual pattern of shipping, trapping, exploratory, and scientific narratives, in which the foreign visitor observed the region then returned to a home or career someplace else, typically in Europe or on the eastern seaboard of the United States. Robinson, on the other hand, had worked in California since at least 1829, had lived there for many years before the war with Mexico, and had integrated himself into the culture by the time many later writers, such as Richard Henry Dana, first visited.[14] Thus, Robinson appears to be a Euro-American immigrant who not only assimilated into Californio culture but also depended on its customs, on its kin networks, and especially on its financial resources for his livelihood. Indeed, it's fair to speculate about whether Robinson would have survived in California without the connections and extensive property of his wife's family.

Robinson appears well positioned, as a Euro-American insider, to offer a distinctive viewpoint, and in some respects, Robinson's *Life in California* (published in 1846 and revised in 1891) offers the first evidence of a published defense of California culture coming from the Euro-American perspective. Robinson appears to offer the first instance of a Euro-American living in and writing from California with the interests and perspectives of its residents in mind, although there are certainly examples of Californios defending themselves in the late nineteenth-century narratives that

Bancroft recorded for his archives as well as in their self-published histories. His narrative was quite well known in the United States, though it was not as widely read as Dana's *Two Years Before the Mast*.

The main difference between Robinson's narrative and those of other foreign visitors emerges in the adjectives that convey the author's attitude toward the region. Robinson often uses words like "beautiful," "pleasant," "fine," and "magnificent" to describe California. Even the Catholic priests are occasionally described as "kind and generous" and the interior of churches as "imposing" and "attractive."[15] Robinson expresses his attitude early in his narrative. When he arrived in Monterey, for instance, at the moment he "was to look for the first time upon those shores which were to become for some years [his] home," he wrote this description:

> Its external appearance, notwithstanding it was built of adobe or brick, made by the mixture of soft mud and straw, modelled and dried in the sun, was not displeasing; for the outer walls had been plastered and whitewashed, giving it a cheerful and inviting aspect.[16]

While it is not an exclamatory endorsement, this description stands in marked contrast to those of many visitors, such as George Vancouver, who described California using words like "barren," "dreary," "lonesome," "stunted," "groveling," and "sterile." Nor is this an isolated passage. Later, Robinson describes Monterey as "situated on the declivity of a beautiful rising ground, the top of which is crowned with stately pines."[17]

Of course, these isolated examples don't necessarily mean anything about Robinson's overall allegiance. After all, many other writers were perfectly willing to praise the beauty of the natural landscape, then denounce the Native Californians and Californios as lazy, stupid, and ripe for conquest in the next sentence.[18] In other words, a few kind words about a mission or the pine trees do not necessarily alter the overall message of the text. Perhaps the primary difference between Robinson and other writers is his willingness to praise cultural features as well as natural features. Praising the natural environment, something almost all visitors to California did, required no concessions to the abilities of the local inhabitants; indeed, this praise was often part of a strategy to marshal excitement for conquest and depict the inhabitants as unworthy of ownership. On the other hand, praising a church, a tradition, or a mode of living did require the acknowledgement of certain local capabilities. The first kind of praise was much more common than the second, given most writers' arguments about the need for political intervention in California, not to mention their belief in the superiority of their own cultures.

Beyond his penchant for more liberal praise, Robinson also seems genuinely attracted to certain elements of Californio culture, and the argument for his integration gains credibility because of the variety of his comments. The text is filled with anecdotes, many of them humorous, that testify to his daily connection to Californio society. In this sense, the text almost reads like the collected articles of a local journalist's newspaper column. In one instance, a priest, trying to escape another priest in a water fight, grabs a bedpan and "let[s] it fly, contents and all, full into the face" of the other priest.[19] In another, the father at Mission San Luis Obispo regales Robinson with English phrases that he learned from a Scottish traveler, totally unaware that he had been taught insults instead of salutations.[20]

However, these anecdotal passages don't necessarily mean Robinson had completely aligned himself with the Californios. Despite his willingness to praise, there are indications of economic motivations in his attitudes. In part, the attitude suggested by his account of California reflects Robinson's position (at the time of composition) as a member of the elite Californio society, a convert to Catholicism, and a merchant with a financial and social stake in that society's reputation. For instance, Robinson's support of the Catholic missions looks incongruous with his Protestant New England background (and suggests religious assimilation with local culture) until one considers the enormous role the missions played in his financial future: they were the clients who supplied the bulk of his hides and tallow and had the most extensive financial resources for purchasing other products.[21]

In addition, Robinson wrote his share of stereotypical commentary. He blasts the government throughout the text as lacking "sagacity" and "energy" and claims that California "can never be in worse hands than the present."[22] In keeping with the standard discourse on appetites, Robinson says that the typical Californio loves "good eating," gambles on Sundays, and is inclined toward "excessive indolence."[23] He says that some priests, because of a "delicate constitution," cannot perform their duties without their daily ration of chocolate.[24] A military commander is described as a "little dried-up piece of vanity, who made up in boastful words what he lacked in physical proportions."[25] Of course, despite all of these problems, Robinson finds the compassion within himself to praise the women. For him, California surpasses all the rest of Mexico in its "display of female beauty." He writes, "No part of Mexico can show so large a share of bright eyes, fine teeth, fair proportions, and beautiful complexions."[26] Significantly, none of this praise extends beyond the physical. Finally, his assessment of Native Californians is even more condescending than his occasional remarks about the elite of California society. For example, the church is described as "well adapted to captivate the simple mind" of the California Native, who, despite this apparent indoctrination, "indulges to the most criminal excess" in gambling and other vices on the Sabbath.[27] All of this material might have been torn from the pages of a dozen other foreign narratives, including Dana's, the very work he was supposedly chastising for its characterizations of local culture.

Perhaps Robinson sounds like Dana in certain passages because, despite his residence in California, he ultimately wanted the same thing Dana wanted: conquest. In fact, Robinson reveals himself to be far less "assimilated" than he initially pretends, if one assumes that assimilation entails any loyalty to the government of the Californios. At the very least, he much prefers the U.S. government to that of the Mexicans. By the conclusion of the text, Robinson casts off any attempt at disguise or diplomacy and baldly states that California is a "grand region for colonization."[28] He even lists the areas that are "unoccupied" and "attainable" for this purpose,[29] then continues into a rehash of the tropes of Manifest Destiny, claiming, "The northern American population must roll on southward, and overwhelm, not only California, but other more important states."[30]

Robinson saves his most fervent advocacy for the last paragraphs of the book. Here his rhetoric rises to a pitch that alters the tone of the entire text. He imagines, in a classic gesture, the future of California as a political rescue.

> Why not extend the 'area of freedom' by the annexation of California? Why not plant the banner of liberty there, in the fortress, at the entrance of the noble, the spacious bay of San Francisco? It requires not the far-reaching eye of the statesman, nor the wisdom of a contemplative mind, to know what would be the result. Soon its immense sheet of water would become enlivened with thousands of vessels, and steamboats would ply between the towns, which, as a matter of course, would spring up on its shores. [. . .] The whole country would be changed. . . . Everything would improve; population would increase; consumption would be greater, and industry would follow.
>
> All this may come to pass; and indeed, it must come to pass, for the march of emigration is to the West, and naught will arrest its advance but the mighty ocean.[31]

Robinson cleverly fuses the notion of futurity with inevitability, so change in California becomes imminent and inexorable; it happens "as a matter of course." Not only is this change considered inevitable, but it is entirely positive. He implies that the future relies on motion and activity, associated with the conquerors, as opposed to stagnation and indolence, associated with the Californios. All of this, of course, is justified by the rhetoric of progress, though the change that he describes wouldn't mean improvement for everyone involved.

When this kind of commentary is considered alongside some of the more favorable passages, Robinson's usefulness as a counterpoint to colonial and imperial rhetoric in the mid-nineteenth century is diminished. Despite his maritime background and the period of his arrival, Robinson is hardly an example of an immigrant who assimilated into Californio culture, at least not to the extent that he championed the residents' interests and sovereignty in the face of U.S. encroachment. In fact, Robinson sounds like an apologist for empire rather than an acculturated Californio, though, as the next writer demonstrates, those roles weren't mutually exclusive. There may indeed have been a new kind of immigrant in California after 1841, but those who arrived before 1841 often displayed some of the same characteristics as later arrivals.

A Californio's Lament: José Bandini

If most foreign visitors to California in the late eighteenth and early nineteenth centuries described a bountiful landscape suffering under the mismanagement of the Spanish or Mexican government, it is worth asking what newly arrived Spanish-Mexicans thought of these assessments and what they thought of California themselves. While visiting foreigners frequently published accounts of their travels in California, there were few if any publications by locals, whether recent immigrants or long-time residents, a situation that continued until the second half of the century. For a variety of reasons, most accounts of California by Californios were written after statehood.[32] One interesting exception is a short narrative by José Bandini, an undated document probably written around 1828. Bandini's "Decrision de l'Alta California," composed of nineteen handwritten pages, was found in the Bancroft Library and published in the early twentieth century.[33] Though brief, it offers one example of a cultural and political worldview that emerged among some Californios in the early Mexican period and suggests possibilities for the imagination of California by a specific subset of its immigrants.[34]

Little is known about José Bandini's biography, but the little that is available helps to situate him in a specific economic and cultural context that sometimes goes unmentioned in accounts of early California. Bandini complicates the traditional understanding of immigration because, as a Spanish citizen who entered Mexico shortly after independence and embraced Mexican citizenship, he was an "immigrant," despite the fact that he would also be considered a Californio by most historians. Californios, of course, are not typically labeled as "immigrants" in the history of California; rather, they are considered part of the region's colonial culture, people who migrated to

California from another part of Spain or Mexico, often with the support of the government. The friction between these distinctions, and the fact that Bandini seems to fit both simultaneously, reveals the complexity of the situation with immigrants and immigration to California. In fact, designating Bandini as a Californio and an immigrant seems to be the most appropriate description of him and his political sympathies.

Bandini was born in Cádiz, Spain, in 1771 and moved to South America roughly twenty years later, eventually settling in Lima. Sometime during the early 1820s, he retired from the military and moved to San Diego, where he became a wealthy merchant and lived for the remainder of his life.[35] Some might argue that because he was born in Spain, which controlled California as a colony until 1821, he did not actually cross a national boundary. However, Bandini likely arrived in California after separation from Spain was complete. More importantly, according to his own account, he took an oath of allegiance to Mexico and claimed that his ship was the first to raise its flag. Indeed, the fact that he highlights these details suggests exactly the kind of behavior (renouncing old cultural ties and establishing new ones) that immigrants are supposed to exhibit under the old paradigm. Curiously, Bandini often writes in a way that also suggests allegiance with foreign or imperial interests rather than allegiance to his newly adopted culture. A closer look at his particular background reveals why his assimilation may have been more complicated than it initially appears.

Bandini was what Spanish speakers in the Americas would have called a "peninsular" Spaniard, meaning, according to the elaborate caste system prevalent in the Americas, that he was born in Spain and occupied the highest rung on the cultural ladder. Furthermore, as a wealthy male member of this already elite group, Bandini would have moved in the most powerful circles of society.[36] Bandini's elite position, and his investment in maintaining it, illuminates many of the comments in his description of California. The marginalization of Californios after the Mexican-American War has drawn important critical attention to their lamentable treatment by the United States. This situation has at times diverted attention from the vexed relationship that existed between Californios and Native Americans or even between Californios and other immigrants from Mexico, whom they saw as a lower caste than themselves.[37] In one sense, this attitude was common to peninsular Spaniards of this era and was a legacy of the colonial culture throughout the Americas.[38] In another sense, however, Bandini and his group were different than the other Spaniards, not only because they were residents of California who often deliberately forged an identity in contradistinction to Spain *and* Mexico, but because of the way they at times repeated the mantras about geography, Native Californians, and industry common to visiting foreigners. If nothing else, Bandini reveals the complicated racial and cultural boundaries in California, where various groups often sought to leverage their own positions by shaping the depiction of those around them.[39]

Bandini's relationship to the Native Californians, whom he castigates throughout the document, suggests the extent of this racism among the elites and the importance of maintaining distinctions between them. One paragraph, from his discussion of the missions, should suffice to convey the tenor of this rhetoric:

> The Indians are by nature slovenly and indolent, and their powers of understanding are greatly limited. In handicrafts they are imitators, never creators. As their true character is one of vengeance and timidity, they are inclined toward treachery. They do not recognize kindness, and ingratitude is common among them. Their present education is not the most suitable one for bringing out their intellectual powers, but even if it were, I doubt that they would ever be capable of responding to good influences.[40]

The key terms of this passage, "slovenly," "indolent," "timidity," and "treachery," recall earlier descriptions by European and Euro-American visitors and immigrants, not only in their unwillingness to acknowledge Native intelligence but especially in their focus on productivity.[41] Multiple times in the description, Bandini returns to the notion of "industry" or its opposite, "idleness." Perhaps most interesting, however, is that when Bandini uses these terms he isn't always talking about the Native Californians.

The friction between his descriptions of the "Indians" and of the inhabitants of the pueblos demonstrates how important racial designations were to Bandini. He writes, "The inhabitants of these pueblos are white people, and in order to distinguish them from the Indians they are commonly called gente de razón." He also comments that "the white people are robust, healthy, and well-built," and that their "fecundity . . . is extreme." Indeed, the further Bandini describes California, the more it sounds like a rehash of Edenic mythologies that began in the sixteenth century. He notes the very low death rate, and that "an age of eighty or one hundred has always been quite common." Furthermore, he says, "Most illnesses are unknown, and the freshness and hardiness of the people demonstrate the beneficial effect of the climate." In keeping with a tendency to return to gender in narratives of paradise, Bandini adds, "The women in particular always have roses in their cheeks."[42]

All of this fecundity and vigor, however, stands in contrast to the Native Californians, who, Bandini says, are "weak and without vigor."[43] While Bandini acknowledges that "venereal disease" dramatically affects their population, he also argues that "their customs" are to blame and remains invested in the idea that their problems are "innate" rather than learned, a point that he makes more than once.[44] In fact, Bandini remarks in passing, "It should be noted that their constitutions are very susceptible to the contagion," but he never acknowledges the deplorable living conditions in the missions, nor the fact that those "white people" he describes were often responsible for distributing the disease, many times through forced sex.[45]

The necessity of depicting Native depravity and infirmity as innate becomes clear when he continues his treatment of the "white" residents. Despite the picture of health that Bandini locates in the gente de razón, he admits that "most of them live in idleness." He continues in the tradition of Spanish and Mexican stereotypes, claiming, "They exert themselves only in dancing, horsemanship, and gambling, with which they fill their days. In most cases they ignore the arts, and I doubt if there is to be found anyone who practices a trade."[46] Over and over, Bandini returns to this theme, using words like "industrious," "indigence," and "enterprise."[47] As it turns out, these themes of indolence and paradise are not unrelated.

The connection between industry and climate appears most clearly in a section titled "Kingdoms of Nature," where Bandini again evokes the rhetoric of paradise, remarking that the "Vegetable Kingdom of this region cannot be surpassed." His most striking claim appears in this same section, in a statement that echoes with eerie similarity the comments of Dana, who would visit California shortly after Bandini's text was written, and those already written by George Vancouver, William Shaler, and other imperially minded writers. Continuing his enumeration of the fertility of California, Bandini writes,

> Fowls are abundant, and the sea provides the most delicious fish. Among amphibians one finds the rare otter, and the rivers of the interior offer asylum to the useful beaver. What riches could be supplied by such a variety of valuable animals! But, unfortunately, industry is unknown in California.[48]

It was a comment that anticipated not only the strategies of Richard Henry Dana, setting a fecund landscape against the laziness of its inhabitants, but even some of the sentiment in its suggestion of future potential. For instance, Dana's most famous quote, "In the hands of an enterprising people, what a country this might be!" highlights the future potential of California by contrasting it with the torpor of the present.

Bandini, then, may seem to be something of an anomaly in the literature of California in that he appears to appropriate the language of visiting foreigners and direct it at the members of his own community. Given the argument that those visiting foreigners were attempting to drive a wedge between the residents and the land so that they could justify their own calls for conquest, the use of this rhetoric by Bandini might seem inexplicable. One might ask what he hoped to gain by adopting such strategies when he was already a resident, even if a fairly recent arrival; would not need to manufacture a rationale for conquest; and would presumably gain nothing by it. A closer examination of some of his descriptions, as well as their likely audience, suggests that there was in fact much to be gained.

Bandini often repeats the language of visiting foreigners, especially those inclined toward mercantile goals, because he actually has many of their same interests, particularly the expansion and deregulation of markets. His commentary on the missions is revealing in this regard because he characterizes them as voracious and inconsiderate consumers of territory, "always opposing the private ownership of lands" around their own property. Furthermore, he writes,

> They have unfeelingly appropriated the whole region, although for their planting and for the maintenance of their cattle they do not need all they possess. It is to be hoped that the new system of enlightenment and the need for encouraging the resident gente de razón will compel the government to take adequate measures to reconcile the interests of all.[49]

This battle with the church over land that might be profitable in the hands of ranchers is buttressed by a discussion of the overburdened tax system, into which the missions do not have to pay, and an extensive discussion of the problem with regulations on trade, specifically the proposal to close most ports to foreign commerce.[50] In fact, Bandini's "description" of California really amounts to a detailed complaint about government regulation and its consequences. Along the way, he manages to insert details about the Native Californians or the pueblos or the Edenic landscape. Some of his section titles, like "Ports and Commerce" and "Revenue," suggest this inclination, but his conclusion makes his overall intent most clear, in which he plainly lays out the financial goals of his plan.

Thus, given his position and his purpose, Bandini's arguments shouldn't be so surprising. One might argue that Bandini has unwittingly adopted the language of the imperialists or colonizers, despite being an immigrant to Mexico who has assimilated into its society. There is, however, another potential perspective: While he may be using similar language, his response likely originated in his effort to secure additional personal advantages.[51] His description of the Native Californians certainly fits with those aims, as it fortified his position atop the racial hierarchy in California and further undermined the authority of a class of people who performed the bulk of the labor on those industrial ranchos he championed.[52] His adoption of Edenic rhetoric in descriptions of the landscape was likely influenced by circulating descriptions of California, but it also suited his purposes because it highlighted California's potential as a producer of mercantile goods. Even his comments on the indolence of the gente de razón can be interpreted as buttressing his own class position. On closer examination, for instance, he carefully notes, "Almost all [of the families] are the descendants of a small number of individuals who came with their wives from the Mexican mainland."[53] Thus, according to his logic, the so-called lazy people in the pueblo were not really like Bandini because, as a peninsular Spaniard and wealthy landowner, he could safely distinguish himself from them.

Bandini is hardly an example of an "assimilated" immigrant, despite the fact that he arrived in California already possessing the background for rapid acculturation (such as his language, his long residence in Latin America, and his Spanish heritage). Furthermore, his early arrival in California, long before the beginning of overland migrations from the United States, offers an example of an individual who cuts against the grain of the standard narrative. In spite of the way one might imagine Bandini to react in California, given his background and his apparently eager adoption of Mexican citizenship, he did not align himself with the existing culture but instead supported many of the same positions that were voiced by visiting representatives of imperial and colonial governments.

Hugo Reid: Immigrant and Ethnographer

If long-time residents like Robinson and Bandini, men who displayed all the outward signs of acculturation and regional loyalty, changed (or perhaps revealed) their allegiance as the cavalry of empire approached, one could be forgiven for expecting the same of a Scottish immigrant like Hugo Reid. As it turns out, Reid's writing offers an interesting contrast to the prevailing attitudes of foreigners in Mexican California. In the aftermath of conquest, while gold fever still raged, Reid wrote a text advocating not for Anglo supremacy but for the Native Americans of California. Rather than using "liberty" and "progress" as code words for the appropriation of resources by the new elite, Reid agitated for the rights of those who had arrived in California long before the Europeans.

Despite his unusual sentiments, Reid began his life in California as a typical European immigrant. Reid was Scottish and Protestant, an itinerant merchant who had worked in northern Mexico and South America. When he came to California to visit in 1832, long before U.S. control, he fell in love with a local woman and eventually decided to convert to Catholicism so that he could marry her and set up a business in Los Angeles. He became a Mexican citizen and a rancher who managed a significant amount of property in southern California.[54]

At this point, Reid's story sounds similar to that of other immigrants to California before 1841, such as William Hartnell, Henry Fitch, William Heath Davis, Abel Stearns, and Jacob Leese.[55] Unlike these other immigrants, however, Reid married an Indian woman, a member of the Gabrieleno tribe. Victoria Comicrabit was known to be a California Native, though she was living with an established Californio family as an assimilated member of the Spanish-Mexican society. As such, she was subject to the standard prejudices of the time. In fact, Reid was discouraged from marrying her because of her cultural heritage; his friends imagined Reid living in a squalid hut as a "squaw man."[56]

Reid's story was also different because at the end of his life, shortly after the U.S. conquest, instead of becoming antagonistic toward Native Californians, Reid became a public advocate of Native cultures. In the years just before his death, he began to write a series of letters that documented Native culture and advocated for its defense from destruction by encroaching U.S. laws and practices, which he published in the *Los Angeles Star* beginning in February of 1852. These efforts were both a labor of conscience and the work of a genuinely curious person who had no ethnographic education. At least in part from close association with his wife and her people, Reid saw the value in preserving what remained to be preserved of Native culture. This labor, according to his own writing, gave him enormous satisfaction, and when he died he was engaged in trying to write a grammar of the Gabrieleno language.[57] The twenty-two letters reveal the thoughts of a person who showed remarkable compassion and openness to cultures whose beliefs were far different from his own.[58]

Reid's letters also show that immigrants from places quite distant from California could not only appreciate local cultures but also align themselves with the underprivileged against those in power. While marrying into a local family and converting to Catholicism could be explained as calculated gestures with financial benefits for merchants or ranchers like Reid, there were few benefits, whether social or financial, associated with Reid's decision to write letters about the California Natives.[59] In fact, given the local interest in maintaining a docile and cheap workforce, with few protections under law, there were potential dangers in calling attention to Native Californians and treating them as if they were fully human. A writer who stirred up public sentiment in favor of the Natives could undermine the stranglehold ranchers and townspeople had on the Indian workers.[60] This type of action could, at best, force Reid into uncomfortable encounters with those in power. At worst, if the public became sufficiently motivated by calls for better treatment, Reid's advocacy could lead to policy changes that would negatively affect the balance sheets of numerous landholders, which would expose him to potential retribution.

One has only to recall Bandini's description of the Native Californians to understand how important Indian subjection was to the wealthy class, whether Spanish-Mexican or foreign. Furthermore, Robinson's text shows how easily a writer could turn from a position of tolerance to one of bald imperialism when publishing on the eve of the Mexican-American War or shortly after. Reid, though a long-time resident of California, began his project after the war, when the power of the United States was firmly established. It is possible that, at a low point in his life financially and physically, Reid felt that he had nothing left to lose. Furthermore, some have speculated that Reid hoped, with the publication of his letters, to secure the position of inspector of Indian Affairs.[61] Even if both of these suppositions are true, it is still remarkable to consider how Reid, an outsider to Native, Spanish, Mexican, and (to some extent) even U.S. culture, chose to take up the standard for the most embattled group in his adopted home.

A few examples from Reid's text demonstrate just how critical he could be of those controlling the Indians. Commenting on the treatment Indians received at the hands of Padre José María Zalvidea in the years before the war, Reid noted that "he must assuredly have considered whipping as meat and drink to them, for they had it morning, noon, and night."[62] Given their living conditions and this punishment, he remarked, "Indians of course deserted. Who would not have deserted?"[63] These kinds of statements were not without risk, and they did not go unnoticed. In fact, some scholars believe that a few of the original letters were destroyed after their initial publication, presumably by the church, because they were so critical.[64]

Yet, Reid did more than simply castigate the priests for their treatment of the Native Californians. He also made conscientious efforts to reveal the Indians' view of the Catholic religion and Spanish-Mexican culture in general. Glimpses into the Native view of California are extremely scarce, especially in the years before Helen Hunt Jackson's *Ramona* brought widespread attention to California.[65] Thus, the contents of these letters are especially valuable, even if the information is filtered through Reid. Baptism is one issue that is particularly interesting. Reid claimed that the Catholic ceremony "can hardly be said to be a conversion." Despite this, it was "of great advantage to the missionaries, because once baptized, they [Native Californians] lost 'caste' with their people."[66] As Reid points out, the baptism, far from being an empty ceremony, gave the priests remarkable leverage and the ability to coerce and control whole communities.

Baptism, according to the Natives, was "ignominious and degrading," and because of the effect it had on perception among Native Californians, the priests knew that they could manipulate individual families and often whole communities. They typically baptized babies and children first so that, as Reid notes, they had leverage over the rest of the family.

> The consequence was, first, the women consented to the rite and received it, for the love they bore their offspring; and finally the males gave way for the purpose of enjoying once more the society of wife and family. Marriage was then performed, and so this contaminated race, in their own sight and that of their kindred, became followers of Christ.[67]

It is easy to see why this kind of commentary didn't endear Reid to the clergy. Indeed, it is somewhat remarkable that Reid maintained his popularity in local circles after publishing materials that likely would have inspired recriminations.

At other times, Reid's commentary reveals a humorous side to the Natives' view of the arriving Spaniards. For example, he recalls that Indians "refused to eat pork, alleging the whole family to be transformed Spaniards!"[68] In another instance, Reid notes that, after having witnessed the Spanish kill animals, the Indians realized that the newcomers were merely "human beings, of a nasty white color, and having ugly blue eyes!"[69] These examples suggest that Reid was willing to look at European culture without feeling defensive; after all, the Indians were describing someone who looked like Reid himself.

Finally, Reid spent a considerable amount of time on Native culture, especially stories and traditions, which is remarkable given the fact that this was exactly the kind of material that was usually ignored or ridiculed in prior accounts of California. For example, Father Geronimo Boscana repeatedly mocks Native culture in his account of the Indians of San Juan Capistrano.[70] Reid, in contrast, generally presents indigenous traditions in a way that is, if not completely neutral, more even-handed. He discusses marriage, birth, puberty rites, and funerals. He even retells three traditional stories in extended detail.

Because of Reid's personal connection to Native Californians, he didn't romanticize the past the way other immigrant observers often did. For example, there was little of the Edenic paradise in Reid's account of California before the Spanish arrived. He does claim, in a section on laws and government, "Robbery was never known among them. Murder was of rare occurrence, and punished with death."[71] Reid's description of this period, however, lacks the gauzy images of Native Californians lounging in the shade and fattening themselves on the bountiful landscape. For example, the English merchant, Alexander Forbes, who had some contact with Reid in Mexico and who published his *History of California* in 1839, described the Native Californians as "basking, in dreamy inactivity, on the banks of their rivers, or on the shores of the ocean" before the advent of the Spaniards.[72] Instead, Reid sounds like an interested observer, surprised at times by customs different than his own but willing to record those customs with generosity and open-mindedness.

In his assessments of the landscape, he avoids the common urge to imagine a blissful, fertile past that vanishes under the pragmatic and implacable forces of progress. For example, he notes that the site of the mission was "at the conquest of this country, a complete forest of oaks, with considerable underwood."[73] After having been cleared for the mission, Reid remarked that it became a "washed waste of gravel and sand."[74] In this case, Reid's comment sounds more like a frank assessment rather than a paean to an imagined past. Thus, unlike most writers, Reid strikes a balance between extremes: outright denigration of the past or outright adulation, both of which typically serve the self-interest of the writer commenting on the present. For Reid, the present was a reminder of the ways that Indians had been ill-served by the Spaniards, Mexicans, and Euro-Americans.

While most immigrants to California in the years before the Mexican-American War lived in two cultures (that which they carried with them and the Mexican-Spanish culture they saw around them), Reid might be said to have lived in three cultures. As a Scottish immigrant, he moved easily among Euro-American and European traders, especially those from England, as evidenced by his connections with Alexander Forbes in Mexico. Furthermore, as an immigrant to California and a trader with experience in South America, Reid moved fluidly among the Spanish-speaking people of California and Mexico. In fact, his letters themselves are a testament to his very thorough integration into local society; many of the letters are written partially in Spanish, and he constantly peppered his English with Spanish phrases. Finally, Reid traveled in the world of the Native Californians, where he was well known and respected. Reid raised his wife's Native children as his own and, though he never became fluent in the language, learned many Native words.

Despite his remarkable accomplishments, Reid was not a saint. Like many other compelling figures from the early nineteenth century, Reid presents contradictions that are hard to reconcile with his writing. For example, he and his wife, Victoria, kept Indian servants whose lives and wages were essentially regulated with alcohol. Furthermore, there is evidence that, even as Reid was composing the letters that he had long promised Victoria he would write, he temporarily abandoned the family, perhaps out of frustration with his financial reverses.[75] But Reid presents an interesting counter-example, given the frequent stories of foreigners coming to California and embedding themselves in a society principally so they might acquire the leverage to wrest it from those in power. Unlike those men with whom he worked and conversed, Reid was not primarily interested in conquest, and he was unafraid to advocate for the Native Californians even as the new regime sought to undermine their political influence and limit their territory.

Conclusion

Ultimately, all three writers demonstrate that immigrants who arrived in California before 1841 did not always conform to the narrative of assimilation suggested by scholarship on Mexican California, nor did their complex attitudes align with the old paradigms of immigration theory.[76] On the one hand, despite the fact that early migrants willingly adopted some local customs in exchange for access to resources, early migrants were not necessarily more closely allied with California's local culture than the migrants who arrived after 1841, especially considering the former group's advocacy for foreign intervention. On the other hand, these early migrants were not exactly like colonists or imperialists, either, people with no allegiance to Mexico who favored and perhaps precipitated the invasion of California by the United States. Instead, they exhibited a malleable and ad hoc allegiance to their former homes as well as their new home in California. Furthermore, while immigrants may have different attitudes than short-term visitors, a writer's status as an immigrant does not necessarily reveal any patterns about that person's beliefs or reactions to the region. Immigrants to California were as varied and complicated as immigration itself, and an immigrant's religion, place of birth, economic status, or political inclinations do not necessarily predict behavior or allegiance. This was as true for Reid as it was for Bandini and Robinson. Finally, and perhaps most importantly, immigrant attitudes were not static, but often fluctuated based on a multitude of external pressures, which were themselves in constant flux. Immigrants who relocated to California in the decades before the gold rush entered a complex and dynamic cultural system, one that produced various colonial and imperial reactions even as it created opportunities for more locally rooted points of view.

Notes

1. For an overview of immigration to California prior to 1846, see Doyce B. Nunis, "Alta California's Trojan Horse: Foreign Immigration," in Ramón Gutiérrez and Richard J. Orsi, eds., *Contested Eden: California Before the Gold Rush* (Berkeley: University of California Press, 1998). For additional material on immigration in California before 1846, see Douglas Monroy, *Thrown among Strangers: The Making of Mexican Culture in Frontier California* (Berkeley: University of California Press, 1990), especially 154–62; Kevin Starr, *Americans and the California Dream, 1850–1915* (Oxford: Oxford University Press, 1973), especially 11–34. For chapters on specific immigrants from the United States, see Charles B. Churchill, *Adventurers and Prophets: American Autobiographers in Mexican California, 1828–1847* (Spokane: Arthur H. Clark, 1995). Discussions of immigration in northwestern Mexico more generally can be found in David J. Weber, *The Mexican Frontier, 1821–1846: The American Southwest Under Mexico* (Albuquerque: University of New Mexico Press, 1982), 122–46, 179–206. For a wide-angle treatment of the Spanish borderland, see David J. Weber, "Conflicts and Accommodations: Hispanic and Anglo-American Borders in Historical Perspective, 1670–1853," *Journal of the Southwest* 39, no. 1 (Spring 1997): 1–32. For a treatment of immigration to Mexico as a whole, including the early national period, see Jürgen Buchenau, "Small Numbers, Great Impact: Mexico and Its Immigrants, 1821–1973," *Journal of American Ethnic History* 20, no. 2 (Spring 2001): 23–30.
2. It is true that this policy was not evenly enforced prior to 1821 and that there are many instances of illicit trade in California. Furthermore, policies emerging in Mexico City were often slow to arrive in Alta California. Despite these complications, the shift remains significant.
3. Recent scholarship has examined marriages between immigrants and Californios. See Louise Pubols, *The Father of All: The de la Guerra Family, Power, and Patriarchy in Mexican California* (Berkeley: University of California Press, and San Marino: Huntington Library, 2009); María Raquél Casas, *Married to a Daughter of the Land: Spanish-Mexican Women and Interethnic Marriage in California, 1820–1880* (Reno: University of Nevada Press, 2007); Miroslava Chávez-García, *Negotiating Conquest: Gender and Power in California, 1770s to 1880s* (Tucson: University of Arizona Press, 2004); Deborah Moreno, "'Here the Society is United': 'Respectable' Anglos and Intercultural Marriage in Pre-Gold Rush California," *California History* 80, no. 1 (Spring 2001): 2–17.
4. Scholarship on the first overland immigrants can be found in the sources listed above. For a list of overland immigrants who became residents, see Nunis, "Alta California's Trojan Horse," 312. For general material on trappers and trade, see Robert Utley, *A Life Wild and Perilous: Mountain Men and Paths to the Pacific* (New York: Henry Holt, 1997); Le Roy Hafen, ed., *Fur Trappers and Traders of the Southwest: Twenty Biographical Sketches* (Logan: Utah State University Press, 1997); Robert Glass Cleland, *This Reckless Breed of Men: The Trappers and Fur Traders of the Southwest* (Albuquerque: University of New Mexico Press, 1976; rpt. 1950); David J. Weber, *The Taos Trappers: The Fur Trade in the Far Southwest, 1540–1846* (Norman: University of Oklahoma Press, 1971).
5. For material on the 1841 immigrants, see Doyce B. Nunis, ed., *The Bidwell-Bartleson Party: 1841 California Emigrant Adventure: The Documents and Memoirs of the*

Overland Pioneers (Santa Cruz: Western Tanager Press, 1991), and Nunis, "Alta California's Trojan Horse."

6. Roger Daniels, *Coming to America: A History of Immigration and Ethnicity in American Life* (New York: Harper Collins, 1990), 3.
7. See Starr, *Americans and the California Dream*, 21–25, for an example of this distinction.
8. See Oscar Handlin, *The Uprooted: The Epic Story of the Great Migration that Made the American People* (Boston: Little and Brown, 1951); and John Bodnar, *The Transplanted: A History of Immigrants in Urban America* (Bloomington: Indiana University Press, 1985). Handlin's thesis was also critiqued in two important papers that set the trajectory for the next round of scholarship. See Frank Thistlethwaite, "Migration from Europe Overseas in the Nineteenth and Twentieth Centuries," in *A Century of European Migrations, 1830–1930*, ed. Rudolph J. Vecoli and Suzanne M. Sinke (Urbana: University of Illinois Press, 1991), reprint 1960; and Rudolph J. Vecoli, "*Contidini* in Chicago: A Critique of *The Uprooted*," *Journal of American History* 51 (1964): 404–17. Though Handlin, Thistlethwaite, Vecoli, and Bodnar have powerfully influenced early scholarship on immigration, other scholars were obviously part of this conversation. A very brief sample of these early texts might include: John Higham, *Strangers in the Land: Patterns of American Nativism, 1860–1925* (New Brunswick, NJ: Rutgers University Press, 1955); Maldwyn Jones, *American Immigration* (Chicago: University of Chicago Press, 1960); John Higham, *Send These to Me: Immigrants in Urban America* (Baltimore: Johns Hopkins University Press, 1975); Leonard Dinnerstein and David Reimers, *Ethnic Americans: A History of Immigration and Assimilation* (New York: New York University Press, 1977); Maxine Seller, *To Seek America: A History of Ethnic Life in the United States* (Englewood, NJ: Jerome Ozer, 1977); and Thomas J. Archdeacon, *Becoming American: An Ethnic History* (New York: The Free Press, 1983).
9. George Sánchez, *Becoming Mexican American: Ethnicity, Culture and Identity in Chicano Los Angeles, 1900–1945* (New York: Oxford University Press, 1993), 8. Sánchez offers a lucid gloss of the debates in immigration scholarship in his introduction, 3–14.
10. Dirk Hoerder is probably the most well-known proponent of this theory. See *Cultures in Contact: World Migrations in the Second Millennium* (Durham, NC: Duke University Press, 2002). For additional comments on this shift, see Suzanne M. Sinke, "Crossing National Borders: Locating the United States in Migration History," *OAH Magazine of History* 19, no. 3 (May 2005): 59; and David A. Gerber, "Forming a Transnational Narrative: New Perspectives on European Migrations to the United States," *The History Teacher* 35, no. 1 (November 2001): 67.
11. Dirk Hoerder, "Historians and Their Data: The Complex Shift from Nation-State Approaches to the Study of People's Transcultural Lives," *Journal of American Ethnic History* 25, no. 4 (Summer 2006): 85–96.
12. For examples of this tendency to underrepresent the early literature, see David Wyatt, *The Fall into Eden: Landscape and Imagination in California* (Cambridge: Cambridge University Press, 1986), or Stephen Fender, *Plotting the Golden West: American Literature and the Rhetoric of the California Trail* (Cambridge: Cambridge University Press, 1981). Likewise, Lawrence Clark Powell, *California Classics: The*

Creative Literature of the Golden State (Santa Barbara: Capra Press, 1982), and Franklin Walker, *A Literary History of Southern California* (Berkeley: University of California Press, 1950), focus on the mid- or late nineteenth century. Anthologies of literature often reflect this situation, such as Dana Gioia, Chryss Yost, Jack Hicks, eds., *California Poetry: From the Gold Rush to the Present* (Berkeley: Heyday Books, 2004); Gerald Haslam, ed., *Many Californias: Literature from the Golden State*, (Reno: University of Nevada Press, 1999); and Leonard Michaels, David Reid, and Raquel Scherr, eds., *West of the West: Imagining California* (San Francisco: North Point Press, 1989). Most of these collections make an attempt to incorporate the early nineteenth century, but the majority of the texts come from the twentieth. Some anthologies have incorporated older literature, such as John W. Caughey and LaRee Caughey, eds., *California Heritage: An Anthology of History and Literature* (Itasca, IL: Peacock Publishers, 1971); Jack Hicks et al., eds., *The Literature of California: Writings from the Golden State* (Berkeley: University of California Press, 2000); and W. Storrs Lee, ed., *California: A Literary Chronicle* (New York: Funk & Wagnalls, 1968), though many opportunities for expansion remain. This period has not, however, been ignored by historians, who have published frequently on early California. Some editors, such as Rose Marie Beebe and Robert M. Senkewicz, and certain publishers, such as Heyday, have been very helpful in this regard. See Beebe and Senkewicz, *Lands of Promise and Despair: Chronicles of Early California, 1535–1846* (Berkeley: Heyday Books, 2001); Beebe and Senkewicz, *Testimonios: Early California through the Eyes of Women, 1815–1848* (Berkeley: Heyday Books, 2006); and Joshua Paddison, *A World Transformed: California before the Gold Rush* (Berkeley: Heyday Books, 1999).

13. Adele Ogden, "Alfred Robinson, New England Merchant in Mexican California," *California Historical Society Quarterly* 23, no. 3 (September 1944). Material on the de la Guerras can be found in Pubols, *The Father of All*.
14. Dana shipped to California as a common sailor in the mid-1830s, despite being from an elite Boston family, and wrote what is arguably the most famous and influential of the early narratives on California, *Two Years Before the Mast* (1840). The best sources on Robinson are Charles B. Churchill, *Adventurers and Prophets: American Autobiographers in Mexican California, 1828–1847* (Spokane: Arthur H. Clark, 1995), 17–35; and Ogden, "Alfred Robinson, New England Merchant in Mexican California," 193–218. Biographical material can also be found in Andrew Rolle's introduction to Alfred Robinson, *Life in California* (Santa Barbara: Peregrine, 1970); Maynard Geiger, ed., *The Letters of Alfred Robinson to the De la Guerra Family of Santa Barbara, 1834–1873* (Los Angeles: Zamorano Club, 1972); and Adele Ogden, "Business Letters of Alfred Robinson," *California Historical Society Quarterly* 23, no. 4 (December 1944): 301–34. For background on shipping and trade, see Adele Ogden, *The California Sea Otter Trade, 1784–1848* (Berkeley: University of California Press, 1941); Terrence J. Barragy, "The Trading Age, 1792–1844," *Oregon Historical Quarterly* 76, no. 3 (Spring 1975): 197–224; and Bruno Fritzsche, "'On Liberal Terms': The Boston Hide-Merchants in California," *Business History Review* 42, no. 4 (Winter 1968): 467–81. For treatments of the Californio society and marriage, see Pubols, *The Father of All*, 105–47; Albert Hurtado, *Intimate Frontiers: Sex, Gender, and Culture in Old California* (Albuquerque: University of New Mexico Press, 1999), 21–44; María Raquél

Casas, *Married to a Daughter of the Land: Spanish-Mexican Women and Interethnic Marriage in California, 1820–1880* (Reno: University of Nevada Press, 2007); and Moreno, "'Here the Society is United,'" 2–17.

15. Robinson, *Life in California*, 18.
16. Ibid., 7.
17. Ibid., 8.
18. *Native Californians* here refers to the indigenous inhabitants of California, those people who inhabited the region before the arrival of Europeans. *Californios*, on the other hand, is a somewhat flexible regional term that generally refers to Spanish-speaking people who trace their roots in California to the eighteenth and nineteenth centuries.
19. Ibid., 96.
20. Ibid., 74–75.
21. Churchill, *Adventurers and Prophets*, 25, makes a compelling case for the influence of finance in some of Robinson's contradictory remarks. Robinson was most likely financially adept, given his years in the hide trade. See Bruno Fritzsche, "On Liberal Terms," 467–81, especially 475.
22. Robinson, *Life in California*, 11 and 138.
23. Ibid., 55, 67, and 99.
24. Ibid., 65.
25. Ibid., 66.
26. Ibid., 50.
27. Hugo Reid, discussed in the next section, says similar things, but he also elaborates on the social pressures behind such claims.
28. Ibid., 150.
29. Ibid., 151.
30. Ibid., 155.
31. Ibid., 157.
32. There are, of course, letters and municipal documents, but there do not appear to be any published assessments of the region before 1846 by local writers. There were certainly literate people in California, but the printing press was a relatively late arrival to the region, and for those capable of writing about it, publication was not the most pressing concern. Furthermore, many foreigners had the benefit of state sponsorship to fund their often lavish publications. Most of what we know about local attitudes toward foreigners comes from the oral narratives recorded by Bancroft in the late nineteenth century. See David J. Weber, *The Californios vs. Jedediah Smith, 1826–1827: A New Cache of Documents* (Spokane, WA: A. H. Clark, 1990), for an interesting compilation of historical documents that tell another side of the Euro-American story.
33. Published in English as José Bandini, *A Description of California in 1828*, trans. Doris Marion Wright (Berkeley: Friends of the Bancroft Library, 1951). All translations are from this edition.
34. See Doris Marion Wright, introduction to *A Description of California in 1828*, vii. For an excellent history of one Californio family, see Pubols, *The Father of All*. For further material on the Californios, see Rosaura Sánchez, *Telling Identities: The Californio Testimonios* (Minneapolis: University of Minnesota Press, 1995); Genaro Padilla, *My History, Not Yours: The Formation of Mexican-American*

Autobiography (Madison: University of Wisconsin Press, 1993); and Leonard Pitt, *The Decline of the Californios: A Social History of the Spanish-Speaking Californians, 1846–1890* (Berkeley: University of California Press, 1966), a dated but still useful text. Further information can be gleaned from the introductory materials in Antonio María Osio, *The History of Alta California: A Memoir of Mexican California*, Rose Marie Beebe and Robert M. Senkewicz, trans. and eds. (Madison: University of Wisconsin Press, 1996); María Amparo Ruiz de Burton, *The Squatter and the Don*, Sánchez and Pita, eds. (Houston: Arte Público Press, 1997); and *Testimonios: Early California through the Eyes of Women*.

35. Scholarship on José Bandini is extremely scarce. This material comes from Wright, *A Description of California in 1828*, vi–vii. See also F. Arturo Rosales, "Fantasy Heritage Reexamined: Race and Class in the Writings of the Bandini Family Authors and Other *Californios*, 1828–1965," in *Recovering the U.S. Hispanic Literary Heritage*, vol. 2 (Houston: Arte Público Press, 1996), 81–87. There is more material on his son, Juan Bandini, and some general details can be gleaned there.
36. Pubols, *The Father of All*, 14–18. Another revealing detail in this regard is the fact that Bandini's description was written originally for Eustace Barron, the business partner of Alexander Forbes, who would eventually write a widely read history of California, a text that was instrumental in shaping the notion of California as potential collateral for Mexican debt or part of a British colonization scheme. See Wright, *A Description of California in 1828*, vii. Forbes also had a connection to Hugo Reid, to be discussed later.
37. This attitude appears frequently in early texts. Hugo Reid even repeats this sentiment. See Letter 21 in Robert F. Heizer, ed., *The Indians of Los Angeles County: Hugo Reid's Letters of 1852* (Los Angeles: Southwest Museum, 1968), 99. See also David J. Weber, *Myth and the History of the Hispanic Southwest* (Albuquerque: University of New Mexico Press, 1988), 114–15; and Lisbeth Haas, *Conquests and Historical Identities in California, 1769–1936* (Berkeley: University of California Press, 1995), 37.
38. Rosales, "'Fantasy Heritage' Reexamined," 94, correctly points out that the wider context for Californio racism is important and often forgotten.
39. Haas, *Conquests and Historical Identities*, 37.
40. Bandini, *A Description of California*, 7.
41. Examples of this tendency can be found in George Vancouver's *A Voyage of Discovery* (1798), William Shaler's *Journal of a Voyage* (1808), and Richard Henry Dana's *Two Years Before the Mast* (1840).
42. Bandini, *A Description of California*, 9–10.
43. Ibid., 7, 9.
44. Ibid., 6, 7, 18.
45. Ibid., 7. For material on rape and forced sexual encounters, see Steven W. Hackel, *Children of Coyote, Missionaries of Saint Francis: Indian-Spanish Relations in Colonial California, 1769–1850* (Chapel Hill: University of North Carolina Press, 2005), 222–27, and Albert Hurtado, "Sexuality in California's Franciscan Missions: Cultural Perception and Sad Realities," *California History* 71, no. 3 (1992): 370–85.
46. Bandini, *A Description of California*, 9.
47. Ibid., 10, 12, 16.

48. Ibid., 15.
49. Ibid., 7.
50. This complaint mirrors others among the elites of California. See Pubols, *The Father of All*, 165–95.
51. See David E. Stannard, "Recounting the Fables of Savagery: Native Infanticide and the Functions of Political Myth," *Journal of American Studies* 25, no. 3 (1991): 381–417, for a gloss of this argument. Rosales, "'Fantasy Heritage' Reexamined," 94, also contests this explanation.
52. For a discussion of the use of Native labor, see George Harwood Phillips, *Vineyards and Vaqueros: Indian Labor and the Economic Expansion of Southern California, 1771–1877* (Norman, OK: Arthur H. Clark, 2010).
53. Bandini, *A Description of California*, 9.
54. The only biography of Reid is Susanna Bryant Dakin, *A Scotch Paisano in Old Los Angeles: Hugo Reid's Life in California, 1832–1852, Derived from His Correspondence* (Berkeley: University of California Press, 1939). While historians have for decades used his letters as a source, especially on matters regarding Native Californians, few other writers have extensively discussed him as a historical figure. In part because of his marriage to a Native woman, scholars are again turning their attention to Reid himself and his wife, Victoria Bartolomea Comicrabit. See Casas, *Married to a Daughter of the Land*, 63–73; Casas, "Victoria Reid and the Politics of Identity," in *Latina Legacies: Identity, Biography, and Community*, Vicki Ruiz and Virginia Sanchez Korrol, eds. (Oxford: Oxford University Press, 2005), 19–38; and Miroslava Chávez-García, *Negotiating Conquest: Gender and Power in California, 1770s to 1880s* (Tucson: University of Arizona Press, 2004), 77, 134. For nineteenth-century accounts, see William Heath Davis, *Sixty Years in California: A History of Events and Life in California* (San Francisco: A.J. Leary, 1889), 196–97; and Laura Evertson King, "Hugo Reid and His Indian Wife," in *The Annual Publication of the Historical Society of Southern California and Pioneer Register* (Los Angeles, 1898), 111–13. For a discussion of Scottish immigration generally, see Martha Voght, "Scots in Hispanic California," *The Scottish Historical Review* 52, no. 154 (1973): 137–48.
55. Some of these marriages are treated in Casas, *Married to a Daughter of the Land.*
56. Dakin, *Scotch Paisano*, 40, 56.
57. Ibid., 196.
58. These letters emerged, in part, from California's constitutional convention in 1849. See Dakin, *Scotch Paisano*, 187–88, 191. While Dakin includes an appendix with Reid's letters, the most accurate available edition is Robert F. Heizer, ed., *The Indians of Los Angeles County: Hugo Reid's Letters of 1852* (Los Angeles: Southwest Museum, 1968). Quotations from the letters are taken from this edition.
59. There is the possible explanation, discussed later, that Reid wrote the letters hoping to secure a position with the U.S. government as an Indian agent. See Heizer, *Indians of Los Angeles County*, 2.
60. Phillips, *Vineyards and Vaqueros.*
61. Heizer, *Indians of Los Angeles County*, 2.
62. Ibid., 88.
63. Ibid., 80.
64. Dakin, *Scotch Paisano*, 219.

65. Helen Hunt Jackson's *Ramona* (1884) was an enormously popular novel that Jackson hoped would bring attention to the suffering of Native Americans in California, but instead the book had the effect of romanticizing the Spanish-Mexican culture in ways that remain evident even in the twenty-first century.
66. Heizer, *Indians of Los Angeles County*, 74.
67. Ibid., 75–76.
68. Ibid., 88.
69. Ibid., 69.
70. See Geronimo Boscana, "Chinigchinich: An Historical Account of the Origin, Customs, and Traditions of the Indians of Alta-California," in *Life in California*, ed. Andrew Rolle (Santa Barbara: Peregrine, 1970), especially 43, 70.
71. Heizer, *Indians of Los Angeles County*, 15.
72. Forbes, *History of California*, 233.
73. Heizer, *Indians of Los Angeles County*. It is interesting to note that Pablo Tac, who wrote the first known text by a mission Indian, described the changes to the land around Mission San Luis Rey in a similar way. See Pablo Tac, "Indian Life and Customs at Mission San Luis Rey," ed. and trans. Minna Hewes and Gordon Hewes, *The Americas* 9.1 (1952): 91, no. 1.
74. Heizer, *Indians of Los Angeles County*, 73.
75. Casas, *Married to a Daughter of the Land*, 67, 71.
76. See note 1 for a gloss on the standard narrative of immigration to California. This attitude is most evident in Nunis, "Alta California's Trojan Horse." The most nuanced depiction of immigration comes from David J. Weber, "Conflicts and Accommodations: Hispanic and Anglo-American Borders in Historical Perspective, 1670–1853," *Journal of the Southwest* 39, no. 1 (Spring 1997): 1–32.

2

Hell and Heaven on Wheels

Mormons, Immigrants, and the Reconstruction of American Progress and Masculinity on the First Transcontinental Railroad

Ryan Dearinger

American identity has been hotly contested. In the history of the West that identity has often been claimed by the process of "othering." "Othering" was influentially described by literary theorist Edward Saïd in his seminal work Orientalism *in which he charted the ways in which Europeans and Americans had caricatured and stereotyped Moslems and Arabs as the exotic, effete, or corrupt "other." In this chapter, historian Ryan Dearinger shows how Mormon workers and polemicists in Utah caricatured Irish immigrant laborers on the transcontinental railroad as inebriated, unruly, and uncivilized "others." By contrast, they characterized themselves as abstemious, disciplined, and civilized Americans—the epitome of civilized manliness—hoping to deflect attention from distinctive religious doctrines and practices that placed them beyond the pale of respectability in the minds of most Americans. Thereby Mormons, thousands of whom were also immigrants, hoped to narrow the gap between "who we are" and who Americans "said we should be."*

In May 1869, when the Central Pacific Railroad, built primarily by Chinese immigrants, and the Union Pacific Railroad, constructed largely by Irish immigrants, united in the "wedding of the rails," Americans celebrated and claimed this achievement as their own. The illustrious Golden Spike ceremony for the transcontinental railroad shrouded another glaring irony. The definitive moment and symbol of American progress, built by immigrants and outsiders, was completed in what was then seen as the most un-American of American places, the Utah Territory. The transcontinental railroad was central to what Elliott West calls the "Greater Reconstruction" of post-Civil War America. As the country's geographic and political boundaries expanded, its cultural boundaries—what it entailed to be or become an American—contracted.[1] During and after the railroad's construction period, Americans were once again faced with a question as old as the nation itself: could a large republic tolerate a diversity of peoples brought within its borders? The answer was still no.

Even in the Utah Territory, an incredibly homogenous place, the construction of the transcontinental railroad accelerated a new peopling of immigrants and emigrants (from Europe, China, and all parts of the United States) on a wageworkers' frontier that began to mirror the diversity of other western locales in this period. These groups, whose brains and brawn built the railroad, would test the limits of racial democracy in the American West, that place of ostensibly endless opportunities, a proving ground for national progress, and for some, even a site of Americanization. As some scholars have suggested, the building of the transcontinental railroad was not only among the greatest American achievements of the nineteenth century but a definitive episode in western, imperial, and transnational history.[2] The most famous of the several ceremonial "last spikes" driven into a polished laurel tie at the aforementioned 1869 celebration, California's offering, which contained eighteen ounces of pure gold, seemed to echo the idea of a nation transformed. Etched on its side were the words: "May God continue the unity of our Country as this Railroad unites the two great Oceans of the world."[3] The scene at Promontory Summit on the morning of May 10, though exaggerated in several popular accounts to include Indians and Mexicans, featured, according to one eyewitness, "men of every color, creed, and nationality."[4] As historian Mark Fiege notes in his superb chapter on the environmental history of the railroad, "The world had come to America, and America had become, in effect, the world."[5]

Mormon unskilled labor on the transcontinental railroad marked a significant change from earlier labor trends on America's massive transportation projects. It was one of the few times that large segments of a settled Anglo-American community were marshaled to assist in railroad construction. Not only did Mormons of all social classes participate in railroad building, but Mormon workers and leaders found in such labor an opportunity to surmount national prejudices against their religious practices and to discredit allegations of defiant isolationism. Railroad construction labor offered a chance to participate in a work of national importance, gain recognition and the acceptance of Americans, prove Mormon loyalty to the federal government, and secure the economic benefits of the country's most substantial project in western expansion and internal improvement.

Moreover, the Mormon contribution to the transcontinental railroad offers insights into alternate definitions of western work, progress, and manhood. Of particular interest is how Mormon workers and leaders interpreted the role of transient immigrant laborers and the march of "civilization" that supporters of the railroad predicted. In the story of triumph that followed the tracks of the Union Pacific and Central Pacific, Mormons advanced their cultural values, ideas about progress, and definitions of masculinity, all in sharp contrast to the experiences of the railroad companies and their immigrant construction workers.

This study builds on recent literature that explores how working-class men constructed masculinity and confronted challenges to their manhood. In revealing how languages of manhood and notions of manliness shaped class perceptions and work experiences, scholars have demonstrated the importance of gender and identity in America's transition to industrial capitalism in the nineteenth century. More often than not, however, this gendered vision of industrial development focuses on the de-skilling of urban craftsmen, their separation from the traditional workplace, and their loss of control over production. These changes, along with the expansion of immigrant groups into the workplace and political arena and challenges to the structure of patriarchy, precipitated what scholars call a "crisis" in masculinity.[6] As some historians have argued, in the case of workers, this crisis was actually threefold and involved the issues of work, class, and gender. Skilled male workers in various trades responded to social and technological transformations by refashioning the meanings of manhood. They crafted a collective identity of "worker" that was thoroughly raced and gendered. Most importantly, they organized to defend their manly identities.[7] Gregory Kaster argues that in equating manliness with "respectability" and in opposition to femaleness, blackness, and common laborers, "organized skilled white workingmen" in nineteenth-century America articulated an idealized notion of working-class manhood that required continual demonstration and validation, and thus remained unresolved.[8]

Historian Gail Bederman's influential book *Manliness & Civilization* has similarly helped scholars rethink their language in studies of masculine identity. She interprets a distinction between "manhood" or "masculinity" and "manliness" as ideological and historical processes, each of which were socially constructed and tied to one's identity. Bederman critiques historians for not periodizing and unpacking the use of masculinity—as a discourse—by their subjects. She argues that, by the turn of the twentieth century, an evolving discourse of manliness which stressed restraint and self-mastery helped shape middle-class identity.[9] Such a "remaking" of manhood she describes as an "ongoing project." For middle-class men, masculinity alone could not distinguish "bodies, identities, and power," but when reformulated with attention to race and the discourse of "civilization," *manliness* held the potential to shore up and advance white dominance in all facets of American life—public and private, civil and political.[10] This link between manliness, citizenship, and civilization was a salient yet worrisome feature of Latter-day Saint life in the nineteenth century. Race, religion, self-mastery, power, and the notion of a virtuous brotherhood, each reinforced through a new iteration of civilized manliness, certainly applied to Mormon railroad workers; they used these qualities to set themselves apart from the underworld of American progress so often associated with immigrant laborers. The problem with this endeavor, however, was that apparent cultural, political, and religious factors had also placed Mormons beyond the pale of civilization in the minds of most Americans. Countless citizens saw Mormons as neither white nor American.[11]

Another problem complicated by the Mormon experience was a prevailing "army of labor" model of capitalism that governed massive construction projects like the Union and Central Pacific Railroads, wherein, as historian Richard White notes in *Railroaded*, his award-winning business history of America's transcontinental railroads, corporate officers commanded workers to take orders as soldiers. "They had no control over their work, how it was done, or when it was supposed to be performed," White writes. "They became a different kind of being; they were no longer, in workers' terms, men. Their opinions did not matter. They were to do what they were told. Conditions they would never accept in their civic or public life were to be the conditions of their working lives."[12] Because the Union Pacific Railroad contracted directly with Mormon leader Brigham Young (who was also a UPRR stockholder), his construction crews were almost exclusively comprised of Latter-day Saint subcontractors, labor bosses, and workers, often from the same communities and even belonging to the same LDS wards. Such a labor arrangement led to a markedly different experience for Mormon construction crews when compared to their Union Pacific and Central Pacific counterparts, something that this chapter explores in considerable detail.

Although scholars of labor, immigration, and masculinity have often identified the workplace as a key site for the construction of male identity, historical interpretations of the nineteenth-century American workplace unfortunately tend to exclude many workers. This workplace is depicted as primarily urban and dominated by artisans, trade unionists, and labor politics. The challenge is to broaden this picture, incorporating native-born, immigrant, and transient workers, skilled and unskilled, and a workplace that was, quite literally, in motion on remote frontiers of the American West. Historian Gunther Peck, in *Reinventing Free Labor*, argues that immigrant workers' notions of manhood in the American West were unstable due to the transitory nature of their labor, the demands of their bosses (notably immigrant *padrones*), their ties to the Old World, and familial expectations. Though he concentrates on the vicissitudes of a chaotic labor market in relation to state, legal, and business structures, Peck, in this pathbreaking study, interprets the process of masculine identity formation in the West as "manhood on the move."[13] He locates workers' understandings of manhood and solidarity in mobility itself, and thus departs from studies of immigration and migration that highlight the importance of established ethnic enclaves. While much of Peck's study takes place in the twentieth century, he nonetheless illustrates the hollowness of visions of the West as a paradise of "free land" and "free labor."[14]

However, to build on the concept of the "wageworkers' frontier" and explore the meanings of labor and manhood, it is imperative to address the evolution of worker masculinity over space and time.[15] For Peck, "manhood on the move" is related less to workers' notions of progress in contention with American elites than to their memory of ancestral homelands and resistance to the undue control exercised by their immigrant padrones. This chapter differs from Peck's transnational approach, for new ideas of manhood developed in the Mountain West where masculine identity was not simply internal to class and ethnicity but actively contested by different class, ethnic, and religious groups. On these frontiers of progress, construction laborers grafted new identities to old as they battled to brand both manhood and progress. Moreover, workers' claims to masculinity were contested not only by their counterparts and employers but by the public at large. Throughout this period, American citizens as well as immigrants used railroads and the wilderness that they ostensibly conquered to reconstruct boundaries of citizenship and manhood and lay claim to history in the making. Beyond men in motion, these were communities in contestation.

Generations of historians have assessed the transcontinental railroad's impact on Utah and the Great Basin region. Mormon-focused research has addressed the "railroad threat" in Utah, but most of these studies concentrate on what political and economic change meant to Utahns and the Church of Jesus Christ of Latter-day Saints.[16] Despite the historical importance of the transcontinental railroad and its impact on Utah and the American West, scholars have done little to explore the contours and contestation of railroad progress. Nowhere do unskilled construction workers figure into the story. Thus, in examining Utah's transportation frontier, of special concern is how laborers understood their work; how dignitaries, writers, and local residents perceived it; and how the meaning of productive work, community, and respectable masculinity informed the Mormon response to railroad progress and "civilization."[17]

This story cannot be told from the workers' perspectives alone. Immediate contact among Mormon, Irish, and Chinese laborers was rare, and unskilled construction workers were ignored in company records. The perspectives of Mormon and non-Mormon leaders, politicians, editors, travelers, and community residents cast light not only on these invisible agents of railroad progress but on the meaning of American progress, manhood, and citizenship. For Utah's Mormons, the discussion also entails competing narratives of national belonging. In the eyes of non-Mormon, native-born American citizens, the Mormons were "profligate outcasts," perhaps even more threatening than the Irish and Chinese immigrants with whom they shared the task of completing the transcontinental railroad.[18]

Mormon workers on the railroad marked a turning point in Latter-day Saint history. Whether born in the United States, British Isles, or Scandinavia, mid-nineteenth-century Mormon converts had to overcome a unique set of prejudices that placed them below even the most despised foreign immigrants. As historian W. Paul Reeve recently put it, "In the nineteenth century they were denigrated as not white enough."[19] In building the transcontinental, Mormons sought acceptance as citizens, national belonging, and much more. They sought not only to shape the contours of American progress but to claim the credit, benefits, and the history of such progress as their own. In Mormon hands, the history of railroad progress became part of a masculine pioneer epic that both included and set them apart from American civilization.

As early as 1866, Utah and its citizens became the focal point of a track-laying contest between the Union Pacific and Central Pacific Railroads, each hoping to bring "civilization" to a wilderness environment that some called the American Desert. The 1862 Pacific Railway Act granted each company ten square miles of public land on each side of the track, and authorized government bonds at the rate of $16,000 per mile of track laid in nonmountainous regions, up to $48,000 over and within the Sierra Nevada Mountains and Rocky Mountains, and up to $32,000 for track laid between the two ranges.[20]

While financing became easier, the task of constructing a transcontinental railroad remained unchanged. Common, unskilled laborers were still the critical agents of progress. As the Central Pacific, with the help of over ten thousand Chinese laborers, built eastward from Sacramento, California, the Union Pacific, employing upwards of eight thousand Irish, German, and Italian immigrants, built west from Omaha, Nebraska.[21]

The federal government's assumption that the rails would intersect at the first feasible location underestimated the power of greed. Soaking up subsidies of cash and land grants that were awarded for each mile of railroad completed, the Union Pacific and Central Pacific companies deliberately refused to meet and instead built parallel roads for several hundred miles, from eastern Nevada to southwestern Wyoming. Finally, in April 1869, just one month prior to the Golden Spike celebration, the U.S. Congress, in a joint resolution, selected Promontory Summit, a location north of Utah's Great Salt Lake, as the spot "at which rails shall meet and form one continuous line."[22]

Perhaps the choice of Promontory Summit was not fortuitous. Utah and the Mormons had long raised problems for Americans and the federal government. Thousands of Mormons were immigrants but even if native-born, their fellow Americans considered Mormons incapable of citizenship and without character. Like the early Irish and the Chinese, the Mormons could not claim the rewards of their deeds. They were uncivilized others, the antithesis of American progress, beyond the American pale.

While many supporters of the transcontinental railroad predicted that it would "civilize" the Mormons by forcing them out of isolation and into the expanding world of goods, peoples, and ideas, others praised the choice of Promontory (as opposed to Salt Lake City) for establishing yet another partition that excluded Mormon outlanders from the immediate benefits of this celebrated project—despite promises that the railroad would unite the nation's inhabitants. To exclude Utah's Mormons from America's continental empire, railroad proponents in and outside of Congress proposed removing them from its map. As Patricia Limerick argues, "Conquest basically involved the drawing of lines on a map . . . and the subsequent giving of meaning and power to those lines." The American West featured "an ongoing competition for legitimacy," a contest not limited to property or resources but one for "cultural dominance" that remained unresolved.[23] The contest to build, claim, and celebrate the railroad mirrored this process.

Mormonism was reviled by a majority of nineteenth-century Americans, who viewed it as an unorthodox and authoritarian religious movement, hostile to conventional values and traditions. Not only did its religious peculiarities draw the ire of critics, but Mormons' aggressive proselytizing posed a threat to mainstream American churches.[24] Moreover, like Roman Catholicism, Mormonism was perceived as an un-American and antidemocratic religion whose members were under the dominion of an autocratic leader, Brigham Young, who dictated how believers should live, act, and vote in the secular world. Critics, such as Methodist minister Daniel P. Kidder, argued that even writing on the "low and groveling" subject of Mormonism "elevated [it] . . . to a rank it never deserved," for it was a "delusion" that inflicted "spiritual blindness and misery . . . upon its successive victims."[25] Other commentators, such as Reverend Robert W. Beers, claimed that among patriotic American citizens, Mormonism was "acknowledged to be the Great Modern Abomination, the most pernicious heresy of this century."[26] Preaching "a doctrine of exclusivity" while in self-isolation from American society, Utah's Mormons combined their spiritual mission with communalistic economic practices. This provoked critics, who deemed Mormonism a mysterious cult that was determined to accumulate illegitimate authority, preventing non-Mormons from fulfilling the American dream of individual and democratic self-improvement.[27] According to dissenting Mormon journalist T. B. H. Stenhouse, the church was thoroughly anti-American and endeavored to "overthrow all stable governments, in order to make way for the advancement and growth of the Mormon Kingdom."[28]

Most abominable in the eyes of Americans was the Mormon practice of polygamy. With the proliferation of plural marriage, Mormonism threatened to subvert the custom of monogamy that Americans viewed as an essential bulwark against immorality and the primary tradition for the control of sexuality. Popular, political, and even religious precepts held American men responsible for guiding their energies toward financial success and respectable masculinity.[29] Those who argued that Mormons posed a danger to American democracy and manhood pointed to polygamy as evidence of a weakness of character, for it undermined nineteenth-century precepts that valued the control of masculine passions as much as it did control of households.[30] Polygamy reinforced the notion that Mormonism was an authoritarian and cultish religion established by "lustful" men who sought unrestrained illicit sexual relationships with young women.[31]

While distancing Mormons from respectable manhood and mainstream American values, polygamy also racialized them as a "peculiar people."[32] Brigham Young's sexual prowess (over sixty wives) was seen as a threat to civilized masculinity, and Americans transferred the allegedly aggressive sexuality of blacks and Indians to Mormons.[33] Anti-Mormon commentators argued that practices such as polygamy had turned "the civilized world against them" and "classed [them] with Pariahs and lepers."[34] Popular American journalists and illustrators coupled Mormons with seemingly savage Indians, brutish African Americans, drunken Irish, and heathen Chinese immigrants in periodicals such as *Harper's Weekly* and *The Wasp*.[35] Mormonism, an evil "Viper on the Hearth," was a menace to American progress, manhood, and national identity.[36]

Figure 2.1. "Uncle Sam's Troublesome Bed Fellows," *The Wasp*, February 8, 1879, in "Cartoons on Current Topics." Courtesy of The Bancroft Library, University of California, Berkeley, No. 142: 441.

Ridiculed as a nonwhite and uncivilized race in a cartoon titled "Uncle Sam's Troublesome Bed Fellows," published in *The Wasp* at the height of the anti-Chinese movement, Mormons had yet to shake their inferior status as racial and cultural outsiders (see Figure 2.1). In this illustration, Uncle Sam boots the Chinese immigrant to the floor, where he joins the Mormon polygamist. The savage Indian pokes at Uncle Sam while the blackface "Jim Crow" African American smiles in approval. The Irish immigrant appears passed-out drunk. Prominently displayed on the footboard is the emblem of the Union, which doubled as the logo of the Union Pacific Railroad, though this scene suggests depravity and disunion.

Harsh criticisms of Mormon practices and Brigham Young's theocratic rule over the Utah Territory had often reverberated in the halls of Congress and on the national political stage. The 1856 platform of the new Republican Party stipulated that Congress could not only prohibit slavery in the western territories, but polygamy as well, for these were the "twin relics of barbarism."[37] Illinois Senator Stephen Douglas, arguing that the Mormons deliberately resisted federal authority and collaborated with Indian groups in robberies and murders, declared that "the knife must be applied to this pestiferous, disgusting cancer which is gnawing into the very vitals of the body politic."[38] If military measures against the Mormons failed, he recommended that Congress dissolve the Utah Territory, for Mormons "are alien enemies and outlaws, unfit to be citizens of a territory."[39] On the issue of polygamy, Douglas thought the federal government should make every effort to cut this "loathsome ulcer" out of American society.[40] In signing the 1862 Morrill Anti-Bigamy Act, President Lincoln did just that; the act criminalized polygamy in the territories, annulled all polygamy-supporting legislation in Utah, and restricted the LDS Church's ownership of property.[41] When Mormons defied the antipolygamy law, their detractors' verbal attacks grew fiercer. In a debate with Utah's territorial delegate to Congress in 1863, New York representative Fernando Wood argued that Mormons were "profligate outcasts . . . hostile to the moral and political institutions of the United States."[42]

Even the boundaries of the Utah Territory, through which the railroad would pass, became a target of anti-Mormon legislation. Taking up the cause of Stephen Douglas and others to dissolve Zion, Ohio representative James M. Ashley, chairman of the U.S. House Committee on Territories and staunchly anti-Mormon, steered a bill through the house in 1866, which shifted Utah's western border fifty miles to the east, the land given to Nevada for mining interests.[43] In 1869, Ashley went further and introduced a bill designed to "blot out the Territory," reducing Utah to 22,000 square miles (roughly the size of West Virginia) and thereby eliminating Mormon political power and halting the church's expansion in the Great Basin.[44] Although the bill never came to a vote, it generated popular debate on the best way to deal with "the Mormon Problem." The editor of the *San Francisco Call*, informing readers of Ashley's plan to "despoil the Mormons" by "cutting up their territory and dividing it among the neighboring powers and territories," nonetheless considered the bill "ill-advised." Political solutions such as Ashley's, the editor argued, would only "create new complications, jealousies, and disturbances." Conversely, "the Pacific Railroad" will effect a "peaceful settlement of the Mormon difficulty," based on the "impetus which will be given to inland commerce and immigration."[45]

In fact, Mormons in the Great Basin region had long promoted the construction of a national railroad through the Utah Territory. As early as 1851, the territorial legislature petitioned Congress to construct a railroad to the Pacific and suggested that the tracks pass through Weber Canyon into Salt Lake City and proceed south around the Great Salt Lake to California. In 1862, as a gesture of good will toward the Union Pacific Railroad Company, Brigham Young, on behalf of his church, bought five shares of stock for five thousand dollars and was subsequently made a director of the company. The LDS Church would eventually use the railroad for its missionary and immigration programs while it spurred the development of the territorial mining industry. Having long predicted such success, Brigham Young, as the tracks traversed what he termed "the unsettled plains and deserts" and approached Utah in 1867, argued that "the completion of this gigantic work will increase intercourse, and it is to be hoped, soften prejudices, and bind the country together."[46]

Faced with the onslaught from politicians and newspaper editors, Mormon leadership answered the railroad challenge by reframing the road as an economic civilizer while simultaneously pointing to the "uncivilized" nature of some of its accompanying social consequences. Mormon letters, editorials, and sermons published in the years following the initiation of Union Pacific construction in 1865 show a positive view of the railroad as an impetus to reap both converts and consumers for many of Utah's cash-starved producers. In response to allegations that railroad men and "civilization" threatened the church, Young wrote to overseas missionaries that "we want the railroad, [and] we are not afraid of its results," and that Mormonism "must . . . be a damned poor religion, if it cannot stand one railroad."[47]

In post-Civil War America, however, the national media refused to let Brigham Young and the editors at the church-owned *Deseret News* define westward expansion. With memories of the Utah War (1857–1858) and the Mountain Meadows Massacre (1857) still fresh, and polygamy having supplanted slavery as America's evil institution, newspapers such as the *Nebraska Republican* predicted that, with the coming of the Union Pacific, the "dissolution of Mormondom" was indeed "inevitable."[48] Echoing this theme, the *Providence Journal* claimed that "the cohesive power of Mormonism will soon be subjected to stern practical tests," and "no regulations it can enact will keep out Gentile emigrants."[49] The editor continued: "[Mormonism's] remoteness from civilized States has, hitherto, been an effective safeguard. Brigham Young has been a supreme ruler, and any troublesome Gentiles were easily removed either by threats or force. . . . But the Pacific Railroad is to pass through the heart of Utah, and . . . Mormonism can no longer be isolated. . . . Utah will soon lie open to thronging crowds of emigrants, and if Mormonism has not better elements of life than is commonly supposed, it must gradually succumb to higher civilization, or migrate to a new home."[50]

Confronting anti-Mormon sentiment, the *Deseret News* reprinted an editorial from the *Chicago Republican* entitled "Mormonism Doomed," which argued that "frontier" railroad towns led by "adventurous classes" would "spring up with magical swiftness . . . and ripen into cities." The *Republican* editor reevaluated Irish immigrant traits that had been judged uncivilized east of the Mississippi River to claim them as patriotic, Christian behaviors in Utah. Armed with the accoutrements of civilization, he argued, this advance guard of "Gentiles" who feared "neither the world, the flesh, nor the devil," would "swarm into every part of Utah," set up a free press, and "open [their] batteries daily upon the iniquity of harem life."[51] Like many of his colleagues, George Q. Cannon of the *Deseret News* responded by using Chicago's village-to-metropolis model to craft a narrative of uncivilization that distanced "temporary work" and its supposed vices from the more righteous and permanent "industry" and settlement that was Utah:

> Our [Mormon cooperative] system has already endured some very severe tests. We should be disappointed if we did not have to come in contact with these hostile influences and civilizing (?) agencies which he describes. Border ruffians [and] adventurers may come and go . . . [but] we shall neither tremble nor object. Our readers who are familiar with Chicago—the most notoriously corrupt city of its size in the Union—can imagine what a change is foreshadowed by the promised introduction of such civilization![52]

Mormon leaders sought to diminish the railroad threat by first defining and then limiting the manner in which socioeconomic progress would unfold in Zion. It was not the railroad itself, but the men who built it, that posed the greatest danger. In frequent meetings at the Salt Lake tabernacle in 1867 and 1868, a narrative of "successful progress" was crafted according to the cultural values of Utah's "relatively self-sufficient . . . equalitarian, and homogenous" Mormon citizenry.[53] Church elders and editors contrasted Utah's cooperative system of work, based on agricultural production, permanent settlement, family values, sobriety, and community improvements, such as small-scale irrigation canals, with the transience, violence, drunkenness, immorality, and "pandemonium" that allegedly prevailed in railroad camps along the transcontinental route.[54] An editorial in the Mormon *Millennial Star* titled "The Great Railroad of the West" suggested that, with "God's help," "Utonians" had the "power to make Utah a most disagreeable spot for the vile and lawless rabble whose only glory is destruction and infamy."[55] According to the writer, "The railway will no doubt bring some of that class of bipeds to our mountain State, but the same line will take them away again."[56]

Both the image and reality of such reckless progress figured prominently in Utah, where Mormons interpreted the railroad as both a threat and an opportunity. Under Brigham Young's leadership, the church responded to the railroad dilemma by transforming its School of Prophets (originally a priesthood gospel study group) into an economic organization that successfully maintained Mormon solidarity in the face of socioeconomic "revolution." In particular, the school's system of "protection" sought to minimize the influx of railroad employees and "hangers-on."[57] It was the railroad's immigrant laborers and their accompanying vices that posed a threat to the essential structure, function, and morality of the Mormon community. According to one school member, this system promised to inhibit "the swarms of scalawags that the construction of the railroad would bring" from infesting Zion.[58]

European-born converts to Mormonism echoed this perceived danger as they crossed the Atlantic and traveled by train from New York to end-of-track locations in the Wyoming Territory en route to Salt Lake City in the mid- to late 1860s. After six weeks at sea on the packet ship *John Bright* where she "was seasick before the tug boat went back . . . [and] from shore to shore," in August 1868, Liverpool native Celestial Roberts Knight's company of Saints reached the Union Pacific's end-of-track west of Laramie, where they were excited to see "mule and horse teams" waiting to transport them to Salt Lake City. As Knight's interviewer noted, the company was immediately "counseled . . . to drive out around the railroad camps and . . . not stop day or night till they got out of the way of the camps and thus they would avoid the rough element that is generally found around the railroad camps. . . . No one was to walk."[59] Similar descriptions of non-Mormon Union Pacific camps would serve as negative reference points for Mormon construction camps that soon dotted this landscape of progress.

The chance to contribute to American progress by building the transcontinental railroad offered Mormon men an opportunity to shift attention from their conspicuous earmarks of difference and present themselves as patriotic, entrepreneurial, and morally upright Americans. While working on the railroad, Mormons could present themselves as both American citizens and men of character. This work helped facilitate the construction of a Mormon American manhood that redefined the very meaning of railroad labor and progress. At the same time, Mormons would build their holy community, securing it politically and economically. This effort left the power of the church's leadership untouched in all matters temporal and spiritual.

Still, the opening of Zion for "great national work" was no easy decision. The Mormon response, in fact, was similar to reactions in nineteenth-century communities where the presence of immigrant "improvement" labor ostensibly threatened social, religious, and familial stability.[60] Utah's Saints marked outside railroad labor in general as foreign and savage, and railroad laborers in particular as a violent, heathenish, and repugnant army. George Reynolds, a church official and member of the School of Prophets who had immigrated to Utah from England, confided to a missionary friend in England that he feared "what the result would be to our cities and settlements of 5,000 or 6,000 Irish . . . and other laborers crowding through our peaceful vales."[61] Mormons exacerbated this perceived sense of difference by arguing that immigrant laborers were "idle" and "unproductive."[62] British immigrant and *Deseret News* editor Cannon often mocked anti-Mormon editorials by borrowing their titles, such as "The Coming Railroad," for his own pieces, in which he argued that mere "hard work" did not transform men and allow them to inherit the Promised Land and claim citizenship. It was the greater good of the work and the honorable behavior of the worker that did.

Religion and community would thus act as bulwarks against the "other," as Mormons demonstrated the dual process of community building and protecting, endeavors that were both inward and outward looking. Mormon leaders and followers not only critiqued but redefined railroad "civilization," portraying railroad construction workers as "dreaded rowdies," "gamblers," "patrons of drinking saloons," and "idlers" who, "too lazy to earn their own living," were "bound to have it, if they have to steal it." Progress, according to the Saints, meant "making a living by honest industry" and was limited to "peaceable, virtuous, [and] law-abiding men."[63] Broadcasting themselves as respectable men, Mormons working on the railroad would teach the nation a lesson in citizenship.

While it was easy to project an otherness on the Chinese workingman, who, according to an Ogden editor, was as a "copper-colored incubus" belonging to an "inferior and alien race," less frequent contact with this immigrant group led to a host of different interpretations.[64] Mormons reserved particular revulsion, however, for transient Irish railroad workers; the Book of Mormon even declared their Catholic Church "the mother of harlots."[65] According to the leading scholar of Irish immigrants in the West, "To understate considerably, the Irish did not find Utah congenial. They did not go there if they could help it and did not stay there any longer than they had to."[66]

In anticipation of a Mormon grading contract with the Union Pacific, Brigham Young called a special meeting in early June of 1868 to address the benefits of, and Utah's role in, the transcontinental railroad. Held at Salt Lake City's recently built tabernacle, this "Mass Meeting" featured an "enthusiastic audience" of over three thousand men, including both church dignitaries and "common" citizens.[67] The June assembly sought to demonstrate wide support for the railroad amid national accusations that the "isolationist-minded" Mormons opposed commercial and cultural intercourse with outsiders and thus feared the coming of the rails. An elected committee that included Brigham Young (president), Colonel F. H. Head, elder John Taylor, apostle and *Deseret News* editor George Q. Cannon, and Judge Thomas Marshall spoke passionately on the subject but from different perspectives. Since Leonard Arrington, scholars of Mormon history have emphasized the committee's four resolutions on the railroad question to debunk the notion that Utah's Latter-day Saints were hostile to national internal improvements and "Gentile" influences. The resolutions, which were forwarded to the directors of the Union Pacific and Central Pacific, welcomed the railroad and "more intimate relations" with East and West. They proposed that the Central Pacific and Union Pacific intersect south of the Great Salt Lake (thus closer to the city) and demanded that such "great national work" be performed "for the people's benefit and not for private profit or personal speculation."[68]

A closer examination of this report and others, however, reveals varied nuances in Mormon visions of the railroad, "progress," transient immigrant laborers, and the meaning of productive work. Brigham Young was not only exceedingly optimistic about the railroad project, but confident in the fortitude of his Saints to coexist and act as "co-laborers" with workers from both railroad companies in Utah. According to Young, "large cities" would likely follow the track routes and, rather than gold and silver, the "only capital required to build cities is bone and sinew," for "laboring men are the ones who build the cities."[69] F. H. Head articulated the railroad in terms that would surely have pleased company officials, arguing that "the business of building railroads . . . has undergone remarkable change[s]" such that only "the highest order of statesmanship and profoundest knowledge of political economy" could meet such a task. He insisted that Union Pacific officials were interested in world commerce, not in "building up temporary shingle cities like Cheyenne."[70] Elder Taylor made railroad building consistent with Mormon work practices. Mormon workers, he argued, "have always been the advocates of improvement." Nonetheless, the British-born Taylor curiously omitted the primary workforces on both the Union and Central Pacific—Irish and Chinese laborers, each of whom were then grading and laying track near Utah's borders. Instead, he drew a parallel to the Mormon experience and spoke of "the Englishmen, the Frenchmen, the Saxon, the Dane, and the Norwegian who are to-day with bare arm, strong muscle, and busy brain . . . piercing the hitherto supposed impenetrable cañon, filling up the valleys, leveling the hills and preparing a pathway for the 'iron horse.'"[71] According to Taylor, these men were partners in the process, as Mormonism united proud Anglo-American classes. Yet, for Mormons, religion, manhood, race, and ethnicity, not social class, were the key variables.

Apostle and editor George Q. Cannon arrived late to the mass meeting, but was no less enthusiastic, maintaining that "we have arrived at that point in our history when the building of the railroad is a necessity." Disputing allegations that Mormons were "secretly adverse to the construction of this railroad," Cannon noted that anyone who was familiar with Utah's citizens "know[s] full well that whatever our peculiarities may be, we are not opposed to progress." While he conceded that Mormons "may view progress from a different stand point to many others," Cannon remarked that "upon matters of great national importance," there existed a "union of feelings." Yet, Cannon saw other important benefits that would result from Mormon labor on the transcontinental railroad. "Four years with the railroad," he predicted, would end in Utah achieving statehood in 1872 and its citizens having the chance to cast presidential ballots. More broadly, the railroad would provide a "common platform" on which Mormons could stand with their "fellow-men," who, in Cannon's experience, interpreted "Mormon" to signify "a creature from another planet," with "horns or a cloven foot" or other "distinguishing peculiarit[ies]" that were "different from other men."[72] The railroad, he suggested, would create Mormon *American* men.

For LDS Church leaders, the railroad was as much a commemoration of the past as it was about dreams of the future. Young, returning to the podium to close the mass meeting, noted that when the Mormon pioneers fled Nauvoo, "we left naked and barefoot. We left our property, and with the old, broken down horses and cows, and broken wagons that could pick up, we commenced our journey into the wilderness."[73] On this epic errand into the wild, Young recalled, "I do not suppose we traveled one day from the Missouri River . . . through the cañon, or . . . over the dividing ranges," without "look[ing] for a track where the rails could be laid with success, for a railroad . . . to the Pacific Ocean."[74]

Though the goal of the mass meeting was to "express popular feeling" concerning the railroad, Young and his colleagues went further and sought to link Mormon history to future progress. Such a narrative crafted pioneers as both refugees and amateur railroad surveyors. Though forcibly ejected from the United States, Mormons were also crafted as the ostensible vanguard of American progress. Thus, Mormons' westward migration, a story of courage and resilience in the face of extreme persecution, came to symbolize a masculine pioneer epic that was both quintessentially American and yet superior to any equivalent American story of triumph over adversity. The railroad enabled them to contrast their culture with that of immigrant "others" and stake a claim to whiteness, manhood, and Americanism above Irish, Chinese, and non-Mormon workingmen. Mormon leaders' different visions suggest the variety of ways in which progress was defined in the community. Yet, affirmation came quickly as the church band performed numbers such as "Railroad Polka" and "Hard Times Come Again No More" and the audience shouted its huzzahs.[75]

By late spring of 1868, regularly scheduled trains were running as far west as Laramie, Wyoming. Although construction to this point had gone relatively smoothly, Union Pacific crews prepared for a more arduous stretch of building through the rugged Rocky Mountains. After extensive surveying, Union Pacific superintendent Samuel P. Reed concluded that perhaps the most difficult area of construction would be through the canyons of Utah's Wasatch Mountains. This region was unlike any other on the route, for the Mormon communities of northern Utah could perform immediate grading work with construction provisioned locally. Superintendent Reed signed a contract with Brigham Young in May of 1868 calling for up to five thousand Mormon workers organized into several hundred teams, to perform over 150 miles of grading, tunneling, and bridge masonry, beginning at the head of Echo Canyon through Weber Canyon and to the shores of the Great Salt Lake. This grading contract was worth $2,125,000, and the majority of the work was scheduled to be completed by November of 1868.[76] According to President Young, "this contract is viewed by the brethren of understanding as a God-send."[77]

Earlier that year, Apostle Wilford Woodruff had written in a letter to Franklin D. Richards that as "the great National Railroad is making rapid strides to meet in Utah, [o]ur enemies have great hopes of soon trapping us." Woodruff claimed that Zion's Gentile enemies "are looking for our destruction," and yet, "they will be woefully disappointed," as Brigham Young planned to seize this opportunity to rebound from hard economic times, pay debts, and "gathe[r] means to bring out the Saints from abroad" to build up the Kingdom. Woodruff informed Richards that Young was prepared "to remove the whole Church from England, Elders and all," as part of this "great exertion" to build the railroad.[78] Non-Mormon newspapers corroborate this. On July 12, 1868, the *New York Express* reported that the steamer *Minnesota* landed at the port of New York, carrying at least 531 Mormons, "a very motley group of young and old, male and female . . . from the manufacturing districts of England and Wales." That same evening, the ship *John Bright* arrived, carrying another 700 Mormons, and the editor noted that "3,000 to 5,000 more are expected this season." The "able-bodied men" of these groups informed the newspaper that they were "engaged to work on the Pacific Railroad, under Brigham Young's contract."[79]

Returned missionary Joseph Smith Horne's company, which included 45 emigrants from Switzerland, Bavaria, Württemberg, and the Netherlands, and 412 from the British Isles, departed on June 24, 1868, from Liverpool on the ship *Constitution* and arrived at Castle Garden in early

August.[80] As Horne noted, a customary route was from the port of New York to Albany, Rochester, Detroit, Chicago, and Omaha to Benton, Wyoming Territory, which was at that time the Union Pacific terminus. "Here," he stated, "men and teams from Utah waited our arrival, and on Sunday [August] 16th we were taken by wagons to 'Mormon Emigration Camp' 4 miles distant," prior to traveling by wagon train or on foot to Salt Lake City.[81] Foreign-born Mormon emigrants were incentivized by a cheaper passage rate if they opted to work on Union Pacific construction crews in the Intermountain West. Joining Elder Horne on the *Constitution* was thirty-one-year old John Lazenby, a Mormon convert from Hull, England, who noted that upon arriving at the head of Echo Canyon on September 14, "I bid adieu to my wife and boy and went to work for John W. Young upon the railroad, which I had agreed to do on arriving at New York for which I received a free pass from Omaha to the end of the track. I received 2 dollars per day and board. Stayed at work six weeks and then came on to Salt Lake City."[82]

European-born Mormon emigration accounts, though valuable and voluminous resources, are typically inward looking and relatively silent on the subject of interethnic encounters with non-Mormons. That said, records from the late 1860s reveal a common occurrence: steamships full of both Mormon converts and Irish immigrants. The same was true of trains bound for the Union Pacific's westernmost depots, as both groups were headed west and contact was inevitable. Jens Iver Jensen, aboard the steamer *Manhattan* in the summer of 1867, documented six hundred Scandinavian Saints and "also a lot of Irish people not Mormons."[83] When seventeen-year-old Emily Pickering, an English-born Mormon convert who crossed the Atlantic with over five hundred Saints on the steamship *Minnesota* the following summer arrived in Laramie, Wyoming Territory, she was startled by a group of teamsters who surrounded the train. "I was very frightened," she noted, "thinking that we were surely captured, when they quickly explained that they were the Mormon boys . . . driving the horses for us." As the company trekked toward Utah, Pickering recalled that "the Mormon boys were working in the middle of Echo Canyon building the railroad. My husband was among them, but I was not aware of it then."[84] Though Elder Zebulon Jacobs, who was also aboard the *Minnesota*, commented that the sight of Salt Lake City from Parley's Canyon "seemed like a dream," the long journey to Zion was a harrowing one. He calculated 631 Saints aboard the steamship "in the forward steerage," most of whom kept their distance from the "mixture of all nationalities (with enough Irish to keep them lively)" who were situated "in the other part" of the vessel.[85] At sea or on land, Mormon emigrants such as Pickering and Jacobs found it necessary to contrast the dangers of strangers with the honorable qualities of more familiar Saints, especially the "Mormon boys" along the railroad's right-of-way. If Saints and non-Mormon immigrants were each laboring to bring progress to the West by virtue of the iron horse, Mormon labor, by 1868, had assumed a decidedly more civilized air.

These unskilled immigrants were armies of progress of a different sort. In taking up the national task, the Saints softened public perceptions of Mormonism. Yet, their mission was to build Zion, not America. An 1868 editorial in the *Millennial Star* argued that Mormon labor on the transcontinental railroad would place the "prognostications" and threats of anti-Mormon commentators "in the heap of rubbish where lie buried so many unfulfilled predictions of the overthrow of 'Mormonism.'" Wishing "God speed to the great railroad of the West," the writer hailed that in the Saints' construction of the railroad, "Zion may be built up and adorned and beautified. . . . [T]he State of Deseret may be enriched and developed, and that the way may be prepared for the consummation of the latter-day Work!"[86]

The editors of the Mormon *Deseret News* were overjoyed with the news of Brigham Young's grading contract and celebrated it with editorials that assessed the impact of Mormon work on the transcontinental: "How such people will be disappointed when they know that our citizens expect to do all in their power this Summer to grade the road for the rails at the head of Echo Cañon and this valley! It is gratifying to think that we have such an opportunity offered to us. . . . [T]he grading of this road . . . [will] disabus[e] the public mind respecting us and our views."[87] The grading contract would enable struggling Mormon farmers to survive recent crop failures due to grasshopper invasions and eventually return to their fields. Mormon leaders and workers considered *their* railroad labor a temporary yet honorable occupation and emphasized the need to continue farming in order to support the community and provision future railroad workers.[88] This was a case of farmers working overtime to build a railroad, but for Mormons the "public good" was a holy endeavor. A writer for the *Deseret News* reminded readers that, despite the coming of the railroad, "Latter-day Saints" must never look "to the outside world . . . for their bread." To this end, he noted that Saints' "labors on the railroad" ought "not prevent . . . [the] sow[ing] of a wide breadth of fall grain."[89]

Immediately, Brigham Young enlisted his sons, Joseph A., Brigham Jr., and John W. to subcontract the grading work to church dignitaries and ward bishops. John Sharp and Joseph Young were awarded the largest parts of the grading contract, and they employed crews to perform grading, bridge, and trestle work and to build two tunnels of three hundred and five hundred feet in

Echo and Weber Canyons.[90] A detailed list of jobs and wages for the Union Pacific contract was published twice during the spring and summer of 1868, and the figures indicate that Mormon wages were equivalent to those of the Union Pacific's other construction employees. The jobs and wages shown are based on data published in the *Deseret Evening News* on May 21 and June 9, 1869.

Type of labor	Payment (per cubic yard)
Earth excavation, either borrowed from embankment, wasted from cuts, or hauled not exceeding 200 feet from cuts into embankment	$.27
Earth excavation, hauled more than 200 feet from cuts into embankment.	$.45
Loose rock	$1.57
Solid lime or sand rock	$2.70
Granite	$3.60
Rubble masonry in box culverts, laid in lime or cement	$5.85
Rubble masonry, laid dry.	$5.40
Masonry in bridge abutments and piers, laid in lime mortar or cement, beds and joints dressed, drafts on corners, laid in courses	$13.50
Rubble masonry in bridge abutments and piers, laid dry.	$7.20
Rubble masonry in bridge abutments and piers, laid in cement.	$7.65

The challenge of determining payment in this pre-labor union era of transient railroad construction is assuaged by the fact that Utahns received little of their promised wages and instead were given church tithing credit, travel vouchers, and railroad bonds.[91] While several thousand Mormons worked to complete the grading, tunneling, and bridge building, Union Pacific officials stalled to avoid payment. Not until October 1868, four months after Mormon crews began digging, did the Union Pacific approve the contract.

Though frustrated by the lack of payments and the daily grind of railroad construction, Mormons both inside and outside of the construction camps focused on their investment in this "great national project." Patriotic and honorable labor was the means to gain national respect and to distinguish themselves from the faceless "armies" of immigrant tracklayers who were fast approaching Mormon work sites in Weber and Echo Canyons. Bishops Sharp and Young (the aforementioned subcontractors) and their laborers were under strict instructions to report their progress and the conditions of camp life to local editors and church leaders. An anonymous laborer in Bishop Sharp's camp at Devil's Gate (Weber Canyon) wrote in June of 1868 that his camp of 120 men witnessed no "angry or profane word[s]," always remembered their prayers, and "strictly [observed] the third commandment." Overall, he insisted that "a better set of boys I don't believe will be easily found."[92] Two letters from Echo Canyon reiterated similar themes. In the first, Adolphus Noon, a clerk for subcontractor E. F. Sheets, mentioned that since bookkeeping was almost useless along the line, "I made up my mind to lay hold of the pick and shovel and 'clerk' with that." Even then, Noon argued that digging was "not near so formidable a job as was generally anticipated." Mocking Irish dialect, he then assured readers that the conduct of "our Mormon Boys" was praiseworthy and that, although "we have no whiskey shebangs 'or sich' here yet . . . just as soon as anybody sticks them down we will stick them down . . . deep in the creek."[93] The second letter from Echo City, sent by an anonymous worker, praised the cooperative system upon which Mormons based their railroad camps:

> The railroad is coming. Already it is estimated, one half, if not more of the track down Echo Canyon is ready for the ties and rails. . . . All classes of profession, art and avocation, almost, are represented. Here are the ministers of the gospel and the dusky collier laboring side by side. Here may be seen the Bishop on the embankment and his "diocese" filling their carts, scrapers and shovels from the neighboring cut. Here are the measurer of tapes and calicos and the homoepathic [*sic*] doctor in mud to their knees or knecks [*sic*]. . . . Here the man of literature deciphers hieroglyphics in prying into the seams of sand rock. . . . [S]uch an illustrious corps of practical railroad makers must surely leave their mark.[94]

Advertisements for railroad construction workers in the *Deseret News* enticed able-bodied men in the Salt Lake Valley with guarantees of "the highest wages . . . in cash, [paid] monthly," and directed them to "apply

Figure 2.2. "Mormon contractors advertise for workers," *Deseret News*, September 9, 1868. Courtesy Special Collections, J. Willard Marriott Library, University of Utah, Salt Lake City.

immediately at the Mouth of Weber Kanyon."[95] Yet, as evidenced in the call for workers by Bishops Sharp and Young (figure 2.2), Mormon subcontractors had a certain audience in mind. If desperate for "500 men," they also stressed that "None but Good Men need apply."

Despite the grueling nature of canyon grading and trestle and tunneling work, reports from the Mormon work camps frequently expressed complete and efficient command over tasks—and a general mastery of the environment. Moreover, letters mentioned camp oaths against swearing, brawling, gambling, and alcohol consumption. Writing from "the Head of Echo" in late July of 1868, a *Deseret News* correspondent stated that "'the boys' enjoy themselves, albeit they have plenty of hard work."[96] The proximity and conduct of Bishop E. F. Sheets's and John W. Young's construction camps, he argued, made them "the best . . . encampment[s] I have yet seen in the Cañons. Order governs, harmony reigns, and the best of feelings exist."[97] Workers, contractors, editors, and church dignitaries referred to the Mormon men grading the railroad as "boys" in contrast to the Irish and

Chinese track layers, the "company men," who, by the fall of 1868, were working near the Saints.[98] Such language was perhaps meant to contrast wholesome and innocent manliness with the "rough" varieties commonly associated with transient immigrant workers.[99]

In August 1868, the Central Pacific entered into contracts with Brigham Young and other Mormon leaders to grade sections of the roadbed from Ogden northwest to Monument Point. Young remarked that, for his Mormon boys, "These contracts give us many advantages, besides furnishing money for labor to those whom the grasshoppers have left but little to do, and who could not well otherwise supply themselves with food until another harvest." Additional grading was performed in the vicinity of Promontory, Utah. A second contract with Leland Stanford and the Central Pacific followed in September 1868, when Mormons were called upon to grade roughly two hundred miles of roadbed from Humboldt Wells, Nevada, east into Weber Canyon. Interestingly, Stanford paid manual and "skilled" laborers fairly equal wages, three to six dollars per day, whereas wagonmen earned ten dollars a day. In light of his disappointing experience with the Union Pacific, which had failed to meet monthly payment quotas and had since decided to build its road north of the Great Salt Lake, Brigham Young required that the Central Pacific compensate Mormon laborers and contractors with a cash down payment.[100]

In late 1868 and early 1869, when concerns about the transcontinental junction point had escalated, the Union Pacific's and Central Pacific's Mormon subcontractors and their unskilled graders worked side-by-side along the east slope of Promontory and often in the vicinity of Irish tracklayers. John Casement, the Union Pacific's chief construction supervisor (and of Irish descent), wrote to his wife in Ohio as his largely Irish track-laying crews entered the "wild looking country" that was Utah. With clear disdain, Casement noted: "Brigham Young sent me word that he would like to see us lay track . . . [and] I sent him word all he would have to do would be to come where we were at work and open his eye. He came here but I think so little of him and his pretensions that I did not stay to receive him."[101]

Mormon grading contracts at one point during the transcontinental construction brought them in the vicinity of Irish and Chinese immigrants, mainstays of the Union and Central Pacific workforces. In this context, the boys/men, sober/inebriated, peaceful/violent narratives that the Saints had crafted took on new meaning. In episodes of self-definition, these encounters enabled Mormons to distinguish their manhood and interpretation of progress from those of the railroad companies and their immigrant workers.

Mormon leaders, workers, and residents championed an ordered, community-minded manhood. Contributing to this "great national project," they portrayed themselves and were perceived as peaceful and hard-working; their labor on the railroad was based on a higher moral ground than were the efforts of immigrant "company men."[102] On the other hand, the Irish and Chinese laborers on the Union and Central Pacific were painted by Mormons as outsiders and derided as foreign-born "strangers." Undisciplined, violent, immoral, these transitory laborers were unconcerned with the "public good."[103]

In an 1868 letter to Apostle Franklin D. Richards, Samuel Richards, anticipating "heavy rock work" and an "attack . . . upon the 'Devil's Gate'" at the mouth of Weber Canyon, discussed the plans of Mormon contractors to dominate the work: "This [work] will make a call for that portion of the community not necessarily engaged in farming labor . . . [and] will obviate the necessity of some few thousands of strangers being brought here, to mix and interfere with the settlers, of that class of men who take pleasure in making disturbance wherever they go. . . . It will show that we are interested in forwarding the great national project." "The people," Richards noted, "feel like taking off their coats and going at it."[104] In sum, Mormon workers were building a holy community, and transient immigrants were subjects of the profane world. This helps explain how and why Mormons considered railroad "company men" as less productive, less concerned about permanent settlement, and less civilized than their righteous "boys."

When immigrant track-laying gangs occupied former Mormon construction camps such as Echo City, Uintah, Wasatch, and Kelton, Mormon leaders and local editors characterized these landscapes as "the most wretched communities in the world," and "nests of everything vile and abominable."[105] Others, such as Corrine and Blue Creek, were "the toughest place[s] on the continent . . . morally nearest to the infernal regions of any town on the road."[106] This symbolic transformation of the landscape highlighted the "uncivilized" behavior of immigrants and distanced their role in building the transcontinental and contributing to western progress. Unlike Mormon "boys," these "company men" detracted from, rather than enhanced, the civilizing venture of the Union and Central Pacific.

While railroads opened up new markets, reduced the price of freight, and offered struggling farmers a source of employment and income, Utahns soon had misgivings about the social cost to be paid for "outside world" endowments. A Mormon elder described Bear River City (just beyond Utah's northeast border) as "several hundred tents, wagons and shanties . . . erected for the sale of whiskey and for gambling and dance houses."[107] One scholar has argued that short-lived construction camps such as this one, often dubbed "Terminopolis," did not even survive long enough for "serious disorder" to occur.[108] Yet, not content with documenting only the "hell on wheels" in their midst, the *Deseret News* featured reports from church missionaries at more populated, "demoralized" frontier outposts. The writings of Mormon missionaries and journalists were in fact essential to the creation of "hell on wheels" images that dominate our understanding of the first transcontinental railroad. Bishop W. Seeley's trip to Laramie and Cheyenne, Wyoming, in late 1868 offered the following example as representative of uncivilized versions of progress:

> This town, with another on the other side of the river, has been called into creation by the building of the railway, and they are without exception the most demoralized places I ever saw. Life is of no value here. At least one man per day has been the average of murders. Women, a disgrace to the name, offer themselves openly, and, in fact, I am informed, they have printed invitations affixed to their dwellings to catch the unwary and foolish. Almost every other house is a whiskey mill, gambling hole, or a house of ill fame, and sometimes all three. This description of one city will suffice for all. . . . Such is so-called civilization![109]

Although per capita rates of alcoholism, violence, and "rowdyism" are unknown, many Utahns were convinced that Union and Central Pacific shantytowns were merely sites of "floating populations" of unproductive "roughs."[110] Mormon letters and editorials drew a clear line to separate the benefits of settlement from the consequences of transience. The meaning and significance of productive work differed drastically based on the men who performed it.

To position themselves as far as possible from the "rough" manhood that predominated among transient and immigrant work camps, Mormon men focused on the organization and the spiritual, moral, and physical health of the camps. Observers claimed that Brigham Young's subletting of contracts was a "very superior" system compared "to that usually employed for construction." A group of workers, typically from the same LDS ward, would "combine together, take their sub-contracts, and work it as partners." Unlike immigrant company men, Mormon railroaders "did not tie themselves to hours, nor did they endeavor to kill time by doing as little as possible," for the Saints "had as deep an interest in the completion of the job as the 'boss.'" As a result, one witness remarked that "I have not heard of a strike on President Young's contract since the commencement of the work."[111] A Mormon railroad grader in working in Echo Canyon noted that the workers "drew up and signed a cooperative agreement, and a system of rules, the strict prohibition of

Figure 2.3. Mormon grading party, Union Pacific Railroad construction, deep cut no. 1, Weber Canyon, 1868. Andrew J. Russell Photograph. Used by permission, Utah State Historical Society, all rights reserved.

profane language being one of them." Demonstrating a manly control over their jobs, this worker noted that "the dirt is beginning to fly," and soon the Mormons' "cuts, dams, and grading" were being "repeatedly referred to by the Engineers in speaking to other companies, as fair specimens of how they want the work done."[112]

Transforming Utah's canyons with their virtuous labor, "the brethren" created railroad working environments that were strikingly different from those of the Union Pacific's Irish immigrants, whose "camps . . . give birth to the towns along the track, which are the nests of everything vile and abominable."[113] According to an 1868 article in the *Deseret News*, when

Figure 2.4. "Rocky Mountain Glee Club," drawn from the ranks of Mormon Union Pacific Railroad workers, 1868–1869. Andrew J. Russell Photograph. Used by permission, Utah State Historical Society, all rights reserved.

unconfirmed reports that his Mormon graders had "struck for wages" while performing "heavy work" in Weber Canyon reached Bishop Sharp, the contractor "gave his most unqualified denial." "The brethren," noted the writer, "have the best of feelings, and work with good spirits and with a desire to do all that is asked of them."[114] A surviving photograph of the "heavy work" performed by Mormon crews in Weber Canyon captures the writer's sentiment (see Figure 2.3).

Further evidence suggests that the Saints carried out railroad labor for the Union and Central Pacific with even more zeal than they did in local cooperative projects, particularly since railroading in 1868 and 1869 put them in the national spotlight. The members of the "Rocky Mountain Glee Club," drawn from the ranks of Mormon construction workers, dressed in coats and ties to perform for and with the men in their camps. While very little is known about the Glee Club and no record of its songs has survived, an Andrew J. Russell photograph (see Figure 2.4) depicts these Mormon railroad workers as the essence of masculine civility, with their boots polished and white dress shirts perfectly starched. These laborers were both building and refining the filthy transportation frontier.

Clearly, the glee club was attuned to the meaning of Mormon labor on the railroad and the need to exhibit—and perform—difference from its uncivilized immigrant counterparts.

While not a member of the Rocky Mountain Glee Club, James Crane, a grader from Sugarhouse, in Salt Lake City, undoubtedly shared their sentiments. In 1868, Crane wrote the following "ditty" to describe the Mormons' righteous railroad work. The song is noteworthy, among other reasons, for its marked difference from the songs of immigrant transportation workers that often expressed an abhorrence of wage labor in "free" America and a longing for home:

(CHORUS)
Hurrah! Hurrah! For the railroad's begun!
Three cheers for our contractor, his name's Brigham Young!
Hurrah! Hurrah! we're honest and true,
For if we stick to it's bound to go through.

Now there's Mr. Reed, he's a gentleman true,
He knows very well what the "Mormons" can do;
He knows in their work they are lively and gay,
And just the right boys to build a railway.

Our camp is united, we all labor hard;
And if we work faithfully we'll get our reward;
Our leader is wise and industrious too
And all things he tells us we're willing to do.

The boys in our camp are lighthearted and gay,
We work on the railway ten hours a day;
We are thinking of fine times we'll have in the fall,
Then we'll be with our ladies and go to the ball.

The great locomotive next season will come
To gather the Saints from their far distance home;
And bring them to Utah in peace here to stay,
While the judgments of God sweep the wicked away.[115]

In another 1868 song, "The Utah Iron Horse," Mormon workers expressed both self-deprecating humor and self-evident racism in anticipating the impact of the transcontinental railroad. The song exulted that "the iron horse is coming, with a train in its wake," and went on:

We have isolated been; but soon we shall be seen;
Through this wide mountain region, folks can learn of our religion;
"Civilized" we shall be, many folks we shall see,
Lords and nobles, tramps and beggars, anyhow we'll see the niggers;
Saints will come, sinners too, we'll have all that we can do,
For this great Union railroad it will fetch the Devil through.[116]

Immigrant track-laying camps, like mining camps, were allegedly littered with men whose character sharply contrasted with Mormons who labored in (and for) communities. According to historian Robert Athearn, Mormons feared transients and desired farmers, "handscraftmen," and persons likely to settle comfortably into already established villages.[117] Here, Mormon values resembled those of the native-born residents in eastern and midwestern canal towns during the antebellum period. But in the context of internal improvement work, a profound difference is apparent. A great majority of American farmers in the antebellum era prided their status as "independent" far too much to work on canals and railroads. This type of work was seen as degrading, for "gang" labor conjured up images of black slavery, and was thought to strip men of their self-sufficient status by marking them as beholden to another. Such a reaction on the part of America's native-born in part necessitated the employment of large numbers of working-class immigrants throughout the nineteenth century. Mormons, while partial to an agriculturalist and permanent settlement-oriented worldview, chose to leave the comforts of home, farm, and profession to work—in gangs and under the cooperative principle—on the Union Pacific and Central Pacific railroads. They had been called to this holy work by the prophet, another feature of cooperative labor in Zion. This fact, too, distinguished them from their non-Mormon counterparts elsewhere in the nation.[118]

In late September 1868, a broadside entitled "Work and Good Wages for All" appeared in the *Deseret News*. It encouraged able-bodied and willing men to report immediately to "Weber Cañon" to complete grading for the Central Pacific, 150 miles westward from the mouth of the canyon. Writing from the construction camp, the author claimed that Mormons were "gaining a national reputation by our labor on the railroad" and in the process "disabusing the minds of hundreds of thousands who have been falsely impressed concerning us." Mormon railroad builders, he noted, had dramatically transformed the typically rough-edged environment of transportation labor: "In our grading camps there have been no drunkenness, blasphemous language, nor any of those disgraceful sights and sounds which have abounded in the grading camps farther east [in the Wyoming Territory]. We should take a pride in sustaining this reputation." Moreover, the writer argued that "it would be cheaper, too, for us to build the road for nothing and make a present of it to the company, than to have our Territory cursed and our settlements polluted with the scum that infest the line east."[119] A prominent church member echoed this theme, insisting that it would be better "for the Saints to do the work for nothing . . . than to let outsiders do it, as it would cost us more to preserve our cattle and horses from thieves, and our family from insult, than to roll up our sleeves and go and do the work ourselves."[120]

Thus, daily work and experiences on the transcontinental railroad—its companies, employees, and overall mission—solidified Mormon perspectives on the benefits and dangers of progress. Faced with the threat of immigrant work camps in their midst, Mormon workers and their superiors sought to "other" themselves from the evils of progress and to "other" the Union Pacific and Central Pacific "company men" from the benefits of the "great national work" in which they, too, were engaged. Mormons crafted themselves as a unique people, best able to execute the manifest work of civilizing a nation. Moreover, the "other" in their midst confirmed to Mormons the holiness of their leaders and the godliness of their mission. Theirs was a peoplehood superior to the nationhood promised by the railroad.

Constant references to "the East" not only were emblematic of the defensive mentality of the Saints but also indicated that Irish and not Chinese workers were more often the focus of "hell on wheels" descriptions and stories. The *Deseret News*, in fact, occasionally blamed Central Pacific officials, not their "celestial" armies, for the uncivilized conditions on the railroad:

> We have seen it urged against the Chinese that they are bound fast in the swaddling clothes of superstition, from which they show no disposition to emancipate themselves. But who can expect them to do otherwise under the treatment they receive? Cling to their Heathenism? They would be little less than idiots not to do so under the circumstances. Men may prate to them about American civilization, free and enlightened institutions, the spirit of progress and Christianity until doomsday, but they [the Chinese] will fail to respect or attach any value to these high-sounding phrases and professions while they are treated like wild beasts.[121]

In contrast, the *Union Vedette*, Utah's first anti-Mormon newspaper, spoke admirably about Central Pacific officials who marshaled "the indomitable spirit of American enterprise" and yet heaped even more praise on its Chinese graders and track-layers, whose "labor and determination" qualified them for the "herculean task" of building over the High Sierras.[122]

The *Deseret News* criticized California's politicians and citizens for being "particularly hard" on the Chinese, who "are treated like dogs. They are chased, abused, robbed and abominably maltreated . . . and even the dogs are set upon them and taught to bite them." What bothered the *News* reporter the most, however, was that the Californians who "torture this race call themselves Christians" while they "mock and denounce [the Chinese] as idolators [*sic*] and heathens." Taking the high ground, the Mormon editor argued that the "true and only correct" solution to this dilemma was to treat the Chinese workers "as human beings" and "grant them the rights of citizenship" if they "can prove themselves capable." He continued: "These Asiatics are willing to work, and work cheap at any kind of drudgery. If the Anglo-Saxon is the superior being which he affects to be, he can with safety assume the direction of this class of laborers. . . . If he treat them kindly, and pay them honestly, he will do more to convert them to his religion and ways than years of preaching with a contrary practice would do, and he need not be afraid that their degradation, vices, or barbarism will hurt him."[123]

The Mormons, busy in building "the Kingdom," did not engage in Chinese-baiting. The Chinese posed no threat to the civic, political, and religious life of Utah's Mormons, and church leaders often distanced themselves from the American majority on the Chinese "problem."[124] As such, a sympathetic, even humanitarian stance is noticeable in the columns of the *Deseret News*. Californians, the editors argued, should not worry, for the "force of circumstances" would gradually "push" Chinese workers to distant frontiers of wage labor, so long as they remained content in "work[ing] for less than a dollar" per day in various industries.[125] At the very least, Chinese immigrants were of great value to the country as a cheap source of labor. The presence of Chinese immigrants "in large numbers in the Western States and Territories," argued the editors, "will inevitably work a great revolution in labor." Unlike the "European laborer" who "will not work for less than two or three dollars a day," the Chinese are "frugal and patient, and as industrious as a beaver." Willing to "live where one of the so-called superior race would starve," the Chinese worker could subsist on merely "a little rice," "eats meat but seldom . . . indulges in no dissipation," and in general, "is simple, abstinent, and very economical."[126] Few in number, transitory, and with no desire to confront, the Chinese did little to distract Mormons from their mission.[127]

Census data is problematic because railroad construction labor was transient labor, thus presenting census enumerators with continually moving targets or none at all. As David Emmons notes, "building a railroad was not the same as working for one."[128] Yet numbers, proximity, and contract obligations likely influenced Mormons' sympathy for the plight of the

Chinese. Immigrants from China made up only one-half of 1 percent of Utah's official population in 1870, and only one Chinese immigrant was counted in the 1870 census for Salt Lake City, compared to 157 Irish immigrants in Salt Lake and 502 in the state. Moreover, Mormons performed more extensive labor for the Union Pacific than for the Central Pacific and were in closer proximity to the former's Irish workers, who worked near the Mormon capital for a longer period of time—based on the UPRR's end-of-track dates for Evanston, Wyoming Territory (December 4, 1868), and Echo City, Utah Territory, January 15, 1869). However, attitudes in Utah changed a decade after the completion of the railroad and amid the debates surrounding Chinese exclusion, as Utah's newspapers began to echo the sentiments of anti-Chinese westerners.[129]

During the construction period, Union Pacific's Irish workers were an altogether different story. Local correspondents for the *Deseret News* seized on accounts that demonstrated the cultural superiority of Mormon workers in the canyons. Non-Mormon contractors Joseph Nounan and "Miller & Patterson," apparently fed up with their own "strikers," were "anxious to hire workmen from Utah." According to one report, these contractors "declared that they would discharge every man of the regular [Irish] navvies in their employment, who are always dissatisfied and give a great amount of trouble because of their intemperate and riotous habits." Miller and Patterson informed the writer that they sought "workmen from this Territory, in preference to the regular railroad hands." Summarizing this railroad work "in the Cañons," the *Deseret News* noted that the Saints, despite their "little experience" in railroading, have "satisf[ied] [the contractors] of the superiority of Utah men as workers," for "they are sober, quiet, orderly, and do their work without any trouble, giving satisfaction in performing it." Moreover, according to church leaders, strikes among Mormon workers were "not to be thought of," and the "absence of profanity, disorder, or quarrels in the camps was highly gratifying."[130] Contact with the "other" had the effect of strengthening the resolve of Mormon communities and clarifying their ideas about proper manhood and productive progress.

The specter of cross-cultural interaction that railroad labor produced coincided with the thirty-eighth semiannual LDS Church Conference in 1868. The railroad now nearing completion, a major theme of the conference centered on the potential impact of Gentile-Mormon trade in Utah. Participants voted to "withdraw the hand of fellowship from all those who persisted in the policy of sustaining our enemies" and agreed to limit economic intercourse with Gentiles to "absolute necessities."[131] Once the evils of progress were made apparent to Mormons, economic self-defense measures aimed at "the rapidly approaching dangers of outsiders, coming in with the Pacific Railroad, who are avowed enemies of Mormonism" made sense.[132] Though it did "increase intercourse," Brigham Young's earlier argument that the transcontinental railroad would "soften prejudices, and bind the country together," was realized neither by Mormons nor by their avowed cultural enemies working in the Great Basin region.[133]

As camps of Irish graders and track-layers entered Utah, the pious Mormon laborers feared the worst. In December 1868 and January 1869, Union Pacific officials replaced Mormon tunnel workers in Echo and Weber Canyons with Irish crews, "outsiders" imported from Bear River City, Wyoming, and equipped with nitroglycerin.[134] These seasoned construction workers were meant to relieve the Mormons of their "hardest and heaviest work" in canyon tunnels.[135] According to a letter from an anonymous Mormon laborer working below the mouth of Echo Canyon, the entrance of the Irish, "direct from [a] scene of hostilities at Bear River [City]," frightened the Mormon graders. The writer discussed how, unbeknownst to him, "the Celts" had relieved Bishop Sharp's grading crew to speed up tunneling work:

> Not fully aware of such change, this evening as I passed down, everything tunnelward seemed unaccountably metamorphosed. Not one familiar face; a demented stare instead of a friendly eye, a thud-thud stalk instead of the elastic tread, and broken noses, blackened eyes and the "crayther" predominant. . . . [They claim that] they can "put her through" [the tunnel] within six weeks; which, if accomplished, will be doing more in that space of time than has been done during the past summer and fall.[136]

Mormons, whose bodies had often been racialized and dehumanized by detractors who suggested they appeared as "creatures from another planet," complete with "horns or a cloven foot," could nonetheless reciprocate in the presence of Irish immigrants.[137] As this Mormon worker noted, the Union Pacific "company's swarms of 'Ould Ireland's' sons" were unrefined, animalistic "craythers" [creatures], bruised and broken from the strain of heavy construction and as a result of their rough lifestyles.[138] Their mere presence at "Tunnelville" had "metamorphosed" this construction environment. Their pace of labor and style of living held a dangerous and foreign quality, more primitive and out of control than was common in the cultured construction communities of the Saints.

Yet, in February, the near-completed work at Echo and Weber Canyons was transferred back to the Mormon contractors to finish, and Brigham Young noted with satisfaction that "the big tunnel which the company's men took off from our hands to complete in a hurry has been proffered

Figure 2.5. Golden Spike Ceremony, Promontory Summit, Utah Territory, May 10, 1869. Fifteen minutes after ceremonial "last" spikes had been driven, under the direction of photographers Andrew J. Russell and Charles Savage, the special trains were positioned facing each other. Accordingly, the Central Pacific's Jupiter (left) and the Union Pacific's No. 119 touched pilots. Chief Engineers Samuel Montague (left) and Grenville Dodge shook hands, champagne was distributed, and the ceremony's participants posed for what would become the most famous photograph of the nineteenth century. Andrew J. Russell photograph, no. 227. Courtesy of Yale Collection of Western Americana, Beinecke Rare Book and Manuscript Library.

Figure 2.6. Frank Bellew, "Does Not Such a Meeting Make Amends?" Wood engraving, *Frank Leslie's Illustrated Newspaper*, May 29, 1869, 176. Note the savage Indians and other wilderness inhabitants fleeing this "civilizing" scene. Courtesy of Library of Congress, Prints and Photographs Division, LC-USZC2-747.

Figure 2.7. "The East and the West," *Crofutt's Trans-Continental Tourist's Guide*, 5th Vol., 4th Annual Revise (New York: George A. Crofutt, 1873), 118. Two Chinese workers appear in this illustration, on the far left near the train, marked by their silk skullcaps and a single long braid, or queue, hanging down their backs. Courtesy of Yale Collection of Western Americana, Beinecke Rare Book and Manuscript Library.

back again." Young seized this opportunity to contrast the two workforces. He maintained that the Irish crews, who had at least a four-to-one worker advantage over the Mormon crews, "withal, have not been doing over two-thirds as much work." Admitting that nitroglycerin's superiority over powder would allow Bishop Sharp's and Joseph Young's men to blast through the 772-foot "Tunnel 2" at the head of Echo Canyon, the Mormon leader went further, arguing that "the sobriety, steadiness and industry of our men gives us a marked advantage."[139]

Scholars have argued that throughout modern history, masculinity has symbolized courage, physical toughness, virtue, honor, order, and the best hopes and ideals of civilized society. Some have pointed to the rough, martial, and even degenerative variants of masculinity. In this case, Mormons suggested that their immigrant and native-born counterparts on the railroad had weakened ideal manliness in their transiency, combativeness, drinking, and even in their language. Mormon workers, on the other hand, had sharpened western masculinity in their arduous yet honorable and faith-based labor in Utah's canyons. Regenerating masculinity on the wage-workers' frontier, Mormons depicted themselves as hardy, civilized, and worthy specimens of a triumphant nation. Yet so principled and superior was their labor that they stood apart from—and above—the native-born and immigrant men whose work had come to represent the culture of American progress.[140]

When Mormons celebrated the progress of their railroad construction workers, they did so in a manner that denied the work of "uncivilized" railroad crews in which violence, drunkenness, and disorder were thought to hinder any sense of worthy production. Historians studying internal improvements and national public works have found that canal and railroad construction laborers were often distanced by civic and community leaders, moral reformers, and politicians. In this case, however, it was Mormon workers who, in their actions, writings, and communities, denigrated the contributions of their counterparts by perpetuating images of reckless, unmanly, and uncultured progress.[141] Mormons clearly exaggerated the threat of violence and the pervasiveness of alcohol abuse in an occupation that often encouraged masculine camaraderie—even its rough variants.

In completing the transcontinental railroad, Mormons were introduced to the frontier of transportation labor and the threats of "higher civilization" leveled by their detractors. Work on the railroad thrust the Saints into the national spotlight and provoked a host of responses in and outside of the Mormon community. In many ways, the "progress" that the Union Pacific and Central Pacific brought to Utah was no different than the social and economic developments that accompanied the "Iron Horse" in other locations. What was different, however, was the manner in which Mormons selectively adopted, resisted, and redefined such progress.

Relatively few Mormons actually attended the transcontinental railroad celebration at Promontory, although their work helped complete the project. Brigham Young, who declined an invitation, sent as his emissaries Bishop John Sharp, Ogden mayor Lorin Farr, and Chauncey West, who, as Young's contractors, had completed their work for both companies and had received $2 million, less than half of what was owed. Charles Savage, an official Union Pacific photographer at the event (and a devout Mormon), commented, in reference to the U.P.'s Irish construction workers, that "the company [did] the country a service in sending such men back to Omaha—for their presence would be a scourge upon any community." Moreover, he noted that "at Blue River [*sic*] the returning demons . . . were being piled upon the cars in every stage of drunkenness. Every ranch or tent has whiskey for sale. Verily the men earn their money like horses and spend it like asses."[142]

Along with Andrew J. Russell's famous photograph of the 1869 Golden Spike ceremony, popular representations of the Promontory celebration published in *Frank Leslie's Illustrated Newspaper*, *Croffut's Trans-Continental Tourist's Guide*, and in other periodicals crafted a dramatic, nationalistic scene. Some of these carefully constructed visual commemorations incorporated Chinese, Irish, Mormon, and American construction workers—and even fictional representatives of the "warlike" Indians of the Great Plains—into the transcontinental pageant of American development. Perhaps their participation in the event was didactic: an object lesson for uncivilized others in the consequences of western expansion. "Progress" would soon mean territorial dispossession, Chinese exclusion, and a federal attack on Mormon authority.

Nonetheless, the Golden Spike ceremony echoed the original mission of the transcontinental railroad: to civilize a wilderness and bind a country together. Mormons, in their labor on the line, exposed the inherent contradictions of such "great national work." The railroad had neither "civilized" nor "doomed" Mormons in the ways their detractors had hoped. Instead, it offered Mormon workers, leaders, and followers an opportunity to help raise the banner of American progress. In the process, the Saints civilized the railroad's rough edges, transformed notions of labor masculinity in their "productive" work, created negative reference groups to amplify their righteous contribution, and refashioned American progress to suit the goals of their Great Basin Kingdom.

A separate celebration honoring the completion of the transcontinental railroad took place in Salt Lake City on May 10, 1869. The *Salt Lake Daily Telegraph* noted that "a large congregation assembled in the Tabernacle," and after an Ogden band played music and the chaplain offered a prayer, "Professor W. Burton" gave a stirring address. As this railroad "spans the continent," Burton noted, it "tender[s] to the world an opportunity of a better acquaintance with the people of Utah and their peculiar institutions, which will . . . correct the base calumnies that have been circulated from the pulpit and press." Gesturing panoramically to the crowd, he remarked that "land, but a few years ago was covered with sagebrush, half devoured by the crickets and the grasshoppers," had been transformed by "one of the greatest tasks ever undertaken by man." Burton then posed a rhetorical question: "Who is it that produced this mighty change? The misrepresented citizens of Utah, through the blessings of God. Jesus said that a corrupt tree could not bring forth good fruit. Then come, ye Christians of every land, and come and see and taste the fruit that the Mormon tree has borne."[143]

Though Mormon labor on the transcontinental railroad did little to divert public attention from the practice of polygamy, it kept Mormons in regional and national news that increasingly centered on the "race" to further American progress. Mormons not only endeavored to frame this news according to their cultural values but crafted themselves as both the visionaries and executors of railroad progress. Mormon dignitaries and workers contested their negative public image with manly and courageous labor on the transcontinental railroad. At the same time, they contested the character and pace of progress within the borders of Zion. Beyond laboring for recognition as Americans, Mormons worked to prove the ascendancy of their men, culture, and holy community. In reaching to heaven and manhood, they positioned themselves as superior while denying mortal and immortal rewards to their fellow workers.

For these poor, stereotyped, "profligate outcasts," the transcontinental railroad was a heaven on wheels. Working on the railroad, in theory, held out the chance of national acceptance. Yet in practice it produced a renewed sense of cultural superiority. As Mormons toiled to complete the railroad, they also constructed a Mormon American identity and a Mormon masculinity by setting themselves apart from the underworld of progress and the heathen world of immigrant workers.

Notes

1. Elliott West, *The Last Indian War: The Nez Perce Story* (New York: Oxford University Press, 2009), 319. For an extended analysis, see West, "Reconstructing Race," *Western Historical Quarterly*, 34, no. 1 (Spring 2003): 7–26.
2. Gary Y. Okihiro, *Common Ground: Reimagining American History* (Princeton: Princeton University Press, 2001); see chapter 1 in particular. While many historians have examined the role of the transcontinental railroad in completing America's continental empire, few have attempted to connect it to endeavors and developments beyond the West and the nation; namely, the centuries-long quest to reach the Orient. America's transcontinental railroads achieved this by establishing ownership of (and operating) steamship companies which served Asia from ports on the West Coast. For a recent study that conceptualizes and situates the West transnationally, see Richard V. Francaviglia, *Go East, Young Man: Imagining the American West as the Orient* (Logan: Utah State University Press, 2011).
3. California's golden spike remains on display at Stanford University's Cantor Arts Center, http://museum.stanford.edu/.
4. Quoted in John Hoyt Williams, *A Great and Shining Road: The Epic Story of the Transcontinental Railroad* (Lincoln: University of Nebraska Press, 1996), 264.
5. Mark Fiege, *The Republic of Nature: An Environmental History of the United States* (Seattle: University of Washington Press, 2012), 229.
6. For studies of masculine "crises" and American masculinities, see Judith A. Allen, "Men Interminably in Crisis? Historians on Masculinity, Sexual Boundaries, and Manhood," *Radical History Review* 82, no. 1 (January 2002): 191–207; Mark C. Carnes, *Secret Ritual and Manhood in Victorian America* (New Haven: Yale University Press, 1989); Ava Baron, "Technology and the Crisis of Masculinity: The Gendering of Work and Skill in the US Printing Industry, 1850–1920," in *Skill and Consent: Contemporary Studies in the Labour Process*, ed. Andrew Sturdy, David Knights, and Hugh Willmott (New York: Routledge, 1992), 67–96; Michael Kimmel, *Manhood in America: A Cultural History* (New York: Free Press, 1996); Calvin Thomas, *Male Matters: Masculinity, Anxiety, and the Male Body on*

the Line (Urbana: University of Illinois Press, 1996); Ava Baron, ed., *Work Engendered: Toward a New History of American Labor* (Ithaca: Cornell University Press, 1991); Ava Baron, "Masculinity, the Embodied Male Worker, and the Historian's Gaze," *International Labor and Working-Class History* 69 (Spring 2006): 143–60; Gregory L. Kaster, "Labour's True Man: Organised Workingmen and the Language of Manliness in the USA, 1827–1877," *Gender and History* 13, no. 1 (April 2001): 24–64; Steven Maynard, "Rough Work and Rugged Men: The Social Construction of Masculinity in Working-Class History," *Labour/Le Travail* 23 (Spring 1989): 159–69; Gail Bederman, *Manliness and Civilization: A Cultural History of Gender and Race in the United States, 1880–1917* (Chicago: University of Chicago Press, 1995); Amy S. Greenberg, *Manifest Manhood and the Antebellum American Empire* (New York: Cambridge University Press, 2005); Kristin L. Hoganson, *Fighting for American Manhood: How Gender Politics Provoked the Spanish-American and Philippine-American Wars* (New Haven: Yale University Press, 1998); Mark C. Carnes and Clyde Griffen, eds., *Meanings for Manhood: Constructions of Masculinity in Victorian America* (Chicago: University of Chicago Press, 1990); E. Anthony Rotundo, *American Manhood: Transformations in Masculinity from the Revolution to the Modern Era* (New York: Basic Books, 1994); and Joshua R. Greenberg, *Advocating the Man: Masculinity, Organized Labor, and the Household in New York, 1800–1840* (New York: Columbia University Press, 2009).

7. Maynard, "Rough Work and Rugged Men," 159–69.
8. Kaster, "Labour's True Man," 26. This chapter is unique in that it does not deal with "organized skilled white workingmen" but rather with unskilled workers (native-born and immigrant) on a remote frontier of the American West.
9. Bederman, *Manliness and Civilization*, see chapter 1 in particular.
10. Ibid., 20–21. The othering of African American men, in particular, was critical to this process, and it is yet another factor that differentiates this article from Bederman's analysis. Moreover, railroad construction workers (whether native-born or immigrant) typically did not identify as, nor were they considered, middle class. Finally, when the terms "manhood," "manly," "manliness," "masculine," and "masculinity" appear in the following study, they do not refer to fixed traits or values, but rather to culturally adaptable ones that immigrant and native-born men transformed and contested over time.
11. As some scholars, most notably W. Paul Reeve, have explored, the apparent differences were not only religious, cultural, and ideological; they were physical. Reeve, *Religion of a Different Color: Race and the Mormon Struggle for Whiteness* (forthcoming from Oxford University Press).
12. Richard White, *Railroaded: The Transcontinentals and the Making of Modern America* (New York: W. W. Norton, 2011), 281–82.
13. Gunther Peck, *Reinventing Free Labor: Padrones and Immigrant Workers in the North American West, 1880–1930* (New York: Cambridge University Press, 2000), 129–45.
14. Ibid., chapters 4–6. For earlier studies of immigration, migration, and labor, see John Bodnar, *The Transplanted: A History of Immigrants in Urban America* (Bloomington: Indiana University Press, 1987); James R. Barrett, *Work and Community in the Jungle: Chicago's Packinghouse Workers, 1894–1922* (Urbana: University of Illinois Press, 1987); and Lizabeth Cohen, *Making a New Deal:*

Industrial Workers in Chicago, 1919–1939 (New York: Cambridge University Press, 1991). Peck's work builds on that of Sarah Deutsch, *No Separate Refuge: Culture, Class, and Gender on an Anglo-Hispanic Frontier in the American Southwest, 1880–1940* (New York: Oxford University Press, 1989). More recently, see Matthew Frye Jacobson, *Whiteness of a Different Color: European Immigrants and the Alchemy of Race* (Cambridge: Harvard University Press, 1999); Moon-Ho Jung, *Coolies and Cane: Race, Labor, and Sugar in the Age of Emancipation* (Baltimore: Johns Hopkins University Press, 2006); Mae Ngai, *Impossible Subjects: Illegal Aliens and the Making of Modern America* (Princeton: Princeton University Press, 2005); Erika Lee, *At America's Gates: Chinese Immigration during the Exclusion Era, 1882–1943* (Chapel Hill: University of North Carolina Press, 2007); and David M. Emmons, *Beyond the American Pale: The Irish in the West, 1845–1910* (Norman: University of Oklahoma Press, 2010).

15. Carlos A. Schwantes, "The Concept of the Wageworkers' Frontier: A Framework for Future Research," *Western Historical Quarterly* 18, no. 1 (January 1987): 39–55.
16. Leonard J. Arrington, *Great Basin Kingdom: An Economic History of the Latter-day Saints, 1830–1900* (Cambridge: Harvard University Press, 1958). See also note 3, this chapter.
17. Following Arrington, historians have emphasized the Mormon Church's seemingly unwavering support for the transcontinental railroad in spite of national attention to the church's "isolationism." Robert G. Athearn focuses on the role that Mormon leaders and missionaries played in identifying both the threats and benefits that the railroad posed to the church's economic control over Utah and its people. See Robert G. Athearn, "Opening the Gates of Zion: Utah and the Coming of the Union Pacific Railroad," *Utah Historical Quarterly* 36, no. 4 (Fall 1968): 292–314. John J. Stewart devotes a chapter to Utah's contribution to the railroad in a study that otherwise describes the foremost role of Union and Central Pacific officials. His brief discussion of Utah's involvement highlights the scandal that prevented Union Pacific officials from adequately remunerating Mormon workers in Echo and Weber Canyon in 1868 and 1869. See Stewart, *The Iron Trail to the Golden Spike* (Salt Lake City: Deseret Book Company, 1969). Clarence Reeder's dissertation maintains a territorial focus, describing Mormon labor on the Union and Central Pacific with emphasis on the various branch line railroads in Utah. Clarence Reeder, "The History of Utah's Railroads, 1869–1883" (PhD diss., University of Utah, 1970). See also Richard E. Kotter, "The Transcontinental Railroad and Ogden City Politics," *Utah Historical Quarterly* 42, no. 3 (Summer 1974): 278–84; Richard O. Cowan, "Steel Rails and the Utah Saints," *Journal of Mormon History* 27, no. 2 (Fall 2001): 177–84; and Craig L. Foster, "'That Canny Scotsman': John Sharp and the Union Pacific Negotiations, 1869–72," *Journal of Mormon History* 27, no. 2 (Fall 2001): 197–214. Confirming, but not building upon, Arrington's work, these scholars see unanimity among Mormon leaders about the nature of progress and the Mormon contribution to it, and describe the challenges the railroad presented in distinctly religious and economic terms.
18. New York Congressman Fernando Wood is quoted in Orson F. Whitney, *Popular History of Utah* (Salt Lake City: The Deseret News, 1916), 194.
19. W. Paul Reeve, "The Wrong Side of White," *Sightings*, May 31, 2012, http://

divinity.uchicago.edu/martycenter/publications/sightings/archive_2012/0531.shtml. As Reeve notes, "The historical arc of Mormonism's racial dance is richly ironic," for by today's standards Mormons are viewed as "too white."

20. Referred to as the Pacific Railway Act, its original title was, "An Act to aid in the construction of a railroad and telegraph line from the Missouri River to the Pacific Ocean, and to secure to the government the use of the same for postal, military, and other purposes." *US Statutes at Large* 12 (1862): 489. An 1864 revision of this act ceded all natural resources on the line to the railroads and empowered each company to "enter . . . purchase, take, and hold any lands or premises," within one hundred feet of the main line, "that may be necessary and proper for the construction and working of said road." *US Statutes at Large* 13 (1864): 356.
21. See David Hayward Bain, *Empire Express: Building the First Transcontinental Railroad* (New York: Viking, 1999), and Maury Klein, *Union Pacific*, vol. 1, *Birth of a Railroad, 1862–1893* (New York: Doubleday, 1987).
22. *US Statutes at Large* 16 (1869): 56.
23. Patricia Nelson Limerick, *Legacy of Conquest: The Unbroken Past of the American West* (New York: W. W. Norton, 1987), 27–28.
24. Terryl L. Givens, *The Viper on the Hearth: Mormons, Myths, and the Construction of Heresy* (New York: Oxford University Press, 1997), 4–5. Peculiarities included ongoing revelation, contemporary prophets, and the doctrines of plural marriage and blood atonement. Though the concept of blood atonement was repudiated by the LDS Church in 1978, in traditional Mormon theology, it refers to sins for which the atonement of Jesus does not apply. In order to achieve the highest degree of salvation, Mormons who have committed such sins must, in the words of Brigham Young, "have their blood spilt upon the ground, that the smoke thereof might ascend to heaven as an offering for their sins." Brigham Young, September 21, 1856, *Journal of Discourses,* vol. 4 (London: LDS Booksellers Depot, 1857), 51–63 ; Young, February 8, 1857, *Journal of Discourses,* vol. 4 (1857), 220–21.
25. Daniel P. Kidder, *Mormonism and the Mormons: A Historical View of the Rise and Progress of the Sect Self-Styled Latter-Day Saints* (New York: G. A. Lane and P. P. Sandford, 1842), 7–8. See also Pomeroy Tucker, *Origin, Rise, and Progress of Mormonism; Biography of its Founders and History of its Church; Personal Remembrances and Historical Collections Hitherto Unwritten* (New York: D. Appleton, 1867).
26. Robert W. Beers, *The Mormon Puzzle and How to Solve It* (New York: Funk and Wagnalls, 1887), 17. Beers then lamented, "But thus far it has successfully withstood even the fiercest opposition."
27. Givens, *The Viper on the Hearth*, 5; see also, 3–13.
28. T. B. H. Stenhouse, *The Rocky Mountain Saints: A Full and Complete History of the Mormons, from the First Vision of Joseph Smith to the Last Courtship of Brigham Young* (London: Ward, Lock, and Tyler, 1874), 497–98.
29. See Rotundo, *American Manhood*, chapters 8–9.
30. See Michael Kimmel, *Manhood in America: A Cultural History* (New York: Free Press, 1996).
31. Megan Sanborn Jones, *Performing American Identity in Anti-Mormon Melodrama* (New York: Routledge, 2009), 53, 63–65. In an 1870 sermon, Brigham Young argued that, as a polygamous husband, his authority extended beyond his family to

"my neighbors and people around me." He continued, "If I am thus controlled by the Spirit of the Most High I am a king, I am supreme so far as the control of self is concerned; and it also enables me to control my wives and children ... [for] [T]hey will be perfectly submissive to my dictates." Young, July 24, 1870, *Journal of Discourses*, vol. 13 (London: LDS Booksellers Depot, 1871), 272.

32. Quoted in Arrington, *Great Basin Kingdom*, 255.
33. Jones, *Performing American Identity in Anti-Mormon Melodrama*, 65.
34. Charles H. Brigham, "The Mormon Problem," *Old and New* 1 (May 1870): 638.
35. See Figure 2.3. Dan Moos, *Outside America: Race, Ethnicity, and the Role of the American West in National Belonging* (Hanover: Dartmouth College Press, 2005), 108.
36. Alfred Henry Lewis, "The Viper on the Hearth, Part 1: Mormonism: Its Plots, Plans, and Intrigues Against American Homes," *Cosmopolitan Magazine* 50, no. 4 (March 1911): 439.
37. Eric Foner, *Free Soil, Free Labor, and Free Men: The Ideology of the Republican Party before the Civil War* (New York: Oxford University Press, 1970), 130.
38. Quoted in Brigham Henry Roberts, *History of the Church of Jesus Christ of Latter-day Saints, Period I*, 5 vols. (Salt Lake City: The Church of Jesus Christ of Latter-day Saints, 1909), 5: 397. See also, Whitney, *Popular History of Utah*, 158.
39. Roberts, *History of the Church*, 5: 397.
40. Quoted in Edward Tullidge, *Life of Brigham Young; or, Utah and Her Founders* (New York: privately printed, 1877), 387.
41. *Congressional Globe*, 37th Cong., 2nd Sess. (Washington, DC, 1862), pt. 2, 1581, pt. 3, 2507, and Appendix, 385. See also E. B. Long, *The Saints and the Union: Utah Territory during the Civil War* (Urbana: University of Illinois Press, 1981), 71–72, and W. Paul Reeve, *Making Space on the Western Frontier: Mormons, Miners, and Southern Paiutes* (Urbana: University of Illinois Press, 2006), 35.
42. Representative Wood quoted in Whitney, *Popular History of Utah*, 194.
43. For the House of Representatives debate over Ashley's 1866 bill, see *Congressional Globe*, 39th Cong., 1st Sess. (Washington, DC: F. and J. Rives, 1866), pt. 3, 2368–70. The best discussion of James Ashley's 1866 bill is in Reeve, *Making Space on the Western Frontier*, 43–46. See also William P. MacKinnon, "'Like Splitting a Man up His Backbone': The Territorial Dismemberment of Utah, 1850–1896," *Utah Historical Quarterly* 71, no. 2 (Spring 2003): 100–124.
44. For Ashley's proposed 1869 bill to remap Utah, see *Congressional Globe*, 40th Cong., 3rd Sess. (Washington, DC: F. and J. Rives and G.A. Bailey, 1869), pt. 1, 363–64. See also, Reeve, *Making Space on the Western Frontier*, 58–61.
45. "After the Mormons," *Salt Lake Daily Telegraph*, January 28, 1869, copying the *San Francisco Call.*
46. Both Grenville Dodge of the Union Pacific and Leland Stanford of the Central Pacific—each of whom benefited from Mormon grading and embankment work on the railroad—delayed informing Young of their decision to link the railroads north of the Great Salt Lake until early in 1868. Utah, *A Memorial to Congress for the Construction of a Great National Central Railroad to the Pacific Coast, Utah Session Laws*, 1st sess. (1852), 225; Utah, *A Memorial to Congress in relation to the Pacific Railway, Utah Session Laws*, 3rd sess. (1854), 30–32; Arrington, *Great Basin Kingdom*, 234–37; *Deseret News*, January 22, 1867.

47. Brigham Young to George Nebeker, November 4, 1868, Brigham Young Collection, Church Archives, Family and Church History Department, Church of Jesus Christ of Latter-day Saints, Salt Lake City; Young to Franklin D. Richards, May 23, 1868, Journal History of the Church of Jesus Christ of Latter-day Saints (hereafter cited as Journal History), Family and Church History Department, Church of Jesus Christ of Latter-day Saints, Salt Lake City.
48. *Nebraska Republican* (Omaha), November 15, 1865.
49. This editorial, titled "Higher Civilization," appeared in the *Providence* (Rhode Island) *Journal* in 1868 and was reprinted in the *Deseret News*, August 12, 1868.
50. Ibid.
51. The article, titled "Mormonism Doomed," first appeared in the *Chicago Republican* and was reprinted in the *Deseret News*, May 13, 1868.
52. *Deseret News*, May 13, 1868, copying the *Chicago Republican*. The punctuation (?) after "civilizing" is in the original.
53. *Deseret News*, June 3, 1868; Arrington, *Great Basin Kingdom*, 236–37.
54. *Deseret News*, June 3, 1868.
55. "The Great Railroad of the West," *Millennial Star* 30 (June 27, 1868): 408–10.
56. Ibid.
57. Arrington, *Great Basin Kingdom*, 234–35, 245–51. Moreover, the School of Prophets raised money to facilitate the construction of branch railroads to serve the Utah hinterland; established the Zion's Cooperative Mercantile Institution (ZCMI) to control the importation and purchase of outside goods; and raised monies for the Perpetual Emigration Fund. Additionally, the "Word of Wisdom," a revelation announced by Joseph Smith in 1833 that called for abstinence from tobacco and "strong drinks" such as hot tea, coffee, and liquor, was reinforced by Brigham Young prior to the arrival of the railroad. Church leaders felt that such abstinence would not only save money to devote to the emigration fund, but would demonstrate Mormon self-control in comparison to the habits of Gentile "outsiders." Arrington, *Great Basin Kingdom*, 249–50.
58. Journal History, May 22, 28, and 29, 1868, quoted in Arrington, *Great Basin Kingdom*, 246. Arrington also notes that the school tried to "minimize the influx of undesirable 'outsiders' by deflating the reports of Utah's mineral wealth," thereby limiting a rush of miners to the territory.
59. Celestial Roberts Knight, "Interview," *Utah Pioneer Biographies*, vol. 17, 131–33, Family History Library, LDS Church, Salt Lake City.
60. For other examples of community reactions to construction workers, see Roger E. Carp, "The Limits of Reform: Labor and Discipline on the Erie Canal," *Journal of the Early Republic*, 10, no. 2 (Summer 1990): 191–219; Peter Way, *Common Labour: Workers and the Digging of North American Canals, 1780–1860* (New York: Cambridge University Press, 1993); Carol Sheriff, *The Artificial River: The Erie Canal and the Paradox of Progress, 1817–1860* (New York: Hill and Wang, 1996); Matthew E. Mason, "'The Hands Here are Disposed to be Turbulent': Unrest among the Irish Trackmen of the Baltimore and Ohio Railroad, 1829–1851," *Labor History* 39, no. 3 (August 1998): 253–272; David L. Lightner, "Construction Labor on the Illinois Central Railroad," *Journal of the Illinois State Historical Society* 66, no. 3 (Autumn 1973): 285–301; and W. David Baird "Violence Along the Chesapeake Canal: 1839," *Maryland Historical Magazine* 66 (Summer 1971): 121–134.

61. George Reynolds to George F. Gibbs, June 4, 1868, reprinted in the *Millennial Star* 30 (1868): 443.
62. "The Coming Railroad," *Deseret News*, June 3, 1868.
63. Ibid.
64. *Ogden Junction*, January 29, 1879.
65. Book of Mormon, I Nephi 13:5, 14:16, quoted in Brigham Madsen, *Glory Hunter: A Biography of Patrick Edward Connor* (Salt Lake City: University of Utah Press), 66.
66. David M. Emmons, *Beyond the American Pale: The Irish in the West, 1845–1910* (Norman: University of Oklahoma Press, 2010), 226.
67. *Deseret News*, June 17, 1868. Speeches from the June 1868 "Mass Meeting" were also reprinted in the *Millennial Star* 30 (July 18, August 1, August 8, 1868): 449–53, 484–88, 499–501.
68. *Deseret News*, June 17, 1868.
69. Ibid.
70. Ibid.
71. Ibid.
72. Ibid.
73. *Millennial Star* 30 (July 18, 1868): 451.
74. Ibid., 499.
75. *Deseret News*, June 17, 1868.
76. Arrington, *Great Basin Kingdom*, 261–62; Stewart, *The Iron Trail to the Golden Spike*, 188–99. Stewart lists the amount of the contract at "one million dollars," with eighty percent being paid monthly according to the progress of the work, and the remaining twenty percent after the Mormons' project was completed.
77. Young to Franklin D. Richards, Journal History, May 23, 1868.
78. W. Woodruff to Franklin D. Richards, January 6, 1868, reprinted in the *Millennial Star* 30 (February 8, 1868): 90–91. Woodruff went on to serve as the LDS Church's fourth president, from 1887 to 1898.
79. The *New York Express* article (n.d., 1868), was reprinted in the *Millennial Star* 30 (September 12, 1868): 590. This emigration strategy, in some ways, mirrored the experience of antebellum Irish immigrants who arrived in New York and were immediately plugged into networks of transportation labor, often on remote frontiers.
80. British Mission Emigration Register, Book #1048, 333–72; "A Compilation of General Voyage Notes," *Millennial Star*, 30:27 (July 4, 1868): 426.
81. Joseph Smith Horne, "Autobiography," *Utah Pioneer Biographies*, vol. 2, 60–61, Family History Library, LDS Church, Salt Lake City.
82. John Thomas Lazenby, "Journal," Ms 6043, 3–5, Church History Library, LDS Church, Salt Lake City.
83. Jens Iver Jensen, "Autobiography," in *Our Pioneer Heritage*, comp. Kate B. Carter, vol. 10 (Salt Lake City: Daughters of Utah Pioneers, 1967), 74–75.
84. British Mission Emigration Register, Book #1041, 1–20, Family History Library, LDS Church, Salt Lake City; "A Compilation of General Voyage Notes," *Millennial Star*, 30 (July 11, 1868): 442–43; Emily Pickering Anderson, "Reminiscences," in *Denmark to Manti: The History of William Anderson and Family*

(Salt Lake City: James L. Anderson, n.d.), 66–69, Church History Library, Salt Lake City.

85. Zebulon Jacobs, "Reminiscences and Diaries," folder. 3, 114–34, Church History Library, Salt Lake City.
86. "The Great Railroad of the West," reprinted in the *Millennial Star* 30 (June 27, 1868): 408–10.
87. *Deseret Evening News*, May 26, 1868.
88. Arrington, *Great Basin Kingdom*, 261–62; Stewart, *The Iron Trail to the Golden Spike*, 190–91.
89. *Deseret News*, September 23, 1868.
90. Besides Sharp and Young, Levi Stewart, Thomas E. Ricks, and John Taylor were prominent subcontractors, as were their counterparts Ezra T. Benson, Chauncey W. West, and Ogden Mayor Lorin Farr on the Central Pacific. See Reeder, "The History of Utah's Railroads, 1869–1883." This study discusses Mormon labor on the UPRR and CPRR, but focuses primarily on the Utah Central, the Utah Northern, the Utah Southern, the Denver and Rio Grande, and other branch lines in Utah.
91. The Union Pacific would later transfer unpaid wages in the form of capital and construction materials for the Utah Central Railroad. See M. Guy Bishop, "Building Railroads for the Kingdom: The Career of John W. Young, 1867–91," *Utah Historical Quarterly* 48, no. 1 (Winter 1980): 66–80; and Reeder, "The History of Utah's Railroads, 1869–1883," 73–75.
92. *Deseret Evening News*, June 23, 1868; the letter was dated June 18.
93. *Deseret News*, July 15, 1868; the letter was dated June 28.
94. *Deseret News*, July 22, 1868; the letter was dated July 13.
95. *Deseret News*, September 8, 1868.
96. *Deseret News*, August 12, 1868.
97. Ibid.
98. *Deseret News*, July 15, 1868; Samuel W. Richards to Franklin D. Richards, May 24, 1868, reprinted in the *Millennial Star* 30 (June 27, 1868): 410–12; Brigham Young to Albert Carrington, Journal History, February 4, 1869, reprinted in the *Millennial Star* 31 (1869): 164.
99. On the "rough" masculinity of transportation workers, see Way, *Common Labour*; Sheriff, *The Artificial River*; and Maynard, "Rough Work and Rugged Men," 159–69.
100. Young to F. D. Richards, August 4, 1868, Journal History.
101. See John Casement to Frances Casement, March 3, 8, and 12, 1869, Folder 15, Box 1, John Stephen and Frances Jennings Casement Papers, Accession Number 308, American Heritage Center, University of Wyoming, Laramie.
102. Samuel W. Richards to Franklin D. Richards, May 24, 1868, reprinted in the *Millennial Star* 30 (June 27, 1868): 410–12; Brigham Young to Albert Carrington, Journal History, February 4, 1869, reprinted in the *Millennial Star* 31 (1869): 164.
103. S. Richards to F. Richards, May 24, 1868, *Millennial Star* 30 (June 27, 1868): 410–12.
104. Ibid.
105. *Deseret News*, September 16, 1868.
106. Joseph A. West, "Construction of the Union and Central Pacific Railroads Across Utah, Fifty-Five Years Ago," *Union Pacific Magazine* (October 6, 1922), 8; J. H.

Beadle, *The Undeveloped West, or, Five Years in the Territories* (Philadelphia: National, 1873), 140, 154.

107. George A. Smith to W. S. Elderkin, April 14, 1869, Journal History.
108. Athearn, "Opening the Gates of Zion," 309–10.
109. *Deseret News*, August 12, 1868, copying the *Providence* (Rhode Island) *Journal*, "Higher Civilization."
110. Ibid.
111. *Deseret News*, August 19, 1868.
112. "How we are Getting on in Echo," *Deseret News*, July 15, 1868. The letter was dated June 28, 1868.
113. *Deseret News*, September 16, 1868.
114. *Deseret News*, June 24, 1868.
115. This song was reprinted in the *Deseret News*, August 12, 1868.
116. Thomas E. Cheney, ed., *Mormon Songs from the Rocky Mountains: A Compilation of Mormon Folksong* (Austin: University of Texas Press, 1968), 92–98.
117. Athearn, "Opening the Gates of Zion," 300.
118. See Leonard Arrington, Feramorz Fox, and Dean L. May, *Building the City of God: Community and Cooperation among the Mormons* (Urbana: University of Illinois Press, 1992); and Dean L. May, *Three Frontiers: Family, Land, and Society in the American West, 1850–1900* (New York: Cambridge University Press, 1994).
119. *Deseret News*, September 16, 1868.
120. George Reynolds to George F. Gibbs, June 4, 1868, reprinted in the *Millennial Star* 30 (1868): 443.
121. *Deseret News*, September 16, 1868.
122. *Union Vedette* (Camp Douglas, Utah Territory), March 12, 1867. Established in 1863, the *Vedette* had a short life-span of four years. In 1872, the *Corinne Daily Reporter* (Corinne, Utah Territory) was established as a successful but opposition newspaper. It, too, was rather short-lived. See Brigham D. Madsen, *Corinne: The Gentile Capital of Utah* (Salt Lake City: Utah State Historical Society, 1980).
123. "Chinese Labor in the West," *Deseret News*, May 26, 1869.
124. For a discussion of widespread democratic support for anti-Chinese legislation in the West, see Limerick, *The Legacy of Conquest.*
125. "Chinese Labor in the West," *Deseret News*, May 26, 1869.
126. Ibid.
127. See *The Statistics of the Population of the United States, Ninth Census, Vol. 1* (Washington, DC: U.S. Bureau of Census, 1870), 373, and Bain, *Empire Express*, 605–7.
128. Emmons, *Beyond the American Pale.*
129. A January 29, 1879, editorial in the *Ogden Junction* argued that "the wages of white men . . . have dwindled to such an extent that there is . . . but a trifling difference between the prices paid for work performed by the white man and that done by the copper-colored incubus. . . . There are unquestionably more workmen than there is work to be performed; and to divide what little work there is with the inferior and alien race, is not a good nor a just policy."
130. "The Railroad in the Cañons, No. IX," *Deseret News*, August 1, 1868.
131. *Deseret Evening News*, October 9, 1868; Athearn, "Opening the Gates of Zion," 304–6.
132. *Deseret Evening News*, October 9, 1868.

133. Young quoted in the *Deseret News*, January 22, 1867. For the LDS Church's efforts at theologizing concepts of race, primarily in relation to their own "Israelite lineage," and in Mormon interactions with American Indians and African Americans, see Armand L. Mauss, "The Children of Ham and the Children of Abraham: The Construction and Deconstruction of Ethnic Identities in the Mormon Heartland," in *Race, Religion, Region: Landscapes of Encounter in the American West*, ed. Fay Botham and Sara M. Patterson (Tucson: University of Arizona Press, 2006), 115–24. See also Mauss, *All Abraham's Children: Changing Mormon Conceptions of Race and Lineage* (Urbana: University of Illinois Press, 2003).
134. Arrington, *Great Basin Kingdom*, 264.
135. Ibid.
136. "Tunnelville, 12 miles below Mouth of Echo," *Deseret News*, January 1, 1869. This letter was dated December 27, 1868, and was written by a Mormon railroad worker who referred to himself as "ANON." See also Golden Spike Railroad Scrapbook, J. Willard Marriott Library Special Collections, University of Utah, Salt Lake City.
137. On "horns" and "a cloven foot," see George Q. Cannon's speech at the 1868 "Mass Meeting," *Deseret News*, June 17, 1868. W. Paul Reeve, "'Nits Make Lice': The Construction of a Mormon-Indian Body," Work-in-Progress presentation, Tanner Humanities Center, University of Utah, November 2007.
138. The word "craythur," sometimes used as a term of endearment in Ireland, was invariably utilized in a dehumanizing context during immigrant encounters. See Fiona Bateman, "Defining the Heathen in Ireland and Africa: Two Similar Discourses a Century Apart," *Social Sciences and Missions* 21, no. 1 (2008): 89.
139. Brigham Young to Albert Carrington, Journal History, February 4, 1869, reprinted in the *Millennial Star* 31 (1869): 164.
140. See George L. Mosse, *The Image of Man: The Creation of Modern Masculinity* (New York: Oxford University Press, 1996). On martial masculinity, see Hoganson, *Fighting for American Manhood*.
141. Interestingly, in light of the achievement at Promontory just eight months previous, Utah's Saints depicted the Utah Central Railroad from Salt Lake to Ogden as more honorable and influential. After the completion of this branch line in January 1870, John W. Young's loyal workers returned thanks, a rare occurrence in a field of labor as filthy and oppressive as railroad construction. Despite enduring the difficulties of construction and receiving little or no wages, the workers did not flee or protest but praised their boss in a joint letter to the *Deseret Evening News*: "We the brethren employed in laying track on the Utah Central Railroad, take this present occasion of congratulating you on the speedy and successful termination of the greatest enterprise of the age, which we feel is mainly due to the energy and spirit displayed by you." *Deseret Evening News*, January 11, 1870. See "The Utah Central and Other Railroads," *Treasures of Pioneer History*, ed. Kate B. Carter (Salt Lake City: Daughters of Utah Pioneers, 1952), 1.
142. Charles R. Savage Journals, May 7, 1869, L. Tom Perry Special Collections, Harold B. Lee Library, Brigham Young University, Provo.
143. *Salt Lake Daily Telegraph*, May 11, 1869.

3

Japanese Immigrants and the Dillingham Commission

Federal Immigration Policy and the American West

Katherine Benton-Cohen

Japanese immigration to the United States in the nineteenth and early twentieth centuries was largely a western phenomenon. Many newcomers settled in ethnic neighborhoods in the West's cities; others inhabited segregated boarding houses in mining camps or near canneries, or fanned out in rural districts where they worked as agricultural laborers, amassing capital to purchase or lease their own land. In some places they experienced intense prejudice while in others they were largely accepted. Their presence attracted little concern in Congress or the White House—President Theodore Roosevelt called it a "purely local" concern—until San Franciscans alienated the Japanese government by discriminating against Japanese residents. In this chapter Katherine Benton-Cohen of Georgetown University brings the state back into the study of Japanese immigration, linking race relations on the West Coast to diplomacy between Japan and the United States and to national immigration policy. She shows that the influential Dillingham Commission's investigations of immigration, which led to major restrictions on immigration, were sparked in part by developments in San Francisco. The West thus influenced federal immigration policy in a way that has seldom been recognized. At the same time, the commission's careful documentation of Japanese labor activism and land holding offers a rich corpus of data for historians.

Japanese immigrants in the American West were surprisingly central to the national fight over immigration policy in the early twentieth century. For decades, historians of immigration restriction focused on the far more numerous eastern and southern Europeans and their opponents in elite universities and the halls of Congress. These scholars told the story as one about the eastern United States.[1] More recently, scholars like Mae

Ngai and Erika Lee have pushed the narrative of restriction back to the anti-Chinese campaigns in 1870s California and their culmination in the federal Chinese Exclusion Act of 1882—the first law to bar immigrants by race and class (by forbidding Chinese laborers from entry).[2] Yet for most chroniclers of immigration policy, Asian exclusion then fades again into the background.

In the first years of the twentieth century, new geopolitics and rising immigration from Japan to the United States rekindled anti-Asian campaigns. These campaigns were strongest on the Pacific coast. A focus on this region reveals the importance of western immigrants—and especially those from Japan—in the trajectory from "open borders" to the age of restriction. The role of the Japanese in this transition appears in a new look at the United States Immigration Commission—better known as the Dillingham Commission for its chair, Sen. William P. Dillingham (R-Vt.). The Immigration Act of February 20, 1907, created the United States Immigration Commission, which produced forty-one detailed reports.[3] The commission's impact was significant: its findings and recommendations led to the 1917 literacy test, a permanent ban on Asiatic immigration, and the national-origins quota system cemented in 1924—which effectively ended mass immigration to the United States until 1965.

The Dillingham Commission is often associated with its study of eastern and southern Europeans, and with the industrial cities of the Midwest and Northeast. Yet the commission's legislative origins were in a crisis with Japan created by California politics. Because of the commission's influence, the relatively small and regionally isolated Japanese immigrants are far more important to the history of immigration than has been previously recognized.[4] Three volumes of the Dillingham Commission's influential reports examined Japanese immigration to the American West as a source of both curiosity and anxiety. The reports revealed what policymakers thought about the Japanese, but their extensive interviews also allowed many Japanese immigrants to express how they saw themselves—as strivers and achievers, who hoped in vain for the right to American citizenship. These visions of the Japanese—by policymakers, social scientists, and the immigrants themselves—are the subject of this article. Ultimately, it argues that both the American West and Japanese immigrants deserve a more central place in the history of immigration policy, and, at the same time, that the story of the Japanese on the Pacific coast puts to rest any Turnerian clichés about the West as a welcoming place for immigrants.

The Dillingham Commission's origins in the Japan crisis reveal the deep interconnections among regional politics, immigration restriction, and foreign policy in the age of empire. The commission's era was one in which the United States emerged as a world power. The commission's most prominent members—among them Massachusetts Republican senator Henry Cabot Lodge—were among the nation's leading imperialists. Diplomatic politics and imperial ambition became the backdrop for the study of immigration. The reports of the Immigration Commission expressed not just the racial science of the age, for which they are well known, but also confidence and anxiety about the United States as an immigrant nation in an era of emerging imperial powers. After the Russo-Japanese War, these nations included Japan.

In 1906, a local act of unvarnished racism became the accidental catalyst for the creation of the Dillingham Commission. In October, the San Francisco school board issued a resolution that ordered principals to "send all Chinese, Japanese, and Korean children to the Oriental Public School."[5] The announcement was the culmination of events that had begun in 1900, when San Francisco labor leaders and other nativists held mass meetings demanding a renewal and expansion of the Chinese Exclusion Act that would apply to Japanese immigrants.[6] In 1905, a Japanese and Korean Exclusion League organized by over a hundred white labor unions and a group calling itself the Native Sons of the Golden West held fiery meetings and sent dozens of petitions to Congress.[7] The league was a weird alloy of leftists (the socialist-leaning Building Trades Council funded it) and the conservative press, especially the *San Francisco Chronicle*.[8] The Exclusion League pressured the San Francisco school board for months to craft a segregation order. Then, on April 18, 1906, San Francisco's cataclysmic earthquake—followed by a devastating fire—upended race relations in the era's largest and most important western city. "Taking this as a God-given opportunity," as one Japanese scholar put it in 1925, the school board issued its announcement six months later.[9] The decree applied to just ninety-three Japanese schoolchildren scattered across twenty-three public schools.[10]

The diplomatic crisis that unfurled from a local act affecting fewer than one hundred children led, in the winding manner of political compromise, from popular agitation to local legislation to political arm-twisting of ambassadors and congressmen. The result was a compromise bill that established the U.S. Immigration Commission and made possible the Gentlemen's Agreement with Japan, which ended most immigration.

Time has blunted the horror of San Francisco's earthquake and subsequent fire. Just after five a.m. on an April day, San Franciscans woke to the earth roiling underneath them—hard enough to be felt from Oregon to Los Angeles. In the three days afterward, exploding gas mains ignited at least thirty fires that destroyed much of what the earthquake had not. The loss of human life was at least double Katrina's hurricane and flood in 2005, and the economic impact was similar. Direct damages were perhaps $400 million (approximately $10 billion in 2010 dollars). More than half the city's population of four hundred thousand were left homeless. Few people had easily accessible savings, and many were immigrants with shallow roots in this country. The city's fire chief died in the quake. The firemen who survived created firebreaks by dynamiting buildings, but in their inexperience they destroyed twice as many structures as was necessary. Between the quake and fire, perhaps twenty-eight thousand buildings were lost. With no formal system of disaster relief, the U.S. Army took control of the response, but private relief—including $246,000 from Japan, the largest donation from a foreign nation—provided the bulk of assistance.[11]

Japan and its immigrants got little thanks. Not all crises worsen race relations, but, like Katrina a century later, the San Francisco fire exacerbated and exposed the racism and social divisions of ordinary urban life. After the fire, an influx and rapid organization of Japanese immigrants in San Francisco increased their visibility at a time when nerves were already frayed. San Francisco's Japanese population had grown more than six-fold in the years surrounding 1906, from 1,781 in 1900 to 11,380 in 1907.[12] Violent assaults against Japanese skyrocketed.[13] Most victims belonged to the largely working-class population, but a mob also assaulted and stoned two professors visiting from Tokyo's Imperial University. They had come to study the disaster recovery.[14]

America's new imperial ambitions heated up the social friction created by the earthquake and an influx of Japanese immigrants. Although Japan had informally discouraged emigration to the United States beginning in 1900, the American annexation of Hawaii in 1898 meant that Japanese workers there could use the islands as a "stepping stone" to the U.S. mainland.[15] The Japanese already in Hawaii were not technically immigrants, and there was no way to restrict them from the continental United States. Japanese emigrants, almost all of them men, had begun going to Hawaii—usually as contract labor—after the Chinese Exclusion Act of 1882 closed that labor supply.[16] The few Japanese who came in via Mexico and Canada represented less than 5 percent of the total.[17] Hawaiian newspaper advertisements and broadsides lured Japanese to California. The Japanese there suffered, as one Hawaiian newspaper put it, from "American fever"—an expression that underscored Hawaii's status as not quite part of the nation proper.[18] In 1906 alone, of the 17,000 Japanese who entered the mainland United States, two-thirds were from Hawaii.[19] By 1909, more than half of the Japanese in the United States lived in California, where they made up as much as seven percent of the male working class.[20] This percentage was unfathomable in other parts of the country, where only a handful of

Japanese lived. In all, about 250,000 Japanese immigrated to the United States from 1899–1924, with almost all before 1907 and along the Pacific coast. Perhaps 24 million Europeans—almost a hundred times as many as the Japanese—came during the same period.[21] And yet, this small group of Asian migrants to the Pacific coast would create far more diplomatic problems than the supposedly much-maligned southern and eastern Europeans.

The San Francisco schools imbroglio became the first serious crisis in U.S.-Japan relations—worse, in President Roosevelt's words, than "any of the other rather stormy incidents" during his presidency.[22] San Francisco nativists foisted segregation onto Roosevelt's agenda at a time when good relations with Japan were especially crucial. In 1905 Japan had trounced Russia in the Battle of Tsushima, demonstrating itself as a martial empire worthy of wary admiration. The next year, Roosevelt won the Nobel Peace Prize for his role in brokering an end to the Russo-Japanese War.[23] After 1906, the United States and Japan had firmly established themselves as the dominant Pacific powers. The last thing Roosevelt wanted was to be at odds with a potential competitor for control of the Philippines, Guam, and Hawaii.[24] Imperialism had given the US more to lose in the Pacific. Roosevelt, Secretary of State Elihu Root, and Secretary of Commerce and Labor Oscar Straus (whose department included the Bureau of Immigration) wanted to make sure Japan remained an ally. All three men had been strong supporters of Japan in its conflicts with both Russia and China—albeit in the race language of the era.[25] Straus remembered laughing with Roosevelt about a quip he had heard that "the Japs were yellow-skinned, but the Russians were yellow all the way through."[26]

Roosevelt had been on good terms with Japan, but he needed all the goodwill he could muster as news about San Francisco's segregation order broke in Japan.[27] Within ten days of the proclamation, U.S. ambassador to Japan Luke Wright wired the State Department, "All newspapers here publish dispatches from the United States giving accounts of agitation in San Francisco for exclusion of Japanese." The London *Times* reported on it, too.[28] The telegram caught Secretary Root off guard, because, as he told the ambassador, the "trouble was so local" he had not heard about it until his staff scoured the papers. Roosevelt echoed that it was "so purely local that we never heard of it here in Washington."[29] To the Japanese, however, it was anything but a local matter.

The Japanese government maintained that the Treaty of 1894, which granted Japan a status equal to most favored nation, made the school board's segregation measure illegal. Japanese in San Francisco boycotted the new Oriental School, using the legal opinion as justification.[30] The State Department's chief lawyer, James B. Scott, doubted this argument could succeed and predicted, "What happened to the Fourteenth Amendment may well happen to the Treaty of 1894." He was referring to the *Plessy v. Ferguson* case of a decade earlier, when the Supreme Court had interpreted the Fourteenth Amendment's promise of equal protection to be consistent with "separate but equal" accommodations for African Americans. Coming from a Republican lawyer who presumably opposed the *Plessy* ruling, Scott's statement expressed pessimism about whether Japan's argument would work.[31]

As Scott's comparison to *Plessy* suggested, the racial implications of the boycott were not lost on policymakers. Roosevelt called the people of San Francisco "idiots" and "infernal fools" for "insult[ing] the Japanese recklessly."[32] The president's private writings throughout 1906 and 1907 revealed his increasing awareness that for San Franciscans (unlike himself and Straus who, like other elites, viewed the Japanese with something like awe and the Chinese with mere contempt), race was at the root of the problem. By early February 1907, Roosevelt had decided that the San Francisco schools controversies were "partly [about] labor, and partly a deep-rooted racial antipathy, the extent of which fairly astounds me."[33] Many upper-class Americans—including Roosevelt, Root, and Straus—read middle-brow articles that characterized the Japanese as racially superior to the almost universally denigrated Chinese.[34] The Dillingham Commission's *Dictionary of Races or Peoples* would claim that the Japanese's "Mongolian traits are much less pronounced" than that of the Chinese. "What nonsense it is to speak of the Chinese and Japanese as of the same race!" Theodore Roosevelt had written to diplomat John Hay in 1904. "They are of the same race only in the sense that a Leventine Greek is of the same race with Lord Milner."[35] Likewise, some scholars argued that the Japanese were not Mongolian at all, and had "white blood" in them.[36]

Roosevelt was worried enough about Japan's reaction to the schools crisis to address the matter directly in his December 1906 message to Congress. In it, he claimed, "To shut them [the Japanese] out from the public schools of San Francisco is a wicked absurdity."[37] Roosevelt and his close friend Henry Cabot Lodge (member and later chair of the Senate Foreign Relations Committee), had long discussed how to restrict Chinese and Japanese immigration while preserving diplomatic relations. Roosevelt assailed the "criminal stupidity" of San Francisco anti-Asian activists, even as he supported in principle a ban on Chinese laborers and the Japanese.[38] Like many other diplomatic and intellectual elites, including Straus and Root, the president also favored granting Japanese immigrants the right to naturalize—and said so in his December address to Congress. Popular sentiment on the Pacific coast remained adamantly opposed. Roosevelt and Root resolved that federal action would be needed to quell the Japan crisis.

Passing the Law

While San Francisco recovered from natural disaster and agitators seized on the issue of Japanese exclusion, in Washington both houses of Congress were mired in debate over new immigration legislation. A pending bill raised entry fees and requirements, but its most notable feature was a literacy test to be given to incoming immigrants in a language of their choice—a pet cause of Senator Lodge's since the 1890s. In late May 1906, the Senate passed a bill containing the test and introduced by William P. Dillingham of Vermont, who chaired its Committee on Immigration. The bill was then sent to the House, where it was sponsored by Lodge's son-in-law, Augustus Gardner (R-NY).

Gardner's initial version also contained the literacy test, but the House was a tricky place to negotiate immigration legislation. On one hand, the House was "decidedly restrictionist," in the approving estimation of Immigration Restriction League official Joseph Lee.[39] On the other, dozens of members relied on immigrants for their seats. The powerful House Majority Leader Joseph Cannon (R-IL) was an ardent foe of restriction.[40] In June 1906, one of Cannon's political lieutenants introduced an amendment to the House bill to replace the literacy test with a commission to study immigrants in the United States and to propose policy.[41] With Cannon's pressure, the new version passed in the House without a literacy test. The commission plan was the classic tactic of delaying action by studying a problem, but it was also a genuine reflection of the Progressive-era enthusiasm for "expertise." Cannon had initially opposed the commission (because he hated reform and reformers), but he changed his mind when he saw he could use the commission as a way to defeat the literacy test.[42]

Roosevelt had privately favored a commission, too—there was some discussion of the idea in his earlier correspondence, and he wrote to several people, including U.S. Commissioner of Labor Charles P. Neill (later named to the commission) about conducting such a study.[43] Roosevelt played both sides against the middle. Whether out of conviction or for political reasons (immigration reform, then as now, was not an issue that divided along partisan lines), Roosevelt and even Lodge had begun to distance themselves from the literacy test. Yet the impasse over the literacy test left the bill languishing in conference committee for six months.

By the end of December 1906, crisis with Japan was becoming a top priority. The necessary ingredients to peace with Japan appeared to be an end to San Francisco's segregation order, an agreement that the Japanese government would not issue passports to laborers bound for the United States (what became the Gentlemen's Agreement), and federal legislation to close immigration from Japan through Hawaii, Canada, and Mexico. Roosevelt saw the stalled immigration bill as a vessel for resolution.[44] Cannon and Lodge fashioned an amendment to the immigration bill in conference that included these components, and substituted the Senate's literacy test with the House's Immigration Commission. From December 1906 until the final moments before the Immigration Act of 1907 passed in mid-February, the president and his allies horse-traded with California politicians and cajoled angry members of Congress to vote for a revised version of the immigration bill. South Carolina's fire-brand (and white supremacist) senator Ben Tillman complained that "the conferees were harassed and bedeviled . . . lectured and censured here for three whole days" by Lodge and other supporters.[45]

Roosevelt, Straus, Root, and Lodge all saw the immigration bill as foreign—not domestic—policy. "You can well imagine," Straus remarked to his brother after a cabinet meeting on the subject, "that foreign relations are quite closely connected with Japanese and Chinese immigration matters."[46] For protesting members of Congress, couching the issue as foreign policy veiled an unacceptable expansion of federal power.[47] Senator Charles Culberson of Texas complained that Roosevelt was holding "this authority as a club to compel the San Franciscans to admit Japanese children to their schools, refusing to exclude the Japanese coolies unless the Californians come to time on their end of the bargain"—that is, the deal to end segregation in the schools in exchange for the gentlemen's agreement limiting Japanese immigration.[48]

Supporters of states' rights saw the action as federal bullying of local officials. Many policymakers believed that Asian segregation and even exclusion were legitimate domestic, even local, prerogatives to protect the "American standard of living" with which other countries had no business interfering.[49] Even some politicians sympathetic with Japan hesitated to interfere in San Francisco's local school governance.[50] Henry Millis, a Stanford University economist who oversaw studies of Japanese immigrants for the commission and later republished them as a book, explained, "The Japanese government looks to the [U.S.] federal government to prevent discriminatory treatment of its subjects, [yet] . . . our political organization is a poor one for dealing with international questions. States may do things of serious international importance, and the federal government does not have power to stay their hands."[51]

Presidents have tended to avoid binding immigration legislation passed by Congress. Those who are seeking reelection are loath to antagonize ethnic voters, and, from a policy perspective, they tend to prefer to use executive power to bend policy when diplomacy demands it. Rutherford Hayes vetoed an early Chinese exclusion measure; Cleveland, Taft, and Wilson all vetoed literacy tests (Wilson twice).[52] Many members of Congress felt differently. In 1907, some nativists resented the impermanent nature of the proposed Gentleman's Agreement, which could be changed at the discretion of the chief executive. One senator complained, "The proposed legislation as a permanent proposition would not be worth the paper upon which it is written."[53] Others, conversely, complained that the measure conceded too much to Japan. Senator Edward Carmack of Tennessee thought that Japan had pulled a fast one on the United States: "I believe, speaking in plain words, that a foreign power has browbeaten the Government of the United States and browbeaten a sovereign State of this Union into a surrender of its rights to control its own affairs."[54]

Southerners made states' rights arguments that invoked white supremacy. Senator Williams of Mississippi explained, "I am with the Californians. . . . I want the Pacific slope kept a white man's country [applause], as I want all of this land, as far as it can be, a white man's country. . . . [T]his is our land—the land of our traditions, the land of our ideals—and I knew that the influx of another and a radically different race . . . means another race problem for another portion of this Republic."[55] Some San Francisco activists had made the same dire prediction and comparison to the South.[56] One of the ironies of regional comparisons, however, was that in San Francisco black children attended school with whites, as one newspaper noted, "and no protest has been raised by politicians or newspapers."[57]

Debates over states' rights and executive power reflected partisan divides exacerbated by Roosevelt's enthusiasm for the big stick. Congressman William Burnett, an Alabama Democrat who chaired the House Immigration Committee and was later appointed to the Dillingham Commission, saw the power vested in the president to shape immigration policy as

> obnoxious to any man who does not believe in investing the President with the autocratic powers embraced in the proviso. . . . Any man who believes in the right of local self-government and in the autonomy of the States, notwithstanding all the good features of this report, is in duty bound, as I see it, to vote against the report. The big stick which it permits the President to hold over the States may sometime be wielded to the overthrow of the most sacred institutions of the South [that is, segregation]. This constant trenching on the reserved rights of the States is *becoming more dangerous with every Republican Administration*.[58]

Likewise, Mississippi's Senator Williams pointed out that California's delegation included not one Democrat. "Had there been, this craven surrender of California's representatives in Washington to White House and foreign influence would not have been unanimous.[59]

Although the Mississippian Williams acted as though Californians had one voice, many Californians supported the compromise. Even as San Francisco launched a global salvo with its school segregation measure, Los Angeles coolly proceeded with Asian integration. The *Los Angeles Times* proclaimed, "Chinese and Japanese laborers are a blessing rather than a menace." The Los Angeles school superintendent called Japanese students "quiet, well behaved pupils, who set a good example to the others," and promised that there was "no Japanese question here." After the 1906 earthquake, many Japanese in San Francisco moved to Los Angeles.[60] The commission's own reports would later conclude that attitudes about the Japanese varied considerably in the western states—from the epicenter of anti-Japanese efforts in San Francisco to Colorado, where "opinion . . . varies all the way from extreme race antagonism to extreme favor," to the "extremely cosmopolitan" Wyoming coal fields, where "few race antipathies are present."[61] The commission's own analysis of the Bay Area school controversy concluded that "in most localities Japanese pupils and the pupils of other races associate with little or no friction."[62] There was no one model for race relations in the American West.

Because of opposition in Congress and the delicacy of negotiations with the San Francisco school board and Japan, the deal went down to the wire. Petitions poured in from all sides—from groups like the Alliance of German Societies and the Republican League of Clubs, who both favored a commission, to the "citizens of Battle Mountain, Nevada," who protested "the little brown men from Japan."[63] Throughout late January and February, Roosevelt held secret meetings with Root, committee members, and, eventually, the San Francisco school board and mayor—out of jail on bail for corruption charges.[64] Meanwhile, Japanese laborers from Hawaii continued to arrive at San Francisco ports.[65] On February 15, Straus and Root dined with the Japanese ambassador and his German wife.[66] The next day, Roosevelt wrote to his son, "Slowly and with infinite difficulty and frequent setbacks, I am getting both the Californians and Japan into an attitude that will permit of a solution."[67]

Finally, on February 18, the revised Immigration Act of 1907 passed both houses, and the president signed it two days later. Roosevelt immediately issued an executive order refusing admission to Japanese and Korean laborers with passports to Mexico, Canada, or Hawaii—that is, the Gentlemen's Agreement.[68] Within weeks, plans for the commission were underway.[69]

The Commission and Its Priorities

Commissions were a popular new form of governance during the Progressive Era, because they operated as a hybrid between democratic oversight and expert management. Federal commissions took on everything from railroad arbitration to Ellis Island to the meatpacking industry. Echoing some critical members of Congress, newspapers across the country made note of the Dillingham Commission's unusually robust powers and long reach beyond the nation's borders. "The law places no limit on the time the Commission shall consume in making its inquiries or on the expense it may incur," the Kentucky *Berea* reported. "The provisions of the law under which the commission will operate are broad."[70] The *Washington Post* noted, "The commission is authorized to go anywhere in this country and abroad," and could ask the president to "call an international conference, or to send special commissioners to any foreign country to regulate by agreement the immigration of aliens and to do a number of other things."[71] In its four years of work, the commission spent at least three-quarters of a million dollars—a large and controversial amount at the time.[72] Three hundred staff members researched everything from crime to children's physiology to women's "fecundity" and white slavery. The series on immigrants in industry alone took up twenty volumes.

The law specified that the commission be made up of three members of Congress appointed by the Speaker of the House, three senators appointed by the vice-president (as President of the Senate), and three presidentially appointed "experts." Seven commissioners were Republicans, and two were Democrats, although their views on immigrants were not defined by party. Dillingham and Lodge represented the Senate, along with a succession of three southern Democrats (two died in office). In the House, appointees were Reps. Benjamin Howell (R-NJ), John Burnett (D-AL), and William Bennet, a Manhattan Republican from a heavily immigrant district. Bennet was the only member to oppose most restrictions. The three men appointed by Roosevelt included federal commissioner of labor and Catholic University professor Charles P. Neill, Cornell economist Jeremiah Jenks, and San Francisco businessman William R. Wheeler (who was named assistant secretary of commerce and labor a year later, making him, like Neill, a member of the Roosevelt Administration). Neill, whose parents were Irish immigrants, was the only Catholic. No commissioner was an immigrant, and none were from southern or eastern European stock—much less Asian. As Straus explained to one Jewish inquirer, Roosevelt wanted no one "who may be regarded as the representative of any special interest; that is to say, he does not intend to take anyone to represent Jewish immigration, Italian immigration, or any of the streams of immigration, for if he makes an exception in one direction he will have to do so in other directions."[73] The staff did include immigrants, as well as many women, and employed prominent economists, sociologists, and anthropologists. Three members (Lodge, Jenks, and Neill) also held PhDs.

In 1907, it was clear that the commission and the Japan controversy were closely linked. News articles referred to the legislation that created the commission as the "Japanese Immigration Bill" because of its so-called "coolie measure" restricting Japanese laborers.[74] The commission's Pacific coast volumes described in detail the San Francisco controversies and their resolution in 1907, although without mention that the commission itself was a product of the same law that created the Gentlemen's Agreement.[75] In 1911, economist Henry Millis, the superintendent of the western reports, summarized the "three immigration problems" that the commission believed needed legislative remedies. The first was European immigration; the other two pertained to excluding Asians.[76] A closer look at the contents of the reports reveals that the Japanese crisis in the American West shaped the study in important ways.

Japanese in the Reports

The commission's origins in the Japan crisis left their first mark in a special report it produced called "Immigration Conditions in Hawaii." The short report reflected interest in the Japanese in particular (in 1900, 36 percent of Hawaii's population had been born in Japan),[77] and in the relationship between imperialism and immigration in general. Congressional debates over the immigration bill had included discussions of the impact of Japanese immigration on the colonies of Hawaii and the Philippines. Some people wanted to bar Japanese immigrants from Hawaii, while others wanted to restrict them just from the mainland. One Idaho senator complained, "Under this bill Japanese can go to Hawaii, to the Philippine Islands, and our other possessions. There is no adequate restriction upon them.... I think we ought to guard the Filipino as much as we guard our own people against this class of labor."[78] His comments reflected ongoing controversy over how residents of the colonies would assimilate into the American population, and whether the same immigration rules would apply to them and their homelands.

Out of such concerns came the commission's decision to include a study of Hawaii. The Hawaii report's prominent placement in the second volume, which contained the commission's policy recommendations and abstracts of the other reports, guaranteed broad readership. Other details reveal its significance. Senator Dillingham (who had previously served on the Senate Committee on Territories) traveled personally to Hawaii to contribute to the study. Critics derided his trip as a Vermonter's tropical junket. Perhaps it was, but it was also a sign of financial and personal commitment. The commission members, as well as Straus, met with the governor of Hawaii while he was in Washington.[79] Secretary Straus undertook his own investigation of Hawaii at the same time—a sign of its importance to immigration policy at the time.[80]

The author of the Hawaii immigration report also exemplified the close links between immigration and imperial policy in the early twentieth century. Economist Victor Clark enjoyed a cosmopolitan career as a globe-trotting colonial bureaucrat, with postings in Puerto Rico, Cuba, the Philippines, the U.S.-Mexico border, and contract work in New Zealand.[81] Like many early advanced-degree holders, Victor Clark spent a year in Germany doing graduate work before receiving a PhD from Columbia University in 1900.[82]

In 1906 Clark moved to Hawaii to serve as the Commissioner of Labor and then Immigration. In this capacity, he wrote the Hawaii report for the Dillingham Commission. He described Hawaii as a place where the competition between Japan and Russia continued, now in the form of immigrant recruitment and settlement. Through the late nineteenth century, labor in Hawaii was predominantly contract peonage. Although debt peonage was illegal in the United States, these laws did not apply to Hawaii prior to annexation.[83] "The system resulted," Clark explained, "in making the population of Hawaii predominantly oriental." The joint resolution to annex Hawaii in 1898 specifically excluded the continued importation of Chinese workers there but did not mention the Japanese—who had begun to replace the Chinese.[84] American annexation ended penal contracts in Hawaii, and after 1905, as Japanese began to leave for the United States mainland in large numbers, Hawaiian employers attempted to recruit family groups. They also appealed to Puerto Ricans and Filipinos, in part because as colonial subjects they did not count as "immigrants." But their preference was for Europeans, so much so that Clark described theirs as a "white immigration policy."

Dissatisfaction with Asian laborers (who began to organize and protest) sent recruiters to Siberia in search of settlers. Clark noted that Hawaiian and "federal officials, from the President down, showed a strong interest in the effort to domicile in Hawaii a larger proportion of Caucasians."[85] The term "domicile" connoted family and permanent settlement. "From the first, however," the Europeans got better pay, "partly in consideration of their higher standard of living and partly because these European immigrants brought their families with them, while the Orientals were mostly single men."[86]

Luring Siberians to Hawaii was not as easy as it might sound. Wages—even the higher ones—were still too low to appeal to many Europeans. The shift from Asian recruitment to trying to get Russian families reflected a preference for family settlement in Hawaii, though Clark admitted this goal was a difficult one. The plots of land available to potential settlers were too small to farm, the climate iffy for general cultivation, and immigrants were far from home. As a result, the "flowing out of the Caucasian population almost as rapidly as it is recruited is one of the most serious problems met by the Territory in its present immigration policy."[87] Those Russians who left Hawaii had no intention of returning, and those who stayed could not promote more immigration by word-of-mouth because they did not return home to circulate news. "The authorities of the Territory," Clark noted, "look forward to the Panama route as the channel through which European immigrants will reach Hawaii." He concluded the report by reiterating the language of home and family in expressing the territorial government's desire for Europeans to replace Japanese: "The minor industries call for a home-owning domiciled citizenship population, and it is from this population that the labor needs of the plantations will ultimately be supplied. The formation of this population," he concluded, "is the present immigration problem before the Territory."[88]

Back in Washington, the Japanese crisis had also led directly to the appointment of commission member William R. Wheeler and to the three volumes on the American West for which he took responsibility. Roosevelt's nomination of Wheeler, a Californian, was an olive branch to the anti-Japan vote in California—the choice, according to the *Washington Post*, of "practically the entire Congressional delegations from the Pacific Coast."[89] "I much desire to see California represented on this commission," Roosevelt wrote to Wheeler upon his nomination, "and feel that you will be rendering a public service if you find yourself able to accept."[90] Then, too, Roosevelt fashioned himself a westerner, and it makes sense he would consider the region's interests in forming the commission. Wheeler took credit—likely accurately if not modestly—for the very existence of the Pacific coast investigation. In early 1909 he explained to the new president, William Howard Taft, that given "the interest which the Pacific Coast has in the immigration problem, particularly oriental immigration, the [Dillingham] Commission, on my motion, authorized a Pacific coast investigation, making me chairman of the sub-committee." Wheeler felt the commission's Japanese investigation was particularly important because "the state of California [was] about to attempt a similar investigation." Wheeler opened a branch office for the commission in San Francisco.

Wheeler underscored to Taft what he saw as the crucial relationship between immigration and foreign policy. "In view of the present attitude of the Japanese people toward the state of California," he wrote, Japan is not going to consider "data furnished by the state authorities" as a valid basis for diplomacy. "On the other hand," he went on, "I believe that data furnished by a federal body such as The Immigration Commission cannot but be accepted as authoritative. With San Francisco as my present base of operations I am in close touch with the progress of this investigation and in a position to give it close and personal supervision."[91] In other words, his work was a diplomatic necessity.

The title of the western volumes—"Japanese and Other Races in the Pacific Coast and Rocky Mountain States"—testified to the outsized impact of a relatively small immigration population. Mexican immigrants—though far from numerous—outnumbered the Japanese by two to one, and were the largest immigrant population in several western states.[92] But it was the proposed research on Japan that at least one news story called "likely to be the most important" because of potential "trouble with Japanese immigration . . . looming ahead."[93] In private meetings, the commission described the volumes, which were nominally about several groups, as "confined principally to a study of the Japanese and Hindus."[94] The first of the three published volumes began with the statement that "special emphasis was placed on Japanese immigration." In August 1907 the commission's most active member, Jeremiah Jenks, met personally with Rep. E. A. Hayes of California, an ardent Asian exclusionist who had called Japanese immigration a "gigantic race problem, as ugly and dangerous as the negro question in the South."[95] The commission considered an investigatory trip to Asia.[96] The commission's three volumes on the American West shared a five-page table of contents, which listed several sections on the Japanese, as well as entries for "East Indians," Scandinavian, Danish, German-Russian, Armenian, Italian, and Portuguese immigrants. In contrast, it did not contain a single listing for Mexicans, the West's largest immigrant group, even though the studies included the southwestern states of California, Arizona, New Mexico, and Colorado. In 1909 budget cuts spared studies of "Japanese and Hindus," but eliminated most of those on Mexicans—who outnumbered Japanese immigrants by two to one.[97]

The attention to Japanese immigration made for a very thorough study. In addition to using census statistics, the commission's agents secured their own data on 13,307 Japanese, around 5 percent of the total population, and believed their data about the Japanese to be "superior to those collected for most other races" in the western states.[98] The commission studied every industry in which the Japanese participated. In Washington State, for example, it investigated all but two of the eighteen canneries on the Columbia River, and nineteen of twenty-three in Puget Sound.[99]

The commission made every effort to be "objective," and the Pacific coast study was no cover-up for restriction propaganda. Henry Millis, the director of the Pacific coast study, favored Japanese immigrants' right to naturalization, and thought it understandable that their ineligibility discouraged them from developing civic pride and commitments to the community. He noted in the reports and later publications that the Japanese learned English with alacrity in comparison to Mexicans and other competitors. Their achievement was all the more impressive, according to the reports, because "they work together in 'gangs' of their own race very largely and come into little contact with English-speaking people," yet "make use of every opportunity" to learn the language.[100] He also reported that Japanese immigrants kept more money in the United States than did many other immigrants, and that they explicitly expressed a desire to become citizens.[101] In 1915, Millis republished the Japanese studies for a Christian organization largely sympathetic to the Japanese.[102]

Japanese Self-Defense

As Millis's words suggest, the western reports went beyond dry statistics to offer a glimpse at the lives and aspirations of the Japanese in the United States. Japanese laborers, even in the most degrading work situations, found ways to protest their plight. California farmers at first recruited Japanese men to break strikes or simply because they assumed them to be docile hard workers, but evidence from Hawaii might have warned them otherwise. In Hawaii resistance and strikes by Japanese plantation workers stretched back into the nineteenth century.[103] In March 1907, after Roosevelt ordered that Japanese in Hawaii no longer come to the mainland, Japanese immigrants in Honolulu staged a mass protest, shouting "It enslaves us permanently to Hawaii's capitalists!"[104]

A survey of wages reflected the varied treatment of the Japanese in the West. Although Japanese had a reputation for being the lowest-paid workers, in fact their wages ranged considerably from place to place. On one railroad line in Nevada and Utah, Italians made $1.50 per day, while the Japanese made just $1.10. But on two other railroads, "the Japanese are paid the same wages as all white men, $1.45 per day, and in one case more than the Mexicans."[105] In the year after the Gentlemen's Agreement, the investigators noticed that the wage differential between Japanese and white workers dwindled with increased labor demand.[106] But employers did not like "races" who pushed for better wages, even as white wageworkers like those in San Francisco did not like when Japanese accepted lower wages and lowered the standard of living. Both groups used these facts against the Japanese. The reports found that employers often compared Japanese favorably as workers to Mexicans, but considered them inferior as wage laborers, because they were more likely to demand better pay. The Japanese, according to one employer, were "more alert, more progressive, and more temperate than the Mexicans, who, when of the peon class, are generally deficient in these qualities."[107]

Across the West, Japanese agricultural workers found strength in numbers as growers began to rely on them. One employer described the Japanese as more likely than Mexicans to make "organized demands for higher wages and better conditions."[108] In California, the commission recorded several instances of increasing assertiveness. Ranchers who once had "praised [the Japanese] for their industry, quickness, adaptability, and eagerness to learn American ways" changed their tune. Now "complaints are heard that they are less accommodating and do less work in a day; they have become very independent and hard to deal with; by strikes and threat of strikes and boycott they have raised wages; and they can not always be depended upon to perform their contracts."[109]

A commission study of the agricultural center of Vaca Valley, California, offered an account of how these assertions of rights developed over time and in relation to other immigrant laborers. Research for the California studies was conducted and perhaps written by Stanford student and Japanese immigrant Yamato Ichihashi. Ichihashi had an acute awareness of Japanese aspirations and opposition—but he could also be an acerbic critic of his fellow countrymen. Both employers and commission agents held contradictory and complicated views about the Japanese. Over the course of several seasons in Vaca Valley, Japanese workers had outnumbered Chinese and white competitors. "No sooner had this control become an established fact, however, than it became unsatisfactory to the ranchers. In the first place, the wages of the Japanese have risen," in part because of well-ordered demands of the Japanese.

> Though, so far as known, no union has been organized by them, concerted effort, occasional strikes, and regard for one another's "jobs" have become almost as characteristic of the Japanese as laborers as of a trade union. Their tendency for several years has been to increase rather than to lower [their] wages. They are never paid less than the Chinese, and they are usually paid as much as the white laborers employed on the same ranches. . . . [But] it is said that the Japanese will not do as much work as formerly; in fact, will shirk and loaf when paid by the day; that much supervision is required to have work done properly; that the Japanese are arrogant and intractable; that they are dishonest.[110]

Ichihashi recognized that the story had two sides, and that the actions of the Japanese reflected a deliberate strategy. The Japanese did not formally organize, but they recognized their effective collective bargaining power.[111] "Whatever the truth of these matters may be," his report noted, "it is true that the Japanese are ambitious, and being naturally shrewd as to methods to employ have made the most of the situation," and "the ranchers have come to feel that they are oppressed." "The leasing of much land by the Japanese," has made "the situation . . . worse from the ranchers' point of view," because now they "competed for laborers with these [Japanese] tenants."[112] Ranchers, in short, complained that the Japanese refused to be the obedient, docile laborers they had sought. Although the commission focused mainly on ethnic solidarity strikes, in 1903 Mexican and Japanese farmworkers in Oxnard, California, cooperated in a massive—and ultimately successful—strike.[113]

In Wyoming, the commission documented a stunning example of cross-ethnic cooperation involving the Japanese. In 1907 the United Mine Workers came to the state to organize coal miners. Normally, Asian workers were the *object* of union opposition, but in this instance "a delegation of Japanese was sent to the convention of the union [in Denver] . . . to present their side of the case, with the result that a special dispensation was granted, and the Chinese and Japanese who were on the ground were allowed to become members of the union on an equal footing with other races." As a result, the Japanese earned wages equal to all other workers—$3.10 per day for wage workers and equal piece rates for mining and loading. After 1907, Japanese coal miners in Wyoming made better wages than any others in the West.[114] The vestiges of ancient Japanese caste distinctions, which reserved coal mining for the most undesirable social groups—"for criminals or the lowest of the low," as one migrant put it—made their wage successes and alliances with non-Japanese workers all the more meaningful.[115]

The Wyoming story did end with some skepticism about Japanese workers' ability to be true "free laborers." "Though they are members of the union," the passage noted, "the individual Japanese are not masters of their own affairs." A Japanese contracting agency in New York City assigned them to the work, just as Japanese bosses tended to control Japanese railroad and agricultural workers.[116] Some employers preferred this practice because they could negotiate directly with a contractor, who took care of managing the employees and arranging their room and board (which, unlike for most white workers, was not included in their compensation).[117] In much of California agriculture, white men were employed individually, whereas "Japanese 'bosses' were the most numerous labor agents." A gang system first introduced by the Chinese was adopted for Japanese workers. They received no board, and got the housing that whites refused.[118] These arrangements contributed to a suspicion that Japanese workers—like Chinese—were not really "free." In addition, any work Japanese did, according to the reports, the "'American' laborer comes to acquire a contempt for," because "he regards it as too servile for an American to engage in. Thus an odium is attached to much of the work done by Japanese. It is not regarded as 'white man's work.'"[119] Even some employers disliked the Japanese gang system—what they called "the evil of subcontracting." In Utah, sugar beet growers and Japanese workers cooperated in trying to get rid of Japanese bosses.[120]

Japanese asserted their rights in other ways, according to the reports. Japanese immigrants leased land whenever and wherever they could, as they did in Vaca Valley.[121] They did so to escape exploitation from Japanese and white bosses alike, and, perhaps, to escape the vestiges of low status in Japan. According to one scholar, Japanese immigrants found it rude to ask one another personal questions that might reveal an outcaste status obscured by upward mobility.[122] "Alien land laws" in several western states and local disapprobation often made it impossible for Japanese to buy land. They also could not file homestead claims, which were limited to people eligible for citizenship.[123] In Vaca Valley, the commission reports recount, "the number of Japanese desirous of leasing has been large. In their anxiety to obtain possession of land they not only have bid high for it, but in several authenticated cases have made threats that if the land was not leased as desired no Japanese labor would be had when wanted." They were willing, in other words, to threaten strikes to get access to land. "But why should the Japanese wish so strongly to lease land rather than to work for wages?" the reports asked. Ichihashi, who likely authored this section with Millis's oversight, was an astute observer:

> In the first place, the Japanese seem to take a great deal of pride in controlling the land on which they work. At home [in Japan] the wage system is young. In fact, it is scarcely known in the rural provinces, from which nearly all the Japanese have come. There they have controlled the land and worked for themselves; here they have wished to do the same. In the second place, the fruit-growing industry and the conditions surrounding it are new to the Japanese, and they have had exaggerated ideas as to the profit which may be made.... In the third place, the Japanese in this country are speculative in their instincts. A large winning outweighs all losses. As a matter of fact, the losses sustained by the Japanese have been great, but it is a notorious fact that a disastrous year has not materially diminished the number who want to lease land. Possibly the fact that most of the Japanese in this community are from two provinces and the life and industries in one of them have always been hazardous has something to do with this. In the fourth place, the Japanese are ambitious and, like other ambitious men, want the fullest opportunity to make money.[124]

The passage underscored the motivations of Japanese immigrants. In it, the Japanese were more than mere abstractions; they were striving entrepreneurs and human beings trying to improve their lot—either by demanding better wages or by securing their own (or at least leased) land where they could raise crops—and families. The discussion of the immigrants' origins also hinted at an escape from low caste status. Some observers speculated that the West attracted low-caste Japanese eager to remake themselves—a sort of Japanese version of the frontier thesis.[125] The shift to farming helped explain the fact that, according to the commission, almost eighty percent of Japanese women in California had arrived in the last five years.[126] (The 1908 Gentlemen's Agreements had made an exception for women—which launched concerns about "picture brides.")

Women's presence was important, because the school protests of 1906 had had a sexual undercurrent to them. The San Francisco school board's proclamation claimed segregation was not just to alleviate overcrowding in the schools, but also for the "higher end" of keeping the "youthful impressions" of their children from being "affected by association with people of the Mongolian race." In newsletters pushing the segregation measure, the Native Sons of the Golden West asked its readers, "Would you like your daughter to marry a Japanese?" "If not, demand that your representative in the Legislature vote for segregation of whites and Asiatics in the public schools."[127] Proponents of the segregation measure complained about adult Japanese men crowding into primary schools to learn English. But the commission reports found that only a handful of students were above appropriate ages, and the two oldest among them were just twenty years old.[128]

Bringing more Japanese women to the United States promised to lessen this seeming threat. Although the proportion of women in the Japanese American population was tiny, they were most likely to appear among farming families. Escaping gang labor gave Japanese men a way to build a family life. In Oregon and Washington, "most of the laborers cannot secure tolerable conditions under which to live with their families, while the farmer and his family can lead a normal family life." As a result, Japanese laborers turning to farming were willing to pay high rents, and had "displaced" other races—especially white farmers—in some regions. They did well: of 647 Japanese farmers interviewed in the Pacific Northwest, 432 had made a profit, and 101 broke even.[129]

The Japanese farmers must have seen their actions as those of good Americans—indeed, as yeoman's work that might show they were deserving of citizenship. Ironically, as a commission report on the mass meetings in San Francisco explained, critics wanted to exclude the Japanese "not only on the grounds set forth in the policy of Chinese exclusion but because . . . the assumed virtue of the Japanese—i.e., their partial adoption of American customs—makes them the more dangerous as competitors."[130] They had families, a hallmark of citizenship. Moreover, "a comparative large

Figure 3.1. Commission agents were surprisingly sympathetic to Japanese farmers, but to little avail. Courtesy Library of Congress, Printed Photographs Division, LC-DIG-ggbain-12867.

number of the farmers and business classes expressed a desire to become naturalized and expressed regret at the discrimination against persons who did not belong to some white race."[131] Many Japanese had achieved financial independence, and "seldom have the Japanese become public charges or been charity patients at public hospitals"—in large part because their own fraternal organizations took care of the indigent.[132]

The Dillingham Commission's sympathetic portrayal of Japanese farmers must have pleased Japanese authorities. The Japanese consulate had offered its "fullest cooperation" and "every assistance" to the study.[133] Cooperation, the Japanese government might have believed, would demonstrate their loyalty and friendship, and help show Japanese immigrants in a positive light. Consider the case of four Stanford undergraduates, part of the tiny cadre of Japanese students in the United States,[134] who worked as interpreters for the commission (unlike their Euro-American counterparts, they did not receive credit by name in the reports).[135] Until the school board controversy (when they were already at Stanford, although Ichihashi recalled staying out of San Francisco public school during agitators' first calls for segregation in 1900),[136] their homeland and the United States had enjoyed good relations. They were not members of the barred "laboring classes." They had the confidence and connections to study in the United States. Perhaps they hoped, as the consular officials would have, to communicate the assimilation and progress of their countrymen. "Bringing about a better understanding between the West and East," Ichihashi wrote Stanford president David Starr Jordan in spring 1908, is the "object of my life."[137] Ichihashi and the others likely knew business owners and small farmers, who had risen painstakingly from the laboring classes. By 1909, there were as many as five thousand Japanese-owned businesses in the western states—ranging from a sake brewery to a shingle mill.[138] The translators themselves embodied and expressed the positive spirit of assimilation and progress.

Anti-Japanese racism would eventually darken their experiences of the United States, however. Ichihashi went on to Harvard for a PhD based on his research for the Dillingham Commission. At Harvard, he studied with eugenicist William Z. Ripley and none other than Frederick Jackson Turner.[139] Ichihashi returned to Stanford to teach in 1913 and became a prominent scholar. In 1932 he published a definitive history of Japanese immigration, based in part on the Dillingham reports, and continued a productive research career.[140] In 1941, after the attack on Pearl Harbor, Ichihashi supported the United States and bought Liberty Bonds. David Starr Jordan, another famous eugenicist who had defended the Japanese during the crises of 1907, endorsed his continued employment there. But in spring of 1942, Ichihashi and his wife were interned first at Santa Anita racetrack (where families were housed in horse stalls) and later in the desolate Tule Lake camp. Ichihashi kept diaries of his experience, but became reclusive and never published again.[141] Later scholars—both Japanese and American—have blamed the controversies of 1906–1907 and the Gentlemen's Agreement for tension between Japan and the United States that would eventually erupt in war and institutionalized racism.[142]

The Dillingham Commission's origins in the crisis with Japan reveal the centrality of the American West to diplomacy and immigration politics in the age of empire.[143] After orchestrating the deal for the Gentlemen's Agreement and the commission in February 1907, Roosevelt's "Great White Fleet" began its round-the-world show of naval force that December. It docked at San Francisco in July of the following year, in the Philippines in early October, then Yokohama, Japan, in October 1908. Cheering Japanese crowds greeted the fleet, eager to show their friendship with the United States. At the same time, the commission was undertaking its studies of the Japanese along the Pacific coast—home of vicious anti-Japanese campaigns.

In the early twentieth century, much of the political and academic writing about the Japanese emphasized the tension between the international aspects of immigration and those who insisted it was only a domestic concern. After World War I, Japan introduced an amendment to the Versailles

Treaty calling for racial equality between nations. It spoke to the troubled history of its relations with erstwhile allies like the United States. The proposal was defeated.[144] In the aftermath of Versailles, immigration reverted to an insistently domestic policy. U.S. senator James D. Phelan offered perhaps the most insistent example. His 1920 campaign posters proclaimed, "Keep California White." In 1924, he wrote in the *North American Review*, "You know, of course, that immigration is conceded to be a domestic question and is not a proper subject for international discussion, nor has the United States any treaty with any other nation affecting immigration. The so-called 'Gentlemen's Agreement' with Japan is wholly exceptional."[145] In spite of the striving of Japan and Japanese Americans, the Immigration Act of 1924 barred any "alien ineligible for naturalization" (all Asians, in other words) and those already in the states could not pursue citizenship. Japanese newspapers called the day the law went into effect "National Humiliation Day."[146] The moderating voice of Millis and of the Japanese themselves could not save them from draconian legislation and a denial of civil liberties for some time to come.

Notes

The author would like to thank the members of the Redd Center workshop who created this volume, especially organizers Jessie Embry and Brian Cannon; the participants in the Georgetown Department of History Faculty Workshop, especially Michael Kazin, Chandra Manning, and Jordan Sand; Warren I. Cohen, and Hal R. Cohen.

1. Examples are too numerous to cite, but paradigmatically, see, for example, John Higham, *Strangers in the Land: Patterns of American Nativism 1860–1925* (New Brunswick, NJ: Rutgers University Press, 1955), and Barbara M. Solomon, *Ancestors and Immigrants, and Changing New England Tradition* (Chicago: University of Chicago Press, 1956).
2. Mae Ngai, *Impossible Subjects: Illegal Aliens and the Making of Modern America* (Princeton, NJ: Princeton University Press, 2004), Erika Lee, *At America's Gates: Chinese Immigration during the Exclusion Era, 1882–1943* (Chapel Hill: University of North Carolina Press, 2003).
3. Google Books has digital copies of the reports. The reports cited in this chapter are Henry A. Millis, *Immigrants in Industries*, Vol. 23, *Japanese and Other Immigrant Races in the Pacific Coast and Rocky Mountain States*, Reports of the U.S. Immigration Commission (Washington, DC: Government Printing Office, 1911), and Henry A. Millis, *Immigrants in Industries* Vol. 24, *Agriculture*, Reports of the U.S. Immigration Commission (Washington, DC: Government Printing Office, 1911). Hereafter I have referred to them as Vol. 23 and Vol. 24. Many scholars list forty-two reports, but the forty-second proposed volume, an index, was never published.
4. See, for example, Thomas J. Archdeacon, *Becoming American: An Ethnic History* (New York: Free Press, 1983); Robert F. Zeidel, *Immigrants, Progressives, and*

Exclusion Politics: The Dillingham Commission, 1900–1927 (DeKalb: Northern Illinois University Press, 2004); Maldwyn Allen Jones, *American Immigration* (Chicago: University of Chicago Press, 1960; 1992), esp. 152–57; Desmond King, *Making Americans: Immigration, Race, and the Origins of the Diverse Democracy* (Cambridge, MA: Harvard University Press, 2000); Roger Daniels, *Coming to America* (New York: Perennial Books, 1991; 2002); Roger Daniels, *Guarding the Golden Door* (New York: Hill and Wang, 2004); Charles Jaret, "Troubled by Newcomers: Anti-Immigrant Attitudes and Action during Two Eras of Mass Immigration to the United States," *Journal of American Ethnic History* 18, no. 3 (Spring 1999): 9–39; Lawrence H. Fuchs, "Immigration Reform in 1911 and 1981: The Role of Select Commissions," *Journal of American Ethnic History* 3, no. 1 (Fall 1983): 59–89. Even a recent Korean article placed its emphasis on the commission's obsession with southern and eastern Europeans. Young-Ho Soon, "Reports of the Dillingham Immigration Commission: An Analysis of the Findings," *Mguk-sa Yongu* 20 (November 2004): 89–117. By contrast, see Elliott Robert Barkan, *From All Points: America's Immigrant West, 1870s–1952* (Bloomington: Indiana University Press, 2007), chapter 12.

5. Raymond A. Esthus, *Theodore Roosevelt and Japan* (Seattle: University of Washington Press, 1967), 134.
6. Vol. 23: 67.
7. Examples of the petitions can be found in HR59A–H8.1, Committee on Immigration and Naturalization/Chinese Immigration, Box 404, Records of U.S. House of Representatives Center for Legislative Archives, RG 233, National Archives I, Washington, DC [NADC].
8. See, for example, John P. Irish, U.S. Customs Service, Port of San Francisco, CA, to Secretary of Commerce and Labor Oscar Straus, March 29, 1907, Folder March 16–31, 1907, Box 6, Oscar Straus Papers, Library of Congress Manuscript Division, Library of Congress, Washington, DC. On the crisis's roots in leftist San Francisco politics, see Michael Kazin, *Barons of Labor: The San Francisco Building Trades and Union Power in the Progressive Era* (Urbana: University of Illinois Press, 1987), 162–69.
9. Kiyo Sue Inui, "The Gentleman's Agreement: How It Has Functioned," *Annals of the American Academy of Political and Social Science* 122 (November 1925): 188–98, quotation on p. 188.
10. Eldon R. Penrose, *California Nativism: Organized Opposition to the Japanese, 1890–1913* (San Francisco: R and E Research Associates, 1974), 27.
11. Esthus, *TR and Japan*, 133; Charles Scawthorn, John Eidinger, and Anshel Schiff, eds., *Fire Following Earthquake* (Reston, VA: ASCE, NFPA, 2005); numerical data from the United States Geological Survey, accessed December 30, 2011, http://earthquake.usgs.gov/regional/nca/1906/18april/casualties.php, and currency conversion based on the Inflation Calculator, accessed December 30, 2011, http://www.westegg.com/inflation/infl.cgi.
12. Vol. 23: 191. The overall population increased perhaps only 15 percent, based on estimates by the U.S. Census, accessed October 10, 2011, http://www.infoplease.com/spot/sanfranearthquakecensus.html.
13. I have not calculated whether the increase in violence was proportional to the population increase.

14. Esthus, *TR and Japan*, 133. In contrast, the San Francisco fire was somewhat of a boon for the Chinese community. Most of the birth records were destroyed, allowing Chinese to claim "paper sons," children of legal Chinese immigrants. These children were technically U.S. citizens, so fraudulent "birth certificates" became a way to immigrate to the United States and/or become a citizen, by claiming a father who was a legal resident. See Ronald Takaki, *Strangers from a Different Shore: A History of Asian Americans*, updated and revised (New York: Little, Brown, 1998), 234–37.
15. Vol. 23: 6, 13.
16. It was a pattern that would repeat itself with each successive restriction law. Filipino and Mexican migration increased after the restrictions on European immigration in 1921, 1924, and 1927.
17. Both the Bureau of Immigration and the Dillingham Commission examined these immigrant flows as well. Vol. 23: 15. Marcus Braun, an agent for the Bureau of Immigration, did a report on the subject.
18. The *Hawaiian Star*, quoted in Takaki, *Strangers*, 147.
19. Esthus, *TR and Japan*, p. 146; also see Oscar Straus to Mr. Secretary (Elihu Root), December 22, 1906, Letterbook 7, Box 20, Straus Papers.
20. Vol. 23: 21–22.
21. Archdeacon, *Becoming American*, 118.
22. Roosevelt, quoted in Esthus, *TR and Japan*, 128, preface.
23. See ibid., 76–96.
24. Michael Auslin, *Pacific Cosmopolitans: A Cultural History of U.S.-Japan Relations* (Cambridge, MA: Harvard University Press, 2011), 87; Esthus, *TR and Japan*, 106.
25. On Straus's views, see *Under Four Administrations* (Boston: Houghton Mifflin, 1922), 218–30. See Esthus, *TR and Japan*, on overall views, as well as Daniel J. Tichenor, *Dividing Lines: The Politics of Immigration Control in America* (Princeton: Princeton University Press, 2002), 128–32.
26. Straus, *Under Four Administrations*, 180.
27. Esthus, *TR and Japan*, 143.
28. Ibid., 148–49.
29. Ibid., 132, 139. And see Masuda Hajimu, "Rumors of War: Immigration Disputes and the Social Construction of American-Japanese Relations, 1905–1913," *Diplomatic History* 33, no. 1 (January 2009): 1–37.
30. Vol. 23: 162.
31. Esthus, *TR and Japan*, 144. For two views, see "Olney Disagrees with Roosevelt Over Japan," *New York Times*, February 6, 1907, and "The Real Questions Under the Japanese Treaty and the San Francisco School Board Resolution," Presidential Address at the First Annual Meeting of the American Society of International Law, Washington, DC, April 19, 1907, in Elihu Root, *Addresses on International Subjects*, collected and edited by Robert Bacon and James Brown Scott (Freeport, NY: Books For Libraries, 1916; 1969), 273–86.
32. Esthus, *TR and Japan*, 139, 156. It should be pointed out, however, that TR was working to increase naval appropriations at the same time, so it made sense for him to emphasize the military aspect of the conflict.
33. Ibid., 166.

34. On Root's views, see Philip C. Jessup, *Elihu Root* (1938; reprint, New Haven, CT: Archon Books, 1964), 1:458; on Straus, see Straus to Charles Bonaparte, U.S. Attorney General, January 30, 1907, Letterbook 7, and Wilber F. Crafts to Straus, August 27, 1907, Folder August 1907, Box 7, Straus Papers, and *Under Four Administrations*, 221, 225.
35. Roosevelt to John Hay, September 2, 1904, quoted in Warren I. Cohen, "From Contempt to Containment: Cycles in American Attitudes toward China," in John Braeman et al., eds., *Twentieth Century American Foreign Policy* (Columbus: Ohio State University Press, 1971).
36. David Folkmar and Elnora Folkmar, *Dictionary of Races or Peoples*, Vol. 5, *Reports of the U.S. Immigration Commission* (Washington, DC: Government Printing Office, 1910), esp. 98, 147. On "white blood," see quotations from David Starr Jordon in Gordon H. Chang, *Morning Glory, Evening Shadow: Yamato Ichihashi and His Internment Writings, 1942–1945* (Palo Alto: Stanford University Press, 1999), 19–20.
37. Esthus, *TR and Japan*, 145–47. As pernicious as segregation was, Roosevelt was exaggerating, since the Oriental School was, of course, public.
38. Theodore Roosevelt to Henry Cabot Lodge, marked confidential, July 10, 1907, in *Selections from the Correspondence of Theodore Roosevelt and Henry Cabot Lodge, 1884–1918*, Vol. 2, ed. Henry Cabot Lodge (New York, 1925), 274–75.
39. Ibid.
40. Robert Zeidel offers a good argument for this in the opening chapter of his book, *Immigrants, Progressives*.
41. The commission was modeled on an earlier version: See H.J. Res. 161, "Joint Resolution to create a commission to examine the subject of immigration," May 22, 1906, Folder 15 Committee on Naturalization and Immigration Administration Papers 1 of 2, Box 347, Records of the House of Representatives, RG 233, 59A, The Center for Legislative Archives, NADC.
42. Zeidel, *Immigrants, Progressives*, 31.
43. Ibid., 33–35.
44. On heightened importance of the issue, see Oscar Straus's diary entry "First Cabinet Meeting—December 18," Diary 1906–7, Box 22, Oscar Straus Papers.
45. "Restriction of Immigration," *Congressional Record* 41:59 (February 16, 1907), p. 3089.
46. Oscar Straus to Isidor Straus, December 19, 1906, Letterbook 7, Box 20, Straus Papers.
47. "Restriction of Immigration," 3218.
48. "Senate Passes Coolie Measure," *New York Times*, February 17, 1907.
49. Kornel Chang, "Circulating Race and Empire: Transnational Labor Activism and the Politics of Anti-Asian Agitation in the Anglo-American Pacific World, 1880–1910," *Journal of American History* 96, no. 3 (December 2009): 678–701.
50. Esthus, *TR and Japan*, 159.
51. H. A. Millis, *The Japanese Problem in the United States: An Investigation for the Commission on Relations with Japan Appointed by the Federal Council of the Churches of Christ in America* (New York: Macmillan, 1915), 211.
52. Christopher Mitchell, ed., *Western Hemisphere Immigration and United States Foreign Policy* (State College: Pennsylvania State University Press, 1992), Introduction, 13.

53. "Restriction of Immigration," 3097.
54. Ibid., 3098.
55. Ibid., 3222.
56. Kazin, *Barons of Labor*, 164.
57. Quotation from *The Wasp* [San Francisco], December 8, 1906, quoted in Doremus Scudder, "The Japanese Question," unpublished paper, in Wilber F. Crafts to Oscar Straus, August 27, 1907, Folder August 1907, Box 7, Straus Papers.
58. "Restriction of Immigration," 3227 (emphasis added).
59. Ibid., 3222.
60. Scott Kurashige, *The Shifting Grounds of Race: Black and Japanese Americans in the Making of Multiethnic Los Angeles* (Princeton: Princeton University Press, 2008), 18, *Los Angeles Times* quotation on p. 20.
61. Vol. 23: 73, 55; also see 97.
62. Ibid., 162.
63. All petitions in Sen61A-J39, Folder April 21, 1909–January 10, 1911, Box 132, Records of the United States Senate, RG 46, Center for Legislative Archives, NADC.
64. Jessup, *Elihu Root*, 13.
65. Esthus, *TR and Japan*, 160; also see "Jordan Explains President Was in Bad Temper," *San Francisco Call*, February 16, 1907; Andrea Geiger, *Subverting Exclusion: Transpacific Encounters with Race, Caste, and Borders, 1885–1928* (New Haven: Yale University Press, 2011), 105.
66. Straus diary, 215.
67. Esthus, *TR and Japan*, 152–60, quotation on p. 160.
68. In addition to the Japan measure and the commission, the new law excluded new categories of immigrants and raised a head tax for immigrants, the revenue from which was used to fund the Commission. I am indebted to Zeidel, *Immigrants, Progressives*, 26–34, for this account.
69. The jockeying for appointments to the Commission began nearly right away. See the letters of the Immigration Restriction League, for example, Stuart Hall to James Patten, February 4, 1907, File J. Lee Immigration Restriction League Correspondence, Jan.–Apr. 1907, Carton 1, Joseph Lee Papers, Massachusetts Historical Society, Boston; also see February 1907 correspondence, Letterbook 7, Box 20, Straus Papers.
70. "Nation Aroused," Kentucky *Berea*, April 25, 1907.
71. "Coast Man Selected: W. R. Wheeler, of Oakland, on Immigration Body," *Washington Post*, March 27, 1907.
72. See Zeidel, *Immigrants, Progressives*, 81–85.
73. Oscar Straus to Adolf Kraus, March 13, 1907, Letterbook 7, Box 20, Straus Papers.
74. "Senate Passes Coolie Measure," *New York Times*, February 17, 1907, p. 1; John Lund, "Boundaries of Restriction: The Dillingham Commission," *UVM History Review* 6 (December 1994), available at www.uvm.edu/~hag/histreview/vol6/lund.html (accessed August 31, 2009); Tichenor, *Dividing Lines*, 128–32. For the centrality of the passport measure to congressional debates, see "Restriction of Immigration," esp. 3083–99.

75. See Vol. 23: 162–70.
76. *Bulletin of the American Economic Association*, 1911, 246–47.
77. Victor Clark, "Immigration Conditions in Hawaii," 700, in U.S. Immigration Commission, *Abstracts of Reports on the Immigration Commission*, Vol. 2, *Reports of the U.S. Immigration Commission* (Washington, DC: Government Printing Office, 1911).
78. "Restriction of Immigration," 3084.
79. "Immigration Commission Records 1907–1910," December 14, 1909, p. 105, William W. Husband Papers, Chicago Historical Society.
80. See H. C. Stevens, Acting Private Secretary, to "Sir," July 1, 1907, Folder July 1-15, Box 7, Straus Papers.
81. On the Philippines report, see James A. LeRoy, American Consular Service, Durango, Mexico, to Dr. Victor S. Clark, Bureau of Labor, Washington, DC, January 31, 1905; and on New Zealand, Edward Treagor to Victor Clark, April 8, 1904; and see Clark to James LeRoy, January 4, 1906, all File: Personal File, Correspondence 1890–1929, Box 1, Victor S. Clark Collection, Library of Congress Manuscript Division, Washington, DC. Victor S. Clark, "Mexican Labor in the United States," *Bureau of Labor Bulletin* 78 (1908): 466–522.
82. On this common academic path, see Daniel T. Rodgers, *Atlantic Crossings: Social Politics in a Progressive Age* (Cambridge: Harvard University Press, 1998).
83. Clark was a bit of an expert on the subject; in 1906 and 1907 he went to the American South to investigate debt peonage of immigrants and African Americans. See Straus to Bishop Gailor, January 13, 1908, Scrapbook 3, Box 20, Straus Papers.
84. Victor Clark, "Immigration Conditions in Hawaii," 700. "Joint Resolution Annexing Hawaii to the United States," Resolution No. 55, known as the "Newlands Resolution," of July 7, 1898: 20 Stat. 750: 2 Supp. R. S. 395, available at http://www.hookele.com/non-hawaiians/newlands.html (accessed January 6, 2012).
85. Clark, "Immigration Conditions," 702. His use of the term "Caucasian" in this context was doubly confusing, because the Dillingham Commission's *Dictionary of Races or Peoples* classified Siberians as "Caucasians" but also criticized the term for its confusion, see pp. 98, 147.
86. Clark, "Immigration Conditions," 700.
87. Ibid., 712.
88. Ibid., 722.
89. "Coast Man Selected."
90. Roosevelt to William R. Wheeler, March 19, 1907, quoted in Wheeler to William Howard Taft, April 21, 1909, Microfilm Reel 351, Series 5, William Howard Taft Papers, Library of Congress Manuscript Division, Washington, DC.
91. Ibid.
92. Archdeacon, *Becoming American*, 118.
93. "Secondary Topics: The Immigration Problem," *The National Tribune* [Washington, DC], April 25, 1907. See also "Substitutes for Asiatics," *Los Angeles Times*, May 8, 1908.
94. "U.S. Immigration Commission Records 1907–1910," Notebook, p. 87, W. W. Husband Papers, Chicago Historical Society.
95. "Warns Jenks of Brown Peril," *Los Angeles Times*, August 17, 1907.

96. See, for example, "Immigration Investigated," *Los Angeles Times*, November 10, 1907.
97. These tables of contents were compiled in the summer of 1910; the abstracts (volume 1), compiled in December, *did* list Mexicans in a simplified table of contents organized around national origin. On the cuts, see Zeidel, *Immigrants, Progressives*, 82–85.
98. Vol. 23: 3–4.
99. Ibid., 3, 48.
100. Vol. 24: 59.
101. Vol. 23: 141, 148–9, 160; Vol. 24: 59.
102. Millis, *Japanese Problem*.
103. Takaki, *Strangers*, 143.
104. Ibid., 148.
105. Vol. 23: 41.
106. Ibid., 4, 41; Vol. 24: 228.
107. Vol. 23: 43.
108. Ibid., 40.
109. Ibid., 67.
110. Vol. 24: 186.
111. Ibid.
112. Ibid., 187. A special report on the small East Indian population in California (largely Punjabi) was included in the same volume, and they were described in the Japanese reports as "a filthy, ignorant, and despised race . . . considered the least desirable immigrants in the state." Vol. 24: 28.
113. Among many discussions of this strike, see Takaki, *Strangers*, 198–99, and Tomas Almaguer, *Racial Fault Lines: The Historical Origins of White Supremacy in California* (Berkeley: University of California Press, 2008).
114. Vol. 23: 54–55.
115. Geiger, *Subverting Exclusion*, 17, 66–70, quotation on p. 67. Some Japanese diplomats blamed prejudice in the American West on the preponderance of lower-caste Japanese there, pp. 56–57.
116. Vol. 23: 55, 57.
117. Vol. 24: 36.
118. Ibid., 21.
119. Ibid., 29.
120. Ibid., 141.
121. See, for example, Vol. 23: 80–82. In some places, though, there were no Japanese farmers; in Colorado, for example, where general opinions of the Japanese were higher than in California, "only one Japanese landowner—a half breed with a white wife—was reported." Vol. 24: 123.
122. Geiger, *Subverting Exclusion*, 70.
123. Vol. 24: 236. In 1909, the California Assembly came close to passing an alien land law forbidding Japanese from owning land, but President Roosevelt intervened with the governor, who managed its narrow defeat. It succeeded in 1913, however.
124. Vol. 24: 189.
125. Geiger, *Subverting Exclusion*, 56–57.
126. Vol. 24: 56.

127. Quoted in Takaki, *Strangers*, 201.
128. Proclamation cited in Vol. 23: 162. These fears would animate anti-Japanese attacks for years to come. In 1913 hearings to promote an alien land act, one white California farmer testified, "Near my home is an eighty-acre tract of as fine land as there is in California. On that tract lives a Japanese. With that Japanese lives a white woman. In that woman's arms is a baby. What is that baby? It isn't Japanese. It isn't white. I'll tell you what that baby is. It is a germ of the mightiest problem that ever faced this state; a problem that will make the black problem of the South look white. All about us the Asiatics are gaining a foothold." Quoted in Takaki, *Strangers*, 204. Ichihashi himself appears to have lied about his age in high school to avoid criticism, Chang, *Morning Glory*, 14.
129. Vol. 23: 82–88.
130. Report of mass meeting in San Francisco, May 8, 1900, cited in ibid., 167.
131. Ibid., 160.
132. Ibid., 164.
133. Ibid., 3.
134. I am indebted to conversations with Paul Kramer and Alicia Ratterree about the world of Asian university students in the United States.
135. I found their names in payroll reports in William Jett Lauck Papers, Small Library, University of Virginia, and Husband Papers.
136. Chang, *Morning Glory*, 17.
137. Ibid., 22.
138. Takaki, *Strangers*, 186, and Vol. 23: 131, 48. The shingle mill story was a disheartening one—the shingle workers faced opposition from white unions, so they worked to buy their own mills, only to find they could not get insurance for their mills when one burned down. Vol. 23: 48.
139. Gordon, *Morning Glory*, 20.
140. Yamato Ichihashi, *Japanese Immigration, Its Status in California* (San Francisco: The Marshall Press, 1915); Yamato Ichihashi, *Japanese in the United States* (Stanford: Stanford University Press, 1932; New York: Arno Press, 1969).
141. On horse stalls, see http://encyclopedia.densho.org/Santa_Anita_(detention_facility)/ accessed June 30, 2014; Gordon H. Chang, "We Almost Wept," *Stanford Today* (November/December 1996) accessed January 6, 2011, http://news.stanford.edu/stanfordtoday/ed/9611/9611fea401.shtml; Chang, *Morning Glory*.
142. See, for example, T. C. Rhee, "A Postscript on the Japanese-American 'Immigration' Dispute, 1868–1924: A Diplomatic Tinderbox," *Asian Quarterly, no. 2 (*1973): 135.
143. A growing new literature on the links between foreign policy and immigration policy is nicely encapsulated in Donna Gabaccia, *Foreign Relations: American Immigration in Global Perspective* (Princeton: Princeton University Press, 2012).
144. Erez Manela, "Imagining Woodrow Wilson in Asia: Dreams of East-West Harmony and the Revolt against Empire in 1919," *American Historical Review* 111, no. 5 (December 2006): 1327–51; Naoko Shimaza, *Japan, Race, and Equality: The Racial Equality Proposal of 1919* (London: Routledge Books, 1998).
145. Phelan, "Letter to a Japanese Gentleman," in *Japanese Exclusion*, comp. Julia E. Johnsen (New York: H. W. Wilson Co., 1925), 126.
146. Geiger, *Subverting Exclusion*, 188.

4

The Specter of Nations
Immigration, Gothicism, and Transnational Mimicry in Two Post-Revolutionary Mexican American Novels

D. Seth Horton

D. Seth Horton explores the complex logic of Mexican emigration and immigration to the United States throughout the Mexican revolution by examining the relationships between Francisco Madero's political treatise, La sucesión presidencial en 1910, *and two post-Revolutionary Mexican American novels, Conrado Espinoza's* El sol de Texas *and Daniel Venegas's* Las aventuras de don Chipote, o cuando los pericos mamen. *Utilizing postcolonial theory, Horton argues that these novels transformed Madero's usage of Gothic imagery and mimicry through the spectrum of immigration and emigration, thereby highlighting some of the ways in which Mexican American immigrants responded to the contradictions of American citizenship in the 1920s. Horton suggests Espinoza described Texas as "a kind of Gothic hellscape" that exposed the racist challenges that many new immigrants to the United States had to confront. Moreover, employing a strategy that literary scholar Homi Bhabha has termed "mimicry," Horton argues that Venegas investigated his protagonist's relationship to power structures in the United States, which ranged from Public Health Service disinfecting stations on the border to subject formation in Los Angeles, thus constructing a narrative of the American West that included the previously marginalized story of Mexican American immigration.*

In response to President Porfirio Díaz's announcement in 1908 that Mexico was ready to embrace democracy, Francisco Madero wrote *La sucesión presidencial en 1910*, a political treatise that became a highly influential bestseller and effectively launched his political campaign for the presidency.[1] Madero argued that Díaz's despotism was the latest historical example of the militarism that had plagued Mexico since the Colonial Era, and thus a transformation more radical than simply a presidential change was needed. He called on his compatriots to form a political party dedicated to the principles of "real suffrage" and "no re-election," and later codified these ideas in the "Plan de San Luis Potosí" (1910), a short document released while he was exiled in San Antonio that served as a blueprint for the government he was attempting to assemble. Madero was finally elected president in 1911, but his short term in office was characterized by an inability to govern effectively. Many of his supporters felt betrayed when he was unable to initiate the social, political, and economic reforms they were anticipating. They began to see him as an impractical ideologue, and he was assassinated on February 22, 1913.

Although most historians have focused on the foundational relationship between Madero's text and the Mexican revolution, his work can also be read as a literary precursor to a pair of post-Revolutionary Mexican American immigrant novels, Conrado Espinoza's *El sol de Texas* (1926) and Daniel Venegas's *Las aventuras de don Chipote, o cuando los pericos mamen* (1928).[2] Two of Madero's most significant tropes, namely, the employment of Gothic imagery and his rhetorical usage of what I will call "transnational mimicry," became transformed in the texts of Espinoza and Venegas, respectively, through the prism of immigration.[3] While these novels are not in ideological agreement, they are both situated within the U.S.-Mexico borderlands, and thus need to be historically understood not only as narratives that document the experiences of immigrating to the United States, but also as responses to the mass emigration caused by the Mexican revolution. Reading these near contemporaneous texts against Francisco Madero's *La sucesión presidencial en 1910* therefore reveals the multiple logics of Mexican emigration and immigration in the aftermath of the revolution. Furthermore, by disclosing the transnational trajectory from Madero's political treatise to the novels of Espinoza and Venegas, my essay highlights the ways in which these Mexican American novelists responded to the paradox of citizenship, and in the process reveals how Mexican American immigrant literature began to theorize the borderlands and the American West as alternative spaces of nationalist critique.

Though Madero explicitly condemned absolute power in *La sucesión presidencial en 1910*, he nevertheless faced a rhetorical requirement to justify his qualifications for the presidency, a conflict that he resolved by constructing a modernist persona wherein he became *the* leading populist messenger who would guide Mexico toward a new and utopic future. Madero's political vision was thus liberatory; he believed that the establishment of his political party would help to insure the "salvation of our institutions, of our freedom, and perhaps even our national integrity" (19).[4] *La sucesión presidencial en 1910* contains a dozen other occurrences of the terms "salvar" and "salvación," and thus Madero constructed for himself a Christ-like persona in his rejection of absolute power, concern for the poor, and willingness to die for the Mexican people. This implication was reinforced by the ever-present references to blood throughout the text, which were usually employed to signify either the victims or perpetrators of Mexico's revolutions. The first sentence, for example, reads in part, "I dedicate this book to the heroes who won the independence of our country with their blood" (1). Madero's ubiquitous references to blood throughout the text gradually transform it into a multivalent symbol, for not only did blood remind his readers of the violence that Díaz would like to bury from Mexico's collective memory, but it simultaneously reemerged as a symbol for the Christ-like redemption that Madero offered in the guise of political salvation.

If Madero was *the* redeemer, Díaz was a "semi-dios" (85) who functions throughout the text as an uncanny doppelgänger. "To see him, even in a photograph, one can discern the appearance of a sphinx; it seems that he is enclosed within a great mystery; that he hides carefully in the depth of his soul a thought, a fixed idea, which will only become manifest through the transcendental events that control his entire life" (112). Madero's representation of Díaz as a "great mystery" relied on a linkage between the president and the haunted history of Mexico, a Gothic past marked by a troubled hybridity between colonizers and the colonized. In his discussion of the inter-American Gothic, Jesse Alemán has argued, "In much the same way that the 'Africanist presence' accounts for the U.S. Gothic, the inter-American Gothic emerges when the hemispheric horrors of the Spanish conquest of Mexico return in narratives, such as Prescott's [*History of the Conquest of Mexico*], that sense how the United States stands to inherit the monstrous race war hidden beneath the romantic veneer of Mexico's history" (84).[5] A similar disinterment, albeit a strictly nationalist one, is at work in Madero's text, which intimated that when Díaz repeated the transgressions of the Spanish conquest, for example by deporting and enslaving the Yaqui from Sonora, he became possessed by the moral excesses of Mexico's colonial history.[6] While Madero acknowledged the horrors of that history, his treatment was rather concise, as if he were unwilling or unable to envision the full devastation experienced by generations of indigenous persons in Mexico. He instead relied on Gothic imagery as a way simply to gesture toward these transgressions, thereby quickly allowing him to assure his readers that unlike Díaz, he would not repeat them.

By representing Díaz as a "great mystery," a socially invisible individual, isolated and cut off from his fellow countrymen, Madero not only rendered him indifferent to the plight of the Mexican people, but more subtly, Díaz also became a spectral embodiment of the country's social inequality. In *Specters of Marx* (1994), Derrida positioned the figure of the specter, which is neither dead nor alive, neither present nor absent, as a central figure in his theory of hauntology, a philosophy of history that resists the linear progression of time by asserting that the present is saturated with the past.[7] As Frederic Jameson has explained, spectrality suggests that "the living present is scarcely as self-sufficient as it claims to be; that we would do well not to count on its density and solidity, which might under exceptional circumstances betray us" (39).[8] The present is thus disrupted by the reemergence of past events, a position that parallels Gothic concerns with the ways in which the past returns through the repressed, disallowed, or buried. Spectrality thus subverts those secrets that the present refuses to acknowledge. Understood in this way, the Díaz presidency, as described by Madero, was a specter of the economic conditions that continued to plague the country. This might seem like a counterintuitive argument given the modernization in late nineteenth-century Mexico, including capital investments in science, technology, manufacturing, and mining. The infrastructure of the country admittedly improved, especially the roads, railroads, and ports, and there were also gains made in education as well as a growing middle class. However, as Robert M. Buffington and William E. French point out, despite a remarkable 8 percent growth between 1884 and 1900, most Mexicans, perhaps as many as 90 percent, did not experience a general improvement in economic conditions.[9] Elites mostly profited from Díaz's agenda of modernization, which is why Madero was rhetorically able to portray him as an apparition, a president in absentia who was entirely unconcerned with the plight of most Mexicans.

The distinction between Díaz's embodiment of a Gothic past and elitist present with Madero's populist salvation and democratic path to a utopic future reveals a teleological argument rooted in Madero's foregrounding of the temporal over the spatial, which is not surprising given his rhetorical objective, namely, to attain Mexican unity and support for his transition into the presidency. However, as Mexican immigrants began to flee the chaos of the ensuing revolution by crossing over to the United States, Madero's strategies of Gothic representation became spatialized. Instead of differentiating between a Gothic past and a modernist future, Conrado Espinoza's *El sol de Texas* depicts Texas as a kind of Gothic hellscape for heterogeneous groups of Mexicanos, including immigrants who remain permanently in the United States, those who intend to return to Mexico, and Texas Mexicans with deep historic roots in the state.[10] For Espinoza and other Mexican emigrants, Gothic conditions were not merely remnants of a colonial past, but were rather encountered throughout the hegemonic and "bedeviled" spaces, to use José E. Limón's term, of the borderlands and the western United States that had once belonged to Mexico (187).[11]

Espinoza's novel opens with the García family crossing into "Laredo gringo" (8) to escape the tribulations of the revolution. On their way to San Antonio, they befriend Don Serapio and his two sons, Matías and José, and while everyone is optimistic about the future, Espinoza alludes to the landscape in Gothic terms to foreshadow the journeys that await them: "Deep down there in their heart of hearts, they all felt a suspicion, an inexplicable fear that rose with the view of that mountainless land without the rapid and prodigious variations of their native country" (10). The landscape unnerves them precisely where American civilization is most present, and they become even more afraid upon actually encountering Anglos. Espinoza then describes San Antonio's Spanish ruins in detail, supporting his cultural excavation by subsequently interpreting the Mexicans in Haymarket Square to be incarnations of various characters in *Don Quijote de la Mancha*. The nostalgic linkage between lost land and the lost Spanish Golden Age effectively marks San Antonio as a haunted space, where the city's Spanish roots have not been expunged despite the continued encroachment of Anglo society and its nativism.

Once the two families arrive in San Antonio, they find an employment contractor, a fellow Mexican, and stand before him like "skeletons" (22). Though they are reliant on his cultural and linguistic knowledge, he nevertheless makes them feel uneasy, which they attempt to "bury under their effort to overcome adversity" (21). This is a clear indication that Espinoza's narrative will resist the cultural processes of assimilation, and he goes on to critique the man's role as a mediator by describing him as a deformed devil who misspells even the most basic words. Economic conditions soon force the two families to separate, a reminder that the bonds between immigrant communities in the United States are fragile. While the Garcías barely subsist doing odd jobs around San Antonio, at one point even falling into homelessness, Don Serapio and his sons leave to work on the railroad. However, tragedy soon befalls them when José is crushed by a train: "For a moment, haloed by an intense flash, they [the workers] saw José's silhouette above the tracks, then nothing" (33).

José's silhouette is a Gothic image in its allusion to the metaphysical differences between life and death, a point later strengthened by the description of a pair of starving musicians as two "ungainly shadows" (53), but Espinoza also complicates this distinction by envisioning his characters as silhouettes of one another. For example, when Don Serapio and Matías leave their railroad jobs "in the darkness of the night," unable to walk along the train tracks because Don Serapio was haunted there by the final scream of his son, they do so as "grief-stricken silhouettes" (39), which is to imply that they have become shadows of José. Similarly, when the families reunite back in San Antonio, a city that after José's death now appears "disfigured" (46), Matías sees Juana García as a mere shadow of Toribia, the young woman in Mexico whom he hopes one day to marry.

Silhouettes and shadows allow Espinoza to conceive of uncanny resemblances to the identities of certain characters, but the imagery of these concepts—dark shapes against light backgrounds where the border between the two is distinct—can also be read as a spatialization of Gothic attributes. For example, San Antonio was a hub of Mexican immigration, and through the return of Don Serapio and Matías to the city, Espinoza characterizes it as a place to which immigrants "would always return" (40).[12] San Antonio in particular, and Texas in general, are thus shadows of Mexico in that they constitute a second, albeit denigrated, homeland. Similarly, the Mexican immigrants who pass through and live in these areas struggle terribly to become more than mere shadows in American society. The racial component of this image becomes clear when both families get jobs picking cotton near Houston, a city "completely ornamented with vivid points of light" (89). Quico, the patriarch of the Garcías, "dreamt of harvesting a lot of cotton, filling sack after sack with that rich whiteness, living a soft life, as soft as those cotton balls" (64). Whiteness here denotes economic and racial advantage, and it contrasts with the "dark tragedies" (64) that engulf the lives of immigrants as they are forced to toil "under that fiery sun, on that burning land, between those [Anglo] men who know only how to despise and squeeze out life" (5). The comparison between brownness and whiteness exposes Quico's naiveté about the United States, a place Espinoza suggests is primarily concerned with exteriority because one's character is often buried beneath a binary system of supposedly discernable racial attributes.

Again, the spatialization of Gothic imagery is significant, for it reinforces the strict racial bifurcation of the text. Irrationally fearful of being murdered by immigrants (41), most Anglo characters force Mexican Americans to survive on the periphery of society where they are to remain hidden from view until they are needed for cheap labor. Their fears are manifestations of a racist ideology, but they also signify that the presence of Mexican Americans subverts the "American Dream," a national metanarrative that envisions the United States as having the potential to become a kind of New World promised land. On the other hand, for Mexican Americans who slowly realized that they would be permitted neither social nor economic advancement, the United States became a place of Gothic encounters, a hellish nightmare where white men were "devils" (59) and the fate that awaited them after all of their work was death, or at best, mere subsistence living where poverty and even emaciation, a particularly apt image given its gesture toward invisibility, were inevitable (68). While many Anglos continued to view Mexico as a premodern country trapped in a Gothic past, Espinoza's novel suggests that it is the "modern" United States that most tenaciously evokes death. The Gothic tradition and its focus on repressed crimes thus becomes a useful model through which to examine the trauma inflicted upon Mexican Americans throughout the American West.

As the novel reaches its conclusion, the families separate one final time; their divergence is geographical, but it is cultural as well, and their differences contrast so sharply that they imply yet another level to Espinoza's figurative use of shadows. Quico finds a relatively high-paying job at an oil refinery in "Poraza" (Port Arthur), a "strange place" (96) that left him and the rest of the García family feeling disconcerted despite their considerable economic improvement. These Gothic insinuations presage the family's final tragedy, for by the end of the novel, Quico's older children have become so thoroughly Americanized that he considers them to be lost. His son, Doroteo, has become a lazy drunkard, and Juana, his daughter, has run away with a man out of wedlock and might eventually be reduced to working in a brothel. Ironically, it was Quico, more so than any other character, who had previously celebrated cultural hybridization, refusing, for example, to continue smoking cigarettes rolled in corn husks, and then gleefully demanding that his wife serve him "sirope," "jat queiques," and "bisquetes" for breakfast (76).[13] Espinoza's message here is a rather didactic one: Mexicans who assimilate into the United States, including flappers and pochos, will become moral and cultural degenerates, or to put this assessment in the Gothic articulation of the novel, they are to be left for dead. "He [Quico] had one wish: his little children. He would watch over them. If he could manage to save them, if he knew how to point them in a better direction, then perhaps they would return to their homeland. The others [Doroteo and Juana] already were dead" (110).

In contrast to the Garcías, Don Serapio and Matías are unsettled by José's death and eventually decide to return to Mexico. However, they first want to mark José's grave with a tombstone but are shocked to discover that the Mexican cemetery has been desecrated; crosses have been removed, corpses dismembered. Espinoza uses this act of racial hatred to challenge U.S. nativism in the Southwest, which defined American civilization against the alleged barbarism of Mexicans and various Native tribes. Furthermore, the scene also functions as the apex of the Gothic storyline: for immigrants, the United States is a place of such horror that they are unable to find peace even after being segregated in death. Don Serapio and Matías exhume José's body and carry the remains back to Mexico. Quico meets them in Laredo to say goodbye one final time, and he accompanies them across the border. Don Serapio and Matías prepare to take a train back to their home in Michoacán, a mode of transportation they had refused to use in the United States after José's death. Like Don Quijote, their journey has left them disillusioned, and the novel ends with them watching Quico return north to the United States to chase, much like Sancho Panza once did, his materialistic ambitions: "In the darkness of the night, his silhouette was lost like just another shadow" (110).

For Espinoza, class and racial differences are characterized by the ever-present threat of Gothic violence. His narrative solves a double problematic in that both families attempted to escape the horrors of the Mexican revolution only to encounter a different set of horrors in the United States. The solution in *El sol de Texas* is tenuous: given the economic necessity of leaving Mexico at the beginning of the novel, it remains unclear how Don Serapio and Matías will survive after they return, which is perhaps why the novel concludes on the border. If Gothic texts reveal those secrets that society tries to ignore, then the secret of Espinoza's *El sol de Texas* is that there were tragic situations in Mexico and the United States that could not be escaped by movement after the advent of the revolution. By envisioning U.S. culture and geography through the attributes of the Gothic novel, Espinoza constructs a border that is more complex than a mere delineation of national boundaries, marking instead the place where Mexicans would trade one set of horrors for another. This partially explains the references to *Don Quijote*, a metatext for *El sol de Texas*, in that Espinoza's characters "lived epically" (81) by enduring what amounted to a series of heroic battles, and it also accounts for how the spatialization of the Gothic imagery of the text assists in the construction of a strict binary logic that resists hybridity.

Although Espinoza's novel is more concerned with exploring race and identity than experimenting with formal innovation, by reading its rich exploration of ethnic and linguistic contact zones as a response to Madero's *La sucesión presidencial en 1910*, the text's modernist features become clearly discernible, most notably concerning the issues of spatiality and the underlying anxiety over the permeability of the Gothic body across national lines.[14] The unease that permeates Espinoza's exploration of immigration and emigration also constitutes a historical extension on the work of Cuban revolutionary poet and essayist José Martí. During the final fourteen years of his life, Martí mostly lived in New York, where he wrote numerous essays and columns about the United States for various Latin American publications. Although he was initially impressed with U.S. democratic institutions, he soon became disillusioned with capitalist economic exploitations against the working classes, and he also grew anxious about the imperialist threat posed by U.S. interests in Latin America and the Caribbean. In his final, unfinished letter, written one day before he died in battle, he famously wrote: "It is my duty—inasmuch as I realize it and have the spirit to fulfill it—to prevent, by the independence of Cuba, the United States from spreading over the West Indies and falling, with that added weight, upon other lands of our America. All I have done up to now, and shall do hereafter, is to that end. . . . I have lived inside the monster and know its entrails–and my weapon is only the slingshot of David."[15] Like Espinoza, Martí's characterization of Anglo-America as monstrous derived from his lived experiences, and thus his writing is a precursor to the Gothic elaborations found in *El sol de Texas*.

Espinoza's narrative occurs within a strictly nationalist framework, resulting in representations of Mexican American subject positions that remain rigid throughout. His racial and nationalist divisions begin to be unfixed through Daniel Venegas's use of transnational mimicry in *Las aventuras de don Chipote*. Mimicry serves a dual function, for just as one copies those in power in order eventually to access that power, it can also be a subversive act to mock and resist hegemony. As Homi K. Bhabha has observed, this oscillation between repetition and rebellion "does not merely 'rupture' the discourse, but becomes transformed into an uncertainty." (86).[16] Mimicry therefore constitutes an ambivalent act, and in Venegas's novel, this ambivalence has transnational characteristics. To be more specific, his utilization of transnational mimicry both echoes the mimicry in Madero's text in ways that undermine its implied utopia while simultaneously resisting the hegemony faced by Mexican immigrants to the United States, resulting in an ambivalence toward both nation states. In other words, just as Espinoza's text engages with the Gothic imagery of Madero through the optics of immigration and emigration, Venegas similarly reorients Madero's use of mimicry so that it becomes more transnational in scope.

To return briefly to Madero, the two principles at the center of his texts, "real suffrage" and "no re-election," had previously been articulated by Díaz during his presidential run in 1876. Furthermore, just as Díaz had published the "Plan de Tuxtepec" after he had "lost" the 1876 presidential election to Lerdo de Tejada, Madero responded to the presidential election of 1910, which was similarly fraudulent, with his "Plan de San Luis Potosí." Both documents upheld the constitution of 1857, declared the governments of their rivals to be null, and called for an end to reelections. Madero's mimicry served to mock Díaz's inability to follow through on his political ideals while also implying a historical trajectory to his hopeful followers, for just as Díaz obtained eventual success when he declared himself president on November 29, 1876, so, too, did Madero want to suggest that he would ultimately win the presidency. However, once this event finally occurred and Díaz was removed from power, Madero was no longer able to craft a persuasive political message; the ambivalence of his discourse consisted in the necessity of using Díaz as a political foil. Ironically, without Díaz, Madero had little to say.

There are also transnational aspects within the mimicry of the text. Influenced by the procedural democracy of the United States, Madero implied in *La sucesión presidencial en 1910* that he wanted to imitate American jurisprudence: "The increasing greatness of the United States is very well known to us, and we should imitate its practices, above all that attachment to the law, which its officials exemplify, in order to become as great as it is" (50). As the undertone of this passage reveals, Madero was anxious about the possibility of yet more U.S. expansion into Mexican territory, and he asserted that the best way to prevent such an invasion would not be through military fortification of the northern border, but rather through increased education and democracy. Such a development would rupture U.S. colonial discourse that attempted to justify territorial expansion by postulating the existence of fundamental differences between the United States, Mexico, and their respective citizenries.

There is, however, an inconsistency here, for while Madero used the strategy of mimicry on a national level to resist further U.S. colonial expansion, he seemed unable to recognize its rhetorical importance for individuals crossing the Mexico-U.S. border, despite his own period of exile in San Antonio. In fact, he was silent on the issue of Mexican emigration except to note that they endured humiliation because of the potential for financial gains, a situation that he intended to reverse upon taking office by improving the socioeconomic conditions of the country. Madero's elision of Mexican emigrants from his text was due in part to his running for president, an office that seemingly demands from its candidates an allegiance to nationalism, but it also marked the limits of his political vision. Just as Madero needed to differentiate himself from Díaz, he also needed to distinguish Mexico from the United States, thereby making it impossible for his political philosophy to include those emigrants who challenged his strict nationalist ideology.[17]

These elisions can be understood as structural components of mimicry, for as Bhabha perceived, "the visibility of mimicry is always produced at the site of interdiction. It is a form of colonial discourse that is uttered *inter dicta*: a discourse at the crossroads of what is known and permissible and that which though known must be kept concealed; a discourse uttered between the lines and as such both against the rules and within them."[18] If Madero's primary political message was a promise to actualize Díaz's 1876 platform via the rearticulation and celebration of an American-style democracy, then what needed to be concealed consisted, first of all, of an ambivalence of identities, for Madero's political persona was dependent in its construction on Díaz; and secondly, Madero's strictly nationalist ideology, which was threatened by the fluid geographical and cultural borders between Mexico and the United States. These concealments in Madero's transnational mimicry became increasingly visible after he was removed from the presidency. He was not only unable to enact his political platform, but more importantly, the violence and economic deterioration of the Mexican revolution caused a sharp increase in emigration to the United States. This gap in Madero's transnational mimicry is precisely where Daniel Venegas's novel intervenes.

There have primarily been two critical responses to *Las aventuras de don Chipote*, both of which stem from Nicolás Kanellos, who first discovered the text in the National Library of Mexico and subsequently edited it for publication in both Mexico and the United States. The first has sought to map out the relationships between Venegas's novel and the subsequent boom in Chicano literature that began in the 1960s.[19] The second has contended that Venegas's novel satirized the processes of cultural hybridization and that he was therefore espousing the principles of El Mexico de Afuera, a movement of Mexican exiles in the United States who maintained their Mexican citizenship and attempted to keep their culture free from Anglo influence in the hopes of one day returning to their homeland.[20] Unfortunately, the latter approach is unable to deal with the linguistic novelty of the text, much of which was written in a vernacular style that contains extensive use of Anglicisms in order to capture the dialect of Mexican American laborers in the 1920s. For example, soon after Don Chipote and his friend Policarpo cross the U.S.-Mexico border, they must rely on Chicano intermediaries with a knowledge of "toquingles" (39) to help them order a meal at an El Paso restaurant. Afterward, on the street and in search of a job, they ask a person who "looks Mexican" (42) if he knows where they can find work. The man responds, "Ai du no tok spanish" (43), and proceeds to make fun of the "poor compatriots" (43), an expression that highlights both the economic and linguistic disparities between the men. Venegas's narrator then offers a critical assessment of those who use their knowledge of "tok inglis" (43) to disparage braceros, many of whom have only recently arrived to the United States in search of employment. However, the lexical differences between "toquingles" and "tok ingles" in this particular scene indicate a fissure in the text's representation of Mexicano intermediaries; whereas the former term is a lexeme that signifies the possibility of translation, the latter is bifurcated with a velar stop and visually marks the occasion of an unbridgeable cultural divide.

The distinction between "toquingles" and "tok ingles" suggests an alternative reading of *Las aventuras de don Chipote*. The repetitive pronunciation of these homophones alludes to a kind of sonic mimicry, which is reflected in the reference to parrots in the subtitle of the novel, "Or When Parrots Breast-Feed." Similarly, just as the name "Don Chipote" alludes to "Don Quijote," it also, as Rita E. Urquijo-Ruiz notes, derives from the Nahuatl word, "xipotli," which means the resulting bump caused by a blow to the head (65).[21] Don Chipote is thus situated between the classical and the bawdry, the European and the Native, the epic and the comic, and this trope of hybridization is developed throughout the novel as the protagonist increasingly attempts to mimic Los Angeles culture.

Interestingly, this process is related to spatiality, for Venegas rescripted subject formation based on political issues in the three American locations where he successively set his novel: the medicalization of the border in El Paso, labor on "el traque" in Arizona, and the cultural mimicry that finds its fullest articulation in the Mexican American theaters of Los Angeles. Thus, eleven years prior to the publication of John Steinbeck's *The Grapes of Wrath*, Don Chipote's journey from Texas to California allowed Venegas to revise what it meant for an individual in the United States to move westward. No longer was the West to be seen simply as the space wherein individualistic Anglo men grew into larger-than-life heroic symbols of empire. Instead, the West became a space through which Venegas's theory of transnational mimicry could achieve its dual project of articulating a cultural hybridity that resisted both Mexican and U.S. nationalism, while simultaneously rupturing U.S. nativism and its helixing together of race and nationality.

Although Venegas's novel shares similar features with Espinoza's *El sol de Texas*, including a comparable plot and metatextual allusions to *Don Quijote*, one of the key differences is that the novel's comic tone allows Venegas to mock the ways in which his protagonist mimics U.S. culture. For example, at the end of an already grueling day, Don Chipote thinks it is still his turn to work the pushcart, and thus he becomes an unknowing volunteer. This scene depicts him as a victim of exploitative working conditions, but it also provides comic relief in the face of economic adversity. Yet Venegas's novel is not simply a comedy, for it also relies on the form of the picaresque novel and the Hispanic theatrical tradition. The narrator's interpretive viewpoints are therefore in flux, which are reflected in his descriptions of Don Chipote and Policarpo; on the one hand they are los "verdes," but elsewhere they are referred to as "paisanos." These shifts are a sign that Venegas was redefining what it meant to be a Mexican American immigrant by creating representational flexibility in the subject formation of his characters.

The novel opens in Mexico, but instead of suggesting, as Espinoza does, that the revolution is the primary reason why his protagonist must emigrate, Don Chipote is instead deceived by a neighbor's false accounts of his recent journey to the United States, which he embellishes for several days in order to obtain as many free meals as possible. Don Chipote's journey to the United States therefore acts as a corrective narrative. When it is time for him to say goodbye to his family, "he cried with hanging snot [from his nose]" (22). From the very beginning, Venegas eschews a histrionic portrayal of the Mexican immigrant experience, a rhetorical strategy that was helpful in reimagining subject formation in the American West.

When Don Chipote tries to cross from Ciudad Juárez to El Paso, a U.S. official directs him into a disinfecting station where he must shower while his clothes are sanitized. He seemingly enjoys "the first humiliation that the gringos force Mexican emigrants to suffer" (27). The passage reveals a distance between the narrator and the protagonist, and it also suggests that Don Chipote, though perhaps unrefined, nevertheless remains self-possessed when encountering Anglo hegemony. However, the humiliation continues: he is eventually refused entry into the United States because he is illiterate and cannot pay the eight-dollar fee. He considers the possibility of returning home, but instead hires a coyote and simply crosses the Río Bravo to El Paso.

By depicting the relative ease with which Don Chipote is able to cross the border illegally, Venegas was undermining the "disinfection" practices instituted by United States Public Health Service (USPHS) officials shortly after the Mexican revolution entered its second and more violent phase with the assassination of Madero in 1913. U.S. health and government officials were fearful of a typhus epidemic, which could have spread by body fleas or lice; prior to the development of the first vaccine in the 1930s by Rudolf Stefan Weigl and the refinements later made by Harold Cox, the bacterial disease had historically reached epidemic levels following certain wars, famines, and other events that caused mass casualties. While typhus had been in Mexico since Spanish colonists first introduced it in the sixteenth century, it was not until the Mexican revolution displaced large portions of the population, some of whom crossed the border into the United States, that USPHS officials began classifying the disease as a public health threat.[22]

In 1916, Claude C. Pierce, a surgeon with the USPHS, was sent to El Paso to oversee the renovation of a building that had originally been designed simply to provide showers for those who crossed into the United States.[23] The government spent six thousand dollars on the installation of boilers and other equipment in order to streamline what would soon become a mandatory process of "disinfection." In January 1917, Pierce announced the implementation of a quarantine that would be required for anyone entering the United States from Ciudad Juárez because, as he wrote in a report just two months later, they were "considered as likely to be vermin infested" (427).[24] Although fewer than ten people from El Paso had died from typhus between 1915–1917, Pierce nevertheless justified the new policy by arguing that "the disturbed political conditions in Mexico for the past five years and the consequent migration of refugees, soldiers, and their families, with the attendant misery, poverty, and absolute lack of sanitary measures, have resulted in spreading typhus fever to all parts of Mexico, its prevalence in border towns near the States being a recognized menace."[25]

The medical inspections that Pierce initiated required men and women first to be separated, and then stripped naked. Their clothes were laundered with hydrocyanic acid, and U.S. attendants checked the scalps, armpits, pubic areas, and anuses for lice. For any man who was found to have lice, his hair was shaved; for women, their hair was treated with a mixture of vinegar and kerosene. The border crossers were subsequently required to take showers where they were sprayed with water, soap, and gasoline, and then if it was deemed necessary, they were forced to be vaccinated against smallpox. They were then allowed to dress, but still had to undergo a general medical exam where they might yet be denied entry for any number of physical or mental "deficiencies," including a low I.Q., clubbed feet, or trachoma, which required medical examiners to invert the eyelids of border crossers. The medical exam, which Don Chipote fails, also constituted psychological profiling, as the Immigration Act of 1917 stipulated that anyone suspected of "psychopathic inferiority," such as vagrants, liars, and homosexuals, were sent back to Mexico.[26] In order to continue crossing into the United States, Mexicans were required to undergo this process of "disinfection" every eight days, and thus, unlike Ellis Island, the medical assault on their bodies was continuous. Furthermore, the procedure constituted sexual assault; less than one month after the inspections had begun, Pierce informed his superiors in Washington, DC, that he was investigating reports of women being photographed while nude.

In June 1917, Pierce reported that there had been no new cases of typhus in El Paso since the quarantine began in January. However, as Alexandra Minna Stern notes, there were only thirty-one cases of new typhus reported throughout the entire United States during this period; despite the actual low threat of a typhus epidemic, the number of people affected by the quarantine was quite large: through June, 871,639 bodies were inspected, and 69,674 were forced to be "disinfected."[27] For the entire year 1917, the *El Paso Herald* reported that 127,174 bodies were "sanitized."[28]

The reason why there was such a substantial disjunct between actual and perceived threats of contamination was that the U.S.-Mexico border underwent important transformations during the Mexican revolution. Rather than the nineteenth century's abstract and often meaningless line of demarcation, the border became a modern construct, a kind of membrane separating the body politic of "healthy Americans" from the threat of Mexican bodies, which came to be understood as little more than embodied sites of potential disease and infection. By medicalizing the border, Anglos were able to utilize a scientific rhetoric whereby their fears of being both culturally and bacteriologically contaminated could be cleansed. For this model to work, it did not require empirical evidence about, for example, whether or not typhus posed an actual epidemic threat; rather, it necessitated an ideological system of exclusion that fetishized bodily difference as if race and nationality were biological entities. Intertwined with the eugenics movement, this cultural technology attempted to transform diseased bodies into desired laborers by relying on a process whereby government officials examined, counted, racialized, and classified the bodies of potential entrants.

Xenophobia along the border was not, of course, novel; the term "greaser" had been used since the mid-nineteenth century.[29] However, never before had racism manifested itself through the medicalization of power, which resulted not only in the use of pseudo-scientific discourse to mark Mexicans as contaminants, but also involved the physical transformation of the border through the dual processes of industrial development and bureaucratic oversight.[30] For Mexicans, the physical and cultural construction of the border constituted a new set of obstacles. A "here" and a "there" now existed, an "us" and a "them," and just as it became more difficult to pass the physical border, it similarly became more difficult to pass the cultural borders congealing around concepts of race and cleanliness. Whereas there once had been freedom of movement, getting to *el otro lado* now required repeatedly passing through a space characterized by violating medical procedures.

Lisa Lowe's *Immigrant Acts*, a groundbreaking study of Asian American cultural politics, is concerned with an archive separate from the one considered here, but her methodological and theoretical insights are nevertheless helpful in addressing issues related to Mexican American immigration. She writes of the "*contradictions* of Asian immigration, which at different moments in the last century and a half of Asian entry into the United States have placed Asians 'within' the U.S. nation-state, its workplaces, and its markets, yet linguistically, culturally, and racially marked Asians as 'foreign' and 'outside' the national polity."[31] Asian Americans were economically admitted into the nation, but they were simultaneously excluded from citizenship along racial lines. This distance prevented Asian American entry into American national culture, resulting in an alternate set of cultural expressions where the contradictions of immigration were performed.

Mexican American immigrants faced a similar situation, for they were also both of and not of the nation. Shortly after the turn of the century, large numbers of Mexican immigrants began entering the United States, their labor being essential to agriculture and infrastructural development. As they initially tended to remain in isolated regions of the Southwest, most Anglos remained unaware of their presence. However, their numbers grew dramatically after the Mexican revolution, reaching a peak of ninety thousand in 1924, the result of a limited domestic economy coupled with the U.S. need for cheap labor after its entrance into World War I in 1917, and they eventually entered the urban centers of the East and Midwest in larger numbers.[32] With the advent of the depression, there was an Anglo xenophobic backlash that led to the Great Relocation where hundreds of thousands of Mexicans and Mexican Americans were forcibly relocated to Mexico throughout the 1930s.[33] And as the concluding chapters of *El sol de Texas* and *Las aventuras de don Chipote* reveal, a number of Mexicans simply left the United States after enduring racial discrimination and exploitative economic conditions.

That Don Chipote was able simply to evade the authorities, then, constitutes an important counternarrative to U.S. attempts to medicalize the border.[34] Like Espinoza, who recognizes the Alamo as a site of U.S. triumphalism in order to resist it with an account of the connections between San Antonio and Spain, Venegas similarly acknowledges the existence of "disinfection stations," but then quickly renders them completely ineffective in that they could not even prevent the foolish Don Chipote from entering the country. Later in the novel, Venegas further undermines the power structure involving American medical bureaucracy and Mexican bodies when Don Chipote stays for an extended period of time in a Los Angeles hospital, a point I will return to shortly.

In El Paso, Don Chipote and Policarpo are hired to work on the Santa Fe railroad, or "el traque," and soon they are packed onto a train with other workers and sent to a small camp in northwest Arizona. Along the way, the men take turns singing corridos, and when it is Don Chipote's and Policarpo's turn, they choose a corrido that relates many of the odd things that they have encountered. In Ethriam Cash Brammer's English translation, this includes the line, "But the one thing I ain't never seen/Is a parrot that could breast-feed" (63).[35] As Paul Fallon rightly points out, the original

Spanish language version of the text does not contain these words (117).[36] One assumes that Brammer's addendum is an attempt to connect this part of the text with the last line of the novel where Don Chipote comes to the realization that "Mexicans will become rich in the United States WHEN PARROTS BREAST-FEED" (159), which is, of course, to say never. Rather than attempt to find unity in a text that actually eschews it, not out of aesthetic shortcomings but because such an approach allows for greater flexibility in the representation of subject formation, a more accurate approach to this scene would be to recognize that Venegas was subtly revising modernism's association between trains and trauma in order to allow for human bonding amongst various members of the working class, including Mexican immigrants and African Americans. Although their community is short-lived, for Don Chipote is injured and taken to a hospital in Los Angeles, it is an important step in Venegas's unfixing of the subject positions available to Mexican Americans, and it also revises the individualism that had become fetishized in the westerns of the late nineteenth and early twentieth centuries.

Like *El sol de Texas, Las aventuras de don Chipote* initially expresses anxiety about railroad travel. This is not surprising, for such unease was ubiquitous in modernist texts. Lynne Kirby has added a nuanced psychological component to Wolfgang Schivelbusch's classic, *The Railway Journey: The Industrialization and Perception of Time and Space*, arguing that early twentieth-century films often focused on railroad accident victims because of the cultural anxiety that still surrounded the dangers of train travel.[37] Unlike other forms of hysteria, which many Freudians thought affected only women, the shock and trauma of the train collision was experienced by filmgoers of all genders, and thus it was emblematic of the dislocation associated with modernism. If trains were an unstoppable modern invention, death by train was one of the great modernist fears.

Whereas Espinoza's depiction of José's death in *El sol de Texas* entirely supports the modernist linkage between trauma and displacement, Venegas's narrative, after acknowledging this fear, goes on to envision train travel as a site through which new cultural connections can be created. Toward the end of the corrido mentioned above, Don Chipote's dog, who was hiding in a knapsack because the contractor didn't allow workers to bring their animals with them, joins in the singing. The contractor threatens to throw the dog off the train, but the other workers warn him that he would suffer a similar fate were he to follow through on such a vow. Because trains imply displacement and the formation of new communities, they constitute a type of space through which immigrants have the power to resist racism and hegemonic working conditions.

In spite of this important revision, the narrative is still operating within the logic of "tok ingles" wherein the disjunct between working-class Mexican American immigrants and the cultural intermediary, in this case the work contractor, is severe. However, unlike Don Serapio and Matías in Espinoza's *El sol de Texas*, the cultural and linguistic separations are temporary. The transition begins to occur after Don Chipote accidentally drives a pick into his foot while working on "el traque." Bleeding profusely, he becomes delirious and goes into shock; the foreman decides to put him on the next train to Los Angeles so that he can acquire proper medical attention. Policarpo accompanies him, and they travel ahead together "at full speed" (81). The narrative temporarily shifts to Policarpo's point-of-view because Don Chipote's untreated injury keeps him rather sedated, but again, this constitutes a novel development from the shock and trauma that had been associated with train travel: "With half-closed eyes, Policarpo saw the passing stations, the towns, and the cities. In the stations, he saw his fellow Mexicans doubled over, axes in hand, working like camels, raising their sight only to see the passing train" (83–84). For Mexican American immigrants, train travel initially registers not as emblematic of psychological illnesses, but rather as a manifestation of class distinctions, a point strengthened when the other Anglo passengers refuse to sit with Don Chipote and Policarpo. The latter, however, befriends an African American cook en route, and thus Venegas's text not only satirizes Anglo conceptualizations of Mexican American immigrants through the caricature of Don Chipote, he also undermines nativist ideology about the American West by revealing the similar social positions of working-class African Americans and Mexican immigrants, suggesting sympathy between these groups. Don Chipote's journey westward is thus a movement from the fixed cultural bifurcation of "tok ingles" and the El Paso/Ciudad Juárez border to "toquingles" and the possibilities for cultural translation and the radical new subject formations that Los Angeles offers.

In Los Angeles, Don Chipote is hospitalized for an extended period of time, and his experiences there sharply contrast with the medical procedures instituted by the USPHS along the U.S.-Mexico border. The hospital proffers an abundant time to recover, which allows him to rest, probably for the first time in his life. After he is finally released, he looks for work and eventually finds a job as a dishwasher, earning enough money to begin routinely attending the Spanish-language theaters and cinemas.[38] Ignoring his family back in Mexico, he begins a one-sided attempt to court an Anglo flapper. One of the major reasons he is unsuccessful is that while he tries to mimic American popular culture, he is nevertheless unable to accurately reproduce it: "as the readers have understood, although Don Chipote thought he looked very elegant, in reality he looked ridiculous" (126). In order to impress this woman, he goes on stage at one of the theaters and performs for her in a talent show. However, his wife and their children, who have traveled from Mexico to Los Angeles in order to find him, happen to be in the audience. At first, many of the spectators believe the resulting confrontation between Don and Doña Chipote is simply part of the vaudeville act and they enjoy it immensely, but once they realize that what they are witnessing is a real argument, they expect the theater management to intervene. The entire family is arrested and eventually deported back to Mexico, and the last line of the novel is a reminder that neither wealth nor contentment are guaranteed to U.S. immigrants.

As Martín Rodríguez has noted, because the overall novel is more concerned with urban Mexican American immigrants than with Mexican society, the ending "should not be taken literally, since it is clearly undermined by Venegas's solidarity with those who have been uprooted from Mexico" (49).[39] While I agree with Rodríguez that the novel is more concerned with addressing the wrongs done to Mexican immigrants than with supporting Mexican nationalism, I would add that although the racism that Don Chipote overcomes makes much of his narrative a laudable one, the novel nevertheless accomplishes more than a mere portrayal of those racist practices that were rampant in the United States during the 1920s.[40] If Don Quijote is about a man who cannot adapt to the modern world, *Las aventuras de don Chipote* tells the story of how one person deals with the complexities of immigration and begins to embody different subject positions through his growing infatuation with American popular culture.[41] Of course, Don Chipote's assimilation is not complete, but that is hardly the point. Although he fails to completely remake himself, at the end of the novel he nevertheless remembers his journey to the United States, which provides him with a mental respite as he endures the drudgery of hard labor back in Mexico. These memories, which seem like a movie to Don Chipote, are the only significant characteristics that distinguish the first chapter from the epilogue. So while he is still poor, he is not bitter about his economic plight because he is now able to imagine a different identity for himself, one that is mediated by his movie-like journey to Los Angeles.

Again, many critics have interpreted Don Chipote's attempt to forge a new identity through the process of mimicry to be a failure, but as Paul Fallon has noted, the conflicting features of the text resist a single point of view.[42] The narrator's pronoun usage slips throughout the text; at times, he aligns himself with the reader through a "nosostros," though at other times he speaks from the position of the sole subject. He also calls himself both Mexican and Chicano, and seems to use these terms interchangeably.

The text thus shifts between linguistic tones and registers just as the narrator changes his points of view because Venegas's narrator spoke for a social group that was undergoing radical cultural changes.

To return to an earlier point, the separation signified by "tok ingles" never fully morphs into the cultural fluency of "toquinglis" within the character Don Chipote. However, by constructing a novel rich in the lexical switching between English and Spanish, which is set in both Mexico and the United States and alludes to classical literature and the pop culture of the cinema, Venegas was able to create a transnational character who both mimics and mocks the nationalist sentiments of both the United States and Mexico while simultaneously revising the story of the West to include the economically disadvantaged Mexican American immigrants. Were we simply to point out the myriad ways in which Don Chipote fails to reproduce American culture, we would be committing a similar interpretive error that the theater's audience makes when they reject the Chipote family the moment their struggles become genuine, for we would be focused only on the performance of Don Chipote. Again, Bhabha asserts that the discourse of mimicry includes that which must remain concealed, and in the case of *Las aventuras de don Chipote*, this hidden discourse is metafictional: despite the limitations of the protagonist, the novel itself achieves such cultural and linguistic fluency that it challenges strict nationalist bifurcations. While Don Chipote and the other characters remain trapped in a "tok inglis" binary, the novel itself operates within the logic of "toquinglis." The novel's great achievement is the articulation of this hybridity, for it effectively unfixes the rigid subject positions that had previously been available to Mexican American immigrants throughout the 1920s.

Following Andrew Thacker, who argued that modernist texts created metaphorical spaces that tried to make sense of modernity's changing material spaces, my reading of Espinoza's *El sol de Texas* and Venegas's *Las aventuras de don Chipote* suggests that in the aftermath of the Mexican revolution, the borderlands and the American West became alternative, transnational spaces that allowed for rich possibilities in linguistic novelty and identity formation.[43] Part of the reason these novels can be put in fruitful dialogue with one another is that they both function to reveal cultural insights that would have otherwise been ignored or forgotten; Espinoza's use of Gothic spatialization demonstrated that the suffering caused by the Mexican revolution couldn't be escaped simply by immigrating to the United States, and Venegas's transnational mimicry articulated a complex and entirely novel form of cultural hybridity. Yet, as the writings of Manuel Gamio should remind us, a note of caution is needed here.

From 1926–1927, Gamio, one of Mexico's first anthropologists, conducted fieldwork on Mexicans and Mexican Americans living in the United States. His research led to the publication of two books, *Mexican Immigration to the United States* (1930), an ethnography infused with a Mexican nationalist ideology and concerned with the issues of repatriation, and *The Mexican Immigrant: His Life Story* (1931), a transcribed collection of biographical narratives as told by immigrants themselves.[44] José E Limón has rightfully noted the inconsistencies in these narratives, for Gamio's nation-building project was undercut by the heterogeneity in his informants' points of view.[45] Although many protested the racial obstacles that they encountered in the United States, and although many maintained a proud and patriotic attitude toward Mexico, many nevertheless remained doubtful that the political and economic conditions at home would improve to an extent that would allow them to return. My point here is not to criticize Gamio, for as Limón has observed, he effectively provided a platform for early twentieth-century Mexican American immigrants to tell their stories, even when these narratives challenged his own nationalist project; rather, I want to highlight the methodological problems that arise when one tries to account for the complexities of Mexican American immigration with a single metanarrative.[46]

While my essay has sketched out a historical trajectory from the cultural segregation of Conrado Espinoza to the exploration of cultural hybridity by Daniel Venegas, I want to emphasize that this is not a universal model for approaching all Mexican American immigrant texts from the period. The multiplicity of subject formations represented in this diverse literature demands heterogeneous interpretive approaches. Rather than offer an exhaustive history of Mexican American immigrant literature in the aftermath of the Mexican revolution, my reading has attempted instead to develop a methodology of location that rethinks and revises issues of genealogies, affiliations, and periodizations associated with the borderlands and the American West, their interstitial spaces, and their patterns of uncontainable change and discontinuity.

Notes

1. Francisco I. Madero, *La sucesión presidencial en 1910. El Partido Nacional Democrático* (San Pedro, Coahuila, 1908), http://www.archive.org/stream/lasucesinpresid00madegoog#page/n8/mode/2up.
2. Conrado Espinoza, *El sol de Texas*, Edición Bilingüe (1926; repr., Houston: Arte Público Press, 2007); Daniel Venegas, *Las aventuras de don Chipote, o cuando los pericos mamen* (1928; repr., Houston: Arte Público Press, 1999).
3. By the term "Gothic," I intend to reference a strategy of representation that has its roots in the attention to mysterious circumstances and fascination with horror

as developed throughout the eighteenth and early nineteenth centuries that subsequently became characterized in various guises and genres by its focus upon the return of repressed Otherness.

4. All translations throughout this essay are my own.
5. Jesse Alemán, "The Other Country: Mexico, the United States, and the Gothic History of Conquest," in *Hemispheric American Studies*, ed. Caroline F. Levander and Robert S. Levine (New Brunswick, NJ: Rutgers University Press, 2008), 75–95.
6. For a discussion of Mexico's wars with the Yaqui, Seri, Mayo, and Apache tribes, see Miguel Tinker Salas, "'The Repose of the Dead': Conflict and Power on the Frontier," in Salas, *In the Shadow of the Eagles: Sonora and the Transformation of the Border during the Porfiriato* (Berkeley: University of California Press, 1997), 58–78.
7. Jacques Derrida, *Specters of Marx: The State of the Debt, the Work of Mourning, and the New International*, trans. Peggy Kamuf (New York: Routledge, 1994).
8. Frederic Jameson, "Marx's Purloined Letter," *Ghostly Demarcations: A Symposium on Jacques Derrida's Specters of Marx*, ed. Michael Sprinker (New York: Verso, 2008), 26–67.
9. Robert M. Buffington and William E. French, in "The Culture of Modernity," *The Oxford History of Mexico*, ed. Michael C. Meyer and William H. Beezley (Oxford: Oxford University Press, 2000), 397–432.
10. For an analysis of the diverse categories of immigrants in Mexican American literature, see Nicolás Kanellos, "A Schematic Approach to Understanding Latino Transnational Literary Texts," in *Imagined Transnationalism: U.S. Latino/a Literature, Culture, and Identity*, ed. Kevin Concannon, Francisco A. Lomelí, and Marc Priewe (New York: Palgrave Macmillan, 2009), 29–46.
11. José E. Limón, *Dancing with the Devil: Society and Cultural Poetics in Mexican American South Texas* (Madison: University of Wisconsin Press, 1994).
12. Indeed, after escaping his Porfirian captors in 1910, Francisco Madero spent most of his time in exile in San Antonio, where he composed his "Plan de San Luis Potosí."
13. I.e., syrup, hotcakes, and biscuits.
14. For an argument that *El sol de Texas* should be read as a realist/naturalist novel, see Ethriam Cash Brammer de Gonzales, "'Keeping it Real': The Translation of *El sol de Texas*," in *Recovering the U.S. Hispanic Literary Heritage*, Vol. 7, eds. Gerald E. Poyo and Tomas Ybarra-Frausto (Houston: Arte Público Press, 2009), 154–67.
15. José Martí, epigraph to *Inside the Monster: Writings on the United States and American Imperialism*, ed. Philip S. Foner, trans. Elinor Randall (New York: Monthly Review Press, 1975).
16. Homi K. Bhabha, "Of Mimicry and Man: The Ambivalence of Colonial Discourse," in Bhabha, *The Location of Culture* (New York: Routledge, 1994), 85–92.
17. Of course, the enthusiasm with which Madero articulated his nationalism must also be seen as a response to the criticism that he had received for relying too heavily on foreign assistance during the revolution.
18. Bhabha, "Of Mimicry and Man," 89.
19. Nicolás Kanellos, "*Las aventuras de don Chipote*, obra precursora de la novella chicana," *Hispania* 67, no. 3 (Fall 1984): 358–63. For an expansion on this

interpretation, see Patricia Cabrera, "Dialogismo y carnavalización en la primera novela chicana," *The Americas Review: A Review of Hispanic Literature and Art* 22, no. 1 (Spring–Summer 1994): 168–78. For an argument that Venegas's novel is a direct precursor to the post-1965 Chicano novel, see A. Gabriel Melendez, "Camellando en los Estamos Sumidos: Review *oi Las aventuras de don Chipote o Cuando los pericos mamen* by Daniel Venegas," *Bilingual Review* 13, no. 3 (September–December 1986): 87–93. For the connections between *Las aventuras de don Chipote*, Miguel Méndez's *Peregrinos de Aztlán*, and Antonio Arreguín Bermúdez's *Miel Quemada*, see Sergio M. Martínez, "Movimientos migratorios masivos de México a Estados Unidos en tres novellas chicanas escrita en español," *Confluencia: Revista hispánica de cultura y literatura* 26, no. 1 (Fall 2010): 34–45. For the ways in which Venegas and Paredes are linked to subsequent Chicano writers, see Spencer R. Herrera, "The Pocho Palimpsest in Early 20th Century Chicano Literature from Daniel Venegas to Américo Paredes," *Confluencia: Revista hispánica de cultura y literatura* 26, no. 1 (Fall 2010): 21–33.

20. Nicolás Kanellos, Introduction to Daniel Venegas, *Las aventuras de don Chipote, o Cuando los pericos mamen* (Houston: Arte Público Press, 1999). For an analysis of how Venegas's novel functions as a form of cultural resistance, see Sergio Reyna, "La resistencia cultural en la novela de inmigración mexicana a los Estados Unidos," in *Recovering the U.S. Hispanic Literary Heritage*, Vol. 6, ed. Antonia I. Castañeda and A. Gabriel Meléndez (Houston: Arte Público Press, 2006), 160–81. For an argument that Venegas employed what Mikhail Bakhtin called "the carnivalesque" to subvert the American dream, see Gabriela Baeza Ventura, "El aspecto carnavalesco en *Las aventuras de don Chipote, o Cuando los pericos mamen*," in *Recovering the U.S. Hispanic Literary Heritage*, Vol. 4, ed. José E Aranda Jr. and Silvio Torres-Saillant (Houston: Arte Público Press, 2003), 145–53.

21. Rita E. Urquijo-Ruiz, "Estudio onomástico de los personajes en *Las aventuras de don Chipote o Cuando los pericos mamen*," *Nerter: Una revista dedicada al arte la literatura y el conocimiento* 5–6 (Spring–Summer 2003): 64–67.

22. Elinor G. K. Melville, "Disease, Ecology, and the Environment," in *The Oxford History of Mexico*, ed. Michael C. Meyer and William H. Beezley (Oxford: Oxford University Press, 2000), 213–43.

23. My discussion of "disinfecting" plants along the border is largely indebted to the following sources: Yolanda Chávez Leyva, "There is Great Good in Returning: A Testimonio from the Borderlands," *Frontiers: A Journal of Women's Studies* 24: 2/3 (2003): 1–9; Howard Markel and Alexandra Minna Stern, "Which Face? Whose Nation? Immigration, Public Health, and the Construction of Disease at America's Ports and Borders, 1891 to 1928," In *Immigration Research for a New Century: Multidisciplinary Perspectives*, ed. Nancy Foner, Rubén G. Rumbaut, and Steven J. Gold (New York: Russell Sage Foundation, 2000), 93–112; David Dorado Romo, "The Bath Riots: Revolt of the Mexican Amazons at the Santa Fe Bridge," in *Ringside Seat to a Revolution: An Underground Cultural History of El Paso and Juárez: 1893–1923* (El Paso: Cinco Punto Press, 2005), 223–244; Alexandra Minna Stern, "Buildings, Boundaries, and Blood: Medicalization and Nation-Building on the U.S.-Mexico Border, 1910–1930," *The Hispanic American Historical Review* 79:1 (February 1999): 41–81.

24. C. C. Pierce, "Combating Typhus Fever on the Mexican Border," *Public Health Reports* 32, no. 12 (March 23, 1917): 426–29.

25. Ibid., 426.
26. Immigration Act of 1917, Pub. L. No. 301, Ch. 29, Sec. 2, 875.
27. Stern, "Buildings, Boundaries, and Blood," 47.
28. "Labor Agents in Juarez Jai," *El Paso Herald*, March 7, 1918, home edition, http://chroniclingamerica.loc.gov/lccn/sn88084272/1918-03-07/ed-1/seq-3 (quoted in Romo, *Ringside Seat to a Revolution*, 229).
29. For more on the history and meaning of this term, see Steven W. Bender, *Greasers and Gringos: Latinos, Law, and the American Imagination* (New York: New York University Press, 2003).
30. For an argument that medical perception does not constitute pure knowledge, but is rather based on cultural attitudes that contain interests in power, see Michel Foucault, *The Birth of the Clinic: An Archeology of Medical Perception*, trans. A. M. Sheridan Smith (New York: Vintage Books, 1994).
31. Lisa Lowe, *Immigrant Acts: On Asian American Cultural Politics* (Durham, NC: Duke University Press, 1996), 8 (italics in the original).
32. Mark Reisler, "Always the Laborer, Never the Citizen: Anglo Perceptions of the Mexican Immigrant during the 1920s," In *Between Two Worlds: Mexican Immigrants in the United States*, ed. David G. Gutiérrez (Wilmington: Scholarly Resources, 1996), 23–43.
33. Francisco E. Balderrama and Raymond Rodríguez, *Decade of Betrayal: Mexican Repatriation in the 1930s* (Albuquerque: University of New Mexico Press, 2006).
34. Four other primary texts offered similar resistance. As far as I have been able to discover in my research, Olga Beatriz Torres was the first published writer to depict the process of being "disinfected" along the U.S.-Mexico border during the Mexican revolution. See Olga Beatriz Torres, *Memorias de mi viaje/Recollections of My Trip*, trans. Juanita Luna-Lawhn (Albuquerque: University of New Mexico Press, 1994). For a novelistic account of an "Old Western" cowboy who assists a Hispanic family suffering from diphtheria, which was published during the same year as Espinoza's novel, see Eugene Manlove Rhodes, *Pasó por Aquí* (1926; repr., Norman: University of Oklahoma Press, 1973). For an account of an American physician who assisted in caring for wounded insurrectos, see Ira Jefferson Bush, *Gringo Doctor* (Caldwell, Idaho: Caxton Printers, Ltd., 1939). Finally, for a feminist and transnational approach to nursing during the Mexican Revolution, see Leonor Villegas de Magnón, *La Rebelde*, ed. Clara Lomas (Houston: Arte Público Press, 1994). The author also wrote a different version of her life story in English; see Leonor Villegas de Magnón, *The Rebel*, ed. Clara Lomas (Houston: Arte Público Press, 2000).
35. Daniel Venegas, *The Adventures of Don Chipote or, When Parrots Breast-Feed*, ed. Nicolás Kanellos, trans. Ethriam Cash Brammer (Houston: Arte Público Press, 2000).
36. Paul Fallon, "Staging a Protest: Fiction, Experience and the Narrator's Shifting Position in *Las aventuras de don Chipote o Cuando los pericos mamen*," *Confluencia: Revista hispánica de cultura y literatura* 23, no. 1 (Fall 2007): 115–27.
37. Lynne Kirby, "Male Hysteria and Early Cinema," *Camera Obscura* 6, no. 2 17 (May 1988): 112–32.
38. For an analysis of the growth in the early twentieth-century Mexican American theater in Los Angeles, see Nicolás Kanellos, in "Los Angeles," *A History of*

Hispanic Theatre in the United States: Origins to 1940 (Austin: University of Texas Press, 1990), 17–70.

39. Manuel M. Martín Rodríguez, "Textual and Land Reclamations: The Critical Reception of Early Chicana/o Literature," *Recovering the U.S. Hispanic Literary Heritage*, Vol. 2, eds. Erlinda Gonzales-Berry and Chuck Tatum (Houston: Arte Público Press, 1995), 40–58.
40. It should also be noted, however, that *Las aventuras de don Chipote* also suffers from sexist and anti-Semitic rhetoric.
41. For more on the relationship between Don Quijote and Don Chipote, see Erlinda Gonzales-Berry and Alfred Rodríguez, *"Las aventuras de don Chipote: De lo quijotesco a lo carnavelsco," Cuadernos Americanos* 55 (1996): 110–17.
42. Fallon, "Staging a Protest," 116.
43. Andrew Thacker, *Moving Through Modernity: Space and Geography in Modernism* (Manchester: Manchester University Press, 2003).
44. Manuel Gamio, *Mexican Immigration to the United States* (1930; repr., New York: Dover Publications, 1971); *The Life Story of the Mexican Immigrant: Autobiographical Documents Collected by Manuel Gamio* (originally published as *The Mexican Immigrant: His Life Story*, 1931; repr., New York: Dover Publications, 1971).
45. José E. Limón, "Nation, Love, and Labor Lost: Katherine Anne Porter and Manuel Gamio," *American Encounters: Greater Mexico, the United States, and the Erotics of Culture* (Boston: Beacon Press, 1998), 35–71.
46. Ibid., 60.

5

Converting the Civilizing Mission

American Catholics, Mexican Immigrants, and the Taming of the West in the Early Twentieth Century

Anne M. Martínez

While many anti-immigration groups in the early twentieth century viewed Catholics as the "other" and non-American because of their feared allegiance to the Pope and the Vatican, Anne Martínez shows how U.S. Catholics saw themselves as both Americans and Catholics in a Protestant world. This was especially true as Mexicans migrated to the Southwest following the 1910 Mexican Revolution. Through a widely circulated Catholic magazine, Extension, *writers told stories of Catholic missionary service in the American Southwest, including their attempts to encourage the newcomers to bolster their Catholic faith despite Protestant proselytizers' schools, meetings, and welfare services. These stories not only pointed out that Mexican Catholics could be Americans in the Southwest, but they also created an American Catholic identity for those throughout the United States who read about the church's missionary efforts in the Wild West. In claiming an American identity for themselves, writers stressed the historic presence of Catholics in the region and pointed out that the Protestants were relative newcomers.*

In the fall of 1913, the Second American Catholic Missionary Congress took place in Boston, Massachusetts. Catholic priests, bishops, and laypeople from across the country met for three days to discuss Catholic home missions—that is, missionary work within the United States. Archbishop John Baptist Pitival, of Santa Fe, New Mexico, represented the leadership of the "wild and wooly west."[1] In a speech repeatedly interrupted by bursts of applause, Pitival compared the ornate cathedrals he had seen in Boston with the sacred buildings that surrounded him in the Southwest. "It is the picture of another glorious edifice, hoary with age, cemented with the blood of many martyrs, with the sweat of countless apostolic men—the picture of the older Church in our great country, but now crumbling into ruin, disintegrating pillar by pillar—nay, stone by stone, moreover exposed to the fierce attacks of a relentless foe. It is our Catholic Church in the Southwest." Pitival continued his comparison of Catholic life in the East versus the West: "Occasionally I hear from your churches and cathedrals the peal of mighty organs, the strains of heavenly music in praise of the Most High, but it is drowned in the far-off cry of the dark skinned sons of my western desert: 'Behold, our children are crying for the bread of God's Word and there are none to break it to them.'[2] Behold, *we* are being dispossessed of *our* lands; *we* are a doomed and vanishing race." The archbishop seemingly embodied Mexicans or American Indians of the Southwest. He continued, "The white man [presumably referring to Protestants from the East] is enjoying the fruit of the land that *we* inherited from *our* fathers," subtly transitioning from the Mexican or Indian "we" to the Catholic "we." "After being robbed of our earthly heritage, are we to be deprived of our heavenly birthright also?"[3] Pitival began by invoking the seemingly familiar image of the West in the mind of the Northeasterner but ended by reminding his audience that this territory, in fact, had a Catholic past, and the Protestants were taking the land "we inherited from our fathers." This embrace of the Spanish Catholic past was an important part of building an American Catholic missionary ethos in the early twentieth century. The other major factor shaping this narrative was immigration, particularly Mexican immigration following the start of the Mexican Revolution in 1910.

At a session dedicated to immigration, Bishop Peter Muldoon of Rockford, Illinois, reported, "The action of the Protestant sects in the South and West towards the Mexicans, who are coming to our country in no inconsiderable numbers . . . should make us very apprehensive of the future of the faith of many Mexicans." Echoing reports from priests in the field, Muldoon noted the substantial funds Protestant sects were spending on churches, schools, and social work "to attract the Mexican laborer and his children."[4] The bishop proposed the formation of a Catholic Immigration Bureau to centralize Catholic efforts and prevent the loss of immigrant souls to the lures of the proselytizers and socialists recruiting at every turn.

The Missionary Congress was the creation of Francis Kelley, president of the Catholic Church Extension Society in the United States of America. Kelley's work as editor of *Extension Magazine* sustained a national Catholic conversation about immigration and the West. Kelley's audience here, and at the congress, was people who for generations were treated as foreigners. Now they had the chance to declare themselves 100 percent American by carrying out the American agenda but in a distinctly Catholic way. The influx of Mexican immigrants into the Southwest after 1910 gave northeastern and midwestern Catholics the opportunity to reframe the message of Protestant uplift and civilization into a Catholic taming and civilizing of the West. This, combined with a recuperation of the Catholic history of the Southwest, allowed for the manifestation of an American Catholic destiny. The conditions in the West in the American imagination in the early twentieth century gave the Catholic Church Extension Society, through *Extension Magazine*, the chance to move away from being "the immigrant church" in the East, to being part and parcel of the American narrative of taking the West and civilizing her peoples. The testimonials, short stories, and images presented in *Extension Magazine* demonstrate the work of Francis Kelley to cultivate an American Catholic discourse that did not simply mimic Protestant efforts. Rather, Kelley wove the Spanish Catholic past into a deeper historical understanding of the United States, particularly the West, as naturally and inherently Catholic. I begin with the Extension Society's founding and establishment in a still anti-Catholic United States, consider the context of the Mexican Revolution, and then analyze the image of the West in *Extension Magazine*, the role of immigration in this narrative, and finally the Catholic claim on the West to show the Catholic project of taming the West as an affirmation of the inherent American-ness of Catholicism.

Francis Clement Kelley, born in 1870 in Prince Edward Island, Canada, became one of the most influential Catholic priests in the United States in the first half of the twentieth century. During his first assignment in Lapeer, Michigan, Kelley found that his own and surrounding rural parishes suffered from a lack of funding to sustain churches and schools. In 1905, he approached Archbishop James Quigley of Chicago with a plan to support such struggling rural parishes by calling on more affluent, mostly urban parishes for financial support. The Extension Society was established in 1905 to serve remote populations throughout the United States, with Kelley as president its first nineteen years.

The society was a joint effort of the archbishop of Chicago, the archbishop of Santa Fe, the bishop of Wichita, and several Illinois Catholic leaders. Catholic leadership from the East was noticeably absent from this project. Chicago, the largest and most stable diocese in "the West," was the natural home for the Extension Society. As part of the thriving Archdiocese of Chicago, Extension was able to gain a national and even international audience, giving Kelley national and international stature as a Catholic spokesman and statesman.

At the turn of the twentieth century, mission societies were being created in the United States, and American provinces of foreign orders were established to serve the great geographic expanse that needed attention. As early as 1909, Kelley sought to establish a Board of American Catholic

Missions to coordinate and oversee the varied Catholic missionary efforts. The board did not win approval of the U.S. bishops until 1919, and was formally inaugurated in 1925 with Kelley, then bishop of Oklahoma, as a member. Through *Extension Magazine*, Kelley did manage to centralize much of the reporting on U.S. Catholic missions, and distributed funds widely in the name of American Catholics. In some dioceses, Extension was the only domestic missionary organization allowed to visit to raise funds or have special collections.[5]

Years later, Kelley wrote that the society was formed to "assist small missions, embryo parishes, chiefly located in pioneer sections, to secure the necessary Church buildings which are required for the Holy Sacrifice, the education of children and the residence of a priest."[6] In its first thirteen years, the society focused on building churches and schools—an amazing seventeen hundred structures from 1905 to 1918. Extension purchased pews, chalices, altars, and whatever else was needed to turn a "dry goods box with a cross" into a church.[7] It also provided railroad and motor chapels to those dioceses which had Catholics spread far and wide—particularly in the Plains states and the Far West. Extension worked collaboratively with dioceses and orders to man the mobile chapels and serve as many Catholics as possible.

Extension Magazine, the official organ of the Catholic Church Extension Society, had a rapidly growing audience in its first decade, largely east of the Mississippi River. U.S. Catholic history in this era is largely described as a history of urban immigrants and their national parishes. Francis Kelley drove urban Catholics to invest in Catholicism in the West. By 1910, the magazine had more subscribers than *National Geographic* and *The Atlantic Monthly* combined. *Extension Magazine* frequently contained short stories, which produced narratives of faith and conversion of morally impoverished populations in the South and West. Kelley fancied himself a novelist and sought to cultivate a cadre of young Catholic writers. He soon found, however, that the most compelling stories came from those "in the field." Priests in remote parishes, some reachable by railroad cars, motor chapels, or even horseback, wrote detailed narratives and shared testimonials of service to the most needy of American Catholics. *Extension Magazine* featured articles and photos of these communities and the heroic priests who served them. Testimonials from those serving remote communities throughout the United States reported the quantity and quality of Catholics in their assigned territories. Missionaries described in painstaking detail the lack of appropriate liturgical goods, let alone churches or schools necessary to sustain the faithful. Extension priests and brothers requested funds for projects such as building or repairing churches, or attracting an order of sisters to start a school. *Extension Magazine* was designed to raise funds for the Extension Society, a key mechanism in maintaining the Catholic populations in both the West and East. Eastern Catholics reveled in the chance to chart the American future in the West. They also affirmed their own Catholic identity through their boosterism.[8] Extension was financially independent from the Archdiocese of Chicago and enjoyed tremendous growth under Kelley's stewardship.

Kelley took a keen interest in "the Mexican situation" and later described it as "in many respects, the most interesting event in the Society's life."[9] After the Mexican Revolution began in 1910, Mexican immigrants entered the Southwest in increasing numbers. Their status as immigrants was enhanced, from the Catholic perspective, by the fact that they were escaping an anticlerical revolutionary uprising. Mexico's "religion question" and the arrival of those fleeing the revolution were complicated by the history of Catholics in the United States. Catholics had come a long way since the U.S.-Mexican War, when their loyalties were assumed to be with Catholic Mexico against a Protestant United States, and violence against Catholics in the United States was openly tolerated. Even so, in the early twentieth century, the Catholic Church was still perceived as the immigrant church. Anti-Catholic fervor was focused on the later Catholic immigrants from southern and eastern Europe in the East, and Mexico in the West. As newer immigrants and as Catholics, these immigrants were considered un-American on two counts—they were culturally and racially suspect and were perceived to be loyal to the Pope before their new home, the United States. The anticlericalism of the Mexican Revolution, and the public perception of the U.S. government's tacit support for such activity, contributed to a revival and strengthening of anti-Catholic sentiment in the United States.

In a sense, the U.S. government was called upon to keep the peace between and even within U.S. Catholic and anti-Catholic populations. H. M. Andrews, a self-proclaimed Catholic Democrat, reported to President Woodrow Wilson's secretary, "I am enclosing you a pamphlet . . . being sent broadcast from Chicago all over the country. . . . Don't you think for the good of the party some action of refutation should be taken?"[10] Catholic publications called for U.S. action to combat the outrages—actions against Catholics and the Catholic Church in Mexico—while Protestant publications encouraged the administration to ignore the cries of Catholics in the United States. A decade later, for instance, *The Congregationalist* opined, "To the suggestion that the United States ought to intervene in Mexico to pull Roman Catholic chestnuts out of the fire, every Protestant in this country should present the most uncompromising opposition." In this era, in particular, the repression against Catholics in Mexico was violent and extreme. Still, there was little sympathy in the United States. The editors of *The Congregationalist* continued, "Romanism inherently denies us all rights to our faith and freedom. . . . If Roman Catholic control were as absolute in this country as it has been in Mexico in days gone by, it would seek to prevent the exercise of these rights in exactly the same way as it sought to suppress all non-Romanistic exercise of religion in that country."[11] Clearly, anti-Catholic sentiment had hardly subsided; it had become less violent and perhaps less public, but it was still present and politically charged. The perceived Catholic threat in the United States was considered very real.

Most correspondence from anti-Catholics was of this nature, suggesting censure of some kind or lobbying against intervention. Occasionally, however, U.S. citizens saw *Washington in the Lap of Rome*, as the 1888 book described it. For example, J. A. Miller of Lincoln, Nebraska, wrote to Secretary of State William Jennings Bryan in 1914 suggesting the certain defeat of President Wilson for a second term, since "too many appointments have been made of those who are Romish and acknowledge first an implicit obedience to the Foreign Potentate on the Tiber."[12] For the strongest anti-Catholics, any public Catholic presence in the United States was proof that Romanism was ruling the day. And, for most, it was the perceived allegiance of Catholics to the Vatican before the United States that was most offensive.

In the early twentieth century, U.S. Catholics struggled to establish themselves as both "American" and Catholic in a Protestant-dominated nation. Immigrants faced challenges to their legitimacy as Americans. As Catholics, the prejudice against them multiplied. Catholic bishops in the United States faced pressures from the Vatican and from the American public in the late nineteenth and early twentieth century. Until 1908, the United States was considered "mission" territory by the Vatican, meaning it had received the gospel relatively recently. Still, there was concern that a peculiar form of Catholicism was developing in the United States. Pope Leo XIII's 1899 apostolic letter to the U.S. Catholic hierarchy, *Testem Benevolentiae Nostrae*, cautioned U.S. Catholic leaders that "Americanism" was threatening the unity of the church and confusing earthly liberty with the eternal version offered through the faith. Bishop Muldoon reported at the Missionary Congress, more than a decade later, the expectation that the Catholic Church in the United States attend to not only the spiritual needs but the material needs of immigrants.[13] Within the church, Americanists sought assimilation of immigrants and embraced the constitutional protection of religious freedom as an opening for the Catholic Church. Conservatives were more cautious and wanted to protect the flock from the dangers to the soul lurking in the United States. *Extension Magazine* came into being in 1906, in the midst of this ongoing tension.

Early issues of *Extension Magazine* brought the unkempt and unruly West, in story form, to northeastern and midwestern Catholics. Chicago novelist Mary Lupton wrote of a trip to Colorado, which she hoped would provide "local color" for her new novel. Lupton recalled for her New York friends her adventures in the Rocky Mountains.

> There, just about a stone's throw from me, rode a girl—a beautiful, young girl, mounted also on a burro, and followed by a score of more rough looking individuals—miners, evidently, judging from their dress. "What a curious sight!" I thought. "Where can they be taking her or she taking them. I'll follow to be near, lest they try to do her an injury." . . . I saw myself, single-handed, fighting off those brawny sons of the mountains, and escaping to some ancient castle with my rescued prize.[14]

Extension Magazine certainly dealt in rescue narratives, but this was an unexpected take on it: a New York woman imagined rescuing a young girl in the West from the presumed riff-raff lurking there. Lupton continued, "I saw the mysterious procession stop in front of a rude wooden structure and the men file in one after the other. . . . I certainly was not prepared for the shock I received on entering, for I actually found myself inside a Catholic Church."[15] This rendering precisely fit the goals of *Extension Magazine*: Lupton brought the righteous news of a ramshackle Catholic Church in the wilderness, catering to miners and maidens alike, to her friends in the East. It showed the struggling, but determined, effort to sustain the church in the West. Equally important, it solidified the Catholic presence in the East; Lupton was civilized, assimilated, and sophisticated—more than worthy of saving the innocent young girl, in both the sacred and secular senses of the word. Stories such as these demonstrated the importance of Extension's work, taking the faith to the far corners of the burgeoning national landscape. They also assured American Catholics that they had a place in this landscape, even far from the Catholic cities dotted with immigrant national parishes.[16]

As early as 1907, Mexicans appeared in *Extension Magazine.* Richard Aumerle wrote a fictional piece, "Juanita," which told the story of John Barr, an Irishman tramping the Southwest for fifty years, traveling with a young Mexican girl, Juanita. "Where or by what queer ways Juanita had come to be his, does not appear. It would have required an extravagant stretch of imagination to have fancied any relationship between them," Aumerle wrote. And yet, from the time she was two or three years old until she was eighteen, Juanita accompanied Barr on his travels. She was portrayed

Figure 5.1. The odd couple of the young Mexican girl and the Irish-American frontiersman, Juanita and John Barr, in their early years together. Story by Richard Aumerle, 1907. Courtesy of Loyola University Chicago Archives and Special Collections.

as shy, wild, and impulsive while Barr was moody and unsociable. When Father Corbin came to town, Barr suggested the priest make his way back to whence he came.[17]

Barr was "the old West, dying fast," and Corbin was determined that Barr ought not die without knowing the church. Barr rebuffed the priest on multiple occasions, but it was clear to him that he was the past and the Catholic town being established down the hill was the future. Barr also came to understand that the time had come for him to "free" Juanita. When he broached this topic with her, she was angry and realized Father Corbin was the influence pushing for change. Juanita was determined to eliminate Corbin, even if it meant killing him. Predictably, Corbin and Juanita met on either side of a river, with a log bridge between them and rising rapids below. In dramatic fashion, Juanita shot Corbin, fell into the river, and was rescued by the wounded priest. "Juanita did not quite understand it to be looking up into the forgiving eyes of this man whom a moment ago she had wanted to kill." Barr's response, having witnessed the incident: "We're needin' you Father."[18] And thus, both Juanita and the old West were saved.

Aumerle's Father Corbin bore a striking resemblance to an Extension Society priest.[19] "The Bishop had given him this corner of the state—territory enough for two eastern dioceses—to do what he could for stray Catholics, to put up a little church here and there with what the miners could give him and what assistance he could get from the East."[20] The illustrations accompanying these stories, or featured on the cover of the magazine, reflected the heroic, yet lonely, nature of Extension life.

Kelley sought to develop Catholic writers and published a range of stories, which stumbled upon the faith in far off and unexpected places. As *Extension Magazine* developed its voice, however, Kelley recognized the power of testimonials. Priests from throughout the West reported the disrepair of churches, the ills of those fallen from the faith, and the constant threat from Protestant proselytizers.

Figure 5.2. Father Corbin suggested Barr let Juanita go when she reached adulthood. Juanita confronted the priest at the river crossing. Courtesy of Loyola University Chicago Archives and Special Collections.

Extension greeted increasing numbers of Mexicans who came north during the Mexican Revolution, prompting the society to face a different challenge: "converting" the civilizing mission from Protestant Americanization to a re-embrace of Catholicism with a distinctively American bent. This American Catholic project was twofold: fending off Protestant poachers encroaching on Catholic immigrants, and returning the landscape itself to its natural—pre-United States, and hence pre-Protestant—form. U.S. Catholics were provoked into action by the work of Protestant proselytizers with Mexican immigrants in the Southwest. For American Catholics, the anticlericalism in Mexico was a significant threat to their own faith, which transcended national boundaries: a blow to Catholicism anywhere was a personal attack. The home mission work of the Extension Society

Figure 5.3. Extension priests took on classic western heroic form, as seen in this May 1907 *Extension Magazine* cover illustration. Courtesy of Loyola University Chicago Archives and Special Collections.

gave them an outlet to address the Mexican situation and affirm their own identities as American Catholics.

By mid- to late 1913, Mexican immigrants appeared regularly in *Extension Magazine.* The August number offered brief reports out of Galveston and Brownsville on the spiritual needs of immigrant Mexicans, who had fled the anticlerical Mexican Revolution. E. de Anta, an Oblate missionary in Galveston, remarked, "How sad is their lot in this country! They crossed the Rio Grande in search of comfort, but all they have found is nothing but labor and sufferings." De Anta noted the material reality of Mexicans, laboring in Texas and beyond, before moving on to the more base experience of Mexican immigrants. "They came, hopeful of finding respect and love," he wrote, "but there is no love—only contempt and hatred. 'Greasers' they are called, and looked down upon and considered pariahs."[21] The Oblate missionaries, committed to working with the poorest of the poor, took a particular interest in working with Mexican immigrants in Texas.

In the same issue, the vice president of the Extension Society, Emmanuel Ledvina, in a field report on one of Extension's motor chapels near Brownsville, wrote, "We of the United States have a grave duty toward these poor Mexican people. Their souls will be on our consciences if we let them fall prey to the systematic efforts of the proselytizer," referring to Protestant missionaries in the area. Ledvina knew this was cause for alarm, especially among Catholic populations. "I would like to tell the Catholic people of our land what a great charge we have on our hands right now within the borders of our own country. We took the State of Texas from the Mexicans," Ledvina wrote, hinting at the Catholic past of the region, "and now every effort is being put forth by the Protestants of the United States to rob them of their Religion, and we Catholics are quietly and indifferently allowing proselytizers to steal these children from before our very eyes."[22] It is unclear whether "these children" were indeed young people or Mexican immigrants as a community, but the message was clear: these are *our* Catholics, who are being perverted by proselytizers. Ledvina's desperate plea marked the beginning of a wave of concern on the part of American Catholics for the souls of their Mexican brethren. An appeal in September presaged the early twenty-first century recognition that Mexican Catholics would be the future of the Church. "Two thousand Mexicans are living in a town in Arizona with a small number of American Catholics. Fine prospects for the future but a chapel must be built."[23] Extension's persistence was rewarded by the constant flow of funds to support such appeals.

The following month, the anticipation built for the Second American Missionary Congress, with an article previewing the gathering in Boston. "At this meeting also, the greetings of the Hierarchy of Mexico will be presented by the Most Rev. Archbishop Gillow, of Oaxaca, who will speak, in particular, on the Mexican Immigration Problem in our own country."[24] Ultimately, the panel on immigration did not include Mexican representation, though the American bishops did comment on Mexican immigrants in a number of sessions at the congress. Their discourse glorified the Catholic history of the American continent and selectively scorned and embraced the Catholic practices of contemporary Mexicans, in both Mexico and the United States. In addition, it cast Protestants as the dastardly forces corrupting the Catholic purity, or pagan simplicity, of Mexican immigrants. Extension demonstrated the need for its presence, without denigrating the needy.

Bishop Muldoon wove together an American Catholic identity and a concern for immigrants in his opening remarks on the immigration panel at the Congress. He called immigration "a most important subject, whether we consider it as American citizens, interested in the growth and permanent welfare of our country, or as Catholics who love their Church and are happy only when her tents are extended, and who believe that it is their bounden duty to welcome the foreigner of every nationality."[25] With this, Muldoon affirmed the quintessentially American nature of the Catholic missionary project. Saving the fictional Mexican child, Juanita, however, was very different from serving Mexican immigrant families in the flesh.

Mexicans, particularly those in Texas, challenged Extension missionaries. One 1915 report read, "The more I have to deal with these Texan Mexicans the more I doubt their former practices," casting aspersions on their native Mexican exercise of Catholicism. "Brought up in the States bordering either side of the Rio Grande, they are far less religiously inclined than those I knew for years farther south in the interior of Mexico."[26] Whether these were Mexicans who had come across the border in response to the revolution or those who had been in South Texas for generations, the message was clear, and was repeated by others; this adulterated practice of the faith was not a form of Catholicism that was embraced by the missionaries. This made all the more dire the circumstances, and thus the need for donations to support this important mission work.

By this time, in the face of anticlericalism present in many factions of the Mexican Revolution, Extension was expending considerable resources in support of Mexican Catholicism. In *The Book of Red and Yellow: Being a Story of Blood and a Yellow Streak*, Kelley described in excruciating detail the harrowing experiences of Mexican clergy and the actions taken by various revolutionary governments in Mexico, based on affidavits from priest and nuns who had fled Mexico. According to Kelley, the Constitutionalists destroyed three-fourths of the churches in Mexico by forcing priests into hiding or out of the country. Exiles of all stripes have been known to exaggerate the circumstances of their departures. For Kelley's purposes, the more dramatic the stories, the better, in order to convince American Catholics of their duty to protect the Catholic Church in Mexico.[27]

Priests and nuns fled Mexico, most of them headed for Cuba or Texas. Father Henry Constantineau, OMI, of San Antonio, Texas, was harboring many of the exiled Mexican priests and Mexican immigrants. In need of assistance and support, he sought out the Archbishop of Chicago "who promptly sent [Kelley] to the border with orders to go to Vera Cruz or anywhere else [he] was needed."[28] The exiled priests reported to Kelley their efforts to avoid imprisonment, death, or the sacrifice of their parishioners. Kelley accepted the mission of educating the American public, particularly American Catholics, about "the Mexican situation." He reported on the journeys of priests across the border to seek refuge from the violence, the coercion, and the "kidnappings." Describing the work of Carrancistas, Kelley wrote:

> They caught an archbishop, bishop or pastor. The more this victim had endeared himself to the people, the more valuable he was to the robbers. Forthwith they "tried" him, and sentenced him to pay a fine which might be only twenty-five thousand pesos, but which more likely might be one hundred thousand. . . . Of course the victim had no such sum of money. That made no difference. He might collect it from the people who had already been robbed.[29]

Kelley charged Protestants in Mexico and the United States with aligning with anti-Catholic forces to defeat the church. "It may seem strange, but yet it is quite true, that many of the most outrageous stories told by lying Protestants—I use the adjective advisedly—were actually believed by Catholics in America, even by members of the clergy."[30] Kelley conducted an all-out effort to draw church and public attention to the plight of the exiled priests and nuns. Kelley housed Mexican bishops in exile in his own residence in Chicago. The Extension Society funded churches, motor chapels, and priests throughout Texas and the Southwest to work with Mexican Catholics in exile during the revolution. Extension even funded a seminary in Castroville, Texas, just west of San Antonio, to train Mexican priests while seminaries in Mexico were not operating, from 1915 to 1917. Extension donors had the crucial responsibility of keeping Mexican seminarians engaged in their studies to sustain the Mexican Church in exile and upon its return home. By October 1918, Extension had expended over $74,000 "for the unfortunate Church in Mexico."[31] On occasion, Extension received large donations, such as the $2,500 oilman Edward Doheny provided to help return priests to Mexico in 1919. However, the great majority of the funds came in small amounts from Catholics across the country, in response to reports and testimonials in *Extension Magazine*.[32]

Kelley's greatest contribution to the Mexican cause by far was his writing, which appeared in Catholic and other publications across the nation, and his editorial control of *Extension Magazine*. The early narratives of the Spanish past were very much like "American" narratives, though Spain was presented as hero, not villain. As Extension found its audience and refined its point of view, the "special work" of the society gave it an edge to claim both an American and a Catholic identity.

Mexicans in Texas, whether they had been present for generations or were recent immigrants fleeing the revolution, were cast in a questionable light. The following year, another missionary in Texas noted the poor Catholic credentials of Mexicans. "The ignorance of these poor Mexicans is appalling. Pictures of saints seem to mean religion for them," echoing a generations-old complaint of assimilated Catholics against immigrant Catholics. "A priest is lucky if he finds them acquainted with the Apostles' Creed, the Ten Commandments of God and the precepts of the Church."[33] Mexicans were Catholics, who must be kept in the fold but who also must be reformed. American Catholics must bring these Catholics into the twentieth century and did so by donating to the Extension Society.

The photographs accompanying these testimonials told a story, as well. Photos of Euro-American missions generally showed neat, little chapels or schools built with Extension funds, while those of Mexican missions almost always focused on the people, in their Sunday best, illustrating how civilized they had become with proper attention. On occasion, they were in front of the Extension-funded altar, church, or school. The message in the photos, in concert with the testimonials, was that Catholic missioners were taking ragged, rough Mexicans and polishing them into upstanding American Catholics.[34]

Appeals from Extension-supported priests often noted the elaborate or modern churches, schools, and services available from Protestant proselytizers in their areas. They emphasized Protestant support of their missionaries, challenging Catholics to contribute to the upkeep of Catholic home missions. The pressure to keep Protestants at bay fed pleas to *Extension Magazine* readers, as illustrated in the case of Clifton, Arizona. Rev. Emile Barrat reported, "My Bishop has sent me here experimentally to see whether it is possible for a priest to remain and live, and so keep the people from falling away from the Faith."[35] Barrat outlined his costs and his income, which made clear his need for additional funds. He warned *Extension Magazine* readers

Figure 5.4. Interior of St. Patrick's Chapel, Bynum, Montana. Missionary priests in white communities took photos of Extension Society–funded churches and altars to appear in *Extension Magazine*. Courtesy of Loyola University Chicago Archives and Special Collections.

Figure 5.5. St. Patrick's Chapel, Bynum, Montana. Courtesy of Loyola University Chicago Archives and Special Collections.

Figures 5.6. Church in San Antonio suburbs with congregation. Missionary priests working with Mexicans most often showed their congregations, in their Sunday-best clothing, in front of their churches. Courtesy of Loyola University Chicago Archives and Special Collections.

Figure 5.7. St. Phillip's Church, San Antonio. Courtesy of Loyola University Chicago Archives and Special Collections.

that if he were to leave, the Protestants would assure the Mexicans fell away from the faith. "The Protestant minister has his residence about 100 yards away from mine. . . . He is a Mexican, and should I go away would no doubt carry on a successful campaign of proselytizing among my poor, uneducated people." The call for funds to compete with Protestants was constant. It was not often the Protestant minister lived near the Catholic priest and even rarer that the minister was Mexican. "I will certainly be grateful for whatever help I may receive from the Catholic Church Extension Society," Barrat continued, and noting his understanding of the principle of Extension, "later on, if I have charge of a larger parish I will point out what the Society has done for this mission." Barrat noted the poverty of the Mexican miners and that even his best families were unreliable in attendance, unfamiliar with Mass Intentions, and likely to leave for a "more prosperous place" after a short stint mining in Clifton.[36] Barrat, an immigrant from France, was seemingly unaware of the labor migration patterns Mexican immigrants had traveled for decades. In addition, Mexican immigrants discovered better wages and less prejudice farther from the border.[37]

Mexican immigrants were portrayed as weak in the face of proselytizing by Protestant missionaries. Extension was fairly aggressive in its attacks on Protestant missionaries poaching "our Catholics" and doing a weak job of keeping former Catholics in the Christian fold. In Texas, a Passionist missionary wrote that if they "had the zealous support that the Protestant proselytizers receive from their missionary societies in the North, many difficult phases of Catholic life would be solved. In fact we could help establish real Catholic life in a real Catholic community."[38] Where the Protestants succeeded in "perverting" Mexicans, such as in Banquete, Texas, Extension priests noted the ultimate failure of the proselytizers' work. Rev. Isidore Dwyer wrote in 1915 that American Bible Societies "can not make good Protestants out of Mexicans; they can transform them into indifferent Christians."[39] Dwyer condemned Mexicans who had left the church as unworthy: "By claiming the name Catholic they brought much more dishonor than they ever did credit to the Church. . . . [A]nything they may become hereafter, in the way of members of some sect . . . will hardly be a step down from their former condition of worthlessness."[40]

Dwyer's contempt for Mexicans was unusual. Most Extension priests considered Mexican immigrants savable, particularly as they were already Catholic. "Being as he is, easily led to good or evil by his surroundings, the Mexican in the United States finds himself exposed to every influence calculated to pervert his mind, estrange him from all religion, and unleash his every vicious inclination."[41] This was in stark contrast to Ledvina, who also saw Mexicans being lured away by proselytizers but viewed the circumstances quite differently. "Their hearts are not easily won by the gift-offering proselytizers, but their poverty and their great pride in their children . . . drives them to secure like advantages for their own offspring, blindly accepting inducements at the sacrifice of their Faith."[42] Ultimately, Dwyer and others painted a fairly consistent picture of Mexican immigrants in the Southwest: without the intervention of American Catholics, Mexicans were at risk of being lost to the church. This situation allowed U.S. Catholics the opportunity to affirm their American identity through claiming and saving the Mexican immigrant. Extension's attention to the Southwest allowed for an even stronger case to be made for an American Catholic identity.

A 1907 *Extension Magazine* article, "Some Notable Catholic Landmarks," informed readers of the Catholic past on the continent, at risk of destruction in the early twentieth century. "Neglect has lost to America many of her most precious historical relics, the Catholic missions, which marked, like milestones, the progress of the pioneers in every quarter of the continent," wrote Thomas O'Shaughnessy, a *Chicago Daily News* artist. He warned of further neglect and reminded the reader that Catholics were here first: "To the indifference of the present generation may be charged the destruction of two of the first fourteen churches built in America, San Yldefonso and Santa Clara, which were standing . . . when the first protestant colonist set foot upon this hemisphere."[43] O'Shaughnessy was driven by both the preservation of the missions and the overwhelming desire for Americans to acknowledge "the sublime story of the Catholic parentage of America" buried in the ruins of Spanish missions, which "were all standing in 1617, three years before the first non-Catholic had set foot on America."[44] Of course, by non-Catholic O'Shaughnessy meant Protestant, as there had been non-Catholics in the hemisphere for centuries before the Spanish arrived. Still, he clearly staked his claim for an American Catholicism "indigenous" to the continent or at least antedating the Protestant presence.

This claim made Catholics legitimate heirs to the heritage of the United States. Catholics were not the interlopers, Protestants were. In the nineteenth century, Irish Catholics faced challenges in populating the West; the structures and hierarchy of the Roman Catholic Church did not allow a community to simply hire a priest and build a church. In spite of this reality, Josiah Strong, a Congregationalist pastor, described Romanism as a peril to the future of the nation in his 1885 book *Our Country: Its Possible Future and Its Present Crisis*. This threat was most striking in California, where Catholics outnumbered Protestants four to one. Immigration likewise posed a danger to the United States, as far as Strong was concerned. In the early twentieth century, Mexicans in the West were the

Figure 5.8. San Yldefonso. Thomas O'Shaughnessy lamented the loss of the San Yldefonso and Santa Clara Missions. Courtesy of Loyola University Chicago Archives and Special Collections.

"possible future" Strong feared: Romish and immigrants, let alone non-white immigrants.[45]

The Black Legend of Spanish cruelty in the American historical imagination leaves little doubt why American Protestants had no interest in invoking the Spanish past. Carey McWilliams writes of the Spanish legacy in the Southwest, "It is only natural that the monuments and ruins should later acquire a piquant antiquarian interest and that the figures of the earlier scene should assume heroic proportions in the imagination of a later period." Kelley used this antiquarian interest to bridge the Catholic Southwest with the Catholic Northeast and Midwest.[46] The civilized past of the Spanish friars gave American Catholics deed to this territory and this work. One 1922 article by a California missionary made explicit the link between the Spanish past and Kelley's contemporary project. "To associate the work of the Extension Society with this land of fantasy would seem incongruous, for it is a far cry from the modern deluge of Eastern Catholic tourists and home-seekers to the days of Father Junipero Serra and his first Extension Society among the Indians. And yet his modern Chicago successor," the missionary wrote, referring to Francis Kelley, "has found arid spots in this land of milk and honey upon which to rain its gifts, and this appeal is voiced that a forgotten corner of the Golden State may not become spiritually what it is materially, a desert waste." Kelley, exchanging "pastoral vestments for imperial robes," produced a strictly Catholic inheritance for *Extension Magazine* readers, as always, designed to raise funds for U.S. Catholic missions.[47]

Kelley was as concerned with the image and role of the West in the eastern imagination as he was the West itself. "Western history," Patricia Limerick writes, "has been an ongoing competition for legitimacy—for the right to claim for oneself and sometimes for one's group the status of legitimate beneficiary of western resources." For Catholics in the early twentieth century, rearticulating a Catholic history of the West legitimized their claim to Americanness. American Catholics had a place in the epic legacy of the West, not just historically, but in the present, as well.[48]

The natural Spanish Catholic past was also gauged in the peoples of the Southwest. Those present-day Catholics who could demonstrate Spanish ancestry were admired and held up as examples for Mexicans. One Catholic brother, Lawrence, reported from Louisiana that his mission was divided into three groups.

> The first and smallest division is composed of descendants of the original Spanish colonists, who have preserved the purity of their blood and their racial integrity. . . . Those of mixed Spanish and Indian blood constitute the second and largest division; and the last division and by far the most miserable, consist of those of pure Indian blood, descendants of the aboriginal inhabitants.[49]

The "Americans," as Lawrence called the Protestants, referred to all of these groups "contemptuously" as Mexicans, "though neither they nor any ancestor of theirs ever saw Mexico. They are accorded less social and civil recognition than negroes."[50] Lawrence dramatically simplified a diverse and complex social system in an area that had seen more imperial hosts than most parts of the present-day United States. The hierarchy, however, was clear: Mexicans—at least in Lawrence's eyes—were at the bottom. His observations of the Spanish legacy are not unlike what was found in New Mexico, where Reverend A. Estvelt reported on the land struggles of the Spanish Dons in Union County in 1917. These Spaniards, likewise, were seen as upstanding, God-fearing, and reserved—meaning not Mexican.[51]

Rev. Isidore Dwyer, writing of Bluntzer, near Corpus Christi, Texas, reported the similar Spanish past and, more notably, the efforts of the early colonial families to stem the tide from the unnamed North. "The pioneer settlers of this neighborhood were sturdy Catholics, who were brought over by Spain in the early part of the last century, as an English-speaking element to hold the territory against the anti-Spanish settlers from the North, who were trenching on Spanish domains, and working to wrest territory from Spain."[52] No doubt they were likewise wresting souls from the Catholic Church. Extension's "special work," then, was not unlike that of these pioneer settlers—holding off the Protestant proselytizers who were trying to poach Catholics from along the contested religious borders at the edges of civilization—the U.S.-Mexico borderlands.

The enduring influence of the early, hardy Spanish families on subsequent Mexican immigrant settlers was significant, according to Dwyer. "Several generations of Mexicans were born, have lived and died in the service of the same families of Catholic ranchers.... The effects of such Catholic influence surrounding them, the sympathy shown them, were evidenced in the fervor with which they attended services, some of them driving six miles each night for the privilege."[53] As was seen in Clifton, Arizona, Mexicans at this time were perceived as not inclined to attend Mass regularly. Ranch work was more sedentary than mine work, so these *Tejanos* could settle in to the Spanish patronage system and be kept safe from proselytizers. The Arizona miners, on the other hand, had little protection for their jobs or their souls. Embedded in the Spanish narrative were claims about the indigenous in the United States and Mexico, all of whom were saved by Spanish missionaries in centuries past.

Thomas O'Shaughnessy drew extensively on the work of Charles Lummis—a non-Catholic, he noted—who was doing justice to the heroic deeds of Spanish missionaries. Lummis, a journalist, photographer, and adventurer, was "the most active exponent of Southwest culture" of his era. He wrote extensively of his travels in the West for assorted newspapers, sharing his views of the people, the natural scenery, and the Spanish missions with those still anchored in the East. Lummis was not always well regarded, but his knowledge of the Southwest was well established.[54] O'Shaughnessy's use of this "authority" on the American Southwest bolstered *Extension Magazine*'s claim to an inherently American Catholic story. The taming of the Indians who spilled "the blood of martyred priests" was intimately tied to this American Catholic history. These "churches had been built and the . . . Indians won to civilization and to the Church not without sacrifice. While in pursuance of this task forty priests had been put to death by the Indians in the pueblos." However, once the Indians had been claimed for Christianity, they guarded the missions zealously.[55] There was little history, as told by *Extension Magazine* chroniclers, between these Spanish colonial stories and the present-day Mexicans. Perhaps Ledvina described it best:

> One can imagine what inspired the early missionaries who labored so perseveringly among the aborigines of this land.... The childlike simplicity of the people and the characteristic devotion of these descendants of the Aztec Indians of Mexico disclose the inspiration of the early *padres* who penetrated the wilds of Mexico and of the Rio Grande valley and along the Pacific coast in California, to bring them the glad tidings of the Christian Faith.

At times it is unclear if Ledvina was speaking historically or about the Mexicans he encountered in Texas a few weeks earlier. The same themes resound, however: the heroic priests sacrificing to bring the Indians and Mexicans along in the Faith. Ledvina continued, "Conditions in Texas . . . emphasize strongly the necessity of erecting and maintaining Catholic schools; and that, too, without delay. The Protestants are cunningly concentrating their whole efforts in establishing schools." There was hope, however, and the Extension Society could deliver it: "If we Catholics would erect Catholic schools, though only humble buildings, and supply Catholic teachers, the Mexicans would prefer to come to the Catholic schools."[56] Without a doubt, the future of Mexican immigrants rested solidly in the hands of Catholic missionaries, dependent entirely on the good will of U.S. Catholics and the hard work of Extension Society priests and missionaries. Funding Extension, then, was the way to save Mexican immigrants and the West.

A century later, we might imagine that the influx of Catholic immigrants in the 1910s and 1920s prevented the U.S. Catholic Church from shaking its immigrant church moniker. On the contrary, the immigration of Mexicans in the Southwest allowed eastern and midwestern Catholics, through *Extension Magazine*, to create a narrative of uplift and civilization to compete with the decades-old Protestant model of conversion and uplift. The special emphasis on the West and the ways Catholics could play a role in the American taming of the West enhanced this narrative. Mexican immigrants in particular gave U.S. Catholics the opportunity to save them from an anticlerical government in their native land, as well as Protestant proselytizers in their new home, the United States. Though U.S. Catholics embraced the Spanish Catholic past of the Southwest, Mexicans hardly felt that they were "returning" home. They were outsiders both as Mexicans and as Catholics. Mexican immigrants allowed the Extension Society to convert the civilizing mission to an eminently American Catholic mission. To further this narrative, *Extension Magazine* editors invoked the deep Spanish past of the West and Southwest to assert a prior Catholic claim to the territory. The weaving of these narratives solidified an American Catholic identity for urban Catholics in the Midwest and East.

Acknowledgments

My thanks to Erika Bsumek, Gaye Theresa Johnson, and participants in the Redd Center Seminar on Immigration in the Far West for their comments on earlier versions of this paper. I am also grateful to the anonymous reviewer and the no longer anonymous David Emmons for their feedback on this piece.

Notes

1. Pitival first used this phrase, which was repeated by others throughout the Congress. Like many of the Catholic clergy in New Mexico Territory and the State of New Mexico in this era, he was an immigrant to the West. Pitival was born in St. Genis-Terrenoire, France, in 1858 and ordained in Santa Fe in 1881. He died in Denver, Colorado, in 1928, having spent the majority of his life in the American West. He was one of over one hundred French priests who served this region in the first half of the twentieth century. His name appears as Jean Baptiste Pitaval in some sources.
2. Drawing on Lamentations 4:4, "The little ones have asked for bread, and there was none to break it unto them." Holy Bible, Catholic Edition (Cleveland: The World Publishing Company, 1954), 782.
3. John Baptist Pitival, untitled address in *Official Report of the Second Catholic American Missionary Congress* (Chicago: J. S. Hyland & Company, 1914), 246, my emphasis.
4. Peter J. Muldoon, "Immigration to and the Immigrants in the United States," in ibid., 144.
5. For more on U.S. Catholic missions, see Angelyn Dries, *The Missionary Movement in American Catholic History* (Maryknoll, NY: Orbis Books, 1998). In a 1916 letter, Archbishop of Chicago George Mundelein explained that the diocese would only permit the Extension Society to conduct appeals for domestic Catholic missions, and the Society of the Divine Word to appeal for international Catholic missions. Mundelein to Rt. Rev. Peter Joseph Hurth, DD, Bishop of Segovia, Holy Cross College, Brookland, Washington, DC, October 30, 1916, Provincial Correspondence, St. Monica's (Chicago), File 2, Robert M. Myer Archives, Society for the Divine Word, Techny, Illinois.
6. Most Reverend Francis C. Kelley, Chicago, to Benedict XV, Vatican City, October 18, 1918, 4 1918 C 62, Madaj Collection, Archdiocese of Chicago Archives and Records Center (hereafter, ACARC), 1–2.
7. As testimony to Kelley's lasting influence, the 2002 Catholic Church Extension Society Family Appointment Calendar glorified his name. The back of the calendar read, in part, "In America, some of the first ripples of 'this new evangelization' [referring to missionary work as described by Pope John Paul II] began nearly a hundred years ago, when a penniless priest embarked on a cross-country begging circuit. . . . He found he wasn't the only pastor stationed at a church described as a 'dry goods box with a cross.'" Catholic Church Extension Society Family Appointment Calendar, 2002.
8. *Extension Magazine* was first issued in June of 1906 as a quarterly publication. It became a monthly the following year. Circulation numbers for selected monthlies in 1910 show the size of Kelley's audience compared to other sacred and secular publications: *American Messenger* (Evangelical), 45,000; *Baptist Home Mission Monthly*, 21,095; *National* Geographic, 49,900; *Atlantic Monthly*, 25,000; *Extension Magazine*, 78,444. N. W. Ayer and Son, *N. W. Ayer and Son's American Newspaper Annual and Directory* (Philadelphia: N. W. Ayer and Son, 1910), 601–2, 111, 362, 158. Thomas A. Tweed shows that donating became a crucial form of religious participation for American Catholics in the early twentieth

century. Tweed, *America's Church: The National Shrine and Catholic Presence in the Nation's Capital* (New York: Oxford University Press, 2011), 245. On the development of a Catholic middle class, see Dierdre M. Moloney, *American Catholic Lay Groups and Transatlantic Social Reform in the Progressive Era* (Chapel Hill: University of North Carolina Press, 2002).

9. Francis C. Kelley, *The Story of Extension* (Chicago: Extension Press, 1922), 179.
10. H. M. Andrews, Columbus, Ohio, to Secretary Joseph Tumulty, Washington, DC, November 1, 1916, File 52, Document 2, Records of the Department of State Relating to the Internal Affairs of Mexico, 1910–1929, Record Group 59, National Archives and Records Administration (hereafter referred to as Internal Affairs of Mexico). Andrews likely was referring to an Extension Society publication but the enclosure was not in the file. Robert Mitchell of Detroit, Florence Griswold of San Antonio, and J. Webb Saffold of Cleveland sent similar correspondence, tattling on local Catholics. There was a revival of this sort of correspondence in the Cristero years, 1926–1929. See Robert Mitchell, Detroit to Frank B. Kellogg, Washington, DC, August 30, 1926, Internal Affairs of Mexico; Florence J. Griwsold, San Antonio, to Secretary of State, Washington, DC, May 16, 1928, Internal Affairs of Mexico; and J. Webb Saffold, Cleveland, to Everett Sanders, Washington, DC, May 28, 1929, Internal Affairs of Mexico.
11. "No Affair of Our Government," *The Congregationalist*, August 12, 1926, 196. "Roman Catholicism and Religious Liberty," ibid., 197.
12. Justin D. Fulton, *Washington in the Lap of Rome* (Boston: W. Kellaway, 1888). Fulton's book includes fabulous illustrations depicting the dominance of the Jesuits in Washington, DC. J. A. Miller to William Jennings Bryan, Lincoln, Nebraska, October 1, 1914, File 52, Document 4, Internal Affairs of Mexico.
13. Muldoon, "Immigration to the United States," 133.
14. Mary J. Lupton, "Lost in the Western Mountains," *Extension Magazine* 1, no. 12 (May 1907): 6. Lupton was also city editor of *New World*, the official organ of the Archdiocese of Chicago.
15. Ibid.
16. As John T. McGreevy demonstrates in *Parish Boundaries: The Catholic Encounter with Race in the Twentieth-Century North* (Chicago: University of Chicago Press, 1996), the national parish system reinforced the racial and ethnic segregation so pervasive in many northern cities. Catholics continued to live in rural and remote areas of the United States but have received scant attention in the historical literature. The Extension Society and *Extension Magazine* bridged these distinct U.S. Catholic bodies.
17. Richard Aumerle [Richard Aumerle Maher, O.S.A.], "Juanita," *Extension Magazine* 2, no. 4 (September 1907): 18.
18. Ibid., 19.
19. I use "Extension Society priest" or "Extension missionary" to refer to those who, regardless of order or diocesan affiliation, wrote pieces in *Extension Magazine* and/or received funds from the Extension Society to support their mission work.
20. Aumerle, "Juanita," 19.
21. E. de Anta, OMI, "Missionary Work in the Diocese of Galveston," *Extension Magazine* 8, no. 3 (August 1913): 6.

22. Emmanuel Ledvina, "The Motor Chapel Car at Work in the Field," *Extension Magazine* 8, no. 3 (August 1913): 9.
23. Francis C. Kelley, "An Appeal to All Good Extensionists," *Extension Magazine* 8, no. 4 (September 1913): 3. "Application No. 46." In this snapshot of appeals, Kelley presented snippets from "applications" written by missionaries across the country.
24. Francis Clement Kelley, "The Second Catholic Missionary Congress," *Extension Magazine* 8, no. 4 (September 1913): 24. A number of speakers at the congress addressed immigration, but the *Official Report of the Second American Catholic Missionary Congress* does not list Archbishop Eulogio Gillow y Zavala or other representation from Mexico on the roster of participants.
25. Muldoon, "Immigration to the United States," 132.
26. A Passionist Missionary, "A Glimpse of Missionary Conditions in Texas," *Extension Magazine* 10, no. 5 (October 1915): 9.
27. Francis Clement Kelley, *The Book of Red and Yellow: Being a Story of Blood and a Yellow Streak* (Chicago: The Catholic Church Extension Society of the United States of America, 1915). It is not clear how Kelley measured the destruction of the church in Mexico.
28. Kelley, *The Story of Extension*, 180. Emmanuel Ledvina, Chicago to Archbishop George William Mundelein, Chicago, March 21, 1919, 5 1919 M 150, and A. E. Burke to President Wilson, March 4, 1919, attachment to 5 1919 M 150. Madaj Collection, ACARC.
29. Kelley, *The Story of Extension*, 180–81. Carrancistas were followers of Venustiano Carranza, active from 1913 until Carranza's assassination in 1920.
30. Ibid., 182.
31. Francis Clement Kelley, Chicago, to Pope Benedict XV, Vatican City, October 18 1918, 9, Madaj Collection, ACARC.
32. Francis Clement Kelley, Chicago, to Edward Doheny, Los Angeles, June 21, 1919, Doheny File, Kelley Papers. Doheny, a California-based oilman, had significant investments in Mexico. He was also Catholic, and committed to supporting Kelley's work after meeting him in Europe during the settlement talks after World War I. Donations were a crucial form of boosterism among Catholics—all the more significantly among wealthy Catholics.
33. M. A. Dombrowski, "On the Texas Plains," *Extension Magazine* 10, no. 11 (April 1916): 6.
34. Blacks, Indians, and Eskimos were treated much like Mexicans in the pages of *Extension Magazine*.
35. Emile Barrat, "An Experiment in Parish Work," *Extension Magazine* 2, no. 10 (March 1908): 1.
36. Ibid.
37. Barrat was one of over one hundred French priests assigned to the New Mexico Territory in the early twentieth century. In 1916, he was assigned to a parish in Costilla, New Mexico, where he fought for land and water rights for members of his congregation. On Mexican labor migration in this region, see Rodolfo F. Acuña, *Corridors of Migration: The Odyssey of Mexican Laborers, 1600–1933* (Tucson: University of Arizona Press, 2007).
38. A Passionist Missionary, "A Glimpse," 9.

39. Isidore Dwyer, "Missionary Work on the Motor Chapel 'St. Joseph,'" *Extension Magazine* 10, no. 5 (October 1915): 17.
40. Ibid., 18.
41. Ibid., 41.
42. Ledvina, "Motor Chapel Car," 9.
43. Thomas A. O'Shaughnessy, "Some Notable Catholic Landmarks," *Extension Magazine* 1, no. 12 (May 1907): 14. O'Shaughnessy, both an artist and a practicing Catholic, later created a series of stained-glass windows in Old St. Patrick's Church in Chicago, which are considered the best known examples of Celtic Revival Art. See http://www.encyclopedia.chicagohistory.org/pages/652.html
44. O'Shaughnessy, "Some Notable Catholic Landmarks," 14.
45. On Irish Catholics in the West, see David M. Emmons, *Beyond the American Pale: The Irish in the West, 1845–1910* (Norman: University of Oklahoma Press, 2010). Josiah Strong, *Our Country: Its Possible Future and Its Present Crisis* (New York: American Home Missionary Society, 1885). Strong identified eight "perils" that endangered the nation: immigration, Romanism, religion and public schools—under which secularism and Romanism were both threatening education, Mormonism, intemperance, socialism, wealth, and the city. See chapters 4 and 5 on immigration and Romanism, respectively. Ferenc Morton Szasz notes that Catholics were the largest denomination in many western states. Szasz, *Religion in the Modern American West* (Tucson: University of Arizona Press, 2000), 4–5.
46. William Hickling Prescott (1796–1859) and his contemporaries advocated the Black Legend, based on details described by Bartlomé de las Casas in his 1552 *Brevísima relación de la destrucción de las Indias*, and widely promoted by Dutch and English Protestant writers from the sixteenth century onward. The Black Legend cast the Spanish as exceptionally cruel and intolerant in their interactions with the indigenous in the New World. Spain was characterized as outside of the European Protestant mainstream in its interactions both within Europe and in the Americas. On the Black Legend, see Richard L. Kagan, "Prescott's Paradigm: American Historical Scholarship and the Decline of Spain," *The American Historical Review* 101, no. 2 (April 1996): 423–46. On representations of Spain in U.S. historiography, see Frederick B. Pike, *Hispanismo, 1898–1936: Spanish Conservatives and Liberals and Their Relations with Spanish America* (Notre Dame, IN: University of Notre Dame Press, 1971). American Protestants had little interest in the decaying missions, but did seek a Spanish architectural inheritance. See Matthew F. Bokovoy, *The San Diego World's Fair and Southwestern Memory, 1880–1940* (Albuquerque: University of New Mexico Press, 2005), 225. Richard L. Kagan documents the reproductions of the Giralda, originally part of a mosque in Seville and later a tower attached to a gothic cathedral, across the United States. Kagan, "The Spanish *Craze* in the United States, Cultural Entitlement and the Appropriation of Spain's Cultural Patrimony, ca. 1890–ca. 1930," *Revista Complutense de Historia de América* 36, no. 2 (2010): 37–58. See also Phoebe S. Kropp, *California Vieja: Culture and Memory in a Modern American Place* (Berkeley: University of California Press, 2006); William Deverell, *Whitewashed Adobe: The Rise of Los Angeles and the Remaking of Its Mexican Past* (Berkeley: University of California Press, 2004), and Carey McWilliams, *North from Mexico: The Spanish-Speaking People of the United States* (Westport, CT: Greenwood Press, 1968),

20. Pitival represented one of the few cities in the West that was still discernably Catholic, but for the purposes of his presentation, the "wild and wooly west" was a better representation of his archdiocese. On Santa Fe, see Michael J. Sheehan, *Four Hundred Years of Faith: Seeds of Struggle, Harvest of Faith* (Santa Fe: Archdiocese of Santa Fe, 1998), and Chris Wilson, *The Myth of Santa Fe: Creating a Modern Regional Tradition* (Albuquerque: University of New Mexico Press, 1997).

47. Emmons, *Beyond the American Pale*, 189.
48. Patricia Nelson Limerick, *The Legacy of Conquest: The Unbroken Past of the American West* (New York: W. W. Norton & Company, 1987), 12. John T. McGreevy demonstrates that the national parish system reinforced the racial and ethnic segregation so pervasive in many northern cities. McGreevy, *Parish Boundaries*.
49. Brother Lawrence, TSA, "One Mission School That Needs Help," *Extension Magazine* 10, no. 9 (February 1916): 20.
50. Ibid., 20.
51. Rev. A. Estvelt, "Where Danger Threatens," *Extension Magazine* 11, no. 9 (February 1917): 5.
52. Rev. Isidore Dwyer, CP, "Missionary Work on the Motor Chapel 'St. Joseph,'" *Extension Magazine* 10, no. 7 (December 1915): 17.
53. Ibid., 18.
54. James W. Byrkit, ed., *Charles Lummis: Letters from the Southwest: September 20, 1884–March 14, 1885* (Tucson: University of Arizona Press, 1989), xi. See Charles F. Lummis, *Some Strange Corners of Our Country: The Wonderland of the Southwest* (New York: The Century Co., 1903), Lummis, *A Tramp Across the Continent* (New York: Charles Scribner's Sons, 1913), for Lummis reports to newspapers of his travels. See also Turbesé Lummis Fiske and Keith Lummis, *Charles F. Lummis: The Man and His West* (Norman: University of Oklahoma Press, 1975).
55. O'Shaughnessy, "Some Notable Catholic Landmarks," 5.
56. Ledvina, "Motor Chapel Car," 9.

6

"Something Fearful and Wonderful"
Immigrant Children, Americanization, and Public Education in Los Angeles, 1900–1929

Eileen V. Wallis

The traditional model of assimilation developed in the 1920s by the Chicago School of Sociology posited that immigrants progressed in linear fashion toward assimilation. However, as later generations of social historians carefully examined the experiences and views of immigrants and recognized immigrants as historical actors with agency, they discovered that assimilation was a far more convoluted and contested process. Like the ethnoracial status of whiteness, the social category of "American" was both a social and political construct with multiple possible interpretations.

During the Progressive Era, as anxiety mounted over the welter of nationalities pouring into the United States, many reformers turned to public education and outreach by private charities to assimilate them. They were motivated by a desire to enrich the lives of immigrant children and a compulsion to check supposedly insidious cultural traditions. This Americanization campaign was particularly intense in the West. In this article, Eileen V. Wallis, associate professor of history at California State Polytechnic University, Pomona, explores the efforts of a variety of organizations including the Los Angeles Board of Education, the YWCA, the Los Angeles Civic Association, and the Daughters of the American Revolution to provide immigrants in Los Angeles with a foundation for American citizenship. Immigrant parents responded to these efforts in a number of ways ranging from genuine gratitude to cooptation and resistance.

In 1918, the *Los Angeles Times*, intrigued by the changing face of public schools in the city, sent a photographer to Utah Street School on the city's east side. The photographer snapped photos of children carting their younger brothers and sisters to the on-site day nursery, of children hard at work in a manual training classroom, and of a cross-section of the student body balancing on a seesaw. In a strategy no doubt designed to validate the article's title, "The Little Stranger Within Our Gates," the paper then

Figure 6.1. "The Little Stranger within Our Gates." Courtesy of the *Los Angeles Times.*

identified the children on the seesaw by name and ethnicity or country of origin. The *Times* identified the boys on the left side of the seesaw as Italian, Austrian, French, Mexican, Russian, Negro, American, Indian, and Spanish. The girls on the right side were identified as English, French, Spanish, Syrian, Jewish, Japanese, and Italian.[1]

While the photo was in all likelihood staged, the demographic changes it reflected were very real. By 1900, schools in Los Angeles found themselves facing a crisis. Rapid population growth was putting unprecedented pressure on the local education system. The population of the Los Angeles metropolitan area would be five times as large in 1920 as it had been in 1900. Los Angeles also encompassed more ethnic diversity within its boundaries than more established cities like Boston, New York, or even Los Angeles's rival city to the north, San Francisco. This meant that Mexican and Mexican-American, Italian, Russian, French, German, Armenian, Japanese, and Korean children were attending (or trying to attend) public schools alongside Anglo children.

This article focuses on elementary schools in and around downtown Los Angeles in the first three decades of the twentieth century.[2] It explores how public schools struggled to adapt to this changing school population. The school district combined forces with private groups to shape the education and Americanization of immigrant children both within the public schools and in the surrounding communities. At times, however, schools became a contested ground between immigrant families and Progressive Era educators in early twentieth-century Los Angeles. Americanization programs could be found throughout the American West in this era. However, according to historian George J. Sanchez, "California's program was the most complete attempt to bring together government, business, and private citizens to deal with the 'problem of the immigrant' in a scientific and rational fashion." Within California, Los Angeles, I argue, offers us the most fully developed portrait of the range of these activities in the American West as well as the problems inherent within them.[3]

Public Education in the Urban American West

Americanization in the public schools in the early twentieth century was in large part a product of Progressivism, the social and political movement then taking hold across the country. Progressives supported causes as varied as political reform, women's suffrage, and temperance. Glen Gendzel points out that "what Progressives had in common was an ideology of positive statism," a belief that individuals and governments could and should create positive change in society.[4] "Juvenile justice, playgrounds, pensions for widowed mothers, health care, housing, even child labor laws received almost unanimous support from the various branches of the Progressive movement," James Marten writes. "As innocent victims and as the hope for America's future, children had to be protected. They represented all that was good about the country, and the way they were treated reflected the nation's values and priorities." All children were supposed to enjoy the same opportunities and advantages, regardless of where they had been born.[5] Progressives thus saw public education as an important tool for "molding students into 'worker-citizens' and integrating them into the new industrial order."[6] Definitions of Americanization varied, as did notions of when and how a given immigrant would finally become American. But most reformers and educators agreed that fluency in English, a basic working knowledge of American government, and a commitment to American cultural values and ideals, however vaguely defined, were key.

To many observers, the stakes seemed highest in the American West. Western states like California wanted to grow economically as quickly as possible and to catch up with the East. Employers and politicians recognized that growth required more manual and agricultural labor than the region possessed. Immigrants, and later their children, it was hoped, would fill that gap.[7] By the turn of the twentieth century that seemed a very real possibility. Large populations of the foreign-born and their American-born children could be found in every western state. By 1900 North Dakota, South Dakota, Nebraska, Montana, Wyoming, Colorado, Utah, Nevada, Washington, and California all exceeded the national average for white foreign-born residents and their native-born children. That year North Dakota led the West with 35.4 percent of its population white foreign-born. Montana held the second place slot with 27.6 percent, and California ranked third with 24.7 percent of its white population born outside the United States.[8]

At the same time the growing population of non-Anglo, non-Western European immigrants in the region fueled anxieties about the dangers they might pose to growth if they did not "conform to the American industrial order," as George J. Sanchez has put it.[9] These anxieties had deep roots in the nineteenth century but peaked during the First World War. In 1916, the California state superintendent of education argued that unassimilated, unnaturalized immigrants "may become dangerous and threatening in the extreme to the very life of the republic." To some, immigrants thus had the potential to become dangerous barriers to progress.[10]

Many Anglo-Americans thus concluded that the only way to ultimately avoid such conflicts was to assimilate immigrants and their children into local society as quickly as possible. Americanization seemed to be the solution. Programs aimed at immigrants and their children were not an entirely new idea: Frank Van Nuys argues convincingly that the first such program actually appeared in San Francisco in 1856. Nor was Americanization through education a purely western phenomenon. In 1901 New York City began offering night schools, designed to provide the basics of an elementary school education for individuals who worked during the day. Chicago followed in 1903, as did Detroit in 1906. But given its large immigrant population, the West pursued Americanization with a zeal seldom seen elsewhere. In Colorado mining companies offered night schools for adult employees. In Kansas immigrant parents were encouraged to participate in elementary school activities with their children and then return in the evenings to learn themselves. In 1919 the state of Utah authorized school districts to offer evening classes for immigrants to help prepare them for citizenship.[11] Thus Americanization work, as Judith Raftery explains, served two purposes: it furthered the narrow aims of cultural hegemony, and it fulfilled the broader needs of immigrant communities.[12] At the same time, however, Van Nuys reminds us that such programs did at least offer "a seemingly objective and benign educational approach to the problems posed by immigration," particularly when compared to the harsher options of restriction or repression that had preceded and would later follow the era of Americanization.[13]

Ethnic Diversity in Los Angeles

Education became compulsory for all children in the state of California in 1903.[14] In downtown Los Angeles and much of the city's east side this meant that the student population in public schools was increasingly multiethnic and multiracial. Mark Wild explains that "attempts to segregate schools within mixed-ethnic areas of the city . . . remained rare and ineffective, especially in light of those districts' rapid demographic changes."[15] Angelenos recognized that something extraordinary was happening. For the first time, every child in the city, including immigrant, non-Anglos, would, by law, receive an elementary school education.

The first educational challenge in the city stemmed from the racial and ethnic divisions already present in the community. Established residential patterns had a direct impact on the city's public schools. No laws required residential segregation in Los Angeles. However, neighborhood racial covenants and other exclusionary practices kept non-Anglos from settling in some parts of the city. Early twentieth-century Los Angeles's economic structure also promoted residential segregation. Anglo-Americans accelerated this trend by increasingly abandoning downtown and the east side for the west side and white-collar suburbs. As the number of non-Anglo residents grew, working-class, immigrant, and non-white Angelenos began to cluster in several neighborhoods across the city: Chinatown; the Plaza; Lincoln Heights; Boyle Heights; Chavez Ravine; and so on.[16] These housing patterns ensured that the bulk of the city's immigrant children were clustered in the handful of schools closest to downtown: Ann Street, Amelia Street, Castelar, Macy Street, and Utah Street.[17]

The Utah Street School provides an excellent example of the extreme diversity of the student body in some of Los Angeles's schools. Utah Street had eleven rooms, six of which were devoted to first-grade work. It only had four grades because most parents pulled their children out of school to work as soon as legally possible. "There is no more cosmopolitan school in the city than this one, a single department of which boasts eight nationalities, Polish and Russian Jews, Italians, French, Spanish, Mexicans, Irish, Germans, and Americans," the *Los Angeles Times* noted. "In one room not a single scholar can comprehend the English language, and the pantomimes enacted in that particular room are something fearful and wonderful."[18]

Studying the children posed on the seesaw and in other photos taken at Utah Street School in 1918 sheds some light on these issues. Johnny Etchart and his younger sister Mary, who had been posed on opposite ends of the seesaw, had both been born in Colorado. Their father, Miguel, was described in census records as "French Basque" or French; their mother, Lazara, as "Spanish."[19] Miguel had originally been a stock raiser in Colorado; what brought him to Los Angeles is unknown. The family lived on North Soto Street, only a few blocks from the Utah Street School. Another child, Sanford (mistakenly spelled "Stanford" by the *Times*) Galt, was a member of the Morongo Band of Mission Indians. He lived with his adoptive mother, Matilda, on East First Street. Rosie Harris was the California-born daughter of Russian parents. Although Yiddish was the family's first language, both parents and all three of their daughters also spoke English. Rosie may have enjoyed a slightly higher economic status than some of her classmates because her father, Sam, owned a grocery store.[20]

Several Utah Street pupils came from families that had already moved multiple times in their children's short lives. Tome Ito had been born in Japan but had immigrated with her parents to Washington State, where her younger sister was born. Her tailor father then moved the family to Los Angeles. Teresa Condidi had been born in Italy, but among her seven siblings, some had been born in New Jersey; others, in Pennsylvania or California. This suggests that the Condidi family had been working their way West for years before arriving in the city.[21] Even African American David Floyd had parents from out of state. His father, David Sr., had been born in Georgia; his mother, Rose, hailed from Virginia. In 1910 David Sr. worked for the railroads as a waiter, suggesting it may have been economic opportunity that had brought the family to Los Angeles.[22] Deena Dallas was photographed not on the seesaw with her classmates but in Utah's manual training class. She had been born in Arizona to a mother from Greece. The seven children in her family survived on their widowed mother's income as a rag picker and their uncle's income as a peddler.[23]

In 1905 Los Angeles had become the center of yet another new immigrant community. The Russian Molokans were peasant pacifists who had fled Russia with the onset of the Sino-Japanese War and the Russian Revolution. Pegged by area social workers as the most reclusive and clannish of all the city's ethnic communities, some three to five thousand Molokans settled in the area, particularly in a ravine known as Fickett's Hollow.[24] The Russian Molokans had been attracted to the region as a refuge from religious persecution at the hands of Russian authorities. Americans sometimes called them "Jumpers" as a way to mock the Molokans' physically exuberant form of worship. The Molokans concerned city fathers because both their social structures and values seemed particularly foreign in contrast to those of Progressive-era Americans.[25] None of the 1918 students can be definitively identified as Molokan, but the most likely candidate was Vera Galitzen. She, too, had been photographed in the manual training class. The Galitzen family, immigrants from Russia, lived in a large extended family. In 1920 that included Vera, her parents Joe and Hazel, her six brothers and sisters, one sister-in-law, and her maternal grandmother. In spite of their Anglicized first names, the Galitzen family fits the typical employment profiles of Molokans. Joe worked in a lumber yard; the family's oldest son worked as a laborer for an ice company; and the family's oldest daughter worked as a packer at a biscuit company on Utah Street. The Galitzens' native language was Russian, not Yiddish. This makes them much more likely to have been Molokan rather than Russian Jews like the Harris family.[26] If Vera was indeed Molokan she was in good company at Utah Street: by 1918 the school's student body was forty percent Molokan.[27]

The teaching staff at Utah Street did not reflect the racial or ethnic diversity of their students. According to school records from 1916, there were forty-four teachers and administrators assigned to Utah Street School. Six of those taught in the night school, one teacher taught in both, and the rest worked only during the day. Utah Street day school's principal, Alice J. Cushing, was perhaps better positioned than many of her teachers to understand her students' experiences. Cushing was born in California to parents who had emigrated from Ireland. She and her eight brothers and sisters grew up in the small town of El Monte outside of Los Angeles. Her career began as a teacher at the Amelia Street School before working her way up to principal, first at Macy Street and then at Utah Street. Five other teachers at Utah were American born but had at least one parent born in another country, usually Germany, Scotland, or Ireland. Only one teacher at Utah Street was an immigrant herself: the music teacher, Mildred Stone, had emigrated with her husband from England in 1909 and been naturalized in 1914. The teachers did at least provide a bit of geographic diversity, having been born in states ranging from Massachusetts to Alabama.[28]

The teachers may have come from backgrounds very different from their students. But most of these men and women, aided by a wide range of public and private programs, still demonstrated a Progressive-spirited commitment to helping children reach their full potential as "Americans." It is to the programs those teachers supported (and in some cases created and implemented) that we now turn.

Programs in the Public Schools and Surrounding Communities

Out of sheer necessity Los Angeles's public schools and private charitable groups developed a symbiotic relationship as they crafted programs to accommodate so many children from all over the world. "Rarely did the school themselves initiate the services," Judith Raftery explains. "But once a service proved successful, only an institution like the public schools had the money and influence to keep the program running."[29]

Organized welfare programs in Los Angeles hoped that by reaching out to young children they would create both better future citizens and better future workers. The local Young Women's Christian Association (YWCA) took the lead. Women had founded the YWCA of Los Angeles in May 1893 to encourage the spiritual development of young women.[30] But in the years after the turn of the century, the YWCA increasingly devoted itself to the improvement of the social and economic conditions of women and children across the nation. With a history of cooperation with local businesses and politicians, the YWCA proved particularly well suited to the task.[31]

The Los Angeles YWCA raised enough money to build and dedicate its own building downtown. The YWCA offered educational classes in its new building, and the program eventually expanded to offer everything from arithmetic and English to shorthand, millinery, and sales training.[32] When it came to immigrants, the YWCA believed that they should be Americanized. But the organization rejected demands for immediate assimilation in favor of a more gradual approach. It recognized the social and economic difficulties often facing new immigrants and worked to ameliorate the worse effects of immigration. Remaining sensitive to the immigrants' historical and cultural traditions, however, was often a struggle.[33]

In 1913 the YWCA founded an International Institute for the Foreign-Born on Utah Street, near the elementary school. Originally developed in New York City by Edith Terry Bremer, a veteran of the Chicago network of social workers and reformers, the YWCA expected the International Institutes to serve functions similar to those of the settlement houses. Unlike the settlements, however, the institutes tried to hire foreign-born and first-generation American women as case workers whenever possible. Institutes offered formal and informal classes in English, American history, government, and homemaking. In 1913 the Los Angeles Institute operated a special summer school to teach English to Dutch, German, Swedish, Russian, Italian, French, and Yiddish-speaking Angelenos.[34] English language instruction and literacy were often at the center of Americanization efforts. Here again an examination of the class of 1918 can be useful. Census data indicates that most of the children's parents could speak English even if they did not do so at home. But this did not always translate into literacy in any language. The two Etchart children, for example, came from a family in which neither parent was a native English speaker. This was common among Utah Street students. Neither Miguel nor Lazara Etchart could read or write. Nor could Deena Dallas's Greek-born mother.[35]

Private charitable organizations such as the YWCA that had previous experience working with immigrants became an invaluable ally to the public schools and the backbone of the welfare programs that were created in Los Angeles.[36] The YWCA case workers, for example, often understood more about the challenges facing immigrant students and their families than teachers and principals did. For example, YWCA case worker Frances Jouromsky tried to educate the schools and the community about Molokan family structure. She stressed that many Molokan women had to work outside the home, and this created problems inside and outside the public schools. "Children who should be in school have to remain home to care for the little ones while the mother is working. And the mothers come home tired and worn out, only to find that they have all the housework to do," Jouromsky told the *Los Angeles Tribune*.[37]

Other Los Angeles charities also developed a variety of programs determined to reshape immigrant family life, work, and even culture. One of the most striking cases of this was the day nursery for immigrant babies created at Utah Street School. Alice J. Cushing, principal of the Utah Street School, remembered that so many Molokan children had to bring their infant brothers and sisters to school while their mothers went to work that "the third-grade teacher had as many as six and eight infants crawling all over the classroom while she carried on instruction." When it was time to sleep, the babies were tucked into kindergarten tables whose raised sides prevented the infants from rolling out. To keep them quiet the older children fed the babies cold tea and gave them pickles to suck on. For two years Cushing tolerated the situation. Finally a private charitable group known as the Mother's Congress offered her a practical solution to this problem. They funded the construction of a new nursery building on campus. "[We] were able to secure the service of a Molokan young woman, a reliable and conscientious worker," Cushing later remembered. "She was married and had a baby of her own attending the nursery." Cushing believed that Molokan mothers trusted the school to care for their infants only because a member of their own community worked there.[38] By 1912, the nursery served forty to sixty babies a day, "sturdy little Russians, dark-eyed Spanish and Italian babies, flaxen headed 'Deutchers,' curly-haired Lithuanians, and now and then an American or colored youngster," reported one newspaper. The city of Los Angeles contributed thirty dollars a month to help maintain the program and then raised it to fifty so an additional aid could be hired. The First Street School later opened its own nursery modeled after Utah Street's.[39]

The school district's penny lunch program grew out of another collaboration, this time with the Los Angeles Civic Association. Concerned that immigrant schoolchildren suffered from inadequate diets at home, and that hungry students could not concentrate in the classroom, the schools sought to provide an affordable lunch option on site. The Civic Association took the lead in starting the program, paying for supplies and for women helpers. The school lunches were first available at the Custer Avenue, Ann Street, Castelar, and Macy Street Schools. Ann Street staff decided to make the program pay for itself by charging a penny for a hot meal, usually vegetable soup, rice with sugar and milk, and a piece of bread. Children without a penny were still fed, however. At Castelar students from the cooking classes often helped with the food preparation, thus learning another useful skill. "Many little foreigners are learning here not only how to cook, but what to cook and how to serve food," the local papers reported. "The children do the dishes and help clean up, too, and are thus gaining practical experience which is of almost as great value as the nourishment to the underfed bodies." In her study of the penny lunch programs, Raftery found no evidence parents were ever consulted about such programs or what kind of food they offered, even though some, like Molokans and Orthodox Jews, followed strict dietary laws in their own homes.[40]

Like the Molokans, Mexican immigrants also triggered acute anxiety among some educators in the city. Economic and political upheaval in Mexico, particularly the land reforms of the Diaz regime, compelled thousands of Mexican immigrants to also search for a better future in the United States. The collapse of the Diaz regime in 1910 and a subsequent war fueled the trend. So many Mexicans migrated to Los Angeles in the early years of the twentieth century that they quickly swamped the smaller population of native-born *Californios*. By the mid 1910s Los Angeles had probably the largest urban colony of immigrant Mexicans in the United States. Immigrant Mexicans now supplanted what many Anglos considered the "declining" and "decadent race" of Californios.[41] As ever-increasing numbers of Mexican immigrants arrived in Los Angeles, both reformers and politicians worried about how best to assimilate them into American culture. Unlike the Swedes, Italians, or even a clannish group like the Molokans, Mexicans seemed to be inherently flawed. Anglo-Americans viewed them as lazy, shiftless, and thriftless. "The Mexican laborer is unambitious, listless, physically weak, irregular, and indolent," Victor S. Clark noted in a 1908 report he drafted for the United States Department of Commerce and Labor.[42]

Thus educators within the school district created programs intended to "train" Molokan, Mexican, and other immigrant children for menial jobs in the American service economy.[43] The Los Angeles Board of Education itself added a system of "model bungalows" to the public schools. Los Angeles's public schools had mandated the teaching of cooking in some schools as early as 1899. School gardens had been introduced in 1906. But the model bungalows were something entirely new. The board placed the bungalows under Ella Flagg, supervisor of domestic science for the district. Flagg argued that many of the immigrant children had "absolutely no idea of housekeeping according to American standards." Utah Street, Amelia Street, and several other schools built small, three-room bungalows to teach students cooking and cleaning skills. Reformers hoped these model schools would train pupils for their future: "At the Utah Street School the rising generation will be taught to forget the ways of their parents and to housekeep in the American style." But by teaching girls cooking and sewing and boys gardening and carpentry work, reformers made it clear that they expected immigrant children to fill only the city's need for manual and domestic labor.[44]

Teachers at the Amelia Street School got even more creative when it came to inculcating domestic skills in their pupils. They purchased a doll the students named "Tina." Little girls clamored to take the doll home for the evening. The lucky child allowed to do so would be expected to give the doll a bath, wash its hair, and wash and iron all its clothes before returning it to school. If the doll's condition was not up to snuff that child would not be permitted to take her home again. An evening with the much-coveted plaything thus reinforced in little girls those domestic skills their teachers considered desirable both for future mothers and for future servants.[45]

Campus gardens served a similar purpose. "It is entirely likely that the practical result will be the turning out of skilled gardeners. The Russian boys take especially well to gardening," a *Los Angeles Times* reporter noted, "while the Mexicans and Spanish have, in some cases, shown particular predilection for it." The district also hoped that the gardens would keep the children occupied and off the streets.[46] The district even added trade schools at both Macy Street and Utah Street where "Little Dorritts" made and sold clothing, rugs, furniture, and more. This was the beginning of a system of social and vocational stratification in the public schools that would eventually try to divide students of different ethnicities into what teachers and administrators felt were the most suitable careers.[47]

The district also fretted about young people who had to leave school to work, particularly if they had not gained fluency in English. In 1909, it launched the city's first evening schools. The first four were located within existing elementary schools in heavily immigrant neighborhoods, at the Utah Street, Olive Street, Castelar Street, and Fourteenth Street Schools. Anyone over the age of fourteen could attend. In 1914, private groups (including the YWCA) received the school district's blessing to offer their own evening schools taught in public school buildings. The most common offering was English language lessons for nonnative speakers. Demand was so high that the district began to expand its own Elementary Evening Schools' offerings. "By 1916, fourteen schools offered classes in Americanization," Raftery points out, "and Los Angeles became the first city to have its Evening Schools' work accepted in the courts in lieu of an examination for citizenship."[48]

The connection between public schools, private charity, and the government came full circle in 1913 with the creation of the California State Commission on Immigration and Housing. It performed its work under the leadership of former school teacher Mary Gibson. With her background in teaching, suffrage, and the Friday Morning Club, Gibson brought to her work an elite, Anglo-American, Protestant orientation. She focused on the power of education and moral leadership to reshape immigrant domestic life. Under her guidance, Gibson's hometown, Los Angeles, became an enthusiastic proponent of Americanization programs. The cornerstone of Gibson's system, home teachers, often entered immigrant homes on the pretext of making sure the children attended school regularly. Once there, however, the teacher attempted to persuade the foreign-born women of the household to attend classes in English, civics, and domestic science. Proponents of these Americanization programs, like those in the school district, hoped that domestic science would provide women with skills they could then apply to finding work as servants. Home teachers neither expected nor wanted such training to instill any more ambition in a woman or child than needed for her to become unskilled or semiskilled labor in the local economy. By 1918, the state of California employed twelve full-time home teachers.[49]

Not wanting to be left out, the Daughters of the American Revolution (DAR) also sought to contribute to local public schools. They sponsored a home teacher named Amanda Matthews Chase who then volunteered her services to the public schools. Most of her time was spent at the Amelia Street School. The DAR even hosted a visit from eleven "foreign" mothers from the Avenue 19 School who entertained DAR members with folk dances, songs, and recitations.[50]

The same state act that authorized the hiring of home teachers also called for the creation of so-called "neighborhood schools." A variation on the settlement house movement, the plan was to adapt public schools in heavily immigrant areas into specialized campuses that served community needs at the same time they educated children.[51] Utah Street became one of the best known of the neighborhood schools in the area. Utah Street already had the model cottage and day nursery. It also offered a penny lunch program, a medical and dental clinic supported by the Parent Teacher Association, and even bathtubs if they were needed.[52] In his study of East Los Angeles, Ricardo Romo found that Macy Street School performed a similar function: it handed out clothes to adults and children in need, provided recreational activities, and even occasionally gave out home furnishings and stoves to local families.[53]

Parents and Teachers: Uneasy Alliances

What did the parents whose children filled these schools make of such programs? This side of the story is much more difficult to recover. As we have seen, many of these families moved frequently. Many others had limited English language skills that made it unlikely they would leave many records behind them. But it is nonetheless clear some parents successfully made the patchwork system of schools and charities work for them.

Language instruction was one focus of parent activism within the school district. For example, in 1908 the Molokans asked for and were granted the use of a Utah Street classroom for after-hours Russian-language instruction. The community raised the funds for a teacher, and the program was so popular a second classroom was later added. Other immigrant groups lobbied the board for classroom spaces where they could teach their children Italian, German, French, Hebrew, and Yiddish.[54] Spanish-speaking parents also felt strongly that their children should be bilingual rather than English-only speakers. "Speaking in English was viewed by many in the *colonia* as tantamount to acceptance of Anglo mores and society," Ricardo Romo notes. "Mexican parents ideally hoped that their children could grow up bilingual and learn to appreciate both Mexican and American culture."[55] The district also loaned out school classrooms after hours for cultural instruction. The local Armenian community, for example, held its own evening classes at First Street School.[56]

There seems to have been relatively little socializing between parents and teachers, hardly a surprise given the gaps in language, education, and experience between them. To try to bridge that divide, Utah Street created a Child Study Circle that met on campus. It offered a range of educational lectures and entertainment for local mothers. On one occasion, mothers from the Russian community offered their own program, featuring "a magnificent, shining samovar," tea served in "the Russian fashion," and cake. Children from the school then sang in both Russian and English for the attendees.[57]

Some of the teachers were more popular with parents than others. Alice J. Cushing, principal of the Utah Street School, and Nora Sterry, principal of Macy Street, seem to have been particular favorites. Both women were single, without children of their own, and both spent the bulk of their working lives in the local public schools. Cushing, so integral to the development of the Utah Street School, was so loved in the Molokan community she was remembered years later by them as "little mother." Parents at Macy Street felt the same way about Nora Sterry. In 1911 they petitioned the school board to try to get her appointed as principal of Macy Street's new night school as well as its day school. The school board refused. Sterry, who, unlike Cushing, came from a well-to-do family, won further renown in the community during Los Angeles's plague outbreak in 1924. Although safely outside the area when illness struck, Sterry insisted on entering the quarantine area and reaching the Macy Street School. "All my children are in there," she told reporters. From the school's kitchen she helped feed people until supplies ran out, and she made visits to local homes. After the quarantine was lifted her students and their parents feted her with songs and flowers and gifted her with a tiny gold medal.[58]

Parents' interest in language instruction, and their affection for Cushing and Sterry, suggests that they paid close attention to their children's education. This is reinforced by the fact that parents loudly objected to school programs that seemed to be trying to usurp the parents' roles. For example, when the Amelia Street School installed a bathtub in the school and tried to establish a regular bathing schedule for students, local parents complained to the school administration. Staff had to settle for making the baths purely optional. School nurses were another irritation. When her children were repeatedly sent home for having lice in their hair, one mother was pushed past her limits. "I did everything I could, everything," she complained, "but [the lice] still stick to their heads. What am I to do? Chop their heads off?"[59] Parents also resented when educators intervened in matters of discipline. One member of the Molokan community remembered:

> Children need discipline. God chastises those whom he loves. Beating should be our last resort. At first there was no complaint, but soon these kids were told by our neighbors, welfare workers, and teachers, that this was a free country and a father couldn't beat his children. I'll never forget when a father was taken over to the police station for strapping his boy . . . Ivan Ivanovitch, a kind-hearted man, arrested—for beating his youngster into obedience! Well, that was a strange thing. But we had to take notice of it. Ivan Ivanovitch has not beaten another one of his little bums as hard. He is afraid of them now, and they know it. They hold the upper hand over him. "I'll give you a thrashing." "I'll have you arrested," settled it all.[60]

Parents often expressed similar concerns that American-style education was driving a wedge between immigrant parents and their children and between children and their native cultures. This gap only grew wider as children reached young adulthood.[61]

Recreation was another sore spot. Some parents felt that the schools encouraged idleness in children who should be working to support the family. "Ball playing does not help you in life," one parent groused to an interviewer. "It's baby stuff." One form of recreation parents did approve of, however, was making sure their children had access to school playgrounds after school and on the weekends. In the tight quarters of these downtown neighborhoods, school playgrounds were often the only open space available. "The little ones are always safe there," the anti-ball-playing parent conceded. The Molokan community approached the school board in 1916 asking for after-hours playground access to be granted. It was. Parents also hoped that the availability of playgrounds would help them keep their older children off the streets and out of trouble.[62] Elsewhere in Los Angeles parents petitioned the Board of Education for kindergartens, library reading rooms, free transportation for their children, and more. "The list appeared endless," Rafferty writes, "and the schools were ill-equipped to grant all the requests that flooded in from so diverse a clientele."[63]

Still other parents flatly rejected the public schools' overtures to them and their children. Their reasons varied.[64] When Pauline Young studied the Molokan community in the 1920s she found that only younger girls attended classes at the YWCA's International Institute. Their mothers and older sisters shunned such participation. Young found that of the five hundred immigrants enrolled in the institute, very few were adult Molokans, and there were no Molokan women enrolled in parenthood classes, baby welfare, cooking, sewing, fancy work, or swimming classes. Some Molokans worried that Americanization and education in general would take young people away from the close-knit community. "The children are being slowly and subtly lured into the outside world by irresistible attractions," Young observed, "yet the older generation is still practically confined within the invisible walls of the Molokan sect."[65]

One young Molokan woman explained that she had to defy her family's wishes in order to remain in school as long as she did:

> My mother was dead set against my plans, and she would say: "Well, look what happens when we send our children to school. All they learn is to despise us. Look how they talk back to us." They gossiped about me in the Colony: "What does she want to go back to school for, to be a young kid all over again?" I paid no attention to any of them, and carried on my school work the best I could. My father now realizes the value of an education, and he wants my brothers to go through high school, but he does not make enough to support all the boys.[66]

Mexican immigrants also seem to have resisted many aspects of these programs. George J. Sanchez has argued that Americanization programs failed with this community for two reasons: first, because many Mexican immigrants never fully committed to them; and second, because the programs themselves held limited appeal to immigrants.[67] In times of trouble Mexican immigrants may also have preferred to turn to local *mutualistas* rather than to the public schools or Americanization teachers.[68] An even more popular option may have been greater Los Angeles's six Catholic social service agencies. The Catholic Church in Los Angeles recognized the need to respond effectively to Mexican immigrants' practical as well as spiritual needs.[69] Had the leaders of Americanization programs recognized the significant role of other aid organizations in immigrant life and adapted their efforts accordingly, they would perhaps have met with more consistent success.

Attitudes held by Anglo-American teachers exacerbated the situation. In the case of the Molokans, for example, many teachers had little patience for the "odd" cultural behavior of this self-segregating group. "Most teachers know little about Molokan culture, and what they do know about it does not appeal to them as worth fostering and promoting. They laugh up their sleeves about the 'Jumpers,'" one retired Americanization teacher remembered. "They [the teachers] have so little to offer that is of immediate practical value to these people that few of them see any use in bothering about school." Teachers were particularly appalled at parents who encouraged their children to leave school as soon as possible for work. "The homes undo so much that the schools are trying to instill in these children that our efforts seem futile," another teacher recalled. Social agencies often failed to coordinate their efforts, and heavy caseloads and a high turnover of social workers plagued relief agencies working in immigrant neighborhoods.[70]

The End of Private-Public Partnerships in Americanization

In spite of the efforts of teachers, reformers, and some parents, Americanization programs had only limited success in Los Angeles. In fact, even Americanization teachers both inside and outside of the school district were not certain what success would look like. Was success merely preparing immigrant children for low-level positions in the local labor force? Was it transforming those children into Americans? If so, what, exactly did American mean?[71]

One thing it evidently did *not* mean was adopting American citizenship. Progressives were consistently disappointed in how few eligible immigrants actually became citizens. By 1920, only one in five immigrants living in Los Angeles had become citizens.[72] How much Americanization training children ultimately retained is also an open question. As we have already seen, immigrant families in Los Angeles moved frequently. Since not every school or every community offered similar programs, this in turn made it difficult to maintain and practice whatever new "American" skills a child might have learned, assuming he or she even wanted to do so.[73]

Recognizing this, and faced with a rising tide of anti-immigrant sentiment, the school district began to abandon many of these programs in the 1920s.[74] State funding for programs like Gibson's were slashed and then slashed again by conservatives in the state legislature. In 1923 the incoming governor of California, Republican Friend Richardson, eliminated any further funding for Americanization in the public schools. Conservatives like Richardson not only felt Americanization programs had been prohibitively expensive and ineffective, but that they often coddled dangerous immigrants, including "Wobblies and communists." Growing anti-immigrant sentiment, particularly against the Japanese and their American-born offspring, led to calls up and down the state for tighter restrictions on immigration, on access to citizenship, and on the privileges citizenship conferred. The economic collapse of 1929 finished off any interest in public investment in such programs. This pattern repeated itself across the American West in the 1920s and 1930s.[75]

By the end of the 1920s the secular Americanization programs and all but two of the settlement houses designed to serve Mexican immigrants in Los Angeles had shut down. But individual immigrant communities, the Catholic Church, and private organizations such as mutualistas continued to provide community support and social services to immigrants.[76] In the 1930s, a new wave of demographic and residential changes in the city created schools with much more homogenous populations than before. Although some public schools, particularly on the east side, would remain diverse for a few more decades, city schools increasingly mirrored the racial and spatial segregation of Los Angeles. The heyday of the multiethnic neighborhood school had, at least for the time being, come to an end.[77]

Conclusion

During the Progressive Era, roughly 1890–1920, the pressure on Los Angeles's schools to both educate and Americanize immigrant children was intense. Without the experience that private charitable organizations such as the YWCA brought to the table, the public schools in Los Angeles would have faced far greater hurdles than they did. As the *Los Angeles Times* put it in 1925, "American citizens of tomorrow—what will they be like? These children have many of them grown away from the teachings of their parents and the advice they receive in school and the information they glean from the scare heads and from their hours on the streets does not always agree," the paper argued. "Self-reliant, skeptical, not very docile, they are an even more important factor in the making of the Los Angeles of tomorrow than are the flour, the candy, the soap, and the other products which are keeping many people busy near at hand."[78]

The perceived need to Americanize immigrant children as quickly as possible was certainly not unique to the American West in this era. All across the United States school districts grappled with the changing demographics of American students and instituted a wide range of programs to try to reach them. But what does make efforts in the American West, and in Los Angeles in particular, stand out is the intense drive of Americanizers there. Many western cities were already embracing Progressivism and Progressive politics. Thus, proponents of Americanization found a level of community, political, and financial support for their work not often seen elsewhere. That organizations as diverse as the YWCA, the DAR, and the Civic Association cooperated with and supported the Los Angeles Unified School District in this era speaks to how deeply Progressive ideas about education and child development had rooted themselves in the community.

The population dynamics at work in western schools also help us to understand why the stakes seemed so high at the time. In the years before the onset of the Great Depression, public schools in western cities were increasingly multiethnic and multiracial. Many westerners would no doubt have agreed with the stance taken by teachers and Americanization activists in Los Angeles that, if properly educated, these children would grow up to become productive members of the labor force and thus would support future economic development. If not properly educated, these children would only be a drag on the region's future growth. Whether immigrant and first-generation children became a help or a hindrance, so the argument ran, depended in large part on what happened during their school years.

But Americanization programs also had a dark side. Public schools often saw little or nothing worth preserving in immigrant cultures, instead opting to try to replace them with an ill-defined "American" culture as quickly as possible. Such programs explicitly supported and reinforced the low position of non-Western European immigrants in the regional economy. If not handled with sensitivity Americanization policies, programs, and attitudes could and did trigger conflict between immigrant parents and the public schools, and between immigrant parents and their children. This led in turn to pushback and resistance from immigrant parents themselves.

Today the United States continues to face the challenge of educating new generations of children who are either immigrants or the children of immigrants. Los Angeles's experience provides a valuable case study of how public schools a century ago fought the same battle. The city's schools were child-centered and open to experimentation. But at the same time they were also often dismissive of immigrant culture and of immigrant parents. Studying this period reminds us that terms like "education," "assimilation," and even "American" are and always have been socially and politically constructed and socially and politically contested. Though never perfect, Progressive-era public schools have lessons to teach us, lessons that are surely still worth learning.

Notes

1. "The Little Stranger within Our Gates," *Los Angeles Times*, February 3, 1918.
2. In this paper the term "elementary school" will be used to describe schools that focused on providing only basic academic skills: reading, writing, and so on.
3. George J. Sanchez, "'Go After the Women': Americanization and the Mexican Immigrant Woman, 1915–1929," in *Unequal Sisters: A Multicultural Reader in U.S.*

Women's History, 2nd ed., ed. Vicki L. Ruiz and Ellen Carol DuBois (New York: Routledge, 1994), 288.

4. Glen Gendzel, "What the Progressives Had in Common," *The Journal of the Gilded Age and Progressive Era* 10, no. 3 (July 2011): 333.
5. James Marten, *Childhood and Child Welfare in the Progressive Era: A Brief History with Documents* (Boston: Bedford/St. Martin's, 2005), 3, 4.
6. John M. Nieto-Phillips, *The Language of Blood: The Making of Spanish-American Identity in New Mexico, 1880s–1930s* (Albuquerque: University of New Mexico Press, 2004), 198.
7. Sanchez, "Go After the Women," 287.
8. Note that because of how the census defined "white" in this era, these numbers included immigrants of Mexican ancestry but not those of Asian ancestry. If Asians had been factored in, the percentages would no doubt be even higher. Frederick C. Luebke, "Introduction," in *European Immigrants in the American West: Community Histories*, ed. Frederick C. Luebke (Albuquerque: University of New Mexico Press, 1998), ix–xii.
9. Sanchez, "Go After the Women," 284.
10. Letter from Edward Hyatt to school superintendents of California, *School and Society*, June 24, 1916, pg. 931, quoted in Frank Van Nuys, *Americanizing the West: Race, Immigrants, and Citizenship, 1890–1930* (Lawrence: University Press of Kansas, 2002), 3.
11. The program, consisting mainly of an adult school, was short-lived. Van Nuys, *Americanizing the West*, 33, 37, 92–93, 132. For more on immigrants in the American West more generally, see Elliott Robert Barkan, *From All Points: America's Immigrant West, 1870s–1952* (Bloomington: Indiana University Press, 2007).
12. Judith Raftery, "Progressivism Moved into the Schools: Los Angeles, 1905–1918," *California History* 66, no. 2 (June 1987): 94.
13. Van Nuys, *Americanizing the West*, 5.
14. Raftery, "Progressivism Moved into the Schools," 94.
15. Mark Wild, "'So Many Children at Once and So Many Kinds': Schools and Ethno-racial Boundaries in Early Twentieth-Century Los Angeles," *Western Historical Quarterly* 22, no. 4 (Winter 2002): 456.
16. Mark Wild, *Street Meeting: Multiethnic Neighborhoods in Early Twentieth-Century Los Angeles* (Berkeley: University of California Press, 2008), 30–31, 54–56, 61.
17. There were two incarnations of the Macy Street School. One was on Macy Street at its junction with Bridge Street and Brooklyn Street: this was the school where Alice J. Cushing worked before moving to Utah Street. It was closed in 1904. The New Macy Street School on Macy Street and adjacent to Avila Street then became known simply as the Macy Street School. It is this school I discuss in this article. Memo to Mr. Kersey, Superintendent, Los Angeles City Board of Education, from Mr. Tritt, Assistant Secretary, Subject: Macy Street School, June 23, 1937, Los Angeles Unified School District Art and Artifact Collection/Archives, Los Angeles, CA.
18. "The Babies and the School Children," *Los Angeles Times*, May 17, 1908; "Little Tots Wield Spade," *Los Angeles Times*, March 4, 1906.
19. "John Etehart [John Etchart]," *Fourteenth Census of the United States, 1920* (Washington, DC: Government Printing Office, 1920), n.p. In this era, the term

"Spanish" was ambiguous. Mrs. Etchart may indeed have been born in Spain. She might have been Basque like her husband; she might have been born in Mexico; or she might have been born in the United States to parents from Mexico. Surviving records are unclear. For more on this, see Eileen V. Wallis, *Earning Power: Women and Work in Los Angeles, 1880–1930* (Reno: University of Nevada Press, 2010), 25–26, 59–61.

20. "Sanford Galt" and "Rose Harris," *Fourteenth Census of the United States*, n.p.
21. "Tome Ito" and "Teresa Condidi," *Fourteenth Census of the United States*, n.p.
22. "David B. Floyd, Jr.," *Thirteenth Census of the United States, 1910* (Washington, DC: Government Printing Office, 1910), np. The census did not record which railroad company employed David Sr. For more on African-American railroad workers in Los Angeles in this era see Douglas Flamming, *Bound For Freedom: Black Los Angeles in Jim Crow America* (Berkeley: University of California Press, 2005), 73.
23. "Deena Dallas," *Fourteenth Census of the United States*, n.p.
24. Pauline V. Young's extensive interviews with members of the Molokan community, conducted in the 1920s, remain the single best primary source on Molokans in Los Angeles. Young, "The Russian Molokan Community in Los Angeles," *The American Journal of Sociology* 35, no. 3 (November 1929): 393–94.
25. Traditional Molokan society had only two formal social organizations: the family and the church. Anglo-Americans did not understand the Molokan church, either—the Molokan church or *sobranie* was much more akin to a Quaker meeting than a Protestant, Catholic, or even Greek or Russian Orthodox service. Molokans rejected any form of formal religious practice because they associated them with the Orthodox Church. There were no social classes. Instead, Molokans based their social hierarchy on age, personal merit, and religious activity. In times of crisis they relied on mutual aid from inside the community, not civic agencies. Pauline V. Young, *The Pilgrims of Russian-Town* (Chicago: University of Chicago Press, 1932), 1, 12, 30; Young, "The Russian Molokan Community in Los Angeles," 396–97.
26. "Vera Galitzen," *Fourteenth Census of the United States*, n.p. For more on employment markers for Molokan immigrants in Los Angeles, see Wallis, *Earning Power*, 138–40.
27. Judith Rosenberg Raftery, *Land of Fair Promise: Politics and Reform in Los Angeles Schools, 1885–1941* (Stanford: Stanford University Press, 1992), 42.
28. *Directory of the Los Angeles City Elementary and High School Districts, November 1916*, Los Angeles Unified School District Art and Artifact Collection/Archives, Los Angeles, CA; "Alice Cushing," "Ramona Block," "Ella Vollstedt," "Kathryn Johnson," "Mildred Stone," "Elizabeth McKelvey," "Hazel Robinson," "Esther Hofert," "Sue Perry," *Fourteenth Census of the United States*, n.p.
29. Raftery, *Land of Fair Promise*, 45.
30. "A Short Historical Sketch of the Los Angeles Y.W.C.A.," Series I, Administrative Records 1894–1972, YWCA of Los Angeles Collection, California State University, Northridge [CSUN].
31. Sarah Heath, "Negotiating White Womanhood: The Cincinnati YWCA and White Wage-Earning Women, 1918–1929," in *Men and Women Adrift: The YMCA and the YWCA in the City*, ed. Nina Mjagkij and Margaret Spratt

(New York: New York University Press, 1997), 87; Unidentified newspaper clipping, January 20, 1906; "Volunteer Rally for Campaign to Aid Girls," unidentified newspaper clipping, c. 1910, Publicity Files, YWCA Collection.

32. "A Short Historical Sketch of the Los Angeles Y.W.C.A."; "How do you plan to spend your evening this winter?" c. 1914, and "Vocational Schools at the YWCA Hill Street," c. 1914, Records of Branches, 1909–1976, YWCA Collection, CSUN; "YWCA Teaches Girls to Make Living in Pleasant Line of Work," *Los Angeles Record*, November 19, 1912.
33. Robyn Muncy, *Creating a Female Dominion in American Reform, 1890–1935* (New York: Oxford University Press, 1991), 9, 13–14; "YWCA Work for Newcomers," *Los Angeles Times*, October 18, 1914; Raymond A. Mohl, "Cultural Pluralism in Immigrant Education: The YWCA's International Institutes, 1910–1940," in Mjagkij and Spratt, *Men and Women Adrift*, 114.
34. Mohl, "Cultural Pluralism in Immigrant Education," 119.
35. "Miguel Etehart [Miguel Etchart]," *Fourteenth Census of the United States*, n.p.; "Deena Dallas," *Fourteenth Census of the United States*, n.p.
36. Raftery, "Progressivism Moved into the Schools," 95.
37. "Woman Angel of Cheer to Slaves; Labor of Love Instructing Poor; Russian Colony Is Scene of Work," *Los Angeles Tribune*, December 3, 1914; Young, *The Pilgrims of Russian-Town*, 149, 153.
38. "The Babies and the School Children," *Los Angeles Times*, May 17, 1908; "Day Nursery Meets Need," *Los Angeles Times*, April 10, 1910; "Woman Angel of Cheer to Slaves"; Young, *The Pilgrims of Russian-Town*, 149, 153.
39. "Show World Our Ways of Child-Education," *Los Angeles Times*, May 19, 1912.
40. Ibid.; "Pupils Suffer from Pie Diet," *Los Angeles Times*, May 4, 1910; "Babies and School Children—Striking Pictures and Points Here and There," *Los Angeles Times*, March 14, 1909; Young, *The Pilgrims of Russia-Town*, 20; Raftery, *Land of Fair Promise*, 39.
41. Phoebe S. Kropp, *California Vieja: Culture and Memory in a Modern American Place* (Berkeley: University of California Press, 2006), passim; Victor S. Clark, "Mexican Labor in the United States," Department of Commerce and Labor, Bureau of Labor Bulletin No. 76 (1908), 507.
42. Decades of economic and social discrimination had reduced Los Angeles' Mexican and Mexican-American population to the status of second-class citizens. One survey of more than one thousand Mexican families living near the Plaza found that, while 60 percent had lived in the city for more than three years, 55 percent of men and 74 percent of women could not speak English. Literacy rates were even lower. G. Bromley Oxnam, *The Mexican in Los Angeles: Los Angeles City Survey* (Los Angeles: Los Angeles City Survey, 1920), 9–12; Gayle Gullett, "Women Progressives and the Politics of Americanization in California, 1915–1920," *Pacific Historical Review* 64, no. 1 (February 1995): 82; Clark, "Mexican Labor in the United States," 496.
43. In his influential article "Go After the Women," Sanchez argues that Americanizers targeted adult Mexican women for much the same reason (289).
44. Raftery, "Progressivism Moved into the Schools," 103; "Needle and Saucepan," *Los Angeles Times*, September 2, 1899; "School Grounds Will Bloom," *Los Angeles Times*, January 16, 1906; Gullett, "Women Progressives and the Politics of Americanization," 82; Sanchez, "Go After the Women," 251–63; "Plans Model

Bungalow," *Los Angeles Express*, November 8, 1910; "Macy School Children Make Efficient Workers," *Los Angeles Express*, September 17, 1914; "Trade Union Movement Helps to Americanize," Los Angeles *Citizen*, May 5, 1916.

45. "Doll an Aid to Teacher," *Los Angeles Times*, November 4, 1906.
46. "Big Tree Makes Babies Shriek," *Los Angeles Times*, December 16, 1910; "Crisp Lettuce Ready Today," *Los Angeles Times*, May 13, 1906.
47. "In the Public Schools," *Los Angeles Times*, June 15, 1913; Wild, "So Many Children," 464.
48. Raftery, "Progressivism Moved into the Schools," 102; "May Go to Night School," *Los Angeles Times*, September 15, 1909.
49. Gullett, "Women Progressives and the Politics of Americanization in California, 1915–1920," 79, 81, 85–93.
50. Chase later used her experiences in the public schools as a basis for a series of short stories, often featuring immigrant schoolchildren, published in the *Los Angeles Times* in the early 1920s. Van Nuys, *Americanizing the West*, 124; "Women's Work and Women's Clubs," *Los Angeles Times*, February 17, 1918. For Chase's writings see, for example, "Minerva and the Muse," *Los Angeles Times*, August 28, 1921 and "Chon the Bold," *Los Angeles Times*, February 5, 1922.
51. Wild, "So Many Children," 462; Van Nuys, *Americanizing the West*, 117.
52. Raftery, "Progressivism Moved into the Schools," 101.
53. Ricardo Romo, *East Los Angeles: History of a Barrio* (Austin: University of Texas Press, 1983), 133; "Designed for Young and Old," *Los Angeles Times*, May 2, 1915.
54. Raftery, "Progressivism Moved into the Schools," 101; Raftery, *Land of Fair Promise*, 43.
55. Romo, *East Los Angeles*, 142.
56. Raftery, *Land of Fair Promise*, 43.
57. "High Schools Ballot Week," *Los Angeles Times*, March 18, 1906.
58. Raftery, *Land of Fair Promise*, 42; "Citizens Made as They Wait," *Los Angeles Times*, September 12, 1911; "Medal Given to Teacher," *Los Angeles Times*, November 14, 1924.
59. "A Daily Dip for the Kids," *Los Angeles Times*, January 14, 1904; Young, *The Pilgrims of Russian-Town*, 224.
60. Young, *The Pilgrims of Russian-Town*, 138.
61. For a discussion of these divides in the Mexican and Mexican-American populations, see Sanchez, "Go After the Women," 294–95, and Vicki Ruiz, *From Out of the Shadows: Mexican Women in Twentieth Century America*, 10th ed. (New York: Oxford University Press, 2008), chapter 3.
62. A "well-equipped and well-supervised" playground, this one funded by the Los Angeles Playground Commission, was built in the neighborhood in 1926. Young, *The Pilgrims of Russian-Town*, 141.
63. Raftery, *Land of Fair Promise*, 21.
64. Gullett, "Women Progressives and the Politics of Americanization," 79, 81, 85–93.
65. Young, *The Pilgrims of Russian-Town*, 21, 230–31.
66. Ibid., 168.
67. Sanchez, "Go After the Women," 293.
68. These were self-support groups originally developed in Mexico and then adapted in the United States by Mexican Americans. *Mutualistas* argued that, due to

racism on the part of Anglo-American officials, Mexican men and women often could not rely on local social services for help in times of crisis. Each mutualista offered different benefits to its members. These could range from low-cost insurance and funeral benefits to low-interest loans and social services. Nelson A. Pichardo, "The Establishment and Development of Chicano Voluntary Associations in California, 1910–1930," *Aztlan* 19, no. 2 (Fall 1988–1990): 93–95, 110, 117; Kaye Lynn Briegel, "Alizanza Hispano-Americana, 1894–1965: A Mexican American Fraternal Insurance Society," (PhD diss., University of Southern California, 1974), 53, 208; Cynthia E. Orozco, "Beyond Machismo, La Familia, and Ladies Auxiliaries: A Historiography of Mexican-Origin Women's Participation in Voluntary Associations and Politics in the United States, 1870–1990," *Perspectives in Mexican American Studies* 5 (1995): 13; Jose Amaro Hernandez, *Mutual Aid for Survival: The Case of the Mexican American* (Malabar, FL: Robert E. Krieger Publishing Company, 1983), 9.

69. Before the 1910s, Mexican attendance at local Catholic churches had been on the decline. Attendance rebounded in the 1910s and 1920s. Jay P. Dolan and Gilberto Miguel Hinjoso, *Mexican Americans and the Catholic Church, 1900–1965* (Notre Dame, IN: University of Notre Dame Press, 1994), 137, 155.
70. Young, *The Pilgrims of Russian-Town*, 146, 154, 226–27.
71. For more on the ambivalence Americanization workers often felt about the process, see, for example, Mohl, "Cultural Pluralism in Immigrant Education," 114–99; Gullett, "Women Progressives and the Politics of Americanization," 85–93.
72. Raftery, *Land of Fair Promise*, 102.
73. See, for example, the discussion of mobility in the Los Angeles Mexican community in Sanchez, "Go After the Women," 295.
74. Romo, *East Los Angeles*, 90; Gullett, "Women Progressives and the Politics of Americanization," 85–93.
75. Japanese-born immigrants, like other Asian immigrants, were already barred from citizenship. But during the 1910s, new laws limited their ability to own or lease land and even outlawed guardianship by Japanese for their American-born children. Van Nuys, *Americanizing the West*, 66, 180; Sanchez, "Go After the Women," 294–95.
76. George J. Sanchez, *Becoming Mexican American: Ethnicity, Culture, and Identity in Chicano Los Angeles, 1900–1945* (New York: Oxford University Press, 1993), 159.
77. Sanchez, "Go After the Women," 258; Wild, "So Many Children," 474; see also Charles Wollenberg, "Race, Nationality and Segregation in California Schools," *California Historical Quarterly* 53, no. 4 (Winter 1974): 320.
78. "Unique School Teaches Tots from All Nations," *Los Angeles Times*, November 1, 1925.

7

Locally Made
Immigrant Whiteness in Montana's Copper Communities

Matthew Basso

For immigrants in the Progressive Era, racial-ethnic identity was central to the question of "who we were." In this chapter, Matthew Basso investigates how racial-ethnic and gender identities coalesced and how they affected power relations in two Montana copper communities, Butte and Black Eagle. What most people today think of as nationality or ethnicity was commonly called race in the nineteenth century. By 1900, race had come to mean skin color as well, and many Americans subdivided European nationalities into three racial-ethnic categories: Nordic, Alpine, and Mediterranean. On the basis of these subdivisions, some Americans, including the Irish who themselves had earlier been the butt of racist jokes, questioned the fitness or "whiteness" of southeastern Europeans.

With admirable clarity Basso illustrates the importance of local power structures, residential patterns, religious affiliations, and population profiles in shaping the racial-ethnic status and experiences of immigrants in the West. Although both Butte and Black Eagle were Montana copper towns, the experiences of immigrant residents in the two communities differed markedly. Basso describes how over time panethnic bonds developed that linked "white" workers of various nationalities in opposition to African American and American Indian labor.

From the last half of the nineteenth century until well into the twentieth century, the Far West was defined as much by its immigrant population as any of its now more famous features. In Montana, for example, just before World War II, persons of foreign birth or of foreign or mixed parentage still made up over 45 percent of the state's entire population. They included Germans, Norwegians, English, Catholics from "the Irish Free State," Swedes, Russians, "Jugoslavs," Scots, Danes, Italians, Finns, Czechs and Slovaks, Protestants from Northern Ireland, and Welsh. This essay explores the experiences of European immigrants in two Montana towns, Butte and Black Eagle, from the 1880s through the 1930s. Specifically I examine the question of the racial identities of Butte and Black Eagle's immigrants and the social politics that emerged from those identities. The largest immigrant groups in Butte and Black Eagle—the Irish, English, Welsh, Finns, Italians, and the Croats, Slovaks, and Serbs who together made up the "Jugoslavs"—have been of deep interest to scholars studying the development of white racial identity as part of the larger history of race and power in the United States. The central debate among these scholars of "whiteness" is often framed as a single question: were these immigrants and their descendants considered "white"?[1] In the work of the best of these scholars, however, that question emerges as a point of interest only insofar as it relates to a deeper set of questions: how did racial identities form and operate during this era, and how were relations of power affected? My answer to both of these questions forefronts the importance of being attuned to local forces and local circumstances.

While acknowledging the impact of forces like national popular culture and the ideas immigrants brought from their home countries, the immigrant histories of Butte and Black Eagle show that racial, ethnic, and gender identities were generated in a definitive way locally through interactions among immigrants and their descendants in the workplace, the union hall, and the community, and between them and working- and middle-class white Americans, including management. Underscoring the necessity of employing a "local" lens, I contend that the dynamic of identity among immigrants was different in Butte than Black Eagle because the mix of immigrants and the local history of ethnic interaction were different. Irish and Irish Americans dominated Butte and in the process marginalized the city's large southeastern European population, among others. In contrast, southeastern Europeans, especially Croats and Italians, comprised the largest part of Black Eagle's population. Sharing Catholic faith and values brought these two ethnic communities together earlier and more completely than what occurred among European immigrants in Butte. I will argue that in both of these places the differences in these ethnic relationships substantially impacted local social politics. I will further contend that both the presence and the relative absence of the other racial–ethnic groups that characterized the unique human geography of Butte and Black Eagle—and also defined a number of other towns and cities in the West—shaped the sense of group identity in each of these places.[2] Although the number of African Americans in Montana dropped between 1900 and 1930, blacks figured especially significantly in the local process through which immigrant groups in Butte and Black Eagle came to be defined and define themselves as white. Likewise, American Indians, who comprised a notable percentage of Montana's population during this period, were crucial to the process through which Black Eagle's immigrants in particular were able to assert their own whiteness and eventually claim an identity that is commonly known today as "ethnic."

A century ago, Butte, Montana, was one of the most remarkable—and remarked upon—cities in the nation. The contradictions that defined Butte meant that disagreements about its character abounded. Mark Twain, who visited Butte at the height of its prosperity, thought it surprisingly urbane. Dashiell Hammett, who experienced it during the tumultuous period around World War I, described it as a corrupt, ugly place. To those seeking their fortunes, Butte's astonishing copper deposits made it the "Richest Hill on Earth." To the workers, who organized virtually every sector of the local economy so as to keep some of the vast wealth their labor created, Butte was America's "Gibraltar of Unionism." For its residents, Butte was also a city of neighborhoods with distinct characteristics and specific, though not exclusive, ethnic affiliations.[3]

Where a person came from made an enormous difference in Butte just as it did in the rest of America. Workers originated from as many as fifty different nations and from most parts of the United States. Figures from 1910 show that almost 3,000 "Austrians" (mainly Serbians and Croatians), 2,500 Germans, 1,600 Italians, and 1,500 Finns called Butte home. They toiled alongside immigrants from across Europe as well as from Mexico, China, Syria, and Afghanistan.[4] Until the end of the nineteenth century, English immigrants, especially from Cornwall, outnumbered other foreigners; their Protestant faith and Republican Party leanings meant they tended to assimilate easily. But the culture and politics of Butte were dominated by the Irish, stalwarts of the Catholic Church and the Democratic Party. By 1900, the Irish population in metropolitan Butte stood at 12,000, or 26 percent of the total, surpassing all other racial-ethnic groups.[5] The Irish made their power felt in a myriad of ways, both large and small. Rug merchant Mohammed Akara's decision to change his name to "Mohammed Murphy" for what he called "business reasons" provides an apt illustration.[6] Historian David Emmons's conclusion that Butte "belonged to the Irish in almost the same way Salt Lake City belonged to the Mormons" makes the point succinctly.[7]

The power of the Irish made Butte's racial-ethnic politics distinctive from the national and regional picture, as well as from Black Eagle. In the United States, for much of the nineteenth century, when an individual's "race" was mentioned it often referred to her or his "nationality," not the color of her or his skin. Racial theorists placed each of these nationalities into a hierarchy based on their sense of the merits of particular languages, religions, and national histories. With the increase in Irish immigration to the United States following the potato famine, influential American commentators echoed their counterparts in Britain by deriding the Irish "race" for its Catholicism, its Gaelic language, and its supposedly uncivilized peasant culture. By the latter part of the century, although Irish immigrants still faced prejudice, their place on the American racial hierarchy had been elevated based on a number of factors including their ability to speak English as well as Gaelic and nativists' growing antipathy toward the new immigrants from southern and eastern Europe.[8]

Around this time, the sense of race as nationality and race as color grew entangled. Prominent thinkers placed national races into three categories, Mongoloid, Negroid, and Caucasoid, with virtually all Europeans located in the last of these. Spurred by their antagonism to immigrants from southern and eastern Europe, some theorists argued that Caucasoid did not distinguish important differences between the European races. Madison Grant, who saw European immigrants as divided into Nordic, Alpine, and Mediterranean groupings, represented perhaps the most influential early twentieth-century development of this idea of race. Grant produced a complicated taxonomy that used pseudoscientific reasoning to bolster the argument about the superiority of "white" northern and western Europeans. The specificity of these theories did not dampen their racist core and, ultimately, mattered little to a general public—including Butte's Irish—who typically referenced simplified versions as they argued for the inferiority of new immigrants. The overarching precept was that southern and eastern Europeans fell outside the Nordic identity, and, as lower racial-ethnic groups, were on the margins of whiteness and should not have access to the full material and psychological "wages" that it brought.[9]

One of the reasons the Irish were able to secure power in Butte earlier and more fully than in other places was because employers there did not have an anti-Irish bias. Some western mine owners grouped the Irish with immigrants from southern and eastern Europe whom they considered of lesser intelligence, ability, and worth than "American" men. Others called them "Irish Mexican greasers," rhetorically linking them with another stigmatized group. In both cases part of the purpose was to promote competition and animosity between workers of different nationalities so as to drive down wages and make union organizing more difficult. But beginning with Marcus Daly, that was not the common practice in Butte. Daly, the head of the Anaconda Copper Mining Company [ACM] and the most powerful man in the city during its formative period, was himself an Irish immigrant. Daly sought out Irish workers and helped place a substantial number in positions of authority in both the mines and the town. William Andrews Clark and Fritz Heinze, two of the other Copper Kings, were also favorably disposed toward Butte's English-speaking workers. Even though it arguably went against their economic interests, they publicly declared their opposition to non-English-speaking workers, especially southeastern Europeans.[10]

Butte's Irish also developed a set of local institutions, especially associations, Catholic parishes, and the Butte Miners Union (BMU), that enabled the enclave to grow and prosper. Miners started the BMU in 1882, the same year Daly recognized the richness of Butte's copper lode. Other workers followed the miners' lead, and Butte became one of the most fully unionized cities in the country; pundits called it "the strongest union town on earth." As the most powerful local union in the copper industry and one of the largest and most influential locals in the United States, the BMU wielded considerable power. Although it was organized along industrial instead of craft lines, a rarity in late nineteenth-century America, the BMU was firmly under the control of settled Irish miners and was less responsive to others in the diverse workforce.[11]

The BMU championed racial politics that sought to shore up the privileges of whiteness of native-born and northern European immigrant workers by excluding or marginalizing groups considered nonwhite or of lower racial-ethnic status.[12] Butte's miners, like their peers elsewhere in the region, initially focused not on southeastern Europeans, but on Chinese "Mongoloid" workers as the most likely threat to the jobs and reasonable wages they had secured. Chinese who entered mining during the California Gold Rush, often under the control of a boss, patron, or contractor, found their way to other western mining towns during the late nineteenth century. Chinese faced racist opposition, including violence. In Butte, according to a local newspaper, a "disheartened, yet patriotic" miner lynched "a "Chinaman" in 1868. The city's 1882 mayoral race was won by a candidate who championed the ouster of "Cheap Chinese labor," registering the level of ongoing anti-Chinese sentiment and the relationship between racial prejudice and workplace concerns.[13]

By the 1890s, the question of whether southeastern Europeans and African Americans would be allowed to mine in Butte had overshadowed the Chinese question.[14] Small numbers of Italians, Serbians, and Croatians came to the Mountain West to work in the copper industry before 1890. After that their numbers rose rapidly and peaked in the first decade of the twentieth century. In response, northern European and other miners in Butte, as well as their allies, mounted a concerted campaign against the "Dago" and the "Bohunk." An 1897 editorial in the *Butte Bystander*, the official newspaper of the BMU, argued that southeastern Europeans were "three centuries behind northern Europeans in intelligence" and the prospective miners from that region were "brutish, ignorant men" who willingly accepted wages that no "American could live on."[15]

The battle over the employment of southeastern Europeans in the mines began in earnest in the early twentieth century. As an increasing number of southeastern Europeans arrived in Butte, Irish workers' influence with the company dissipated following the death of Daly and the emergence of less Irish-friendly management policies as officers of Standard Oil, who at that point owned the ACM, exerted their power over the mines.[16] Around 1910, the Immigration Commission sent to inspect the situation in Butte and other hard-rock mining towns in the Mountain West reported that non-English-speaking immigrants had a reputation for deflating wages, hampering unionization, and hindering efforts to improve the relationship between employer and employee. According to the commission, these new immigrants facilitated managers' use of "race competition" to maximize profits. In 1897, Butte had stood outside much of the rest of the industry because bosses protected English-speaking workers from the threat posed by non-English-speaking immigrants. A decade later, some managers in the mining city were behaving much more like their peers elsewhere. One North Butte Mining Company official nicely summarized their attitude: "I don't like to see too many of one nationality put together. I would rather keep them mixed. . . . I think you get better results if you don't have all your employees belonging to one clan or nationality." Local labor leaders' contention that Marcus Daly would have barred the new immigrants from the mines drew applause from workers but only served to highlight the changing ethno-racial politics in the mines.[17]

A long exposé in the July 1910 *Butte Evening News*, entitled "The Story of the Butte Bo-hunk—The Dark Skinned Invader," reflected the use of racial rhetoric around immigrants as well as an increasing conflation of nationality and color in conceptualizations of race. It began: "This story tells of the bohunks, three thousand strong, who are driving the white man slowly but surely out of the camp." Pointedly referring to the older immigrant and native-born miners as "white men" or "Americans" rather than specifying their ethnic backgrounds, the article reinforced a sense that they were racially acceptable and well within the national mainstream. It described southeastern Europeans as "some mysterious form of foreigner" and as "low grade" foreigners. The "Bohunk miner" was similar to "a Chinaman." Collectively, these "black men from across the water" threatened the city with "a black peril" akin to the old "yellow peril."[18]

By using these racial terms, the article ascribed a form of enervated masculinity to southeastern Europeans. In contrast—indeed, in opposition—to the masculinity of the upright, family-centered white miners who were Butte's "bread-winner[s]," Bohunk men were "ready to slip into every job where a white man is laid off." Even worse in the eyes of Butte's independent-minded miners with their advertised ethic of battling the boss, a Bohunk was willing to "buy his job from the foreman and pa[y] him for keeping it." Union men should be especially alarmed because Bohunk men lacked both a sense of working men's independence and a sense of class solidarity.[19] Suggesting the cross-class affinities between settled northern European and native-born miner masculinity and local middle-class masculinity, the paper asserted that Bohunk men failed to support the community by patronizing local businesses. Instead, they spent their earnings at their own groceries and bakeries, because "the bohunk does not eat white bread." For Butte, the paper asserted, the Bohunk invasion would lead to the exodus of white mining families. "Every train that dumps these foreigners off as it pulls in takes just as many old-timers aboard as it pulls out. . . . Up the gulch, 'mother and the kids' watch daily for the postman to see if father has found a place where a white man can live and earn his living. Up the gulch, boys who were born and raised there are kissing their grey-haired mothers good-bye and are leaving for pastures new."[20]

The *Evening News* exposé put pressure on the "padrone" practices that saw the poorest of these southern European immigrants come to Butte and other western mining districts under contractual control of a labor boss, with the result that their numbers decreased briefly.[21] They were replaced by other southeastern Europeans who also faced some resistance to their presence. However, unlike African Americans, another group of overtly racialized workers, Bohunks were still allowed to labor in Butte's mines indicating that the language of color, like "black peril," deployed against these men did not bar them from the most important privilege of whiteness in this local space.

Like the debate over allowing southeastern Europeans into Butte's mines, the discussion about employing African Americans started in the 1890s. But the ACM categorically barred blacks from their mines. The *Helena Colored Citizen*, one of a number of African American papers in Montana, first publicized the ACM's stance on September 24, 1894. In "The Anaconda Company Employs Only White Men and Dagoes," the *Colored Citizen* bemoaned exclusionary employment policies and the racial order they reflected, while also championing the prowess of African American workers. "Montana has just right to feel proud of its . . . colored citizens," wrote editor J. P. Ball. "They are the brawn that has unfettered and exposed to the sunshine of our unsurpassed clime the treasured wealth of ages."[22]

The exclusion of African Americans from mining had a profound effect on the interdependent race and gender order of the city.[23] Black men were not allowed to demonstrate their equality with whites by working in the city's best-paying, most masculine working-class job. Soon this bar became self-perpetuating, as racist logic concluded that black men were unable to handle hard-rock mining because none toiled in the mines. By barring African Americans from the mines while it hired southeastern Europeans, the ACM, in effect, used blackness to whiten suspect immigrants. Although they grumbled about it, the willingness of English, Cornish, Irish, and other "white" miners to work next to "Bohunks" and "Dagoes" solidified, if sometimes slowly, the bond between white miners of different racial-ethnic backgrounds. A critical part of this bond between miners involved their joint role in exercising and protecting the privileges of whiteness in the mines by actively supporting the ongoing exclusion of black miners.

The Irish continued to be the dominant group in Butte during the 1920s and 1930s, but evolving attitudes driven by generational change marked the city's racial-ethnic relations producing conditions that bolstered a *developing* panethnic bond. Once the cornerstone of the city's immigrant separatism, northern, southern, and eastern European ethnic lodges began to use English and to socialize with each other. Southeastern Europeans still sometimes found themselves referred to as "garlic eaters" or even more derogatory terms, and fights still broke out between them and the Irish. However, they enjoyed growing acceptance as a core part of Butte society. According to a WPA assessment, by the latter 1930s they were seen as "some of the camp's most respected citizenry."[24] In contrast, Butte's chilly racial climate and economic difficulties drove most blacks to leave the city in the late 1920s and early 1930s.[25]

The immigrant history of Black Eagle, the least well known of Montana's copper communities, differed in fascinating ways from Butte. Black Eagle began as a collection of "shanties" for workers helping construct the nearby reduction works and smelter built by the Boston and Montana Consolidated Copper and Silver Mining Company on the north bank of the Missouri River across from Great Falls. Initially inhabited by northern European immigrants from Norway and Sweden but, notably, not from Ireland, it soon attracted large numbers of Croatians and Italians, most from rural areas, who were pushed to leave their countries by economic and political problems tied to the global process of industrialization.[26]

Black Eagle was markedly more friendly toward the immigrant groups that in Butte were derided as "Bohunks" and "Dagoes." Notably, most of the Croatians and Italians that emigrated to Black Eagle came from the northern regions of their countries.[27] That all but two of the twenty-plus members of Black Eagle's famed "Croatian Nightingale Band" came from Bribir, a town near the northern reaches of the Adriatic "not far from the Italian border," was not an anomaly. Walt Valacich, a local historian, estimated that 75 percent of the original Croatian migrants came from Bribir. Black Eagle's Italian immigrants did not display a chain migration pattern quite as focused on one town, but a substantial number originated in the north–central province of Lucca, particularly the town of Santa Maria Del Guidice.[28] These ties to place played a crucial role in shaping Black Eagle. Like what occurred in Butte with the Irish, Croatians and Italians who had put down roots offered new arrivals from their homeland a network with access to housing, work, and familiar culture. Each wave of immigrants from Bribir and Lucca reminded earlier immigrants of the shared values of their sending communities, bolstering the immigrant identity of Black Eagle and, through their growing numbers, increasing the power of Italians and Croatians to shape their world.[29]

By the early twentieth century, although a number of other racial-ethnic groups were found in Black Eagle, Croatians and Italians so dominated the town that it was called Little Chi (for Chicago) or Little Milwaukee, both places known for their large numbers of southeastern Europeans. As it expanded up the northwestern bank of the Missouri River and spread out from its central axis of Smelter Avenue, Black Eagle acquired many of the trappings immigration historians associate with immigrant enclaves in larger cities. Unlike Butte, where Austrians were criticized for patronizing un-American markets that offered goods like dried meats and brown bread, Black Eagle businesses catered to them. Amelia Polich remembered, "The butcher man would go up the street in his wagon. You'd go out and buy your meat, if you wanted to." Some merchants would speak Croatian to her mother, so she did not have to learn to speak English. Black Eagle residents, Italian and Croatian alike, fondly remember walking down the town's dozen or so streets and hearing Italian operas being sung by men and women out gardening or emanating from phonographs that seemed to be playing day and night.[30]

Here, unlike the densely packed urban neighborhoods we associate with early twentieth-century immigrants, these songs did not echo within tenement house courtyards but were carried by the fierce winds that blew across the northern plains. The proximity of open spaces allowed residents to partake of elements of rural life, especially subsistence production. Black Eagle's relatively low density made it comparable to many immigrant enclaves in midwestern and western towns. In fact, a substantial number of Black Eagle's immigrant residents had already failed at farming on the Great Plains.[31]

Black Eagle's immigrants forged unusually close ties based in part on their experience living as neighbors, a contrast to the spatial dynamics of Butte where racial-ethnic segregation defined most immigrant neighborhoods.[32] Language differences, one of the most typical obstacles to bonding between immigrant groups, did not pose a significant barrier to forging relationships between first-generation Croatians and Italians. Some knew each other's language because they had worked in the others' country before emigrating, evidence of the often forgotten cosmopolitanism of some immigrants to the United States. Others learned Croatian or Italian so they could communicate with their workmates and neighbors, whether to complain about the climate—as one disgruntled immigrant put it, "when [you] g[o]t up in the morning it was so cold . . . shoes [were] frozen to the floor"—or to gripe about work and the prejudice they faced as immigrants.[33]

Schooling reinforced the social ties between immigrants as well. Black Eagle residents thought of the Hawthorne School, first called "Copper Smelter School," as one of the centers of the community. The connection between Black Eagle's two dominant groups strengthened into a panethnic bond as the second generation learned English at Hawthorne. While children in Butte reverted to racial-ethnic neighborhood allegiances once they left school, sharing the same classrooms and neighborhoods cemented the solidarity among youth in Black Eagle. Beginning in 1917, when immigrant adults began to attend night classes in "English, civics, and other subjects essential to citizenship," it did the same for their parents.[34] Notably, the local public school curriculum in Black Eagle did not erase racial-ethnic identity.[35] Claire Del Guerra recalled that Fanny Collins, who taught and then served as principal of Hawthorne, "reinforced more than ever for us the fact that we were fortunate, we were somebody because we had our heritage."

While schooling helped knit together the town's immigrant fabric into a panethnic fabric, other aspects of immigrant life in Black Eagle reflected the cultural fissures apparent in Butte and many American cities. Associations based on nationality strengthened ties based on a shared homeland, created a network that in the case of Butte and Black Eagle kept each community apprised of the racial-ethnic politics in nearby towns, and theoretically blocked interimmigrant bonding.[36] Like many such associations, Black Eagle's chapter of the Croatian Brotherhood provided life and health insurance. But its best-known activities focused on conviviality. It built a Croatian Hall so the community would have a place to gather and regularly sponsored festivals and dinners to celebrate "old country" holidays.[37] Yet, rather than allow it to only bolster allegiance to the Croatian community, Black Eagle's Croatians invited their Italian neighbors, and those from other racial-ethnic backgrounds as well, to partake in Mesopust with them. This was only one of many occasions throughout the year in Black Eagle when the celebrations of one immigrant group built ties among them all.[38]

Socializing at each other's associations was important in establishing the panethnic sensibility and shared value system that defined Black Eagle, but Catholicism served as an even more essential connection between Italians and Croatians. In Butte, the Catholic Church operated in part as a vehicle for Irish power. In Black Eagle, the communally written town history underscores the importance of "*common* faith" in linking the "contrasting languages and customs" of immigrant settlers. Black Eagle residents remember that Blessed Sacrament, the church Croatians and Italians built together in 1922, became the center of panethnic community life for both children and adults.[39] While Catholicism trumped racial-ethnic divisions and bound Black Eagle together, church doctrine reinforced gender divisions. Local norms placed women in the home and privileged men as breadwinners and heads of household.[40]

During these formative decades, immigrant men gained status within the community by being their family's sole breadwinners. However, the evaluation of immigrant working-class masculinity involved much more than a man's ability to form and provide for a family. Religiosity; racial-ethnic identity; sexuality; muscularity and other bodily matters; wealth; education; military, union, and associational experience; and the type of work he did all contributed to the assessment of a man's masculinity. Neither the evaluation nor performance of these aspects of immigrant masculinity can be made sense of without carefully considering context. Numerous studies have shown that immigrant working-class men were at various times and in various places seen as meeting, and perhaps even setting, the standard for American manhood. During other times and in other places they were perceived as lacking the crucial characteristics of manhood, either because of the ways gender was read through their ethno-racial identity and/or because of their subordinate class position.[41] Locally, though, the convergence of the gender order of Black Eagle's immigrants and that of Great Falls in regard to masculine expectations reinforced these men's standing.

Employment in the smelter was central to men's claims to breadwinner status. The smelter's refusal to employ women in production jobs enabled Italian and Croatian men to maintain and promote their sex-segregated view of the world. Black Eagle's immigrant men did not control the smelter as they did the rest of the town. There was no guarantee that the panethnic sensibility that defined the ethno-racial order in the community would prevail in the workplace. In Black Eagle, as in Butte, racial-ethnic relations proved critical to how gender worked.

Racial-ethnic identity framed certain production jobs in Black Eagle but not others. Charles Micheletti remembers work at the zinc plant as punishing: "Not many smeltermen worked there long." Immigrant men of any nationality could claim significant masculine status by being tough enough to work in a place like the zinc plant.[42] The tank house, on the other hand, was tied to a particular group. "The type of work that they had to do" there, commented smelterman Clarence Silloway, who notably was neither Italian nor Croatian, "it was hard to get a white man to do it." But the "husky" Austrians and Croatians were willing to do it. In contrast, Silloway claimed, the Italian men made sure they did "higher-class labor."[43] By doing "higher-class" labor, Italian men signified both their whiteness and their masculinity. Racialized masculinity, in this local scenario, echoed what occurred in Butte between the Irish and southeastern Europeans whom the *Evening News* described as the "black men from over the water." The ideology embedded in Silloway's comment that "it was hard to get a white man to do it" was deeply rooted in a notion of labor that emerged with industrialization and was contrasted to slavery. In American labor discourse, skill, honor, independence, and a stance against degrading tasks defined white man's labor. At Black Eagle and other production sites across the United States, specific tasks or entire categories of labor were interpreted through a racial and gender lens that in Silloway's reading seemed to place Italians inside and Croatians outside white masculinity.[44]

Yet in Black Eagle the connections between racial identity, skin color, and job hierarchies were nothing if not complex and mutable. Croatian immigrant William Tonkovich recalled that "being dark complected I'd slip in" to the Italian Lodge's Columbus Day Dance. "They thought I was one of the Italians."[45] A local Italian contended that the northern Italian character of the town's Italian residents trumped the national common sense about Italians' racial status. Citing her brother's blond hair and nickname, "Ole the Swede," she argued that "people never thought we were Italians, see, we weren't dark." According to her, Black Eagle's Italians did not suffer from the "bad reputation" Italians had in the United States, because it was applied mostly to Sicilians and Neapolitans who were "dark" and "a different type."[46] Clearly the relationship between color and race was an issue of some importance to local immigrants as it was for immigrants across the nation.[47] But in the Anglo-dominated national imagination, shaped more by Anglo-controlled popular culture and intellectual currents than by the maneuvering of individual immigrant groups, Italians and Croatians were by and large equally suspect racially.

Both Italians and Croatians pointedly recall being "treated like a minority" on the Great Falls side of the river. Adults and children often heard themselves referred to as "bohunks," "wops," or "dagoes."[48] Great Falls, founded in 1884 by the visionary entrepreneur Paris Gibson as a hydroelectric and commercial center, had become Montana's largest city by the

1950s, and Black Eagle was swallowed up by the burgeoning military and industrial conurbation.[49] But until the end of World War II, Black Eagle's residents saw their small town as a discrete place with a distinct culture, and residents of Great Falls saw themselves as markedly different from the immigrants across the river.[50] Immigrants' experiences in Black Eagle and Great Falls were quite different from their counterparts in Butte, which were controlled by immigrants and their children.

The ACM's employment policies served as a crucial counterbalance to the effort by some Great Falls residents to define Black Eagle's immigrants as nonwhite. The company had prompted immigrants to move there and saw the continued growth of that labor supply as essential to their production plans. Many employers across the United States saw southern and eastern European immigration as a plentiful source of hard workers. Language differences, job competition, and the practice of separating racial-ethnic groups in the workplace made collective action by immigrants difficult to organize, keeping wages low and profits high. In the smelter, however, workers of different racial-ethnic backgrounds were not segregated, nor were native-born and immigrant workers pitted against one another.[51]

Instead, southeastern European immigrants and native-born workers together feared employers would introduce African Americans to the workforce. Immigrants who found themselves placed further down the racial hierarchy sought to avoid being associated with black workers for fear of the degradation that a nonwhite identity entailed.[52] By the early twentieth century, when the Great Northern Railroad, one of the area's largest industrial employers, had hired a number of black workers, there were enough African Americans in Great Falls for employers to consider hiring them as a way of dividing the working class. But, even though the other large industrial employer in the area had done so and the ACM employed black workers at other company facilities, the Anaconda Company had a de facto policy barring the employment of African Americans in Black Eagle just as they did in Butte. Eugene Cox, personnel manager at the Black Eagle smelter, remembered: "Over here . . . I was just simply told don't hire 'em. And that come from [the head office in] Butte."[53]

The way race worked in the smelter changed around World War I when the ACM hired not African Americans but "a lot of Indians" to replace men who had been drafted. Great Falls' "Landless Indians," from which the majority of the smelter's Indian workers came, had varied tribal affiliations. Some were Métis, of mixed French and indigenous ancestry. Others had ties to the Turtle Mountain Band of the Chippewa, or the Little Shell Band of the Chippewa, or, through intermarriage, to other tribes and to the white community. No matter their individual background, each member of the community shared a history of dispossession.[54] Why did the ACM bar African Americans, even when many other employers turned to them during World War I, but hire Indians to work at the Black Eagle smelter? Why did Black Eagle's immigrants not seek to block the employment of this community of color? Black Eagle managers, for their part, shared aspects of the worldview of local liberal elites, including Charlie Russell whose paintings portrayed Indians as noble victims of modernity. Most whites in the West still exhibited racial hostility toward Indians, but liberals sought to "help" them. Coupled with the demand for labor at the smelter, this racial ideology motivated ACM managers to offer Landless Indians jobs.

Immigrants' willingness to work alongside Indians potentially stemmed from a number of sources. It could have resulted from still vibrant working-class radicalism reflected by the presence of the Industrial Workers of the World (IWW, or Wobblies) in Montana's copper communities during the World War I period.[55] Like the more famous case of Butte workers, some men in Black Eagle responded positively to the IWW's calls for class-based militancy. It is unclear whether they received the Wobblies' message of interracial cooperation in the same way that some in Butte did. Significantly, however, the mob that lynched Frank Little, an IWW organizer, in Butte in 1917 targeted a mixed-race Indian.[56] But more probably, immigrant men might simply have lacked the power to prevent the employment of Indians in the smelter. During the World War I period, when immigrants and especially those accused of radicalism came under attack, immigrant workers across the United States lost power in their workplaces. Fractures in Montana's labor movement exacerbated this loss of power.[57] In Black Eagle, these circumstances and the company's continued antiunion activities harmed the relationship between immigrant workers and smelter management, sapping the ability of immigrant workers to use collective bargaining to better their lot or to fight against changes at the smelter they opposed, like the employment of Indians, for a decade and a half.

The relationship between Black Eagle's immigrant workers and the plant's managers became more cordial toward the end of the 1920s, the same time that a drought struck the northern plains, driving more Indians toward Great Falls.[58] At the onset of the Great Depression, the Landless Indian community occupied shelters in an area just below and less than a mile west of Black Eagle along the banks of the Missouri River.[59] It was at this Landless Indian camp and at the smelter that the next critical moment in the formation of immigrant racialization occurred. On May 7, 1932, the ACM instituted what the plant's manager called a "mass shut down." The question became not how many men could share the work but whether the smelter would employ anyone at all. By the end of the year, operations had once again resumed, but the smelter employed only 684 men, the majority of whom were working even fewer shifts than before, down from 1,400 workers before the shutdown.[60]

No matter how much they appreciated the corporate welfare initiatives that helped prompt the change in the relationship between workers and managers in the 1920s, the shutdown tested the faith of the immigrant smelter men who remained on the rolls. At this very moment, management helped solidify immigrants' claims to white identity: employees and employer joined to force Indians from the smelter. Nearly simultaneously, whites burned the riverside camps to the ground. We know more about their exclusion from employment than about the attack on their community, though burning down Chinatowns was a popular tactic across the West and perhaps served as a template for this assault. One Black Eagle worker's recollections hint at the all-too-familiar mechanism of accusation blended with stereotype used to remove Indian workers from the plant: "The Indians, they stole too many things. In fact they cleaned out one of the welding shops for the Zinc plant. They had all the stuff, but [the company] found it. Finally we just had to eliminate the Indians, that was all. I'll never forget it."[61]

Although competition for work in lean times also caused tensions among Black Eagle's European immigrant groups, Croatian and Italian workers "never forgot" the power they exercised in the ouster of Indian workers. They also used the incident to assert that honesty and hard work, the hallmarks of white masculine labor, were intrinsic to their character.[62] Equally compelling for their claim to whiteness, they displayed their ability to mobilize one of the principal tools of white privilege: control over property and access to jobs.

Ironically for the ACM management, which colluded with workers in the removal of Indians from the smelter and the community, the sense of mutuality that the expulsion reinforced was instrumental in securing an even greater level of worker control over jobs as a result of the plant's first major strike on June 7, 1934. The 950 daily wage men employed at the smelter banded together in opposition to the ACM-controlled company union that had been in place for over a decade. Like their fellow copper workers and ACM employees in Butte and Anaconda, and indeed like workers across the United States, Black Eagle's workers drew inspiration to strike from the National Industrial Recovery Act (NIRA), which offered federal support for collective bargaining. Butte-based activists took the lead in reestablishing Mine Mill in Montana's major copper production facilities.[63] Mine Mill's renaissance served to bring working men together across regional and racial-ethnic lines. In Black Eagle the resurrection of the union along with collective antipathy to American Indian workers appeared to end years of low-level tension and even occasional violence between Black Eagle men and the smelter workers of Great Falls.[64] This solidarity bolstered white and white ethnic men's power to control access to scarce jobs. The ability to bring home a decent paycheck during these difficult times, though still sporadic, bolstered both the masculinity and whiteness of Black Eagle's immigrant men. The unusual relationship between immigrant workers in Black Eagle and the company they worked for was essential in shaping racial and gender formation for the next decade.

By the mid-1930s, the growing panethnic sensibility in Butte and Black Eagle, the support of first- and second-generation immigrant copper men, and the reemergence of Mine Mill under progressive leadership suggested that local ideologies about race were changing dramatically. Butte's and Black Eagle's copper workers reinforced this perception by providing major funding for Mine Mill's organizing campaigns among African American workers in the Southeast and Mexican and Mexican American workers in the Southwest and by seeming to support Mine Mill's broader interracial platform.[65] In reality, as World War II would show, these developments served to obscure the continuation of fraught relationships between local immigrants and race. That Butte and Black Eagle copper workers handled the war's challenges to their identity differently than not only other groups of first- and second-generation European immigrant men, but also each other, further underscores the importance of being attuned to the "locally made" aspects of immigrant identity, especially in that most fascinating and complex of regions, the Far West.

Notes

1. A fuller treatment of the topics considered in this essay, and an exploration of the interrelated process of gender formation, appears in Matthew Basso, *Meet Joe Copper: Masculinity and Race on Montana's World War II Home Front* (Chicago: University of Chicago Press, 2013). *Meet Joe Copper* also examines the immigrant history of Anaconda, the third major copper town in Montana. Scholarship on white racial formation includes: David R. Roediger, *The Wages of Whiteness: Race and the Making of the American Working Class* (New York: Verso, 1990); Noel Ignatiev, *How the Irish Became White* (New York: Routledge, 1995); Matthew Frye Jacobson, *Whiteness of a Different Color: European Immigrants and the Alchemy of Race* (Cambridge: Harvard University Press, 1998); Thomas Guglielmo, *White on Arrival: Italians, Race, Color, and Power in Chicago, 1890–1945* (New York: Oxford University Press, 2003).
2. The aspect of identity that around World War II came to be called "ethnicity," prior to that was called "race." Beginning locally in the 1880s, the rhetoric of racial ranking—found in terms like "bohunk," "dago," and "wop," for example—was

deployed against and by European "immigrants" as part of a larger effort to create and enforce a hierarchy of races that had material and psychological effects. The idea of someone being part of a "race," however, also bonded groups of immigrants. Being Italian or Croatian or Irish was a key part of identity that the vast majority of immigrants discussed in this study were not keen to shed. My use of the term "racial-ethnic" throughout this essay is meant to reference both this range of meanings and this history.

3. Joe Navarro's characterization of Butte's neighborhoods—"the Dublin Gulch was Irish, and Broadway Street was all Finlanders. Meaderville was strictly Bohunks and Italians"—is echoed by numerous sources. Joe Navarro, interview by Laurie Mercier, March 25, 1983, Montana Historical Society Research Center (hereafter MHSRC); "Montana State Guide—Butte," June 15, 1938, Folder 27, Box 26, WPA Records, MC77, MHSRC; Pat Kearney, *Butte Voices: Mining, Neighborhoods, People* (Butte: Skyhigh Communications, 1998), 161–258.
4. Writers Project of Montana, *Copper Camp: The Lusty Story of Butte, Montana, The Richest Hill on Earth* (1943; Helena: Riverbend Publishing, 2002), 11.
5. David Emmons, *The Butte Irish: Class and Ethnicity in an American Mining Town, 1875–1925* (Urbana: University of Illinois Press, 1989), 13, 63; Michael P. Malone, *The Battle for Butte: Mining and Politics on the Northern Frontier, 1864–1906* (Seattle: University of Washington Press, 2006), 64–67.
6. Writers Project, *Copper Camp*, 11.
7. Ibid., 6, 11, 61, 222; Emmons, *The Butte Irish*, 13, 63.
8. Matthew Guterl, *The Color of Race in America, 1900–1940* (Cambridge, MA: Harvard University Press, 2001), 15–19; Kevin Kenny, "Race, Violence, and the Anti-Irish Sentiment in the Nineteenth Century," in *Making the Irish American: History and Heritage of the Irish in the United States*, ed. J. J. Lee and Marion R. Casey (New York: New York University Press, 2006), 364–78; Matthew Frye Jacobsen, *Barbarian Virtues: The United States Encounters Foreign Peoples at Home and Abroad, 1876–1917* (New York: Macmillan, 2001), 180–95; Ignatiev, *How the Irish Became White*.
9. Madison Grant, *The Passing of the Great Race; or, The Racial Basis of European History* (New York: Charles Scribner's Sons, 1916), 86, 107–11. On the popularity of Grant and more generally on racial thinking during this time, see Guterl, *The Color of Race*, 32–55.
10. Ronald C. Brown, *Hard-Rock Miners: The Intermountain West, 1860–1920* (College Station: Texas A&M University Press, 1979), 134; Emmons, *The Butte Irish*, 246–47.
11. Writers Project, *Copper Camp*, 33; Emmons, *The Butte Irish*, *passim*; Murphy, *Mining Cultures*, 136–68.
12. Emmons, *The Butte Irish*, 223–31.
13. Robert R. Swartout Jr., "Kwangtung to Big Sky: the Chinese in Montana, 1864–1900," *Montana: The Magazine of Western History* 38, no. 1 (Winter 1988): 42–53; Stacy A. Flaherty, "Boycott in Butte: Organized Labor and the Chinese Community, 1896–1897," *Montana: The Magazine of Western History* 37, no. 1 (Winter 1987): 34–47. More generally, see Erica Lee, *At America's Gates: Chinese Immigration during the Exclusion Era, 1882–1943* (Chapel Hill: University of North Carolina Press, 2004); and Henry Yu, *Thinking Orientals: Migration,*

Contact, and Exoticism in Modern America (New York: Oxford University Press, 2002).

14. Mark Wyman, *Hard Rock Epic: Western Miners and the Industrial Revolution, 1860–1910* (Berkeley: University of California Press, 1979,) 37–41; Writers Project, *Copper Camp*, 48.
15. Emmons, *The Butte Irish*, 224. Isaac F. Marcosson, *Anaconda* (New York: Dodd, Mead & Company, 1957), 90–119; Emmons, *The Butte Irish*, 245, 257; Malone, *The Battle for Butte*, 69.
16. Ibid.
17. Emmons, *The Butte Irish*, 245, 257; Malone, *The Battle for Butte*, 69. Further unsettling Butte's social politics, Irish BMU leaders were facing a significant shift within the union's core membership. Malone, *The Battle for Butte*, 65.
18. Writers Project, *Copper Camp*, 140–44; Richard White, *It's Your Misfortune and None of My Own* (Norman: University of Oklahoma Press, 1993), 289; "The Story of the Butte Bo-hunk—The Dark Skinned Invader," *Butte Evening News*, July 24, 1910.
19. Ibid.
20. Ibid; Writers Project, *Copper Camp*, 141–44.
21. On the Padrone system, see Gunther Peck, *Reinventing Free Labor: Padrones and Immigrant Workers in the North American West, 1880–1930* (New York: Cambridge University Press, 2000).
22. On Butte's African American community, see Matthew Basso, "Metal of Honor: Montana's World War II Homefront, Movies, and the Social Politics of White Male Anxiety" (PhD diss., University of Minnesota, 2001), 104–50; Perdita Duncan, Walter Duncan, William Fenter, Elmo Fortune, and notes made by Mrs. Lena Brown, interview by Laurie Mercier, March 24, 1983, MHSRC; Rex C. Myers, "Montana's Negro Newspapers, 1894–1911," *Montana Journalism Review*, 16 (1973): 17–22; Lucille Smith Thompson and Alma Smith Jacobs, *The Negro in Montana 1800–1945: A Selective Bibliography* (Helena: Montana State Library, 1970). For a masterful overview of the African American experience in the West, see Quintard Taylor, *In Search of the Racial Frontier: African Americans in the American West, 1528–1990* (New York: W. W. Norton and Company, 1998).
23. Black residents recall that discrimination was an ever-present part of life in Butte. Duncan, Duncan, Fenter, Fortune, Brown, interview; Taylor, *In Search of the Racial Frontier*, 194–96.
24. Murphy, *Mining Cultures*, 113, 151, 152; Writers Project, *Copper Camp*, 144. On panethnicity between Irish and other immigrants, see David Roediger and James Barrett, "Making New Immigrants 'Inbetween': Irish Hosts and White Panethnicity, 1890 to 1930," in *Not Just Black and White: Historical and Contemporary Perspectives on Immigration, Race, and Ethnicity in the United States*, ed. Nancy Foner and George M. Frederickson (New York: Russell Sage Foundation, 2004), 167–96.
25. Duncan, Duncan, Fenter, Fortune, Brown, interview.
26. "Shack Towns on River Near New Town Spur Hill into Action," *Great Falls Leader*, Nov. 11, 1959; Walter Valacich, interview by Laurie Mercier, July 17, 1986, MHRSC. On the debate over the character of immigration and what forces compel it, see Gary Gerstle, "Liberty, Coercion, and the Making of Americans," *Journal of American History* 84, no. 2 (September 1997): 524–58. Regarding the

Irish in Black Eagle, the Garrity family, proud of their Irish heritage like many in Montana, recall in their family history that when they arrived in Black Eagle in 1929 they "were the only ones at the time of Irish descent and speaking only one language, English." Their Croatian and Italian neighbors welcomed them warmly and invited them to participate in their culture, but the strongest bond was the church. Black Eagle Book Committee, *In the Shadow of the Big Stack: Black Eagle* (Black Eagle, MT: Black Eagle Book Committee, 2000), 109.

27. Black Eagle Book Committee, *In the Shadow*, 6–12.
28. Walt Valacich, "First Croats and Slovenes Came to Area in 1890 to Work at Smelter," *Great Falls Tribune*, March 25, 1984; "[Photograph of "Croatian Nightingale Band" from 1908]," *Great Falls Leader*, November 11, 1959; Jennie Signori, interview by Laurie Mercier, April 23, 1987, MHSRC. Black Eagle residents noted that Bribir was "not far from Italian border." Black Eagle Book Committee, *In the Shadow*, 43.
29. For a cogent rendering of networks and push and pull factors, see Lucie Cheng and Edna Bonacich, eds., *Labor Migration under Capitalism: Asian Workers in the United States before World War II* (Berkeley: University of California Press, 1984).
30. Valacich, "First Croats"; Olanda Rinari Vangelisti and Claire Vangelisti Del Guerra, interviewed by Laurie Mercier, July 16, 1986, MHSRC; Amelia Polich, interviewed by Laurie Mercier, March 13, 1986, MHSRC. Swedes and Germans also had a presence in Black Eagle. Joan Earl, interviewed by Laurie Mercier, January 19, 1988, MHSRC. On chain migration to Montana's copper communities by southeastern Europeans, see Anne Prebil, interviewed by Laurie Mercier, July 10, 1986, MHSRC; Emelia Tabaracci Qunell, interview by Laurie Mercier, February 6, 1986, MHSRC; Black Eagle Book Committee, *In the Shadow*, 24–27; Kathleen Conzen, "Mainstreams and Side Channels: The Localization of Immigrant Cultures," *Journal of American Ethnic History* 11, no. 1 (Fall 1991): 5–20.
31. On enclaves, see John Bodnar, *Workers' World: Kinship, Community, and Protest in an Industrial Society, 1900–1940* (Baltimore: Johns Hopkins University Press, 1982), 63–66.
32. Vangelisti and Del Guerra, interview. Smelterman William Tonkovich lived on a typical block; it housed Croatians, Italians, Dalmatians, and some Norwegians. William Tonkovich, interviewed by Laurie Mercier, February 27, 1986, MHSRC. Some Black Eagle residents saw Butte as an example of ethnic segregation. Qunell, interview. For one account that details such traditional splits, see Ronald Bayor, *Neighbors in Conflict: The Irish, Germans, Jews, and Italians of New York City, 1929–1941* (Baltimore: Johns Hopkins University Press, 1978).
33. Polich, interview; Qunell, interview; Black Eagle Book Committee, *In the Shadow*, 109, 319, 388; Prebil, interview; Nancy C. Carnevale, *A New Language, A New World: Italian Immigrants in the United States, 1890–1945* (Urbana: University of Illinois Press, 2009); Philip Gleason, *Speaking of Diversity: Language and Ethnicity in Twentieth Century America* (Baltimore: Johns Hopkins University Press, 1992).
34. Black Eagle Book Committee, *In the Shadow*, 433–35.
35. Desmond S. King, *Making Americans: Immigration, Race, and the Origins of the Diverse Democracy* (Cambridge, MA: Harvard University Press, 2002), 29–30, 35, 44; Johnathan Zimmerman, "Ethnics against Ethnicity: European Immigrants and

Foreign-Language Instruction, 1890–1940," *Journal of American History* 88, no. 4 (March 2003): 1383–1404.

36. Richard Jules Oestreicher, *Solidarity and Fragmentation: Working People and Class Consciousness in Detroit, 1875–1900* (Urbana: University of Illinois Press, 1989). On the history and practice of associational life in Montana, see Emmons, *The Butte Irish*, 94–132; and Murphy, *Mining Cultures*, 136–62. Nationally, see Mary Ann Clawson, *Constructing Brotherhood: Class, Gender, and Fraternalism* (Princeton: Princeton University Press, 1989).
37. Valacich, "First Croats"; Black Eagle Book Committee, *In the Shadow*, 27–29, 39, 501.
38. Tonkovich, interview; Signori, interview; Black Eagle Book Committee, *In the Shadow*, 27–28.
39. "The History of Blessed Sacrament Parish, Black Eagle, Montana," n.d., and "The Church History of the Black Eagle Parish for the 50th Anniversary of the Blessed Sacrament Church," December 16, 1972, both in Diocese of Great Falls–Billings Archives. Vangelisti and Del Guerra, interview; Tonkovich, interview; Qunell, interview; Earl, interview; Black Eagle Book Committee, *In the Shadow*, 5, 27, 34, 424–26.
40. Qunell, interview; Signori, interview. For a fuller picture of the relationship between immigrants, Catholicism, and gender formation, see Colleen McDannell, "True Men as We Need Them: Catholicism and the Irish Male," *American Studies* 27, no. 2 (Fall 1986): 19–36; Colleen McDannell, "Catholic Domesticity, 1860–1960," in *American Catholic Women: A Historical Exploration*, ed. Karen Kennelly, CSJ (New York: MacMillan Publishing Company, 1989), 48–80; Robert A. Orsi, *Thank You, St. Jude: Women's Devotion to the Patron Saint of Hopeless Causes* (New Haven: Yale University Press, 1996), 71–94.
41. See, for example, McDannell, "True Men"; Kevin Murphy, *Political Manhood: Red Bloods, Mollycoddles, and the Politics of Progressive Era Reform* (New York: Columbia University Press, 2008), 38–103.
42. Edward Reynolds, "Anaconda," in *Men at Work: Stories of People at Their Jobs in America*, ed. Harold Rosenberg, unpublished manuscript, "Writers' Program, Work Projects Administration," 1941, folder 1 and 2, box A-852, WPA Records, Library of Congress.
43. "Story of the Butte Bo-hunk"; Clarence Silloway, interview by Laurie Mercier, July 15, 1986, MHSRC; Cox, interview.
44. For a fuller description of areas in the plant, see Black Eagle Book Committee, *In the Shadow*, 9–11. Eric Foner, *Free Soil, Free Labor, Free Men: The Ideology of the Republican Party before the Civil War* (New York: Oxford University Press, 1970); Roediger, *The Wages of Whiteness*.
45. Tonkovich, interview.
46. Signori, interview; Guterl, *The Color of Race*; Guglielmo, *White on Arrival*.
47. Fights did occur occasionally between Croatians and Italians. Silloway, interview; Guglielmo, *White on Arrival*.
48. Great Falls was home to a large Anglo population, as well as a substantial number of first-, second-, and third-generation immigrants, a small African American community, and a sizable Native American community. Del Guerra says that ethnics in Black Eagle "were much closer as a community because of the pressure

to abandon" their culture and assimilate. Vangelisti and Del Guerra, interview; Valacich, interview.

49. Richard B. Roeder, "A Settlement on the Plains: Paris Gibson and the Building of Great Falls," *Montana: The Magazine of Western History* 42, no. 4 (Autumn 1992): 4–19.
50. Godlewski, interview; Valacich, interview; and Tonkovich, interview. Valacich claims that Black Eagle's immigrants were refused work in Great Falls.
51. Cox, interview; Black Eagle Book Committee, *In the Shadow*, 119.
52. David Roediger, *Working Toward Whiteness: How America's Immigrant Became White: The Strange Journey from Ellis Island to the Suburbs* (New York: Basic Books, 2006).
53. Residents suggested that the company saw Black Eagle's ethnic groups as "valuable people to society and the community." Vangelisti and Del Guerra, interview; Silloway, interview.
54. Tessman, interview. A precise historical accounting of the shifting population of Great Falls' Landless Indian community is virtually impossible, but the following sources are enlightening: "Population of Hill 57 Tribal Affiliation," November 6, 1955, available in Hill 57 Vertical File, MHSRC; "Large Percentage of Hill 57 Residents Originally Turtle Mountain Chippewa," *Great Falls Tribune*, September 6, 1955.
55. Valacich, interview. On the connection between the IWW and Indian employment, see Silloway, interview; "Montana State Guide—Great Falls," folder 28, box 26, WPA Records, MHSRC.
56. Melvin Dubofsky, *We Shall Be All: A History of the Industrial Workers of the World* (New York: Quadrangle Books, 1969), 369; Philip S. Foner, *History of the Labor Movement in the United States, World War I, 1914–1918* (New York: International Publishers Co., 1987), 247; Michael Punke, *Fire and Brimstone: The North Butte Disaster of 1917* (New York: Hyperion, 2007), 202.
57. Malone, *The Battle for Butte*; Emmons, *The Butte Irish*.
58. During the 1920s the Anaconda Company, which had joined employers across the United States in utilizing an oppositional management style during the World War I era, shifted toward the "kinder and gentler" but no less coercive style of labor relations called "paternalism." Lizabeth Cohen, *Making a New Deal: Industrial Workers in Chicago, 1919–1939* (New York: Cambridge University Press, 1989); Gerald Zahavi, *Workers, Managers, and Welfare Capitalism: The Shoemakers and Tanners of Endicott Johnson, 1890–1950* (Urbana: University of Illinois Press, 1988); Tom Dickson, interview by Laurie Mercier, May 30, 1986, MHSRC.
59. Ties to immigrant identity were also maintained into the World War II period by shopping at Black Eagle's local ethnic markets. The continuation of this practice put Black Eagle outside of national trends. Black Eagle Book Committee, *In the Shadow*, 406–7.
60. R. B. Caples to W. B. Daly, January 11, 1932, folder 1, box 219, ACM Co. Records, MHSRC; "Notice to Employees," April 23, 1930; and "Share the Work" worksheet, December 20, 1932, folder 8, box 229, folder 8, ACM Co. Records, MHSRC.
61. Silloway, interview.
62. Black Eagle's second-generation immigrant children "played Indian" during this

same period, a practice, as Philip Deloria has argued, that was part of claiming whiteness. Black Eagle Book Committee, *In the Shadow*, 441; Philip Deloria, *Playing Indian* (New Haven: Yale University Press, 1998), 95–107.

63. Black Eagle's workers joined the strike a month after Butte miners initiated it. Ward Kinney, "Montana Challenges the Tyranny of Copper," *The Nation*, July 25, 1934, 98–99; Polich, interview; "Montana State Guide—Great Falls," June 17, 1938, folder 28, box 26, WPA Records, MHSRC; U.S. Department of Labor to Anaconda Copper Mining Company, Great Falls, June 16, 1934, folder 8, box 229, ACM Co. Records, MHSRC; Deloria, *Playing Indian*.
64. For this dating see Tonkovich, interview; Michael Denning, *The Cultural Front: The Laboring of American Culture in the Twentieth Century* (New York: Verso, 1997); "Montana State Guide—Great Falls."
65. Mercier, *Anaconda*, 31. On smelter men's cross-ethnic male bond, see Sister Gilmary Vaughan, interview by Laurie Mercier, July 30, 1986, MHSRC; Robin D. G. Kelley, *Hammer and Hoe: Alabama Communists during the Great Depression* (Chapel Hill: University of North Carolina Press, 1990).

PART II

Why We Came and What We Made of It

Jessie L. Embry and Brian Q. Cannon

Why have immigrants come to the American West? There have been almost as many reasons as immigrants. Some were seeking adventure, escaping an old way of life, or desiring a change. Others moved to join family. Some sought the company of those with similar beliefs or left because of poor economic or political conditions.

It is equally difficult to cite a single example of how immigrants experienced the Far West, or what they achieved or made of their experiences. Some came with established careers that they were able to continue in their new location, but others had to work in jobs far below their experience and education because of language difficulties. Some came with nothing and worked at menial jobs. While they did not improve their economic status, they provided greater opportunities for their children. Others came with nothing and left with nothing. Some found greater political freedom; others found life restrictive in the United States. There have likely been as many outcomes as there were reasons for immigrating.

This introduction provides a contextual overview of why immigrants came and what their lives were like in the American West. We first outline theories that social scientists have developed to explain migration. Next, we briefly identify variables that affected immigrants' achievements in America, including group identity and dynamics, drawing upon theories that scholars have developed to explain how groups adjust to their new surroundings. Finally, we relate illustrative stories of individual immigrants, exploring their reasons for coming and how they adapted to life in the United States.

Theoretical Insights Regarding Why We Came

Many scholars refer to "push" and "pull" factors when explaining why people moved to America. The idea that immigrants came to the United States because they were "pulled" by upswings in the American economy was proposed by economist Harry Jerome in 1926. In 1935, Dorothy Swaine Thomas used the theory for the first time in a study of European immigrants.[1] Some economists, including Brinley Thomas in 1954, correlated the pull of an expanding American economy with the push of a contracting economy in immigrants' native lands. Historians also referred to factors abroad that pulled immigrants to America. Writing in 1940, Marcus Lee Hansen, sometimes viewed as the "father of immigration history," saw America as "a huge magnet of varying intensity, drawing the people of Europe from those regions where conditions made them mobile and from which transportation provided a path."[2] Philip Taylor used the same image in his 1971 study *The Distant Magnet.* With regard to the United States, he wrote, "Economic growth [and] the freedom built into its institutions . . . possess[ed] advantages that no other overseas land could rival."[3]

By that time, some historians were questioning the United States' exceptionalism as an immigrant destination, or the "pull" part of the push-pull equation. After explaining that European immigrants moved to many countries including Argentina, Canada, Australia, and New Zealand, British historian Frank Thistlethwaite concluded in 1964, "We are a long way from a simple case of America fever."[4] In 1985 John Bodnar trenchantly questioned the allure of the United States as an overriding pull factor: "If immigration was caused largely by the lure of America, then we would expect that struggling people everywhere would come here in relatively equal numbers with common intentions and . . . backgrounds." Since that did not happen, Bodnar argued, push factors in the immigrants' homelands such as the dislocations wrought by agricultural modernization and industrialization must have brought most people to the United States.[5]

Some scholars have approached push and pull factors in the context of international capitalism, dividing the world into dominant economic core nations and dependent peripheries.[6] Economists proposed that workers respond to the laws of supply and demand and rational choice by relocating to places where work is abundant in order to maximize their economic prospects. They also pointed out that international capitalist investment displaces residents of third-world nations and compels migration.[7] Historians Gilbert G. Gonzalez and Raul A. Fernandez showed how those factors especially influenced Mexican immigration in light of Mexico's economic relationship to the United States.[8]

Other studies expanded on push and pull forces and discussed other considerations. In 1966, Everett S. Lee listed four factors that impelled immigration. The first two are essentially push and pull. But Lee described them as "factors associated with the area of origin" and "factors associated with the area of destination," rather than using those value-laden terms, which imply negative conditions in the homeland and positive conditions in the country of destination. Lee's other two reasons for immigration were "intervening obstacles" and "personal factors." Intervening obstacles include the distances to be traveled and physical barriers such as mountain ranges or oceans, legal restrictions on immigration, the cost of moving, and the presence of dependents whose needs must be accommodated by the migrant. Lee underscored the importance both of actual conditions and of how prospective migrants perceive those conditions.[9]

Sociologists Alejandro Portes and Rubén G. Rumbaut identified two additional preconditions for migration: the migrants' knowledge that workers are needed, and workers' perception that moving will be advantageous. They theorized that the impetus for migration to the United States changed during the twentieth century. Early in the century, the nation was industrializing rapidly and needed workers, "but because its lifestyle was not a global standard and its economic opportunities were not well known, it had to resort to direct recruitment." For example, railroads, mines, and smelters in the American West needed workers and hired recruiters to find people who were willing to come. As American economic opportunities became better known, recruitment was no longer necessary. Migration became "self-sustaining and virtually unstoppable" as "family imperatives, transnational entrepreneurial opportunities, and other considerations linked to the web of transaction between sending areas and their expatriate communities [took] over as engines of the movement."[10]

In addition to influence from these factors, migratory decisions are influenced by personal considerations such as age, stage in lifecycle, personal disposition, and agency. Children often immigrate involuntarily when their parents decide to move; independent young adults may be more likely to emigrate than people who are more established. Some migrants are easily dissatisfied or may desire a new adventure even if conditions are very good in their native lands. As Lee explains, "The decision to migrate . . . is never completely rational."[11]

Conceptualizing What We Made of It

Just as it is hard to generalize about "what we came for," there is no single generalization for "what we made of it." As Elliott Barkan observed, "whether we speak of the 1870s, 1920s, 1970s, or early 2000s," immigrants generally have sought economic stability and adjusted the "balance between integrated, translocal, and transnational life styles" with stability in mind. In their quest for material progress, most immigrants have accommodated "the unifying elements within the host (or settlement) society" in terms of language, group membership, and daily interaction, sometimes at the expense of "homeland ties."[12]

Sociologist Ewa Morawska identified several variables that affect immigrants' opportunities and fortunes in the United States. These include the timing of their arrival in America, the region in which they settle, the jobs they obtain, and the class-based ties and identity politics in their workplace and marketplace.[13]

In their efforts to shape their lives in America, immigrants are empowered or constrained by their "human capital," or their skills and abilities, including education, literacy, health, occupational skills, and language abilities. Portes and Rumbaut distinguished between four types of modern immigrants with varying degrees of human capital: professionals, entrepreneurs, laborers, and refugees. Professionals come with high educational and occupational capital, assets that are valued by U.S. immigration policy. Entrepreneurs come with the skill, ambition, and savings or access to credit necessary to start businesses. Most immigrants come as laborers. The final category, refugees and asylees, often come to escape political problems in their own countries. These four categories of immigrants differ markedly in their experiences. Many professionals find it relatively easy to adjust, especially if they also have high English proficiency. However, language barriers or licensing requirements in the United States impede others. Entrepreneurs sometimes start out as peddlers or small business owners in America, but they often expand their businesses. Laborers face higher risks of injury on the job and job loss. Nevertheless, over time many laborers manage to gain more education and move up the economic ladder. As they vacate their entry-level manual labor jobs, new immigrants fill those positions. Refugees and asylees often come with nothing and receive special legal status and protection.[14]

Historically, "what we made of it" depended not only on individual choices and assets but on ethnic group dynamics and constraints, particularly for those who settled in ethnic neighborhoods. Ethnic clustering did not always arise purely by choice. Sometimes the dominant society barred newcomers from settling next door through laws, restrictive covenants, or intimidation.

Ethnic neighborhoods provided advantages and disadvantages for immigrants. In his study of Mexican Americans in Los Angeles, George J. Sanchez summarized the key benefits and shortcomings of residential clustering for Mexican Americans: "At times, the barrio was for some a stifling, restrictive environment. Strong cultural norms were enforced which kept the community at least outwardly familiar to most newcomers from Mexico. More often than not, however, the barrio provided a haven for Mexican immigrants and American-born Chicanos. There they could adapt to American society while still retaining in their daily lives much of the flavor of Mexico."[15]

Economic opportunities varied in ethnic neighborhoods. Most immigrants from southern and eastern Europe between 1890 and 1914 worked in established American factories owned by old-stock Americans but lived in ethnic neighborhoods and patronized social institutions ranging from mutual aid societies to parish schools. Some ethnic neighborhoods became "ethnic enclaves" in which immigrants themselves owned most of the businesses which were staffed almost exclusively by their compatriots.[16]

While some immigrants remained in these ethnic neighborhoods and enclaves, many immigrants or their descendants integrated socially and economically and eventually moved away. By the second and third generation, this caused many ethnic communities that were not infused with new waves of immigrants to decline. While increasing residential integration was the dominant pattern for second- and third-generation immigrants, there were exceptions. Some groups and individuals assimilated more slowly and some groups remained tightly segregated in order to achieve cultural or religious objectives.[17]

The fact that immigrants moved away from ethnic neighborhoods did not necessarily indicate that they had lost their ethnic group identity. Kathleen Neils Conzen pointed out that many pre–World War I German out-migrants lived in heterogeneous neighborhoods, spoke English, and appeared to assimilate, but they returned to their ethnic neighborhoods periodically as a cultural reference point and as a source of ethnic services. They retained a "kind of biculturalism in spite of structural assimilation." This ended when repression during the war made the cost of bicultural identity too high.[18]

Whether they live within ethnic neighborhoods or in the larger community, immigrant groups acquire and deploy many types of capital to shape life in their new setting. The first immigrant members of an ethnic group come with few, if any, social ties to others in the area. Those who follow depend on these pioneers for support, and the ethnic group's social capital develops over time. Those who settle in ethnic neighborhoods network with their new neighbors. They cultivate additional ties with coworkers and employers. Immigrants also find common experience and network with the larger community through sports, religion, and other interests.

Political culture and influence can be another type of capital. As immigrants in the past faced new economic and social challenges in the United States, some drew upon political culture and views from their collective past to promote change. A minority of immigrants from Europe and Asia were skilled workers who had experience with unions and a "well developed working-class movement." These immigrants included skilled Germans, Finns who worked in mining towns and logging camps, and Jews who led the unionization of textile workers. These workers often turned to strikes and civil disobedience in an effort to improve their working and living conditions. However, most immigrants in the early twentieth century were politically inexperienced peasants. Strikes often failed to stop production because of the constant flow of new arrivals. New immigrant groups were brought to work as strikebreakers and took over the unfilled jobs, an action that led to ethnic resentment. Eventually some strikebreakers also recognized a need for change. In some places, the different nationalities combined forces to stage strikes. The degree of interethnic cooperation depended on how many and which ethnic groups were represented in a community.[19]

In time, most immigrant groups in the twentieth century adapted to the American political system and even used it to their advantage, especially on the local level, where they elected their own as aldermen and mayors. Some immigrants coalesced in panethnic political movements based upon common concerns and based partly upon the fact that the U.S. government and many Americans lumped immigrant nationalities together by referring to them as Asian Americans, Polynesian Americans, and Hispanic Americans. For example, immigrant workers called for "A Day Without Immigrants" on May Day 2006 to show the importance of these groups in the U.S. economy.[20] Latinos and supporters refused to go to work or make purchases to show how important immigrants, including undocumented ones, were to the U.S. economy. Jaime Contreras, president of the National Capital Immigrant Coalition, used the 1965 Selma, Alabama, slogan: "Today we march, tomorrow we vote."[21]

Another type of collective social capital that immigrants possess arises from affiliation with a religious community. For the most part, religion was not the reason immigrants came to the United States and did not structure the reception they received once they arrived. However, as Portes and Rumbaut explained, religion smoothed the transition for religiously active immigrants and sometimes shielded newcomers from nativist attacks. In these respects, religious capital was something that many immigrants mobilized to enhance their experience. Churches supported immigrants by providing three things: "refuge, respect, and resources." First, they offered a refuge from "the traumas of resettlement" by providing "comfort and protection." Second, churches gave newcomers "a sense of self worth." And finally, churches helped immigrants to claim moral respectability, discipline, and the attendant economic benefits.[22]

Religious capital also helped second-generation immigrants. By providing private schools, religious programs, and health facilities, the Catholic Church enriched the lives of Irish, Italian, and Polish immigrants' children. Religion tied generations together and sometimes helped the second generation avoid criminal activity, drugs, and gangs.[23] Portes and Rumbaut concluded, "Because religion has proven to be one of the resilient elements of immigrants' culture across generations, the beliefs and organized activities carried out by foreign groups in this realm can be expected to be a trademark of their long-term incorporation into American society and, simultaneously, a key force guiding the character of this process" for all religions including Protestants, Buddhists, Hindus, and Muslims.[24]

Why We Came and What We Made of It—Individual Stories

The sagas of individual western immigrants illustrate how broad structural forces, individual choice, personal disposition, and human capital shaped migratory decisions and outcomes. As Elliott Barkan observed in his history of immigration, "These specific narrative portraits . . . can frequently convey in concrete, personal ways the dynamics only sketched on the broader group-oriented canvases."[25]

The story of Aaron Meier, a German Jewish immigrant, illustrates how persistence, luck, capital, and social networks built some immigrants' fortunes. Meier joined his brothers in 1855 at age twenty-four in Downieville, California, where he worked in their dry goods business. Two years later, he moved to Portland, Oregon, which had been established only thirteen years earlier. The conditions seemed right for an entrepreneur to start a business, so he opened a dry goods store with a partner. Meier returned to Germany in 1864 after his father died. There he married Jeanette Hirsch and returned to Portland, only to discover that the store had failed. But Meier was not dissuaded: he started a new store and later forged a partnership with Emil Frank, a German immigrant he met on a buying trip to San Francisco. The two families grew closer when Emil's brother Sigmund Frank emigrated from Germany, worked at the store, and married Meier's only daughter, Fannie. When Aaron died in 1889, Sigmund became company president and expanded the store operation. Eventually, Meier and Frank became the largest retail outlet west of the Mississippi and one of the largest stores in the United States. Julius Meier served as Oregon's governor from 1930 to 1934. The two families ran the business until the 1960s when it was sold to the May Department Stores.[26]

"Minnie" Fazzio Bonacci's story illustrates the familial dynamics of immigration, the role of immigrant labor in western extractive industries, the prejudice encountered by some ethnic groups, and the importance of religious affiliation for some immigrants and their children. Minnie's father and mother hailed from Decollatura, Italy. After they married there, her father, Rosario Fazzio, "migrated four or five times." He would go to America to work for a year and then return home, only to go back again when he needed more money. Finally her mother, Filomena, said, "If you're going back [to America] again, don't come back anymore." So in 1908, Rosario brought his wife and three children to Sunnyside, Utah. Filomena was pregnant at the time, and Minnie was born a few months after the move. Rosario was a coal miner; Filomena was a homemaker. Most of the Fazzio daughters worked in the house, but Minnie liked to work outside. Life was often hard, especially during the 1922 strike and the Depression. Minnie married Vito Bonacci, an immigrant, when she was sixteen. Vito was a coal miner, and they moved between coal camps. She recalled how the "mines were a constant worry" for her. She prayed every day that her husband would return home safely. During World War II, her oldest son was in the military. Someone reported that the FBI spied on her husband. She remembered, "I don't think we deserved it. I told one [fellow worker], 'He got his mother, father, brothers, and sisters in Italy. He is working here and buying United States government bonds so the army can go and kill his parents and you are feeling him around? It makes no sense.'" After her children were in school, Minnie worked at a factory and later at a laundry. After Vito retired, Minnie worked as a custodian at a country club. She was active in the St. Anthony's Catholic Parish in town and organized fundraisers for the Notre Dame Catholic School. The parish named her "woman of the year" for her services in 1985.[27]

A young second-generation immigrant's account illustrates how complicated questions of identity and assimilation could be. This individual was born in San Francisco in 1909 to Chinese immigrants. He first attended Chinatown language schools and then went to American high school. He enrolled in the University of California in 1928 but failed his exams. He explained that "he couldn't find time to study; too many distractions in Chinatown." After three years he quit college and got a job driving truck for a Chinese butcher. He was fired from that job and several others "because he was not polite enough" in his morning greetings, by Chinese standards. Then he sorted potatoes with a Chinese "gang." His thirty dollars a month gave him "just enough for spending money," so he had to stay with his parents. He was among the first Chinese hired to work for the Civil Works Administration in 1933, where he "found the work swell" and felt he was "treated like a white-man." However, when the CWA closed a year later, he could not get a job with the State Emergency Relief Administration projects because his family had too much money. In 1935, he was working as an elevator boy in a hospital, but his job was threatened since all Chinese workers were to be let go so their jobs could go to "white" people. Pardee Lowe, who recorded this story in the 1930s, concluded from his observations and research that this man's predicament was "fairly typical" of youth in Chinatown who were caught in between Chinese and American identity. "His freedom of action [was] definitely limited." He could not make a life for himself outside of his parents' home in Chinatown. Despite these limitations, "he seems, or gives the impression, of being wholly enamored of American ways. He is ashamed of the old culture and makes every effort to be as American as possible."[28]

Under the Bracero Program, thousands of Mexican migrants worked in fields throughout the West between 1942 and 1964. Their experiences highlight dimensions of immigration within an international capitalist framework, with its admixture of relative economic opportunity and exploitation. One bracero, Jesus Campoya Calderon, came from San Diego, Chihuahua, and traveled to an American-run "trocadero," or processing center, in Chihuahua City. He passed an initial interview, was hired, and signed a contract. He and other workers were then taken to the border. Calderon went from Ciudad Juarez to El Paso, and then to a processing center in Fabens in the El Paso Lower Valley. There they were sprayed with a white powder "to kill the Mexicans fleas" and given baloney sandwiches for dinner. Calderon recalled, "After several days without food, the sandwich tasted like glory." He was selected by a farmer to pick cotton, but he did all the work on the farm. He received $2.10 for 100 pounds of cotton. Once a week he went to the "big town" for groceries and cigarettes. Calderon saved all of his money, since he did not trust the bank, and went home with "almost $300." For Calderon, "those were very good days."[29]

Like Calderon, most braceros earned more than they could have made in Mexico, but many complained about substandard housing and overwork. Alfredo Gutierrez Castaneda recalled, "They'd get us up at four in the morning . . . then a truck arrived to take us to the fields. They'd put a bucket of water at each end of the field trench and we couldn't drink water until we finished hoeing the trench. And you couldn't rest, if you did they'd get after you. And that was every day."[30]

The experiences of Jubilee Lau and her family illuminate assimilation and identity formation and illustrate how the places where immigrants settle, an important part of social context, can shape their experiences profoundly. Lau moved with her family to California in 1983 when she was six years old. She explained in an essay that she wrote in 1996, "My parents left Hong Kong, our longtime home, with high hopes to 'make something of their lives.'" They settled in an apartment near San Francisco's Chinatown, and although a relative tried to teach them to shop at the American malls, they went to Chinatown at least once a day because they felt comfortable there. She attended a school for new immigrants trying to learn English. She struggled with the language and refused to speak English after a teacher laughed at her when she asked, "Do you know the toilet?"

When she refused to learn the language and insisted on only watching Chinese television at home, her parents decided to move to Nampa, Idaho, and buy a restaurant. Lau described it as "the worst day of my life" because "Idaho was everything that I had feared. There was no Chinatown for us to 'hide,' no Asians, and nothing but farms, cows, and the 'English people.'" Three days after arriving, her parents put her in a school where the principal greeted her, saying, "You are the only Asian we've ever had in this school, and we hope you'll feel right at home." The principal spoke slowly, and Lau was surprised she could understand. She "could sense the friendliness all around me." Her schoolmates accepted her and wanted to know about her Chinese culture. She concluded, "My family really benefitted from our decision to move to Idaho. My parents not only had a steady business, but they also learned to speak English a lot better by constant practice with customers at the restaurant. I realized that not all Americans look down on the new immigrants who can't even pronounce the simplest English. Idaho made me see a completely different side to the American culture." She still considered herself a Chinese-American, returned to the University of California–Berkeley for college, and settled in Santa Clara where there were more Chinese. She concluded, "I will always be a hyphenated American because I am from Hong Kong, my ancestors are from China, and I will always be Chinese."[31]

As these examples show, newcomers' experiences vary drastically. Even if newcomers possessed the same levels of skill, education, and motivation, variables beyond their control would still affect their destiny, such as legal status, employment options, and economic ups and downs. As Portes and Rumbaut pointed out, "The most hardworking individuals may . . . end up in poor jobs simply because they perceive no alternatives or none are available; others may rise to the top, riding in the wake of a lucky set of external circumstances. Social context renders individualistic models insufficient because it can alter, in decisive ways, the link between individual skills and motivations and their expected rewards." But the stories also suggest immigrants bring their own agency to bear in negotiating structural forces.[32]

The chapters that follow illuminate the experiences of Jewish, Irish, English Mormon, Italian, Boer, and Hispanic immigrants to the American West. They illustrate the complexity of reasons for migration. They also show the variety of ways that the immigrants made something of their new lives as they developed and brokered economic, social, civic, political, and religious capital.

Notes

1. Jason McDonald, *American Ethnic History: Themes and Perspectives* (New Brunswick, NJ: Rutgers University Press, 2007), 39.
2. Quoted in ibid., 39.
3. Quoted in ibid., 40; John W. Briggs, *An Italian Passage: Immigrants to Three American Cities, 1890–1930* (New Haven, CT: Yale University Press, 1978), 1.
4. Quoted in McDonald, *American Ethnic History*, 40–41.
5. Quoted in ibid., 41. For further discussion of the reasons immigrants left their countries and came to the United States, see the introductory essay for "Why We Came and What We Made of It" in this volume.
6. McDonald, *American Ethnic History*, 43, 46; Ewa Morawska, "The Sociology and Historiography of Immigration," *Immigration Reconsidered: History, Sociology, and Politics*, ed. Virginia Yans-McLaughlin (New York: Oxford University Press, 1990), 192–93.
7. Siroj Sirojudin, "Economic Theories of Emigration," *Journal of Human Behavior in the Social Environment* 19, no. 6 (2009): 702–12; Barry R. Chiswick, "Are Immigrants Favorably Self-Selected? An Economic Analysis," in *Migration Theory: Talking Across Disciplines*, ed. Caroline D. Brettell and James F. Hollifield (New York: Routledge, 2008), 63–65; see also Mimi Kimi, "The Political Economy of Immigration and the Emergence of Transnationalism," *Journal of Human Behavior in the Social Environment* 19, no. 6 (2009): 675–89, and Edna Bonacich and Lucie Cheng, "Introduction: A Theoretical Orientation to International Labor Migration," in *Labor Immigration under Capitalism: Asian Workers in the United States before World War II*, ed. Lucie Cheng and Edna Bonacich (Berkeley: University of California, 1983), 1–56.
8. Gilbert G. Gonzalez and Raul A. Fernandez, *A Century of Chicano History: Empire, Nation, and Migration* (New York: Routledge, 2003), 59.
9. Everett S. Lee, "A Theory of Migration," *Demography* 3, no. 1 (1966): 50; Alejandro Portes and Rubén G. Rumbaut explain that rarely the poorest leave their home country because they lack the requisite financial resources. Portes and Rumbaut, *Immigrant America: A Portrait* (Berkeley: University of California Press, 2006), 19–34.
10. Lee, "A Theory of Migration," 50; Portes and Rumbaut, *Immigrant America*, 17–18; Elliott Robert Barkan, *From All Points: America's Immigrant West, 1880s–1952* (Bloomington: Indiana University Press, 2007), 139–40.
11. Lee, "A Theory of Migration," 51.
12. Barkan, *From All Points*, 20, 34.
13. Morawska, "The Sociology and Historiography of Immigration," 212–13, 218.
14. Portes and Rumbaut, *Immigrant America*, 19–34.
15. George J. Sanchez, *Becoming Mexican American: Ethnicity, Culture, and Identity in Chicano Los Angeles, 1900–1945* (New York: Oxford University Press, 1993), 150.
16. Alejandro Portes and Robert L. Bach, *Latin Journey: Cuban and Mexican Immigrants in the United States* (Berkeley: University of California Press, 1985), 31–42; Kenneth L. Wilson and Alejandro Portes, "Immigrant Enclaves: An Analysis of the Labor Market Experiences of Cubans in Miami," *American Journal of Sociology* 86 (September 1980): 295–319.
17. Barkan, *From All Points*, 19–21.

18. Kathleen Neils Conzen, "Immigrants, Immigrant Neighborhoods, and Ethnic Identity: Historical Issues," *Journal of American History* 66 (December 1979): 613–14.
19. See Barkan, *From All Points*, 137–54.
20. Maria Herrera-Sobek, "Transnational Migrations and Political Mobilizations: The Case of *A Day Without a Mexican*," in *Imagined Transnationalism: U.S. Latino/a Literature, Culture, and Identity* (New York: Palgrave Macmillan, 2009*)*, 60–73. Quotes on 62–63, 72.
21. Benita Heiskanen, "A Day Without Immigrants," *European Journal of American Studies* (2009), http://ejas.revues.org, accessed April 30, 2012. The rallies promoted a nativist "backlash" more than helping the immigrants. Critics of "A Day Without Immigrants" blamed the immigrants for creating problems. The founder of the Minutemen Civil Defense Corps, Jim Gilbert, protested, "When the rule of law is dictated by a mob of illegal aliens taking to the street, especially under a foreign flag, then that means the nation is not governed by a rule of law—it is a mobocracy." Pat Buchanan called the day "a strike against America," and conservative spokeswoman Michelle Malkin said it was a "Mexican conspiracy to 'reconquer' the U.S. southwest." John Tanton, part of the Federation for American Immigration Reform (FAIR) went so far as to call the immigrants "bacteria" because of their high birthrates who would "take over" the United States.
22. Portes and Rumbaut, *Immigrant America*, 301.
23. Ibid., 318.
24. Ibid. 341.
25. Barkan, *From All Points*, 34.
26. William Toll, *The Making of an Ethnic Middle Class: Portland Jewry Over Four Generations* (Albany: State University of New York Press, 1982), 12; internet sites on store.
27. Leslie G. Kelen and Eileen Hallett Stone, *Missing Stories: An Oral History of Ethnic and Minority Groups in Utah* (Salt Lake City: University of Utah Press, 1998), 275–80; Obituary of Filomena "Minnie" Bonacci, *Deseret News*, August 20, 1998, http://www.deseretnews.com, accessed September 9, 2013.
28. Pardee Lowe, "Second Generation Dilemmas (1930s)," in *Chinese American Voices: From the Gold Rush to the Present*, ed. Judy Yung, Gordon Chang, and Him Mark Lai (Berkeley: University of California Press, 2006), 165–68.
29. "Testimony from a 'bracero,'" http://www.farmworkers. Org/testimony.html, accessed October 8, 2013.
30. http://www.farmworkermovement.org/media/video/flyersoldiersinthefields1.pdf; see also Gilbert Gonzalez and Vivian Price, *Harvest of Loneliness: The Bracero Program* (New York: Films for the Humanities and Sciences, 2011), and Juan Ramon Garcia, *Operation Wetback: The Mass Deportation of Mexican Workers in 1954* (Westport, CT: Greenwood Press, 1980), 35–61.
31. Jubilee Lau, "Chinese and Proud of It," in Yung, Chang, and Lai, *Chinese American Voices*, 363–67.
32. Portes and Rumbaut, *Immigrant America*, 19, 28–34, 102.

8

Social Capital and Frontier Community Building

The Case of Immigrant Jews in Nineteenth-Century Los Angeles

Karen S. Wilson

Traditional scholarly treatments of Jewish immigrant communities stressed their residential and social segregation and their emphasis upon mutual assistance within their own communities. That had been their tradition in many European nations where law and custom produced segregated quarters. Using the techniques of social network analysis, a mode of investigation first developed by sociologists that maps the ties, or links, between nodes, or individuals, Karen S. Wilson, the Sady and Ludwig Kahn Post-Doctoral Research Fellow at UCLA's Center for Jewish Studies, shows the ways in which Jewish immigrants to nineteenth-century Los Angeles—long before the Hollywood era with its outward-looking Jewish movie moguls—developed associational ties with other social groups. While early social historians found it natural to aggregate individuals into groups based upon the categories employed by the census including race, ethnicity, or class, Dr. Wilson shows the limitations of this approach. Nationality, religion, and education did exert an influence on associational ties, but so did common needs, interests, and concerns. Jewish immigrants developed multiple identities through their associational networks. These multiple identities served them well in securing or improving work, generating commercial opportunities, or finding spouses.

In nineteenth-century Los Angeles, social capital facilitated the creation and sustenance of religious and social institutions that transformed a frontier town of "mutual strangers" into a community of mutual supporters. Social capital, that is, individual and collective advantages secured through social relations, made it possible for Catholic Californios, Protestant Americans, and Jewish Europeans to surmount the challenges of geographic isolation, thin population, limited services, and weakened family ties that characterize frontiers. As the case of Jewish Angelenos illustrates, individuals embedded in diverse local networks leveraged the value of social connections for the benefit of particular communal institutions, which, in turn, helped stabilize the emerging society. In aspiring to establish institutions of Judaism, immigrant Jews not only extended religious diversity in the American West but also assisted in instigating a custom of interfaith cooperation and mutuality that was critical to the eventual flourishing of all three faith traditions in the city.[1]

Along with the rest of the world, Jewish Europeans came seeking El Dorado in the Gold Rush that transformed California. They secured something less legendary and more valuable. Epitomized by men such as Levi Strauss, they found opportunity and success not in mining, but in supplying the miners. As the mining quickly industrialized and the competition in commerce intensified in the overwhelmed cities of Sacramento and San Francisco, other western towns attracted Jewish merchants looking for less volatility and more security. Despite having a population of less than two thousand people, Los Angeles became such an alternative. In the early 1850s, Jewish immigrants began to settle there, establishing stores and other businesses, starting families, and instituting the structures of Judaism. Frontier conditions were magnified for Jewish settlers as they were a continent and an ocean away from their homelands and families, never more than 3 percent of the local population, and bereft of the resources of an established Jewish community. In the fluid, transforming American West, though, the willingness and ability of Jews to be part of diverse networks brought stability to their own communal institutions as well as those of the larger community. Displaying a confidence in the collective in coping with the conditions of the frontier, Jews acquired the social capital necessary to transform strangers into friends, émigrés into Angelenos. Embedded advantageously in broad and dense social networks, Jews contributed and received tangible and intangible resources that sustained Jewish and other religious institutions and stabilized the fluid frontier created by Spanish colonialism, Mexican republicanism, and American expansionism.

The significance of understanding the role of social capital in frontier community building is twofold. First, it reopens a window onto the dynamic processes of community formation and reformation instigated by the acquisition of the Far West by the United States, a subject once at the center of American western history. Second, it situates those processes in the webs of interpersonal relations that developed between residents and newcomers from many nations, cultures, and classes, all of whom were attempting to re-create familiar worlds in an unfamiliar universe. The convergence of those various worlds brought interaction between existing traditions and imported social forms, exchange and adaptation of customs and values, and negotiation over the structures and meanings of community.[2]

Recent historical study of social relations in the American West has focused most frequently and familiarly on people in conflict and on the move. With its emphasis on conquest and migration, the myth and history of the American West rarely attends to the mundane and ordinary processes of settling in and making community. Cities and towns in the nineteenth-century West often have been seen as temporary, chaotic, and dangerous, created to service individual, corporate, and national agendas. In the words of historian Anne Hyde, "People assembled such communities more often to convenience distant economic forces than to enhance the quality of human life." The isolation of the western frontier ironically made community more important there and made the region more urban than other parts of the United States. While its isolation made migration there an exceptional and risky choice, its urban character made persistence there a viable option for those who valued community. Faced with limited social and economic options in their home countries, Jewish Europeans found the open and fluid American West especially attractive for permanent resettlement.[3]

Relationships sit at the center of this examination of community building. Rather than assuming that groups defined by race, class, or nationality were the building blocks of frontier society, this essay offers documented social ties as a way to understand how strangers became familiar with each other. Rather than assuming that attributes of individuals, such as religion or education, sufficiently explain social behavior, social network analysis points to how and when such attributes became important variables in addressing the individual and collective challenges of life on the frontier. Specifically, this essay describes how Jewish immigrants became embedded in networks, what was significant about their presence and positions in those networks, and how networks produced Jewish and other communal institutions in Los Angeles.

Angelenos by Association

Jews and other Angelenos were part of economic, proximity, and affiliational networks that served as efficient structures of negotiation between mutual strangers on a fluid frontier. The transformation of California from Mexico's northern frontier to the United States' western frontier was done virtually with the stroke of a pen with the signing of the Treaty of Guadalupe Hidalgo, which ended the Mexican-American War in 1848. But the incorporation of Los Angeles into American society took a few decades, requiring not only external efforts to connect the West Coast with the rest of the nation but also internal efforts to forge ties between people from diverse societies. Through the existence and effects of personal connections, the local economy diversified, a new social order arose, and Los Angeles became the urban center imagined by its Spanish colonizers. Networks functioned first to bring together people of disparate cultures and later to keep together people of common interests. Among the most critical social networks were those that supported the religious and social welfare institutions that responded to the realities of life on the American frontier.

Frontier circumstances required that people create and adapt institutions necessary to individual and collective survival and growth. Jews and others who came to nineteenth-century Los Angeles redefined and reinforced particular institutions as they settled into their new home. The realms of religion, ethnic and national identity, political activism, and communal responsibilities, among others, were spheres of negotiation as diverse peoples asserted their particular visions of community. Most visibly through participation in voluntary organizations, Jewish immigrants engaged in negotiations that helped determine the nature and degree of their integration into the social landscapes as well as the trajectory of the emerging society. Through belonging to a variety of voluntary associations, Jews became embedded in networks that ranged across much of the cultural diversity of Los Angeles.

Jewish immigrants added to that diversity, emigrating from thirteen different European states, with the largest number coming from Prussia and other German-speaking countries. Jews from France, Poland, and England settled as well. The substantial presence of other German- and French-speaking immigrants encouraged many Jews to assert a strong connection to their European roots.[4] By 1870, Jews numbered 357 in the county or 2.33 percent of the total population. Typical for frontier societies, adult men outnumbered adult women by roughly two to one. However, the presence of a large number of growing families was moving the population toward gender parity (56 percent male and 44 percent female), while the split between European-born adults and American-born children remained about even.[5]

The path for social incorporation that Jewish immigrants chose, as evident from their behavior, privileged community over individualism, connection over insularity, and Jewish continuity over assimilation. They added English, Spanish, and even some Chinese to their linguistic repertoires. They lived next door to former African American slaves and future Confederate officers. They cultivated long-term business ties with Americans and Mexicans. Further, by creating, joining, and leading a variety of organizations, Jewish immigrants established the foundations of Jewish community while simultaneously helping to define broader communal institutions. As with any people seeking to find their place in a society, they navigated their way through the opportunities and challenges of preserving values, asserting identities, and forging relationships with people holding different values and expressing different identities. In that process, Jews were exposed to various options for living on the California frontier. Those options ranged from the celebrated individualism of the "self-made man" to the disciplined insularity of the Latter-day Saints, from the Yankee dons who adopted the Californio culture as their own to the American Southerners who took offense at the mixture and social mixing of races in the region. In following a path that embraced the multiculturalism of Los Angeles, Jewish immigrants secured social incorporation and communal stability. Their early, persistent, and diverse engagement with the thick democratic associational life that characterized nineteenth-century Los Angeles was the most visible aspect of their commitment to communal collaboration.

As in many frontier settlements, voluntary associations in Los Angeles usually originated as "first responders" to public safety needs, as guardians of ethnic and religious traditions, and as organizers of public and private lifecycle events and social occasions. They reinforced national and religious identities while also facilitating new and deepening identities as Angelenos. Because of overlapping members, associations were nodes on both broad and narrow social networks, some structured around ethnicity, religion, or class, while common interests and civic concerns defined others. The variety of organizations that emerged over the first decades of the American era encouraged individual expressions of values, opinions, identities, and free and unfettered association. Angelenos of different ethnicities, cultures, and religions exercised their individualism by joining voluntary associations, displaying what has come to be seen as a characteristic American propensity for energetically seeking the company of others for prayer, play, politics, protection, and persuasion.

The world of associational life began early in the American era and steadily gained momentum. Angelenos associated in lodges, volunteer fire companies, and sewing circles. Californios joined Americans and Europeans in cross-cultural endeavors and in creating their own mutual benefit and political societies. Jews, Protestants, and Catholics formed the first Masonic lodge in the city in 1853.[6] Irish John Downey, French Jew Solomon Lazard, defender of Mexican California Andres Pico, and Tennessee native Benjamin Wilson were among the twenty-six men who initiated Democratic Party politics in the region in 1854. French, German, and Spanish Angelenos followed the precedent of Jewish immigrants in establishing

TABLE 8.1. RATE OF GROWTH, LOS ANGELES ORGANIZATIONS, 1855–1892

Type of Organization	1855	1872	1883	1892
Secular Associations	6	16	29	173
Religious Congregations	2	7	22	74
Total	8	23	51	247

Notes: Secular associations included fraternal and sororal organizations, mutual benefit societies, social clubs, militias, volunteer fire companies, and other such groups. Religious congregations included organizations created to provide religious services and sanctuary to followers of particular faith traditions. Both types of organizations had voluntary memberships and were included in the broader terms of associations and associational life.[7]

their own social and charitable organizations. By the 1870s, women were organizing their own associations. Well before urbanism, industrialization, and immigration became challenges to Angelenos, they had created spaces in which to join with others based on many different commonalities.

Contemporary scholars of nineteenth-century associationalism have seen it as a panacea or a problem, a strategy of community building or of asserting self-interests. Recent debate over the meaning and role of associationalism in the United States falls along two main contentions: (1) associations are a necessary and positive force in unifying Americans and guarding the ideas of democracy, a position most notably championed by political scientist Robert D. Putnam, and (2) associations are vehicles for social differentiation and expression of self-interest, the argument made by historian Mary P. Ryan among other scholars. Despite their different conclusions, the two sides of the debate over associationalism share an assumption that the challenges of nineteenth-century immigration, industrialization, and urbanization were key motivating factors in the American embrace of joining. Reacting to the disruptive forces of these elements, Americans resorted and retreated to factions of common interests. Putnam preferred to see defense of democratic ideals as the organizing principle with the creation of public goods being the result. Ryan, on the other hand, saw a kind of Manichean society stemming from the proliferation of voluntary organizations, with societies and clubs serving as battalions of troops engaged in social combat. Based substantially on studies of well-established cities in the eastern half of the country, the underlying assumptions for these perspectives did not account for the fluidity of the frontier, the significance of people who belonged to several different organizations, or a gradual process of transformation in which associations and the networks they engendered changed in purpose and influence over time.[8]

In each decade following American statehood, the number of lodges, mutual benefit societies, charities, civic groups, and religious congregations

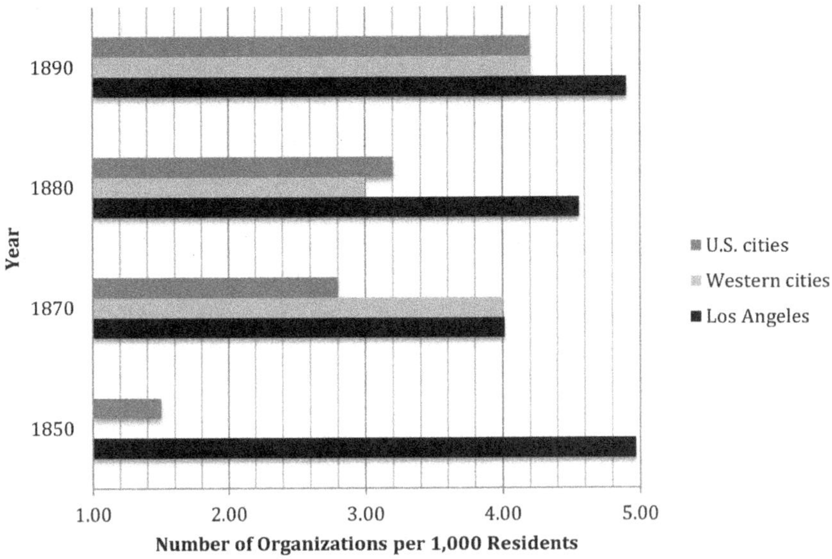

Figure 8.1. Organizational Density for Los Angeles, Western Cities, and United States Cities. Sources: Calculations for Los Angeles based on U.S. Census data and figures drawn from notices and articles in the *Los Angeles Star* newspaper, 1854–1855, from Engh, *Frontier Faiths*, 19 and Appendix, and from counts of associations listed in the following directories: *The First Los Angeles City and County Directory, 1872*; *Los Angeles City and County Directory for 1883–1884*; and *Los Angeles City Directory and Gazetteer of Southern California 1892*. Figures for U.S. and Western cities from Gamm and Putnam, "Growth of Voluntary Associations in America," 524, Fig. 1, and 536, Fig. 4.

in Los Angeles grew exponentially (see Table 8.1, Rate of Growth, Los Angeles Organizations, 1855–1892). In the mid-1850s, with a population of less than five thousand in the county, there were at least six voluntary organizations actively enrolling members. In the 1870s and 1880s, the rate of organizational growth exceeded that of population growth in the city, in line with a national trend in associational growth rates. *Maxwell's Los Angeles City Directory for 1896* listed 393 associations to which Angelenos belonged, an increase of over six thousand percent in forty years. The rate of growth reflected the national embrace of associations.[9]

In distinction to national averages, though, Los Angeles sustained an exceptionally high number of associations relative to its population. In 1850, American cities and towns nationwide averaged 1.5 organizations per one thousand residents. In sparsely populated Los Angeles during that decade, the ratio was close to five associations for every one thousand residents (see Figure 8.1, Organizational Density for Los Angeles, Western Cities, and United States Cities). About twenty years later, the ratio in the city had dropped slightly to 4.6 organizations per thousand, yet still exceeded the national average (2.5) as well as the average for other Western towns (3.0). In the early 1890s, the national and regional ratio moved closer to the Los Angeles case but did not overtake it. Even after the decade in which its population jumped from about eleven thousand to over fifty thousand residents, Los Angeles maintained an extraordinarily dense level of organizations.[10]

By the same measures, the enthusiasm for associational life was strong in Los Angeles's Jewish community. The growth trends for associations organized by and for Jewish Angelenos matched those for general organizations in the city, while the ratio of organizations to the Jewish population exceeded such ratios for the whole population. Established in 1854 to acquire a cemetery, provide burial services, and take care of the needy in keeping with Jewish custom and law, the Hebrew Benevolent Society was the first Jewish organization as well as the city's first mutual benefit society and charity and its first organization formed predominantly by immigrants. Four decades later, there were nine specifically Jewish organizations. By comparison, in the early 1890s, German-speaking Angelenos, who numbered at least twice the Jewish population, had ten organizations, only one more than Jewish Angelenos had. The ratio of organizations per one thousand Jewish residents grew from 6.2 in the 1850s to almost 12 in the 1870s and 1880s. In contrast, the ratio of German organizations per one thousand German-speaking residents declined from 3.2 in 1872 to 2.3 in 1892. In the robust and dense world of association that made Los Angeles unique even among Western cities, Jewish organizations made a distinctive contribution to that standing.[11]

Jewish immigrants helped bolster and sustain associational life by belonging to organizations in high numbers and in disproportion to their size in the population. The thirty men who founded the Hebrew Benevolent Society represented about half of the estimated Jewish population at the time. In 1870, the membership numbers for the Hebrew Benevolent Society, still an all-male organization, and the Ladies Hebrew Benevolent Society, its all-female counterpart, totaled 103, or 56 percent of the adult Jewish population.[12] Congregation B'nai B'rith was founded in 1862 by thirty-two families, a figure that very likely represented all the nuclear Jewish families present at the time.[13] Despite accounting for less than 2 percent of the adult male population in 1850, Jews accounted for 8 percent of the members of non-Jewish associations established by 1855. In a sample of organizations active in the early 1860s, among the members of fourteen different associations were thirty-five Jews, nearly 40 percent of the estimated adult Jewish population in 1860 and a third of the adult Jewish population in 1870. In the 1870s, Jewish Angelenos could be found in over 60 percent of the

Table 8.2. Disproportionate Jewish Participation in General Organizations, Los Angeles County and City, 1854–1895

	Total Members	Number of Jewish Members	Percentage of Members = Jewish	Percentage of Adult Population = Jewish
All General Organizations (Number)				
1850s First Organizations (6)	102	8	7.84	1.64 (a)
1860s Second Wave Organizations (16)	357	48	13.45	4.67 (b)
1872 Organizations (14)	71	19	26.76	5.95 (c)
1895 Private Social Clubs (3)	200	75	37.5	—
Masonic Lodge Los Angeles No. 42				
1854	23	5	21.74	1.64 (a)
1860	66	13	19.7	5.29 (d)
1870	67	16	23.88	5.95 (c)
1880	88	18	20.45	—
1890	169	30	17.75	—

(a) Based on 1850 U.S. Census, white males only. (b) Based on 1860 U.S. Census, white males and females only. (c) Based on 1870 U.S. Census, white males only. (d) Based on 1860 U.S. Census, white males only. Sources: Membership numbers for general organizations drawn from newspapers, directories, and organizational histories cited in text and in notes to tables of organizations. Figures for Masonic Lodge Los Angeles No. 42 from "Journal of Proceedings of the Grand Lodge of the State of California."

Notes: Membership figures for the 1872 Organizations are for officers only. Except for 1895 clubs, membership figures do not include those of Jewish communal, religious, and fraternal organizations. Figures for the 1895 clubs include the Concordia Club, founded by Jewish elites who also were among the founders of the other two clubs, the California Club and the Jonathan Club.[14]

associations listed in the city's first directory, well beyond what would be expected from a population of less than 400 men, women, and children. Thirteen percent of Jewish men were members of Masonic Lodge No. 42 in 1870, compared to 3 percent of all white adult males in Los Angeles. In 1895, Jewish men constituted 37.5 percent of the members of the three leading private clubs (see Table 8.2, Disproportionate Jewish Participation in Los Angeles Associations, 1854–1895).[15] Jewish involvement with organizations boosted the overall proportion of Angelenos belonging to associations. It also increased the collective Jewish presence in the resultant networks of clubmen and charity ladies, reflecting a persistent and shared inclination toward connection over insularity.[16]

With their disproportionate participation, Jewish immigrants were distinctive from other Europeans in associational life. Among the originators of the earliest organizations with known places of birth, all but two of the European immigrants were Jewish.[17] Among the officers of sixteen organizations in 1872, European immigrants accounted for over 70 percent of the leaders, reflecting the increased number of foreign-born Angelenos. Two-thirds of those officers were Jewish immigrants, reflecting their continued enthusiasm for associational life.[18]

Jewish Angelenos embraced the lively, evolving associational life of Los Angeles with what could be called Western zeal and Jewish communalism. Jews were engaged in the proliferation of organizations that turned strangers into lodge brothers, brought relief in the wake of illness and disaster, promoted and created civic improvements, and established various faith traditions on the California frontier. In the process, Jewish joiners demonstrated civic responsibility, exercised multiple identities, and experienced unity as well as rivalry with other Jews, other immigrants, and other Angelenos. Through their participation, they helped to shape the transforming society in which immigrants and natives with diverse and mutually unfamiliar backgrounds overcame social distance and fashioned egalitarian webs of relations. When Jewish immigrants established the Hebrew Benevolent Society and later other communal institutions, they were adapting ancient traditions of diaspora Jews to a new frontier and era of Jewish settlement.[19] When they joined non-Jews to sustain other organizations, they were exercising opportunities of free association rarely available to them in the past and in Europe except for the price of abandoning Jewish identity through religious conversion or secularism and assimilation.[20]

Contrary to assumptions that grew out of a later attachment to Reform Judaism by Jews further removed from their European roots, the Jewish immigrants who settled in Los Angeles attempted to follow Jewish traditions and law. The congregation they formed was an unusual example of Jews of diverse origins finding common ground in association. Bavarian, Prussian, French, Polish, and American Jews recruited Polish native Rabbi Abraham Wolf Edelman from San Francisco to be the spiritual leader of the congregation. The first bylaws of the congregation stipulated that *minhag Polin* (Polish custom) was the ritual of the congregation and that prayers were required to be in Hebrew. In San Francisco a decade earlier, Bavarian and Polish Jews established two separate congregations rather than put aside differences of class, culture, and custom. Despite the challenges of leading an observant life in the hinterlands, a group of up-and-coming Jewish Angelenos founded what was, in its day and in America, a traditional synagogue imbued with the tolerant spirit of Los Angeles.[21]

With their enthusiastic participation in various associations, Jewish Angelenos were persistently embedded in extended affiliation networks. Every voluntary organization created a small network among its members, with each member having a direct tie to every other member based on their common affiliation. Through the act of joining an association, individuals increased their social connections. As new members joined, the network grew, with popular organizations producing many ties. Individuals who were especially engaged in associational life accumulated more ties with each organization they joined. Further, these individuals brought the small, single-group networks into a larger affiliation network by being a common link between multiple organizations. Joining an association was an active and significant step toward turning strangers into friends. Individuals who were positioned in the network to link associates from one group to associates in another group multiplied the effect of joining; that is, they reduced the social distance between people.[22]

Because of their tendency to belong to multiple organizations, Jewish immigrants often were in the position of linking different groups together. In the 1850s and 1870s, Jewish immigrant men on average held 2.4 memberships each. In the 1880s, middle-class Jewish women commonly held memberships in the Ladies Hebrew Benevolent Society and the nonsectarian Ladies Benevolent Society. Some even belonged to a third organization, the German Ladies Benevolent Society. Through their multiple memberships, "super" joiners enlarged their own personal networks quickly while simultaneously creating bridges between separate organizations and expanding the affiliation network.

A dramatic early example of Jewish Angelenos creating bridges and reducing social distance is that of Solomon Lazard, a merchant from Alsace. Lazard arrived in Los Angeles apparently not knowing anyone. In addition to connections with his neighbors on Bell's Row where his store was located and his customers, his first social relations were formed through membership in organizations. Four years after his arrival he sat at the center of the earliest affiliation network. Whether motivated by interests, identity, or religious values, Lazard typified the Jewish embrace of associationalism and acquired a growing personal network as a result.

As a founder of the Hebrew Benevolent Society, Lazard was connected to each of the other founders, and each of them to him, by virtue of their association in the society (see Figure 8.2, Lazard Affiliation Network, ca. 1855). Lazard's engagement with the county's Democratic County Convention as a delegate connected him to the other twenty-five Democrat delegates and each of them to him. Further, all members of HBS and all the county delegates were linked indirectly to each other through their shared member, Lazard. With each organization he joined, Lazard added another set of direct ties with members of the group and another set of indirect ties for everyone else in his existing network. Because of his affiliation

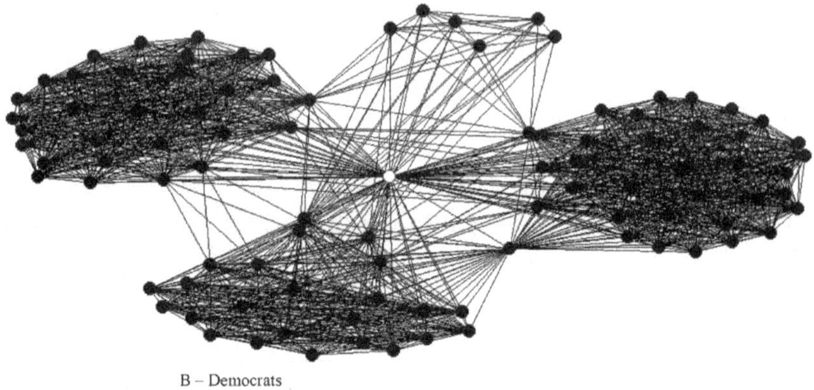

Figure 8.2. Lazard Affiliation Network, ca. 1855. Legend: White Circle = Solomon Lazard; Black Circle = other members of groups; Lines = ties between individuals. Source: S. P. Borgatti, NetDraw Graph Visualization Software, Version 2 (Harvard Analytic Technologies, 2002).

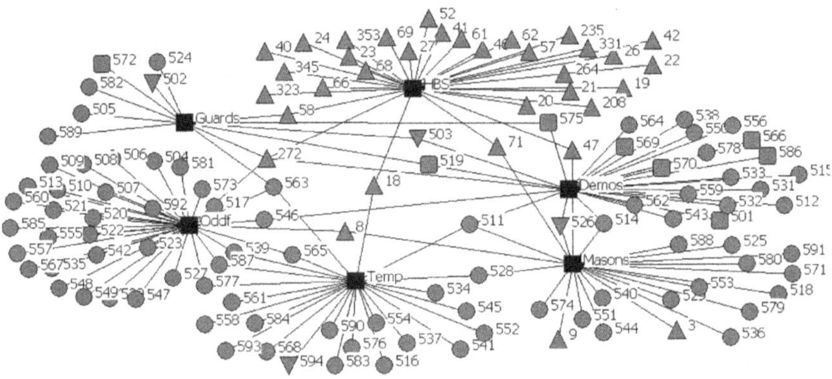

Figure 8.3. First Los Angeles Affiliation Network, ca. 1855. Legend: Numbers are identification labels for individual members. Symbols: Black Squares = organizations; Up Triangle = Jew; Down Triangle = non-Jewish European; Rounded Square = Californio; Circle = U.S.-born or unknown; Lines = ties between individuals and designated groups. Organizations: Guards = Los Angeles Guards; HBS = Hebrew Benevolent Society; Demos = County Democratic Party; Masons = Los Angeles Lodge, No. 42; Temp = Sons of Temperance; Oddf = Odd Fellows, Lodge No. 35. Note: The ties between members of each individual group have been eliminated for clarity. Source: S. P. Borgatti, NetDraw Graph Visualization Software, Version 2 (Harvard Analytic Technologies, 2002).

with HBS, the Democrats, the Los Angeles Guards, and the Odd Fellows, Lazard had direct ties to ninety-four individuals.

The overlapping memberships of Lazard created a network of four organizations. Some members in this network also belonged to two other groups, the Masons and the Sons of Temperance, which expanded the affiliation network to six organizations (see Figure 8.3, First Los Angeles Affiliation Network, ca. 1855). Because of those overlapping memberships, Lazard was embedded in a network of 127 other individuals, 33 more than were in his personal network. Belonging to four organizations gave Lazard direct ties to a large number of people, made him a potential broker through which others within the network connected, and expanded his possible social relations to individuals beyond his religious, political, and personal associations.[23]

Composed of the original six organizations to be established in the American era, the first affiliation network reflected the enthusiasm of a few men (the network consisted exclusively of male organizations) to join several organizations and the tendency of most men to join only one organization. With few overlapping memberships, there were few direct ties among the 128 men in the network. Less than 20 percent of the possible ties were actually present. Most men only had direct ties to other members of a single organization. Those men who belonged to two or more organizations had more direct ties, bridging the distance between the separate organizations. The affiliation network formed around and through the connections of "super" joiners, creating a core of brokers and a periphery of individuals attached to one of the six organizations.

Bavarian Esther Neugass Hellman was another "super" joiner, active in all three ladies benevolent societies and serving as treasurer for the nonsectarian Ladies Benevolent Society for thirteen years. As was the case with other Jewish middle-class women, the wife of merchant-turned-banker Isaias Hellman devoted considerable time and energy to organizations intent on bolstering education and helping the less fortunate. In addition to her work with the benevolent societies, she was a charter member of the Kindergarten Association, serving as its vice president in 1886 and 1888 when the organization successfully lobbied the Los Angeles public school system to add kindergarten classes. She also actively supported the Orphans' Home Society, the Boy's Home Society, and the Flower Festival Society, which started a boarding house for young, single, and older working women. Her membership in these organizations placed her in an extended affiliation network of women activists and philanthropists.[24]

Between the 1850s and 1890s, associational networks in Los Angeles changed in size, cohesion, and density, reflecting initially the fluidity of the frontier and later the emergence of a new social order. The earliest affiliation network was comparatively small in terms of individuals and ties, with low density and reliance upon a few brokers for its breadth and heterogeneity. It reflected limited trust among mutual strangers but also the significant role of enthusiastic joiners in creating connections across a variety of identities and interests. Affiliation networks in the 1860s and 1870s were comparatively more fragmented, with greater distance between members and much less density of ties. They reflected the expansion of associational life in the city, as different groups arose in response to demographic and economic changes. These networks were more open to the emergence of powerful brokers who could bridge gaps between various ethnic and religious groups. By the late 1880s, affiliation networks were significantly different from the earlier networks. In the case of arguably the four most prominent organizations of the decade, the networks were much higher in density and more cohesive with nearly twice as many actors and ties as any of the earlier affiliation networks (see Figure 8.4, 1880s Affiliation Network).

A striking consistency of associational networks across the period and changes was the centrality of Jewish Angelenos. While the particular individuals changed, the presence of Jews in the center of the networks remained the same. Rooted in both religious obligations and concepts of community and magnified by the thinness of frontier networks, Jewish participation in associational life placed Jews in between significant numbers of other people. It made them brokers who linked disparate groups

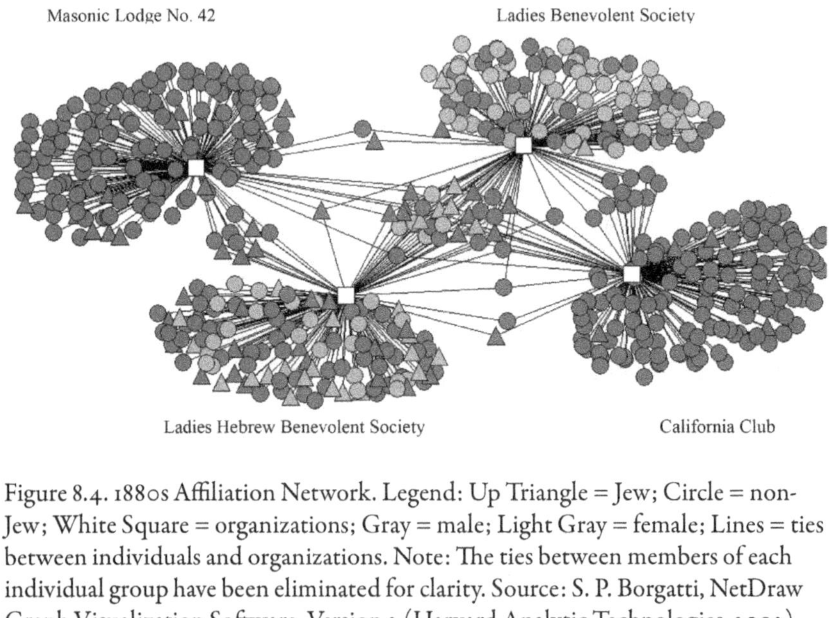

Figure 8.4. 1880s Affiliation Network. Legend: Up Triangle = Jew; Circle = non-Jew; White Square = organizations; Gray = male; Light Gray = female; Lines = ties between individuals and organizations. Note: The ties between members of each individual group have been eliminated for clarity. Source: S. P. Borgatti, NetDraw Graph Visualization Software, Version 2 (Harvard Analytic Technologies, 2002).

together, adding to the breadth of networks, who reduced the distance between individuals, creating efficiency in flows, and who increased the density of ties, bringing more cohesion and facilitating dispersal of common values. Persistent and outsized association by Jews kept them at the center of networks across the decades and changes. That distinctive embrace of associationalism put them in advantageous positions; that is, it generated social capital.

In its most succinct form, the crux of social capital theory is a simple assertion: relationships matter. Whether viewed as an asset of groups or of individuals, social capital emerges in the structures and functions of networks, the direct and indirect links between people. Through family ties, as well as those between neighbors, merchants and customers, and members of religious congregations and charitable societies, people are embedded in networks that shape their social opportunities and constraints. Network influence can range from the mundane (e.g., the spread of a cold virus) to the profound (e.g., the engagement in war by political allies). Networks create international trade routes and convert chains of émigrés into generations of native-born residents. People use networks to find jobs and marriage partners, expand businesses, get elected to public office, care for young children and elderly parents, and many other activities. Social capital encapsulates the potential assets of networks. Like other forms of capital, social capital, when used, changes the dynamics of relationships and the circumstances of people.[25]

As an asset of individuals, social capital is "the advantage created by a person's location in a structure of relationships," in the words of theorist Ronald S. Burt. It consists of resources embedded in a social network that are accessed and used by individuals for purposive action in a position to do so. The resources are an attribute of the network, while accessing and using such resources is a function of individual behavior. Advantage attaches to positions in a network and is actualized only when an individual acts to use the benefit. Like other forms of capital, social capital requires advantage and action to have effect.[26]

Individual behavior is necessary to create the potential for capital and to actualize that potential. In the nineteenth century, a store clerk saving a portion of his salary eventually could create the financial capital to open his own dry goods store. A child learning to read and write created the human capital necessary for competing for jobs off the farm or beyond the storefront. An immigrant joining the local benevolent society initiated a set of social ties that could have resulted in the social capital needed to find a business or marriage partner. In each case, when the individual could recognize the potential advantage of using his resource (financial, human, social), then acted to employ the advantage to enhance his well-being, the resource became capital, "investment of resources with expected returns in the marketplace."[27]

The accrual and exercise of social capital was not due to an inherent or immutable characteristic of Jews, but rather due to the behavior of individuals who saw value in connectedness and community, whether motivated by altruism or selfishness, by tradition, adaptation, or innovation, by practicality or ideology. The more ties Jewish immigrants created with diverse Angelenos, the more likely they were to accrue social capital and have opportunities to benefit from it. Because of the notably distinctive participation in associations by a large number of Jewish Angelenos, the networks in which Jews were embedded facilitated acquiring diverse and numerous social connections that often placed Jews at the center of broad and dense networks.

Not only did Jews persist in the center of affiliation networks, but they also maintained a consistent level of connection even as the size of networks changed and the specific Jews in central positions changed. Centrality is determined by how a member is situated within the network in relation to other members. Number of ties, distance between an individual and all other members, and how many pairs of people an individual sits between are relevant measures of centrality. With many ties that created closeness with a large portion of the network, Jews frequently were on many paths between pairs of other actors. Over four decades of affiliation networks, Jews were always found among the top five central actors. In those different networks, they connected between a quarter and a third of pairs of actors, creating links that otherwise would not have been present and increasing the density of the network (see Table 8.3, Central Actors in Affiliation Networks, 1855–1889, column labeled "Normalized Broker"). In addition to demonstrating the direct effects of their own enthusiasm for joining, the centrality of Jewish immigrants over time and in different affiliation networks reflected an enduring acceptance of their presence in well-integrated broker positions.

The significant disparity in centrality measures between Jews and non-Jews further reinforces the sense that Jewish behavior was distinctly prosocial, influenced by a valuing of collaboration. In each affiliation network, a Jew was the most centrally positioned actor, with a betweenness index at least one and one-half times higher than the most centrally positioned non-Jew (see Table 8.3, column labeled "Normalized Betweenness"). A Jew also had the highest broker index among the five most central actors. In other words, the person in each network who was on the most paths between other actors and who most expanded the number of links present in the network was a Jewish immigrant. In three of the networks, three or more Jews were among the top five actors in that similar position and role. In the earliest network, three immigrant Jews and two Americans held the top

Table 8.3. Central Actors in Affiliation Networks, 1855–1889

	Normalized Betweenness	Normalized Broker
1855 Affiliation Network		
Solomon Lazard	24.664	0.34
James R. Barton	8.912	0.32
Morris L. Goodman	0.067	0.24
Joseph J. Labatt	6.456	0.25
Myron Norton	5.036	0.28
1860s Affiliation Network		
Maurice Kremer	19.931	0.35
Jean Louis Sainsevain	8.855	0.24
Damien Marchessault	8.495	0.25
John M. Brite	6.704	0.19
Thomas A. Mayes	6.704	0.19
1872 Affiliation Network		
S. Julius Meyer	29.526	0.37
Simon Benjamin	26.844	0.34
Samuel Prager	19.849	0.26
C. C. Lips	16.55	0.27
Charles Gerson	10.97	0.25
1880s Affiliation Network		
I. W. Hellman	6.914	0.35
Eugene Germain	6.914	0.35
Walter S. Moore	4.098	0.32
Leopold Harris	3.49	0.31
Edward Germain	2.325	0.24

Notes: The italicized names are those of Jewish Angelenos. For each affiliation network, the five individuals with the highest Betweenness indices are listed. Betweenness centrality measures how frequently a given individual sits on a path linking other individuals in the network. The Broker measurement indicates what percentage of pairs in a network is connected by a given individual.[28]

spots. In the 1860s network, a Jew was joined by two Frenchmen and two Americans, in that order. In the 1872 network, Jews held four of the five top spots, reflecting their tendency to take leadership roles in more than one organization at the same time. In the 1880s network, Jews once again claimed most of the top spots, indicating their thorough integration into the most prominent middle-class organizations.[29]

By several measures of centrality, Jews were top ranked across different affiliation networks and periods. The centrality of Jews was not concentrated among a handful of elites but extended to more and more Jews over time. The high level of centrality made Jews key actors within the networks, influencing the size and density of the networks themselves and potentially influencing flows of information and exchanges of resources between members. Centrality gave Jews channels to and from many different people and groups in Los Angeles. It increased their potential to tap and be tapped by a wide range of individuals for information, expertise, votes for public office, or cash for charity. The change in network structure over time made the persistency of Jewish centrality significant as a factor both in the evolution of the structures and in the extent of Jewish incorporation. Jewish immigrants influenced and were influenced by the networks in which they were embedded.

Social Capital and Community Building

Positioned advantageously in their social networks, Jewish Angelenos were able to access and deliver resources on par with other Angelenos in similar positions. They were fully embedded in a world best captured in the phrase "mutually-made men." Coined by historian Judith A. McGaw to describe the relations between paper manufacturers in early nineteenth-century Massachusetts, it is applicable to relations among members of the elite and middle class of Los Angeles with the addition of two words—"and women." In contrast to the notion of being self-made men that some attached to their recollections of life on the frontier, upwardly mobile Jews and other Angelenos—men and women—made each other successful and respectable with resources that were accessed and delivered through networks. It was also through networks that they created and sustained the institutions of religion and social welfare which made the city an attractive home to respectable people.[30]

Due to characteristics of the California frontier, including a highly mobile population and the disruption of Spanish-Mexican institutions with the American takeover, Angelenos seeking the stability of religious congregations were a distinct minority. Catholics, Protestants, and Jews each faced the challenges of scarce resources as they worked to unite coreligionists and follow the tenets of their faith. The Catholic Church struggled in the transition from Spanish-Mexican leadership to American leadership. Protestant clergy found it difficult to muster and sustain a sufficient number of congregants to justify their permanent residence in the city. It took Jewish Angelenos eight years after the first Jewish organization was created to establish a formal congregation and hire a rabbi. With a common tradition of attending to the less fortunate, each group also sought to provide services and assistance to coreligionists and others in need, such as orphans and widows. To compensate for frontier limits, individuals within each faith tradition used their social capital to obtain tangible support for their congregations and causes.

Networks of women often were the conduits of what became customs of mutual support, beginning with the activities of the Catholic Sisters of Charity. With remarkable tenacity and success, nuns from the order of St. Vincent de Paul established, operated, and sustained a girl's school, orphanage, and the County Hospital beginning in the late 1850s. Although administered by Catholics, none of these institutions were restricted to Catholics and all received financial backing from non-Catholics. Because of their ecumenical service and their ability to engage others in their mission, the sisters developed broad support within the transforming community that extended far beyond the Catholic population. Annually, the sisters called upon women of other faiths to assist in staging a fair to raise funds for the orphanage. Particularly admired by Jewish Angelenos, the sisters' work provoked donations from the Hebrew Benevolent Society, loans from the Farmers and Merchants Bank headed by Bavarian Jew Isaias Hellman, and notable bequests from the community's first rabbi. In their work and involvement with the diversity of Los Angeles, the Sisters of Charity set a precedent for cooperation and collaboration emulated by other women-organized efforts.[31]

Fundraising by women was critical to the stabilization of a number of religious congregations. Although the impulse to form congregations came with some of the earliest settlers, their numbers were generally too small to support such ambitions as paid clergy and permanent houses of worship. The broader community became an abiding and necessary source of help to attain those resources. While they solicited their fellow congregants, male and female, Jewish and Protestant women regularly reached out through their networks of relatives, neighbors, and associates for support as well, especially for construction projects.

From its founding in 1862, women members of Congregation B'nai B'rith organized dances, dinners, and concerts to supplement the dues paid by member families. In 1869, as the *Los Angeles Star* reported, "the ladies of the [Jewish] congregation assembled for the purpose of devising means to raise funds to purchase a lot and erect a suitable church building." The account further remarked, "We are glad to know that the [non-Jewish] ladies of the city have very generally tendered their co-operation in the matter, thus at once securing the projected festival as a success," calling attention to the critical role of women and interfaith support in such efforts. When the synagogue was dedicated in August 1872, it was the third house of worship constructed in the city, joining Our Lady of the Angels Church on the Plaza and the Fort Street Methodist Episcopal Church.[32]

Reservoirs of trust developed among Christians and Jews who supported each other's efforts to build brick-and-mortar homes for their respective congregations as well as other institutions. Jewish Angelenos reciprocated the general community's support for its religious establishment with direct support of other congregations and institutions. In 1865, English-born Rosa Newmark, a member of one of the founding families of Congregation B'nai B'rith, organized a women's fair in support of the creation of St. Vincent's College, a Catholic secondary school for boys. In 1869, eight Jews joined ten Protestants in donating to various Catholic projects with specifically sectarian missions, including improvements and renovations of the parish cemetery, church, and schoolhouse. Jews also made financial contributions toward the $75,000 cost of the Cathedral of St. Vibiana, the first such edifice in the Roman Catholic diocese of Monterey–Los Angeles.[33]

While Jews were early and consistent supporters of Catholic institutions, their aid extended to Protestant projects as well. Mrs. Isaias W. (Esther) Hellman, Miss Rachel Kremer, and "Madame Eugene Meyer" contributed several recipes each to *Los Angeles Cookery*, a project of the Ladies' Aid Society of the Fort Street Methodist Episcopal Church. The collection was intended to provide "the house-keepers of the county with a large list of tried and valuable recipes" and "to raise funds to help pay off the indebtedness of the Church." Both aims were deemed "reasonable and worthy," in the introduction to the cookbook by Reverend M. M. Bovard, president of the recently founded University of Southern California, a Methodist institution rising up on land donated by the developers of the surrounding neighborhood, Episcopalian O. W. Childs, Catholic John Downey, and Jewish Isaias Hellman. By helping to create institutions that fostered security and respectability in the place known as "Hell Town," Jewish Angelenos reinforced a custom of interfaith cooperation and religious tolerance.[34]

Through their philanthropic activities, Jewish men and women not only aided their congregation and needy people, but they also influenced the structures, resources, and advantages of their networks. In particular, public fundraising events in which Jewish women participated were venues for expanding networks, developing multiplex relations, and building trust. Through their charity balls and other events, Jewish women attracted the financial support of family members, coreligionists, and non-Jewish friends. In return, they provided a venue in which Jews and non-Jews could become better acquainted, a place where men could observe each other in a context other than the world of commerce and business, and a context in which people could become more individuated to each other. Brought together through bonds of kinship, religion, friendship, and helping a good cause, men and women could build bridges of familiarity and common values while enjoying themselves at dances and concerts. In their public embrace of charity, Jewish Angelenos not only signaled their ethical ideals but also displayed their prosocial behavior and enhanced their reputations for trustworthiness as members of the larger community. Further, they also gauged the trustworthiness of other attendees. People willing to give financial support for the building of the synagogue or for the assistance of Jewish widows were allies in both preserving Jewish distinctiveness and building a stable community.[35]

Exemplifying the existence, exercise, and influence of social capital was an event organized by the Ladies Hebrew Benevolent Society in 1887. Held annually since the founding of the society in 1870, the "grand charity ball" was an occasion worthy of notice in the society column of the *Los Angeles Times*. According to the account, in an Armory Hall decorated with "vines, pepper-branches and brightly colored and lighted Japanese lanterns of fantastic shapes . . . [the cream of the Hebrew society of Los Angeles] first marched, then danced, chatted, ate and flirted, with numerous of their Gentile friends." Among the Gentile friends attending were the sitting mayor of Los Angeles, a state senator, a federal judge, and the medical advisor to the Southern Pacific and Santa Fé railroads. All of these men were part of the "Reception Committee" or what today would be termed the honorary hosts of the ball. Their names, along with those of prominent Jewish businessmen, were featured in advertisements for the event, signaling both an endorsement of the charitable cause and an invitation to other Jews and non-Jews to lend their presence and support. Of the 158 ball attendees listed in the *Times* article, little more than a third were Jewish, evidence of broad support for the Ladies Hebrew Benevolent Society beyond the coreligionists of its members. The significant presence of Gentiles at a Jewish-sponsored event was the result of social capital acquired and exercised through diverse social networks.[36]

A Western Difference

What may account for the centrality of Jewish immigrants in nineteenth-century Los Angeles? A shared confidence and comfort in the power of collective efforts, rooted in Jewish values and customs, explains in part the consistent and persistent actions by individual Jewish immigrants that made them integral to the emergent society. That Jewish distinction was a necessary element to their incorporation and to the stabilizing of the frontier community, but it was not sufficient to create the valuable social capital they wielded. Although the evidence is mainly suggestive, a case can be made that a critical factor was place. A distinctive custom and culture of comingling and contention found in the American West was particularly receptive to the Jewish approach to community building.[37]

Living on the Western frontier completed the equation for Jewish immigrants and allowed them to exercise a higher degree of influence over their own integration than their coreligionists in other regions of the United States. The upheaval instigated by American sovereignty and the Gold Rush undermined the relatively young institutions of Mexican California. The fluidity of a new frontier defined by indigenous diversity and international migration allowed Jews (and other newcomers to the region) to encounter and cross multiple national, racial, and religious boundaries not found elsewhere. Multiculturalism arose from the absence of a singular cultural norm and the presence of contending, dynamic visions of Los Angeles. Bridging social distance became essential for individual and collective survival, obvious in ways long obscured in the established urbanity of the Eastern Seaboard and the slave-based economy of the American South. In the West, volatility and diversity shaped the odds and alternatives for existence.

A scarcity of historical studies that formally analyze social networks in other American regions in the same era makes it difficult to confirm a Western distinction. One recent work argued persuasively that German Jewish immigrants in late nineteenth-century New York City were included in the Gentile-dominated economic networks of the world of finance and banking, but they were excluded from the associational networks that strengthened the bonds of business. Long-established social hierarchies inhibited the creation and advantages of diverse networks, preventing the development of trust between cultural strangers. Such restrictions on social relations not only were absent in the West but, given the circumstances, they would have been detrimental, if not devastating, to community development, as the Los Angeles case demonstrated.[38]

Alternatively, studies of associationalism help make the case that the West was different. As discussed earlier, Gamm and Putnam uncovered distinctive rates of associationalism for the region as compared to other parts of the United States. Western cities and towns sustained a higher number of associations per capita than their more established, more densely populated counterparts in the eastern and southern regions of the country. Los Angeles matched or exceeded those regional associational rates during the second half of the nineteenth century. That record at least raises the possibility of a correlation between the town's prolonged instability and varied citizenry and its reliance on voluntary association to transform mutual strangers into friends and neighbors. Studies of Jewish participation in Masonic lodges in nineteenth-century San Francisco and Portland, Oregon, suggest that the Los Angeles experience was typical for Jews in the region and period. The western embrace of associationalism combined with Jewish enthusiasm proved to be a productive combination for acquiring and expending social capital in the process of community building.[39]

The coinciding of people and place facilitated unfettered social ties, determined primarily by mutual interest and need, rather than by genealogy, stature, or identity. Instead of an entrenched social hierarchy determining who belonged to what social networks, organic interpersonal ties created social structures that bridged, rather than reinforced, distinctions of race, class, and religion. Given an environment conducive to free association, Jewish immigrants freely associated. Given an opportunity to belong, Jewish immigrants joined. Given a seemingly endless variety of organizations to join and the presence of a population that reflected the diversity of the world, Jewish immigrants displayed the breadth of their interests and identities. Jewish confidence in the collective was a necessary ingredient to Jewish integration, but it had to have a forum in which to thrive, a setting in which broad association was essential to creating and realizing possibilities. On the edge of the West in the throes of political, economic, and cultural reinvention, Los Angeles provided that forum.

Conclusion

Trusting the power of the collective, Jewish immigrants replicated and adapted the formal institutions of Judaism in the California borderland, while embracing customs from the Mexican frontier, the American republic, and their European homelands. Understanding firsthand the necessity and efficacy of people working together in the face of limited options and even hostile conditions, Jewish Angelenos created and sought out opportunities to join others in common purpose. The traditions of ranchero hospitality continued in the fairs and dances that became regular venues for raising funds for orphans, schools, and even the construction of a synagogue. The American enthusiasm for constitutions, democratic deliberations, and popularly elected leaders shaped the structure of groups that Jews founded. Jews threw their lot in with other Angeleno joiners and gambled that their confidence in community would be beneficial all around.

Through chains of communication and purposive actions, networks mitigated the conflict and change that arose on the Mexican-American borderland, transforming mutually suspicious strangers into mutually familiar Angelenos. Through networks, Jews came to know what sort of behavior to expect from their fellow Angelenos, while simultaneously conveying to others what sort of behavior to expect from them. Social networks connected Jews to many others, often in multiple ways and in positions to be bridges between different groups of Angelenos. The social capital Jewish immigrants accrued based on their locations in networks allowed them to assert and maintain ethnoreligious differentiation, while being fully integrated Angelenos at the same time. Individuals able to connect and influence other individuals enhanced flows of information, levels of trust, and exchanges of resources for the benefit of particular groups as well as the broader community. Social capital formed the foundation of immigrant integration and community stability in the Far West.

Notes

1. Quoted phrase from Robert V. Hine, *Community on the American Frontier: Separate but Not Alone* (Norman: University of Oklahoma Press, 1980), 249. Frontier characteristics adapted from Bernard Reisman, "Alaskan Jews Discover the Last Frontier," *Jewries at the Frontier: Accommodation, Identity, Conflict*, ed. Sander L. Gilman and Milton Shain (Urbana: University of Illinois Press, 1999), 111.
2. Richard White, *"It's Your Misfortune and None of My Own": A History of the American West* (Norman: University of Oklahoma Press, 1991), 210; Elliot West, "Thinking West," in *A Companion to the American West*, ed. William Deverell (Malden, MA: Blackwell Publishing, Ltd., 2004), 36–37.
3. Anne Hyde, "Transients and Stickers: The Problem of Community in the American West," in *A Companion to the American West*, ed. Deverell, 307. On influential studies of the American West, see Don Harrison Doyle, *The Social Order of a Frontier Community: Jacksonville, Illinois, 1825–70* (Urbana: University of Illinois Press, 1978); Hine, *Community on the American Frontier*; John Mack Faragher, "Open-Country Community: Sugar Creek, Illinois, 1820–1850," in *The Countryside in the Age of Capitalist Transformation: Essays in the Social History of Rural America*, ed. Steven Hahn and Jonathan Prude (Chapel Hill: University of North Carolina Press, 1985), 233–58; Patricia Nelson Limerick, *The Legacy of Conquest: The Unbroken Past of the American Wes*t (New York: W. W. Norton, 1987); Richard White, *The Middle Ground: Indians, Empires, and Republics in the Great Lakes Region, 1650–1815* (New York: Cambridge University Press, 1991); and Stephen Aron, *American Confluence: The Missouri Frontier from Borderland to Border State* (Bloomington: Indiana University Press, 2006).
4. Among European immigrants living in Los Angeles County in 1870, those from Germany and other German states were the largest in number (635), accounting for nearly 15 percent of all foreign-born residents. German-speaking Jews numbered 127, or 74 percent of Jews in the county. French immigrants numbered 317, or 7.3 percent of foreigners, with 15 Jews included or about 9 percent of the Jewish Europeans. By way of comparison, immigrants from Ireland, the largest foreign population in California at the time, accounted for about 11 percent of the Los Angeles foreign residents. Mexico was the country of origin for the largest foreign-born group, accounting for over 43 percent of the foreign population. Population data drawn from study sample and U.S. Bureau of the Census. *Ninth Census, The Statistics of the Population of the United States, 1870*, Volume 1. URL: http://www.census.gov/prod/www/abs/decennial/1870.html.
5. Jewish population data is based on the study sample drawn from an analysis of 1870 federal census manuscripts for Los Angeles County accessed on http://www.ancestry.com. Jews were identified through a manual search of the census manuscripts, using multiple attributes, such as a distinctive Jewish name, particular European birthplaces, and certain occupations, for preliminary identification. Jewish

identity was further confirmed by locating individuals in membership records of Jewish organizations, in cemetery records, or in family genealogical records. No one who could not be confirmed by two or more attributes was counted as Jewish. In the 1870 U.S. Census for Los Angeles County, 357 individuals were confirmed as Jewish, while 39 others were considered possibly Jewish but could not be confirmed. All statistics and calculations presented here are based only on the confirmed individuals.

6. In keeping with national Catholic policies, in the 1860s and 1870s Catholic participation was guided by regulations issued by the local bishop that prohibited membership in secret societies and groups that engaged in mixed social outings, reflecting concern over the "Protestantization" of Los Angeles. Many Catholic Angelenos adhered to the local bishop's prohibition against joining certain kinds of organizations, while some did not. See Michael E. Engh, *Frontier Faiths: Church, Temple, and Synagogue in Los Angeles, 1846–1888* (Albuquerque: University of New Mexico Press, 1992), chapter 8, for a detailed discussion of how this "withdrawal" from associational life contributed to the displacement of Hispanic Roman Catholics from civic life.
7. Figures for 1855 were drawn from notices and articles in the *Los Angeles Star* newspaper, 1854–1855 and from Engh, *Frontier Faiths*, 19. Figures for 1872, 1883, and 1892 were based on Engh, *Frontier Faiths*, Appendix, and on counts of associations listed in the following directories: The First Los Angeles City and County Directory, 1872; Los Angeles City and County Directory for 1883–84, Containing a Complete List of Names, Places of Business and Residences of All Adult Citizens (Los Angeles 1883); and Los Angeles City Directory and Gazetteer of Southern California for 1892 (Los Angeles 1892). None of the directories had a complete list of all extant organizations in Los Angeles at the time of publication (for example, the city's first directory listed only two churches when there were five other active congregations and both the 1883 and 1892 directories omitted the Hebrew Benevolent Society and the Ladies Hebrew Benevolent Society although both organizations were well-established at the time), so the figures here generally can be considered lower than the actual numbers.
8. Robert D. Putnam, *Bowling Alone: The Collapse and Revival of American Community* (New York: Simon & Schuster, 2000); Mary P. Ryan, *Civic Wars: Democracy and Public Life in the American City During the Nineteenth Century* (Berkeley: University of California Press, 1997); Jason Kaufman, *For the Common Good? American Civic Life and the Golden Age of Fraternity* (New York: Oxford University Press, 2002).
9. *Maxwell's Los Angeles City Directory and Gazetteer of Southern California 1896* (Los Angeles: 1896), 36–46; Gerald Gamm and Robert D. Putnam, "The Growth of Voluntary Associations in America, 1840–1940," *Journal of Interdisciplinary History* 29, no. 4 (1999): 514.
10. National and regional density ratios from Gamm and Putnam, "Growth of Voluntary Associations in America," 524, 536. Kaufman's estimates of organizational density, based on a similar methodology, more or less matched those of Gamm and Putnam; see *For the Common Good?*, 43–45. Los Angeles figures were calculated using counts of organizations derived from newspapers and city directories and U.S. Census figures. See Figure 8.1, Organizational Density for Los Angeles, Western Cities and United States Cities, for specific sources.

11. Ratios of organizations to population were calculated using population figures from the nearest decennial census and organization counts from city directories published in the years cited.
12. While the 1850 Census listed only eight identifiably Jewish men, one estimate put the population by 1855 at sixty, mostly men, of which thirty signed the original constitution and by-laws of the Hebrew Benevolent Society. The 1855 membership figure for HBS is from the published *Constitution and By-Laws of the Hebrew Benevolent Society of Los Angeles* (Los Angeles, 1855), Benjamin Hayes Scrapbooks, Scrapbook 47 Southern California Los Angeles County V Local History 1851–1861, Bancroft Library, University of California, Berkeley. The 1870 membership figure for HBS is from *The First Los Angeles City and County Directory, 1872*, 30. Twenty-seven LHBS members were named by Max Vorspan and Lloyd P. Gartner, *History of the Jews of Los Angeles* (San Marino, CA: The Huntington Library, 1970), 63n90; Sarah Newmark, the founding vice president and inexplicably not listed as a member by Vorspan and Gartner, brought the total to twenty-eight. For estimates of the total Jewish population in Los Angeles, see Appendix 1 in Vorspan and Gartner, *History of the Jews of Los Angeles*.
13. In a preliminary analysis of the 1860 Census that identified 161 Jews in Los Angeles, twenty-six families can be discerned based on common last names and domiciles. The figure of thirty-two families is cited by Marco R. Newmark, "Wilshire Boulevard Temple: Congregation B'nai B'rith (1862–1947)," *Historical Society of Southern California Quarterly* 38, no. 2 (1956). Norton B. Stern, "Probable & known Jewish residents of LA, listed in US Census of 1860," Norton B. Stern Materials, Small Collections, SC-7437, American Jewish Archives, Cincinnati.
14. Membership numbers for general organizations drawn from newspapers, directories, and organizational histories cited in text and in notes to tables of organizations. Figures for Masonic Lodge Los Angeles No. 42 from "Journal of Proceedings of the Grand Lodge of the State of California."
15. All the statistics presented here were based on membership data collected for organizations active at three different times: the mid-1850s, the early 1860s, and 1872. In each case, the organizations were included in the analysis because at least some data on their membership were available and because they were founded or active in the respective periods. Jewish and non-Jewish associations were included, with the presence of Jewish members not being a selection criterion. The data on members for each period are incomplete.
16. There were 184 Jews age eighteen and over in the 1870 U.S. Census for Los Angeles County. Jewish men belonging to the California, Concordia, and Jonathan private clubs were identified in lists of members for each organization published in the *Los Angeles Blue Book, 1894–95* (Los Angeles: Fitzgerald Murphy, 1894).
17. Places of birth are known for 62 out of 128 individuals who have been identified as members of the first six organizations. Jews with known places of birth were from Prussia, Bavaria, Poland, and France, while the two non-Jewish Europeans came from England and Ireland.
18. Of the fifty-six officers with known places of birth, forty were European-born, with twenty-six of those being Jewish.
19. The oldest references to what is now termed a synagogue (a Greek term), a physical place of assembly and worship for Jews, appear in inscriptions from

third-century B.C.E. Ptolemaic Egypt. Some scholars have speculated that the notion of a Jewish place of assembly other than the temple in Jerusalem originated in Babylon, with the Jewish captives taken there after the destruction of the First Temple in 587 B.C.E. See Lee I. Levine, *The Ancient Synagogue: The First Thousand Years* (New Haven: Yale University Press, 2005), 22–23, and Ben-Sasson, *A History of the Jewish People*, 173. In Hellenistic and Roman cities, Jewish communities "established places for study, worship, and burial, [and] provided material help to indigents, especially widows." Robert M. Seltzer, *Jewish People, Jewish Thought: The Jewish Experience in History* (Upper Saddle River, NJ: Prentice-Hall, Inc., 1980), 176–77.

20. Associationalism in the nineteenth-century American West was part of a larger, international trend toward embracing many different types of voluntary organizations. Jews in France created in 1860 the Alliance Israélite Universelle to fight anti-Semitism and help modernize Jews. In German-speaking states, by the 1830s, Jewish women's charitable societies were well established in a number of urban and rural communities. European Jews who settled in Los Angeles in midcentury likely would have been familiar with such organizations and probably would have seen them as a mark of modernity, a condition with which they and their fellow Angelenos aspired to be associated. In the United States, Jews were not confined to Jewish-only organizations and so they were active in cross-cultural, nonsectarian associational life some two decades before middle-class Jews in Imperial Germany became so engaged. Only at the beginning of the twentieth century were the levels and breadth of Jewish participation in German nonsectarian organizations comparable to those of Jewish Angelenos in the 1870s. Marion Kaplan, "Friendship on the Margins: Jewish Social Relations in Imperial Germany," *Central European History* 34, no. 4 (December 2001): 471–501; Benjamin Maria Baader, "When Judaism Turned Bourgeois: Gender in Jewish Associational Life and in the Synagogue, 1750–1850," *Leo Baeck Institute Yearbook* (2001): 114.

21. To term Congregation B'nai B'rith a "traditional synagogue" is to characterize it as being a product of the efforts of the local Jewish population to follow the tenets of Judaism within the context of American democracy and pluralism. From the appointment of a rabbi to the architecture of its first synagogue, it is evident that the congregation intended to be seen as one of the mainstream religious institutions of the city. Notably, while the divisions among the Jews in San Francisco were in line with Jewish communities elsewhere in the United States at the time, Jewish Angelenos embraced a single congregation for three decades. The congregation was led by elected laymen who hired a rabbi to conduct religious services and educational programs. Unlike the European custom in which community and synagogue were synonymous, membership in Congregation B'nai B'rith was voluntary, reflecting a practice that American Jews had adopted earlier in the nineteenth century. Similar to many religious bodies, at times it struggled to stay relevant and appealing to successive generations and newcomers. Because American Judaism was, in the words of Jonathan Sarna, "more democratic, free, diverse, and competitive" than the monolithic Judaism of Europe and colonial America, members of the congregation followed tradition and customs that fit their understanding of Judaism and local circumstances. The congregation resisted the early overtures of Isaac Mayer Wise to become part of his Reform movement, following their own timeline and

modernization process with formal affiliation with the movement not coming until 1903. Rooted in customs of Jewish community and practices of American religion, the congregation known today as the Wilshire Boulevard Temple established a tradition of independence and reinvention that became characteristic of many Jewish organizations in Los Angeles and elsewhere in the American West. On the history of Congregation B'nai B'rith, see Vorspan and Gartner, *History of the Jews of Los Angeles*, 54–62, and Marco R. Newmark, "Wilshire Boulevard Temple: Congregation B'nai B'rith (1862–1947)," *Historical Society of Southern California Quarterly* 38 (May 1956). On Isaac Mayer Wise's attempt to recruit the congregation to join the Reform movement, see William M. Kramer, ed., *The Western Journal of Isaac Mayer Wise, 1877* (Berkeley: Western Jewish History Center, Magnes Museum, 1974), 56, 76, n141. On the founding of San Francisco's first Jewish congregations, see Fred Rosenbaum, *Cosmopolitans: A Social and Cultural History of the Jews of San Francisco* (Berkeley: University of California Press, 2009), 14–16. On the characteristics of American Judaism that emerged in the early nineteenth century, see Jonathan D. Sarna, *American Judaism: A History* (New Haven: Yale University Press, 2004), 59–61.

22. In social networks, distance refers to the shortest path between any two actors over which information or other resources could flow. In the case of a single membership organization, the shortest path is always the same distance between any two members (one step), while in the case of a network of several organizations, the shortest path varies depending upon a number of factors. One factor is the density of ties. Density is the measure of the number of actual links compared to the number of possible links. In a single association, density is 100 percent, as all members are linked to all other members by virtue of their common affiliation. In a larger affiliation network of several organizations, density is less than 100 percent, with the percentage dependent upon the number of individuals with multiple memberships. As networks grow from a single membership organization to multiple organizations, measures of distance and density provide insight into network cohesiveness, or efficiency of flows, and the extent to which given individuals are positioned with advantage or constraint within a network. Short paths between actors increase the potential of network effects, while low density increases the potential for brokers to be highly influential over network flows. Low redundancy of ties can improve the opportunity for innovations to enter a network, but it also can indicate a low level of familiarity and trust, or fragmentation, among network members. High redundancy of ties can signal a network closed to outsiders, but it also can suggest a high level of homophily and trust, or cohesion, among network members. As networks change, distance and density are key characteristics in determining their functions and effects. Stanley Wasserman and Katherine Faust, *Social Network Analysis: Methods and Applications* (Cambridge: Cambridge University Press, 1994), 101, 110.

23. As with all networks reconstructed for this study, Lazard's network was inferred from a variety of sources that confirmed association with particular organizations at a particular time. It is assumed that he connected with other members through attending meetings and other events related to the organizations' activities. The completeness of the network is limited by the sources, some of which only provided names of officers or were somewhat removed from the period under

study. Every effort has been made to draw upon the most reliable and complete sources. Nevertheless, the networks are necessarily incomplete as to all members who Lazard may have known and the degree of familiarity (e.g., actual contact, frequency of contact, etc.) that may have existed. Even in the case of observed networks, where all connections theoretically are captured through individuals reporting and characterizing their ties, there is always an element of incompleteness or missing data in social network analysis. Consistency in sources, reconstruction, and analysis still produces useful patterns of structures and understandings of network effects.

24. Hellman was treasurer of the Ladies Benevolent Society (LBS) from 1877 to 1890. The Kindergarten Society was organized in 1884 by Caroline M. Severance, the nineteenth-century activist for women's rights and social justice who prior to her residency in Los Angeles had founded the first women's club in the United States, earning her the title "the Mother of Clubs." In 1886, while treasurer of LBS and vice president of the Kindergarten Society, Hellman also was president of the Ladies Hebrew Benevolent Society. Martha Burton Woodhead Williamson, *Ladies' Clubs and Societies in Los Angeles in 1892, Reported for the Historical Society of Southern California, Compiled and Edited by Mrs. M. Burton Williamson, March, 1892* (Los Angeles: E. R. King, 1892), 22; Frances Dinkelspiel, *Towers of Gold: How One Jewish Immigrant Named Isaias Hellman Created California* (New York: St. Martin's Press, 2008), 121.

25. John Field, *Social Capital* (London: Routledge, 2008), 1, 14. The literature on social capital and its various definitions is vast. Most scholars and theorists acknowledge the pioneering work of sociologist Pierre Bourdieu and James Coleman as foundational to the current interest and popularity of the concept. As with any appealing concept, their theories and definitions of social capital have been challenged and transformed across many disciplines, which has led to a diffusion of applications and controversy over appropriate units of analysis. The main divide between scholars of social capital centers on whether it is an asset of individuals or of communities, a personal, private advantage or a collective, public good. Useful summaries and discussions of the history of the concept and the individual versus community debate include Alejandro Portes, *Economic Sociology: A Systemic Inquiry* (Princeton, NJ: Princeton University Press, 2010), chapter 3; Nan Lin, *Social Capital: A Theory of Social Structure and Action* (New York: Cambridge University Press, 2001), chapter 1; and David Halpern, *Social Capital* (Malden, MA: Polity Press, 2005), introduction.

26. Quote from Ronald S. Burt, *Brokerage and Closure: An Introduction to Social Capital* (Oxford: Oxford University Press, 2005), 4. See also Lin, *Social Capital*, 25.

27. Social capital can work in four ways to influence outcomes of actions. It can facilitate the flow of information, bringing efficiency to exchanges of tangible and intangible goods. It may exert influence on other actors who have important roles in the expected outcomes of actions, shaping norms of behavior. It may represent an individual's social credentials and stature, signaling to others the range and depth of an individual's access to network resources. Social capital also can reinforce identity and recognition of an individual's value and worth to the network, supporting a person's emotional well-being as well as strengthening network ties. Through a combination of identifying positions within networks that

were advantageous and effects that stemmed from such positions on actions, the existence, use, and value of social capital can be assessed and analyzed. Lin, *Social Capital*, 20.

28. Sources: S.P. Borgatti, M.G. Everett, and L.C. Freeman, UCINet for Windows Software for Social Network Analysis, Version 6 (Harvard Analytic Technologies, 2002).
29. In the 1860s affiliation network, the three most central actors had in common their membership in the French Benevolent Society, the largest of the fourteen associations in the network, plus at least one of the other two large groups, the Masons and the Democrats. Being members of large associations increased their centrality. In the 1880s affiliation network, the two most central actors were connected to all four organizations in the network. Being members of all organizations increased their centrality. In both cases, the key act was becoming connected to multiple organizations.
30. McGaw phrase quoted in Naomi R. Lamoreaux, "Rethinking the Transition to Capitalism in the Early American Northeast," *The Journal of American History* 90 (September 2003): 449, and in Pamela Walker Laird, *Pull: Networking and Success since Benjamin Franklin* (Cambridge, MA: Harvard University Press, 2006), 15.
31. Engh, *Frontier Faiths*, 75–76, 79–83, 149–51, 155, 159; Dinkelspiel, *Towers of Gold*, 59; Stern and Kramer, "Jewish Padre to the Pueblo," 221. For a recent and thorough examination of the effectiveness and influence of the Sisters of Charity, see Kristine Ashton Gunnell, "Without Regard to Race or Creed: The Daughters of Charity and the Development of Social Welfare in Los Angeles, 1856–1927" (Dissertation, Claremont Graduate University, 2010).
32. *Los Angeles Star*, March 27, 1869; June 5, 1869; June 12, 1869. For other editorial examples, see Engh, *Frontier Faiths*, 84.
33. Engh, *Frontier Faiths*, 93, 160.
34. The 1883 building campaign of the First Congregational Church also received support from a number of nonmembers, including Methodists, Episcopalians, Roman Catholics, and Jews. Michael Engh argued, "Religious cooperation among pioneer settlers developed out of necessity and retained its vigor as long as primitive conditions prevailed." By his account, the motivation of "necessity" was diminishing by the late 1860s, as "local Protestants were increasingly able to sustain, by themselves, both a well-regulated society and their respective denominations." Further, "by 1890, Los Angeles so resembled communities in the Midwest that many citizens would forget its formerly distinctive religious heritage." His characterization is well supported by a variety of evidence, but his chronology ignores the networks of personal relationships among the pioneers, their children, and even grandchildren in some cases that continued to foster interfaith support. While the scale of collaboration and support certainly changed as the city grew and the number of religious institutions increased, the custom of interfaith support of Los Angeles did not disappear as rapidly or as completely as Engh suggests. For several months in 1928 and 1929, the First Congregational Church temporarily housed the services and classes of Congregation B'nai B'rith as it awaited the completion of its new synagogue on Wilshire Boulevard. At the beginning of the twenty-first century, Jewish Angelenos contributed financially and in other ways to the construction of a new Catholic cathedral, with a sense of civic pride perhaps

not unlike that of the pioneers who aided the erection of the city's first cathedral. These two examples, nearly a century apart and well beyond Engh's era of religious cooperation, stand in for numerous others that suggest that legacy has not been lost in Los Angeles, but, rather, obscured. Engh, *Frontier Faiths*, 84, 93–95, 99–100, 178–79; Fort Street Methodist Episcopal Church Ladies Aid Society, *Los Angeles Cookery* (Los Angeles: Mirror Printing and Binding House, 1881), Introduction, 11, 50, 51, 21, 22, 43, 44; Marco R. Newmark, "Wilshire Boulevard Temple," 175; *Los Angeles Times*, November 15, 2001, "$2.5 Million Given for Fountain at New Cathedral—Gift: A Jewish philanthropist donates the money in recognition of Jewish-Catholic relationship," http://articles.latimes.com/2001/nov/15/local/me-4360, accessed 02/28/11.

35. On the relationship between charitable behavior and perceptions of trustworthiness, see Sebastian Fehrler, "Charity as a Signal of Trustworthiness," *IZA Discussion Paper No. 5299* (2010). Accessed 12/21/10 at SSRN: http://ssrn.com/abstract=1708745.
36. Classified advertisement, *Los Angeles Times*, October 26, 1887; "Society," *Los Angeles Times*, November 11, 1887; Harris Newmark, *Sixty Years in Southern California, 1853–1913, Containing the Reminiscences of Harris Newmark* (Los Angeles: Dawson's Book Shop, 1984), 367.
37. For the now-classic discussion of the American West as a distinctive place defined by continuous battles for dominance and its diversity, see Limerick, *The Legacy of Conquest*, 26–32.
38. Susie Pak, *Gentlemen Bankers: The World of J. P. Morgan* (Cambridge, MA: Harvard University Press, 2013).
39. Gamm and Putnam, "The Growth of Voluntary Associations in America," 524, 536; Tony Fels, "Religious Assimilation in a Fraternal Organization: Jews and Freemasonry in Gilded-Age San Francisco," *American Jewish History* 74, no. 4 (1985): 369–403; William Toll, *The Making of an Ethnic Middle Class: Portland Jewry over Four Generations* (Albany: State University of New York Press, 1982).

9

Greening the Silver Saloon
Building Irish Community in the Mining West

Michelle A. Charest

Americans think they know something about Virginia City, Nevada, from reading Mark Twain's Roughing It *and watching the television series* Bonanza. *But archaeological digs in the city's National Landmark District reveal a more complex lifestyle than the shoot-it-up Wild West image. Virginia City was a boom-and-bust town like many western mining towns. It also attracted immigrants who brought their traditions, businesses, and cultural values. Chinese and Irish immigrants especially left their mark on the city. By carefully analyzing remains in the buildings and checking written records, archaeologists can piece together what these immigrants valued. Michelle Charest's discussion of the Irish Hibernia Brewery Saloon joins a number of studies that look at material culture to understand life in Virginia City.*[1] *Through her careful study of artifacts found by University of Nevada–Reno research teams, she is able to determine that the saloon was not only a place to drink but also a place to socialize, serving as a foundation of Irish-American community life. Her study reinforces the conclusion that other historians and social scientists have reached that the tools and techniques from many disciplines can help scholars understand migration and its effects on a community.*

This chapter explores the ways in which nineteenth-century Irish residents of the American Mining West created and maintained community by embracing the saloon as a site for the translation of the traditional Irish pub abroad. The following discussion examines in particular the case study of the mining boomtown of Virginia City, Nevada, and the archaeological excavations of the Irish-identified Hibernia Brewery Saloon. Research focuses on the early decades of the town, from 1859–1890. Archaeological analysis is emphasized as an essential source of historical data on a subject, nineteenth-century Irish-American Western saloons, which has a very limited presence in the contemporary documentary record. This research in turn reveals the vital role played by the Irish saloon in fostering the reification of a shared Irish identity among immigrants on the Comstock, an identity intimately linked to memories of community life in Ireland. Not only does this research contribute to a more complete understanding of the immigrant experience in the American West, it also addresses the translation of the Irish pub, the heart of community in nineteenth-century Ireland, into a parallel foundational institution of Irish-American community life, providing context for understanding the overall development of community in modern American culture.

Virginia City, Nevada, was a mining boomtown that sprang up in 1859 following the discovery of the Comstock Lode, the first major discovery of silver ore in United States history. During the twenty years following the discovery of the lode, the Comstock, composed of Virginia City and the adjacent town of Gold Hill, grew from nothing into a thriving minimetropolis with a population of over twenty thousand, seemingly dropped into the desert mountains of Nevada.[2] A significant portion of this population was foreign born, accounting for 36 percent of the population of Virginia City in 1860, with that proportion increasing over the remainder of the century to 50 percent in 1870 and 45 percent in 1880.[3] The largest numbers of foreign-born residents of the Comstock hailed from Ireland, Germany, Britain, and Canada, though a hugely diverse array of other origins were represented within the population including Mexico, Scandinavia, France, China, and Italy.[4] The largest group of immigrants in Virginia City was the Irish, accounting for approximately 11 percent in 1860, and then approximately 18 percent from 1870 on.

Above all, nineteenth-century Virginia City, Nevada, was a mining boomtown. Beyond that, among the myriad characterizations of the town emerge two key factors to this discussion: Virginia City had a very large Irish population, and the town was filled to the brim with saloons. Yet what, if anything, did these two aspects of Virginia City have to do with one another? Contemporary descriptions of the relationship between the Irish/Irish-American community and the saloon in the late nineteenth century were replete with vehement anti-Irish stereotypes and cultural misunderstanding at worst and complete disinterest at best.[5] Historical research on the subject, while certainly having moved well beyond the negative attitudes of the turn of the century, has still taken a limited interest in the relationship between the Irish community and the saloon. Most typically, the Irish have been addressed as a mere component of the overall "saloon culture" of the late nineteenth and early twentieth century, with little detail beyond a few tidbits regarding their supposedly minimalist saloons and hard-drinking ways.[6] In the limited number of studies providing more in-depth details of the Irish relationship with the saloon in America, the saloon has still figured as only a more minor aspect of a different story and one that largely takes place on the East Coast.[7] Still, by and large, the relationship between the Irish community and the saloon in the late nineteenth-century West has remained largely unexplored.

The research presented here helps to establish the key role of the saloon as a community center among Irish immigrants to the West, much in the way that the pub traditionally served as the center of the community in Ireland.[8] Research is grounded in the discipline of historical archaeology, which employs a methodological approach that incorporates a wide range of sources to provide information about the past. Thus, in addition to all strands of evidence from the documentary and oral historical record, historical archaeologists also examine the material remains of past human activities to provide insight into aspects of historical experience that are not detailed in the historical record.[9] In the case of the Irish saloon, the documentary record is extremely limited, even nonexistent, with regard to much of what actually went on in these saloons, and thus in the social lives of saloon patrons. As such, the archaeological record may provide the only detailed insight into how these spaces were used among the Irish communities of the West, contextualized by a broader documentary record.

Irish Traditional Community Abroad

The story of nineteenth-century Irish immigration, centered around the Great Famine (1845–1852), is one that has already been well told in great detail elsewhere.[10] However, in order to frame a discussion of the presence of traditional Irish community in the mining West, it is nevertheless pertinent to briefly examine the relationship between nineteenth-century Irish immigration and Irish traditional culture. The Great Famine had served as a catalyst for large-scale cultural change in Ireland, particularly due to the loss of 40 percent of the Irish population as a result of death and emigration.[11] This population decline was particularly large among those groups that were typically most strongly invested in conserving Irish traditional values: the elderly, the Irish-speakers, and the traditionalist peasants.[12] As a result, there were significantly fewer people available to pass on Irish traditional culture. Furthermore, the growth of the British-run public education system and increasing antitraditionalist attitudes of the Catholic Church over the course of the century both aided in effectively quashing many traditional practices and beliefs throughout the Irish populace.[13] At the same time, a modern capitalist, industrialized, and internationalized worldview was gradually overtaking Ireland. Irish traditional culture was being subsumed, either willingly or unwillingly, by a more generic Anglicized culture more in keeping with the increased reliance on international markets and ideals, particularly those of Britain and America.[14]

Although perhaps counterintuitive, for some post-famine Irish a possible solution to this loss of traditional culture may have been found in the act of emigration. America was an ideal destination for the Irish emigrant seeking a place in which to rebuild an Irish traditional culture. While the United States could hardly be confused with pre-famine Ireland, it provided a social environment that allowed for the development of Irish enclaves composed of those who remembered Ireland and whose nostalgia for traditional Irish cultural values would allow those cultural practices to carry on.[15] The American West was particularly suitable for such purposes as it was seen as a blank slate, a fresh place where settlers could, according to White, "re-create familiar worlds" and per Gjerde, "reestablish and embellish upon former patterns of life."[16] In addition, the West presented the added opportunity for the Irish to be among the first nonnative settlers in an area,[17] which was far from the case in the East where the Irish were relative newcomers. This in part allowed those who settled in the West to more readily avoid the anti-Irish and anti-Catholic sentiments and discrimination often exhibited in the well-established eastern cities,[18] placing the Irish at the same level as any other group of European heritage in America.

Any discussion of Irish traditional community would seem to necessitate discussion of the Irish Catholic Church. The relationship between the two has become naturalized to the extent that Catholicism is popularly seen as one of, if not the primary, central identifying characteristic of the Irish people in all historical contexts.[19] Yet in reality, this association did not arise until fairly recently in Irish history, and in fact, the church was far from a major player in the lives of much of the rural and working-class Irish population even at the middle of the nineteenth century. Miller has suggested that large numbers of Irish peasants that emigrated during the famine and the years immediately following would have been considered to be "merely nominal or customary Catholics" rather than active, devoted Catholics, describing their faith as "at best imperfectly internalized."[20] In particular, the rural Irish did not always attend church, and many not at all—less than half of the prefamine Catholic population of Ireland attended church.[21] When they did, they most likely attended a local church that did not claim association with Catholicism at all. The influence of the Catholic Church in rural Irish lives was not fully realized until the general cultural shift and identity crisis that occurred gradually following the country's recuperation from the famine. During that period, often referred to as a "devotional revolution" with reference to the church, Ireland saw great increases in numbers of professionalized clergy, cathedrals, churches, convents, and an overall increasing dominance of Catholic Church ideology over Irish culture at the end of the century.[22]

However, since research indicates that the majority of Irish immigrants in Virginia City came from a rural Ireland on the early cusp of this cultural shift,[23] it is likely that the majority of Irish immigrants living in Virginia City would not have had a background that made the Catholic Church a pivotal component of their lives and their sense of community. Rather, they were instead part of the demographic group of "nominal Catholics" described above, a group whose religious affiliation was "in danger of disintegrating in [the] unfamiliar environments" of America, where the existing church infrastructure, particularly in the West, was not able to accommodate the Irish population influx until the last quarter of the century.[24] As a result of these factors, "tens of thousands of Irish-Americans in the meantime drifted into indifference or apostasy."[25]

Likewise, many Irish-Catholics in Virginia City during the period from 1860–1890 did not attend church on a weekly basis. Echoing larger infrastructural issues experienced throughout the country, the Catholic Church in Virginia City was not nearly physically large enough to accommodate the Catholic population of the town, even if it offered several Sunday and weekday masses.[26] Furthermore, workers in the mining town regularly chose to work instead of attending mass. Timothy McCarthy, a mine worker in Virginia City, wrote in his diaries on numerous occasions that he had failed to attend Sunday Mass because he had to work.[27] Although McCarthy's diaries clearly indicate he was concerned with his faith and that he desired to attend mass, especially as he grew older, his experience of being made to work on Sunday could hardly have been a singular one. Similarly, diarist and Irish-American resident of Virginia City Mary Mathews commented that "as far as work is concerned, there is no Sabbath there. The mills, mines and machine-shops are always going. You will see all sorts of teaming going on the same as any other day."[28] An Irish reporter visiting the mining West as late as 1894 even wrote back to his readers in Dublin, about the Irish "exiles" in America who had "lost touch with the old religion, their children went in search of false gods, and drifted into other creeds and other associations, and where they should have reverenced they scoffed."[29]

However, even if there were large segments of the Irish population of Virginia City not actively participating in the Catholic Church, it is likely that a considerable number of the parishioners who could not attend mass had not completely given up on their faith. They may have instead practiced their Catholicism at home or prayed to St. Patrick. Many may have thought of themselves as Catholic, and conveyed their religious faith as Catholicism, all without having a particularly strong or self-defining association with the religion. Even of those who did attend church, they may not have been doing so for purely devout or even community-seeking reasons. For example, Mathews also wrote, "The people of Virginia City are more dressy than any place I ever lived in. I candidly believe many of them go to church simply to show their fine costumes."[30] Of course, Mathews's observations on such matters are hardly fact. Still, while there is strong evidence that many of the Irish Catholics of Virginia City did not actively practice their religion, this should not be seen as a denial of those who strongly identified as Catholics. Mary Mathews attended Sunday mass, and so did Timothy McCarthy when he could, and yet even with the increased insight into these two individuals' lives it is difficult to determine the degree to which Catholicism and the Catholic community figured in their own identities. Even Mary Mathews rarely discussed church and did not ever talk about her Catholicism specifically throughout her highly detailed narrative of life in Virginia City.

The key point here is that without the backbone of participation in actual church ceremonies and activities by the vast majority of the Irish in Virginia City, it seems unlikely that those who did not attend service had developed much of a sense of a Catholic social community. As such, it is hard to imagine that the Catholic Church could fulfill the need for social interaction among the Irish in Virginia City. Sociality would have had to have been sought elsewhere.

Although lacking a prominent church-based community, there is nevertheless strong evidence suggesting that there was a true Irish social community in Virginia City, not simply a coresidence of Irish people. For the sake of this paper, the term *community* refers to a group of people who maintain a shared history, a feeling of togetherness, common interactions, and ties to place, wherever that place may be.[31] These characteristics appear to be strongly present in many aspects of the social life of the Irish in Virginia City. Outside of their neighborhoods and homes, the Irish and Irish-American residents had a variety of regular, formal, Irish-associated activities. Irish-themed commercial entertainment was quite popular at venues such as Maguire's Opera House and the Black Crook Melodeon. Such entertainment might include plays, musical recitals, lectures, Irish University benefits, and even exhibitions of paintings, as in *The New Hibernicon*, representing a tour through Ireland.[32]

In addition to this very public entertainment, the Virginia City Irish community also participated in a number of Irish social and cultural organizations, such as the Irish-American Benevolent Association, the Sons and Friends of Ireland, and the Ancient Order of the Hibernians; military organizations such as the Emmet Guard; and political organizations such as the Fenian Brotherhood and Fenian Sisterhood.[33] These formal groups gathered regularly to fundraise for Irish causes such as Irish university endowment and famine relief, as well as for frequent grand banquets, balls, and lectures on a range of Irish topics.[34] These groups, and others, all contributed to impressive St. Patrick's Day festivities in Virginia City, including balls, banquets, and an outstanding parade.[35]

While most of the Irish social activities were essentially available to all classes of Irish and Irish-American residents of Virginia City, there were certain economic limitations placed upon those who wished to participate in many of those activities. Irish-oriented balls, for instance, were lovely events, but they were typically held for either charity or for profit, and tickets were often pricey. For example, a ticket to the Annual Fenian Ball in 1865 cost three dollars, or the equivalent of one hundred pounds of good potatoes, twelve pounds of pork, thirteen and a half pounds of sugar, or thirty drinks at the local saloon.[36] And that was merely the entrance fee. While the cost of attendance was not necessarily prohibitive, it would have required budgeting for the average working-class Irish couple to attend. Even if the average Irish resident of Virginia City was not able to participate in all the fine Irish community social events of the town, this did not mean that there was no opportunity for an Irish social community among the working class. There was always the saloon.

Although the Catholic Church did not gain its powerful foothold on rural Ireland until at the earliest the second half of the nineteenth century, the pub's role in the community had been well established even at the turn of the century.[37] In fact, by the beginning of the nineteenth century, the licensed public house had become a fixture in the Irish community, on par with the local (non-Catholic associated) church as its social center.[38] Even when compared to the church, though, there were characteristics of the pub that made it an ideal place for creating community bonds. Kearns describes it as the "only type of public building used by large numbers of ordinary people where their thoughts and actions are not arranged for them."[39] Pubs might not have been the only gathering space, but they were the only spaces in which folks could do what they pleased in an unstructured and unmanaged fashion. This was a very different sort of space from the church. The pub was the only place where a working-class man could be himself. Share goes even further in discussing present-day Irish pubs to convincingly argue for the position of the pub as Oldenburg's "third place," a neutral public place that is neither work nor home[40]—an attribution which would seem to be just as accurate with regard to the nineteenth century. Share identifies key attributes—including an atmosphere of playfulness, and the presence of regulars and conversation—contributing to the social use of the pub as a place of comfort which would likewise contribute to the feeling of community solidarity which Kearns refers to as "the heart of the pub."[41] From a historical perspective, the centrality of the pub in Irish community life is equally evident, and descriptions of rural villages in the writings of the day make it clear that the pubs were the only social space available to rural people.[42] These pubs were valuable, essential social spaces for the nineteenth-century Irish community—spaces with easy surrogates in the saloons of the American West.

A Saloon Community

Mythologized perceptions of the American Western boomtown tend to heavily project the image of an overall rowdy, drunken world with the saloon as its epicenter.[43] And while the early mining camps certainly had a chaotic and even dangerous character at times, once the camps developed into permanent communities with families and businesses, the West was really no more chaotic and dangerous than anywhere else in the country at the time, even if saloons were present in high numbers.

In Virginia City, saloons were typically the most numerous commercial establishments in town, often far outnumbering any other variety of business. In 1876, William Wright claimed in his historical sketch of Virginia City, *The History of the Big Bonanza*, that there were one hundred saloons in the town at the time of publication.[44] Eliot Lord in his 1883 *Comstock Mining and Miners* repeated this same number as true in 1880.[45] Mary Mathews claimed in 1877 that along the main commercial street, every fourth door was a saloon.[46] Although it is likely that these numbers were merely estimates, they do not appear to be very far from the truth. Using local directories and newspaper advertisements and articles, it has been possible to determine the minimum number of saloons that were in operation in Virginia City during the period from 1862 through 1890, shedding light on contemporary estimates of the saloon presence in the town.[47] This research has shown that as early as 1864, Virginia City had ninety-three known saloons. With an estimated population of approximately 4,250 at the time, this meant that there was a saloon for every forty-six people, incidentally the highest number of saloons relative to the total population in the history of the town.

To place the saloons of Virginia City in context with those of other cities during this time, this data can be compared to that of Duis's examination of saloons in Chicago and Boston in 1885. Duis found that Chicago had approximately one saloon for every 203 people, and that Boston had a saloon for every 500.[48] Contrast these numbers with Virginia City in 1884 (the closest year with reliable saloon numbers) which had a minimum of one saloon for every 161 people including children. Compared with an earlier Virginia City of 1864, there was a minimum of four and a half times as many saloons per person in Virginia City as in Chicago in 1885, and eleven times more than Boston in that same year. The high numbers of saloons in Virginia City represented a very widely available public gathering space, but these saloons also served as an ideal space for community maintenance through their incorporation of the commensal acts of drinking and eating.

Although these saloons were businesses first, this designation does not preclude the saloons from having a greater cultural value within society. While it would take many decades of social research before an awareness of the social value of drinking came to be generally accepted among scholars, there was nevertheless some awareness even at the turn of the twentieth century that the saloon itself had some redemptive social value, even if perhaps the drinking that was done there was still seen as socially displeasing. Raymond Calkins in 1901 wrote a report addressing alternatives to the saloon as a potential solution to the perceived "liquor problems" of the time.[49] The general premise of the report, though, was importantly that the saloon played an integral part in American social life and as such could not be simply done away with; a substitute that provided the same social role had to be provided as an alternative.

The need for a space in which a social community could be created was one felt particularly strongly among two groups that are of central interest to this discussion: immigrants and boomtown residents. With specific regard to Irish immigrants in America there was a desire to seek out the comfort of one's own countrymen,[50] with the saloon acting as one of the few social gathering spaces available. Immigrants in general faced the particular challenge of finding community in a world where they were very likely outsiders, a completely different sort of scenario than they would have encountered in their homelands. This issue would have been greatly magnified in the case of a mining boomtown like Virginia City with its incredibly diverse foreign-born population. Furthermore, boomtowns inherently incorporated stressors which would have strongly encouraged their residents to seek out comfort in their social surroundings. As West put it, in "societies of chance and change, [and] life with few moorings, many of the members could be expected to seek out the ready fellowship of the bottle."[51]

Virginia City's number of saloons may have been relatively higher than Boston and Chicago, but this did not necessarily mean that Virginia City was a town of drunks. In this context, it is important to consider that there is more to drinking than just getting drunk, and there is more to drinking establishments than just providing a space in which to do so. In fact, the social act of drinking alcohol together, commensally, and in public settings—both characteristic of saloons—has been anthropologically shown to be particularly conducive to the establishment and maintenance of social relations.[52] Essentially, the social nature of drinking helps to build communities. As such, the social consumption of alcohol has been linked to the development of identities associated with this social act, leading to distinctions among class, gender, age, nation, ethnicity, occupation, and religion.[53] In other words, group identities are often shaped by how that same group goes about the act of drinking—what is consumed, who participates, where the drinking occurs, what activities coincide with the drinking, and so on. Each of these factors, often repeated on most drinking occasions, will become a part of that group's identity.

The shared consumption of food has been found to have a similar effect on social relationships, helping to cement group ties and to provide an apt social scenario for facilitating interaction.[54] Furthermore, a significant factor in the continuance of a maintained sense of identity among immigrants is the strength of memories of the homeland and of the experiences left behind. In the context of the Irish saloon, an especially pertinent aspect of a perpetuated Irish identity is the impact of what is understood to be a very strong relationship between human memory and food.[55] Anthropological research of immigrant and diasporic communities in particular, a class which would include the Irish of Virginia City, has revealed a strong presence of nostalgic recollections linked to the foods of these communities' homelands,[56] associations which were similarly exhibited within Irish-American saloons as discussed below. Considering that food was often available with drinks at the Virginia City saloons, there would have been quite a potential for community building within their walls.

As the social act of consuming food and drink has been seen to be instrumental in the creation and maintenance of group identity, the same is true in the case of the Irish of Virginia City. The Irish, much as any immigrant group, brought to America certain ideas about the nature of community relations and sociability based upon their experiences in their homeland, including expectations of the social drinking experience that had been fostered in the pubs of Ireland.[57] For many Irish immigrants, America was a place where they could recreate an Irish community in an idealized and often exaggerated fashion.[58] The easy parallel of saloons in the American West would have been the ideal space in which to build a solid community foundation as they were inexpensive, widely available, and inherently promoted community building by providing a space for traditional practices of the consumption of food and drink.

Perhaps telling with regard to the importance of the saloon or pub in Irish community life was the fact that in Virginia City, saloon keeping was one of the most popular professions among the Irish. Ireland was the most common birthplace among all saloonkeepers, disproportionately higher than would be expected based purely upon the total Irish population.[59] This high proportion of Irish saloonkeepers would seem to be related to the conception within the Irish community that such a position was an attainable means of securing economic and social status within the community.[60] Publicans and saloonkeepers were the overseers of the social world which was centered around the pub or saloon. And the economic potential of the position seems to have been a reality in Virginia City as well: according to the United States Census of 1870, Irish saloonkeepers were 40 percent more likely than saloonkeepers in general to have personal real estate and more than 200 percent more likely than men on average in Virginia City.[61]

Archaeological Evidence from the Hibernia Brewery Saloon

Unfortunately, despite the apparent prevalence of Irish-run saloons, the documentary record of the Irish saloon experience in Virginia City is rather limited. In fact, the archival record of the *overall* saloon experience in Virginia City is quite limited, primarily gleaned from advertisements and the odd mention in passing in the newspaper. There does remain one invaluable resource which has become essential for understanding the saloon community of Virginia City, and that is archaeological excavations of saloon sites. To date, excavations of four nineteenth-century saloon sites in Virginia City have been conducted by University of Nevada–Reno archaeological field schools.[62] The first of these excavations was that of the former site of Shanahan and O'Connor's Hibernia Brewery Saloon. The archaeological remains and data gathered from this excavation in turn provide a rare glimpse into the Irish saloon community of Virginia City.

Archaeological excavations of the Hibernia Brewery were conducted over the course of the 1993 and 1994 field seasons under the supervision of Donald Hardesty of the University of Nevada–Reno. The site itself was located under a vacant unpaved lot at the former address of 162 South C Street (Figure 9.1). Over the course of two field seasons a total of thirty-one two-square-meter units were excavated by hand using stratigraphic excavation broken down by arbitrary ten-centimeter levels for precision. Researchers use one-eighth-inch screens for artifact recovery, including faunal remains, with artifacts bagged by stratigraphic context. Preliminary analysis of a portion of the collection, primarily of glass and ceramic remains, was conducted by Ralph Giles upon return from the field, in addition to a full faunal remains analysis performed by Elizabeth Scott.[63] Additional

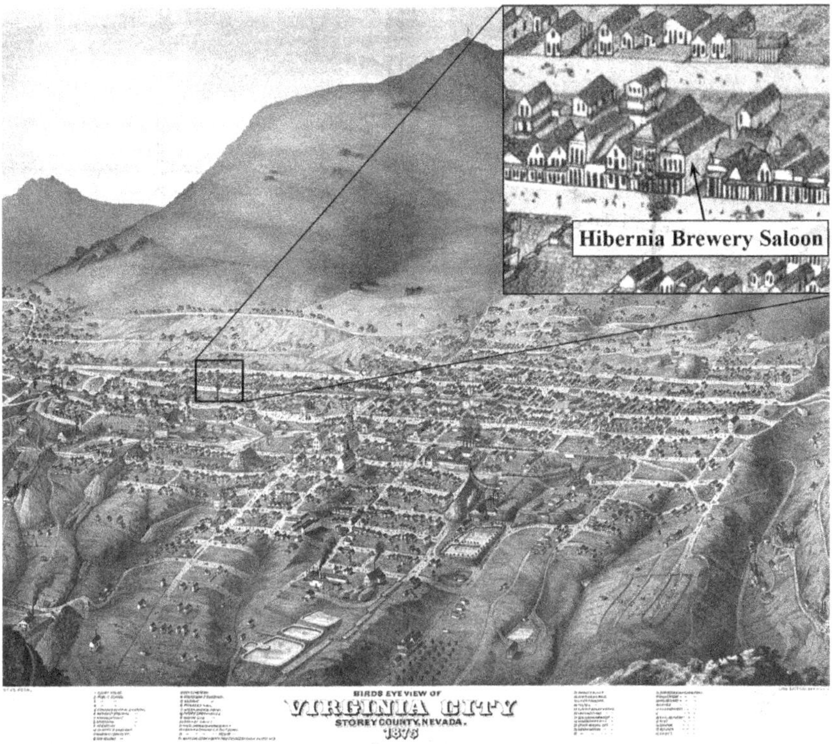

Figure 9.1. Map of Virginia City, Nevada, with detail illustrating the Hibernia Brewery Saloon. Augustus Koch, "Bird's Eye View of Virginia City, Storey County, Nevada" (San Francisco: Britton, Rey, and Company, 1875). Courtesy of Library of Congress, Geography and Map Division.

Figure 9.2. Shanahan & O'Connor saloon advertisement (*The Virginia Evening Chronicle*, November 29, 1878).

reanalysis of the archaeological collection was conducted from 2009–2011 by Michelle Charest.[64]

The Hibernia Brewery was located on the main commercial street in Virginia City, though well outside of the most central part of the commercial district. Nevertheless, the Hibernia was still an easy walk from the center of town or, conversely, from the largest Irish neighborhood. The first mention of the Hibernia Brewery Saloon dates to 1877, referencing the saloon's proprietors, William W. Shanahan and John O'Connor, both Irish natives.[65] The Hibernia was in operation until at least 1884, after which directory listings for the establishment cease, although it may have been in operation through 1886.[66] By the time the 1890 Sanborn map of Virginia City was published, the building had been converted to a livery stable.[67]

Based upon the limited documentary record, including the Sanborn insurance map, advertisements, and contemporary drawings, the Hibernia would appear on the outside to be a fairly typical working-class Virginia City saloon,[68] though one that proudly proclaimed its identity as an Irish saloon with its name "Hibernia." Likewise, this Irish community identity also manifested in a variety of ways in the actual day-to-day community experience at the saloon.

Irish saloons are portrayed in the historical literature as being bare-bones establishments, distinctive if anything for their lack of adornment in comparison with their fellows.[69] Calkins in 1901 even described "poorer kinds of Irish saloons" in New York City as being characterized by "indifference to real comfort" because the Irishman "was born in dirt and he is not afraid of it."[70] The pub in Ireland, in contrast, was a comfortable, homey sort of place—largely because it was actually a part of someone's home, usually just the ground floor of a house.[71] A sudden complete disinterest for the general atmosphere of the space seems an unlikely result of a single ocean voyage. As such, the validity of these statements, and seeming repetition of such negative views in historical research, does not appear to be necessarily grounded in reality.

This sterile décor certainly does not appear to have been the case with the Hibernia. Large quantities of multicolored painted plate glass found at the site provide evidence that at least one saloon window facing the street was painted with an undetermined but elaborate design. Gold paint was particularly prominent along with red, blue, green, pink, and black. Fragments of plaster and wallpaper recovered from the Hibernia site reveal that the walls of the saloon were covered in blue, red, white, and gray paint, along with at least two styles of floral wallpaper—one in blue, red/pink and yellow, and the other in green and pink. Evidence of a range of decorative fittings from the interior of the saloon were also identified including

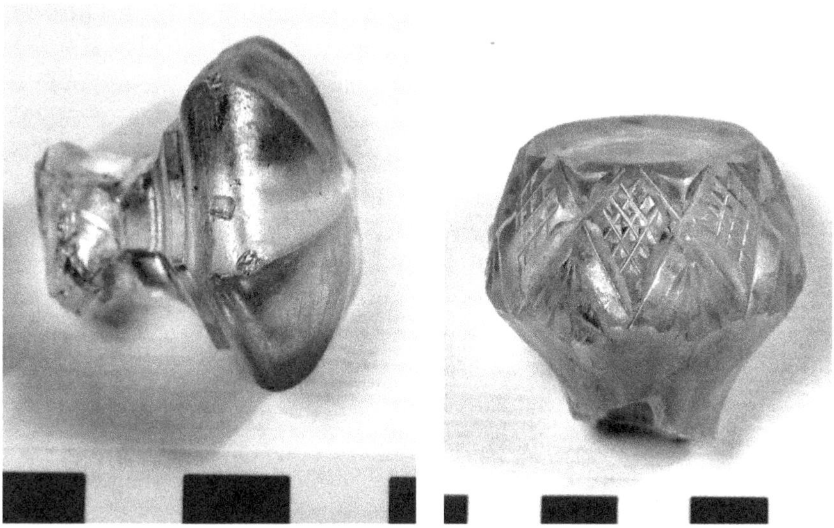

Figure 9.3. Decanter stoppers from the Hibernia Brewery Saloon site. Photograph by Michelle Charest. Scale in centimeters.

Figure 9.4. Brass emblem with international symbol of music from Hibernia Brewery Saloon site. Photograph by Ronald M. James.

brass door knobs, iron coat or hat hooks with acorn heads, curtain rod brackets (suggesting curtains), mirror fragments (suggesting the standard mirror above the bar), a fancy Rockingham glazed spittoon, and even a clock-winding key. Multiple fragments of colored lamp globes in combinations of white and teal, and gold and coral were also excavated. These decorations were well beyond the bare minimum suggested as being typical of Irish saloons in the day.

A total of seven glass decanter stoppers were recovered from the Hibernia site: three green glass stoppers, one black glass stopper, and two decoratively molded clear glass stoppers (Figure 9.3). This was the largest number of decanter stoppers found at any of the four Virginia City saloon excavations. The Hibernia site also revealed numerous examples of quality decorative glass stemware, tumblers, etched drinking glasses, and pressed glass dishes, in addition to more utilitarian vessels. Shanahan and O'Connor cared about the way their saloon was presented to the world, and as part of an effort to make the Hibernia a worthy place in the eyes of the Irish community of Virginia City, for either business or social reasons, they fitted the saloon out in the finest fashion they could manage. By creating an inviting atmosphere with carefully chosen and even sometimes elaborate décor they took their saloon well beyond the minimal expectations of a drinking establishment to make a place worthy of being a community center. And by providing their customers with fine beverage glasses and decorative snack and condiment dishes, they cultivated a feeling that the Hibernia's community was fully deserving of such finery, regardless of their social class. The Hibernia was a fine Irish saloon for a fine Irish community.

The atmosphere of the traditional Irish pub may have also been manifested at the Hibernia Brewery Saloon through the presence of Irish music. Dancing and music were seen as essential components of the traditional Irish pub experience,[72] and ones that were not necessarily present in all types of drinking establishments. For example, the English seemed to think it was incredibly odd that music and dancing would be found in Irish pubs; it was seen as a uniquely Irish aberrant activity.[73] Excavations at the Hibernia uncovered two small brass emblems that appear to have once been fastened to a wooden item (Figure 9.4). On each emblem is depicted a lyre with a wreath of laurel and oak. While it is tempting to identify this symbol as representative of the iconic Irish harp that is the symbol of Ireland, the emblems actually evoke the international symbol for music. These brass objects may in part serve as a "close-enough" reference to Irish symbology, but perhaps more importantly their presence indicates that music was very important to someone at the Hibernia, perhaps as part of the traditional pub/saloon experience, showing that music was an essential component of the Irish atmosphere of the Hibernia Saloon.

Another way in which the character of the traditional Irish pub may have been apparent at the Hibernia is simply through the presence of women at the saloon. Up to now, the saloon in Virginia City, including the Hibernia, has been discussed as a largely male space. And this does appear to have been the case in general—the saloons of Virginia City were predominantly male spaces. Yet, Irish tradition would suggest that the presence of women, and even families, would not have been out of place in the rural Irish pubs that were remembered by significant numbers of Irish immigrants on the Comstock.[74] Unfortunately, in the United States, there was a significant stigma against women who came into contact with alcoholic beverages and who frequented saloons during the nineteenth century, a stigma that even continues in modern historical research.[75]

It is clear from documentary evidence that, at the very least, female family members were often actively and respectably involved in the family saloon business. Irish women in particular seem to have been associated in the saloon trade, as saloonkeepers in particular. Of the saloonkeepers identified in the course of this study, forty were women operating saloons between 1862 and 1887. Intriguingly, in some cases, such as those of Anne Shields and Ellen Byrne, these female saloonkeepers served as the primary breadwinners in their families, providing support for their husbands' more risky business ventures.[76] Of the forty female saloonkeepers in Virginia City, 30 percent were identified as being Irish either through census records or through having clearly Irish names (e.g., McCarthy, Flanigan, etc.). An additional eleven women had potentially Irish names, suggesting that possibly up to 58 percent of the female saloonkeepers were of Irish descent. These percentages are much higher than the general Irish population over the course of the century making the Irish women significantly more likely to become saloonkeepers than would be expected based on the population (ratio of 1.6–1.8:1). In keeping with the trend in Virginia City, Rosenzweig in his study of the nineteenth-century Irish immigrant community of Worcester, Massachusetts, observed that Irish women had played a key role in the mid-nineteenth-century Worcester liquor trade, to the apparent distaste of non-Irish commentators of the day.[77] Archaeological evidence from the Hibernia clearly indicates the presence of women at the saloon through the identification of items such as women's clothing notions including clasps (Figure 9.5); decorative porcelain, shell, brass, rubber, and glass buttons; and glass beads and cabochons.

One category of archaeological remains that often finds its way into discussion of gender in the nineteenth century is teawares. A minimum

Figure 9.5. Decorative brass clasp with shell inlay and incised floral design. Photographs by Michelle Charest. Scale in centimeters.

of fifteen teacups were identified at the site among a large number of nondiagnostic vessel sherds accounting for a much larger assemblage. In addition to simpler styles, the teaware remains included a variety of more decorative examples, like decorative molded designs such as a bamboo-style handle. Another featured a molded scalloped edge with a gold-luster band painted as a rim line. A fragment of one earthenware tea saucer had a hand-painted bluebell design in blue, gold, and green over the transfer print; yet another porcelain teacup handle showed a hand-painted blue line running down the handle with a single line of gold dots down its center (Figure 9.6). A final example of elaborate

Figure 9.6. Top left and top right, pressed-glass dish sherds; bottom right, chinoiserie teacup sherd; bottom left, bluebell design tea saucer sherd; middle left, gold and blue teacup handle. Photographs by Michelle Charest. Scale in centimeters.

teawares at the Hibernia is a very fine chinoiserie hand-painted polychrome landscape scene on a small porcelain teacup sherd (Figure 9.6). The remains of a variety of pressed glass snack dishes were also found at the site (Figure 9.6). That tea and snacks were being served in vessels that had individual character, rather than in plain, inexpensive utilitarian vessels, again speaks to a more personalized and homelike atmosphere being created by the saloon owners to provide the comfort of the traditional Irish pub.

Furthermore, the presence of teacups at the Hibernia site speaks to the role that the saloon may have played in providing meals for their patrons of both genders. Although many may have preferred to drink a beer alongside a meal, for others tea might have been a more appropriate accompaniment—perhaps with a drink after the meal. As the nineteenth century progressed, men began to increasingly join their wives at the tea table at the end of their work day, even in working-class Irish families.[78] The consumption of tea at the Hibernia may represent this shared family meal, then, rather than the formal ritual of tea service. On the other hand, the tea service itself was overwhelmingly considered to be part of the women's sphere even if men were not excluded from the consumption of the actual beverage itself.[79] The teawares at the Hibernia site may also be direct indicators of a female presence on the site. Perhaps they represent the involvement in the family business of Katherine or Johanna Shanahan, sisters to William Shanahan, the saloon proprietor. Both women appear to have been involved in their brother's restaurant in Gold Hill and it is very reasonable that they might also have been involved in the Hibernia Brewery.

A final way in which Irish community identity was encouraged at the Hibernia was through the provision of Irish and Irish-American food and drink. First, while the name Hibernia was a clear reference to Ireland, and one that represented a conscious choice of the saloon owners, the full name Hibernia Brewery Saloon referred to the fact that the saloon was tied to the Hibernia Brewery, an Irish-run brewery in San Francisco.[80] Thus, by default, the beer served at the Hibernia was already imbued with an Irish identity.

In addition, archaeological remains from the Hibernia site indicate a preference for Irish and Irish-American products by the owners and patrons of the saloon. This was particularly evident in the consumption of soda water, several examples of which can be sourced to Irish or Irish-American run companies. These companies include the Empire Soda Works of San Francisco run by John Delehanty, Michael Skelly, and Co., and Casey & Cronan's Eagle Soda Works of Sacramento (Figure 9.7). In addition, the Hibernia apparently imported soda water directly from Cantrell and Cochrane of Dublin and Belfast. The environmental resources of Virginia City necessitated that all saloons either purchase or filter their own soda water. However, there was no real need to make such an extreme effort to obtain soda water as there were multiple water bottling companies within Virginia City. This imported Irish soda water may not have necessarily cost much more for the consumer because shipping rates for overseas bottles would have been fairly competitive with overland freight during the latter part of the nineteenth century.[81] Regardless of price, the convenience of local Virginia City soda water cannot

Figure 9.7. Soda water bottle from Casey & Cronan's Eagle Soda Works, Sacramento, found at the Hibernia Brewery Saloon site. Photograph by Michelle Charest. Scale in centimeters.

be denied. The presence of these Irish and Irish-American soda bottles at the Hibernia would suggest that there was a market for such beverages, that the patrons of the Hibernia Brewery were seeking out products that would evoke the Irish immigrant community or the homeland itself.

Perhaps one of the most iconic of Irish products also made an appearance at the Hibernia site—a bottle of Guinness. This bottle exhibited a lead seal indicating that it was bottled by Blood Wolfe & Co., a Liverpool exporter of Guinness, and that it was part of the 'Z' brand, a variety of Guinness produced between 1864 and 1888.[82] Guinness had previously been sold briefly in Virginia City by two liquor dealers—Kennedy and Mallon in 1865 and Daniel O'Connell in 1869.[83] For the most part, though, Guinness was rather scarce in Virginia City, and its presence at the Hibernia is noteworthy. Further, examination of the archaeological assemblages of the three other non-Irish saloon excavations in Virginia City suggests that there is no evidence of Guinness being found at any other saloon site. The presence of imported beer at the Hibernia may also suggest a higher class of clientele, or at least a class that was willing to pay a bit more for their imported Irish porter.[84] The Hibernia was declaring its Irishness by serving this uncommon, more costly, yet iconic brew. Glassware remains from the site also feature higher concentrations of drinking glasses and tumblers than stemware, for example, which is also well in keeping with established nineteenth-century preferences for beer and whiskey among the Irish.[85]

Examination of the faunal remains from the Hibernia excavations also indicates a preference for traditional Irish foodways. Irish food traditionally relied heavily upon cooking in pots over open fires, resulting in a strong tradition of either boiling or baking food which carried on into the post-famine period.[86] Similarly, deep-set cooking traditions would have carried over to the United States. A particular characteristic of boiled foods—soups, stews, and boiled meat dishes—is that they tend to work rather indiscriminately with whatever meat is available on hand. The same is true from baked main dishes such as meat pies. There is a great deal of disagreement over what exactly constitutes Irish Stew, for example, as a direct result of this attitude. Irish stew relies particularly upon "available ingredients" which may very well vary from person to person.[87] At the Hibernia, faunal remains indicate the supply of meat represented a wide range of species and economic scales which may reflect this more indiscriminate attitude toward the meat used in preparing meals.

Another form of Irish traditional fare is referenced via the high percentage of pig's feet in the pork assemblage at the Hibernia site. Although pig's feet were an inexpensive cut of meat, their high presence at the site may have been less a choice related to economic hardship and more a result of familiarity and preference for this meat cut. Pig's feet, called *crubeens* in Ireland, were a common food item, typically heavily salted for preservation prior to cooking, in which they were boiled and eaten on their own or with cabbage. In particular, though, pubs in Ireland were especially known for boiling enormous pots of crubeens on Saturday nights and fair days, the most popular drinking days.[88] This was done in part because the publicans realized the crubeens were incredibly popular, but also because they knew the saltiness would encourage their patrons to drink more. Perhaps this popular Irish pub fare was being consumed, and also conveniently for little money, at the Hibernia Brewery Saloon.

An additional interpretation of this evidence for Irish foodways—as well as the Irish soda waters, Guinness, and Hibernia beer—is that these items can all also be considered to be forms of embodied material culture.[89] Embodied material culture is material culture that is consumed, thus becoming a part of the human body, with food and drink especially being excellent examples. Due to the incorporation of the material culture into the body, it has a particularly close relationship to the person and is especially influential in the maintenance and symbolization of identity and difference in the construction of the self.[90] Thus, for the patrons of the Hibernia, by drinking beverages from Ireland and eating Irish food this represented an embodiment of their Irish identity—something *of* Ireland was being incorporated into their own bodies. And the shared communal experience of this embodiment would have helped to cement the community ties already inherently engendered by the saloon experience.

Discussion

The overarching goal of this discussion has been the evaluation of the manifestation of Irish identity and community spirit as fostered by the social space of the saloon. To accomplish this, a multipronged approach has been undertaken by first establishing the need for a working-class Irish community in Virginia City based around the saloon, secondly by detailing the cultural expectations of community among Irish immigrants, next by situating the Irish of Virginia City with regard to the saloon community already in place, and finally by investigating the Irish saloon a space for the perpetuation of Irish ideologies and community pride.

For many of the Irish immigrants arriving in the semimetropolitan and positively multicultural western town of Virginia City, it would have been nothing like what they had experienced before. And yet, the high numbers of Irish immigrants in the town meant that there was critical Irish mass capable of sustaining a very strongly Irish-identified community. Nevertheless, while a formal Irish community did exist in Virginia City, it was somewhat exclusive and particular in its expectations of its members. Despite the presence of an Irish Catholic church in Virginia City from very early in the town's history, participation in the Catholic Church would not have been part of the regular routine of large numbers of Irish citizens of the town. Further, although the more formal Irish community provided limited free public activities, primarily in the form of a regular large St. Patrick's Day parade, it failed to offer much in the way of inexpensive community activities to better accommodate the working- and lower-class members of the Irish community.

It was the saloon that would provide the most ready space in which to accommodate that community. The pub in Ireland had served in the role of community center by not only providing the sole public gathering space for the working-class Irish, but by also by serving as a symbol of attainable social and economic growth on a personal level, as well as a source of

Irish identity. The saloon in Virginia City, while not identical to the pub in Ireland, inspired an innate positive association among Irish immigrants in Virginia City as a place in which community building and identity simply made sense.

This study has not intended to suggest that the Hibernia was "the" social center of the Irish working-class community in Virginia City, though. Rather, it has illustrated that the Hibernia was "a" community center for the Irish working-class community. This saloon did not cater to every Irish person in the town—how could it?—but it catered to a group of people who had a connection through the Irish spirit of the establishment. Archaeological evidence has helped to establish the reality of the Irish community experience at the Hibernia Saloon, indicating, for example, that Irish beverages, traditional Irish cuisine, and even traditional Irish pub snacks were being offered by the saloon. Whether this Irish food and drink was something that the Hibernia proprietors chose to offer to their patrons of their own impetus, as a conscious business decision or due to unconscious desire to connect with the homeland, or it was a result of the demand from the local Irish community, there appears to have been a clear effort made to make these Irish items available to the patrons of the Hibernia.

Further, in Ireland, the rural pub had often been linked with a household, often even part of someone's home. It is possible that Shanahan and O'Connor felt the same way about their saloon as indicated by their attempts to make the Hibernia feel more like a home. They did this by adding personal touches to what could have been a very stark saloon environment, such as curtains, decorative glassware, and wallpaper, and by serving meals and tea at the saloon. These efforts all helped to make their patrons more comfortable and to make the place feel more like a home, just like any good cozy pub should. The saloon, then, became a space in which the traditional Irish community could be transformed, accommodating a new understanding of what it meant to be Irish in America and, more specifically, in the American West.

At the same time, through such care with décor and the comfort of their patrons, the Hibernia proprietors were demonstrating pride of place in the saloon they had developed into a community center. Shanahan and O'Connor may have sought out the social status that proprietorship brought them, but they were equally concerned with developing the social status of the Hibernia itself. The Hibernia, and perhaps other Irish saloons just like it, cultivated an atmosphere that was ideal for the maintenance of an Irish community spirit within a broader American cultural world. Perhaps most importantly, it provided space and means for the embodiment of Irish identity through the consumption of Irish food, drink, and material culture as well as the practice of embodied memories of Irish sociality. It was a space where one could be Irish but in a subtler way that might not have screamed "Irish" to outsiders. After all, having an Irish identity in Ireland did not necessitate participation in formal Irish entertainment or putting shamrocks and harps on every item of material culture. In Ireland, being Irish is that day-to-day practice of the simple things, eating and drinking in traditional ways, participating in shared social manners, and experiencing spaces that happen to be Irish in design. It is this second, quieter form of Irish identity that was best accommodated by the Hibernia—to be Irish like a true Irishman.

The Hibernia served in a role that was essential to the Irish community of Virginia City. It can likely never be known whether Shanahan and O'Connor consciously intended their saloon to serve the needs of the Irish community in Virginia City. In the end, though, all that matters is that it did. The Hibernia provided a place where those who wished to embrace their Irish heritage and identity could do so. And in the rapidly changing world of the late nineteenth-century West, the need for a place of comfort and security that was offered by Hibernia was one that would have been felt in many a home, and many a boarding house, and mine shaft, and forge in Virginia City. Ultimately, there would have been many more saloons just like the Hibernia in Virginia City, and in towns throughout the West, that served the exact same role to their own little Irish saloon communities—a foundational influence on modern Irish-American community life.

Notes

1. For a list of these studies and some interpretation of them, see Ronald M. James, *Virginia City: Secrets of a Western Past* (Lincoln: University of Nebraska Press, 2012).
2. Nevada State Census of 1875. For an excellent chronicle of Virginia City's history, foundational to the research presented in this chapter, see Ronald M. James, *The Roar and the Silence: A History of Virginia City and the Comstock Lode* (Reno: University of Nevada Press, 1998); also James, *Virginia City*.
3. U.S. Manuscript Census, 1860, 1870, and 1880. Note that the 1890 U.S. Census was largely destroyed in a fire and thus the data is no longer available.
4. U.S. Manuscript Census, 1860.
5. E.g., John Koren, *Economic Aspects of the Liquor Problem* (Boston: Houghton, Mifflin and Company, 1899); John Francis Maguire, *The Irish in America* (London: Longmans, Green and Co., 1868).
6. E.g., Perry Duis, *The Saloon: Public Drinking in Chicago and Boston, 1880–1920* (Urbana: University of Illinois Press, 1983); Madelon Powers, *Faces Along the Bar: Lore and Order in the Workingman's Saloon, 1870–1920* (Chicago: University of Chicago Press, 1998); Elliott West, *The Saloon on the Rocky Mountain Mining Frontier* (Lincoln: University of Nebraska Press, 1979).

7. Roy Rosenzweig, *Eight Hours for What We Will: Workers and Leisure in an Industrial City, 1870–1920* (New York: Cambridge University Press, 1983); Richard Stivers, *Hair of the Dog: Irish Drinking and Its American Stereotype* (New York: Continuum, 2000).
8. Kevin C. Kearns, *Dublin Pub Life and Lore: An Oral History* (Dublin: Gill & Macmillan, 1996).
9. Ivor Noël Hume, *Historical Archaeology* (New York: Knopf, 1969); Stanley A. South, *Method and Theory in Historical Archeology* (New York: Academic Press, 1977).
10. E.g., Ronald H. Bayor and Timothy J. Meagher, *The New York Irish* (Baltimore: Johns Hopkins University Press, 1996); James S. Donnelly, *The Great Irish Potato Famine* (Phoenix Mill, Gloucestershire: Sutton Publishing, 2001); David M. Emmons, *Beyond the American Pale: The Irish in the West, 1845–1910* (Norman: University of Oklahoma Press, 2010); Kerby A. Miller, *Emigrants and Exiles: Ireland and the Irish Exodus to North America* (New York: Oxford University Press, 1985); Cormac Ó Gráda, *Black '47 and Beyond: The Great Irish Famine in History, Economy, and Memory* (Princeton, NJ: Princeton University Press, 1999).
11. Donnelly, *The Great Irish Potato Famine.*
12. Seán De Fréine, *The Great Silence: The Study of a Relationship between Language and Nationality* (Dublin: Mercer Press, 1978); Miller, *Emigrants and Exiles*, 417.
13. Timothy J. Meagher, *Inventing Irish America: Generation, Class, and Ethnic Identity in a New England City, 1880–1928* (Notre Dame, IN: University of Notre Dame Press, 2001); Miller, *Emigrants and Exiles*, 418.
14. Miller, *Emigrants and Exiles*, 418.
15. Bayor and Meagher, *The New York Irish*; Miller, *Emigrants and Exiles*; Thomas H. O'Connor, *The Boston Irish: A Political History* (Boston: Northeastern University Press, 1995); Ann M. Shea and Marion R. Casey, *The Irish Experience in New York City: A Select Bibliography* (New York: New York Irish History Roundtable, 1995).
16. Jon Gjerde, *The Minds of the West: Ethnocultural Evolution in the Rural Middle West, 1830–1917* (Chapel Hill: University of North Carolina Press, 1997), 7; Richard White, *It's Your Misfortune and None of My Own: A New History of the American West* (Norman: University of Oklahoma Press, 1991), 210.
17. Emmons, *Beyond the American Pale*, 253.
18. E.g., Stephen A. Brighton, *Historical Archaeology of the Irish Diaspora: A Transnational Approach* (Knoxville: University of Tennessee Press, 2009); Meagher, *Inventing Irish America.*
19. E.g., Emmons, *Beyond the American Pale.*
20. Miller, *Emigrants and Exiles*, 331. For further discussion of religious faith and participation by famine emigrants, see Lynn Hollen Lees, *Exiles of Erin: Irish Migrants in Victorian London* (London: Manchester University Press, 1979), 181–87. See also Robert James Scally, *The End of Hidden Ireland: Rebellion, Famine, and Emigration* (New York: Oxford University Press, 1995), 203, 232.
21. Stivers, *Hair of the Dog*, 60.
22. Emmet Larkin, "The Devotional Revolution in Ireland, 1850–75," *The American Historical Review* 77, no. 3 (1972): 625–52. Miller, *Emigrants and Exiles*, 419–21.
23. Demographic analysis indicates the Irish immigrants on the Comstock

predominantly left rural Ireland between the 1830s and early 1850s. Michelle Charest, "Emerald Pub to Silver Saloon: Building an Irish Saloon Community in the American Mining West" (PhD Dissertation, Brown University, 2012).

24. Miller, *Emigrants and Exiles*, 331–32. With more "work" to do in the West in order for the church to minister to the needs of its potential parishioners, it is likely that this accommodation was pushed to even later in the century, especially in rural western areas like Virginia City.
25. Ibid., 332.
26. D. M. & Co Bishop, *Bishop's Directory of Virginia City, Gold Hill, Silver City, Carson City and Reno: Containing a Business Directory Also City Governments, Public Institutions, Churches, Societies, Etc. Etc., 1878–9* (San Francisco: B. C. Vandall, 1878–1879).
27. Timothy F. McCarthy diaries, Comstock Historic District Commission, Virginia City, NV, 1868, 1872, 1889.
28. Mary McNair Mathews, *Ten Years in Nevada: Or, Life on the Pacific Coast* (Lincoln: University of Nebraska Press, 1880 [1985]), 194.
29. O'Farrell, P.A., "Notes from America," *Freeman's Journal and Daily Commercial Advertiser*, Dublin, December 27, 1894.
30. Mathews, *Ten Years in Nevada,* 195.
31. Roxane Caftanzoglou, "The Shadow of the Sacred Rock: Contrasting Discourses of Place under the Acropolis," in *Contested Landscapes: Movement, Exile, and Place*, ed. Barbara Bender and Margot Winer (Oxford: Berg, 2001), 21.
32. See *The Territorial Enterprise*, April 9, 1865; November 10, 1870; June 29, 1867.
33. See *The Territorial Enterprise*, April 27, 1866; March 9, 1869; February 27, 1877; *The Virginia Evening Chronicle*, July 7, 1879. Although labor unions may have played a large part in the Irish social world of other mining towns like Butte and Leadville, Montana, the same was not true in Virginia City. Labor unions in Virginia City were rather quiet presences in the town, readily finding common ground with management, and thus did not need to be particularly active. The unions played little social role in Virginia City among the populace, including the Irish. James, *The Roar and the Silence.*
34. See *The Virginia Evening Chronicle*, December 2, 1879; *The Territorial Enterprise*, June 20, 1868; February 26, 1878; September 30, 1880; November 25, 1880; February 13, 1881; Alfred Doten, *The Journals of Alfred Doten, 1849–1903* (Reno: University of Nevada Press, 1973), 1404 (January 26, 1882).
35. E.g., Doten, *Journals*, 828 (March 17, 1865). *The Territorial Enterprise* March 13, 1868; March 17, 1868; March 14, 1869; March 17, 1877; March 18, 1880.
36. Ball listed in *The Territorial Enterprise*, April 9, 1865; Price list of food, incidentally remarking on the very low prices of the time, *The Territorial Enterprise*, October 5, 1866; drinks priced at one bit, or ten cents.
37. The genesis of the pub in Ireland can be traced back to the development of shebeens, the unlicensed and thus illegal public houses used for centuries as social drinking spaces by the Irish. Very often shebeens were nothing more than the parlor of a local house, whose owner would brew his or her own beer or poitín (illegally distilled Irish whiskey). It was from these shebeens that the institution of the Irish pub evolved. Originally, shebeens, despite their illicit status, were considered to be generally socially acceptable among the Irish people, particularly in rural

areas, due to the difficulty of obtaining licensing for a legal drinking establishment resulting from politically motivated licensing regulations—shebeens were often the only public drinking space available. However, beginning with the passage of popularly accessible licensing laws in the mid-eighteenth century, well before the time period covered in this chapter, the shebeen's illegal underground status contrasted against the alternative legal public house, which led to the shebeen increasingly being viewed negatively as a place serving very low quality alcohol, where respectable people dare not enter. Correspondingly, over time shebeens became spaces associated with the fostering of subaltern community interests, such as political activism. As the discussion of this chapter focuses on the open and public community life found in the legally licensed pub/saloon, the story of shebeen communities is one that must be told elsewhere. Robert E. Connolly, *The Rise and Fall of the Irish Pub* (Dublin: Liffey, 2010), 21; Kearns, *Dublin Pub Life and Lore,* 16; Cian Molloy, *The Story of the Irish Pub* (Dublin: Liffey, 2002), 35–37.

38. Kearns, *Dublin Pub Life and Lore*, 28; Stivers, *Hair of the Dog*, 130.
39. Kearns, *Dublin Pub Life and Lore*, 28.
40. Ray Oldenburg, *The Great Good Place: Cafés, Coffee Shops, Community Centers, Beauty Parlors, General Stores, Bars, Hangouts, and How They Get You through the Day*, 2nd ed. (New York: Marlowe & Co., 1997); Perry Share, "A Genuine 'Third Place'? Towards an Understanding of the Pub in Contemporary Irish Society" (paper presented at the Sociological Association of Ireland Annual Conference, Cavan, 2003).
41. Kearns, *Dublin Pub Life and Lore*, 27.
42. E.g., William Carleton, *Traits and Stories of the Irish Peasantry*, Vol. 1 (Dublin: William Frederick Wakeman, 1834); E.g., Isaac Weld, *Statistical Survey of the County of Roscommon* (Dublin: R. Graisberry, 1832).
43. West, *The Saloon on the Rocky Mountain Mining Frontier*, 1.
44. William Wright, *The History of the Big Bonanza* (San Francisco: American Publishing Company, 1876), 354.
45. Eliot Lord, *Comstock Mining and Miners* (Berkeley, CA: Howell-North, 1959 [1883]).
46. Mathews, *Ten Years in Nevada*, 169.
47. Charest, "Emerald Pub to Silver Saloon."
48. Duis, *The Saloon*, 28, 31.
49. Raymond Calkins, *Substitutes for the Saloon* (Boston: Houghton, Mifflin and Co., 1901).
50. Miller, *Emigrants and Exiles*, 328.
51. West, *The Saloon on the Rocky Mountain Mining Frontier*, 10.
52. Michael Dietler and Brian Hayden, *Feasts: Archaeological and Ethnographic Perspectives on Food, Politics, and Power* (Washington, DC: Smithsonian Institution Press, 2001); Mary Douglas, ed., *Constructive Drinking: Perspectives on Drink from Anthropology* (Cambridge: Cambridge University Press, 1987); Thomas M. Wilson, *Drinking Cultures: Alcohol and Identity* (Oxford: Berg, 2005).
53. E.g., Jed Levin, "Drinking on the Job: How Effective Was Capitalist Work Discipline?" *American Archaeology* 5, no. 3 (1985); A. Lynn Martin, "Old People, Alcohol and Identity in Europe, 1300–1700," in *Food, Drink and Identity: Cooking, Eating and Drinking in Europe since the Middle Ages*, ed. Peter Scholliers (Oxford:

Berg, 2001); Maryon McDonald, *Gender, Drink, and Drugs*, English ed. (Oxford: Berg, 1994); Wilson, *Drinking Cultures*.

54. Tamara L. Bray, *The Archaeology and Politics of Food and Feasting in Early States and Empires* (New York: Kluwer Academic/Plenum, 2003); Sarah Delamont, "Lobster, Chicken, Cake and Tears: Deciphering Wedding Meals," in *The Sociology of Food and Eating: Essays on the Sociological Significance of Food*, ed. Anne Murcott (Aldershot, Hants, England: Gower, 1983); Dietler and Hayden, *Feasts*; Marc Jacobs and Peter Scholliers, *Eating out in Europe: Picnics, Gourmet Dining, and Snacks since the Late Eighteenth Century* (Oxford: Berg, 2003).
55. Jon D. Holtzman, "Food and Memory," *Annual Review of Anthropology* 33 (2006): 28.
56. Arjun Appadurai, "How to Make a National Cuisine: Cookbooks in Contemporary India," *Comparative Studies in Society and History* 30, no. 1 (1988): 3–24; David E. Sutton, *Remembrance of Repasts: An Anthropology of Food and Memory* (Oxford: Berg, 2001).
57. Miller, *Emigrants and Exiles*, 320.
58. Stivers, *Hair of the Dog*.
59. U.S. Manuscript Census, 1870, 1880.
60. Elizabeth Malcolm, *"Ireland Sober, Ireland Free": Drink and Temperance in Nineteenth-Century Ireland* (Syracuse, NY: Syracuse University Press, 1986), 207. Stivers, *Hair of the Dog*, 129.
61. U.S. Manuscript Census, 1870.
62. Donald L. Hardesty et al., "Public Archaeology on the Comstock" (Carson City: Nevada State Historic Preservation Office, 1996); Kelly J. Dixon, *A Place of Recreation of Our Own: The Archaeology of the Boston Saloon: Diversity and Leisure in an African American–Owned Saloon, Virginia City, Nevada* (Reno: University of Nevada, 2002); Kelly J. Dixon, ed., *The Archaeology of Piper's Old Corner Bar, Virginia City, Nevada*, Comstock Archaeology Center Preliminary Report of Investigations (Carson City: Nevada State Historic Preservation Office, 1999).
63. Hardesty et al., "Public Archaeology on the Comstock," with contributions regarding faunal remains from Elizabeth M. Scott, and regarding ceramics and glass by Ralph B. Giles.
64. Charest, "Emerald Pub to Silver Saloon."
65. L. M. McKenney, *Business Directory of San Francisco and Principal Towns of California and Nevada, 1877* (San Francisco: L. M. McKenney, 1877). U.S. Manuscript Census, 1880, 1890. There is very little history available on William W. Shanahan and John T. O'Connor. O'Connor is only mentioned in one census record without the "O" which often dropped from the name. There is a little more about Shanahan who is first mentioned living in Virginia City in 1871. He had two sisters, Katherine (Katie) and Josie (Johanna) who worked as dressmakers. William was the proprietor of the Pioneer Restaurant. His sisters and mother, Ellen, assisted in the restaurant and a boarding house in the 1870s. In the late 1870s he switched to running the Hibernia with O'Connor. The Shanahans eventually moved to California. William ran a saloon in Los Angeles in 1900.
66. L. M. McKenney, *McKenney's Pacific Coast Directory for 1883–4 Giving Name, Business, and Address of Business and Professional Men of California, Oregon, Washington, British Columbia, Alaska, Nevada, Utah, Idaho, Montana, Arizona, and*

New Mexico: Together with Sketches of the Different Towns: Complete Alphabetical Lists of 3,000 Cities and Towns (San Francisco: L. M. McKenney, 1883–1884.)

67. Sanborn-Perris, "Fire Insurance Map, Virginia City, Nv," (1890).
68. Koch, "Birds Eye View of Virginia City"; Sanborn-Perris, "Fire Insurance Map, Virginia City, Nv."
69. Duis, *The Saloon*, 152.
70. Calkins, *Substitutes for the Saloon*, 6.
71. Kearns, *Dublin Pub Life and Lore*, 17.
72. E.g., *The Freeman's Journal*, March 14, 1861; Weld, *Statistical Survey of the County of Roscommon*, 552.
73. E.g., "Minutes of Evidence Taken Before the Select Committee on the Drogheda Election Petitions; with the Proceedings of the Committee and Index," in *Reports from Committees of the House of Commons*, 1857 (255), 2:1654–57.
74. E.g., "Minutes of Evidence," 2:4210; Carleton, *Traits and Stories of the Irish Peasantry*, 1:1, 16; *The Freeman's Journal*, July 9, 1861; Meagher, *Inventing Irish America*, 35. Full discussion can be found in Charest, "Emerald Pub to Silver Saloon."
75. A common assumption is that all women associated with saloons were prostitutes, often overly mythologized in the context of the Old West. E.g., Catherine H. Spude, "Brothels and Saloons: An Archaeology of Gender in the American West," *Historical Archaeology* 39 (2005): 89–106; Marion S. Goldman, *Gold Diggers & Silver Miners: Prostitution and Social Life on the Comstock Lode* (Ann Arbor: University of Michigan Press, 1981). While many women were prostitutes, in many cases extensive genealogical research by the author has indicated that there is no real supporting evidence of prostitution and often evidence to the contrary. See Charest, "Emerald Pub to Silver Saloon."
76. Charest, "Emerald Pub to Silver Saloon."
77. Rosenzweig, *Eight Hours for What We Will*, 42.
78. E.g., Heather J. Griggs, "*Go gCuire Dia Rath Agus Blath Ort* (God Grant That You Prosper and Flourish): Social and Economic Mobility among the Irish in Nineteenth-Century New York City," *Historical Archaeology* 33, no. 1 (1999): 87–101; Adrian Praetzellis and Mary Praetzellis, "Mangling Symbols of Gentility in the Wild West: Case Studies in Interpretive Archaeology," *American Anthropologist* 103, no. 3 (2001): 645–54; Diana diZerega Wall, "Examining Gender, Class, and Ethnicity in Nineteenth-Century New York City," *Historical Archaeology* 33, no. 1 (1999): 102–17.
79. E.g., Diana diZerega Wall, *The Archaeology of Gender: Separating the Spheres in Urban America* (New York: Plenum Press, 1994); Susan Williams, *Savory Suppers and Fashionable Feasts: Dining in Victorian America* (New York: Pantheon Books, 1985).
80. McKenney, *McKenney's Pacific Coast Directory for 1883–4*.
81. Julian H. Toulouse, "High on the Hawg, or How the Western Miner Lived, as Told by the Bottles He Left Behind," *Historical Archaeology* 4 (1970): 60.
82. David Hughes, *"A Bottle of Guinness Please": A Colourful History of Guinness* (Berkshire: Phimboy, 2006), 113.
83. E.g., *The Territorial Enterprise*, April 12, 1865; August 10, 1869.
84. Jane Russell Armstrong, "Glassware," in *Historical Archaeology at the Golden Eagle Site*, ed. Adrian Praetzellis, Mary Praetzellis, and Marley Brown (Rohnert Park,

CA: Cultural Resources Facility, Anthropological Studies Center, Sonoma State University, 1980), 30.

85. Carleton, *Traits and Stories of the Irish Peasantry*, Vol. 1; Hughes, *"A Bottle of Guinness Please,"* 21; Malcolm, *"Ireland Sober, Ireland Free,"* 2.
86. Regina Sexton, "Ireland," in *The Penguin Companion to Food*, ed. Alan Davidson (New York: Penguin Books, 2002), 485.
87. Darina Allen, *Irish Traditional Cooking* (Lanham, MD: National Book Network, 2005), 98.
88. Ibid., 130.
89. Dietler and Hayden, *Feasts*.
90. Michael Dietler, "Alcohol: Anthropological/Archaeological Perspectives," *Annual Review of Anthropology* 35 (2006): 232.

10

"Saints in the Pit"

Mormon Colliers in Britain and the Intermountain West

Mindi Sitterud-McCluskey

While early American immigration history focused on just the newcomers' experiences in the United States, more recent studies have recognized that scholars also need to understand immigrants' experiences in their homeland. Mindi Sitterud-McCluskey fits that pattern with her discussion of coal miners who joined the Church of Jesus Christ of Latter-day Saints (Mormon or LDS) in Great Britain because the LDS missionaries offered temporal and spiritual assistance to the working class that other religions no longer offered. They chose to move to the American West because church leaders encouraged them to gather to Zion. But they also came because the coal industry suffered economic downturns and they sought a better economic life where they could cooperate with members of their faith.

After setting the stage in Great Britain, Sitterud-McCluskey explains that the miners faced new challenges in the Mormon West. Her study of their economic struggles and religious faith gives a clearer picture of the impact of the Mormon Church on the Intermountain West. Sitterud-McCluskey shows that the colliers did not always find the economic or spiritual peace that they sought. Most still depended on the spiritual gifts they had learned of in England. When some moved to work in mines in Wyoming, they created a Mormon presence in the area. Some struggled with their faith because Zion was not perfect, but they appreciated their new home. Besides showing the relationship between the immigrants and the Mormon settlers, Sitterud-McCluskey explains how immigration history has to entail more than just the relationships between the majority and the newcomers when she discusses the concerns that the British miners had with the Chinese in Wyoming.

On May 12, 1852, Elder W. S. Philips of the Merthyr Tydfil, Wales, branch of the Mormon Church sat down to pen a sorrowful report to Samuel Richards, the president of the British Mission:

> Dear President Richards—I am sorry to inform you of a very dreadful occurrence, which occurred in this neighborhood last Monday morning, in a coal-pit, at Cwmbach.... There were about one hundred men at work in the pit when the damp took fire and blew, burnt, and killed sixty-nine of them, and in that number were killed nineteen brethren.

Within the darkness, debris, and noxious gases that streamed through the tunnels in the aftermath of the explosion, the surviving Saints sought one another out and, according to Philips, "had been praying much." One Mormon collier reportedly shouted encouragement to his brethren: "There are Saints in the pit and I feel the spirit of God here." He instructed the men to pray and then to "pray again." When nearly three dozen workers in a different section of the pit seemingly gave "themselves up to be smothered," another Mormon collier determined that he was going to live to see the Mormon "Zion" then being established in the Intermountain West: "I am not going to die, I must go to Zion first, so I am going out." He then wetted the bag that had carried his lunch, plastered it over his mouth, and "walked out well."[1]

Following the establishment of the British Mission in 1837, missionaries for the newly established Mormon faith fanned out across England, Scotland, and Wales with a message of hope and empowerment, a return to the primitive gospel of old, and the prospect of building Zion, a "New Jerusalem," on the fringes of the North American frontier. By the end of the nineteenth century, Mormonism had garnered over one hundred thousand converts in the British Isles. While the vast majority of these individuals arrived from the industrial poor and working classes, a high percentage earned their livelihoods in collieries like Cwmbach. In fact, of the some thirty-eight thousand converts who traveled to the Mormon homeland as part of church-sponsored emigration parties between 1840 and 1870, those who described themselves as "colliers," "miners," and "pitmen" comprised perhaps the single largest occupational group.[2] For this reason, the stories told by British Mormon colliers offer a valuable window through which to observe the complex dynamics of religion and class in the lives of ordinary people as both the British Isles and the American West underwent a dramatic period of industrial expansion, social unrest, spiritual fervor, and experimentation.

Though separated by thousands of miles and vastly different developmental and cultural pasts, the British Isles and the American West share modern histories shaped heavily by the production of coal. Even as the first Mormon missionaries crossed the Atlantic Ocean to impart their faith, the

British Isles was in the midst of a revolution that transformed the manner in which people labored as well as how and where they lived and conceived of themselves and the larger world. At the center of these great changes was coal. Only one hundred years prior to the advent of what would become known as the Industrial Revolution, Britain had faced an energy crisis as its population dramatically expanded in time with soil depletion and deforestation. Found in remarkable abundance throughout the Isles, coal proved a viable substitute for wood in iron production, home heating, and cooking. Over the course of the nineteenth century, coal also supplied the energy behind steam-driven machinery and fueled the expansion of the iron and steel industries, all of which helped to make Britain the world's industrial powerhouse. Britain's remarkable economic growth and progress, however, contained the propensity for violent market swings and periodic slumps. Deemed the "hungry forties," perhaps the worst of these downturns occurred even as the first wave of Mormon missionaries began conjuring images of a refuge from both spiritual and temporal want on the fringes of the North American frontier.[3]

Seeking to build a self-sufficient religious kingdom in the Intermountain West, the Mormon people also eagerly sought coal resources to rescue their growing settlements from an energy crisis and fuel the type of manufacturing base upon which prosperity and autonomy might be built. Typically educated in the coal trade since their boyhoods, convert colliers carried to the Mormon homeland their advanced knowledge of sinking pits, blasting and boring tunnels, pumping water, ventilating fresh air currents and noxious gasses, reading signs in nature, and carving minerals from the precarious bowels of the earth. Thus, in their efforts to build Zion, achieve a measure of personal success and fund the migrations of loved ones, Mormon colliers played an essential role in developing many of the industrializing West's early coal works.

In their emigrations beyond the Rocky Mountains and travels throughout the Intermountain West, Mormon colliers had much in common with thousands of other labor migrants from Britain, Finland, Italy, Greece, Japan, China, eastern Europe, and other places of origin. Having histories of economic hardship and aspirations for security and upward mobility, Mormon colliers banded together, engaged in mutual aid, and used ethnoreligious associations to better navigate the instabilities of a miner's life in a developing country. These men also drew on familial, village, and church ties in the homeland to engage in chain migrations and often sent remittances to ease the financial burdens of loved ones left behind and facilitate additional transatlantic voyages. As members of a distinctive religious faith and colonization movement, however, Mormon immigrants from the

British coalfields experienced the Intermountain West in ways that differed markedly from other laboring men of transnational origins.

Indeed, even as the Mormon people looked to coal to power their aspirations for a self-contained religious homeland, this same fossil fuel ushered in a host of non-Mormon, or "Gentile," settlers, influences, and authority structures. By the early 1870s, for example, several hundred Mormon colliers could be found toiling in mines owned by the great railroad interests of the day and, thus, firing the engines that were at the forefront of American westward expansion. In the shadow of this progress and unprecedented opportunity for some Saints waned dreams of an independent Mormon kingdom and sanctuary from the world's market instabilities, inequalities, and vice.

Bringing together the histories of the British Isles and the American West, this study examines the intersection of religion, labor, and class in the lives of Mormon colliers from England, Scotland, and Wales. After looking at some of the ways in which early Mormonism spoke to the particular anxieties, aspirations, and experiences of colliers, this study demonstrates the role coal mining played in the emigration of a surprisingly large number of these men and their families. It then follows several Mormon colliers as they continued to draw on their trade and their faith to navigate the realities of the rapidly changing Intermountain West. Although transcendent religious experience certainly should not be discounted in the conversion and migration of thousands of British people to the Mormon homeland, this study emphasizes how the early Mormon faith merged labor and class with the divine and sacred and informed the experiences of convert colliers both below ground and on the surface.[4]

Conversion

The arrival of religious dissenters from the United States in 1837 and the strong appeal Mormonism generated among laboring people, particularly in the collieries, speaks to a broader narrative about religion and class in the British Isles. It was in front of a crowd of several thousand colliers at Kingswood, England, that George Whitefield preached his first open air sermon in 1739. Having been denied a pulpit, and deeply concerned about the poor masses similarly denied pews, Whitefield liberated Christianity from the chapel and sparked a religious movement that led to the establishment of Methodism.[5] Almost seventy years later, Hugh Bourne and his congregation of nearly one hundred colliers in the Black Country of Staffordshire attempted to recapture the original spirit of this nonconformist faith by staging a revival on the top of Mow Cop Hill. From the condemnation this plebian festival garnered among more privileged church leaders arose a new dissenting sect called the Primitive Methodists.[6] Generally considered the most thoroughly working-class denomination in the British Isles during the first half of the nineteenth century, the Primitives, or "Ranters," sought to cleanse Christianity of class privilege in favor of spiritual authenticity and a truer adherence to the teachings of the New Testament. The rebelliousness that was implicit in being a Primitive Methodist and this faith's concern with the plight of common people often made "Ranter" preachers natural leaders in local trade union activities and political movements such as Chartism. Not unlike the denomination from which it dissented, however, Primitive Methodism underwent a power shift away from the working class within a relatively short period of time.[7]

That early Mormonism helped to fill the void left by the Primitive Methodists' turn toward reconciliation with the established order can be witnessed in the significant number of former congregants who embraced the new American faith. In 1840, for example, apostle-missionary Wilford Woodruff baptized some three hundred former Primitives in the vicinity of Worcestershire, Gloucestershire, and Herefordshire, England.[8] John Purdy, a Nottinghamshire collier, baptized several of his children in the Primitive Methodist Church before converting to Mormonism and emigrating to the coalfields of southern Wyoming.[9] Alfred Summerill, a collier from Kingswood, where Whitefield began his open-air preaching career, also claimed to have been a devout Ranter before encountering Mormonism in the 1860s and migrating to the Intermountain West.[10]

Typically plainspoken, simply dressed, and of laboring origins themselves, early Mormon missionaries, like the early Methodists and Primitive Methodists before them, preached wherever a crowd might gather and promoted a return to the principles and practices of the apostolic Christian church as described in the New Testament. Thus, a reoccurring theme that runs through the written testimonies of convert colliers during this period is the appeal of biblical literalism and doctrinal simplicity. Entering the coal pits at the age of twelve, Thomas Hunt of Derby, England, for example, claimed that early in life he "had a desire to be religious but never could fix on no society. They diferd so much from the scriptures which I always believed to meane what they sead." After a fellow collier "got killed in the pit," Hunt became more concerned about the condition of his soul and subsequently gave audience to an itinerant Mormon missionary. Hunt recorded in his diary that he "liked [h]is preaching very well . . . he brought forward a deal of scripture which was wat I believed."[11] Of his first encounter with a Mormon missionary, Scottish collier Matthew Rowan similarly recalled, "The great difference that I observed in his preaching, to that of the other sect's preaching was that I could understand it. I saw it ran beautifully coincident with the other scriptures."[12]

Possessing personal histories of hardship and physical toil, many early Mormon missionaries also appealed to collier communities on the basis that they could understand and articulate much about the anxieties, frustrations, and desires of the British working class. By locating oppression and poverty in the flagrant violation of the teachings of Christ, a number of these men further proved adept at spiritualizing the cause and remedy of class-based injustices. Perhaps the most forceful at merging class rhetoric with religious concerns was the apostle-missionary, prophet, and church president Brigham Young. Conditioned by the poverty of his youth and struggles as a migrant farmer, blacksmith, and carpenter, Young was known to rail against the "corrupt wealthy," maintaining that one day the world's "mighty men" would stand accountable to God for their treatment of the poor and domination of the earth's resources. Before a crowd in 1855, Young sardonically declared:

> The capitalists and mighty men of the earth should notify the Lord that He made a mistake when forming the balance of the human family . . . and petition that they be made with bones of iron, sinews, nerves, ligaments and muscles of steel, and flesh of brass. Then they could labor for them without food, rest, or shelter, and would not have to answer for not "multiplying and replenishing the earth"; neither would the magnates then have to account for the terrible oppression they are meting out to their fellows, often depriving them of the enjoyment even of pure air and light of heaven. . . . [W]e suggest to the corrupt wealthy of the world that they consider and practice upon the idea that their fellow beings are flesh and blood like themselves, that they have a right to a fair share of the bounties bestowed by a kind creator, and cease using human beings as though they were made of iron, steel, and brass.[13]

Another beloved preacher in the British mission field, Parley P. Pratt, similarly demonstrated a heightened sensitivity for the plight of the laboring poor. Rooted in the abuses he endured as a hired-out farmhand during his youth, this apostle-missionary often raged against the inequalities, corruption, and oppression he witnessed in the British Isles:

> O God, sweep away all the falsehoods and abuses of power that are in the world! Down with the tyrants, down with the abuses, down with the false nobility, down with the pride, extravagance,

> and idleness of the one class, and down with the hard trials, want, oppression, and poverty that are heaped upon the other class.[14]

Typically delivered by men of common origins and a consciousness of economic inequalities, the Mormon gospel further offered the British working class a sense of empowerment, dignity, and inclusion in a higher spiritual cause. As a layman's religion, Mormonism tended to envelop new converts into the fold rather quickly by bestowing them with leadership roles and responsibilities that transcended the meeting house. In this way, work and religion became closely intertwined in the lives of early converts. Evan Samuel Morgan of Glamorganshire, Wales, for example, entered the coal pits with his father at the age of eleven and learned about the Mormon faith in the same dark spaces five years later. Shortly after a fellow young collier passed him some Mormon literature, which he "read with great delight and pleasure, believing the doctrines they contained to be true," Morgan's older brother returned to his father's home from employment at a distant pit with a copy of the Book of Mormon. By the age of eighteen, Morgan had been baptized and accepted a call to bring other men and women into the new faith. In the company of another convert collier, the young man traveled through the coalfields of south Wales, laboring in the pits by day, preaching the Mormon gospel by night and baptizing new converts wherever he found them.[15]

Notably, colliers were not alone in taking the Mormon gospel below ground. Oscar F. Hunter, an American-born missionary, reported that he had preached a short sermon while "down in a coal pit" and was treated "very kindly."[16] From the collieries of Durham, England, Henry Lunt wrote that he and his companions "have not been content with preaching upon the earth, but have been 600 yards beneath its surface."[17]

Among early Mormonism's strongest appeals certainly must be counted the promise of "spiritual gifts" and the granting of a special ecclesiastical authority called the "priesthood" to all male members who lived in accordance with certain religious principles. True to the biblical literalism of the early church, Mormon missionaries propagated the idea that spiritual gifts, such as the gift of tongues, prophesy, and healing, were not limited to religious movements of the past. Rather, miracles continued to be manifest in the modern world according to one's faith and God's will. "We were taught to believe in, and contend for the Supernatural gifts of the Spirit," recalled Matthew Rowan. While a large number of colliers, including Rowan, found their "tongue(s) loosened" in such a way as to allow them to speak more confidently and compellingly about the Mormon gospel and "pronounce strange words," the gift of healing seems to have resonated with even greater force.[18] Thomas Hunt relished in God working through him to heal sick and broken bodies as he labored and preached throughout Britain's coalfields. On one occasion, a knock at the door awakened Hunt to an incident in the nearby coal pits:

> We found that Brother Wardbe, a (Mormon) priest, had got bad burnt by an explosion of fire in the pit. He desired the ordinance and so great was the pain that he could scarcely contain himself wile I anointed him, but when wee laid our hands upon him he was free from pain, and wee could see the fire go out of his hands and face and in ten minutes he was singing the songs of Zion.[19]

Indeed, diaries, reminiscences, letters, and public testimonials written by collier converts during this period are replete with accounts of a sort of faith-healing through bodily anointments, prayer, and the "laying on of hands," as practiced by holders of the Mormon priesthood.[20] As epidemics and industrial accidents swept through working-class neighborhoods, the power to make broken bodies whole and relieve the pain of the flesh resounded powerfully among laboring people, particularly in the collieries.

In 1849, for example, Robert Brighton testified from Auchene, Scotland, to the power of Mormon priesthood healing rites after an engineer failed to properly fasten the ropes "to let us down to our work." Free-falling with three other colliers to the bottom of the pit, Brighton sustained a crushed leg and other injuries, which caused him agonizing pain "till the following evening" when a teacher in the local Mormon Church "anointed me with oil, according to Scripture, and I was relieved. . . . I feel to attribute all the praise and glory to God."[21] In a letter signed by four eyewitnesses, John Brown reported that he first began attending Mormon meetings after being crushed by a car full of coal below ground. According to Brown, he had been in great pain and unable to move until a neighbor called a pair of Mormon priesthood holders to anoint his body and lay their hands on his wounds. Immediately thereafter, Brown rose to his feet, put on his clothes, and took tea with the men "as heartily as ever I did in this life."[22] Near Pembrokeshire, Wales, Daniel Williams had been toiling in the coal pits when he was called to administer to a fellow Mormon collier by the name of Hughes who had been "smashed by a stone falling on him in the coal work." After "secretly" administering to Hughes below ground and easing his pain, Williams and a fellow Mormon collier carried their injured brother to the home of another church member:

> When we had stripped off his clothes we found that on his kidneys was raised a lump . . . big as a small bason and his head and face were bruised very much. . . . I anointed him with oil in the name of

> the Lord, and the swelth came down while I anointed him and the pains left him. . . . Hughes leaped up, danced & praised the Lord with me, for his mercy.[23]

From Merthyr Tydfil, Wales, David Richards testified that a roof fall crushed his back while "working among the coal. I was carried home, and the doctor who was present said he could do nothing for me, and told those around me to wrap me up in a sheet that I might die. There was a lump on my back as big as a child's head." That night, "Elder Philips" stopped by his home

> and attended to the ordinance of the Church for the sick, and while commanding the bones in the name of Jesus, they came together, making a noise like the crushing of an old basket; my strength returned, and now I am able to go some miles to bear my testimony to this great miracle.[24]

Among the five witnesses who signed Richards's account in a British-Mormon periodical called the *Millennial Star*, Thomas Rees later testified of the miraculous healing of his son. After eleven-year-old Henry became crushed between coal cars, breaking his leg, Rees reported, "I administered to him the ordinance of the gospel (see James 5:14), and he was relieved of all pain instantly and begged me to take the splints and bandages off his leg and let him get up out of bed." After serving as the president of the Merthyr Tydfil branch congregation of the Mormon Church for several years following this event, Rees and his family made their way to the Utah Territory. There, Brigham Young called Rees and another experienced Welsh collier, John Price, to establish the first productive coal work in central Utah, aptly known today as Wales for the large number of Welsh-Mormon miners recruited by these men.[25]

In addition to divine intervention in illness and injury, many British Mormon colliers believed their faith offered some measure of protection against all too frequent explosions, roof falls, and other calamities in the pits. The origins of this conviction can be located in the spiritual gifts of premonition, dreams, and promptings, as well as the practice of wearing sacred garments under one's clothing.[26] In Lanarkshire, Scotland, for example, William Richardson witnessed the divine protection of the Lord descend upon a pair of Mormon colliers after a young boy had been crushed in a roof fall. As Richardson recalled of the tense situation, no one dared approach the boy to unbury him for fear that more of the roof might come down:

> But whan Brother Fergerson and Robertson came along thay ware not afraid and thay went to work to get that boy out. While thay ware doing so his father came along. When he seen how (who) was traying to get out his boy he could not speak, but went away for he had been a great [enemy] of Brother Fergerson. Now he could see that returning it was good . . . and the men in the pit said so to. Thear was a great many was baptized that spring & summer into the Rutherglen Branch.

By the late 1860s, William Richardson had followed his faith to the Mormon homeland where he continued his mining trade and friendship with fellow convert collier, Andrew Ferguson.[27]

For Thomas Beard of Derbyshire, England, divine protection below ground took the form of a spiritual prompting. While sitting to eat his dinner along a subterranean roadway, Beard heard a soft but forceful voice in his head which he could not ignore:

> There were other miners about a rod way on each side of me . . . something whispered to me in my ear, to move away. I got up and moved about a rod further off. I had no sooner done so, then slate fell in the very place I had been sitting. One of the miners remarked, "Tom, you just moved in time or you would have catched that." Yes, if I had catched it, it would have killed me or crippled me up so I could not have accomplished the object of gathering to Zion.

According to Beard, he had known a great number of other colliers whose lives had been saved by "giving heed to these invisible promptings, which all show that God has His watch and care over His children when they put their trust in Him, though they be in the bowels of the earth."[28]

Joseph Thomas Perkins of Glamorganshire, Wales, credited a dream for his avoidance of a methane explosion. After waking from a nightmare in which the "coal works were on fire," Perkins confided in a Mormon elder with whom he boarded and, consequentially, decided not to go in the pit that day. A few hours later, Perkins opened his door to much commotion,

> and saw men running from the coal pit. My father called on me and said something was the matter at our coal works. I jumped up and dressed . . . and ran with my Father to the top of the coal works and there we found the gas had exploded. . . . [T]here was a young man got up of the pit. He was burned all over, clothes burned off of him. We took him home in sheets, he died that evening. There was a (Mormon) elder named John Pugh there; he was burned and died.

A short time later, Perkins accepted employment at Cwmbach and escaped the 1852 explosion that killed nineteen of his brethren.[29] Having survived the dangers of the British coal pits, both Perkins and Beard later emigrated to the Intermountain West and drew on mining and farming for their livelihoods.

In addition to offering converts a sense of empowerment, a personal stake in the growth of the new religion, and a spiritualized explanation for class oppression and strife, the early Mormon Church proposed an alternative to continually struggling against the social, political, and economic establishment at home. As Brigham Young insisted, "It would certainly seem far better . . . for the poor to constantly plan a scheme to free themselves from the trammels which bind them, and go forth to the wide west where labor meets its reward and element is free and abundant."[30] Though ultimately replete with its own sets of challenges, "Zion," and all of the rhetoric and imagery that accompanied this Mormon gathering place, represented a sanctuary, a more righteous way of life, and the millennial entwinement of the temporal and the spiritual. In emigrating to the Mormon West, converts accepted an invitation to take part in what was believed to be the literal building of a Kingdom of God on earth where the faithful might enrich themselves spiritually and temporally in anticipation of the second advent of Christ. At the same time, doctrine and discourses cast the Mormon homeland as a self-sufficient and cooperative refuge where the Saints could produce their own food, fuel, and material goods and cease to live at the mercy of the world's volatile economic forces. While directed toward a purpose higher than material aggrandizement, the establishment of Zion promised to usher in new values and relationships that would effectively check the rise of poverty and oppression:

> Their message was the beauty of the Utah Zion. . . . They said the Lord would come there to dwell among his people and that poverty and oppression would not be known in that holy land, and urged the Saints to flee to the valley of the mountains for safety. . . . These were cheerful tidings to the Saints in their poor conditions.[31]

Consequently, many church leaders expressed anticipation that in Zion the Mormon gospel and an adherence to higher ecclesiastical values would generate a new type of labor dynamic based on cooperation, brotherly affection, and just dealing. Even as the industrial world seemed bent on class war, Zion proposed to "emancipate the working man" from the industrial slavery of Europe, "heal the wounds of class," and provide "temporal as well as spiritual salvation."[32] According to the prominent church leader, Orson

Spencer, in the Mormon homeland "no ten-hours bill will be needed to mitigate the force of the oppressor's rod."[33] Instead, "the gospel has to remove the cause of every existing wrong, to heal up the wounds of society, to introduce correct feeling, brotherly love."[34]

As a well-planned colonization project, moreover, the colossal plan to build Zion demanded armies of workers well versed in hard physical toil and manual skill. Thus, at a time when thousands of immigrants were making labor migrations to the United States, and technological advancements increasingly rendered certain occupational groups obsolete, Mormon leaders and missionaries further bolstered the merits of Zion with the prospect of available work. "We have a nation to raise," declared an article in the *Millennial Star*, "cities to build, and temples to erect. . . . All who desire it may feel sure of immediate and constant employment at fair wages, comfortable situations and good homes."[35] The physical nature of colonizing the wilderness and creating cities, infrastructure, and home industries almost wholly from muscle and raw materials lent itself to a distinct celebration of labor and productivity by the early Mormon Church. While workers struggled for employment, sustenance, and dignity in Britain, early Mormon rhetoric celebrated laboring people as essential, more valuable than gold and cash currency, and endowed with divine purpose. "Our capital lies in the physical force of this people," declared church leader Ezra T. Benson. "Here is element in abundance all around us, as much as we have a mind to organize, according to their faith, and ability."[36] Even as many British workers saw their abilities to create whole products and pride in craftsmanship whittled away to tasks, or found themselves uprooted from fields and relegated to factories by the advent of the machine, Brigham Young assured believers:

> True capital is labor, and it is confined to the laboring classes. . . . It is bone, sinew, nerve, muscle of man that subdues the earth, makes it yield its strength, and administer to his varied wants. This power tears down mountains and fills up valleys, builds cities and temples, and paves the streets. In short, what is there that yields shelter and comfort to civilized man, that is not produced by the strength of his own arm making the elements bend to his will?[37]

By the mid-nineteenth century, the age of muscle and the artisan had become all but obsolete in industrial Britain, but these same attributes remained essential to the Mormon colonization project on the American frontier.

Arriving at a low point in labor relations and worker empowerment in Britain's coalfields, industrial workers must have relished visions of a place where leaders celebrated the working man and spiritual precepts thwarted oppression and unjustly low wages. In earlier times, "bred colliers" had been able to slow or withhold their labor to effectively influence the value of coal on the market and, by extension, their own earnings. By the mid-nineteenth century, however, an influx of famine refugees from Ireland, surplus agricultural laborers, and displaced workers from other industries greatly undermined this traditional tool of empowerment.[38] Amid ongoing depressions and declining earnings, Mormon collier-missionary William Bowers "joined with others in forming a union for the protection of the miners" in Derbyshire, England. Shortly after being ejected from company housing and "starting with 17 others with a wagon load of furniture . . . drawn by human strength," Bowers and his family sought refuge and spiritual and material uplift in the Mormon homeland. By 1872, Bowers could be found toiling alongside a great number of other Mormon colliers in the southern Wyoming coalfields.[39]

William Gibson, a convert collier from Lanarkshire, Scotland, also embraced the Mormon gospel in the waning strength of miners' associations and the Chartist movement of which he was a part. Orphaned at a young age and subjected to brutal work regimes for much of his life, Gibson believed himself capable of enduring anything but the continued haughtiness, oppression, and mistreatment meted out by Britain's established order: "I have had to labor hard from my boyhood. . . . I have often tasted the 'kindness' of the tyrant and oppressor. Some of them cared more for their horses and dogs then for their fellow man. The first cost them something, the latter, nothing." While preaching to a group of striking colliers in Scotland, Gibson offered Zion as a place where "we might have a part of the soil we can call our own and work it for ourselves and own no master but our God."[40] Such rhetoric proved particularly effective at Fifeshire, where Gibson played an important part in converting nearly an entire pit village. According to convert collier George Cunningham, a native of this region, "Mormonism seemed to take the sway for a long time, the gifts and blessings of the Spirit followed them that believed, as the Lord poured his Spirit out upon them."[41]

In Clackmannanshire, Scotland, William Gibson found a sixty-two-year-old collier by the name of John Sharp in 1847. Rather quickly, Gibson baptized Sharp, his wife, nine children, and a number of extended family members into the Mormon faith. Although the Sharps had dug coal in the Clackmannanshire area for generations, their conversion to the new American religion so threatened the social order that mob harassment, initiated by a colliery owner, expedited their migration to Zion. Being among the first colliers to enter the Salt Lake Valley, the Sharps adapted their hewing skills to stone quarrying for church construction projects and prospered in several areas, including freighting and stock raising. Known as the "railroad bishop," John Sharp's son, John, gained much prominence in the Utah Territory for his dual role as an ecclesiastical leader and businessman. The elder Sharp's grandson, William G. Sharp, became a Mormon bishop as well as the superintendent of the Winter Quarters mine in central Utah's coal belt by the turn of the century.[42] William Gibson, too, made his way to the Mormon homeland where he occupied a number of prominent church and political positions and actively worked to resist encroachments on Mormon autonomy and religious freedom.[43]

Emigration

In 1848, the John Sharp family landed in New Orleans and then traveled by steamboat upriver to the Gravois Coal Diggins' outside St. Louis. Finding a branch of the Mormon Church at the coal works, which included several of their associates from Clackmannan, the Sharp men and boys resumed their trade. A year and a half later, having earned enough money to purchase wagons, oxen, and other needed supplies, the family made its way to the head of the Overland Trail and completed the trek to the Mormon homeland beyond the Rocky Mountains.[44]

While a number of Mormon colliers did arrive in the United States and immediately commenced moving west with other believers as part of well-organized and supervised bodies, others spent months and even years, in essence, coal mining their way to the savings required to continue the journey to the promised land. The earliest American coal works in which a significant number of Mormon colliers took advantage of opportunities to exchange their skills and knowledge for wages were located in the Illinois and Missouri border region. Not only did the first emigration parties disembark at New Orleans and travel through this area as they made their way north, St. Louis housed a large number of refugees after mobs expelled the Saints from their city of Nauvoo in 1845. Even after the Mormons began colonizing the Salt Lake Valley as their new homeland, converts continued to sail up the Mississippi River to reach the head of the Overland Trail. Thus, by the early 1840s, convert colliers could be found digging coal on Rankins's farm on the Illinois Bluffs, Dry Hill near present-day Forest Park, and Gravois just outside St. Louis, among other workings.[45]

Wherever a significant number gathered, Mormon colliers and their families built meeting houses, conducted services, and organized themselves under a lay-leadership body. While some colliers remained at these coal works for only a season, others tarried for a period of years.[46] Edward Moroni Thurmon, of Nottinghamshire, England, recalled that after his mother married a Mormon collier in St. Louis in 1854, the family relocated to a coal camp four miles west of the city. Four years later, the family moved again to the Belleville, Illinois, coal works. It was not for another five years that the Thurman-Perkes family bid farewell to a son who had chosen to enlist in the Union Army and finally departed for the Utah Territory.[47]

Over the course of the 1850s, it became more common for Mormon emigration ships to disembark on the northeastern seaboard. That this entryway into the United States offered relatively easy access to many of North America's coalfields is evidenced in a large number of Mormon collier diaries, reminiscences, biographies, and genealogies. These resources find Mormon colliers laboring in such coal-rich areas as Pennsylvania, Ohio, Iowa, and Illinois as they gradually made their way to the head of the Overland Trail to Zion.[48] Among the most detailed of these accounts of advancing westward by mining coal is that of William Richardson. In need of additional funds after landing at Castle Garden, Richardson and his wife and children rather quickly became enmeshed in what might be described as a mobile community of Mormon miners. Functioning outside the direct oversight of church officials, these colliers and their families engaged in systems of cooperation and mutual responsibility and formed vast communication networks aimed at helping one another continue the journey to the Mormon homeland. By drawing on their advanced understanding of mining coal, some of these Mormon colliers even acquired well-paying supervisory positions east of the Rockies, further expediting the migration process.[49]

An untold number of convert colliers, however, never completed the westward trek. John Thompson, a nineteen-year-old Lanarkshire collier, left home in 1856 determined to earn the wages needed to bring his parents and siblings "out of Babylon." By 1857, this young man could be found drifting among the coal diggings of the Midwest in the company of familiar faces from Scotland and avowing that "Mormonism is true and of God."[50] Yet, beset by ill-fortune, Thompson's optimism steadily began to wane: "Times are very bad here at present. Wages are a doler and turtey five cents pur day but We don't get Study Work.... Dear father & mother you think that I am carles (careless) about you but I am not for I am doing my best to get you here.[51]

Disenchanted by his failure to finance an Atlantic crossing for his family, upset by relationships turned sour in the coalfields, and increasingly aware of the lurid testimonies of apostates and the anti-Mormon press, Thompson rather quickly came to believe that Mormonism "is al humbug" and that he had "helped lofers long anife." Rather than going West, Thompson became "a Cissetion (citizen) of the united Staites of America" and determined that he would fight for "the Best Government under the hivens." During the Civil War, Thompson survived a number of intense campaigns as part of the Union Army. He subsequently achieved a measure of success in the Illinois coalfields, until a mining accident took his life in 1875.[52] Just how many Mormon colliers discontinued their journey to Zion for lack of funds, lack of faith, or a desire to remain where fate placed them will probably never be known.

The Mormon Homeland

Seven years after landing at Castle Garden, New York, William Richardson resigned from the mine foreman position he had acquired in western Illinois, applied his savings to the purchase of a wagon, oxen, and other provisions, and moved his family to the head of the Overland Trail. In spite of being warned that he "wont do so well" in the Mormon homeland, Richardson started west one more time. As he recalled, "It was not for money . . . but it was for the Gospel that I was going thare." By 1870, Richardson had obtained a homestead in the Heber Valley and was drawing on a variety of prospects, including milling, logging, stone quarrying, and dragging road, in an attempt to establish a comfortable livelihood. His faith and hard labors notwithstanding, however, the man failed to earn the capital needed to put his land to productive use. No longer able to watch his family exist in abject poverty, Richardson once again turned to his old trade and set out for the mining frontier of the Intermountain West: "I thought that I would try the mines a while for we had not got much for the family. . . . we had got no clothing & poor living & I was so disharted."[53]

Arriving in the Mormon homeland in the late 1860s, the Richardson family and hundreds of other believers entered a heavily contested space in which the dream of Zion bumped sharply against the realities of the rapidly changing Intermountain West. From the beginning, the Mormon people had been challenged to navigate the complexities of the natural environment and create the kind of manufacturing base upon which a self-contained society might thrive. Yet, by the 1860s, a persistent theme that runs through the records of convert colliers is the difficulties associated with establishing a livelihood amid a dearth of cash resources. While the project of building Zion had rendered work plentiful, church labor was not always paid labor, and the ideal of communalism often faltered in the face of human nature and individual needs. Moreover, the widespread Mormon trade in goods and labor, rather than a cash currency, often led to payments in superfluous commodities rather than the things required to achieve self-sufficiency. As collier John MacNeil suggested to his family in Scotland, agrarian independence in the Mormon homeland increasingly demanded capital investments: "I have been putting Myself in a position to get a Living . . . and it Costs Considerable to do it. Namely to get two horses, a wagon, plough, harrow Cultivator &c &c and at the Same time keep My Family and buy My Land to."[54]

While the steady advance of the nation's westward expansion carried greatly needed supplies and capital, it also functioned to undermine Mormon autonomy and the church's ability to develop the region in accordance with the utopian vision of Zion. Put another way, the ever-increasing influence of outside investors, fortune seekers and settlers, social reformers, and the federal government rapidly led to a loss of Mormon control over much of the territory's natural resources, economic potential, governance, culture, and direction of development. Further compounding this turbulence, great ruptures developed between traditional Mormons who clung to the idea of a self-contained and communitarian, spiritual refuge and more progressive Saints who believed themselves as entitled to the wealth of the Utah Territory as any outside investor. Finding both opportunity and restriction in the confluence of these forces, those Mormon colliers who drew upon their mining skills and knowledge in an attempt to establish a measure of security in the industrializing West navigated a highly precarious landscape to a variety of ends.

Indeed, particularly during the 1860s and 1870s, mining functioned as a sort of battleground on which numerous interests vied for empowerment. Stationed in the northern Utah Territory during the Civil War, Patrick Edward Connor, for example, sought to "Americanize" the Mormon homeland and dilute the power of the Mormon Church by surveying and publicizing the region's mineral wealth. As anticipated, a growing number of silver and copper works, among other mining enterprises, had been opened on the fringes of settlement by non-Mormon investors and miners by the end of the decade. Well before Connor's arrival, the Mormon people had looked to coal to strengthen their hold on the region and achieve a measure of security. In fact, ecclesiastical directives for experienced colliers to locate and develop the Intermountain West's coal resources were part of the Mormon colonization project almost from its beginning. Thus, by 1860, convert colliers at Coalville, Grass Creek, and Wales, or Coalbed, were sending wagonloads of coal through mountain passes and across broad stretches of uneven trails to meet Mormon heating and manufacturing needs.[55]

In an attempt to remedy the impracticalities associated with wagon transport and turn the advancing Transcontinental Railroad to the benefit of the Mormon people, Brigham Young called church members to construct a series of rail lines that might link the northeast coal works at Coalville and Grass Creek to the nearby tracks of the Union Pacific. Having acquired much of the southern Wyoming coalfields, however, the Union Pacific actively worked to curtail production at the Mormon-owned coal mines through a restriction on railroad cars, high shipping rates, buyouts, and coerced contracts. After cutting its way through the heart of the Utah Territory during the 1880s, the Denver and Rio Grande Railroad ultimately broke this transportation monopoly and opened central Utah's massive coalfield to large-scale production. Nevertheless, for nearly two decades, opportunities to mine coal south of the Wyoming border remained limited by the Union Pacific's domination of the rails.[56]

Accordingly, a sizable number of convert colliers turned to the Wyoming coalfields "to make a raise," particularly in the vicinities of Evanston and Rock Springs. Indicative of just how many Mormon men took part in the opening of this region to coal production, John MacNeil wrote glowingly home to Scotland in 1870:

> [Evanston/Almy] is where I am at present and I think this is the place I ought to have went to at first if I had knowed they are Mostly all Mormons that are working here. . . . Laying Mormonism aside this is a better Country for a poor Man than the Old Country ten times over.[57]

Located about four miles north of Evanston, the Almy mining district commenced generating coal for the railroads and market in 1869 with a workforce and managerial staff comprised largely of Mormons from the British Isles.[58] In need of skilled laborers in what was still very much a frontier land, these coal operations initially offered Mormon colliers remarkably high wages in exchange for their expertise below ground. Thus, in addition to finding "mostly all Mormons" like himself at Almy, MacNeil claimed that he earned an average of five dollars per day. Ralph Smith, a Durham, England, born Mormon collier, also reported a significant "raise." For the winter of 1869–1870, Smith recorded in his diary that he had gone "to Evanston Coal Mines. Worked there all winter. Got enough money to pay for my land (and) new wagon."[59]

Much as they had done in the coalfields east of the Rockies, the Mormon colliers at Almy immediately organized themselves into a formal body, put plans in motion to construct a meeting house, and appointed a lay leadership body to guide decision making, conduct church services, and oversee the spiritual and temporal needs and interests of the local congregation. For their first ecclesiastical leader, some 125 Mormon miners of the "Old Wyoming Camp" selected John Jolley, a "bred pitman" with deep roots in Durham, England's Great Northern coalfield. By 1872, members of this growing community had also built a church and a school, established a cooperative livestock company, and began "paying on their own settlements."[60]

In the highly competitive and unstable atmosphere of the industrializing West, however, Mormon prospects at Almy rather quickly constricted. As early as 1872, John MacNeil detected the commencement of these changes when he wrote home about "hundreds of Chinese Working, digging coal for one dollar per day."[61] Very likely, these Chinese men toiled at the Central Pacific–affiliated Almy No. 1 mine. Through an agreement with the Beckwith and Quinn Company, this mine replaced 75 percent of its initial workforce with Chinese contract laborers by 1871 at an average pay rate of $1.25 a day. Through similar arrangements, the Union Pacific mines at both Almy and Rock Springs swiftly followed suit.[62] Thus, the winter of 1873–1874 found MacNeil grappling with significantly reduced wages and "doing no good whatever."

In his letters home, MacNeil railed against the importation of hundreds of Chinese laborers whom he believed "suit masters better than white men" and submitted themselves to being "kicked and cuffed" as a "white man" would not. The Scotsman also acknowledged an influx of Mormon emigrants and miners from the silver works in the wake of the Panic of 1873. This "Emmense Emigration of Chinese and Mormons together," MacNeil reported, resulted in the worst financial prospects he had witnessed since arriving in the Mormon homeland:

> The poor emigrants who have come in this season are running all over the country nearly crazed looking for work & cant find it. I don't know what it will come to. There is hundreds of stout abled bodied men running around who would be glad to work for their grub. We are digging coal for our grub & glad to get that to do & living like dogs in a hole in the Mountains, what we call a Dig Out.

Several days after penning these words, MacNeil received a notice of discharge, in his opinion, "to make room for Chinese."[63]

The precise circumstances surrounding MacNeil's loss of employment are not known. However, Reuben Fowkes, an English Mormon collier from Leicester who accepted a managerial position for the Union Pacific at Almy, recorded in his diary that during this period a miners' strike spun out of growing dissatisfaction with wage reductions. Apparently, Fowkes, who had been recruited from Coalville for his surveying skills and advanced knowledge of mine engineering, warned the men that if they continued to strike, the company would replace them with "Chinamen" who would work for an even lower pay rate. When this prediction proved true, and the company dismissed nearly all of its non-Chinese miners, Fowkes contemplated resigning from his position of authority. Yet, after consulting with a Mormon bishop,

Samuel Pike, Fowkes chose to remain at Almy, believing that he might be "a big help in giving work" to his church brethren in the future.[64]

True to Fowkes's calculations, the retention of several Mormon foremen and skilled colliers functioned to uphold a Latter-day Saint presence in the southern Wyoming coalfields. In 1875, for example, John MacNeil's brother, James, obtained employment at Almy and wrote home about the mining camp's growing Mormon community: "We have a branch of the church here Now & they have had Me up bearing My testimony to this work. . . . I feel a great deal More blissed & More contented & I sincerely hope the Lord will always keep Me so."[65] After rising tensions between "white" and Chinese miners erupted in the tragic Rock Springs Massacre in 1885, leading to tense labor standoffs throughout the Wyoming and Utah coalfields, most of the Chinese workforce evacuated the region.[66] Subsequently, a great number of Mormon miners arrived at Almy and elsewhere to help fill the void left by the Chinese. Of the strongly British and Mormon presence at Almy after 1885, Mormon miner William Moroni Purdy recalled, "Perhaps nowhere could you find a community or a group of communities more closely united, being practically all English speaking, their religious and recreational activities were so closely knit, as to form with few exceptions, one huge family."[67]

Among the more prominent Mormon colliers at Almy during this period was John L. Russell, a Mormon convert from Sterlingshire, who had entered the pits with his father in Scotland at the age of nine. Arriving at Almy to mine coal by the end of the 1870s, Russell held leadership positions within the Mormon Church as well as in Wyoming's growing political arena, including representative at the Ninth Territorial Legislature, delegate to Wyoming's constitutional convention, and state senator. During his political stint, Russell became known largely for pushing forward the first mine safety legislation in the American West and proudly touting himself as first, and foremost, a coal miner: "I work for a living. My people I represent are working people." In 1889, the *Deseret News* applauded the wisdom behind Russell's appointment to the chairmanship of the Committee on Mines and Mining during the state's constitutional convention, describing the man as "a practical coal miner, and yet he is a diplomat—a thinker, a philosopher and statesman, a Scotchman born and bred, a Mormon and a true American." Sadly, Russell's life came to an end ten years later when he was overcome by black damp while battling a mine fire at Diamondville, a short distance from Almy.[68]

Certainly, Russell must have been acquainted with another prominent Mormon collier from Scotland, Thomas Sneddon. Born and raised among the Fifeshire coal pits, Sneddon labored at Almy for fourteen years and then helped open the first coal work at Diamondville, where he quickly rose to the position of superintendent. In addition to claiming membership in the Knights of Labor during the organization's reign in the Wyoming coalfields, Sneddon served in the lower branches of the state legislature and as mayor of Diamondville for three terms. Described as "of heroic build, large-boned and broad shouldered, with rugged, perfect health all his life," Sneddon reportedly earned much respect among both miners and operators for his knowledge of "all phases of the work in and around the coal mines" and determination not to submit his men to dangers greater than he, himself, was willing to brave: "Every one of them would jump to follow Tom Sneddon anywhere in the mine, at any time, having implicit faith at all times in his judgment."[69]

During the latter decades of the nineteenth century, several Mormon families established homesteads in the vicinity of the southern Wyoming coalfields and achieved a measure of security by both working their land and taking advantage of opportunities at the nearby mines. Reuben Fowkes and a number of other Mormons established homesteads in the Bear River Valley, a short distance from Evanston.[70] Star Valley and Bear Lake on the Idaho border also supported sizable Mormon populations, which periodically traveled to the Wyoming coalfields to earn wages as well as sell livestock and agricultural goods.[71] One such family was that of Edward Patterson. A pitman from Northumberland, England, who dug coal in Pennsylvania before pressing on to the Mormon homeland, Patterson made several migrations with his sons between the family homestead at Bear Lake and the coal mines of Rock Springs. Joseph Soulsby, Patterson's son-in-law and fellow convert collier from England's Great Northern coalfield, split his time between farming and serving as a superintendent and Mormon bishop at Rock Springs.[72] Soulsby employed a large number of Mormon miners over the course of his career, some of whom also rose to supervisory positions. For example, after helping to open the Mormon mines at Coalville and Grass Creek, James Robinson, a Nottinghamshire collier, became a foreman under Soulsby. When a mining accident left him hobbled, Robinson fell back on the homestead his mining wages purchased and helped develop.[73]

Indeed, well into the twentieth century, the Mormon colliers who succeeded in establishing a measure of security for themselves in the Intermountain West tended to be those who acquired a piece of land. Neither utterly wage dependent nor fully at the mercy of weather patterns and the natural environment, these colliers quite often migrated to the coal works during the peak production period of winter and returned to their homesteads between planting and harvesting seasons. A piece of land also provided a safety valve when fires, floods, strikes, and company decisions unexpectedly left the mines slack or idle for an indefinite period of time. James MacNeil, for example, reluctantly left the Mormon community at Almy when the mine in which he toiled caught fire and had to be sealed for several months to smother the flames. Lacking a piece of land to turn to for sustenance, MacNeil set out in search of the "raise" he needed to become self-sufficient in the Intermountain West's growing coal, silver, and copper works.

In so doing, MacNeil joined his brother John, William Richardson, and many other Mormon colliers on a broad migratory circuit that extended as far north as Montana and southward to Arizona. At any given time, scores of miners could be found jumping railroad cars, camped along tracks, hiking through mountain passes, and hitching rides on rickety wagons in search of opportunities to trade their labor for wages. Similar to the manner in which he had made his way to the Salt Lake Valley, Richardson reported that he "traveled around for to gate work" with an ever-shifting set of brothers in the Mormon gospel. Existing largely on the fringes of settled community life, and often apart from wives and female family members, it was an overtly male world, requiring a reorganization of gender roles. As John MacNeil explained:

> I am at present time Batching. Perhaps you don't know what that means well Ill tell you: it is 4 men of us . . . cooking our own grub. I can bake bread, make pies & cook anything as good as any woman can. And for sowing, you should see me at that.[74]

Having entered the coal pits of Scotland, England, and Wales typically by the age of twelve, and often reared in villages with deep coal-mining histories, Mormon colliers tended to arrive in mining camps with advanced understandings about the extraction of minerals from the bowels of the earth. The peculiarities of the industrializing West, however, frequently rendered the livelihoods of even the most skilled men quite unstable. Work tended to be seasonal, and periods of opportunity and success were inclined to develop between stretches of slack and misfortune. "It all goes by seasons," wrote James MacNeil, "& you have to work while you can get it," and when one is "in work You have got to work right along at it every day Sunday & all."[75] Particularly in the depressed silver mining districts, slack periods became longer, busts more frequent, and the search for wages more desperate over the course of the 1870s:

> We started for cottonwood with a roll of blankets on each of our backs. We traveled until it got dark then opened our blankets and squatted down among the brush. Got up next morning, got our

> fitting on our backs and started off, but we could not get work. So we started down canyon til dark, and spread our blankets, lay down among the brush. We got back home after five days travel among the mountains. We stayed a week & started again for cottonwood but could find no work to do. I have never laid on a bed but twice . . . and that was on a hay stack.[76]

In addition to encountering a great number of suspended and busted works, miners in the Intermountain West confronted the all-too-frequent prospect of not receiving compensation for labor performed. From Alta in 1875, John MacNeil wrote:

> I have been on the Eve of Leaving this place for the Last 3 weeks but Cant Get My Money for 4 Months work which I did. . . . I would have done very well this Last Eight Months if I had got My pay for My work but there is [a puddle] at Every door.[77]

Reflective of the frequency with which the MacNeil brothers, Richardson, and an untold number of other men spent their strength carving tunnels and picking ore only to be refused compensation, the Utah Territorial Legislature passed an act in 1872 granting miners legal title to their pay. Unfortunately, most laborers did not have the financial resources needed to bring suit.

The Intermountain West's tendency for extreme winter weather further bore down on life on the mining frontier. Notorious during the 1870s for severe snowstorms, which began as early as September, forty-foot snow accumulations, and avalanches that buried whole camps, the Alta mining district presented Richardson and the MacNeil brothers with a host of challenges.[78] Frequently on the move and often without adequate lodging, Richardson recorded several instances in his journal in which he and his companions became engulfed in blinding blizzards. On one occasion, Richardson's boots became so frozen to his skin that blisters and raw swatches hobbled his ability to walk for several weeks.[79]

Existing largely apart from settled Mormon life and frequently wrestling with disappointment and exploitation, many Mormon colliers further experienced acute challenges to their faith. John MacNeil's letters home reveal a man trying to come to terms with the sharp differences he perceived between the congregation through which he first came to know Mormonism in Lanarkshire and the Saints he encountered in the American West. Failing to see cooperation, honest dealings, and egalitarianism on par with all he expected from Zion, MacNeil rather quickly became disillusioned.

As his efforts to build a foundation for himself in Mormondom faltered, the growing class stratification by which he was surrounded and the manner in which certain brethren prospered while others persistently fought for their daily bread nagged the man into a deep sense of bitterness. As early as 1874, John MacNeil concluded:

> The people here are Just the same as at home. Some very good people, but the Majority is both Mean & wicked Like every other place. Religion dont Make No difference to the Natural Scoundral. Heel Still remain a Scoundral & religion Affords him a Cloak for his practice. Mormonism may be right & it may be rong, I don't know. There is one thing I know, the Mormonism of the Old Country has No resemblance to the Mormonism here.[80]

Also on the disadvantaged end of the West's industrial boom, James MacNeil, too, came to believe that at least some of his hardships were rooted in the dishonest dealings of his brethren in the gospel and that good works, righteousness, and honest endeavor weren't always requisites for success. James, however, differed from his brother in his determination not to allow his experiences with some Mormon people to cast a shadow over the Mormon gospel. "Depend on it," the younger MacNeil wrote home in 1875, "I think a great deal too Much of Mormonism for to get disgusted at it through some of them cheating Me & depend upon it I will never turn My back on it because . . . every tub Must Stand on its own bottom."[81] James further reasoned that through his struggles on the mining frontier he was growing stronger and wiser:

> I have got to know a little of the world Since I left home. I have been Studying human nature a little sense I've been here & fancy I have learned a little. An unsophisticated youth like me coming into this country Soon gets to know. . . . I have traveled a hundred & five miles by myself without a Single cent in my pocket. . . but they tell me Ive got to get some thrashed.[82]

Apt to quote the Scottish poet Robert Burns, and clinging to the notion that in the Mormon homeland his faith and hard work would lead to both spiritual and temporal rewards, James MacNeil persistently reminded his family that it is good "to be knocked about in the world," for men are made in overcoming challenges:

> When you get knocked down here at anything you have got to get up & bump at it again until you succeed. It don't do to sit &

> cry over it. It don't pay that (way) nohow. . . . You Must Make up your Mind to Suffer a little at first. But depend on it. You will be better of it in the long run.[83]

Though at times guilt-ridden in his alienation from family and church community, and disenchanted by the hardships he encountered on the mining frontier, William Richardson also resisted blaming Mormonism for his misfortunes. Like the MacNeil brothers, Richardson openly acknowledged that in the Mormon homeland "popel . . . was not all perfect." Instead of equating the spiritual failures of church members with the church itself, however, Richardson seems to have clung more tightly to the higher ideals of his faith. In spite of being one who, by nature, did "not like to say much," Richardson recorded in his journal moments when the spirit inspired him with courage and words beyond his otherwise quiet demeanor. On one such occasion, Richardson had laid out his bed roll among "a good many" miners from Rhodes Valley. After a young man began railing on Brigham Young and other church leaders, and "called them every (thing) that was bad . . . & just went for them," Richardson found himself unable to sit passively:

> I lisned til he was thrue & then asked him if he was doon & he said yes. Then I started to him. I hive it to him & the boys then said well doon Scotty for thay did not [know] my name & I talked til he had verry little to say but we cape on til it was bat [about] bead time & then we went to reast.

In addition to the "gift of tongues," Richardson also continued to believe in the power of premonition and divine protection. Accordingly, a defining moment arrived in this man's life while he was working at Coalville during the winter of 1873. Having experienced a strong "feeling" that he should return to his family, Richardson confided in "Brother Salmon," a local Mormon authority. Although Bishop Salmon advised Richardson that he should heed his prompting and go home, the collier lingered. The emotional gulf between what he "felt" he should do and the shame of returning to his wife and children without a reasonable amount of savings ultimately drove him to his knees:

> I thought that I would not go til I got some money to take with me but I felt that thar was som thing going to happen. that day was the 9 & it was Sabethday & I could not rest all day no whare & when Night came I went out alone & praed [prayed] for the Blessing of the Lord to rest upon me & my Family & that we might live to fill up the [purpose] of our creation. & when I went into the hous I felt a bet better & went to work on Monday & did not think much about it.

Two days later, Richardson's ambivalence about entering the coal mine came to fruition. He had not been hewing longer than two hours when "thare was about 5 or 6 toon of coal fell doon in my place & I was covred over all but the head." Hearing the roof collapse, another Mormon miner rushed into Richardson's room and set to work unburying him and pulling him from the heap of coal to safety. Although his legs had not been broken, "thay war brosed [bruised] a great dale [deal] that I could not walk & thare was some of my rabs brock [ribs broke] & I was hurt across the buck [back]."

Brothers John and Joseph Campbell carried Richardson to his lodging and washed and anointed his body in the tradition of Mormon healing rites. Joseph Campbell, in particular, remained vigilant at Richardson's bedside, visiting his brother in the gospel "three or four times every day" as he struggled to turn himself from side to side without assistance. Also frequently at his bedside were the wife and daughters of the Mormon boarding house owner: "Thay brought me every thing thay thought that I could eat or dring [drink]." For Richardson, the event stood as a reminder of the fellowship that did exist among many members of the Mormon community, even on the mining frontier. It also played out as a lesson regarding the power of premonition and the Lord's capacity for mercy. Although Richardson "hade got hurt & could never be the same agane," there was much wonder in the fact that he had survived at all.[84]

In the Intermountain West, Richardson certainly was not alone in his belief in the entwinement of labor and matters of the spirit. As in the British Isles, religious precepts conditioned experiences below the earth's surface and led to a widespread belief among Mormon miners in the Lord's propensity to provide protection to those who remained faithful and heeded His warnings. Well into the twentieth century, it was not uncommon for Mormon miners to don their garments as they descended below the earth's surface and later testify to the protective power of the sacred clothing. Even as his brother increasingly disassociated himself from the Mormon Church, James MacNeil, for example, informed the people back home that "I Wear My Garments Now all the time & I think it done Me good."[85] From the Almy coal camp, MacNeil further claimed, "We have the gifts & blissings, the power of performing Miracles."[86] In the central Utah coalfields, another Mormon miner credited his and his partner's survival of a large coal mine "bounce" to their sacred garments. After the immense weight of the earth bore down on the roof supports at the Castle Gate mine,

> another terrific bounce occurred which threw down four feet of top coal for over 200 feet along the back entry where we were. The only place where the top coal was not down was where Brother

> Steve and I were standing at the time it occurred. The noise from the bounce was heard for 5000 feet, and men came from a distance to see what happened. I was not able to account for our being saved in that but by one way, and that is we both had our Temple garments on which were given us for the protection of the body.[87]

Like Richardson, many Mormon miners in the Intermountain West also continued to take seriously the power of premonitions and dreams. In addition to offering protection, such spiritual gifts were believed to facilitate rescues and recoveries. Thomas Parmley, a Durham, England-born Mormon collier, claimed to have experienced divine assistance on a number of occasions over the course of his long career in the coalfields of Britain, Iowa, and Utah. In the aftermath of the horrific Winter Quarters explosion, which claimed the lives of at least two hundred men and boys in central Utah, Parmley, who served as both a mine boss and Mormon bishop, led several rescue and recovery crews through gassy and collapsed tunnels. In the years that followed, the local Mormon community told stories about the dreams that led Bishop Parmley to the locations of several missing bodies, including that of his deceased brother.[88] This Mormon mining community also told stories about Benjamin F. Thomas, a local Mormon bishop of Welsh decent who went into the Castle Gate coal mine the morning of the tragic 1924 disaster in spite of a premonition to remain above ground. "He waited and hung back . . . until he finally had to run to catch the mantrip." Having a son to support on a Mormon mission, Bishop Thomas decided to go in the mine that day and, consequently, became one of 171 victims of three violent methane explosions.[89]

For many Mormon colliers, assurances of a measure of protection through faith and adherence to their gospel eased anxieties about entering a place where man stood at the mercy of the forces of nature and few, if any, miners finished their career without witnessing a tragedy. Even so, the miner's life in the Intermountain West tended to take a heavy toll on one's physical and emotional health. Among even those for whom catastrophe remained at bay, body-aches from the grueling nature of the work, headaches caused by accumulations of noxious gas, and injuries from a variety of sources, including the collision of coal cars, rock falls, small and large methane explosions, and sharp picks and other tools, seemed to continually bear down on one's ability to perform hard physical labor. In an attempt to apologize for having not been able to write to his family in Scotland more often, John MacNeil described the effect that mining coal and silver was having on his body by 1876:

> The mining in this country is to rough a life for a man to stand long no matter how stout he is. It is beginning to wear me old already & I've been as stout & tough as any person you ever saw. . . . My wife gives me hell three times a week for not writing to you, but my hands are so big & stiff & clumsy that I hate to take a pen up, but I'll try and write a little oftener.[90]

Likewise seeking forgiveness for the brevity and dearth of letters penned home, William Richardson explained to his wife and children:

> When I rote you last then I was so bad that I could not sit on a chair I rote it standing on my knes I was so bad with my back & side . . . & during that time I would have given any thing if I had been at home with you but I could not gat far. . . . The work has been good . . . & we espect it to be for some time but when it gets dul agane I will come home. . . . I am very lonely.

Certainly, the emotional strains of being away from loved ones and pressures to fulfill familial obligations often compounded the physical cost of a miner's life. Existing within a culture that stressed strong male patriarchs capable of devising the means to hold their families together and providing material support, spiritual guidance, and protection, Richardson tended to descend gloriously from the mountains when his mining ventures paid well and proudly distribute school supplies, shoes, and other gifts among his children. Quite often, however, Richardson's letters and diary entries reveal bouts of shame and avoidance regarding physical injuries and failures to provide adequate remittances to his family. In addition to waiting out periods of slack in the coal and silver districts, rather than returning home empty-handed, Richardson seems to have withheld his letters when he had nothing promising to report:

> I did not want to let you know how I was til I felt better. you wanted to know if I could send you some money that is what I have not got for we did not get much work in January If I will be able to ceap on working I will has a little pay the nest [next] month I am gating very tired I will have to quit do the best you can.

Little is known about how Ann Richardson coped with the absence of her husband during these years and managed to hold the family unit together. William's papers naturally focus on his encounters with nineteenth-century America as a laboring man, British immigrant, and member of the Mormon faith. Yet, within the details of his life story, glimpses of Ann's world can be detected: haggling over her husband's earnings with pay officials in the Salt Lake Valley; overseeing the family's investments and responsibilities at the cooperatively owned mill; hiring out the boys to work cattle and cut timber; balancing available cash with the goods produced on the homestead; working the land; rearing livestock and other animals; coping with snowstorms, floods, and insect infestations; and applying her own ingenuity to the directives given by her often-distant husband. Although William attempted to guide the family's financial decisions and continue to fulfill his obligations as the head of the household, his extended stretches away from home essentially left the farm and immediate matters of survival in the hands of Ann and the boys. Even when read through her husband's record, Ann's loneliness and worry over William's long silences is quite palpable: "You wanted to know why I was so long in riting if I had forgot you," William responded to Ann from the mining frontier, "well I have not forgoting you yet I hope that I never shal."

Remarkably, while other families might have dissolved to pursue individual interests, the Richardson family remained true to their obligations to one another. In fact, during a dark period on the mining circuit, William confided in his diary that his very survival relied strongly on the existence of his family: "I got doon sick with the hurt that I got & I was very bad for over too month & thare was many time I said if it was not for the childring I would rather bee out of the world that I would bee out of my misery." By the end of the 1870s, William Richardson, then in his late forties, was too crippled to continue to take on the mining frontier. Fortunately, his labors, in combination with those of Ann and the boys, succeeded in greatly building up the family homestead in the Heber Valley. At this point, Richardson's diary entries turn from a focus on matters of sustenance to things of a more spiritual and familial nature: church service, experiences as an ecclesiastical teacher and healer, thoughts on religious doctrine and philosophy, grandchildren, and other events that mark the life of a family. Periodically, however, Richardson's journal catches the man sinking pits near his homestead, apparently unable to restrain his collier instincts, and traveling to Coalville and Grass Creek to visit with old friends.[91]

For the MacNeil brothers, distance from loved ones and familial obligations also exacted a heavy toll. While the brothers' early letters reflect a certainty that their efforts would yield the wages needed to bring their parents and siblings to the American West, such optimism waned to "hope" by the late 1870s. "There are Some that do very well here," explained James MacNeil,

> and every Spring that I have been here there has always been two or three poor cusses "Struck it" and made their little pile and it May Come My turn Some Spring. If it does come you May be Sure that

> I will remember you. Nothing would give me so much pleasure as to have you here on a farm.[92]

In spite of the rigid work regimes, the setbacks, and disappointments, the MacNeil brothers astonishingly never indicated in their records a sense of regret for having migrated to the Intermountain West. Although John MacNeil certainly developed an antipathy toward many Mormon people in his new homeland and never fully reconciled himself to membership in a religious community, he consistently tempered his harsh critiques with assertions that, even during the worst of times, prospects in the Utah Territory trumped what was available to a poor man in Scotland:

> I would rather die of starvation in this country than dig coal for a living in the old country. . . . As regards Coming Back to the Old Country to Dig Coal for my Living rest Satisfied that is A thing that Will Never happen. I Might Come back on A Visit to the Old Country Providing I have Enough of Means but I Would Make Sure before I Started that I Had Enough to fetch Me here Again.[93]

James MacNeil concurred with his brother's assessment that, as "curious" and "rough" as mining might be in the Intermountain West, a poor man still had a chance to improve his lot:

> A Miners Life in this country is a hard one but he has A chance to Make A raise Sometime in his life whereas a Man may work all his life there for a bare living Some makes it in no time, others it takes years. There has been a time when I thought I had it. Last Spring I thought I had it sure but it slipped me.[94]

For James MacNeil, life in the Mormon homeland had much in common with the natural environment by which he was typically surrounded as he moved among the coal, silver, and copper works. While at times stern, deceptive, and unsympathetic, the Intermountain West also possessed some of the most beautiful landscapes in the world: "I have seen a great deal of the handy works of the lord here," James MacNeil wrote. "It is rough country and it makes the people rough, but they are kindly people withal. In fact more kindly than I expected."[95]

By 1880, James MacNeil had traveled the mining circuit from the southern Wyoming coalfields, to the silver mines of Alta in northern Utah and Silver Reef in southern Utah, and the copper mines of central and southern Arizona. The year 1883 found him homesteading in Graham County, Arizona, with a Mormon partner by the name of Samuel Alger, freighting for a nearby copper mine where he also functioned as a foreman and writing about a desire to get married and serve a mission for the Mormon Church in Scotland.[96] Sadly, just when he almost seemed to "have it," James MacNeil lost his life moving livestock across a swollen river. After traveling to Arizona to visit his brother's grave and oversee the will and sale of property, John MacNeil returned to the land he had acquired near Bountiful in northern Utah. Still unable to settle fully into a farmer's life, John continued to follow the mining circuit between the coal mines of Rock Springs, the newly developing Winter Quarters coal mines in central Utah, and the silver mines of Park City. While at Park City in 1903, John, then in his fifties, tragically lost his life in a roof fall.[97]

Conclusion

During the mid-nineteenth century, Mormonism arrived in the British Isles as one of several dissent movements, which asserted the worth of common people and their entitlement to various forms of empowerment and quality of life. Unlike Primitive Methodism, Chartism, trade unionism, and other forms of working-class activism, however, the early Mormon Church proposed an alternative to struggling against a seemingly impenetrable established order in the homeland. In addition to offering common people direct access to church gospel and administration through biblical literalism, doctrinal simplicity, lay leadership roles, and other responsibilities, Mormonism put forward the opportunity to build Zion on the fringes of the American frontier. There, the Saints imagined themselves, in essence, "creating the world anew" in such a way as to bring the temporal and spiritual together as one. Self-sufficiency and material well-being would arise from cooperative endeavor and righteous living even as the Mormon gospel generated new sets of values and human relationships capable of restraining oppression and "liberating the laboring man from industrial slavery." Yet, before the Saints could master the trials and complexities associated with building Zion in the Intermountain West, the steady advance of American expansion effectively checked the dream of creating a spiritual kingdom. As in Britain, the "wounds of class" cut sharply through developing settlements, and corruption and the instabilities of the market economy increasingly weighed most heavily on the laboring poor. Some of the ways in which ordinary converts coped with the realities of the Mormon homeland and endeavored to make a life for themselves in the industrializing West can be discerned in narratives written by and about Mormon colliers.

The stories told by William Richardson, John and James MacNeil, and John Thompson reveal an arduous struggle with rigorous work regimes, the environment, exploitation, and unsteady employment which often began well before reaching the Salt Lake Valley. In an attempt to achieve a profitable equilibrium between farming and mining, and send remittances to loved ones left behind, each of these men encountered the deep emotional strains of disappointment and acute challenges to their religious faith. For those who took to the mining circuit of the Intermountain West, tales of achievement typically fell between a host of tragedies, broken bodies, and shattered spirits. However, even among the most disenchanted, a persistent theme that runs through the testimonies of convert colliers is the belief that in the Mormon homeland poor men had a greater shot at a comfortable livelihood than what was available to their class in England, Scotland, or Wales.

Consistent with this notion, the lives of Mormon colliers also present remarkable tales of success and a level of achievement unavailable to much of the laboring poor in the British Isles. Highly valued for the skills and knowledge they acquired in the collieries of the homeland, Mormon colliers could be found holding prominent supervisory positions throughout the coalfields of Utah, Wyoming, Colorado, Illinois, and elsewhere.[98] In the Intermountain West, colliers such as Rueben Fowkes, John L. Russell, Thomas Sneddon, Joseph Soulsby, and Thomas Parmley also occupied important civic and church positions. It was not uncommon, for example, to find the coal camp's local Mormon bishop also functioning as a mine supervisor. That these "bishop bosses" were apt to extend employment opportunities to their brothers in the gospel is quite manifest in the historical record. Similar to the Irish-dominated copper mines of Butte, Montana, relatively stable mining communities developed in parts of the Intermountain West from Mormon bosses delivering coal owners a reliable supply of labor. Thus, one topic that certainly deserves greater exploration is the degree to which "bishop bosses" and their coal-mining congregants mitigated labor strife through job preferences and by holding one another spiritually accountable for favorable working conditions.[99] As in Butte, conservativism and a lack of widespread militancy within a certain ethnoreligious group should not be dismissed as apathy, disempowerment, or subordination.[100]

Consequently, in the continued entwinement of the temporal and the spiritual, elements of Zion did persist in the daily lives of Mormon colliers in the Intermountain West. In addition to religious ties between a number of bosses and employees, the sustained belief in the potential for God's protective influences below ground rendered the workplace and the church house tightly interlaced. As in the British Isles, many Mormon colliers claimed the power to perform priesthood healing rites, and faithfully anointed the injured, broken, and sickly bodies of their brethren and families. Many Mormon colliers also continued to don their protective garments with faith that the Lord watched over "his children though they be in the bowels of the earth."[101] Dreams, premonitions, and promptings also remained a part of Mormon coal camp life. When even the faithful and obedient met tragedy, church narratives assured those left behind that their loved one completed his (or her) earthly mission and had been called to perform heavenly labors. Thus, the spiritual greatly conditioned the temporal in Mormon coal-mining communities and provided a sense of order and divine framework for an occupational life known for its volatility and randomness of tragedy. This intersection of the worldly and otherworldly bound the home, coal mine, and church closely together and shaped labor relations and community life wherever a significant number of Mormons toiled below ground well into the twentieth century.

Notes

1. *Millennial Star*, June 5, 1852, 237–38.
2. Richard L. Jensen and Malcolm R. Thorp, eds., *Mormons in Early Victorian Britain* (Salt Lake City: University of Utah Press, 1989), xi. See occupational surveys in Philip A. M. Taylor, "Why did British Mormons Emigrate?" *Utah Historical Quarterly* 22, no. 3 (July 1954): 249–70; and Philip A. M. Taylor, *Expectations Westward: The Mormons and the Emigration of the British Converts in the Nineteenth-Century* (Ithaca, NY: Cornell University Press, 1960), 18–50; also James Linforth and Frederick Hawkins Piercy, *Route from Liverpool to Great Salt Lake Valley* (Liverpool: Franklin D. Richards, 1855), 16–17. These occupational surveys suggest that second to "laborers," men who clearly designated themselves as "miners," "colliers," and "pitmen" comprised the largest occupational group to migrate to the United States as part of documented Mormon emigration companies from Britain. While "collier" and "pitman" refer to one who specifically labored in coal pits, a "miner" might toil in one of a variety of works, including iron, lead, and coal, or move between a number of extractive industries. In this study, I use the phrase "Mormon collier" or "convert collier" to refer to men from England, Scotland, or Wales who converted to the Mormon faith and whose occupation in the homeland involved the extraction of coal. I do not address Ireland in this study due to the comparatively small number of converts from this nation and the minor role of coal in the Irish economy. However, migrants from Ireland did labor in English, Scottish, and Welsh coal pits and some of these men and their families did convert to Mormonism.
3. Eric Hopkins, *Industrialization and Society: A Social History, 1830–1951* (London: Routledge, 2000), 21–56.
4. In an effort to portray the humanity of my subjects and how these individuals understood themselves and the world in which they lived, this examination aims to empower Mormon colliers to speak for themselves. In so doing, I draw on a methodological approach that elevates belief, feeling, and the authenticity of lived experience over verifiable truth. As a number of oral historians have argued, the value of testimony lies most profoundly in how the subject understood, remembered, and reacted to the forces that marked daily life and the manner in which the

stories they told gave shape to larger historical events and processes. See Alessandro Portelli, *The Death of Luigi Trastulli and Other Stories: Form and Meaning in Oral History* (Albany: State University of New York Press, 2000); Ronald Grele, "Directions for Oral History in the United States," in *Oral History: An Interdisciplinary Anthology*, ed. David Dunaway and Willa Baum (Nashville: American Association for State and Local History, 1984); and Michael Frisch, *A Shared Authority: Essays on the Craft and Meaning of Oral and Public History* (Albany: State University of New York Press, 1990).

5. George Whitefield, *George Whitefield's Journals* (Mulberry, IN: Sovereign Grace Publishers, 2000), 140–50.
6. John Walford, *Memoirs of the Life and Labours of the Late Venerable Hugh Bourne: By a Member of the Bourne Family* (Cambridge: Cambridge University Press, 2011), 62; and John Petty, *The History of the Primitive Methodist Connexion* (London: Richard Davies, 1860), 18–27.
7. Hugh McLeod, *Religion and the Working Class in Nineteenth-Century Britain* (New York: Macmillan Education LTD, 1989), 26–30; and Eileen Yeo, "Christianity in Chartist Struggle, 1838–1842," *Past & Present* 91, no. 1 (May 1981): 109–39.
8. Thomas G. Alexander, *Things of Heaven and Earth: The Life and Times of Wilford Woodruff, a Mormon Prophet* (Salt Lake City: Signature Books, 1991), 90–100, and Grant Underwood, "The Religious Milieu of English Mormonism," in Jensen and Thorp, *Mormons in Early Victorian Britain*, 38–45.
9. Latter-day Saint Ancestral File Number: 1GPK-ZH.
10. Beth J. Baugh, "History of Alfred Summerill 1847–1911 and Elizabeth Lear 1845–1922," Baugh Family History; http://baugh-history.tripod.com/ALFREDSUMMERILL1847.pdf; and Latter-day Saint Ancestral File Number: 1BKH-ZJ. The similarities between the Primitive Methodists and the early Mormons were so marked that historian Ronald W. Walker claims that the former group foreshadowed the latter. See Ronald W. Walker, "Cradling Mormonism: The Rise of the Gospel in Early Victorian England," in *Coming to Zion*, ed. James B. Allen and John W. Welch (Provo, UT: Brigham Young University, 1997), 265.
11. Thomas Hunt Journal, L. Tom Perry Special Collections, MSS 6173, Harold B. Lee Library, Brigham Young University (BYU), Provo, UT. (Hereinafter cited as L. Tom Perry.)
12. Matthew Rowan, "A Concise Historical Account of the Rowan Family," Typed Manuscript, Utah State Historical Society, Salt Lake City; and Matthew Rowan, "Reminiscences and Journal, 1853–1864," MS 8230, Church History Library, History Department, The Church of Jesus Christ of Latter-day Saints, Salt Lake City, UT. (Hereinafter cited as Church History Library.)
13. *Deseret News*, August 1, 1855.
14. Parley P. Pratt in *Journal of Discourses* (London: Latter-day Saints' Book Depot, 1854–1856), January 30, 1851.
15. Evan Samuel Morgan Journal, 1833–1857, L. Tom Perry, MSS 4137.
16. *Millennial Star*, September 1, 1879.
17. Ibid., October 29, 1864.
18. Rowan, "A Concise Historical Account," 1–9, 35.

19. Thomas Hunt Journal.
20. In addition to the accounts discussed, see Orson Pratt, in *Journal of Discourses*, August 8, 1880, 21:240; and Robert Lang Campbell Journal, 1843–1848, L. Tom Perry, MSS 496.
21. *Millennial Star*, January 15, 1849.
22. Ibid., September 1, 1849.
23. Daniel Williams, "Diary and Autobiography, 1847–1852," 61–63, L. Tom Perry, MSS 667.
24. *Millennial Star*, June 15, 1850.
25. Ibid., April 1, 1849; and Jean S. Greenwood, "The Welsh Emigrants," in *Chronicles of Courage* (Salt Lake City: Daughters of the Utah Pioneers, 1995), 331–70.
26. According to the Mormon belief system, these garments function as a reminder of the promises made between the faithful and the Lord, and as a source of both symbolic and literal protection from the evils of the world.
27. William Richardson Journal, L. Tom Perry, MSS 1055; Andrew Ferguson Journal, 1818–1888, L. Tom Perry, MSS 1055.
28. Thomas Beard, "Life of Thomas Beard," in Katherine Lake Andreasen, ed., *Journal of Thomas Beard* (Salt Lake City: privately published, 2006), Church History Library. Also see *Millennial Star*, September 1, 1849.
29. Joseph Thomas Perkins, "Autobiography of Joseph Thomas Perkins," Church History Library.
30. *Deseret News*, August 1, 1855.
31. John R. Gibbs, "My Experiences with the Church in Wales," *Journal of History* 10 (July 1917): 317.
32. *Millennial Star*, March 26, 1859.
33. Ibid., January 15, 1849; January 1, 1849.
34. *Deseret News*, May 27, 1868.
35. *Millennial Star*, December 1, 1850; December 10, 1859; John Kenneth Davies, *Deseret's Sons of Toil: The History of the Worker Movements in Territorial Utah, 1852–1896* (Salt Lake City: Olympus Publishing Company, 1977), chapter 1. Also see Brigham Young in *Journal of Discourses*, June 5, 1853, 1:254.
36. Ezra T. Benson in *Journal of Discourses*, February 16, 1853, 2:350–51.
37. Brigham Young in ibid., June 5, 1853, 1:254.
38. See Alan B. Campbell, *The Lanarkshire Miners: A Social History of Their Trade Unions, 1775–1974* (Edinburgh: J. Donald, 1979); and Robert Colls, *The Pitmen of the Northern Coalfield: Work, Culture, and Protest, 1790–1850* (Manchester: Manchester University Press, 1987).
39. William Bowers Diary quoted in Mabel Brown Blacker, "Within the Walls of Home: Life Story of Herbert Brown," http://lrwaite.net/brown_godber/brown_herbert.htm.
40. William Gibson Journal, Church History Library; Joan Oviatt, "The Gospel According to Gibson," in *More Amazing but True Mormon Stories* (Cedar Fort, UT: Horizon Publishers, 2008), 77–81.
41. George Cunningham, *Autobiography of George Cunningham, 1840–1913*, L. Tom Perry; Pearl Loveless, "Biographical Sketch of George Cunningham," L. Tom Perry, MSS 3288.
42. Ruth H. Barker, "John Sharp and Mary Hunter," http://sites.google.com/site/

emilyfarrer/johnsharp2/john-sharp-and-mary-hunter-by-rhb; Young Men's Mutual Improvement Association, "John Sharp," *Improvement Era* 7 (February 1904): 280–83; James B. Allen, "'Good Guys' vs. 'Good Guys': Rudger Clawson, John Sharp, and Civil Disobedience in Nineteenth-Century Utah," *Utah Historical Quarterly* 48, no. 2 (Spring 1980): 148–74; Craig L. Foster, "John Sharp and T. B. H. Stenhouse: Two Scottish Converts Who Chose Separate Paths," *John Whitmer Historical Association Journal* 17 (1997): 81–93; and Craig L. Foster, "The Canny Scotsman: John Sharp and the Negotiations with the Union Pacific Railroad, 1869–1872," *Journal of Mormon History* 27, no. 2 (Fall 2001): 197–214.

43. William Gibson Journal.
44. Martha Sharp Anderson, "History of Jane Patterson Sharp," http://sites.google.com/site/emilyfarrer/historyofjanepattersonsharp; and "Adam Sharp" in *Conquerors of the West: Stalwart Mormon Pioneers*, ed. Florence C. Youngberg (Scottsdale, AZ: Agreka Books, 1999), 2319.
45. Stanley Kimball, "The Saints and St. Louis, 1831–1857: An Oasis of Tolerance and Security," *BYU Studies* 13, no. 4 (Summer 1973): n38.
46. Mary Joan Boyer, *The Old Gravois Coal Diggings* (Imperial, MO: Tri-City Independent, 1952), 40–41 and 72–86; William Davidson, "Reminiscences of William Davidson," 5–7, Church History Library; Pearl Udall Nelson, *David King Udall, Arizona Pioneer Mormon, His Story and His Family* (Tucson: Arizona Silhouettes, 1959), among other diaries, testimonials, and biographies.
47. Edward Moroni Thurman, "A Life History of Edward Moroni Thurman," http://www.phousley.com/phousleycom/Family.
48. Lezlie Ann Anderson and John M. Brough, "History of Elizabeth Brough and Her Two Husbands," http://www.broughfamily.org/history/brough_tipton.html; "Joshua Salisbury" in Youngberg, *Conquerors of the West*, 2277; "Thomas Lowe (Low)" in Youngberg, 1478; "Joseph Henry Joseph," The Descendants of George Joseph, http://welshmormonhistory.org/index.php?/resources/view/2391; and "James Bryant" in *Our Pioneer Heritage*, ed. Kate B. Carter (Salt Lake City: Daughters of Utah Pioneers, 1958–1977), among other diaries, testimonials, and biographies.
49. William Richardson Journal.
50. John Thompson Letter, November 15, 1857, in *Good Time Coming: Mormon Letters to Scotland*, ed. Fredrick Stewart Buchanan (Salt Lake City: University of Utah Press, 1988), 66–68.
51. Ibid., 68 (August 1858).
52. Ibid., 70, 90–150 (January 16, 1859).
53. William Richardson Journal.
54. John MacNeil Letter, April 20, 1879, in Buchanan, *Good Time Coming*, 223.
55. Leonard J. Arrington, *Great Basin Kingdom: An Economic History of the Latter-day Saints, 1830–1900* (Lincoln: University of Nebraska Press, 1958), 87, 122–27, 275–76, 347–48.
56. M. Guy Bishop, "More than One Coal Road to Zion: The Utah Territory's Efforts to Ease Dependency on Wyoming Coal," *Annals of Wyoming* 60, no. 1 (Spring 1988): 8–16.
57. John MacNeil Letter, March 27, 1870, in Buchanan, *Good Time Coming*, 113–14.

58. Walter R. Jones, "Coal Mine Explosions at Almy, Wyoming: Their Influence on Wyoming's First Coal Mining Laws," *Annals of Wyoming* 56, no. 1 (Spring 1984): 54–65.
59. Ralph Smith Diary and Edward Watkins Smith Diary, GirdlestonesRus featuring Emma Girdlestone, http://westenskow.webspawner.com/anotherversiono/, accessed May 22, 2012; and Andrew Jensen, *Latter-day Saint Biographical Encyclopedia: A Compilation of Biographical Sketches of Prominent Men and Women in the Church of Jesus Christ of Latter-day Saints*, 4 vols. (Salt Lake City: A. Jensen History Company, 1901), 2:73. William Richardson also expressed a desire to follow a pair of Mormon brothers by the name of Watson to Almy/Evanston during this time but was detained in the Heber Valley due to a cooperative milling venture in which he had become involved.
60. Andrew Jensen, "Almy Ward: Uintah County, Wyoming," Microfilm Reel 10591, Church History Library; Alona S. Perkes, "Reuben Fowkes, 1842–1892, and Mary Bacon Fowkes, 1842–1915," Southwick Research, http://www.southwick-research.com/genealogy; Andrew Jensen, *Encyclopedic History of the Church of Jesus Christ of Latter-day Saints* (Salt Lake City: Deseret News Publishing Company, 1941), 13.
61. John MacNeil Letter, May 13, 1872, in Buchanan, *Good Time Coming*, 137–38.
62. Jones, "Coal Mine Explosions," 57; Surveyor General, *Report of Silas Reed*, 19.
63. John MacNeil Letter, December 17, 1873, in Buchanan, *Good Time Coming*, 165–66.
64. Perkes, "Reuben Fowkes," 11–12.
65. James MacNeil Letter, April 1875, in Buchanan, *Good Time Coming*, 201.
66. A. Dudley Gardner and Verla R. Flores, *Forgotten Frontier: A History of Wyoming Coal Mining* (Boulder, CO: Westview Press, 1989), 25–57; and David A. Wolff, *Industrializing the Rockies: Growth, Competition, and Turmoil in the Coalfields of Colorado and Wyoming, 1968–1914* (Boulder: University Press of Colorado, 2003), 31–107.
67. Jones, "Coal Mine Explosions," 58; Jensen, "Almy Ward." A series of mine tragedies at Almy provide further evidence of a sizable Mormon presence by the late 1880s. When an explosion ripped through an Almy mine in 1881, all but three victims were of Chinese descent. In 1886, at least eight of the thirteen miners killed in a No. 5 explosion claimed membership in the Mormon faith. Nine years later, Almy experienced another explosion at its No. 5 mine which killed sixty-one men and boys. This time, the Mormon Church buried thirty-two of its own.
68. Jones, "Coal Mine Explosion," 59–64; Jensen, "Almy Ward"; "Constitutional Convention," *Deseret Weekly*, September 21, 1889, 400; and James F. Willard, *Report on the Archives of the State of Wyoming* (Washington, DC: American Historical Association, 1915), 297.
69. James Morgan, "Miners' Union Movement in Wyoming," *United Mine Workers Journal* 28 (1917): 12–13; *Progressive Men of Wyoming* (Chicago: A. W. Bowen & Co., 1901), 291; and "Thomas Sneddon," *The Anode* 6, no. 6 (June 1920): 12.
70. Perkes, "Reuben Fowkes."
71. See Wilson O. Claugh, "Note on Dialect in the Uintah Mountains of Wyoming," *American Speech* 11 (April 1936): 190–92.
72. Edward Patterson Diary, L. Tom Perry, MSS 1285.

73. Youngberg, *Conquerors of the West*, 2227. After being struck with a pick, Robinson's foot had to be amputated.
74. John MacNeil Letter, March 12, 1873, in Buchanan, *Good Time Coming*, 157.
75. Ibid., 164, 196 (August 31, 1873, and January 14, 1875).
76. Ibid., 162–63 (August 31, 1873).
77. Ibid., 202–3 (May 4, 1875).
78. *The Utah Mining Gazette*, August 30, 1873; and *Salt Lake Tribune*, December 26, 1872.
79. William Richardson Journal.
80. John MacNeil Letter, March 16, 1874, in Buchanan, *Good Time Coming*, 184; see also 175–81.
81. James MacNeil Letter, January 1875, in Buchanan, *Good Time Coming*, 197.
82. Ibid., 171 (January 31, 1874).
83. Ibid., 187 (April 20, 1874).
84. William Richardson Journal.
85. James MacNeil Letter, January 14, 1875, in Buchanan, *Good Time Coming*, 198.
86. Ibid., 201 (April 1875). At testimony meetings, Mormons are encouraged to express their faith. Mormons are also expected to pay a percentage of their earnings as tithing to the church.
87. Christian Hyrum Muhlestein, "Autobiography of Christian Hyrum Muhlestein," Church History Library.
88. Ibid.; Antonione Joseph Delvenne, "Autobiography of Antonione Joseph Delvenne," Church History Library; Nobel Warrum, *Utah Since Statehood, Historical and Biographical* (Salt Lake City: S. J. Clark Publishing Co., 1920), 674–75; *Coal Age* (New York: McGraw-Hill, 1922), 22:285; Ronald L. Lewis, *Welsh Americans: A History of Assimilation in the Coalfields* (Chapel Hill: University of North Carolina Press, 2008), 186.
89. Fay Thacker Oral History, Labor Oral History Project, Charles Redd Center for Western Studies, L. Tom Perry, MSS 1130, 2.
90. John MacNeil Letter, December 16, 1876, in Buchanan, *Good Time Coming*, 218–19.
91. William Richardson Journal.
92. James MacNeil Letter, August 5, 1877, in Buchanan, *Good Time Coming*, 220.
93. Ibid., 155, 138 (February 16, 1873, and August 18, 1872).
94. Ibid., 207 (October 14, 1875).
95. Ibid., 164 (August 31, 1873).
96. Ibid., 254–56 (October 3, 1883). Also see Buchanan, *Good Time Coming*, 235–64. After leaving Arizona, Samuel Alger became one of the founders of Cleveland, Utah, and spent much of the remainder of his life seasonally migrating between his farm in Cleveland and the nearby coal camps of Winter Quarters, Castle Gate, and Sunnyside.
97. Buchanan, *Good Time Coming*, 273–92.
98. In addition to the Mormon mine supervisors already referenced in the text and footnotes, see J. E. Petitt, Andrew Hood, Robert Howard, Oliver Sutch, Peter Forester, William Edward Ruff, William P. Young, James T. Stones, Alexander D. Maclean, Hugh Hunter, Thomas W. Lewis, and William H. Woodhead in Warrum, *Utah Since Statehood*.

99. See Church of Jesus Christ of Latter-day Saints, "Chapter 27: Work and Personal Responsibility," in *Gospel Principles* (Salt Lake City: Intellectual Reserve, 2009), 155–60.
100. See David M. Emmons, *The Butte Irish: Class and Ethnicity in a Mining Town, 1875–1925* (Urbana: University of Illinois Press, 1989). Certainly, disputes with the federal government; open displays of hostility by much of the American public, including miners' unions; and growing class stratification among the Saints, themselves, functioned to blunt prior expressions of working-class consciousness among Mormon colliers in favor of a more cohesive religious identity. Yet, the spiritual intimacies between Mormon bosses and Mormon miners must also account for the "militant hush" among so many former Primitive Methodists, Chartists, and trade unionists by the end of the nineteenth century.
101. Beard, "Life of Thomas Beard." Also see *Millennial Star*, September 1, 1849.

11

The Frontier Thesis in Transnational Migration

The U.S. West in the Making of Italy Abroad

Mark I. Choate

Mark Choate addresses the significance of the American Far West in the Italian diaspora that occurred between the 1880s and World War I. He shows that the West figured prominently as both a destination for migrants and a fanciful image in Italian culture. As millions of Italians embarked for the Americas, the Italian state sought to cultivate ties to those migrants by subsidizing Italian language schools for immigrants' children, facilitating remittances to the motherland through the Bank of Naples, and organizing expositions in Italy to showcase and celebrate Italian immigrants' accomplishments. Moreover, hundreds of Italian societies abroad ranging from literary clubs to sports clubs and self-help groups flourished, often with the blessing and guidance of the Italian state.

Choate's essay shows the ways that a transnational or global focus and "bringing the state back in," or considering the role of government policy in immigration, can enrich our understanding of migration. Choate adopts a global perspective by linking centers of power and influence, including European capitals (the "metropole" or core) to geopolitical "peripheries" like the American frontier. This approach enables him to demonstrate how the American West figured in the Italian government's ideas about Italian expansion. Moreover, Choate shows concrete ways that the language, culture, and politics of Italy remained salient in the lives of Italians in the West. The Italian case supports the transnational hypothesis that many immigrants retain substantial ties to their homelands following emigration, occupying transnational space. This was particularly true for Italian emigrants, over half of whom eventually returned to Italy.

In 1879, a young postal worker in the small town of Lendinara, Italy, decided to emigrate. Adolfo Rossi, twenty-two years old, was discouraged with his prospects in his small town near Venice. Adolfo lived at home with his mother in the heavily populated Polesine valley. Although he had a steady job, he wanted to become a journalist. In Adolfo's words, while taking a walk along the Adige river one night,

> a strange idea struck my mind like a bolt of lightning. I reflected only a moment and committed myself to an audacious resolution. "No, I will not stay vegetating here," I thought. "The world is big, there's America, and New York is a vast metropolis. I will go there, I will study those famous Americans, I will learn English. I will begin as a manual laborer there but, in the land of action and liberty I will learn to better understand life and men and one day I will return to Italy, rich at least with experience. Then it will be easier to dedicate myself to journalism.
>
> I had read some books about the United States the previous month and had fallen in love with North America: this was the only reason I picked New York instead of Sydney or Buenos Aires. My determination and my choice were irrevocable.[1]

As Adolfo Rossi described in his memoir, *Un italiano in America* (1891), he traveled not only to New York City, where he worked as a pastry-maker and hotel doorman and waiter, but on through the Rocky Mountains to Breckenridge, Colorado, where he worked at a restaurant, and to Denver, where he was an administrator for a mining company. He returned to New York to work for the leading Italian-American newspaper, *Il Progresso Italo-Americano*, then returned to Italy as planned after five years in the United States. Rossi then became an important newspaper correspondent for Italy's top newspaper, *Corriere della Sera*, reporting on assignment from the Italian colonies of East Africa. Before his death in 1921 in Buenos Aires, where he was serving as plenipotentiary diplomatic minister in the Italian embassy to Argentina, Rossi had returned to Denver, Colorado, as the Italian consul.

Why, among all the places in the world, did Rossi spend so much time in Colorado? In the global network of Italians abroad, the American West represented freedom and opportunity. New York City was the gateway to the vast continent of North America, but transatlantic migration reached all the way to the Pacific in California and Washington State. Like other immigrant groups, many Italians became trapped in the crowded, high-cost slums of the eastern cityscape. From the Italian perspective of emigration, migration to the American West represented the outside limit of Italian expansion, reach, and influence, more promising than many other destinations in North and South America and more appealing to a dramatic sense of imagination.

Like "manifest destiny" and expansionism in the United States, mass migration for Italy carried symbolic weight beyond its practical economic, social, and demographic consequences. For the Italian state, emigration represented not just physical movement beyond the Italian peninsula, but a cultural and economic enlargement of Italy worldwide. In contrast to the massive Irish, Polish, and Jewish immigrations from multinational empires before the First World War, Italians emigrated from a new nation-state eager to establish its global reputation. At the high point of Italian migration, from 1880 to World War I, the Italian state viewed migration as a form of colonialism, described emigration as irredentism, and developed the economics of remittances and expatriate trade to reach out to emigrants.[2]

Adolfo Rossi is a good example of how individual experiences added up to regional, national, and global trends. In many ways he was a typical Italian emigrant. He was single, male, and from the Veneto region near Venice, which experienced the highest emigration rates of any Italian region. Most strikingly, he never intended to stay in America, and viewed his emigration in terms of his planned career in Italy following his return. Many immigrants saw their plans change, and because of marriage or other reasons, millions did not return home. Nonetheless, more than half of all Italian emigrants returned to Italy within several years, making their emigration temporary rather than permanent. Because of the high rate of return migration, Italy saw migration not only in international terms but as part of its foreign policy, through the perspective of domestic politics and nationalism.[3]

Looking from Italy outward, the Western United States offered the final frontier of freedom, the most wide open and the most American territory in terms of liberty and raw possibilities. A moralizing, progressive coalition in the United States and in Italy aimed to steer Italian migration away from cities on the northeastern seaboard, due to fears not only of a growing, possibly revolutionary proletariat, but also of tuberculosis, organized crime, exploitation, and failed opportunities eventually sent back to Italy. The fears of urban problems returning home to Italy were concrete, not abstract. In 1901 Gaetano Bresci, an Italian anarchist living in Paterson, New Jersey, returned to Italy and assassinated King Umberto in Monza. Italian anarchists celebrated this murderous triumph worldwide. The southern United States was less crowded than the Northeast, but receded as an emigrant destination thanks to widely distributed reports of endemic malaria and the lynching of eleven Italians in New Orleans in 1891.[4] The American West shone in comparison. The many successes of Italian Californians, in banking, arts and architecture, wine production and marketing, and cinema, achieved an enduring fame. Italian writers hailed the expatriate communities in California as the best of the best, because of the extra expense, planning, and organization required for individuals to travel across North America to the Pacific coast. As in Rossi's eureka moment on the banks of the Adige River, emigrant destinations took on a mythical, larger-than-life quality. Maps and geography seemed to shape the challenges and possibilities of a migrant's future.

Viewing migration as both emigration and immigration is one approach to placing regional history in the context of world history. As a nation-state with mass emigration, Italy hoped to link all the scattered Little Italy communities together into a Greater Italy, with the Italian peninsula as the hub of spokes reaching across the world. The vineyards, orchards, fields, mines, and cities of the Rockies and the Pacific coast emerged as destinations connected to a web of personal, social, national, and commercial interests tying North America to the emigrants' madre patria (literally the mother-fatherland). The western frontier thus played a significant role in ideas of the expansion of Italy, not just the expansion of the United States.

Italy's Special Mission in the World: Empire, Irredentism, and Italians Abroad

The ancient nation of Italy became a state only in the nineteenth century. Since the time of Dante and Petrarch, leading Italian philosophers, poets, and intellectuals had called for the reunification of Italy, divided ever since the breakup of Rome. In the nineteenth century, after the nationalism of the Napoleonic era, many intellectuals began to call for Italy's "resurgence" (Risorgimento), as "renaissance" had already been claimed as a moniker for a previous epoch of Italian rebirth. Vincenzo Gioberti, a Catholic priest and politician, called for a reunited Italy to regain its "primacy" in politics, society, and the arts. Before the seven separate regional governments could be united, however, Italian politics faced sharp divisions over religious issues. The anticlerical, visionary republican conspirator Giuseppe Mazzini called for the unification of Italy within her "natural frontiers" ordained by God, in the entire peninsula up to the Alps:

> Italy therefore will be one. Her geographical conditions, language, and literature; the necessities of defense, and of political power; the desire of the populations, the democratic instincts innate in our people, the presentiment of a progress in which all the forces and faculties of the country must concur, the consciousness of an initiative in Europe, and of great things yet to be achieved by Italy for the world; all point to this aim.[5]

Mazzini urged for Italy to stand up against the political rule of the papacy and of the multinational, traditionalist Austrian Empire. As such, Italy would play a world-historical role for the good of everyone: "Italy cannot live, unless she lives for all. We can only live a European life, and can only free ourselves by freeing others. We must be great or perish. . . . What for others may simply be a moral duty, is a law of life for us. . . . The destiny of Italy is that of the world."[6]

Mazzini's visionary and religious appeals echoed the traditions of exceptionalism in the United States. He boldly called for an Italian national mission as unique and universal as the civilization of the ancient Roman Empire.

What actually happened in Italy did not follow Mazzini's republican plans. During the 1848–1849 revolutions, which stretched from Venice to Palermo, Italians fought for unification under a green-white-red flag, in honor of the French Republican and Napoleonic tricolor. The popular revolutions of 1848 were defeated, and Mazzini's Republic of Rome fell to French forces supporting the pope in 1849. Instead of a republic uniting Italy, the king of Piedmont-Sardinia named himself as the king of Italy, unifying Italian regions under his rule in 1859, 1860, 1866, and 1870. The Italian regions of Lombardy and Veneto were torn from the Austrian Empire, as Mazzini had hoped. But this process was abruptly cut short by Bismarck's formation of the Triple Alliance in 1882, linking Germany, Italy, and Austria-Hungary. Italians remained under Austro-Hungarian rule outside the Kingdom of Italy's northern and eastern borders, in Trentino, Istria, and Trieste. Unification was postponed indefinitely, creating a seething discontent underneath the Italian political order.

Italy's truncated national territory created a new political movement of irredentism, named for the unredeemed territories, "le terre irredente," on the Italian frontier. The aim for religious redemption by secular unification was explicit, as the unfinished unification of Italy took on mystical resonance. Trent and Trieste were valuable not only for their symbolism, population, and wealth, but also because of their strategic location. In 1915, Italy controversially entered World War I against Austria-Hungary to win Trent and Trieste in the "third war of Unification." Until this bloody resolution, irredentism was a source of trouble and contradiction. Invested with the legacy of ancient Rome, the Kingdom of Italy struggled to meet the high expectations set by Gioberti and Mazzini, who had predicted that Italy's unification would mean an end to emigration. Beyond the lost territories themselves, irredentism came to apply to all Italians outside of Italy, from California to Australia.

Irredentism carried so much weight because it captured the essence of Mazzini's republican, unifying vision for a strong Italy of the future. The Italians who were not yet even part of Italy promised the best resolution of the kingdom's lingering social and economic problems. Paradoxically, the fringe of Italy was the center of the country's imagined future. The romantic and visionary appeal of irredentism bears a strong resemblance to Frederick Jackson Turner's frontier thesis several decades later, which aimed to explain the core of American history through the history of its periphery.[7]

Political necessity forced a flexible application of irredentist dogmas inside and outside the kingdom. The first irredentist group, Italia Irredenta ("Unredeemed Italy"), had been founded in Italy by republican leaders in 1877. Their radical call to unite all Italians as a nation threatened to undermine the narrow foundations of Italy's Liberal government, and the state responded by banning all irredentist organizations. In their place, in 1889 Ruggero Bonghi founded the "Dante Alighieri Society for Italian Language and Culture outside the Kingdom." Only unofficially irredentist, the society counted many Liberal politicians and ministers among its members. The society chose to name itself after Dante to symbolize the international strength of Italian culture. Under a cultural and literary cover, the society practiced not "political irredentism," but "multiform action." Subsidized by the Foreign Ministry, Bonghi's group publicized the plight of Italians in Trent and Trieste, outside the Italian frontier, and mobilized support and contributions for Italian schools abroad. Bonghi hoped to keep the unredeemed regions within the reach of Italian culture, while waiting for revisions of Italy's political borders.

The society's second president, Senator Pasquale Villari, was a Dante scholar from Naples, who had written influential articles on the social and economic backwardness of Southern Italy compared with Northern Italy. Villari successfully reoriented the society's geographical focus, from the Austrian Alps and the Adriatic to the transatlantic "colonies" of the Americas. Emigrants speaking Italian dialects around the world needed to learn standard Italian, "the language of Dante." Villari asked, "Are not these also unredeemed lands? Are not these our brothers?" He tied emigration to irredentism with a compelling, emotional plea for the future of Italians everywhere. Under his leadership, the Dante Alighieri Society supported the passage of Italy's new Emigration Law of 1901, which created an Emigration Commissariat and an Emigration Fund to subsidize Italian activities abroad, such as Italian schools, hospitals, and charities. Besides 214 committees inside the Kingdom of Italy, 73 Dante Alighieri committees were founded abroad, including in San Francisco, California, and in Washington State, with the express support of the local Italian consuls. Local committees organized and subsidized schools teaching the Italian language to adult emigrants and their children, and sponsored lending libraries aboard emigrant ships. Tying expatriates to Dante's legacy expanded the reach of Italy.

The rhetoric of irredentism attached a powerful symbolism to the cultural status of all Italians outside Italy, even if born abroad. They became adjuncts to Italian culture, politics, and trade. The Italian Foreign Ministry aimed to develop Italy's economic and political interests overseas, by maintaining a permanent Italian identity among expatriates. If Italy's "economic exiles" could remain loyal Italians, redeemed by political, cultural, and social support from the metropole, Italy would reap the benefits of a worldwide network of Italian-speaking enclaves on every continent, buying and selling Italian goods and promoting Italian political interests. Italy thus attempted a strategic opposition to the assimilationist pressures and politics of host nations in Europe and the Americas.

Like the American mission of expanding its culture through westward expansion, Italians across the world were invested with a mix of political, cultural, and social missions as they traveled abroad. Even those who opposed the royal, secular government of Italy carried their ideologies abroad with a missionary zeal. The anarchist Errico Malatesta spread international revolution in Italy but also in France, Switzerland, and Argentina.[8] At the opposite end of the political spectrum, the Catholic Church hierarchy in Rome stubbornly regarded the United States as religiously undeveloped, in need of missionary support. Until 1908 Canada and the United States remained "missionary fields," under the jurisdiction of the prefect of Propaganda Fide in Rome. Struggling against Protestant nativists, American Catholics labored to define themselves as "Americans," not alien imports in a Protestant country.[9]

The secular apostle of nationalism, Giuseppe Mazzini, had thought unification would end emigration and all other problems.[10] But in the end, the geographical basis for nationality, posited as axiomatic by Mazzini, was subverted by emigration. Italy's clearly defined, boot-shaped peninsula became irrelevant to the international meaning of Italy, as Italians spread across both hemispheres, through the interior to the coasts. The different categories of unredeemed Italians, emigrants, exiles, and expatriates blended together under the banner of "Italians abroad." Whether emigrants were aware of this or not, they were invested with the task of representing Italy. Optimistic writers depicted Italian emigration in a narrative of strength, not as an abject failure. Emigration could be the basis for building enduring connections and influence abroad.

Italian Institutions of Culture and Commerce in the American West

The idea of "Italy abroad" was not just talk. With a mix of public and private initiatives, subsidized by the Italian state or supported in kind with books and supplies, regional and local organizations solidified the Italian communities around common interests of commerce, education, and media. The U.S. West provides a good example of the strength and variety of

Italian institutions in their global context. Political initiatives by the Italian government were blocked in the United States as unwanted foreign interference. How could Italy promote and solidify an Italian American community? Cultural identity and economic incentives likely proved more tangible and influential than diplomatic maneuvers in the long run.

The foundation of Italy's outreach to emigrant communities lay in language and culture. As was noted by Leone Carpi in the first study of Italian colonialism, published in 1874, the word *colonìa* in the Italian language is used both for settlements of emigrants and for overseas possessions.[11] Both emigration and African colonialism were under the purview of the Italian Ministry of Foreign Affairs. The powerful prime minister Francesco Crispi declared in parliament in 1887 that emigration would be crucial to the future of Italy's international influence and reach:

> The [Italian] Government . . . must never lose sight of [emigrants] in their new home. . . . Colonies must be like arms which the country extends far away in foreign districts, to bring them within the orbit of its relations of labor and exchange; they must be like an enlargement of the boundaries of its action and its economic power.[12]

Crispi presented to parliament a bold mix of domestic and foreign policy motivations, combining emigration with empire, the Americas with Italian Africa. He envisioned Italy expanding through its emigration, strengthening at the core and at the periphery.

Yet in the countries where Italians settled abroad, whether in Brazil, Argentina, or the United States, immigrants were expected to fuse into their new countries and abandon ties to Italian nationality. Italy responded to assimilationist and nativist pressures with a range of strategic cultural programs. The Italian government relied on culture and religion to brand Italian-speaking emigrants as "Italian." The success of any expatriate colonialism depended upon an enduring ethnic identity, even if subsidized and somewhat artificial. The peninsula, politically divided for a thousand years, was culturally divided into a dozen separate languages. Italian politicians searched for the essence of italianità, which would not dissolve in any immigrant melting pot no matter what pressures were applied. The Italian language became the main ingredient in a theoretically insoluble Italianism. As Giuseppe Prato wrote, "Language is the most solid defense of threatened nationalities, the only salvation and hope of oppressed peoples, the most effective means of expansion for the strongest races and superior peoples." In the words of Ferdinando Martini, "The soul of the fatherland is in language." If first-generation migrants speaking dialects learned standard Italian, the Italian community could unite instead of falling into regional divisions. If second-generation Italians also learned "the language of Dante," they would be moored to Italian culture and society no matter where they lived. The key element to maintaining a "Greater Italy" was reaching this second generation, born abroad. Governmental and semiprivate organizations collaborated in the campaign of the madre patria (mother-fatherland) to reclaim her/his lost children. The Dante Alighieri Society's committees all over the world coordinated local Italian patriotic and educational activities, subsidized by the Italian Foreign Ministry.

The careful cultivation of Italian identities abroad aimed to develop a set of comparable Italian ethnic environments, replicated in locations scattered across the globe, under careful guidance from Italy. Italian cultural groups usually made the local Italian consul a president or chairman ex officio, guaranteeing the groups' political loyalty and permitting their use of Italian royal symbols. The hundreds of expatriate Italian mutual aid societies worked at concrete, local, practical self-improvement, but Italian literary societies and competitive athletic groups aimed to build their reputations as Italians abroad. Speaking Italian and naming their societies "Italian" took on a political meaning outside the cultural frame of their statutory constitution. The Italian National Target Shooting Society of New York refused to join the (United States) National Rifle Association until the NRA made membership a requirement to participate in competitions in the 1890s. The Italians then joined the NRA only after their Italian consul gave permission.[13] With plenty of support from Italy, many Italian patriotic groups in this period attempted to remain as un-American and unassimilated as possible.

The Catholic hierarchy in Italy also wanted to support emigrants in their new environments. The Vatican worried that Italians would lose their religion on the frontier or in remote mining towns because of neglect, or become Protestants in the United States. Coordinated through the Emigration Fund, the Italian state could enlist the open support of Catholic clergy who had no other connections with the normally anticlerical, Liberal state. Italian bishops wanted to redeem their emigrants from these pressures, and collaborated with the Italian state in building schools, hospices, and hospitals for Italian emigrants abroad. Many of the schools subsidized by the Italian state were operated by priests or nuns, although humanitarian organizations organized by reformist Socialists also drew upon the Emigration Fund. The government official in charge of the state's program for Italian Schools Abroad, Angelo Scalabrini, was the brother of Monsignor G. B. Scalabrini, bishop of Piacenza. Monsignor Scalabrini, who favored reconciliation between the papacy and the Italian government, pioneered missionary work among Italians in the Americas, while Monsignor Geremia

Bonomelli, bishop of Cremona, organized a similar effort among Italians in Europe. Both groups of missionaries attempted to keep emigrants speaking Italian, attending Catholic services in Italian, and thinking of their families and friends in Italy. While not sharing the Italian government's political and economic goals for emigration, the bishops accepted government funds to work with similar means toward different ends. Scalabrini defended Italian emigrants' culture and argued that a rapid assimilation would destroy their religion. He called for Italians to resist against the melting pot:

> Not many years ago, in the United States there were enormous efforts to Americanize . . . the emigrants of the various European nations. Religion and Fatherland mourned for millions of their lost children. Only one people knew how to resist this violent attempt at assimilation: the people with this motto on their flag: our church, our school, our language. Let us not forget this fact. Let us also work, each according to his strength, so that all Italians abroad wear the same uniform, with the same steadfastness, the same courage: for Religion and for the Fatherland.[14]

Scalabrini argued for a continuity in the emigrant's intimate relations with God, family, and culture. He argued that being Italian was synonymous with being Catholic, and his missionaries coordinated clerical and lay efforts to support religious, educational, and charitable institutions for Italian Catholic emigrants abroad.

Documenting such efforts encouraged their continuation and inspired imitation. To measure and encourage the success of Italian emigrants, the Italian government subsidized expositions and congresses inside Italy to display the achievements of Italians abroad, including the 1892 Columbus Exposition in Genoa, the 1898 Exposition in Torino, the 1906 Exposition of Italians Abroad in Milan, and the Italian Colonial Institute's First and Second Congresses of Italians Abroad, held in 1908 and 1911 in Turin and Rome. The conjunction between Italian irredentism and emigration strengthened the symbolic and political weight of both movements.

The public display in Italy of each colony's achievements abroad led naturally to comparisons and competition. In the Expositions of Italians Abroad, the Italian community of San Francisco vied with New York City Italians in terms of prestige, wealth, regional influence, and culture. For example, the Italian Chamber of Commerce of San Francisco was very proud that they organized and chartered their group in 1885, two years before the Italian Chamber of New York.[15] Although perhaps the two leading

American coastal Italian communities might have achieved more by working together rather than as rivals, Italians arrived in the United States from a tradition of regional and provincial competition. The continental distances between America's major metropolitan outposts perhaps precluded meaningful cooperation between California and New York; even American Express and Wells Fargo split apart over the vast distances. As a result, the Italians of San Francisco measured themselves against New York as a yardstick, hoping to surpass all other immigrant communities in cohesiveness and achievements.[16]

For the fiftieth anniversary of Italian unification in 1911, the Italian Colonial Institute published an inventory of all Italian community organizations, including those subsidized by the Italian government and those who refused a subsidy. The organizations throughout the American West demonstrated the range, depth, and priorities of Italians abroad organized and linked to the madre patria. Holding pride of place were Italian schools, charged with teaching the second generation of Italians abroad to maintain their Italian language and culture. The Italian government subsidized five schools in California: three in Los Angeles, one in Sacramento, and one in San Francisco; four in Denver, Colorado; one in Portland, Oregon; and two in Seattle, Washington. Many of these were religious schools, for example the orphanages of the Missionary Nuns of the Sacred Heart; but others were secular, as in San Francisco's "Italian school directed by the Committee of the colony." In addition, the Italian Colonial Institute listed the Italian School of the Jesuits in Portland, Oregon, as teaching Italian but not accepting the Italian government subsidy.[17]

Most important for temporary emigrants was a solid and secure method of sending money to family and friends at home. In 1902 the Italian state organized a secure channel for remittances to Italy, administered by the nonprofit Banco di Napoli.[18] The Bank of Naples established a network of correspondent banks, which collected remittances locally and transmitted the money internationally through the Bank of Naples for very low fees. This system not only protected Italian migrants from the abuses and exploitation of unregulated banks, but gave the Italian government a measurement of how much money came into Italy from emigration each year. In the American West, the Bank of Naples correspondents were the Spokane & Eastern Trust Co., in Washington and Oregon; the German American Trust Co. in Denver; Jachetta & Nigro in Pueblo, Colorado; and the Banca Italo Americana San Francisco.[19] When A. P. Giannini began to build his Bank of Italy, later the Bank of America, one of his first goals was to acquire the Banca Italo Americana and its remittances business.[20]

The large number of Italian newspapers and periodicals in the U.S. West not only constituted the solid representation of the Italian language, but also the economic and social interests that held the community together. Local advertisers included importers and exporters, lawyers, doctors, and pharmacists, all catering to Italian audiences and all invested in the continuation of a stable Italian community. The wide variety in the names of the periodicals represents the editors' political priorities and their audiences. Three newspapers published daily were the crowning achievement of Italian American publishing in the West: *L'Italia* and *La Voce del Popolo* [The Voice of the People] in San Francisco, and *La Nazione* [The Nation] in Denver. Weekly newspapers were published throughout Colorado: *Corriere di Trinidad* in the mining town of Trinidad; *L'Unione* [Union] and *Il Vindice* [The Vindicator] in Pueblo; and *Roma*, *La Nazione*, *La Capitale*, and *Il Risveglio* [The Reawakening] in the capital city of Denver. In California, editors in Los Angeles published a weekly, *La Colonia Italiana* [The Italian Colony]; Sacramento produced two weeklies, *La Stella d'Italia* [The Star of Italy] and *La Capitale*; and San Francisco produced four weeklies, representing its hegemony in Italian California: *Il Secolo Nuovo* [The New Century], *Il Topo* [The Mouse], *La Tribuna* [The Tribune], and *La Nuova Elvezia* [New Switzerland]. Two twice-weekly cultural and social magazines were published: *Le Maschere* [The Masks], in Pueblo, and *La Colonia Svizzera* [The Swiss Colony], in Los Angeles. A twice-monthly magazine, *L'Imparziale*, was published in San Francisco; and finally, a monthly commercial magazine, *Rassegna Commerciale: Bollettino mensile della Camera di Commercio di California*, was distributed throughout California by the Italian Chamber of Commerce.[21]

The Italian Colonial Institute also tabulated separately the individual Italian community groups. One network of religious groups serving Italian emigrants, Italica Gens, was coordinated by a prominent lay Catholic organization in Turin, the National Association for Italian Missionaries. In the western United States, several local congregations had joined the Italica Gens: the Jesuits of Portland, Oregon, and Spokane, Washington, at Gonzaga College; the Servite fathers of Denver, Colorado; the Salesians and the Jesuits of San Francisco; the local parishes of Chico and Sacramento, California; and the Salesians of Oakland, California. Beyond local service, these congregations sought an international and transnational tie binding together Italian emigrants around the world. In contrast, the Sister Missionaries of the Sacred Heart did not join the Italica Gens (which had not been sanctioned by the pope), but operated orphanages and schools assisting Italians in Denver, Los Angeles, and Seattle. Two Catholic parishes in San Francisco also listed themselves as serving Italian neighborhoods.[22]

Self-help groups remained the most populist and widespread form of local community organization. In the Italian consular district of Denver, twenty-two Italian mutual-aid societies [società di mutuo soccorso] had been established. Besides groups in Walsenburg and Trinidad, Colorado, seven were formed in Denver alone. Although these seven might have pooled resources and combined into one organization, the Italians preferred to divide themselves among regional, religious, and political lines. Three separate groups were formed in Albuquerque, New Mexico, and four in Kansas, in the towns of Corona, Frontenac, Chicopee, and Weir City. Other Italian mutual-aid groups had been established in Lead, South Dakota; Sunrise and Rock Springs, Wyoming; Coalgate, Oklahoma; Omaha, Nebraska; and Butte, Montana. Based upon subscriptions and contributions, these groups provided insurance and death benefits for their working-class members.[23]

Along the West Coast, sixty Italian organizations showed a much broader range of goals and possibilities. Two Dante Society chapters, in San Francisco and in the state of Washington, demonstrated a cultural and educational focus beyond the hard-scrabble life of mining towns in the mountain West. In addition to many mutual-aid societies, for example, San Francisco proudly displayed a well-rounded roster of organizations, including the Italian Chamber of Commerce, Scholastic Committee for education, and a beneficent committee for charitable works. Italians in Los Angeles also promoted a recreational club and beneficent societies. The sheer number of groups, however, betrayed the deep divisions in Italian society. For example, the Italian mutual-aid societies in San Francisco were divided along religious, royalist, republican, and regional lines: the Circolo Regina Margherita, in loyalty to Queen Margherita, namesake of the mozzarella pizza; the Compagnia Garibaldina, volunteers honoring the great Republican anticlerical war hero; the Società Piemontese, for Piedmontese and other northerners; the Società Meridionale, for all Italian southerners; the Volta and Roma Masonic Lodges; the Giuseppe La Masa Society of Republicans; and the Galileo Grove, Monteverde Grove, Aurora Grove, and Verdi Grove of the United Ancient Order of Druids. Very few causes or movements could unite all the Italians of the West.[24]

Visions of the Western Frontier: *La Fanciulla del West*

Beyond the reality of Italian organizations throughout the American West, the cultural representation of the West influenced continued migration patterns and long-lasting self-perceptions. The West served as the setting for the most prominent depiction of migration in Italian opera: *La fanciulla del West* (1910), by Giacomo Puccini.

One feature of this opera is its outsider's perspective. Although *La Fanciulla* was Puccini's last full-length realist opera, and followed the contemporary standards of verismo, Puccini never visited California, and the opera was produced in New York rather than in California where the fictional story takes place. The opera premiered in 1910 at the Metropolitan Opera in New York City, which had commissioned the work as New York City's first operatic world premiere. The opera represented New York City's coming of age as a major cultural center to rival European capitals. The famed tenor Enrico Caruso starred as the bandit Johnson in the world premiere at the Met, and the opera went on to premiere in other cities, several with strong ties to Italian migration: London (1911), Rome (1911), Buenos Aires (1911), Melbourne (1912), and Berlin (1913), before the First World War. The opera was revived at the Met for its centennial in 2010, yet *La Fanciulla* is performed much less frequently than Puccini's other operas, in part because of its liminal status between American and Italian shores.[25]

In this opera, Giacomo Puccini and his librettists explored the pathos of emigration both directly and indirectly. *La fanciulla del West* (1910) includes important changes from the original source material, David Belasco's play *The Girl of the Golden West* (1905). Unlike the play, the libretto by Carlo Zangarini and Guelfo Civinini opens with a poignant focus on an emigrant's plight. The libretto's printed preface (not performed on stage) quotes Belasco, to emphasize the theme of immigration:

> In those strange days, people coming from God knows where joined forces in that far Western land, and, according to the rude custom of the camp, their very names were soon lost and unrecorded, and here they struggled, laughed, gambled, cursed, killed, loved, and worked out their strange destinies in a manner incredible to us of to-day. Of one thing only we are sure—they lived!

In the first scene, set in a raucous frontier saloon in the Sierra Nevada, a minstrel's nostalgic song on the banjo turns all the miners away from their poker game to thoughts of home, as they sing along with the refrains. The character Jim Larkens breaks down:

> I can't stand it anymore,
> I can't stand it boys! I'm sick,
> I don't know with what. . . . Send me,
> ah, send me home! I'm ruined!
> I'm tired of the pick and the mine!
> I want the plow, I want my mamma!

The miners quickly gather donations as a group to pay for Jim's passage home; Jim thanks them and leaves. In the play, Jim returns home to Pennsylvania; in the opera, however, he returns home to Cornwall, his home across the ocean on the Celtic Sea. This opera of Puccini, Zangarini, and Civinini should be understood as a tale of transatlantic migration, set not in Italy but nevertheless informed by the Italian migrant experience.

At the end of the opera, the main character, Minnie, and her captured bandit lover are set free, redeemed by Minnie's love and forgiveness. They leave the camp to move far away to start a new life together. The drama of emigration, for the individual and the group, is captured in the final lines of the opera, where the California homeland might as well be Italy:

> MINNIE and DICK JOHNSON: Adieu, my sweet land, adieu, my California! Beautiful mountains of the Sierra, o snows, adieu! (Exit scene.) (The crowd is dejected . . . filled with sadness—others sadly wave farewell to Minnie moving further away)
>
> The voices of MINNIE and DICK JOHNSON: (backstage, becoming more distant): Adieu, my California, adieu!
>
> The CROWD: (sobbing) You will never return . . . never . . . never!

Puccini's *Fanciulla* is not considered his best work, and is less known than many of his other operas. Like the Italian emigrants, *La fanciulla del West* had a transient existence. Writing about emigrants for an American audience limited the legacy of this opera by Puccini, and the work became a stranger in a strange land, remembered well neither in the United States nor in Italy. Life on the frontier presented a nontraditional topic for a metropolitan opera and for contemporary and future opera audiences. Nonetheless, the opera presented a memorable and exotic U.S. West, with all the individual pathos, human tragedy, and historic drama of frontier migration on a grand scale. Still today, the cowboys and vast spaces of the American West hold an outsized place in the Italian cultural imagination, and Italian tourists continue to flock to the western national parks of the United States.

Conclusion

The future first elected president of the Republic of Italy, Luigi Einaudi, established his reputation in 1900 with an economics book about emigration. Einaudi chose one industrialist, Enrico Dell'Acqua, as the title character of his work *A Merchant Prince: Study on the Colonial Expansion of Italy*. Einaudi refuted accusations that Italians lack initiative or a sense of solidarity abroad. He also concluded that Italy must not fear competition from established expatriates, in the Italian vineyards of California or in the Dell'Acqua's textile factory in Brazil:

> It is the logic of little minds to believe that every factory established by our compatriots, every piece of cultivated land, every hill planted with vines in America represents a subtraction from our activity, a net loss for Italian exports. In reality, those local products accredit Italian brands and awaken latent desires, and as tastes become more refined the market turns from imitations made by Italians to genuine Italian products.[26]

Einaudi asserted that the California vineyards had aroused a taste in Italian wines "which otherwise would not exist"; likewise, pasta made in New York City cultivated an appetite for real Italian pastas, cheeses, tomatoes, and olive oils.[27] True to his Liberal principles, Einaudi saw no need for economic divisions within "greater Italy." Rather, the Italian government needed to act resolutely to establish trade treaties in the Americas and use diplomacy to bolster the Italian language in the schools, and perhaps in an Italian university abroad. Most urgently, Italy had to build connections to support its expatriates abroad on the expanding frontier, wherever they might be. The logic and sensibleness of Einaudi's appeal strongly influenced Italian legislation, and by extension all other countries who modeled their policies upon Italy's successes.[28]

Not just the broad rhetoric, but the concrete specifics of Italian programs abroad offer a presage to migrants' enduring international connections in culture, economics, and society in an era of international peace. In 1906, before the Great War, Gino Speranza described the transnational context of Italians abroad:

> Commercial interests, the "annihilation of time and space" by improved methods of transportation and the ebb and flow of travel, will render the old distinctions of nationalities and the parochial character of present-day patriotism, more and more an anachronism. The conception of citizenship itself is rapidly changing and we may have to recognize a sort of world or international citizenship as more logical than the present peripatetic kind, which makes a man an American while here, and an Italian while in Italy.[29]

The ease of international connections made new migrant identities not only possible, but attractive, subsidized, and institutionalized. International migration became doubly complicated by the ongoing viewpoint of emigration—people leaving—and of immigration—people coming in. The individual migrants and their families attracted assimilationist and antiassimilationist pressures from near and far, in a contest over which political center would link to the migrant periphery.

The web of connections and interests defied the distances of geography. Emigrants on the Pacific coast of North America, or in the Rocky Mountains, never seemed very distant from Italy due to high rates of return migration. Since so many eventually came home again from mining and agriculture, migration could never be "out of sight, out of mind." Even when Italians abroad adopted foreign citizenship, Italy counted them as responsible for conscripted military service in World War I. Emigrants automatically regained their Italian citizenship after they returned to Italy.[30] Nonetheless, mass emigration remained controversial in Italy, and controversial abroad. What lay in Italy's long-term political interests might not match the interests of immigrant polities, or of the immigrants themselves. While individual migrants created new lives abroad, assimilating to some degree into their local societies, Italy as a sending state could not let go of emigrants as a lost cause. Mass emigration was too important for Italy's economic development and international image.

The Italian institutions created in the American West remain relevant and exemplary for migration in the twenty-first century. Unlike the Poles, Jews, and Irish who came to the Americas a century ago, the Italians emigrated from an established state. This state had every interest in encouraging its citizens to send money back to their families and return home after a profitable career abroad. The Italian state became directly and indirectly involved in the lives of Italian expatriates, through establishing banking channels for remittances, subsidies for cultural and social institutions, and coordination of language education. In these ways, Italy of the late nineteenth and early twentieth centuries was like India, China, and Mexico today in the twenty-first century. Mexico encourages its emigrants to send money home in remittances, to buy Mexican goods and maintain their Mexican culture and heritage, and to return home after earning money abroad. Italy did the same thing, encouraging Italians to send money home, to buy Italian agricultural and industrial products, and to return home after working in the Americas.

International state involvement adds more dimensions to the ongoing history of migration. Mexico has been particularly successful in its creative outreach; recent studies have documented in detail the many issues of dual nationality, and the significant intervention of sending states in the lives of migrants.[31] Thanks to migration, American history is not just for Americans, and foreign states continue to shape the fabric of the American West.

Notes

1. Adolfo Rossi, *Un italiano in America* (Milan: Casa Editrice La Cisalpina, 1899), 4.
2. Compare Anders Stephanson, *Manifest Destiny: American Expansionism and the Empire of Right* (New York: Hill & Wang, 1995); Albert K. Weinberg, *Manifest Destiny: A Study of Nationalist Expansion in American History* (Baltimore: The Johns Hopkins Press, 1935).
3. Mark Wyman, *Round-Trip to America: The Immigrants Return to Europe, 1880–1930* (Ithaca, NY: Cornell University Press, 1993); Dino Cinel, *The National Integration of Italian Return Immigration 1870–1929* (Cambridge: Cambridge University Press, 1991).
4. Richard Gambino, *Vendetta* (New York: Doubleday, 1977); Marco Rimanelli, and Sheryl L. Postman, eds., *The 1891 New Orleans Lynching and U.S.-Italian Relations: A Look Back* (New York: Peter Lang, 1992); David A. Smith, "From the Mississippi to the Mediterranean: The 1891 New Orleans Lynching and Its Effects on United States Diplomacy and the American Navy," *The Southern Historian* 19 (April 1998): 60–85.
5. Giuseppe Mazzini, "On the Unity of Italy," in *Life and Writings of Joseph Mazzini* (London: Smith and Elder, 1891), 1:290.
6. Cited by Gaetano Salvemini, *Mazzini*, trans. I. M. Rawson (Palo Alto, CA: Stanford University Press, 1957), 81–82.
7. Compare Frederick Jackson Turner and John Mack Faragher, *Rereading Frederick Jackson Turner: The Significance of the Frontier in American History, and Other Essays* (New York: H. Holt, 1994).
8. Giampietro D. Berti, *Errico Malatesta e il movimento anarchico italiano e internazionale: 1872–1932* (Milan: F. Angeli, 2003); Vittorio Giacopini, *Non ho bisogno di stare tranquillo. Errico Malatesta, vita straordinaria del rivoluzionario più temuto da tutti i governi e le questure del regno* (Milan: Elèuthera, 2012); Peter H. Marshall, *Demanding the Impossible: A History of Anarchism* (Oakland, CA: PM Press, 2010).
9. Peter R. D'Agostino, "The Scalabrini Fathers, the Italian Emigrant Church and Ethnic Nationalism in America," *Religion and American Culture* 7, no. 1 (Winter 1997): 125–26; Robert J. Wishes, "The Establishment of the Apostolic Delegation in the United States of America" (PhD diss., Pontificia Università Gregoriana, 1981); Robert A. Orsi, *The Madonna of 115th Street* (New Haven: Yale University Press, 1985).
10. Giuseppe Mazzini, *The Duties of Man* (1907; London: Everyman, 1966), 9, 53.
11. Leone Carpi, *Delle colonie e delle emigrazioni d'italiani all'estero sotto l'aspetto dell'industria, commercio, agricoltura e con trattazione d'importanti questioni sociali*, 4 vols. (Milan: Tip. Editrice Lombarda, 1874).
12. Atti Parlamentari, Camera dei Deputati, Leg. XVI, 2a sessione 1887, Documenti n. 85, December 15, 1887, p. 9. See also "Il progetto di legge sull'emigrazione," *Rivista della Beneficenza Pubblica e delle Istituzioni di Previdenza* 16 (1888).
13. Giuseppe Prato, "Per l'emigrazione italiana nell'America Latina," La Riforma Sociale 10, year 7 (1900): 109. *Gli italiani negli Stati Uniti d'America* (New York, 1906), 438.
14. Ferdinando Martini, Pagine raccolte (Florence: G. C. Sansoni, 1912), 811. Giovanni Battista Scalabrini, "L'Italia all'estero," in *Gli italiani all'estero*, ed. Esposizione Generale Italiana (Turin, 1899), 39.

15. *Nel Cinquantenario della Camera di Commercio Italiana in New York. 1887–1937–XVI* (New York: Italian Chamber of Commerce in New York, 1937), preface.
16. Dino Cinel, *From Italy to San Francisco: The Immigrant Experience* (Palo Alto: Stanford University Press, 1982); Vittorio Soldaini, "La raccolta delle rimesse degli emigrati italiani e l'opera del Banco di Napoli: 1902–1913," *Revue internationale d'histoire de la banque* 2 (1969): 137–88.
17. Istituto Coloniale Italiano, *Annuario dell'Italia all'estero e delle sue colonie* (Rome: Tip. Unione Editrice, 1911), 407–22.
18. Francesco Balletta, *Il Banco di Napoli e le rimesse degli emigrati, 1914–1925* (Napoles: Institut Internationale d'histoire de la Banque, 1972); Luigi De Rosa, *Emigranti, capitali e banche (1896–1906)* (Napoles: Edizione del Banco di Napoli, 1980); Soldaini, "La raccolta delle rimesse degli emigrati italiani," 137–88.
19. Istituto Coloniale Italiano, *Annuario*, 390–91.
20. Felice A. Bonadio, *A. P. Giannini, Banker of America* (Berkeley: University of California Press, 1994); Gerald D. Nash, *A. P. Giannini and the Bank of America* (Norman: University of Oklahoma Press, 1992).
21. Istituto Coloniale Italiano, *Annuario*, 461–63.
22. Ibid., 511–14, 518–19, 527.
23. Ibid., 496.
24. Ibid., 496, 500–501.
25. John Russo, "Puccini, the Immigrants, and the Golden West," *Opera Quarterly* 7, no. 3 (Autumn 1990): 4–27; Mark I. Choate, "Italy at Home and Abroad after 150 Years: The Legacy of Emigration and the Future of *Italianità*," *Italian Culture* 30, no. 1 (May 2012): 51–67.
26. Luigi Einaudi, *Un principe mercante; Studio sulla espansione coloniale italiana* (Turin: Fratelli Bocca, 1900), 146, 160.
27. Ibid., 146, 166–68.
28. See Virginia Yans-McLaughlin, ed., *Immigration Reconsidered: History, Sociology, and Politics* (New York: Oxford University Press, 1990).
29. Gino C. Speranza, "Political Representation of Italo-American Colonies in the Italian Parliament," in *The Italians: Social Backgrounds of an American Group*, ed. Francesco Cordasco and Eugene Bucchioni (Clifton, NJ: Augustus M. Kelly Publishers, 1974), 310.
30. Mark I. Choate, *Emigrant Nation: The Making of Italy Abroad* (Cambridge, MA: Harvard University Press, 2008), 203–17.
31. David Cook-Martìn, *The Scramble for Citizens: Dual Nationality and State Competition for Immigrants* (Palo Alto, CA: Stanford University Press, 2012); David Fitzgerald, *A Nation of Emigrants: How Mexico Manages Its Migration* (Berkeley: University of California Press, 2009); Michael Snodgrass, "Patronage and Progress: The Bracero Program from the Perspective of Mexico," in *Workers Across the Americas: The Transnational Turn in Labor History*, ed. Leon Fink (New York: Oxford University Press, 2011).

12

Outlanders and Inlanders

Boer Colonization in the U.S.-Mexican Borderlands, 1902–1905

Andrew Offenburger

Emigrants and refugees from the Eastern Hemisphere seeking economic opportunity and liberty were drawn to Central and South as well as North America. In this chapter, Andrew Offenburger describes the abortive settlement of Boer households on eighty-three thousand acres in Chihuahua, Mexico, between 1903 and 1905, when most relocated to New Mexico's Mesilla Valley. Offenburger masterfully interprets this brief, little-known episode in immigration history to illuminate the connections between the American Southwest and the Mexican North at the turn of the century. His article stresses the permeability of the United States–Mexico border prior to the Mexican Revolution, showing how immigrants and investment capital moved into and across the region, temporarily making northern Mexico a virtual economic extension or "proxy" of the American frontier. Offenburger's article reflects the impact of globalization and transnationalism upon immigration research. He shows that national borders and policies did influence immigrants' settlement decisions. But transportation and communication networks nurtured cross-border ties and complex nationalities. Shifting depending upon time and context, including local circumstances, the immigrants in this study were at various times Boer, African, Mexican, or American. The inclusion of this case study set largely in Mexico in a book about immigration to the far western United States reminds us that regions often transcend national boundaries.

An "exquisite sunset" cast hues of orange across the train depot in Michoacán, Mexico, in October 1902.[1] Members of a brass band warmed their mouthpieces, expectantly, while hundreds of citizens watched a private Pullman car roll to a stop. They were waiting for government officials and three special guests. The first, Willem Snyman, represented a group of Boer émigrés looking for land to colonize.[2] He and his countrymen recently

Figure 12.1. General Benjamin Viljoen and Commandant Willem Snyman, cofounders of the short-lived Boer colony in Santa Rosalía, Chihuahua, 1903–1905. *Congregationalist and Christian World*, December 2, 1905.

suffered defeat by the British Empire in the South African War (1899–1902), and some Boers, like Snyman, faced the death penalty for treason against the Crown. Their republics annexed, their families destitute, and their lands devastated, hundreds if not thousands sought refuge in lands beyond southern Africa.[3] To secure the best contract possible, Snyman traveled with and sought advice from Americans sympathetic to the Boer cause: Marshall Bond, an American mining expert, and Edward Reeve Merritt, a wealthy financier and assistant secretary of the Union Trust Company of New York.[4]

Mexican officials under President Porfirio Díaz courted the Boer veteran of the South African War at many stops on his tour, a "princely pilgrimage of unparalleled luxury."[5] When Snyman stepped from the train that day in Michoacán, Bond wrote, "For a moment we thought we were going to be lynched, when up went a mighty cry of '*Viva Boeros! Viva General!*'" Snyman addressed the crowd, which "went wild" and "hoisted him upon the shoulders of a lot of men, and, amidst screaming and cheering, he was carried to a reserved streetcar."[6] Alongside Snyman's coach "rode caballeros dressed in silver and gold embroidered hats and clothes." Farther behind ran "thousands" of Indians and *peones*.[7] The scene had all the hallmarks of Porfirian Mexico, as the excesses of the elite stood out in relief against the poverty of the masses. While the Boers did not settle in Michoacán, site of this lavish reception, several families did form a small colony the following year near Santa Rosalía, Chihuahua, an agricultural region of great promise, recently connected by rail to markets in the United States and Mexico City. In exchange for tax concessions and low-interest loans, Snyman and the colony's cofounder, Benjamin Viljoen, agreed to relocate fifty families within three years.

To date, a few scholars have acknowledged the history of the Boer colony, although it remains largely unknown.[8] It teeters on the edge of several historiographies—African, imperial, Mexican, and western—and would appear to constitute little more than a quirky episode in the history of the U.S.-Mexican borderlands.[9] But no study has set the Boer colony's history within a broader regional context. Neither has anyone explored the dynamics of daily life in the Mexican colony and explained why, after only two years, most colonists left Chihuahua for southern New Mexico and western Texas. Piecing together the history of this short-lived colony makes two contributions.

First, the Boer colony's history stitches together two literatures—of Latin America and the U.S. West—at a time when capitalist development in the United States influenced its southern neighbor. Thus, the Boers landed in Chihuahua when the development of the American West "turned south" to exploit resources in northern Mexico. With the construction of key railroad trunk lines in the 1880s, as in the American West, trains facilitated the entrenchment of U.S. capital in the borderlands, and they sparked a new era of development. Irrigation expertise, companies, and ditches flourished. American mines and their workers brought new investments to the region. These linear networks of rails, ditches, and veins (human and mineral) connected the borderlands in unprecedented ways. Many people sought glittering riches. Some dreamed of new beginnings. Others fled oppression. Thus, immigrants imbued the landscape with hope of a distinctly western variety. By the time of Snyman's tour, U.S. investors had begun, according to Francisco Almada, a "peaceful invasion" of northern Mexico and the creation of a "semi-colonial economic order."[10]

The Boers settled in Mexico in large part due to this historical push, represented here by Snyman's reception in Michoacán, the Pullman car, the railroad, Bond, and Merritt. The U.S. economic influence south of the border, and the Mexican cultural presence north of it, created similar environments for the everyday life of an agricultural colony, be it in the United States or Mexico. Between 1882 and the breakout of the Mexican

Revolution (1910), farmers could just as easily produce for the market on either side of the border, with one exception: the requirements for immigration. To form a colony in the U.S. West, as the Boers had first considered, U.S. immigration laws required ready cash.[11] Destitute, the colonists needed a less-developed region, one whose state would offer perks for settlement, one that sought rooted settlers. Excepting immigration laws, the Mexican north began to display the processes that created the U.S. West.

Second, the Boer experience in the borderlands reveals the ways that states—and historians—compartmentalize their peoples. As foreigners speaking a strange language, the Boers lived as "outlanders": immigrants not of the Mexican land. Yet as an agricultural colony with state support, the Boers participated very much as "inlanders": those who planted crops to develop the state and to prevent the erosion of its power. Just as Mexico had done before, Díaz recruited colonists to develop Mexico's northern region, part of his ideology of modernization. The Boers thus cultivated the soil and the state, but their lived experiences reveal a persistent negotiation of nationality resistant to a single moniker of "Boer," "African," "Mexican," or "American." Their experience in the borderlands demonstrates the regional fluidity up to the Mexican Revolution of 1910.

Although Snyman surely enjoyed his tours of the countryside and the tremendous *vivas* in his honor, above all else, he and his countrymen sought stability. Ever since the discovery of gold in the heart of the Transvaal in 1886, the independent Boer republics in southern Africa became locked in a struggle with the British Empire.[12] Rural Boers, in an attempt to retain sovereignty amid mass immigration, restricted the franchise from foreigners (*uitlanders*, or "outlanders") who typically worked in the British- and American-led mining industry. While the Crown defended the rights of its citizens, England coveted the mineral wealth in Boer lands and sought any opportunity to strengthen its claim to southern African riches. Their differences were irreconcilable: greed for England, self-determination for the Boers. The South African War resulted in a "flagrant outburst of British imperialism."[13] The war illustrated the limited prospects of independent agriculturalists when faced with large-scale capitalist development.[14] Completely overpowered, the Boers resorted to commando raids and earned the admiration of anti-imperialist leagues around the world. British Lord Kitchener responded with a "scorched earth policy that imperial troops and Afrikaner commandos had been accustomed to using against Africans."[15]

The war left deep wounds in its victims and veterans, and descendants of the Boer colonists still recall how the war affected their extended families. Viljoen, a high-ranking general and cofounder of the Mexican colony, spent several months as a prisoner of war on St. Helena. The British exploited his capture in the press and, according to one descendant, mistreated him while there. Other family members tell of how Snyman's two-year-old niece, Martha, died in a British concentration camp, where an estimated twenty-eight thousand perished.[16] Martha's older sister, Marie, later wrote in a memoir that "a sergeant came to the pup tent we were living in and brought a little black coffin and we went by cab to the cemetery and buried her. There was no one to pray over her grave, but my mother and I sang an old Dutch hymn, 'Praise God in Joy and Sorrow.'" Marie helped to bury up to fourteen children a day when measles passed through the camp.[17] Descendants of the colonists also shared stories of the British tying small children to rooftops and leaving them "baking in the hot sun, no food, no water, to die."[18] Beyond the question of historical accuracy, the survival of these oral histories speaks to how the war seared the colonists' souls, now generations deep.

Willem Snyman, at risk of capital punishment for treason against the Cape Colony, emigrated from British South Africa with Viljoen and his countrymen, "exiled forever." Watching Table Mountain fade over the horizon, Viljoen reminisced, "Two hundred years ago my forefathers [landed at] the Cape of Good Hope. . . . Here was their descendant, two hundred years later, driven from the land they explored and made out of a roaming wilderness into a beautiful country."[19] The dispossessors had become the dispossessed.

The embattled Boers faced two wars: with the military at home and with the press overseas. The South African War captured the imaginations of newspaper readers and writers, who portrayed the war as either the necessary march of the British Empire to bring civilization to a barbarous white race or as the struggle of freedom-loving farmers against the tyrannous John Bull. In southern New Mexico, for example, an article from the *Rio Grande Republican* claimed that Boer "personal habits . . . would shame an Apache Indian. . . . Their underclothing is seldom changed, indeed apparently never till it falls to pieces."[20] Foreign newspaper correspondents such as Winston Churchill and Rudyard Kipling popularized the war, and front pages around the world carried headlines daily from the fronts. Those who participated in or observed key battles often wrote books about their experiences, as did Viljoen, some published before the end of the war.[21] Veterans lectured with Stereoptican images of the war to foreign audiences.

These lectures facilitated Boer immigration. By 1902, while the British held General Viljoen captive at St. Helena, Snyman toured the lecture circuit throughout the United States to garner popular and political support for his cause: in New York, where the Boer anthem opened an evening's presentation, and where Snyman led the 1901 St. Patrick's Day Parade;

Figure 12.2. "A Boer general's reception in the West End: Commander Ben Viljoen's Lecture at Queen's Hall." Drawn by John H. Bacon. *Black & White*, October 25, 1902.

in Boston, where Snyman sat as a guest on the speaker's platform of the Massachusetts State Senate, where he debated citizenship with a British historian at Harvard, and where eight hundred attendees cheered his claim that the "Boers will not be conquered any more than the Americans were"; throughout the eastern states; in Chicago; in Colorado Springs; and at the Transvaal League in San Francisco, among other cities.[22] Each presentation impressed audiences and earned Snyman and later Viljoen reputations as historical showmen working for the benefit of their people. They collected contributions toward the Boer Relief Fund to assist the destitute families who sought a new life free from the English Crown.

Speaking through an interpreter in Mexico City early in 1903, Viljoen told his audience that his warm reception "assures me and my comrades that even in this far-away land there are many hearts that beat warmly for my nation, whose freedom has been taken from her. It may be but a small satisfaction, but to me it is like the sweet dew of the early morn, which freshens the withered, and suffering flowers of the prairie."[23] Viljoen then delivered his traditional speech: a brief history of the Boers of South Africa, followed by his tales from the battlefield, which were often infused with humor and melancholy. In a somewhat defeated manner, he claimed to "endeavor to be impartial because I have no motive in view, other than to let the truth be known."[24] Viljoen's and Snyman's speeches swayed audiences because, in part, of their appeals to authenticity. Audiences were moved by seeing the real veterans, the much-maligned Boers, tell of their past and of their hopes and fears. The veterans on the lecture circuit used to their advantage the minor celebrity status accumulated through the daily reports of the British press.

Their tours were long and successful largely because a significant number of Americans sympathized with the failed Boer "war of independence" and due in part to considerable antipathies for British imperialism. A U.S. House of Representatives' subcommittee on foreign affairs even convened a hearing to consider a statement of support for the Boers.[25] Once the war ended, Snyman's and Viljoen's speeches supported Boer emigration plans rather than military resistance. Viljoen and other renowned rebels began to assemble a troupe of men for a Wild West show, a spectacle of the South African War, for the upcoming St. Louis World's Fair in 1904. It was not the first time that Boers participated in such a production. Twelve soldiers had performed with Buffalo Bill in 1901, before the war had ended, "every one of them [with] one or more wounds to exhibit."[26] The St. Louis spectacle, however, would give the generals a chance to capitalize on their wartime fame more than speaking circuits or book contracts could.

As Viljoen rallied interest in the show, Snyman worked at the future location of the colony. Mexico first appealed to the Boers because of the landscape's familiarity and promise. The terrain on their eighty-three thousand acres in Chihuahua reminded them of the lands of the vanquished Boer Republics.[27] Yet when U.S. Commissioner John Russell Bartlett passed through the area as part of his boundary survey and expedition in 1853, he noted its isolation. On the nearby town of Santa Cruz, Bartlett wrote, "I did not observe a good-looking house in it. Men, women, and children crowded to the doors as we passed, attracted by the cracking of the whips and yells of the teamsters, and seemed to eye us with as much curiosity as though they had never seen a train before."[28] By the Boers' arrival in 1903, though, Chihuahua and the broader region had entered a golden age of development and economic boom.[29] Railroads facilitated the growth of the

Figure 12.3. "There was an affecting scene when the general and a son who has been some time in this country met the boat, and the family was united after a separation of four years." "Snyman's Family Here," *New York Tribune*, June 3, 1903.

cattle industry on both sides of the border, and agriculturalists saw northern Mexico as but an extension of U.S. markets.

For Snyman, May 1903 bloomed with expectation. His sturdy fingers clutched the earth once again, after combat, after exile, after lecture tours and incessant handshakes. With a cousin, Snyman settled at the confluence of the San Pedro and Conchos Rivers in Chihuahua. There he purchased the land with a loan of M$50,000 from the Mexican government and a personal loan of M$150,000 from Enrique Creel, one of the wealthiest men in all of Mexico.[30] For the first time in years, Snyman felt free. He hunted on horseback for three weeks in the region, "one of the finest trips" of his life. "We were out entirely away from towns and cities in the free open country," he told one reporter, "and in a picturesque environment on mountain and plain that made one's heart beat exultantly and the blood course more rapidly through the veins."[31] Snyman felt younger for it, his "face wreathed in smiles." Years of uncertainty and strife finally gave way to the pleasure of knowing that he was securing land for his people. "It's all right," he acknowledged, with a whiff of exuberance.[32] That May, Snyman prepared the land for his countrymen and family, soon to follow. He broke ground with his own hands, planted corn and wheat, purchased angora goats, and irrigated his fields. The newfound freedom, however, must have paled in comparison to the anticipation of reuniting with his wife and six children, who had lived in concentration camps for two years and who had not seen their patriarch for a total of four.

Snyman received his family and began work at the colony. The territory, while significant in other settings (130 square miles), was smaller than forty other landholdings in Chihuahua of the early 1900s.[33] Multimillion-acre estates dwarfed the Boer enterprise in both size and scope. Snyman's family began in poverty, with few possessions and dilapidated buildings. Only the family Bible and his certificate as a Free Mason made the transatlantic voyage, he claimed. Inside their house, nothing adorned the walls save a small piece of paper—a target with holes in the bull's-eye—a souvenir from Snyman's 1902 shooting challenge with Theodore Roosevelt.[34] Near the main house, remnants of a chapel broke the horizon. The adobe and stone walls still supported crossbeams, but wind passed through the roofless and floorless structure.[35]

As devout members of the Dutch Reformed Church, the colonists must have felt culturally and religiously isolated in the Catholic countryside. To their good fortune, a Congregationalist missionary lived in Chihuahua City, fifty miles away. James Demarest Eaton and his wife, Gertrude, worked on behalf of the American Board of Commissioners for Foreign Missions in Mexico, an organization established in the 1880s to convert Catholic peones to the protestant faith. Eaton learned of the Boer colony when news spread of Snyman's presence. The minister often visited Santa Rosalía while riding rounds throughout the state, and before long, the Snymans attended services in the city. Three of the Snyman children belonged to the Eatons' preparatory academy and were members of its Sunday school. Thus, Congregational beliefs and the Boers' adherence to the Dutch Reformed Church produced a tight friendship forged through a spiritual *lingua franca*. When not attending services in Chihuahua, the colonists gathered at Snyman's house on Sundays for "the old fashioned Boer home religious service." Snyman's father-in-law led prayers and hymnal readings with "beautiful, simple faith." Communal singing in Afrikaans, "in that old fashioned style of fifty or more years ago," followed. The image speaks to the seclusion and pragmatism faced by many settler colonies.[36]

The Eatons likewise struggled to find community. James traveled throughout the region and often to the United States for his professional duties, but Gertrude remained close to home with responsibilities for the women's mission school. Eaton's letters and reports convey an isolation felt most acutely by Gertrude, who battled mental illness recurrently. So when the Eatons and Snymans became neighbors, essentially, they connected on many levels. In October 1904, the Snymans stayed with the Eatons in Chihuahua while Willem lectured at the church's social hall, explaining South African current events and describing the war and the infamous concentration camps. In a report sent to his superior, Eaton recalled how Snyman's wife, Sarah, "sat with the tears coursing silently down her cheeks."[37] In short time, the Eatons and Snymans became close enough friends that Eaton lobbied the American Board to assign a Dutch-speaking missionary to locate on the Boer colony's premises.[38] The letters that James Eaton sent to the board's central office in Boston account for one of the only sources to provide a glimpse into daily life in the Boer colony and to explain why, notwithstanding its early success, it failed after just two years.

Despite their isolation and poverty, or rustic charm, the colonists should not be considered small-time peasants receding from the world to subsistence farming. They intended to produce for the market, which made them so appealing to Governor Luis Terrazas and his son-in-law, Enrique Creel. To the Terrazas-Creel political and economic regime, the Boers would have a modernizing influence in the region and produce more goods for the market and regional mining industries. To the Boers, the support of Terrazas and Creel made their colonization scheme possible. At last, the Boers could begin anew. Creel's assistance endeared him to the Snyman family such that the first-born at the colony, a son of Johanna Snyman and Johan Viljoen, carried the name "Enrique Creel Viljoen."

The first year of the colony, which then only consisted of four families, challenged Snyman's optimism. Floods destroyed all corn and wheat, and seven hundred young fruit trees. After the waters subsided, a team of four Boers and fifty-five Mexicans cleaned silt from the irrigation canal—fourteen miles in length—within eleven days.[39] This anecdote raises questions about the relationship between the colonists and the sixty Mexican families living on the premises. None of the Boers spoke Spanish before arriving. Some only spoke Afrikaans and struggled with English. Early attempts to integrate culturally inevitably led to calico phrases of Afrikaans, Spanish, and English, such as, "*Keer die maranas daar*, and *ponga* them back in the *kraal*"—"Stop those pigs, and put them back in the corral."[40]

Initially, it seemed as if the colonists would work and live closely with resident peones. Snyman had arranged with Governor Creel to build and staff a school for local children.[41] In the fields, the Boers reached an agreement with Mexican workers to subdivide the lands into thirty parcels, between twenty-five and sixty acres each. The locals then sharecropped their own portion of lands and gave the Boers half of the harvest.[42] Something soured that first year, though, and several U.S. newspapers reported that the Boers would rely only on themselves for labor, as their "experience with the Mexicans the first year proved that class of labor unreliable and unsatisfactory."[43] One article written in Chihuahua depicts a more hostile situation, where the "native peones on the property are being gotten off as these Boers propose doing their own work."[44] While labor relations became strained in the fields, the women did continue to employ domestic servants. By April 1904, the Boer women had "sufficiently mastered" Spanish to "tell their servants what to do and how to do it."[45] These clues to the cultural climate at the Hacienda Santa Rosalía suggest that the colonists shared a complicated relationship with neighboring Mexican peones. Separated by language, culture, and religion, the Snymans and Viljoens kept Mexican labor at a distance while allowing for intercultural ties within the domestic realm. Race and labor relations slowed intercultural exchanges; only one Snyman child was born to a native Mexican. Unfortunately, no evidence exists to hint of the Mexican tenants' views of their *hacendados*.

While the Snymans established the colony that first year, Viljoen and some 200 fellow Boers, 150 British soldiers, and 40 Africans recreated the South African War at the 1904 World's Fair in St. Louis.[46] It was not without controversy. Many in the media suggested that the Boers were "selling out," cashing in on their wartime fame in a crass, materialistic move. Viljoen, for his part, became embroiled in a romantic scandal.[47] At a time when Viljoen, his collaborators in the show, and his partners in the colony depended on positive public relations, the scandal threatened to halt advances in supporting the Boer cause. By then, however, Snyman and his family had rooted themselves enough in the Mexican north that the colony had a solid foundation, one that could weather a personal controversy three thousand miles away.

By August 1905, the colony appeared to thrive. Snyman's eldest brother, his eldest son, and Viljoen, his parents, his son, five siblings, and their children all arrived at Santa Rosalía, totaling nearly twenty-five families. With no import tax on farm implements, colonists purchased equipment from Texas to produce larger yields, including a thirty-horsepower engine capable of pulling ten plows.[48] Corn and wheat fields and fruit orchards all produced in abundance. The Boers and other farmers profited from the biggest harvest and economic boom in Chihuahua history.[49] In late August, newspapers reported the colony to be prospering and its land to be rich and "brought to a high state of cultivation."[50]

Just as life began to turn around for the displaced families, the colony collapsed in October 1905. Oral histories among the descendants suggest that the colonists abandoned the land when they discovered that government officials had taken it illegally from resident peones.[51] Contemporary newspapers in the United States and Mexico reported that the colony failed due to the inability to "acquire clear titles to their farms and harassed by a series of embarrassments."[52]

Another reporter suggested that "monetary difficulties" caused the failure of the colony.[53] In the press, Viljoen blamed it on the inability to clear individual titles to the land. The truth, however, centered around a disagreement between Snyman and Viljoen on how the colony should secure its lands.

In 1902, Viljoen and Snyman had agreed to split equally the potential profits and losses of the colony, and to divide equally the title to lands acquired.[54] The two cofounders thus embarked upon a communal venture. Upon arriving at the colony from St. Louis, however, Viljoen refused to improve or work the land unless "title deeds for the individual allotments be made out for himself and his relatives."[55] Until that point, all land had been common property, and although Snyman alone signed the contract with Creel and the federal government, the contract "carefully guard[ed] the personal interests of all the colonists."[56] In an attempt to assuage Viljoen's concerns, and at Snyman's request, Creel proposed "to have a committee of a dozen of Chihuahua's best citizens named to look after the interests of the colonists, in order to satisfy Viljoen that there was no danger from the possible deaths of the chief creditors, or even from some change of good will on their part." Viljoen, the prouder of the two Boers, apparently declined. Eaton noted that "Mr. Creel stands by Snyman, and Gen. Viljoen has withdrawn." Eaton felt Viljoen had acted unjustly to Snyman and to the colony, and a mutual friend, the editor of the *Chihuahua Enterprise*, thought Viljoen had been "injured by flattery from those who admired his military prowess, and that he who managed the 'Boer War Exhibition' at St. Louis, wanted to be the manager of the colony."[57] Regardless, Viljoen and his relatives, and those Snymans married to Viljoens, abandoned the colony and moved north to the United States.[58] The extended Viljoen family settled in the corridor between Las Cruces, New Mexico, and Fabens, Texas. Only Snyman and his immediate family remained in Mexico.

Snyman confided to Eaton that he felt "like collapsing," the strain "almost above my strength; more so as this colony was started by myself with the feeling, Here I stand a chance to help my fellow countrymen this side of the ocean; and I am bitterly disappointed. . . . I feel that I have to show now more than ever, with the help of God, my honesty of purpose, and do what is right, now lending an ear to wrong." Still, when Eaton visited Snyman at home, he recalled, "Snyman told me of the outcome of his 'eight years' of attempting to live for ideals—loss and suffering and criticism; and how he could not sleep at night, after a hard day's work in the field, because of his 'worry.'"[59]

Personal dynamics evidently played a role in the separation of the colony, one patriarch remaining on the site, the other migrating north. Snyman and Viljoen would later bicker through the press about South African affairs, and while their families would be forever connected, the two men likely preferred to keep their distance from each other.[60] They seemed to fit the description of their ancestors as "fractious frontiersmen."[61] Looking beyond personalities, the fundamental issue of land divided the colony. Viljoen and the Boers knew well the importance of securing individual title. That the British had stolen theirs only doubled the point. They were, after all, "men without a country." Like millions of immigrants before them, the Boers sought new lands beyond their state, or British, control.

Then, as now, the presence of a Boer colony in Mexico was characterized by its peculiarity, its out-of-place-ness. News of the colony's founding constituted filler material for small papers throughout the United States. In Owingsville, Kentucky, for example, a short news item describing the arrival of colonists in Mexico ran alongside other earth-shattering headlines: "Attacked by an Angry Lion," "His Heart Cut in Two," and "He Killed a Bystander."[62] When looking at the Boer colony in historical perspective, though, its establishment in the borderlands around the dawn of the twentieth century connects the historiographies of Latin America and the U.S. West. The colony moves from its placement in "who'd a thunk it" history to a new location of historical import.

The Boers floated along strong historical currents that had been well established in the borderlands since the 1880s. Following the development of rail lines between the neighboring nations, U.S. investment multiplied especially in the border states. As in the U.S. West, booster materials enticed immigrants and investors to lesser known areas. For the first time, portions of the Mexican North, like the U.S. Southwest, became potentially profitable due to irrigation agriculture. Promoters such as Walter S. Logan, "the apostle of irrigation," advanced an agenda of capitalist development for personal gain.[63] To promote the Sonora and Sinaloa Irrigation Company, Logan made explicit and continuous comparisons to California and western history, calling Sonora "the California of Mexico, and history repeats itself."[64] In terms of investment and immigration figures, Logan's claims fell far short of his goals: few if any colonists bought his message.[65] If one considers the broader economic connections between the U.S. Southwest and the Mexican north, though, then Logan's link between California and Sonora proves prescient.

The U.S. capitalist drive into Mexico exacerbated tensions between small Mexican landholders and large-scale entrepreneurs. Historians of Mexico have debated the correlation between capitalist development and the outbreak of the Mexican Revolution in 1910. John Mason Hart argues that "U.S. elites sought to extend their interests into Mexico by employing the strategies that were so successful for them in the American West."[66]

This certainly holds true for northern Mexico—and the Boer presence fits in line with Hart's analysis—but Alan Knight's two-volume synthesis counterbalances Hart's thesis by showing other historical and regional catalysts of revolution.[67] Showing how the Boers initially landed in Chihuahua as part of a West-turning-south historical progression illuminates how, while still an endogenous movement, the revolution pushed back against frontier patterns that made the American West. Migrations of capital and colonists exacerbated divisions within Mexican society and culminated in the dislocation and dispossession of colonists, of large property owners, and ultimately of the state.

Watching these progressions develop, Mexican journalists and the elite sensed in 1902 the parallels between wartime South Africa and the potential effects of President Díaz's modernization ideology and unrestrained immigration. The South African War provoked debates in Díaz's Mexico on the nature of citizenship, the state, and foreigners. One columnist lamented the loss of the Boer republics, glorified their cause, and placed blame on the *uitlanders*, foreigners who developed Boer mines but were restricted from the vote. The lesson for Mexico was clear: "If the immigrant blends into the dough of our nation, we will have increased national strength, but if the immigrant clings to an independent social circle and has eyes fixed on his homeland, it will have raised a formidable danger. The problem is unavoidable: immigration strengthens, like in the United States, or immigration brings the loss of the state, as in the Transvaal."[68] The discussion on citizens and *uitlanders* resonated in Mexico, particularly in the north where the eyes of imperial Uncle Sam coveted Mexican riches, where early railroad lines linked northern Mexico to continental lines north of the border, and where the transactions between foreign investment and local elites polarized classes.[69]

The news article on outlanders and inlanders raises an important question: how did the Boers view their own relationship with the Mexican state? Little evidence exists to suggest that they felt like anything other than exiles. Separated by language, religion, and culture, the Boers resisted integration with their resident workers. With the northern migration of the majority of colonists into the Mesilla Valley of New Mexico, the Boer colonization scheme came to an end. Only Snyman's immediate family stayed in Chihuahua after selling the colony's lands and purchasing a nearby farm. Those who moved north felt a stronger bond with the United States, as Viljoen's U.S. citizenship affirmed. Upon receiving citizenship, "With tears streaming down his bronzed cheeks," Viljoen "made those about him a stirring little speech in which he declared that for seven years he had been 'a man without a country,' and that this was the proudest moment of his life." Viljoen declared that "every '*oom*' and '*tante*,'" (uncle and aunt), "every man and maid, every boy and girl of them was already loyally American to the core."[70] Descendants of the Viljoens and Snymans confirm the importance of U.S. citizenship to the Boers. Two of the colonists' grandchildren, now of retirement age themselves, recalled their grandfather, John Snyman (Willem's nephew), and his pride at being a U.S. citizen. When attending local high school football games in the 1950s, John would stop kids playing during the "Star-Spangled Banner" by saying, "You are an American citizen! I came from a country where there was not freedom. You stand at attention. Take your hats off. *Your hand on your heart!*" For him, tears often accompanied listening to the song "God Bless America."[71]

Viljoen's and Snyman's nationalities appear to have solidified by 1910: Willem Snyman's family farming and working in local mines, developing the resources of Mexico; and the Viljoens (and some other Snymans) content with an adopted U.S. citizenship. Yet the final years of Benjamin Viljoen's and Willem Snyman's lives suggest that nationality sometimes adjusted to local circumstances. When the Mexican Revolution erupted, Viljoen served as a military advisor to Francisco Madero and, in 1912, joined the diplomatic corps as Mexican consul in Breslau—and filed papers for naturalization in Mexico.[72] Two years later, when two other Boer generals in South Africa attempted to foment rebellion once again in 1914, Viljoen stood ready for the call. Writing from El Paso, he declared, "All Boers in this country will rally to the old flag."[73] Snyman, meanwhile, never applied for citizenship in Mexico. When the revolutionary Francisco "Pancho" Villa attacked Snyman's ranch, he sought protection through the British consulate.[74] Snyman also hoped to one day serve as a "special representative" of the British government on Mexican affairs.[75] Snyman thus considered expedient circumstances when determining allegiance, avoiding British citizenship in South Africa while desiring to serve the Union Jack in Mexico.

Suggesting that some Boer emigrants swapped allegiances when necessary does not somehow tarnish their memory or historical significance. Some of the early colonists (and all descendants today) fully identified with the United States. In contrast to another Boer colony in Argentina, the grandchildren and great-grandchildren of Boer settlers in the Southwest have not retained any Afrikaans beyond *oom*, *tante*, and other miscellaneous words and phrases. Some family members have in storage uncaptioned pictures and occasional documents that hint of their ancestors' journeys. But those descendants who recall a rare secondhand story of life in Mexico, or who retain childhood memories of ranches in the Mesilla Valley, or who have collected extant family archives—these descendants are in agreement that the colonists considered themselves American Boers: Americans first, Boers second. Nationalities may have changed, but

Figure 12.4. George M. "Dogie" Jones with Hector Snyman holding Jones's daughter, Georgia, in León, Guanajuato, Mexico, ca. 1948. Photo courtesy of Jones family.

self-identities did not. Of the existing oral histories, two remain the most vivid, shared between two different branches of the family tree: concentration camps in South Africa and the importance of U.S. citizenship.

As fluid as nationalities may have been, though, the U.S.-Mexican border did exert a notable influence on the Viljoen and Snyman families. Of the descendants in the United States today, only one remembered anything of the Snyman family that had remained in Mexico—and this by pure chance. New Mexican rancher George M. "Dogie" Jones recalled his work for the U.S. federal government in 1948–1949. Jones traveled to Guanajuato to inspect cows for hoof-and-mouth disease. "We were driving around the outskirts of León, Guanajuato," Jones said. He and his Mexican collaborator drove a military vehicle. As they drove down the road, "this fellow was standing there, and he flagged us down. He walked up on my side. I was driving. Of course all the conversation was in Spanish. And he wanted to know if we could test his cows. He had a little dairy." The man gave his last name: Snyman. Jones's Mexican partner fumbled to write the odd last name, and Jones immediately spelled it out, thinking, "My Lord, way down here in Guanajuato? Who the heck is this?" Hector Snyman, the son of Willem and a distant cousin to Jones, smiled. "And I'm not kidding you," Jones said. "[Hector] looked at me, and I got a real weird feeling. He said, 'You've got to be Doreen's boy.'" Purely by accident, and for a brief few days, the northern and southern Boers reunited. Hector Snyman invited Jones to his house and welcomed him "like a son."[76] It was the last time the two branches would meet.

As fluid as the border had been at the establishment of the colony in 1903, its increasing strength after the Mexican Revolution played a role in the separation of Mexican and U.S. citizens of Boer descent. What was once a colony south and north of the border became a fading memory after the deaths of the colony's two patriarchs. Snyman died in 1916 of appendicitis and Viljoen the following year of pneumonia. The second generation remained in touch through family chain letters, but reunions halted after the 1950s. Descendants, dispersed throughout the United States, are aware of their heritage but do not maintain contact with many others (although this has changed somewhat as a result of research into this history).[77] Still, all contact has been lost with any descendants in Mexico.

The Boers—like other immigrants in the borderlands between 1880 and 1910—traveled along historical currents that made the Mexican North a proxy for settlement in the U.S. Southwest. A frontier of development had turned south into the borderlands, but it would soon find resistance as revolution and growing nationalism in Mexico pushed back. Outlanders once again in Mexico, the colonists moved north and were on their way to become inlanders, to become Americanized, and to lose knowledge of life at the Hacienda Santa Rosalía.

Research for this chapter was supported by the Howard R. Lamar Center for the Study of Frontiers and Borders, the Program in Agrarian Studies, and the Beinecke Rare Book and Manuscript Library at Yale University. Thanks to John Mack Faragher and George Miles for their comments on a very early draft of this chapter, and especially to Joann Ganoe, Benjamin Viljoen III, Jeannine Viljoen, Barbara Fonseca, Jackie McLaughlin, Bill Brookreson, George "Dogie" Jones, JoAnn Tessandori, John Stinnett, and several other Boer descendants, as well as their spouses, many of whom generously opened their homes and old papers to me over a period of several years.

Notes

1. Charles de Kay, "Mexico's Latent Wealth Awaiting Development," *New York Times*, Dec. 7 [Nov. 20], 1902.
2. Boers, or Afrikaners in contemporary parlance, were fair-skinned southern Africans of Dutch and French Huguenot descent. I prefer to use the term "Boer" in order to allow for some historical distance between those currently under study with their brethren so strongly associated with apartheid after the rise of the National Party in South Africa in 1948. The South African War has also been called the Boer War, the Anglo-Boer War, and the Second South African War.
3. Brian M. du Toit has written on the history of various Boer colonies. See his *Colonia Boer: An Afrikaner Settlement in Chubut, Argentina* (Lewiston, NY: Edwin Mellen Press, 1995); *The Boers in East Africa: Ethnicity and Identity* (Westport, CT: Bergin & Garvey, 1998); *Boer Settlers in the Southwest* (El Paso: University of Texas at El Paso, 1995); "A Boer Settlement that Was Never Settled: Tamaulipas,

Mexico," *Historia* 49, no. 1 (May 2004): 48–70; and "Boers, Afrikaners, and Diasporas," *Historia* 48, no. 1 (May 2003): 15–54.

4. Merritt was also cousin-in-law to President Theodore Roosevelt, who met with the Boer leaders on occasion. As a partial Dutch descendant, Roosevelt sympathized with their cause but was publicly silent because of political necessity.
5. Marshall Bond Jr., *Gold Hunter: The Adventures of Marshall Bond* (Albuquerque: University of New Mexico Press, 1969), 82.
6. Marshall Bond to Amy Bond, Oct. 27, 1902, Marshall Bond Papers (hereafter MBP), Beinecke Library, Yale University, WA MSS S-2358. Several of Bond's letters are reprinted in Bond Jr., *Gold Hunter*, 89–91.
7. De Kay, "Mexico's Latent Wealth." I use *peones* here to refer to non-landowning agricultural workers.
8. Published works include du Toit's *Boer Settlers in the Southwest*; Lawrence Douglas Taylor Hansen, "La Colonizacion Boer en Chihuahua y el Suroeste de Estados Unidos, 1903–1917," *Historia Mexicana* 52, no. 2 (2002): 449–89; and Dale C. Maluy, "Boer Colonization in the Southwest," *New Mexico Historical Review* 52, no. 2 (April 1977): 93–110. Each of these discusses the colony's residence in the U.S. Southwest in detail but does not offer much in terms of the Mexican colony or the reasons for its failure.
9. The Boers arrived in Chihuahua a little more than fifteen years after Mormon immigrants established a series of colonies in northwestern Chihuahua. The placement of the Mormon colonies in Mexican historiography occupies the same general region of the Boers'. For a brief historical sketch of the two, in conversation with the Mennonite colonies established much later, see Lawrence Douglas Taylor Hansen, "La colonización con extranjeros en el norte de México: El caso de los mormones, los boers y los menonitas," *Vetas: Revista de El Colegio de San Luis* 6, no. 16 (January–April 2004): 107–37.
10. Francisco R. Almada, *Resumen de historia del estado de Chihuahua* (Mexico City: s.n., 1955), 337.
11. "Snyman's Family Here: General Tells Why Boers Did Not Choose America," *New York Tribune*, June 3, 1903.
12. The two independent states were the South African Republic, or *Zuid-Afrikaansche Republiek*, and the Orange Free State, or *Oranjevrijstaat*. For a balanced overview of the war, see Bill Nasson, *The War for South Africa: The Anglo-Boer War, 1899–1902* (Cape Town: Tafelberg, 2010).
13. Leonard Thompson, *A History of South Africa*, 3rd ed. (New Haven: Yale University Press, 2000 [1995]), 141.
14. Donal Lowry, "'The World's No Bigger than a Kraal': The South African War and International Opinion in the First Age of 'Globalization,'" in D. Omissi and A. S. Thompson, eds., *The Impact of the South African War* (New York: Palgrave, 2002).
15. Thompson, *A History of South Africa*, 142.
16. Ibid., 143.
17. Marie Snyman Kroenig, "Minga's Life," Bill Brookreson family archive.
18. Interview with JoAnn Tessandori and John Stinnett, October 22, 2010. JoAnn and John's grandfather, John Snyman, was the brother of Martha and Marie.
19. General B. J. Viljoen, *An Exiled General* (St. Louis: A. Noble Printing Company, 1906), 49–50.

20. F. C. Barker, "Farm & Orchard: The Boer at Home," *Rio Grande Republican*, December 1, 1899.
21. Ben Viljoen, *My Reminiscences of the Anglo-Boer War* (London: Hood, Douglas & Howard, 1902).
22. "Cheers for Boers," *Boston Daily Globe*, March 6, 1901; "Fair Skies for Paraders," *New York Tribune*, March 19, 1901; "Snyman as a Guest," *Boston Daily Globe*, March 28, 1901; "Boer and Briton: Snyman and McVane on Transvaal War," *Boston Daily Globe*, April 27, 1901; "Will Lecture in Boston," *Boston Daily Globe*, February 17, 1901; "Citizens to Aid County Service," *Chicago Daily Tribune*, January 13, 1903; "Santa Catalina Island," *Los Angeles Times*, October 2, 1901.
23. "General Viljoen Delivers Lecture," *The Mexican Herald*, February 3, 1903; also "Un Boero Heroico," *El Pais*, February 3, 1903.
24. "General Viljoen Delivers Lecture."
25. "Mediation for Boers," *Washington Post*, May 6, 1902. The movement stalled for fear of angering England in an age of increasing U.S.-Anglo rapprochement.
26. "Boers with Buffalo Bill," *New York Times*, March 29, 1901.
27. "The Mexican Budget," *Galveston Daily News*, October 19, 1902.
28. John Russell Bartlett, *Personal Narrative of Explorations and Incidents in Texas, New Mexico, California, Sonora, and Chihuahua* (New York: D. Appleton & Co., 1854), 445.
29. See Mark Wasserman, *Capitalists, Caciques, and Revolution: The Native Elite and Foreign Enterprise in Chihuahua, Mexico, 1854–1911* (Chapel Hill: University of North Carolina Press, 1984).
30. "Establecimiento de colonias agrícolas en el Estado de Chihuahua," in *Anales de la Legislacion Federal* (Mexico: Impr. de E. Dublán, 1904), 91–96. He and Viljoen were contractually obligated to locate fifty families within three years, but Snyman, convinced of the colony's success, considered an option of an additional 363,800 acres and reportedly expected a thousand families to immigrate. By 1904 he would reduce this expectation to eighty. "Boer Colony in Mexico," *New York Tribune*, June 1, 1903; "Boers Go to Mexico," *Minneapolis Journal*, May 12, 1903.
31. "Gen. Snyman Back," *Mexican Herald*, December 10, 1902.
32. "Says It's Fixed," *Mexican Herald*, April 20, 1903.
33. Wasserman, *Capitalists, Caciques, and Revolution*, 106–8.
34. "Roosevelt a Crack Shot at Target," *San Francisco Chronicle*, August 3, 1902.
35. Descriptions of the property come from James Demarest Eaton to James Barton, October 14, 1903, Archives of the American Board of Commissioners for Foreign Missions (hereafter ABCFM), Microfilm Edition (Detroit: Gale Group), Reel 731.
36. Details from the family's private religious service come from a contemporary journalist who visited the colony. See "Boers Successful," *Chihuahua Enterprise*, August 12, 1905.
37. James Demarest Eaton to James L. Barton, February 6, 1904, ABCFM, Reel 731.
38. James Demarest Eaton to James L. Barton, August 25, 1904, ABCFM, Reel 731. Eaton saw in the colony the chance to expand his mission work beyond Mexicans—as it had been limited—in the state.
39. "A Boer Colony's Industry," *Deseret Evening News*, March 19, 1904; "Boers Thriving in North Mexico," *Mexican Herald*, March 13, 1904.

40. James A. Honeij, "Boers in Mexico," *Tufts College Graduate* 2, no. 1 (April 1904): 3. Honeij relates details from the colony based on a letter by Lt. W. Malan.
41. James D. Eaton, "The Boer Colony in Mexico: An Interesting Christian Settlement and Its Bearing on the Future," *The Congregationalist and Christian World* 90, no. 48 (December 2, 1905): 807.
42. C. J. Viljoen, *The Huguenot* (June 1948).
43. "Boer Colony is Prospering," *San Francisco Call*, August 22, 1905.
44. "Boers Successful," *Chihuahua Enterprise*, August 12, 1905.
45. Honeij, "Boers in Mexico," 3.
46. Jennie Sutton, "'Transvaal Spectacles': South African Visions at the 1904 St. Louis World's Fair," *Safundi: The Journal of South African and American Studies* 8, no. 3 (July 2007): 271–72.
47. Within a year, Viljoen's wife in South Africa sued him for divorce, his former mistress (and jilted fiancée) published his love letters and publicly whipped him in Chicago, and he remarried an American he met at the fair. For this history, see my forthcoming article in *Amerikastudien/American Studies*.
48. International Bureau of the American Republics, "Monthly Bulletin of the International Bureau of the American Republics," 18 (October–December 1904): 531.
49. Wasserman, *Capitalists, Caciques, and Revolution*, 121.
50. "Boer Colony Prospering," *Los Angeles Times*, August 28, 1905.
51. Interview with Benjamin Viljoen III, May 10, 2010; Interview with JoAnn Tessandori and John Stinnett, October 22, 2010.
52. "Boers Buncoed," *Los Angeles Times*, October 15, 1905.
53. W. W. Crawford, "Boers Leave Ortiz Colony," *Los Angeles Times*, November 7, 1905.
54. Viljoen and Snyman agreement.
55. James Demarest Eaton to James L. Barton, October 28, 1905, ABCFM, Reel 731.
56. "Boers Thriving in North Mexico," *Mexican Herald*, March 13, 1904.
57. James Demarest Eaton to James L. Barton, October 28, 1905, ABCFM, Reel 731.
58. Viljoen and others settled in the corridor between Fabens and El Paso, Texas, and Las Cruces, New Mexico. Families splintered off to all areas of the Southwest after the first generation of immigrants.
59. Quoted in James Demarest Eaton to James L. Barton, October 28, 1905, ABCFM, Reel 731.
60. See, for example, B. J. Viljoen, "The Boer War," *El Paso Herald*, November 11, 1914.
61. Hermann Giliomee, *The Afrikaners: Biography of a People* (Charlottesville: University of Virginia Press, 2009), 45.
62. *Owingsville Outlook*, September 24, 1903.
63. Walter S. Logan, *A Mexican Night: The Toasts and Responses at a Complimentary Dinner Given by Walter S. Logan, at the Democratic Club, New York City, December 16th, 1891, to Senor Don Matias Romero, Mexican Minister to the United States* (New York: Albert B. King, 1891), 32.
64. Logan, "Yaqui Land Convertible Stock," 3–4.
65. Evelyn Hu-DeHart, *Yaqui Resistance and Survival: The Struggle for Land and Autonomy, 1821–1920* (Madison: University of Wisconsin Press, 1984), 129.
66. John Mason Hart, *Empire and Revolution: The Americans in Mexico since the Civil*

War (Berkeley: University of California Press, 2002), 2; see also his *Revolutionary Mexico: The Coming and Process of the Mexican Revolution* (Berkeley: University of California Press, 1987). For the influence of American investments on Revolutionary Yucatán, see Gilbert M. Joseph, *Revolution from Without: Yucatan, Mexico, and the United States, 1880–1924* (Durham, NC: Duke University Press, 1988).

67. Alan Knight, *The Mexican Revolution*, 2 vols. (Cambridge: Cambridge University Press, 1986).
68. "Por qué perdió el Transvaal su Autonomia?" *El Correo de Mexico*, September 8, 1902.
69. On U.S. colonialism and the railroads, see esp. William Robbins, *Colony and Empire: The Capitalist Transformation of the American West* (Lawrence: University Press of Kansas, 1994), 34.
70. "New Mexico Likes Boers," *Los Angeles Times*, March 29, 1909.
71. Interview with JoAnn Tessandori and John Stinnett, October 22, 2010.
72. It appears that Viljoen filed papers in order to counter complaints among Mexican elites that a foreign citizen was acting on behalf of Madero and the government. When Viljoen renounced his post due to health complications, he apparently withdrew his naturalization papers, retaining his U.S. citizenship.
73. "Boer General Eager for War," *Ogden Standard*, September 3, 1914; see also "Boer War Given Start in U.S.," *El Paso Herald*, October 21, 1914.
74. "Snyman Ranch Saved by Official Action," *Mexican Herald*, March 24, 1914; "Alega ahora que esta convencido de la honradez de Snyman a quien habia secuestrado porque compro su rancho," *El Pais*, March 12, 1914; "Villa Saves Snyman Ranch," *Los Angeles Times*, March 11, 1914.
75. Snyman to Bond, July 27, 1916, MBP.
76. Interview with George M. "Dogie" Jones, Watrous, New Mexico, October 20, 2011.
77. The first reunion of Boer descendants in over fifty years took place at the annual conference of the Western History Association in 2010.

13

The Spatial Distribution of Hispanics in the Mountain West

1970–2010

J. Matthew Shumway

Between 1990 and 2010 Hispanics as a percentage of the U.S. population surged from 9 percent to 16 percent. As geographer J. Matthew Shumway indicates in this chapter, that growth is arguably the most significant demographic development of the turn-of-the-century decades in the nation. This chapter illuminates aspects of that consequential development. Growth and economic forces propelled Hispanics into states and counties beyond the Southwest. Although they had traditionally clustered in California, Arizona, New Mexico, Colorado and Texas, by 2010 over half of the nation's Hispanics lived in other states including Nevada and Utah. Using census data for the Rocky Mountain States, Shumway examines the data with a geographer's eye for spatial variation, distinguishing between established counties, high-growth counties and other counties. Shumway focuses on a facet of assimilation of particular interest to geographers: spatial assimilation, or the residential deconcentration of immigrants to reflect the geographic distribution of the general population. To extend his analysis, Shumway calculates the relative dispersal of Hispanics and non-Hispanics using a measure of relative entropy and a Differential Geographic Index. Shumway explores some of the reasons behind Hispanic movement into new counties. Traditionally a sign of social and cultural assimilation, movement into new areas can also be fueled, Shumway points out, by job growth or changes in immigrants' legal status. In an era of electronic social networking and rapid transit, does residential integration have less of an effect upon cultural assimilation than it once did?

One of the most recognizable demographic trends in the United States over the past few decades is the declining population in the small towns of the Midwest and Great Plains regions, some of which has carried over into the Mountain West. The dying towns and rural areas are primarily located away from major transportation corridors, large or even medium-size metropolitan areas, and in regions with few highly desirable and local natural amenities (e.g., mountains, lakes, mild climates). Many of these demographic deserts were built in order to service farming, ranching, mining, and/or logging operations, but as area resources became depleted, as these activities became more capitalized, as the cost of transportation fell, and as regional service centers with big box stores started growing, rural areas began their slow and inevitable march to irrelevance and death—or maybe not. In a 2011 article in the *New York Times*, A. G. Sulzberger pointed out many small towns are being revived by the influx of Hispanic migrants.[1] It isn't just small towns and rural areas that are feeling the influence of increases in Hispanic migration. According to the *San Diego Union-Tribune*, persons of Hispanic origin went from approximately 25 percent of San Diego's population in 2000, to 33 percent in 2010.[2] That is, one-third of the population in San Diego is of Hispanic origin. The anecdotes provided by Sulzberger and others coincide with research using U.S. Census data showing two strong demographic trends: first, the rapid growth of the Hispanic population in the United States; and second, the geographic movement of Hispanics out of and away from the traditional Hispanic heartland of California, Arizona, New Mexico, Texas, and Colorado.[3]

Migration to and within the United States has been and continues to be one of the main driving forces in shaping who and what the country was and will be. The arrival and impact of new immigrants are not surprising phenomena. What is somewhat surprising is the rapidity of the overall growth of migration in the past two decades—the majority of this growth being people of Hispanic origin—and the impact such migration is having on new places. For the United States as a whole, the 15.2 million-person increase in Hispanics between 2000 and 2010 accounted for 56 percent of the 27.3 million increase in total population. This makes Hispanics/Latinos the fastest growing segment of the U.S. population, and in many places, they represent the only population growth that is occurring.[4] While most of the growth in the Hispanic population can be attributed to migration, not all of it can. Some of the current growth and a good deal of the future growth will come as a result of a younger Hispanic age structure and differential fertility rates. Currently, Hispanics/Latinos constitute 16 percent of the total U.S. population. However they make up over 22 percent of those eighteen years and under. Research by Johnson and Lichter shows that Hispanics account for over 40 percent of the natural increase recorded in the United States between 2000 and 2007.[5]

A second demographic trend relative to the Hispanic population is that locations outside of traditionally Hispanic areas in the United States are growing the fastest. For example, between 2000 and 2010 the immigrant (primarily Hispanic) population in the Mountain West grew significantly faster than the immigrant population in the United States as a whole—27 versus 16 percent, respectively (U.S. Census Bureau 2011). The Hispanic/ Latino population in the Mountain West increased from 19 percent of the total population in 2000 to 25 percent in 2010 (these range from a high of 46 percent in New Mexico to a low of 3 percent in Montana). From a geographic perspective, the current increase in the number of Hispanics/ Latinos as reported in the 2010 Census continues the trend first observed in the 1990s of a more dispersed spatial pattern of population growth.[6]

In areas impacted by the growth in Hispanic populations, including areas in the Mountain West region, local populations often view the growth and its impacts as a set of serious issues. In September 2010, the Brookings Mountain West Institute released its Intermountain West Public Opinion Survey. This survey documents responses from residents of the Mountain West (Arizona, Colorado, Idaho, Nevada, New Mexico, and Utah). When asked about the major issues facing this region, 77 percent of the respondents chose immigration as one of the top three issues. Much of the concern expressed can be categorized into three dominant elements: employment/ economic growth and development issues, cultural assimilation (e.g., language, religion) issues, and perceived increases in crime and violence (public security) issues. Such concerns have manifested themselves in various state-level immigration bills sponsored (with some passing) in a number of states, including Arizona, Utah, and Colorado in the Mountain West region. An interesting and ironic note is that the issues expressed by natives concerning immigrants coming into their communities are very similar to the reasons that immigrants have for migrating in the first place: safety, employment, and family (culture). An interview with an immigrant family to Utah illustrates this.

In the early 1980s, Eduardo and his brothers and sisters immigrated with his parents to Los Angeles in order to escape the civil war in El Salvador.[7] Like many Salvadorans who came to the United States during the civil war period, the primary driving force for the move was political violence. Eduardo's family found refuge in what was then a fairly small Salvadoran community in Los Angeles but also as part of the larger set of Hispanic communities in southern California. After coming to the United States, his parents found work and were able to provide a good but modest living for their family as they began their assimilation into U.S. society. Although born in El Salvador, Eduardo identifies himself as an American, and because of the stories his parents told about the violence and poverty of El Salvador, he has no desire to return and live there.

He married an "American" girl and started his own family. As his family grew he became increasingly worried about the gangs and violence that were plaguing his community in southern California. After his son got caught up in a gang shooting, he decided, as his father had many years before, to find a safer place to raise his family. He chose Utah, and when asked why, he replied:

> We moved from Los Angeles because Utah offers better conditions to raise a family and that is very important. Hispanic people, we like to be united with our family. We like to have a strong and united family so you look for the environment where you can be safe, where you feel comfortable, where you feel good, where you don't feel threatened. Something that happened in Los Angeles during 1980s was the gangs. We lived well all the time; everything was peaceful until the gangs started. After that everything changed. We had to not just save our lives but to save our kids too. We needed to save them from that hostile environment.[8]

Eduardo's story is representative of the experience of many immigrants of Hispanic origin living in the United States. Interviews of immigrants from Mexico and Central America, which are the dominant immigrant groups in the Mountain West region, indicate that most immigrants—whether legal or illegal—come for a combination of three main reasons: fear of conflict or violent crime in their home or home countries, economic opportunities for both themselves and their children, and/or to be reunited with family members. In some cases one of the reasons (usually economic opportunities) is dominant, but all three rationales for migrating show up frequently. The purpose of this chapter is to examine the changing spatial distribution of Hispanics in the Mountain West region and to provide a general characterization of the types of places to which Hispanics are migrating.

Migration and the Changing Geography of Hispanics/Latinos in the United States

From the times of earliest European settlement of what is today the United States, those of Spanish descent have been geographically concentrated in the southwestern portion of the country.[9] As time passed, new destinations for both Hispanic migrants as well as new immigrants emerged. Up until 1990, approximately three-quarters of immigrants to the United States lived in just six states: California, New York, Florida, Texas, New Jersey, and Illinois.[10] After 1990, the concentration of immigrants began to become more complex as new immigrants were dispersing away from the traditional immigrant gateways.[11] New areas of settlement emerged in the South and in smaller metropolitan and some nonmetropolitan areas in the West, Midwest, and Northeast.[12] For the Mountain West, the largest source of new Hispanics is California, which had net outflows of migrants to other regions in the West—particularly Nevada, but also Arizona, Utah, Idaho, and Colorado. In addition to the increased dispersal of immigrants across the United States, the total number of immigrants also increased, with over 11 million legal immigrants being admitted to the United States during the 1990s and another 8 million between 2000 and 2010 (although with practically no growth in the number of immigrants in the "Great Recession" years of 2007, 2008, and 2009). In addition to legal immigrants, recent estimates put the number of illegal immigrants in the United States at around 12 million.[13]

Until the early 1990s most Hispanics/Latinos were concentrated geographically in California, Arizona, New Mexico, Colorado, and Texas.[14] Starting in the 1990s and continuing until today, Hispanics/Latinos have been dispersing away from these five states to new destination regions, so that as of the 2010 U.S. census more than half of all Hispanics/Latinos live outside of these traditional gateway states. Most observers attribute the beginning of the dispersal to the 1986 *Immigration Reform and Control Act* (IRCA), which provided amnesty for illegal aliens in the United States, thus enabling easier movement between states.[15] The increased movement of immigrants in general, and Hispanics/Latinos in particular, also coincided with the restructuring of agricultural production into large-scale factory farms (Concentrated Agricultural Feeding Operations or CAFOs), meat-processing plants moving to rural areas, and increased demand for low-wage service and manufacturing workers. These developments encouraged the movement of immigrants to new destinations made up of smaller cities, towns, and rural areas.[16]

Hispanics/Latinos in the Mountain West

Examining the growth of the Hispanic population in the Mountain West is interesting for a couple of reasons. First, Arizona, New Mexico, and Colorado all have counties that are part of the traditional Hispanic core area of the United States. A vital question concerning Hispanic immigration/migration is how it is affecting this traditional Hispanic core. Second, the West, which includes the Mountain West, has traditionally been and continues to be the most ethnically and racially diverse region in the United States. As of the 2010 U.S. Census, approximately 47 percent of the West's population is of minority status (African American, American Indian, Asian, Pacific Islander, or Hispanic).[17] This is significantly more than the South (40 percent), the Northeast (31 percent), or the Midwest (22 percent).

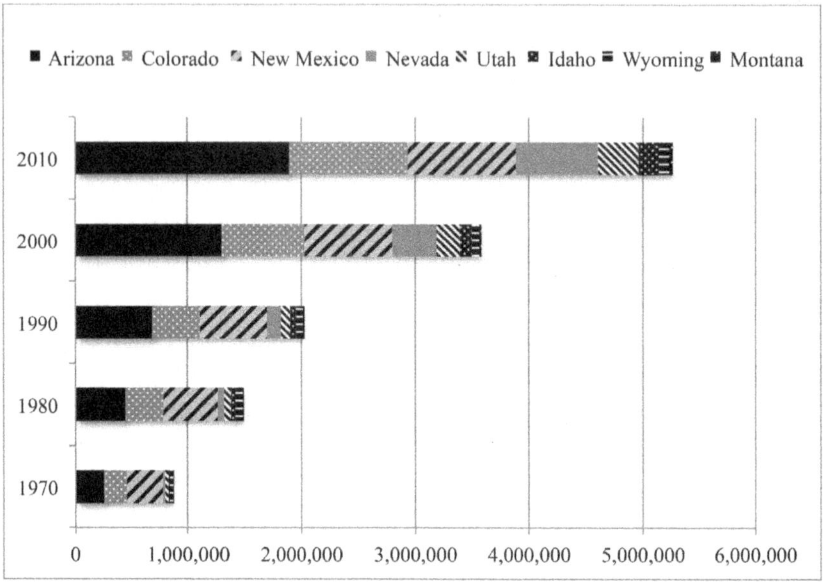

Figure 13.1. Hispanic population size and change by state: 1970–2010.

The 2010 U.S. Census also reports that for the western United States over one-third of the total population is made up of people who report their ethnicity as Hispanic, which is, again, significantly higher than any other region in the United States. In terms of individual states, New Mexico is tied with California with the second highest percentage of its population that is minority (60 percent). Both Nevada and Arizona had two of the fastest growing minority populations, and Utah, Idaho, and Colorado experienced faster than average growth in their minority population—primarily made up of Hispanics. Given the relatively small total population in the Mountain West as well as its being one of the fastest growing regions in the country, it provides a relatively important context for examining the changing size and geographic dispersion of the Hispanic population.

Similar to what happened in both the southeastern United States and other parts of the West and Southwest, the size of the Hispanic/Latino population in the Mountain West increased dramatically after 1990. Using Utah as an example, between 1970 (the first census after the 1965 immigration reform) and 1990, the Hispanic population in Utah only grew by approximately 55,000 people. On the other hand, between 1990 and 2010 the Hispanic population in Utah increased by over a quarter million or five times the previous twenty-year increase. Clearly, something changed after 1990. In examining Figure 13.1, three patterns or trends regarding Hispanic population growth in the Mountain West stand out. First, the total size of the Hispanic population increased from around 800,000 in 1970 to just over five million by 2010. Second, the greatest percentage of the increase in the Hispanic/Latino population came after 1990. Third, a pattern of dispersal is also evident. New Mexico, which had the largest share of the Hispanic population in 1970 and 1980 (for the Mountain West region), dropped to second in 1990 and third by 2010. By far, the largest growth has been in Arizona, which went from around 200,000 in 1970 to almost two million by 2010. Colorado and Nevada (and, to a lesser extent, Utah) have also experienced rapid growth—particularly since 1990.

The original Hispanic core areas found in the Mountain West were concentrated in rural areas, such as the original Spanish settlements in north-central New Mexico and smaller metropolitan areas like Pueblo, Colorado. However, these are not the areas that are growing the fastest or that have the largest increases in Hispanic populations. The greatest increases in absolute numbers are found in large metropolitan areas, while the fastest growing Hispanic populations by percentage are in smaller, micropolitan areas.[18] Micropolitan (micro) areas have the largest share of their total population that are of Hispanic origin. For example, the 2010 U.S. Census shows that almost one in four residents of micropolitan areas in the Mountain West region identify themselves as Hispanic (with approximately one in five in metro areas and one in ten in nonmetro areas). The more traditional Hispanic enclaves in nonmetro and rural areas now have the smallest Hispanic populations and although they are growing, they are increasing at a slower rate than metro- or micropolitan areas (Table 13.1).

Within each metro classification, there are distinct differences in levels of spatial distribution/concentration (bottom panel of Table 13.1). That is, Hispanics are not evenly distributed either across metropolitan categories or within these categories. For example, ten metro counties contain approximately three-quarters of the total Hispanic population (e.g., counties making up the Phoenix, Las Vegas, Albuquerque, Denver, and Salt Lake City metro areas). The proportion concentrated in these counties has not changed much over time, largely because the Mountain West does not have many large metro areas for population dispersal. The story is slightly different for micropolitan counties where the proportion of the Hispanic population has declined from two-thirds in 1970 to just over one-half by 2010. For nonmetro areas the top ten counties contained just more than one-half of the Hispanic population in 1970 but declined to approximately one-third by 2010. What this suggests is that, at least for micro and nonmetro areas, the Hispanic population is becoming less and less concentrated over time. One question that naturally arises from this observation is how the changing spatial distribution of Hispanics

Table 13.1: Hispanics by Metro, Micro, and Non-Metro Classification (based on 2010 Census): 1970–2010

	1970	1980	1990	2000	2010
Number of Hispanics/Latinos					
Metro	596,920	1,085,507	1,545,486	2,925,027	4,425,838
Micro	176,789	252,424	320,609	448,295	573,259
Non-metro	86,696	110,040	125,637	170,365	217,680
Hispanic Share of Total Population					
Metro	7%	11%	12%	15%	18%
Micro	9%	15%	17%	20%	23%
Non-metro	6%	9%	9%	11%	12%
Percent of Hispanic Population in top 10 counties					
Metro	79%	73%	74%	75%	73%
Micro	68%	62%	60%	54%	51%
Non-metro	53%	46%	43%	39%	38%

Date from author based on decennial U.S. Censuses.

compares to the spatial distribution of the overall population in the Mountain West. If the geographic distribution of Hispanics is becoming more similar to the overall population distribution among places, is this an indication of increased assimilation?

Spatial Distribution by County Type and Characteristics

Following a procedure used by Liaw and Frey, counties in the Mountain West region were grouped into three types: Established counties, High–Growth counties, and Other counties based on Hispanic population size and change.[19] Established counties include those where the proportion of the Hispanic population is at least 24 percent, which is twice the proportion of Hispanics in the region as a whole in 1990. High Growth counties are those counties where the increase in the Hispanic population was at least 1.5 standard deviations above mean growth (and were not an established county), and Other counties are the residual group (see Figure 13.2). As can be seen in Figure 13.2, the established counties are only located in New Mexico, Arizona, and Colorado and are part of the U.S. Hispanic core. High growth counties appear to follow the I-70 corridor through Colorado, the I-15 corridor from the Salt Lake City area down to Las Vegas, high-amenity areas in Wyoming and Idaho, and the mining, farming, and CAFO areas of Nevada, Colorado, and Idaho.

In looking at population change at the county level, we include both total population and Hispanic population to see if the rates of change are

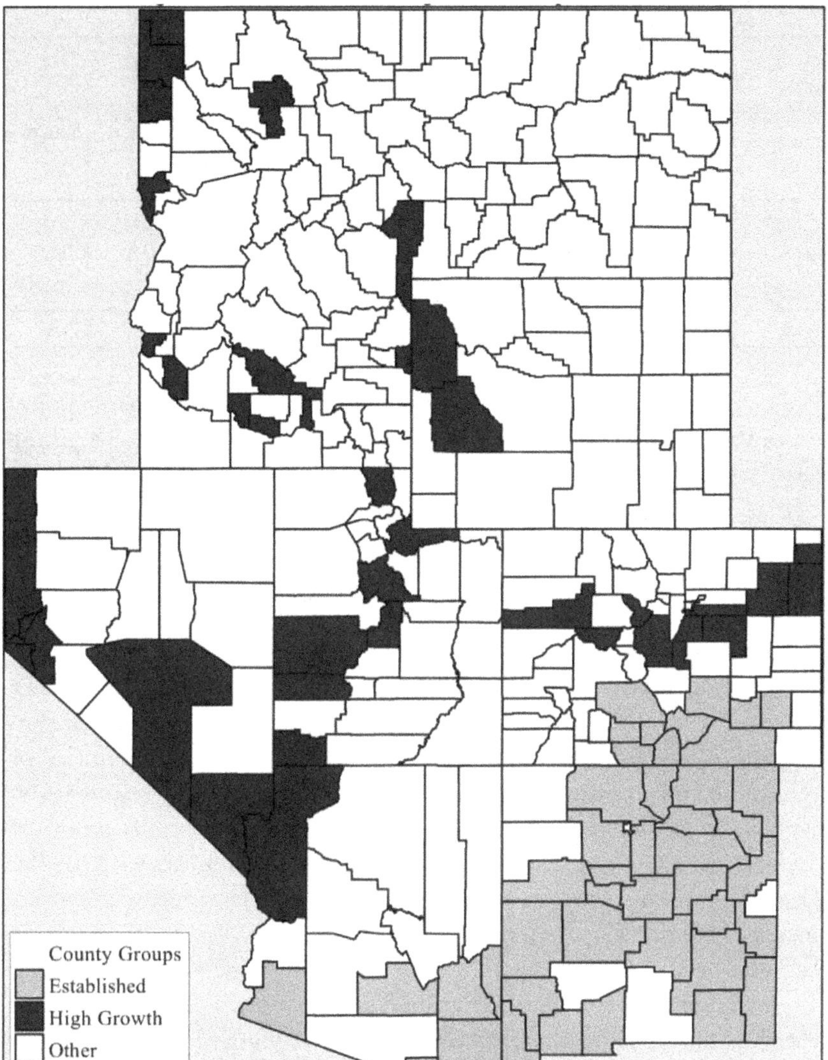

Figure 13.2. Established and high-growth Hispanic counties.

similar. Table 13.2 shows the population change in the high growth period between 1990 and 2010, parsed between the three categories: Established, High Growth, and Other. In examining population change across these categories, three things stand out. First, the Mountain West region is experiencing rapid population growth as total population increased by more than 7.5 million and the Hispanic population increased by almost 3 million. Second, it appears from this data that the Hispanic population is becoming less spatially concentrated (we show this later in more detail).

Table 13.2: Population Change by Hispanic Category, 1990–2010 (population in thousands)

	1990			2010			1990–2010	
	Total Population	Hispanic Population	% Hispanic	Total Population	Hispanic Population	% Hispanic	% Change Hisp Pop	% Change Tot Pop
Other (197)	9,150	1,053	12	13,473	2,788	21	165	47
Established (43)	1,833	749	41	2,578	1,183	46	58	41
High Growth (40)	2,674	166	6	5,251	909	17	445	96
Total	13,657	1,968	14	21,302	4,880	23	148	56

While all three groups of counties increased in total and Hispanic population, the largest increases in both occurred in the High Growth group. Relative to growth rates, High Growth counties have the smallest Hispanic population and thus have the largest percentage increases, which mathematically makes sense, but it also indicates that the Hispanic population *is moving out of or new Hispanic immigrants are not moving to*, the historically Hispanic core. Finally, the dispersal of the Hispanic population appears to be happening away from both large metropolitan and smaller rural areas. The only large metro county that is part of the High Growth group is Clark County, Nevada (Las Vegas). Most of these counties are located in propinquity to larger metro areas or to high-amenity, recreation counties, or are agriculturally dominant counties. From this preliminary examination it appears that there is a rapid increase in the Hispanic population in the Mountain West, the most rapid growth occurring in counties with smaller Hispanic, but not necessarily small total, populations, and the growth is outside of the traditional Hispanic core region.

While it is clear that there has been a significant increase in the overall Hispanic population in the Mountain West between 1990–2010, and that growth is taking place in new areas, this can be more formally measured and mapped. For the entire region, two different measures that provide different perspectives for examining spatial concentration and dispersal are calculated: an entropy measure of dispersal, which, as the name implies, measures the changing degree of the spread of the Hispanic population across all 280 Mountain West counties, and a Geographical Difference Index that measures the distribution of Hispanics relative to the non-Hispanic population.

To characterize the changing spatial pattern of the Hispanic population across Mountain West counties, a measure of relative entropy is used.[20] The value of the entropy measure can never be less than zero, where all Hispanics would be in one county, or greater than log2 (280), when all counties

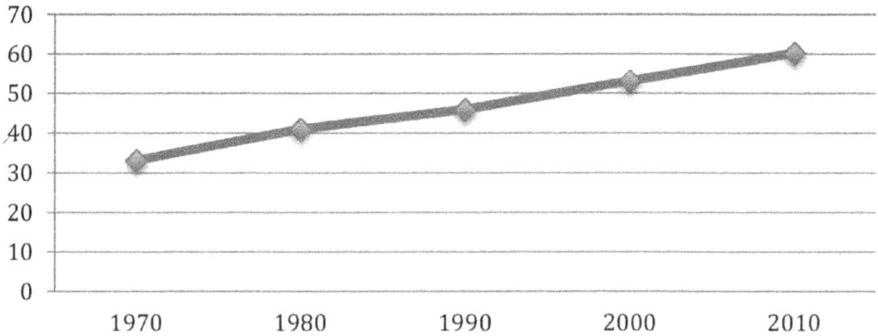

Figure 13.3. Relative entropy of Hispanic population distribution across 280 Mountain West counties: 1970–2010.

would have the same share of Hispanics. The value of relative entropy is bounded between zero percent and one hundred percent. Since the entropy measure depends on the proportional shares of all 280 counties, relative entropy is a measure of *overall dispersal*. That is, an increase in the relative entropy measure indicates an increasing dispersal of the Hispanic population over a greater set of counties. Figure 13.3 plots relative entropy between 1970 and 2010 for Hispanics across counties in the Mountain West. As can be seen in this graph, there is a clear upward trend in the relative entropy measure, thus indicating an increasing dispersal of Hispanics across counties. Between 1970 and 2010, the index increased from 33 percent to almost 61 percent, an increase of over 80 percent. What this means is that not only are Hispanics deconcentrating (i.e., either moving out of or not immigrating into Established counties), they are also dispersing to a wide range of other places. Somewhat surprising is the fact that this increase is rather linear, even though Hispanic population growth was relatively small during the 1970s and 1980s and seems to explode in the 1990s and 2000s. The next question is, how does the changing spatial distribution of Hispanics in the Mountain West compare with the spatial distribution of the non-Hispanic population? In order to measure this, we use the Differential Geographic Index (DG).

The DG index used here is a modified Duncan index also known as the differential geographical index.[21] Like the entropy measure, this index reports a value between zero and one hundred. Zero means that there are exactly the same proportions of Hispanics and non-Hispanics in each county, while a value of 100 would indicate a complete separation of the Hispanic from non-Hispanic, which is highly unlikely. Nevertheless, relatively high values indicate that the proportions of Hispanics to the non-Hispanic population are distributed quite differently among the

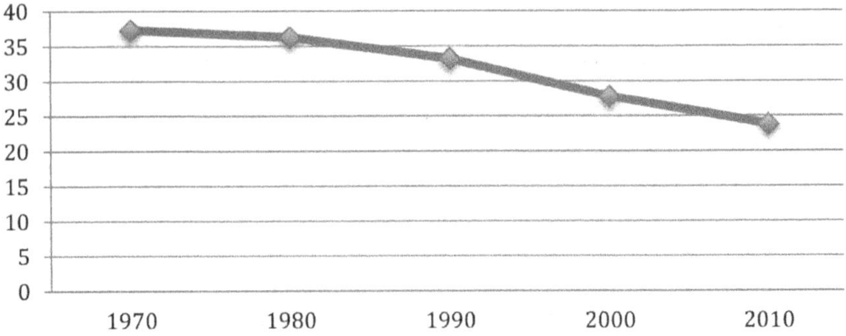

Figure 13.4. Differential Geographic Index Hispanic–non-Hispanic within the Mountain West: 1970–2010.

counties of the region. As stated earlier, the Mountain West has seen significant growth in its Hispanic population, and this population is increasingly found in new locations. The expectation, then, is that these two trends should also lead to an increase in spatial assimilation, i.e., that spatial distribution of Hispanics becoming more similar to the spatial distribution of non-Hispanics, at least at the county level. Figure 13.4 plots the DG index for Mountain West counties between 1970 and 2010 and shows that geographic distribution of Hispanics is becoming more and more like that of the non-Hispanic population. As with the entropy measure, over the past forty years Hispanics are either moving from or not migrating (or immigrating) to Established Hispanic counties. Whether this is maintained at subcounty and within metropolitan areas is unknown (but unlikely—at least to the same extent), but at a regional level the patterns are clear. Unlike the entropy measure, however, most of the decline in the DG has come in the last two decades and is associated with the rapid growth of Hispanics during that same timespan and their movement to new areas.

County Characteristics

Using patterns of Hispanic population growth between 1990 and 2010, all Mountain West counties were categorized into one of five groups based on their standard deviation from mean growth: Very High (+1.5), High (+1), Average (.99 to -.99), Low (-1), and Very Low (-1.5). Various geographic, demographic, and economic characteristics are compared across these categories. These are shown in Tables 13.3, 13.4, and 13.5. A few interesting patterns emerge when looking at county-level characteristics differentiated along lines of Hispanic growth. First, the large and rapid increase in Hispanics in the Mountain West region is not geographically even. Those counties with a population growth at least one standard deviation above the mean only make up 47 out of the 280 counties found in the Mountain West (17 percent). While the largest increases occur in large metropolitan areas—particularly Phoenix and Las Vegas—the most rapid growth in the Hispanic population is found primarily in smaller metro areas (e.g., St. George, Utah), smaller counties within larger metro areas (e.g., Summit County, Utah, as part of the Salt Lake City–Ogden metro area), and nonmetro counties that are either adjacent to large metro areas (e.g., outside of Denver), or adjacent to high-amenity recreation and/or retirement counties (e.g., Teton County/Jackson Hole, Wyoming). Fifty-eight percent of High and Very High growth counties are nonmetro counties of these types, while only 28 percent are metro counties and 14 percent are micro counties. Second, for most micro and nonmetro counties, the highest rates of Hispanic population growth appear to be taking place outside of counties with high concentrations of Hispanics. All of the larger metro counties have relatively large Hispanic populations, and all of them experienced growth in these populations, but only Las Vegas (Clark County) is classified as either a High or Very High growth county. On the other hand, no Established Hispanic counties are found in the High or Very High categories, and only six are present in the Average category.

Economically, the growth in the Hispanic population is, as would be expected, higher in counties with better economies. For example, counties in the Very High and High categories have higher median household incomes, higher housing values, lower unemployment (at the beginning of the period and lower average unemployment over the period), less poverty, and higher employment growth overall and by unskilled/semiskilled economic sectors (agriculture, services, manufacturing, and construction). However, geographically these high growth counties are very diverse places. The map in Figure 13.5 shows the location of the Very High and High counties differentiated by county economic type (as determined by the Economic Research Service [ERS] and metro/micro/nonmetro status). High and Very High growth counties range from the eastern plains of Colorado and Montana, and are associated with agriculture, to the more remote and mountain (and adjacent) counties associated with high-amenity recreation and retirement communities like Sun Valley, Idaho; Jackson Hole, Wyoming; and the Aspen/Vail areas in Colorado. The one underlying characteristic that helps to explain why such diverse counties are all attracting high numbers of Hispanic migrants/immigrants is the availability of relatively low-skill and low-wage employment opportunities in agriculture and services, which can be seen in the data in Table 13.3 where job growth is more than twice as fast in the Very High county group as next-closest category.

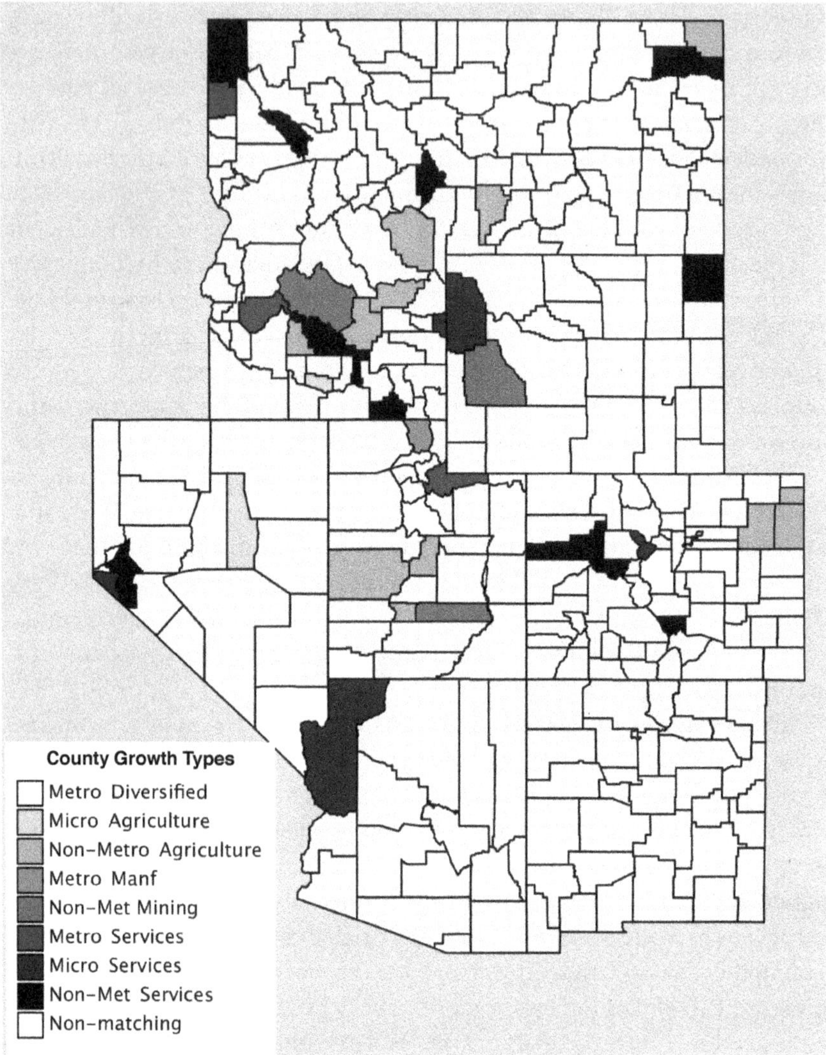

Figure 13.5. High and very high Hispanic population growth counties by economic type and Metro/Micro/Non-Metro status.

Tables 13.3, 13.4, and 13.5 contain data on some socioeconomic and locational information (13.3), population size and change (13.4), and fertility information broken down between non-Hispanic and Hispanic women age fifteen to fifty (13.5).[22] The data contained in these tables confirms much of what was found earlier. For example, Hispanic population growth follows the same pattern of growth across categories as the total population, just at a much higher rate. Only the Very High growth category has a large percentage of metro counties, although as we saw earlier,

Table 13.3: Socioeconomic and Locational Characteristics byHispanic Population Growth Categories, 2000

	% Established Hispanic Counties	Med HH Income ($)	Med House Value ($)	Econ Momentum (%), 90–10	% Job Growth (90–10)	% Metro Counties	% Micro Counties	% Non-Metro Counties
Very High	0	53,260	218,000	139	166	41	18	41
High	0	49,466	237,000	97	67	20	13	67
Average	6	47,183	161,000	74	47	26	21	54
Low	41	42,065	146,000	63	40	20	25	55
Very Low	65	37,159	107,000	37	20	0	20	80

Table 13.4: Population Size & Change by Hispanic Population Growth Categories, 1990–2010

	Total Population (in thousands)			Hispanic Population (in thousands)			Population Under 18		
	1990	2010	Annual % Change	1990	2010	Annual % Change	Total Pop	Non-Hispanic	Hispanic
Very High	188	563	10	5	47	42	3.1	2.3	20.3
High	1,529	3,391	6.1	108	739	29.2	1.8	0.8	18.8
Average	7,024	11,252	3	713	2,370	11.6	0.7	0.1	8.8
Low	4,680	6,541	2	1,049	1,946	4.3	0.1	-0.4	3.1
Very Low	237	263	0.5	95	107	0.6	-1	-1.3	0.1

Table 13.5: Fertility for Non-Hispanic and Hispanic Women, 2005–2009

	Non-Hispanic Women 15–50	Non-Hispanic Births	Non-Hispanic GFR	Hispanic Women 15–50	Hispanic Births	Hispanic GFR (in thousands)
Very High	114,856	7,756	68	10,417	649	62
High	511,732	30,160	58	164,334	12,553	76
Average	1,923,518	105,457	55	581,693	49,724	85
Low	848,151	46,653	55	458,639	34,893	76
Very Low	24,946	1,203	48	24,381	1,754	71

excepting Las Vegas, these tend to be smaller metro areas. In both the High and Very High categories, over one-half of the counties have been identified as recreation and/or retirement destinations, which tend to provide a large number of low-skilled service employment opportunities. Income, housing values, and job growth are all significantly higher in the top two categories, and there are not any counties in these two groups that have been designated as High Poverty counties by the ERS. What is new here is evidence of the potential for future growth of the Hispanic population, which is shown in Table 13.4.

Table 13.4 also includes data on the average annual population change between 1990 and 2010 of the total non-Hispanic and Hispanic populations under the age of eighteen. Assuming that most of the under-eighteen Hispanics stay in the areas where they are currently living, the potential for an increased convergence between the non-Hispanic and Hispanic populations seems probable. Taking the Average group, which has by far the largest population of both non-Hispanics and Hispanics, as an example, the under-eighteen group for non-Hispanics has only been growing at 0.1 percent a year (essentially zero) while the Hispanic population under eighteen has been growing at almost 9 percent a year—that is, an average annual growth of 9 percent per year for twenty years. The comparison is even more dramatic in the High and Very High categories. This pattern differs slightly when looking at recent fertility and is most likely the result of the migration of teenagers and young adults (Table 13.5). For the Very High group of counties, the General Fertility Rate (GFR, or the number of children born divided by the number of women between the ages of fifteen and fifty, multiplied by 1,000) is actually higher for non-Hispanics than for Hispanics (sixty-eight and sixty-two, respectively)—and may reflect the characteristics of the migrants who move to new destinations with fast-growing economies. Perhaps those who move to these new locations are either married, without a partner, or choosing to forego children for whatever reason. It is impossible to determine this with the current data, but finding out is both interesting and important. It is never only about the number of migrants; just as importantly, it is about *who* moves. For each of the other categories, the GFR is higher for Hispanics than it is for non-Hispanics. In looking at the number of births instead of the rates for both the High and Average categories, the Hispanic women are about one-third the number of non-Hispanic women, yet the number of births is more than 40 percent for the High Category and almost 50 percent for the Average category—suggesting that it is not just migration that is fueling the growth of the Hispanic population, it is also higher levels of fertility.

Summary

Julio was born in San Salvador, El Salvador, and lived the first twenty years of his life there. In August of 2009 he left his family in El Salvador and immigrated to Utah. One of his uncles lives in Utah and during one of this uncle's visits back to El Salvador, he invited Julio to come and live with his family. Julio is currently attending a university and hopes to stay in the United States after he graduates. When asked why he wanted to stay, Julio mentioned safety, economic opportunities, and family.

> One of the things I like here is that it is very safe. Once I was calling a friend while I was walking on University Avenue, at midnight and she told me to be careful because they could steal my cell phone. I told her that doesn't happen here. So I like that I can carry my cell phone, my laptop. I like that it is secure and clean. I feel like the people is good; the culture is different. People here is very tolerant. For example, I can't speak the language very well, but they are willing to be patient. I would like my family to live here, my children to grow up here. There are no opportunities back in El Salvador, and there are many opportunities here for economy, job.[23]

As data from the 2010 U.S. Census started being released, many commentators were surprised at how quickly the Hispanic population had grown, which was very similar to what happened after the 2000 Census. During the last twenty years, the dramatic growth of Hispanics is arguably the largest and most important demographic change that has occurred in the United States. In some parts of the Mountain West region, Hispanics were a part of the landscape long before other settlers with a European heritage began to occupy the region. Most of New Mexico, southern Colorado, and southern Arizona are part of the Hispanic geographic core area. Both the Immigration and Nationality Act of 1965 and the 1986 Immigration Reform and Control Act served to change the fundamental nature of immigration and secondary migration patterns in the United States. With the 1965 Act, immigration flows into the United States changed from being primarily European to mostly Mexican, Central and South American, and later Asian—which is still the case today. The 1986 act that opened up a window for legalization of the illegal immigrants who were already in the United States also enabled increased migration flows to new destinations. These two changes in immigration law, combined with the massive economic restructuring that took place after 1970—e.g., the shifting of some manufacturing from urban to rural locations; the development of large factory farms for chickens, hogs, cattle, and dairy; the movement of slaughtering operations to new, rural locations; and the growth of retirement- and recreation-dominant economies all with their demand for cheap labor—created the conditions for both the massive increase in immigrants from Latin America and their flows to new areas of the country.

Because the Mountain West is very geographically diverse, so are its rural and urban economies with their different demands for low-skilled and cheap labor. Whether it is working on one of the largest hog farms in the United States, found in Millard County, Utah; working in low-paying service jobs in and around Jackson Hole, Wyoming; or working in construction in Las Vegas, employment opportunities and the ability to go to new places have encouraged the growth of the Hispanic population in this region. Rapid growth has taken place outside of the Hispanic core, in mostly smaller metropolitan counties, in counties with smaller populations but located within metropolitan areas (and in only one large metropolitan area—Las Vegas), and in rural areas where large CAFOs have been located or there are high-amenity recreation and/or retirement communities. These patterns are representative of the dispersal of Hispanics away from their core area and into areas where, historically, their population has been relatively small. One result of this movement is, as the DG index showed, the spatial distribution of Hispanics increasingly mirroring that of the total population. As the geographic distribution of Hispanic and non-Hispanic populations continues to merge, the potential for increased interactions between Hispanics and other ethnic groups should increase. Increased interaction among different population groups can lead to increases in understanding, acceptance, and assimilation. Because the Hispanic population, at least for the next couple of decades, will increase faster than the non-Hispanic population (due to continuing immigration/migration and significantly higher birth rates among Hispanics), the need for cultural assimilation and acceptance will also need to increase. As this and other research has shown, Hispanic immigrants/migrants generally move to areas for the same reasons as other populations: economic opportunities, safety, and to be close to family. Passing legislation that limits immigrants/migrants' access to jobs, to safer living conditions, or to families in the end will be counterproductive as recent experiences in Alabama has demonstrated.[24]

As with most research, these findings suggest a number of interesting questions that have not been and should be answered. Using geographically weighted regression models could help disentangle the confounding effects of different factors operating differently in various locations. That is, while job growth in services is probably important for high-amenity Park City, Utah, it is less important for explaining growth in Hispanics in the large dairying industry around Twin Falls, Idaho. A second set of questions that needs exploring is associated with spatial scales of analysis. While similar patterns of growth and decline appear to occur across the region, the states, and the counties, the next step would be to explore measures of dispersal and spatial association within metropolitan counties, both large and small, and why they occur where they do. Finally, there are a whole set of interesting questions concerning different migration and settlement patterns of people from different places. That is, do people from Central America, Mexico, and South America immigrate to different places? Are the patterns similar among the various spatial scales? And if so, where and why? And on a more local scale, how are counties that have experienced rapid growth in their Hispanic populations doing—particularly in the smaller metropolitan and micropolitan areas that do not have the same resources as larger urban areas? Examining specific groups and comparing them with the overall Hispanic presence in the Mountain West is an interesting and important research topic that deserves further study.

Notes

1. A. G. Sulzberger, "Hispanics Reviving Faded Towns on the Plains," *New York Times*, November 13, 2011.
2. T. Mannes, "Hispanic Grocers Grab Market Share," *San Diego Union-Tribune*, November 15, 2011.
3. T. Haverluk, "The Changing Geography of U.S. Hispanics, 1850–1990," *Journal of Geography* 96, no. 3 (May/June 1997): 134–35.
4. U.S. Census Bureau, 2010 Census Summary File 1: United States, [machine-readable data files].
5. K. M. Johnson and D. T. Lichter, "Natural Increase: A New Source of Population Growth in Emerging Hispanic Destinations in the United States," *Population and Development Review* 34, no. 2 (June 2008): 327–46.
6. O. Furuseth and H. Smith, "From Winn-Dixie to Tiendas: The Remaking of the New South," in *Latinos in the New South: Transformations of Place*, ed. H. Smith & O. Furuseth (Burlington, VT: Ashgate, 2006), 1–17.
7. Any names are pseudonyms used to protect subjects' identities.
8. Eduardo, personal interview, March 2010.
9. Haverluk, "The Changing Geography of U.S. Hispanics," 134–45.
10. J. S. Passel and W. Zimmermann, *Are Immigrants Leaving California? Settlement Patterns of Immigrants in the Late 1990s*, Research Report, Pub. ID#410287 (Washington, DC: The Urban Institute, 2001).
11. A. Singer, "New Immigrant Gateways," Living Cities Survey Series (Washington, DC: Brookings Institution, Center on Urban and Metropolitan Policy, 2004).
12. D. T. Gurak and M. M. Kritz, "Do the Native Born and Foreign Born Show Differential Migratory Responses to Immigration and Labor Market Conditions?" Paper presented at the annual meetings of the Population Association of America, Boston, April 1–3, 2004.
13. J. R. Weeks et al., "Who's Crossing the Border: New Data on Undocumented

Immigrants to the United States," *Population, Place, and Space* 17, no. 1 (2010): 1–26.

14. D. Arreloa, "The Texas-Mexican Homeland," *Journal of Cultural Geography* 3, no. 2 (Spring/Summer 1993): 56–74.
15. T. Haverluk, "The Changing Geography of U.S. Hispanics," 134–45.
16. D. T. Lichter and K. M. Johnson, "Emerging Rural Settlement Patterns and the Geographic Redistribution of America's New Immigrants," *Rural Sociology* 71, no. 1 (March 2006): 109–31.
17. K. R. Humes, N. A. Jones, and R. R. Ramirez, "Overview of Race and Hispanic Origin: 2010," 2010 Census Briefs, March 2011.
18. The Office of Management and Budget (OMB) and the Census Bureau define a micropolitan area as an urban area based around a core town or city with at least ten thousand but fewer than fifty thousand people.
19. K. L. Liaw and W. H. Frey, "Multivariate Explanation of the 1985–1990 and 1995–2000 Destination Choices of Newly Arrived Immigrants in the United States: The beginning of a new trend?" *Population, Space, and Place* 13, no. 5 (September/October 2007): 377–99.
20. This dispersion measure is produced by taking the proportional (P[h]) share of Hispanics by county, which bounds the resultant value between 0 and 1. Given this, the relative entropy for the spatial pattern of Hispanics is defined as: E = {ΣP[h]* log2 (1/P[h])}/log2 (280) * 100%, where the summation is across all 280 counties.
21. The differential geographical index (DG) at year *y*, is calculated as follows:

$$DG = \sum_{I=1}^{k} \left| \frac{H_c}{H_t} - \frac{G_c}{G_t} \right| * 50$$

    where *I* is the region having *k* counties, *H* is the Hispanic population, and *G* is the non-Hispanic population in the county (*c*) or region (*t*) respectively at year *y*. From S. M. Otterstrom, "Divergent Growth of the Church of Jesus Christ of Latter-day Saints in the United States: Diaspora, Gathering, and the East-West Divide," *Population, Space, and Place* 14, no. 3 (May/June 2008): 231–52.
22. This data comes from the American Community Survey question that asked if there was a child born in the previous twelve months. The survey used is the five-year survey 2005–2009, which averages data over the five years in order to protect the privacy of individuals in areas with small populations but still provide data for these areas.
23. Julio, personal interview, April 2010.
24. P. Constable, "Alabama law drives out illegal immigrants but also has unexpected consequences," *Washington Post*, June 17, 2012. The article explains how the poultry industry has been unable to maintain workers.

14

Hispanic Mormon Immigrants in Provo, Utah

Jessie L. Embry and Meisha Slight

Academic oral history began as an elitist movement at Columbia University in the 1940s when historian Allan Nevins used interviews with leading American politicians to supplement written documents. However, the technique quickly became a way to record the experiences of everyday people. In the 1970s many archives, universities, and public agencies including the Charles Redd Center developed oral history programs in an effort to study history "from the bottom up" by examining and preserving the experiences and perspectives of common people, including immigrants, many of whom were unlikely to leave many written records. In this chapter, Jessie L. Embry and Meisha Slight draw upon oral histories with Spanish-speaking Mormon immigrants who settled in Utah's third-largest city, Provo. Utah's Hispanic population rose rapidly in the 1990s. Even though many of the newcomers to Utah were not Mormons, where there had been only one Spanish-speaking Mormon congregation in Provo and the surrounding communities in 1981, there were thirty-five Spanish-speaking congregations in 2008. As Embry and Slight show, the burgeoning Latino population in the Mormon core region, including many illegal immigrants, raised ethical dilemmas for the church as it struggled to balance respect for the law with compassion for individuals and families. As the LDS Church's policies regarding immigration shifted, so did the church's support for language-based congregations. Embry and Slight reveal some of the dimensions of worship, recreation, and social interaction in Spanish-language congregations. Moreover, they document interaction between Hispanic and English-speaking Mormons at church functions, in the neighborhood, and in the workplace.

State Street (U.S. Highway 89) on the north side of Provo, Utah, looks like any other stretch of American highway. But then just at the bottom of the hill there is a unique strip mall, a little Latino haven. The previous specialty markets have been replaced with a restaurant, a supermarket, and legal services all serving a Spanish-speaking community. Families mingle at the grocery store, Rancho Market, which feels like a store in Latin America. With the *ranchera* music, the Latino soap opera on the television, the constant chatter in Spanish, the Mexican bakery and the small *taquería*, Latin Americans find a home away from home. Here, an Anglo feels like a foreigner.

The same is true at a worship service for the Church of Jesus Christ of Latter-day Saints (LDS or Mormon) on the southwest side of Fifth West across from the Provo Towne Centre. Spanish-speaking Mormons looking for a worship service (sacrament meeting) will find one to attend at nine a.m. in their native language at the East Bay Chapel. A European American who did not speak Spanish or have a Latino/Hispanic background would recognize many common practices but would find the language and culture unfamiliar.

These scenes are not unique to Utah Valley. Similar shopping areas can be found throughout the United States to service Mexican and Central and South American immigrants. Churches of various denominations, including Catholic, Jehovah's Witness, and Seventh-day Adventist, provide worship services in Spanish. This article explores a rarely told story of the experiences and feelings of late twentieth-century and early twenty-first-century Spanish-speaking Latter-day Saints in the middle of the Mormon corridor in the American West. To understand those experiences, the article first explains Mormon immigration policies and compares them to the general U.S. views. It then discusses Mexican and Latin American immigration to Utah, especially focusing on the Mormon experience. The paper uses oral history interviews with Spanish-speaking Latino members to allow them to tell their stories of experiences in Southwest Provo.

Their stories provide a unique Utah/Western American topic because although Latin American Mormons are found throughout the United States, the Latinos who come to the country as Mormons have an expectation that they will be welcomed as Latter-day Saints in the largely Mormon environment in Utah and especially in Provo, the home of Brigham Young University. However, until recently their immigration status has affected how they were accepted by church leaders. That has recently changed so the leaders no longer require documentation to participate in the local congregations. The leaders have also softened their requirements for undocumented immigrants who want to join the church. In addition, the church has allowed the immigrants and their children to worship in Spanish and control the social activities and worship services in language congregations. Despite this institutional acceptance, the Latino Mormons have found that some of their fellow church members are Americans first and have the same prejudices against Hispanic immigrants as others in the United States. While it may seem obvious to some readers that there are cultural differences between Latino Mormons and their neighbors, it was not what some Latinos expected. This case study shows that just being a member of the dominant faith does not mean that these immigrants are insiders.

Provo, Utah, Sources

The main sources that illustrate this story are oral histories with Spanish-speaking Mormon immigrants. The Charles Redd Center for Western Studies conducted interviews with Spanish-speaking Mormons as part of two projects. The first, the LDS Hispanic American Oral History Project, was conducted in 1991 by Latino students.[1] In 2008–2009, the center studied the LDS Provo Utah South Stake. Three Latino students interviewed members of the two Spanish-speaking congregations.[2] Nearly all the interviews used in this article were conducted in Spanish and parts were translated into English.

The interviewers for the LDS Hispanic project asked about early religious life, conversion to the LDS Church, reasons for immigrating to the United States, first experiences in America, experiences as Mormons, and advantages and disadvantages of living in America, Utah, and Provo.[3] In addition to these questions, the interviewers for the Provo Utah South Stake project asked about local church activities. The answers are not uniform since the interviewers directed questions based on what the interviewees discussed. The interviewees for both projects openly discussed good and bad experiences in Provo from their perspectives as Hispanic immigrants.

While not a representative sample, the Spanish-speaking interviewees represented a range of experiences. Of the thirty-eight narrators who were interviewed in their native language (some were interviewed as couples), twenty-five were from Mexico. The other participants came from Peru, Bolivia, Puerto Rico, the Dominican Republic, Honduras, Argentina, Venezuela, and Chile. Most were baptized into the Mormon faith in their home countries. For example, twenty-two of the twenty-five from Mexico were baptized there. Only nine were baptized after immigrating to the United States. The interviewees ranged from twenty to seventy-six years old. The majority were twenty to twenty-nine years old. The average age was forty-seven.

Latino Mormons

Many of the interviewees had been Catholic before they joined the Mormon Church, which might not surprise those who believe the Catholic Church is the predominate religion in Latin America and has deep roots in the people's traditions and lives. While that is mostly true, the religious identity of Latin Americans has shifted. A 1990 study reported Catholics represented only 60 percent of the population in some countries compared to over 90 percent twenty years before.[4] Mormon historian Mark L. Grover explains the change occurred following World War II when political and economic shifts allowed people from all social classes to look for different religions. During that time many moved from rural to urban areas and looked for new support systems. Hispanic scholar Hector Avalos calls "the shift from Catholicism to Protestantism . . . one of the most far-reaching revolutions in the entire history of Christianity." He continues, "Some areas of Latin America may see a majority of the population become Protestant within our readers' lifetimes."[5]

The most rapid growth in Latin America was in evangelical churches. The LDS Church grew more slowly but still increased its membership.[6] Grover explained that changes not only in Latin America but also in the LDS Church led to increased missionary activity in the area. The church expanded its "semiofficial doctrine" regarding the House of Israel, which it felt it was its mission to convert, to include not only northern Europeans but those from southern Europe who settled in Latin America. In the 1960s the church emphasized that the indigenous people of the area were also the descendants of the Book of Mormon people as well as the Native Americans of the United States.[7]

For the most part, the Latin Americans who have joined the LDS Church since the 1960s follow church instructions and stay in their homelands to build the church there. Anthropologist David Knowlton noted third-generation Mormons in Argentina. At the same time, he said that the Mormon Church is not well known in the area or is seen as non-Christian.[8] With this negative response and with a lingering desire to be with other Latter-day Saints, some Mormons ignore the LDS Church leaders' advice to stay at home and instead immigrate to the United States. Besides religious motivations, they also come for educational and economic benefits. It is mainly religion, though, that draws them to Utah rather than to other parts of the United States.

These faithful Latter-day Saint immigrants feel a desire to share the Mormon message with other Latinos who come to the United States for economic and social reasons. The LDS Church leaders also send Spanish-speaking missionaries throughout the United States to proselytize. As a result, non-Mormon immigrants are joining the LDS Church. Latina historian Arlene Sanchez Walsh explains that Mexican Americans are joining Protestant and other churches including the Mormons, Jehovah's Witnesses, and Seventh-day Adventists. She adds that the Mormons have "managed to attract significant proportions of U.S. Latinos" partially because of "a special interest in Latinos for theological reasons."[9]

LDS Church Immigration Policies

The LDS Church's view of immigrants, especially from South America, has not always been as favorable, though. In many ways LDS immigration history mirrors United States policies. In 1830, the church was organized in America, and in the beginning, church leaders encouraged new members either from the United States or northern Europe and England to come to church headquarters in Ohio, Missouri, Illinois, and then Utah. The members felt strength in numbers, but they also gathered to receive saving ordinances in the temples that were only in Utah.

But just as the United States government policy toward immigrants changed over the years, so did the LDS Church leaders' views. In the 1890s leaders started to encourage new members to stay in their home countries and strengthen the church there. As historians James B. Allen and Glen Leonard explain, "The colonization era was over, and economic opportunities for immigrants in Utah were becoming more limited. The original purpose of immigration, filling the region with Latter-day Saints so that the kingdom could not be shaken loose again, had been fulfilled." In 1898, George Q. Cannon, a member of the First Presidency, counseled during a church-wide conference "not to be anxious to break up their homes to gather to Zion."[10] Twelve years later, church president Joseph F. Smith became the first president to travel to Europe and encouraged members to stay where they were even though they did not have temples and other church programs.[11]

Despite these instructions, newcomers continued to come. Over time, the church leaders made no official statements for or against the immigration but encouraged members to obey the laws as they migrated to new countries. Leaders often referred to the church's Twelfth Article of Faith, one of thirteen statements of belief penned by church founder Joseph Smith Jr.: "We believe in being subject to kings, presidents, rulers, and magistrates, in obeying, honoring, and sustaining the law."

That view changed in the mid-1970s. While there are no official statements, it is possible to piece together a changing policy toward illegal immigrants. BYU history professor Ignacio Garcia remembered stake and mission leaders in San Antonio, Texas, often did not keep "tight reign" on missionary activities in the 1950s and 1960s. "So we had people being baptized that were undocumented and no eyebrows were raised."[12] In the 1970s, Texas government officials complained that some Mormon missionaries and immigrant converts lacked document papers. As a result, church leaders asked missionaries not to baptize undocumented aliens.[13] If investigators did not have the proper papers, the missionaries asked them to return to Mexico to be baptized.[14]

With this new policy, missionaries in Los Angeles added a new door approach. After explaining they were from the LDS Church, the missionaries asked if the people had green cards. If the people answered no, the missionaries said they were sorry for the interruption and left. That approach changed, though. According to Rafael N. Seminario, church president Spencer W. Kimball sent a letter in 1976 stating that converts no longer had to be legal in a country. He explained, "Our business is to preach the gospel to every nation in the world and . . . we have no business asking for papers."[15]

While the church did not prevent undocumented immigrants from holding church positions, serving missions, and being baptized, its official position toward enforcing immigration laws in the early twenty-first century was that it had "no position." Church leaders explained in a 2006 press release, "The Church, in fact, has made no comment so far on the immigration debate, recognizing that this complex question is now before Congress and is already being thoroughly aired in the public square." In April 2011, church leaders continued to insist they had no position but supported "an omnibus immigration bill that include[d] a Utah-specific guest worker/amnesty position for illegal aliens."[16]

Ronald W. Mortensen argues that the church moved from that neutral view to a call for compassion.[17] In June 2011 the church issued a new statement on immigration with mixed messages. First, the church discouraged "as a matter of policy" members from "entering any country without legal documentations and from deliberately overstaying legal travel visas." But it continued that with the twelve million undocumented workers in the United States, the church's "bedrock moral issue . . . is how we treat each other as children of God. The history of mass expulsion or mistreatment of individuals or families is cause for concern especially where race, culture, or religion are involved. This should give pause to any policy that contemplates targeting any group, particularly if that group comes mostly from one heritage." As a result, "the Church supports an approach where undocumented immigrants are allowed to square themselves with the law and continue to work without this necessarily leading to citizenship."[18]

How did this policy affect Mormons living in Provo without the proper immigration papers? A Redd Center interviewee referred to some of their legal concerns. He, along with other Hispanics in Provo, was worried after the U.S. Immigration and Customs Enforcement (ICE) officials arrested illegal immigrants in December 2006 at six Swift meat-packing facilities in the United States, including one in Hyrum, Utah. Their fears continued when a smaller raid was made at Universal Industrial Sales in Lindon, Utah, closer to Provo, in February 2008.[19] But there were even greater concerns when the Utah State Legislature passed Senate Bill 81 in

March 2008 that required the government and other employers to check immigration status and not to hire those in the country illegally starting in July 2009.[20]

When he was interviewed in late 2009, this interviewee explained, "For the Hispanics it was in the year 2009 when many of us lived in fear, in desperation, in that state of anguish." He wondered, "What is going to happen? Are they going to take us away or exterminate us like *cucarachas*? Is the police really going to put into effect the laws?" His tension and anxiety built as the enforcement date loomed closer. "Since it was heard that July 1, 2009, was the date when the law was to be put in place, the LDS ward diminished significantly." In October he said, "The benches are empty." The new law going into effect "was a reality that we couldn't hide. The members left because they were illegal, period. They were scared because there isn't tolerance towards diversity. Many members felt affected by this law and decided to leave." In the end, the fears were ungrounded. Using an E-Verify system provided by the Department of Homeland Security, a *Deseret News* reporter found that "only 17 cities, 11 school districts and 5 counties are attempting to obey the law while the rest, more than 300, seem to be ignoring state law."[21]

Even though the law was not enforced, Mormon Hispanics continued to fear deportation. A couple from Mexico explained, "As an immigrant people, the majority of us came illegally. You need to abide by the laws, but on the other hand, you have to survive. You have desires, dreams, and visions. You have a family; you have children." One Hispanic United States citizen asked an attorney before her marriage, "What happens when an illegal Mexican marries an American?" She recalled, "The lawyer told me that for the moment it's a difficult situation and that nothing could be done." With stricter regulations regarding illegal immigration, she felt it was harder to gain citizenship. Her husband did not have a visa, and she lamented, "For the moment we aren't in an economic situation to begin the legal process." While the interviews were conducted in 2009, there is evidence that the fear remains as two local Mormon leaders were deported in June 2011.[22]

One reason that the church has shifted its views of immigration is a change in the Mormon view of Americanization. During much of the nineteenth century, Mormon newcomers were a part of the American melting pot. They were to learn English and to assimilate into the predominant culture. Initially, the church offered non-English language congregations, but the members were expected to also attend English-speaking meetings in the geographical ward (congregation). There they interacted with their neighbors, practiced English, and learned church procedures. The ward was the main building block for developing a Mormon community.[23]

The melting pot ideal started to vanish as early as the 1920s in the LDS Church. The first Mexican Mormons came to Salt Lake City in 1919 and 1920 after the LDS Church leaders had encouraged members to stay in their own country. But the newcomers, three sisters and their husbands, held Spanish-language church meetings in a local store. As more Hispanics arrived, the church leaders recognized a need to serve these members and convert others. Consequently, they formed a Mexican branch (a smaller unit than a ward) in 1925. As more Spanish-speakers from Central and South America came to Utah, the name of the branch was changed to Lucero, meaning Star of the Morning in Spanish but also in honor of Rey Lucero Pratt, an early mission president in Mexico and missionary in Latin America. By 1959, the branch was large enough to be a ward.[24]

The Lucero Branch/Ward was different than other ethnic congregations. The members did not attend a geographical ward; they only attended the Spanish-speaking unit. It was also the only ethnic congregation that was not dissolved during World War II, probably because members were from the western hemisphere and could not be seen as supporting the enemy. When church leaders created a Salt Lake Valley Regional Mission after World War II, they formed two additional Spanish-speaking branches, the Cumorah and the Helaman, in southern Salt Lake Valley along with other non-English branches.[25]

In 1960, church leaders formed the first Spanish-speaking congregation in Provo, Utah. The members were local residents and Brigham Young University students. Initially, there were so few Spanish speakers that the congregation was a dependent branch (a smaller congregation that received support from a ward). But it quickly grew into an independent branch. By 1981 there were enough members for the branch to become a fully functioning ward. These wards continued to function despite efforts by some church leaders to eliminate language units in the 1960s and 1970s and again in the 1990s.[26] While creating new wards does require approval from the church's First Presidency, the leaders recognize the advantages of people worshipping in the language of their heart. A 2008 map shows many non-English language wards in Utah. The number continued to grow. There were thirty-five Spanish-speaking units just in Provo and the surrounding communities in Utah Valley in 2011.

Spanish-Speaking Wards in Southwest Provo

Two of those Spanish-speaking wards were in southwest Provo where the Redd Center interviewees lived. The first Mormons who came to Utah Valley settled near where Brigham Young designated Provo's city center and spread out from there. The southwest part was a working-class area, especially after the railroad depot was built in 1911. Between 1905 and 1959, one-third to one-half of the residents in the current Franklin neighborhood (named after the elementary school in the area) were laborers. Over the years these residents aged, so by the 1960s a quarter to a third were retired or widows. As BYU grew after World War II, so did the number of students in Provo and more settled in the area two miles from campus. In 1971, 21 percent were full-time students (representing 50 percent of the residents younger than thirty).[27]

More changes came in the 1980s south of the railroad tracks. The farms, vacant land, and trailer courts were replaced by townhomes, apartments, and the Provo Towne Centre Mall. The Meadow Apartments complex was a major development. It expanded to Pebble Creek and later became Boulder Apartments with federal funds. In this complex, 386 of the 390 units are mandated by law to be rented exclusively to families who earn below 50 percent of the median income of the county, and most of the residents are on welfare assistance.[28] With these changes, this working-class neighborhood continues to be one of the poorest in Provo. BYU education professor A. LeGrand Richards used block information from the 2000 census to determine the neighborhood's demographics. The average median family income was under $30,000. Over 60 percent of the residents had moved in within the last year. Over 60 percent of the homes were rentals. Most of the city's 950 government rental subsidies and 350 public housing projects were in southwest Provo. According to 1998 figures, that area had the highest number of violent crimes. In 2000, some 75 percent of the children came from low-income families. The 2010 census shows that home costs and rent are lower in the area.[29]

Because of lower rent, Hispanic newcomers became part of this constantly changing community. In 1990, no neighborhood in Provo had over 30 percent Hispanic residents. By the year 2000, between 30 and 35 percent of the residents in parts of southwest Provo were Hispanic. For some census blocks, 50 percent of the households spoke a language other than English at home. The 2010 census shows similar trends. Hispanics represented 13.8 percent of the total Provo population that year. However, 21.2 percent in the 84601 zip code that includes southwest Provo were Hispanic, the highest percentage in the three Provo zip codes.[30]

Hispanic Perceptions of Southwest Provo

The interviewees have mixed feelings about living in southwest Provo. The curriculum specialist for the ESL (English as a Second Language) program in the Provo School District explained, "Many [non-English] people choose/have to choose Southwest Provo because that's what they can afford or that's what was available," adding, "many would rather not be there."[31] According to Richards, who is also president of the Provo South Stake, almost half of the residents in the census district that he and Jessie Embry live in were Hispanic in 2011. He explained that the Hispanics were attracted by the lower rents but also because they wanted to be near other Hispanics. Just as ethnic groups formed Chinatowns and Greektowns when immigrants first arrived in the United States, the Spanish-speaking immigrants wanted to be near people with similar cultural backgrounds.[32]

A couple from Puerto Rico moved to the South Provo "just by chance" because their daughter lived there. A Mormon convert from Guatemala liked living there although drug use in the area scared her. A Mexican convert felt this drug use was a bad influence for children. A couple from Mexico feared arrest because they had darker skin and black hair and the husband was undocumented. A Bolivian woman shared, "South Provo area isn't very ideal for me, but that's how I could begin." A Mexican agreed, "We were looking for an apartment. The last area that we wanted to live was down in Provo because it's kind of a ghetto as you can see. But we found this place that was within our means and we could afford to pay the rent. It wasn't the nicest area in Provo, but it's okay. We've been fine. It's a little dirty outside and noisy with the railroad track and train, but other than that, everything's cool. We had to live here out of necessity."

Although some of the interviewees dislike living in the area, they feel a kinship with other Spanish-speaking people. One couple explained, "We practically only mingle with the Hispanics because we mostly just speak Spanish." One woman admitted that she hadn't "put a lot of effort to learn" English. "I am thankful because I have found a lot of people that have been good to me and I have found even Americans that like to speak Spanish."

The interviewees especially enjoyed worshipping with other Hispanics. Their wards have the same organization of the geographical wards in the area. There are three hundred to four hundred members. The leader of the ward, a bishop, is assisted by two counselors and directs a complex organization of priesthood quorums, a woman's organization (the Relief Society), teenage organizations (Young Men and Young Women), and a children's organization (Primary). Each of these suborganizations has a president and two counselors who supervise teachers and advisors. The ward members meet together for worship and social activities. According to historian Douglas D. Alder, these wards were more than a place where people go to "hear a preacher," but they were not separate units like a monastery.[33] The ward provides an opportunity for people from all walks of life to work together on service projects, staff a congregation, pray, and socialize. Meeting together on Sunday, visiting informally and formally, and attending holiday parties give most Mormons a sense of closeness in their wards that is sometimes referred to as a ward family.

Some interviewees recognize these common elements. A Bolivian who joined the church in the United States felt, "Each ward is the same; the Spirit [of God] is there." A Guatemalan woman who served as the East Bay Second Ward Relief Society president said, "The Spanish wards are like any other ward, normal. You always have a few friends apart from being members of the Church, they become like family. Other members are just members and brothers and sisters in the ward and you don't get to develop a deep friendship like with others."

There are some cultural differences that Hispanics bring to the Mormon Church as they do to other religions. Justo L. Gonzalez explains that a Catholic mass "has become a very significant and enriching worship experience for those who participate" in Spanish. The mass might include mariachis and dancers. While the Spanish and English LDS services would not differ as much, there is, as the example explains above, "much that reminds you of the bembe: the rhythm, the noise, the willingness to release oneself to the consciousness of the group."[34]

A comparison of Spanish and English ward Sunday worship services shows some of the differences. The format in most English geographical wards is very similar. Members arrive barely on time. (There are jokes that Mormon standard time is fifteen minutes late.) Mormon missionaries are often noted for shaking hands, and Mormons in general often use this form of greeting. Sometimes members also hug friends. During sacrament meeting, the members usually sit quietly as the bishop or one of the counselors conducts the meeting. On the first Sunday of the month, members are invited to come fasting and to share their feelings about the church and the gospel extemporaneously. On the other Sundays, members of the congregation are invited to give talks. During the Sunday school hours, members teach lessons similar to school classes. Often the teachers ask for participation, but members raise their hands and wait to be called on before participating. The same arrangement takes place during the third hour, but the men and women meet separately. During the time between the sacrament meeting and the other classes, members visit with each other, but that visiting normally stops at the appointed time to start the meeting. Almost immediately after the closing prayer, members leave for their homes.

The Spanish-speaking ward often brings in Latin culture that differs from the English-speaking Provo ward. As in a geographical ward, Latino Mormons often arrive late. But unlike the English-speaking ward, the meeting does not always start exactly on time. Members greet each other with the traditional kiss on the cheek or *saludo* and chatter during Sunday school lessons about the week's activities. Those commenting on the lessons finish each other's sentences and openly share their insights without waiting for permission to speak. After the meetings are over, many members linger and visit with friends. The worship services become a social event.

A couple from Mexico recognized these differences and explained, "Latinos are very open and we always greet each other and we like to show our feelings. The American wards are a little less, because of their culture. Learning to understand that at first was a little difficult." Another Mexican agreed, "An Anglo is somewhat colder, more than anything because of their personality." An older gentleman from Peru commented, "We are a lot more sensitive, we like to cry a little, we like to chat, we like to tell our stories, our adventures. Not the gringos. For the gringos, everything is direct. In many instances, the division between different groups goes beyond the language barrier."

Ward socials are also different. Geographical wards have traditional parties for holidays such as Valentine's Day, Halloween, and Christmas. There might be an occasional additional program to bring people together. For example, one ward sponsors a monthly "Sunday Sundae" to encourage members to meet and greet outside of the regular meetings. Food is essential. There is not a standard menu, but ham and "funeral potatoes," a cheesy dish often served at a lunch after a funeral, are common. It is always possible that neighbors who do not attend worship services might come. But members of one ward would not attend another ward's party. Other than these parties, the ward members rarely get together to socialize, except with friends. The Spanish-speaking ward is more inclusive. A Mexican commented that Americans are "just polite, they are nice, but that's it. To be included in their circle of daily life is not that easy."

A Spanish ward party takes a great deal of planning. For example, one week the women in Relief Society organized a potluck dinner. They reached a common understanding as to what food to bring when they realized the items were at Rancho Market. They stressed the importance of following through with the food assignments to ensure there would be enough to go around for everybody. It was impossible to tell how many people might show up to a party, but it would not be limited to the ward boundaries. The food served was often from Latin America. One Mexican couple said, "There is always food too, to remember our culture, tamales, carnitas." The early Spanish-speaking wards in Salt Lake City and Provo often held a Noche Latino. The interviewees talk about a similar party that they called Night of the Nations "where every member of the ward, depending on the country where they're from, had the opportunity to bring their customary plate [and] present their culture." This was a celebration of diversity. "Everyone is happy because you can eat from all over Latin America."

Many interviewees saw music and dancing as also essential for a good social. A couple from Mexico said socials "are very animated. We always have music. We love to dance in our ward." In a typical Latino neighborhood or social event, it is common to hear a variety of Latino music genres such as mariachi and salsa. According to a study of Latino dance, these traditions "make a powerful statement of ethnic pride that can help to increase communal feelings among participants."[35] This is also true within Mormon Spanish-speaking wards.

Perceptions of Spanish-Speaking Mormons in South Provo

These worship and social differences are on the surface, but they reflect deeper cultural concerns that sometimes lead to misunderstandings. The interviewees suggest that they see concurrent circles where there is the larger Provo community, the Latin community, and the Mormon community. For the non-Hispanic population, they see separate circles: the larger Provo community, the European American community, the Mormon community, and the Hispanic community. Because of the large number of Mormons in Provo, some interviewees see the European-American community and the Mormon community as the same. However, the European-American Mormons see a distinct difference between their experiences as European Americans and as Mormons, especially in activities such as employment that they do not see as religion-based.

One Peruvian's experience shows that difference. He recalled facing discrimination from his supervisor, an older Mormon American woman, at a factory job. He explained, "From the moment that she saw me, she put me in the worse jobs." Apart from these injustices within the workplace, she did not evaluate this Hispanic worker to receive bonuses. Eventually he decided to quit and invited all of his coworkers, including the supervisor, to dinner as a way to express appreciation and to establish closure. At the dinner, his supervisor explained to him that she had intentionally treated him poorly because she wanted him to quit. The Peruvian felt he would receive better treatment from a fellow church member. The supervisor, however, drew a clear line dividing work and religion.

In a Mormon setting, however, the Latinos and Latinas see their neighborhood in completely separate circles. Since they mainly worship with Spanish-speaking Mormons, they focus on those relationships. They occasionally overlap with their non-Hispanic neighbors who are Mormons in the neighborhood and at church, but these relationships are not as strong as they are within their wards. Part of this is related to the language differences, but part is also related to the Mormon concept of wards. For most Utah Mormons, wards are geographical boundaries where they focus their religious and some of their social activities. The focus on these and family can cause close neighbors to lose contact with each other when ward boundaries place them in separate wards.

Those in geographical wards often do not see the differences in the Spanish-speaking ward. They assume that everyone is the same because they speak the same language. For those on the outside who are unfamiliar with the cultural diversity within Latin America, the Spanish wards probably look like a typical ward, except they speak Spanish and have Latin American activities. But the ward members have many backgrounds. One man saw the ward as "a variety of cultures. It's like grabbing a handful of multi-colored confetti, with all different sounds in the same Spanish language."

Because of the cultural diversity, there are occasionally misunderstandings. A woman from Mexico had to be careful what words she used because in some countries they were offensive. She continued, "I had to be more patient. Even though they speak Spanish, sometimes they have different ideas because of the countries where they grew up." Another couple commented that because they share a common language that doesn't mean it represents one country. There are a lot of different cultures that speak Spanish. They explained, "Many times in daily life you do things that probably bother other people because in their culture it's looked down on." These differences can be found within an English-speaking congregation but would be based on family cultures rather than regional or national boundaries.

Some Spanish-speaking Mormons welcome the cultural differences. One person commented, "I feel very good being surrounded by people of my own language. Even though we are not from the same culture, we are from the same belief and there are good people and I feel very good." These are examples of how people are able to form meaningful relationships despite communication and cultural differences.

The Spanish-speaking wards are not completely separate from the geographical wards in two ways. First, they share a church building with English-speaking wards. When the interviews were conducted in 2009, the Spanish-speaking Freedom First Ward shared a building with two English-speaking wards. The East Bay Second Ward shared another building with an English ward and a ward for single adults (ages eighteen to thirty) who communicated in English, Spanish, and American Sign Language. Members of all groups coordinated to clean the building as well as to open and close the meetinghouse for activities. One member from Mexico said, "In the church where we go, there is an American ward and then us. It was good because we would cross ways in the hall. Even though many times we don't know each other, the members stop and try to say hello and ask us where we are from and what is your name and if we have kids, so that makes me happy."

Several interviewees said with some effort on their part they were able to get along. They made sure to greet each other. One young man from Mexico who first started attending an English ward but then moved to a Spanish ward explained, "At first, when interacting with English speakers, I felt restrained and didn't have a good opportunity to interact with them. [But] they welcomed me and I could feel the love that they share with people, independent of where they are from." He continued, "Americans are very friendly, always smiling. They try to teach and support those who don't know the culture or who are learning the language."

Others sensed more serious problems when interacting with Americans and trying to establish friendly relations with them in the meetinghouse. A man from Venezuela said, "I don't believe I would dare attend an American ward unless someone forced me to attend a ward in English." One couple suggested why. They said they felt they had "good relationships" with the English-speaking wards in the buildings but added that the Anglo Americans got "a little irritated." She went on, "There are some times when, for example, it's our turn to do some sort of activity and sometimes we don't come to an agreement." While she did not explain the activity, possibilities are louder parties and more people. She felt that the irritation was "just temporary." She rationalized, "We think that even though we don't socialize with the American wards, we know they are good members."

The Spanish wards are also members of a stake. There are twelve wards in the Provo South Stake that has geographical boundaries. In Provo, Utah, where there are many Mormons, the Provo South Stake covers about two square miles. Eight of the twelve wards in the stake are English speaking. The two Spanish-speaking units cover the same stake area but overlay the English-speaking wards' boundaries. The stake also has the Utah Valley Deaf Ward and the Franklin Second Ward for Native Americans which cover a much larger geographical area. Most stakes with Spanish-speaking wards have only one ward for the entire stake, but since there are so many Hispanics in south Provo, the ward was split.

For the most part, the stake supports the ward leaders. But it also sponsors occasional worship services and activities that bring all the members together. It does not attempt to provide the closeness of a ward family, but some members do talk about a stake family and hope the larger group can provide spiritual and social assistance. The stake holds conferences twice a year that include a priesthood leadership meeting, an adult meeting, and a Sunday morning worship service that replaces the regular ward meetings. Since members speak three languages—Spanish, English, and American

Sign Language—conferences are a challenge. The Provo South Stake has used two options. One is to have a translator speak through a sound system and those speaking one language, usually the minority language, wear headsets. The second is to have a translator stand next to the speaker and repeat phrases. This takes twice as long to deliver a talk but it usually happens when the talk is in the minority language since there are not enough headsets for all those in the congregation. The stake leaders often have someone speak in Spanish and sing a song in that language.

For example, at one adult session of stake conference there were plenty of headsets given out to those in attendance who needed them. But only twenty out of a congregation of about two hundred were Latinos and used a headset. For the general sessions, there were not always enough headsets. A couple from Mexico said that one time the stake ran out of headsets, so they had to share one in order to understand bits and pieces of the talks given. They felt they had to rush to every stake conference to make sure they got there early enough to get headsets. As a result, one woman from Mexico said that the leaders "try to accommodate Spanish speakers with earphones because of the language barrier, but sometimes they don't have enough. Consequently, many people become irritated and ask, 'Why should I go if I don't understand?'"

Other stake activities present more of a challenge than the conferences. At first the meetings were only in English. One member from Argentina said that she felt "a little lost" because of the lack of translators. But over time the stake has improved. She continued, "Something good now is that there are translators when there is some stake activity." But there were still problems. A special Boy Scout Eagle Court of Honor was held for eight Hispanic young men. Many people were invited from the stake to attend because it was a unique situation to see eight Hispanic youth receive their Eagles. The meeting was originally planned to be in Spanish with translation for the English speakers. However, the majority in attendance spoke English, so only the main welcome was given in Spanish. As a result, the Spanish speakers slowly trickled out of the meeting because they simply didn't understand.

There were even more problems at casual stake socials. The stake Relief Society often held a dinner for all the women before a broadcast of a general church women's meeting. Most women saved seats and sat with friends from their ward. English and Spanish speakers both found it difficult to cross language boundaries. Both could say hello in the others' language, but after that the conversation was over. A Relief Society president from Guatemala noted that the stake Relief Society also had an activity every month, but it was only in English. The majority of the older women in her Spanish-speaking ward didn't speak English so hardly anyone attended.

A stake Pioneer Day celebration also struggled with language and cultural barriers. Most English-speaking members ate dinner and then left. Spanish speakers found nothing to celebrate. One year, those in charge tried to encourage people to stay by playing Mexican-style music. However, few Spanish speakers had come to the dinner and the music was quite loud and difficult to listen to for the older English speakers. In 2012 the stake leaders asked the Spanish wards to provide a breakfast for Pioneer Day. The Hispanics served breakfast burritos. This multicultural approach matched what LDS Church leaders mention when discussing Pioneer Day. The celebration has moved from commemorating Brigham Young's entrance into the Salt Lake Valley to a celebration of all who are pioneers in their families, nations, and culture.

Once the stake sponsored a Hispanic Cultural Fest that all members were invited to attend. It was a memorable event that showcased different Latin American countries, their food, culture, and dance. The activity was scheduled to start at seven o'clock in the evening but began officially about half past the hour. People came in and socialized amiably and offered each other cookies as they waited. Everyone clapped and cheered and enjoyed themselves despite delays. Following the scheduled program, there was a social dance. Most stayed after and moved to the rhythms of salsa, bachata, merengue, and cumbia. One interviewee recalled that the stake "brought a mariachi band." For the Spanish speakers, it gave their children a chance to "understand and value their own native culture." However, just as few Spanish speakers attended many stake activities, few English speakers came to the cultural fest.

For all these activities, language was the major barrier. When Spanish-speaking people did attend stake meetings, they usually sat together. One man explained, "Latinos always polarize together; at meetings we all go to the same bench." When he suggested that they "sit next to the gringos too," the people told him, "No, we feel the Spirit warmer with us." A Mexican agreed, "It's funny because when there's a stake activity, it would be logical to make friends with the other members," but he noted, "Latinos all group together in a corner."

While all of the Spanish-speaking Mormons live in the same area, they do not have an ethnic enclave where they are completely separated from the English-speaking Mormons. Although they are neighbors, communication is a struggle. The English-speaking stake Relief Society president sighed when she said that she tried to say hello but could not communicate beyond that. But some Spanish speakers felt close. One couple commented, "We have always known the neighbors. Most neighbors are older, they speak well of us, treat us well, are friendly. They ask us how we are doing when we're outside and they say hello." A woman from Bolivia said that at church "if I know them and if there is time, then I talk with them." A woman from Mexico said, "We [as neighbors] say hello to each other. I don't think they make many friendships because since I'm Hispanic, many think that I'm not going to understand them. Nonetheless, the neighbor that is closest to me sends her daughter to visit with my granddaughter or she'll invite my granddaughter to go play with her." Yet despite these interactions, she concluded, "No, we don't have many friendships here."

Cultural misunderstandings lead to this lack of friendship. One man was surprised how some European Americans did not know geography. "There are a lot of gringos that don't know anything outside of Utah." Some would ask him, "What part of Mexico is Trujillo? Where is Peru?" He continued, "I tell them, 'Peru is in South America, further down. Mexico is on this side; they are your neighbors.'" Besides not understanding culture, he felt that the whites "take the ideas of some of the stereotypes of the Latino and they judge you sometimes that all the Latinos are like that." Another person agreed, "Many times the Latino image before an American is very degraded because of other people. Sometimes there is prejudice against us, but we aren't all the same."

As a result, one interviewee feared some Americans treated him as a "dirty" Latino. In the fifteen years he had been in the United States, he explained, "I have always felt a little rejected by the people, including members of the Church. They don't even extend their hand to me or when they turned around they looked as if they were looking for something, not acknowledging my presence. They didn't say hello." Consequently, the lack of interaction made him conclude: "They judged me." Prejudice, prejudgment, ignorance, and shallow interactions have made Hispanics feel second-class and have hindered the development of meaningful relationships.

While some interviewees were fixated on cultural and language differences, others felt a need to become a part of the overall Provo Mormon community. One man felt that within his ward there was a focus on learning English and there was an excellent English teacher. One man from Mexico felt coming to the United States to get a better education and learn English was just a "wild dream." But he added, "I've been living here for a long time and I speak the language. I feel comfortable." This individual made the effort to become a part of the community and adopt a new language and lifestyle and make south Provo his home.

Another Mexican went out of her way to become a part of the American community. She "decided to attend the American ward so I could learn and know the people and the culture. I also really wanted them to know me and my kids." A woman from Guatemala who had been living in Utah for thirty years shared, "I like to visit Guatemala but not live there because I am from here." Another woman from Mexico said after living in the United States for more than seven years, "I adapted very quickly to the life here in Provo." These interviewees were able to claim Provo as their home to the degree that they were invested in living in this area. Such assimilation does not disqualify their own nationality and identity, but it does help them feel a greater sense of belonging.

Summary

In June 2011, LDS Church leaders issued a call for tolerance toward those who do not feel they belong. "The First Presidency has for many years taught that undocumented status should not by itself prevent an otherwise worthy Church member from entering the temple or being ordained to the priesthood." Since local church leaders determine worthiness issues, the statement continued, "Church members should avoid making judgments about fellow members in their congregations."[36] While this comment is about illegal immigrants, it also says a lot about how the Mormon Church's views toward immigration have changed over the years. In the nineteenth century, Mormon immigrants to Utah were expected to become English-speaking Americans. In the twentieth century, church leaders discouraged but did not prevent immigration. Those who came were still expected to learn the language. But just as the United States has moved from a melting pot to a salad bowl approach to newcomers, so has the LDS Church focused more on diversity. The Spanish wards are a good example of that willingness to allow differences in language and culture.[37]

Usually the story of immigration is told from a church administrative point of view. By talking to the Spanish-speaking Mormon residents of Provo, it is possible to create a more complete picture of what happens in the salad bowl. These examples show that the interviewees have mixed experiences in southwest Provo. They are very grateful for a place to worship in their native language, but they recognize that although they share the same language, there are cultural differences. Those differences are not as great as those with their English-speaking neighbors. Their expectations that those interactions will be easier with other Mormons are not always realized. They especially sense negative views if they are considered illegal immigrants.

These expectations are not realized because not all Utah Mormons have adopted the salad bowl perspective of immigration. One couple said, "I have heard people complain about the Church, complain about the rudeness of the members, of the people in Utah, the habitants of Utah, the children of the pioneers." This couple believed they would receive better treatment from Mormons because they share a religious belief and because many of the Mormons came from immigrant families. But many residents of Utah feel that since their ancestors adapted, the Hispanics should as well. These debates will not be easily resolved because the perceptions are so firmly rooted. This article gives place to the Spanish speakerss' voices that have often been left out of that discussion.

Notes

1. Jessie L. Embry, *In His Own Language: Mormon Spanish-Speaking Congregations in the United States* (Provo, UT: Charles Redd Center for Western Studies, 1997; Spanish ed., 2007) is based on these interviews.
2. Jessie L. Embry and A. LeGrand Richards, "A Year in the Life of the Provo Utah South Stake, 2008–2009," in *A Firm Foundation: Essays on the Administrative and Organizational History of the LDS Church*, ed. David J. Whittaker and Arnold K. Garr (Provo, UT: Religious Studies Center, Brigham Young University, 2010), 533–51, uses these interviews. All the interviews are housed in the L. Tom Perry Special Collections, Harold B. Lee Library, Brigham Young University. To protect confidentiality, the names of the interviewees are not included in this paper.
3. This was the same outline used for interviews for other ethnic Mormons including LDS African Americans, LDS Asian Americans, LDS Native Americans, and LDS Polynesian Americans.
4. Quoted in Mark L. Grover, "The Miracle of the Rose and the Oak in Latin America," in *Out of Obscurity: The LDS Church in the Twentieth Century, 29th Sperry Symposium* (Salt Lake City: Deseret Book, 2000), 143–44.
5. Hector Avalos, "Conclusion," in Avalos, *Introduction to the U.S. Latina and Latino Religious Experience* (Boston: Brill Academic Publishers, Inc., 2004), 306.
6. Grover, "The Miracle," 144.
7. Mark L. Grover, "South America," in *Mapping Mormonism: An Atlas of Latter-day Saint History*, ed. Brandon S. Plewe et al. (Provo, UT: BYU Press, 2012), 222. For more information on the LDS Church's growth in Latin America, see the articles in *Mapping Mormonism*. According to the article on "Middle America" by Grover and Mormon Mexican historian Fernando R. Gomez, Mexico and Central America constitute one of the strongest areas of the church. The map shows that between 2 and 3 percent of the population in some areas in Guatemala and Honduras and 10 percent of the population in Santa Ana, El Salvador, are Mormons (220–21). The percentages are even more dramatic when looking at Mormon population numbers. According to geographer Samuel M. Otterstrom in his article on "Membership Distribution" in the same volume, 71 percent of the non-U.S. Mormon population lives south of the United States (174). For information on why Latin Americans join the LDS Church, see Mark L. Grover, "The Maturing of the Oak: The Dynamics of the LDS Growth in Latin America," *Dialogue: A Journal of Mormon Thought* 38, no. 2 (Summer 2005): 79–104; and David Clark Knowlton, "Thoughts on Mormonism in Latin America," *Dialogue: A Journal of Mormon Thought* 25, no. 2 (Summer 1992): 41–53. Grover and Knowlton

agree that Latin Americans join the LDS Church because the church represents a change to the middle class, provides lay leadership opportunities, promotes education, and encourages gifts of the spirit. However, Grover looks at the conversions as having more spiritual conviction. Both agree that the LDS Church membership numbers are inflated since many Latin Americans do not continue to attend the LDS Church after they are baptized.

8. Knowlton, "Thoughts on Mormonism in Latin America," 42.
9. Arlene Sanchez Walsh, "The Mexican American Religious Experience," in Avalos, *Introduction to the U.S. Latina and Latino Religious Experience*, 38–39. Other studies suggest that some immigrants were leaving the Catholic Church because it did not meet the needs of Hispanic Americans. Historian Dolores Liptak charged in 1989, "American Catholic leaders were not inclined to recognize the many cultural and spiritual gifts of Hispanic Americans or value their contributions to the American Catholic Church." However, when the Hispanics started to join other churches, local dioceses studied the problem. Dolores Liptak, *Immigrants and Their Church* (New York: Macmillan, 1989), 189. Catholic historian Jay P. Dolan expressed the same fear: "All of . . . the Church should broaden the embrace with which we greet our Hispanic brothers and sisters and deepen our commitment to them. If we do not, then it is certain that the number of Hispanic Catholics will dwindle in the years ahead." Jay P. Dolan, "Conclusion," *Hispanic Catholic Culture in the U.S.: Issues and Concerns*, ed. Allan Figueroa Deck, S.J., and Jay P. Dolan (Notre Dame, IN: University of Notre Dame Press, 1994), 455.
10. James B. Allen and Glen Leonard, *Story of the Latter-day Saints* (Salt Lake City: Deseret Book, 1992), 426–27.
11. Ibid., 471.
12. Ignacio Garcia email to Jessie Embry, October 7, 2011.
13. Chad M. Orton, *More Faith than Fear: The Los Angeles Stake Story* (Salt Lake City: Bookcraft, 1987), 293–94.
14. Ignacio Garcia email to Jessie Embry, October 7, 2011.
15. Rafael N. Seminario Oral History, interviewed by Chad Orton, 1986, LDS Church History Library, 15. Ignacio Garcia expressed similar views. Ignacio Garcia email to Jessie Embry, October 7, 2011. A former bishop in Utah Valley and a member of the Provo Utah South stake presidency said there had not been a policy against teaching and baptizing undocumented immigrants since 1975. He recalled some people mentioning a policy before 1975, but he did not know the source. Victor Rodriguez email to A. LeGrand Richards, May 18, 2011.
16. Ronald W. Mortensen, *The Mormon Church and Illegal Immigration* (Washington, DC: Center for Immigration Studies, 2011), 5, http://www.cis.org/sites/cis.org/files/articles/2011/lds-and-immigration.pdf.
17. Ibid.
18. "Immigration: Church Issues New Statement," http://newsroom.lds.org/article/immigration-church-issues-new-statement.
19. Deborah Bulkeley and Bruce Wallace, "Utah Plant Caught in a Multi-state Immigration Raid," *Deseret News*, December 13, 2006; Linda Thomas and Deborah Bulkeley, "15 Mexican Citizens Are Indicted," *Deseret News*, December 21, 2006; Grace Leong, "Lindon Raid: 30 People May Face Criminal Charges," *Provo Daily Herald*, February 13, 2008.

20. Brock Vergakis, "House OKs Immigration Overhaul," *Provo Daily Herald*, March 3, 2008; "Immigration Bills Passed in Utah," *Provo Daily Herald*, April 16, 2009.
21. Gaylan Stewart, "Ignoring State Laws," *Deseret News*, November 29, 2009.
22. Marjorie Cortez, "2 LDS Branch Presidents in Utah Deported to Guatemala, El Salvador," *Deseret News*, June 15, 2011.
23. Richard L. Jensen, "Mother Tongue: Use of Non-English Languages in the Church of Jesus Christ of Latter-day Saints in the United States, 1850–1983," in *New Views of Mormon History: A Collection of Essays in Honor of Leonard J. Arrington*, ed. Davis Bitton and Maureen Ursenbach Beecher (Salt Lake City: University of Utah Press, 1987), 276–77. See Jessie L. Embry, *Mormon Wards as Community* (Binghampton, NY: Global Publications, 2001), for information on the importance of wards in the LDS Church.
24. Embry, *In His Own Language*, 36.
25. These were dissolved in the 1970s along with other ethnic wards and not restarted in 1977.
26. Embry, *In His Own Language*, 63.
27. These figures were obtained by using the Polk City Directory and checking addresses and occupations listed.
28. A. LeGrand Richards and Jessie Embry, personal observations. The Boulder Apartments has its own police station because of the high crime rate. However, special programs have been developed to work with the residents. The Provo South Stake provides service missionaries to the area. The United Way and government agencies also provide help. Meisha Slight worked with a government youth program in the area during the 2012 summer. For more information on the police station, see Justin Hill, "Provo Setting up Police Substation in Apartment Complex," *Provo Daily Herald*, April 16, 2003.
29. These figures came from A. LeGrand Richards and are based on his block-by-block research of the 2000 census. The figures from the 2010 census come from http://provoinformation.com/Provo_Utah_Demographics.htm, and were based on the zip code data for 84601.
30. Ibid.
31. Katie Barlow, "Teaching English in Schools," Brigham Young University, *Daily Universe*, http://byudailyuniverse.com/immigration/.
32. A. LeGrand Richards, personal observations. For more information on ethnic enclaves, see Mark Abrahamson, *Urban Enclaves: Identity and Place in America* (New York: St. Martin's Press, 1996); Arif Dirlik, *Chinese on the American Frontier* (Lanham, MD: Rowman & Littlefield Publishers, Inc., 2001); and George J. Sanchez, *Becoming Mexican American: Ethnicity, Culture, and Identity in Chicano Los Angeles, 1900–1945* (New York: Oxford University Press, 1993).
33. Douglas D. Alder, "The Mormon Ward: Congregation or Community?" *Journal of Mormon History* 5 (1979): 62–63.
34. Justo L. Gonzalez, "The Religious World of Hispanic Americans," in *World Religions in America*, ed. Jacob Neusner (Louisville, KY: Westminster John Knox Press, 2003), 86, 88, 89.
35. Sydney Hutchinson, *From Quebradita to Duranguense: Dance in the Mexican American Youth Culture* (Tucson: University of Arizona Press, 2007), 86.

36. "Responsibility of Church Members: Avoiding Being Judgmental," http://newsroom.lds.org/article/avoiding-being-judgmental-immigration.
37. That is not to say that there were no problems between immigrants and American Mormons in the nineteenth century, as Mindi Sitterud-McCluskey's article in this volume explains. A popular song by Mormon poetess Eliza R. Snow explained, "Think not when you gather to Zion, your troubles and trials are through," and then goes on to explain that there might be trouble even with the Latter-day Saints. (http://www.hoffmanhouse.com/sheet/eliza/ThinkNotBallad.pdf, accessed May 31, 2013). William Mulder's *Homeward to Zion: The Mormon Migration from Scandinavia* (Minneapolis: University of Minnesota Press, 2000) explains that those immigrants from Scandinavian countries who did not adapt left Utah. The twenty-first-century Mormon Church hopes for more tolerance but not all members share that view as the experiences recounted in this article demonstrate.

Selected Bibliography

Acuña, Rodolfo F. *Corridors of Migration: The Odyssey of Mexican Laborers, 1600–1933*. Tucson: University of Arizona Press, 2007.

Alemán, Jesse. "The Other Country: Mexico, the United States, and the Gothic History of Conquest." In *Hemispheric American Studies*, edited by Caroline F. Levander and Robert S. Levine, 75–95. New Brunswick, NJ: Rutgers University Press, 2008.

Almaguer, Tomas. *Racial Fault Lines: The Historical Origins of White Supremacy in California*. Berkeley: University of California Press, 1994, 2008.

Archdeacon, Thomas J. *Becoming American: An Ethnic History*. New York: The Free Press, 1983.

Attebery, Jennifer Eastman. *Up in the Rocky Mountains: Writing the Swedish Immigrant Experience*. Minneapolis: University of Minnesota Press, 2007.

Balderrama, Francisco E., and Raymond Rodríguez. *Decade of Betrayal: Mexican Repatriation in the 1930s*. Albuquerque: University of New Mexico Press, 2006.

Barkan, Elliott R. "America in the Hand, Homeland in the Heart: Transnational and Translocal Immigrant Experiences in the American West." *Western Historical Quarterly* 35, no. 3 (Autumn 2004): 331–54.

Barkan, Elliott Robert. *From All Points: America's Immigrant West, 1870s–1952*. Bloomington: Indiana University Press, 2007.

Barkan, Elliott R., Hasia Diner, and Alan M. Kraut, eds. *From Arrival to Incorporation: Migrants to the U.S. in a Global Era*. New York: New York University Press, 2008.

Barkan, Elazar. *The Retreat of Scientific Racism: Changing Concepts of Race in Britain and the United States between the World Wars*. New York: Cambridge University Press, 1992.

Barth, Gunther. *Bitter Strength: A History of the Chinese in the United States, 1850–1870*. Cambridge, MA: Harvard University Press, 1964.

Bhabha, Homi K. "Unsatisfied: Notes on Vernacular Cosmopolitanism." In *Text and Nation*, ed. Laura Garcia-Morena and Peter C. Pfeifer, 191–207. London: Camden House, 1996.

Bodnar, John. *The Transplanted: A History of Immigrants in Urban America*. Bloomington: Indiana University Press, 1985.

Brettell, Caroline B., and James F. Hollifield. *Migration Theory: Talking Across Disciplines*. New York: Routledge, 2008.

Buchenau, Jürgen. "Small Numbers, Great Impact: Mexico and Its Immigrants, 1821–1973." *Journal of American Ethnic History* 20, no. 2 (Spring 2001): 23–30.

Carnevale, Nancy C. *A New Language, A New World: Italian Immigrants in the United States, 1890–1945*. Urbana: University of Illinois Press, 2009.

Cheng, Lucie, and Edna Bonacich, eds. *Labor Migration under Capitalism: Asian

Workers in the United States before World War II. Berkeley: University of California Press, 1984.

Choate, Mark I. *Emigrant Nation: The Making of Italy Abroad.* Cambridge, MA: Harvard University Press, 2008.

Cinel, Dino. *From Italy to San Francisco: The Immigrant Experience.* Palo Alto: Stanford University Press, 1982.

Clark, William A. V. *The California Cauldron: Immigration and the Fortunes of Local Communities.* New York: Guilford Press, 1998.

Concannon, Kevin, Francisco A. Lomelí, and Marc Priewe, eds. *Imagined Transnationalism: US Latino/a Literature, Culture, and Identity.* New York: Palgrave Macmillan, 2009.

Conzen, Kathleen. "Immigrants, Immigrant Neighborhoods, and Ethnic Identity: Historical Issues." *Journal of American History* 66, no. 3 (December 1979): 603–15.

———. "Mainstreams and Side Channels: The Localization of Immigrant Cultures." *Journal of American Ethnic History* 11, no. 1 (Fall 1991): 5–20.

Daniels, Roger. *Coming to America: A History of Immigration and Ethnicity.* New York: HarperCollins, 1990.

———. *Guarding the Golden Door: American Immigration Policy and Immigrants since 1882.* New York: Hill and Wang, 2004.

Daniels, Roger, and Spencer C. Olin Jr., eds. *Racism in California: A Reader in the History of Oppression.* New York: Macmillan, 1972.

Deutsch, Sarah. *No Separate Refuge: Culture, Class, and Gender on an Anglo-Hispanic Frontier in the American Southwest, 1880–1940.* New York: Oxford University Press, 1989.

Deutsch, Sarah, George J. Sanchez, and Gary Y. Okihiro. "Contemporary People/Contested Places." In *The Oxford History of The American West,* edited by Clyde A. Milner II, Carol A. O'Connor, and Martha A. Sandweiss, 639–69. New York: Oxford University Press, 1994.

Deverell, William Francis, ed. *A Companion to the American West.* Malden, MA: Blackwell Publishing, 2004.

———. *Whitewashed Adobe: The Rise of Los Angeles and the Remaking of Its Mexican Past.* Berkeley: University of California Press, 2004.

Diner, Hasia. "American Immigration and Ethnic History: Moving the Field Forward, Staying the Course." *Journal of American Ethnic History* 25, no. 4 (Summer 2006): 130–41.

du Toit, Brian M. *Boer Settlers in the Southwest.* El Paso: University of Texas at El Paso, 1995.

Embry, Jessie L. *In His Own Language: Mormon Spanish-Speaking Congregations in the United States.* Provo, UT: Charles Redd Center for Western Studies, 1997.

Emmons, David M. *Beyond the American Pale: The Irish in the West, 1845–1910.* Norman: University of Oklahoma Press, 2010.

Etulain, Richard W., and Jeronima Echeverria, eds. *Portraits of Basques in the New World.* Reno: University of Nevada Press, 1999.

Foner, Nancy, Rubén G. Rumbaut, and Steven J. Gold, eds. *Immigration Research for a New Century: Multidisciplinary Perspectives.* New York: Russell Sage Foundation, 2000.

Francaviglia, Richard V. *Go East, Young Man: Imagining the American West as the Orient.* Logan: Utah State University Press, 2011.

Fuchs, Lawrence. *The American Kaleidoscope: Race, Ethnicity and the Civic Culture*. Hanover, NH: University Press of New England, 1990.
Gans, Herbert J. "Symbolic Ethnicity: The Future of Ethnic Groups and Cultures in America." *Ethnic and Racial Studies* 2, no. 1 (1979): 3–5.
Gjerde, Jon. "New Growth on Old Vines: The State of the Field: The Social History of Immigration to and Ethnicity in the United States." *Journal of American Ethnic History* 18, no. 4 (Summer 1999): 40–65.
Goldman, Marion S. *Gold Diggers & Silver Miners: Prostitution and Social Life on the Comstock Lode*. Ann Arbor: University of Michigan Press, 1981.
Gonzalez, Gilbert G., and Raul A. Fernandez. *A Century of Chicano History: Empire, Nation, and Migration*. New York: Routledge, 2003.
Gonzalez, Gilbert, and Vivian Price. *Harvest of Loneliness: The Bracero Program*. New York: Films for the Humanities and Sciences, 2011.
Gordon, Linda. *The Great Arizona Orphan Abduction*. Cambridge, MA: Harvard University Press, 1999.
Hamilton, Nora, and Norma Stolz Chincilla. *Seeking Community in a Global City: Guatemalans and Salvadorans in Los Angeles*. Philadelphia: Temple University Press, 2001.
Hart, John Mason. *Empire and Revolution: The Americans in Mexico since the Civil War*. Berkeley: University of California Press, 2002.
Handlin, Oscar. *The Uprooted: The Epic Story of the Great Migration that Made the American People*. Boston: Little and Brown, 1951.
Haverluk, T. "The Changing Geography of U.S. Hispanics, 1850–1990." *Journal of Geography* 96, no. 3 (May/June 1997): 134–45.
Higham, John. *Strangers in the Land: Patterns of American Nativism 1860–1925*. New Brunswick, NJ: Rutgers University Press, 1955.
Hoerder. Dirk. *Cultures in Contact: World Migrations in the Second Millennium*. Durham, NC: Duke University Press, 2002.
———. "Historians and Their Data: The Complex Shift from Nation-State Approaches to the Study of People's Transcultural Lives." *Journal of American Ethnic History* 25, no. 4 (Summer 2006): 85–96.
Hutchinson, E. P. *Immigrants and Their Children, 1850–1950*. New York: John Wiley & Sons, 1956.
Iber, Jorge, and Arnoldo de Léon. *Hispanics in the American West*. Santa Barbara: ABC Clio, 2006.
Ignatiev, Noel. *How the Irish Became White*. New York: Routledge, 1995.
Jacobson, Matthew Frye. *Whiteness of a Different Color: European Immigrants and the Alchemy of Race*. Cambridge: Harvard University Press, 1998.
James, Ronald M. *The Roar and the Silence: A History of Virginia City and the Comstock Lode*. Reno: University of Nevada Press, 1998.
Jensen, Richard L., and Malcolm R. Thorp, eds. *Mormons in Early Victorian Britain*. Salt Lake City: University of Utah Press, 1989.
Jiobu, Robert M. *Ethnicity & Assimilation: Blacks, Chinese, Filipinos, Japanese, Koreans, Mexicans, Vietnamese, and Whites*. Albany: State University of New York Press, 1988.
Johnson, K. M., and D. T. Lichter. "Natural Increase: A New Source of Population Growth in Emerging Hispanic Destinations in the United States." *Population and Development Review* 24, no. 2 (June 2006): 327–46.
Kanellos, Nicolás. "A Schematic Approach to Understanding Latino Transnational

Literary Texts." In *Imagined Transnationalism: U.S. Latino/a Literature, Culture, and Identity*, edited by Kevin Concannon, Francisco A. Lomelí, and Marc Priewe, 29–46. New York: Palgrave Macmillan, 2009.

King, Desmond S. *Making Americans: Immigration, Race, and the Origins of the Diverse Democracy*. Cambridge, MA: Harvard University Press, 2002.

Kousser, J. Morgan, and James M. McPherson, eds. *Region, Race and Reconstruction: Essays in Honor of C. Vann Woodward*. New York: Oxford University Press, 1982.

Kurashige, Lon. *Japanese American Celebration and Conflict: A History of Ethnic Identity and Festival, 1934–1990*. Berkeley: University of California Press, 2002.

Lay, Shawn, ed. *The Invisible Empire in the West: Toward a New Historical Appraisal of the Ku Klux Klan of the 1920s*. Urbana: University of Illinois Press, 1992.

Lee, Chris. "Sociological Theories of Immigration: Pathways to Integration for U.S. Immigrants." *Journal of Human Behavior in the Social Environment* 19, no. 6 (2009): 730–44.

Lee, Erika. *At America's Gates: Chinese Immigration during the Exclusion Era, 1882–1943*. Chapel Hill: University of North Carolina Press, 2007.

———. "Immigrants and Immigration Law: A State of the Field Assessment." *Journal of American Ethnic History* 18, no. 4 (Summer 1999): 85–114.

Lee, Erika, and Judy Yung. *Angel Island: Immigrant Gateway to America*. New York: Oxford University Press, 2010.

LeMay, Michael C. *From Open Door to Dutch Door: An Analysis of U.S. Immigration Policy since 1820*. New York: Praeger, 1987.

Lewis, Ronald L. *Welsh Americans: A History of Assimilation in the Coalfields*. Chapel Hill: University of North Carolina Press, 2008.

Liaw, K. L., and W. H. Frey. "Multivariate Explanation of the 1985–1990 and 1996–2000 Destination Choices of Newly Arrived Immigrants in the United States: The Beginning of a New Trend?" *Population, Space, and Place* 13, no. 5 (September/October 2007): 377–99.

Limerick, Patricia Nelson. *The Legacy of Conquest: The Unbroken Past of the American West*. New York: W. W. Norton, 1987.

Liptak, Dolores. *Immigrants and Their Church*. New York: Macmillan, 1989.

Logan, J., R. Alba, and W. Zhang. "Immigrant Enclaves and Ethnic Communities in New York and Los Angeles." *American Sociological Review* 67, no. 2 (April 2002): 299–322.

Lowe, Lisa. *Immigrant Acts: On Asian American Cultural Politics*. Durham, NC: Duke University Press, 1996.

Luebke, Frederick C., ed. *European Immigrants in the American West: Community Histories*. Albuquerque: University of New Mexico Press, 1998.

Massey, Douglas S., and Nancy A. Denton. "Spatial Assimilation as a Socioeconomic Outcome." *American Sociological Review* 50, no. 1 (February 1985): 94–106.

Mauss, Armand. *All Abraham's Children: Changing Mormon Conceptions of Race and Lineage*. Urbana: University of Illinois Press, 2003.

May, Dean L. *Three Frontiers: Family, Land, and Society in the American West, 1850–1900*. New York: Cambridge University Press, 1994.

McDonald, Jason. *American Ethnic History: Themes and Perspectives*. New Brunswick, NJ: Rutgers University Press, 2007.

McWilliams, Wilson Carey. *North from Mexico: The Spanish-Speaking People of the United States.* Westport, CT: Greenwood Press, 1968.

Meier, Matt S., and Feliciano Ribera. *Mexican Americans/American Mexicans: From Conquistadors to Chicanos.* New York: Hill and Wang, 1993.

Miller, Kerby A. *Emigrants and Exiles: Ireland and the Irish Exodus to North America.* New York: Oxford University Press, 1985.

Moloney, Dierdre M. *American Catholic Lay Groups and Transatlantic Social Reform in the Progressive Era.* Chapel Hill: University of North Carolina Press, 2002.

Monroy, Douglas. *Thrown among Strangers: The Making of Mexican Culture in Frontier California.* Berkeley: University of California Press, 1990.

Moos, Dan. *Outside America: Race, Ethnicity, and the Role of the American West in National Belonging.* Hanover, NH: Dartmouth College Press, 2005.

Ngai, Mae. *Impossible Subjects: Illegal Aliens and the Making of Modern America.* Princeton, NJ: Princeton University Press, 2004.

Nugent, Walter. *Into the West: The Story of Its People.* New York: A. A. Knopf, 1999.

Nunis, Doyce B. "Alta California's Trojan Horse: Foreign Immigration." In *Contested Eden: California Before the Gold Rush*, edited by Ramón Gutiérrez and Richard J. Orsi, 299–330. Berkeley: University of California Press, 1998.

Omi, Michael, and Howard Winant. *Racial Formation in the United States: From the 1960s to the 1980s.* New York: Routledge, 1986.

Passel, J. S., and W. Zimmermann. "Are Immigrants Leaving California? Settlement Patterns of Immigrants in the Late 1990s." Research Report, Pub. ID#410287. Washington, DC: The Urban Institute, 2001.

Peck, Gunther. *Reinventing Free Labor: Padrones and Immigrant Workers in the North American West, 1880–1930.* New York: Cambridge University Press, 2000.

Penrose, Eldon R. *California Nativism: Organized Opposition to the Japanese, 1890–1913.* San Francisco: R and E Research Associates, 1974.

Pitt, Leonard. *The Decline of the Californios: A Social History of the Spanish-Speaking Californians, 1846–1890.* Berkeley: University of California Press, 1966.

Portes, Alejandro, and Robert L. Bach. *Latin Journey: Cuban and Mexican Immigrants in the United States.* Berkeley: University of California Press, 1985.

Portes, Alejandro, and Rubén G. Rumbaut. *Immigrant America: A Portrait.* 3rd ed. Berkeley: University of California Press, 2006.

Portes, Alejandro, and Min Zhou. "The New Second Generation: Segmented Assimilation and Its Variants among Post-1965 Immigrant Youth." *Annals of the American Academy of Political and Social Science* 530 (November 1993): 74–98.

Rischin, Moses, and John Livingston, eds. *Jews of the American West.* Detroit: Wayne State University Press, 1991.

Roediger, David R. *The Wages of Whiteness: Race and the Making of the American Working Class.* London: Verso, 1991.

———. *Working Toward Whiteness: How America's Immigrants Became White: The Strange Journey from Ellis Island to the Suburbs.* New York: Basic Books, 2006.

Rogin, Michael. *Blackface, White Noise: Jewish Immigrants in the Hollywood Melting Pot.* Berkeley: University of California Press, 1996.

Romo, Ricardo. *East Los Angeles: History of a Barrio*. Austin: University of Texas Press, 1983.

Sanchez, George J. *Becoming Mexican American: Ethnicity, Culture and Identity in Chicano Los Angeles, 1900–1945*. New York: Oxford University Press, 1993.

———. "'Go After the Women': Americanization and the Mexican Immigrant Woman, 1915–1929." In *Unequal Sisters: A Multicultural Reader in U.S. Women's History*, 2nd ed., edited by Vicki L. Ruiz and Ellen Carol DuBois, 250–63. New York: Routledge, 1994.

———. "Race, Nation, and Culture in Recent Immigration Studies." *Journal of American Ethnic History* 18, no. 4 (Summer 1999): 66–84.

Schaefer, Richard T. *Racial and Ethnic Groups*. Boston: Little, Brown, and Co., 1979.

Schiller, Nina Glick, Linda Basch, and Cristina Szanton Blanc. "From Immigrant to Transmigrant: Theorizing Transnational Migration." *Anthropological Quarterly* 68, no. 1 (January 1995): 48–63.

Schiller, Nina Glick, Linda Basch, and Cristina Blanc-Szanton. "Transnationalism: A New Analytic Framework for Understanding Migration." In *Towards a Transnational Perspective on Migration: Race, Class, Ethnicity and Nationalism Reconsidered*, edited by Nina Glick Schiller, Linda Basch, and Cristina Blanc-Szanton, 1–24. New York: New York Academy of Sciences, 1992.

Sirojudin, Siroj. "Economic Theories of Emigration." *Journal of Human Behavior in the Social Environment* 19, no. 6 (2009): 702–12.

Szasz, Ferenc Morton. *Religion in the Modern American West*. Tucson: University of Arizona Press, 2000.

———. *Scots in the North American West, 1790–1917*. Norman: University of Oklahoma Press, 2000.

Takaki, Ronald. *Strangers from a Different Shore: A History of Asian Americans*. Updated and revised. New York: Little, Brown, 1998.

Thistlethwaite, Frank. "Migration from Europe Overseas in the Nineteenth and Twentieth Centuries." In *A Century of European Migrations, 1830–1930*, edited by Rudolph J. Vecoli and Suzanne M. Sinke. Urbana: University of Illinois Press, 1991.

Tichenor, Daniel J. *Dividing Lines: The Politics of Immigration Control in America*. Princeton: Princeton University Press, 2002.

Toll, William. *The Making of an Ethnic Middle Class: Portland Jewry Over Four Generations*. Albany: State University of New York Press, 1982.

Van Nuys, Frank. *Americanizing the West: Race, Immigrants, and Citizenship, 1890–1930*. Lawrence: University Press of Kansas, 2002.

Vecoli, Rudolph J., ed. *Gale Encyclopedia of Multicultural America*. New York: Gale Research Inc., 1995.

———. "Return to the Melting Pot: Ethnicity in the United States in the Eighties." *Journal of American Ethnic History* 5, no. 1 (Fall 1985): 7–20.

Vorspan, Max, and Lloyd P. Gartner. *History of the Jews of Los Angeles*. San Marino, CA: The Huntington Library, 1970.

Warrin, Donald, and Geoffrey L. Gomes. *Land, As Far as the Eye Can See: Portuguese in the Old West*. Spokane, WA: Arthur H. Clark Co., 2001.

Weber, David J. *Myth and the History of the Hispanic Southwest*. Albuquerque: University of New Mexico Press, 1988.

Weeks, J. B. "Who's Crossing the Border: New Data on Undocumented

Immigrants to the United States." *Population, Place, and Space* 17, no. 1 (2010): 1–26.
West, Elliott. *The Saloon on the Rocky Mountain Mining Frontier*. Lincoln: University of Nebraska Press, 1979.
Wild, Mark. *Street Meeting: Multiethnic Neighborhoods in Early Twentieth-Century Los Angeles*. Berkeley: University of California Press, 2008.
Winther, Oscar O. "English Migration to the American West, 1865–1900." *Huntington Library Quarterly* 27, no. 2 (February 1964): 159–73.
Wyman, Mark. *Hoboes: Bindlestiffs, Fruit Tramps, and the Harvesting of the West*. New York: Hill and Wang, 2010.
Yans-McLaughlin, Virginia. *Family and Community: Italian Immigrants in Buffalo, 1880–1930*. Ithaca, NY: Cornell University Press, 1977.
———, ed. *Immigration Reconsidered: History, Sociology, and Politics*. New York: Oxford University Press, 1990.
Yung, Judy. *Unbound Feet: A Social History of Chinese Women in San Francisco*. Berkeley: University of California Press, 1995.
Yung, Judy, Gordon H. Chang, and Him Mark Lai, eds. *Chinese American Voices: From the Gold Rush to the Present*. Berkeley: University of California Press, 2006.
Zhou, Min. "Segmented Assimilation: Issues, Controversies and Recent Research on the New Second Generation." *International Migration Review* 31, no. 4 (Winter 1997): 975–1008.
Zolberg, Aristide R. *A Nation by Design: Immigrant Policy in the Fashioning of America*. New York: Russell Sage Foundation, 2006.

Contributors

Matthew Basso is associate professor of history and gender studies at the University of Utah. His recent publications include *Meet Joe Copper: Masculinity and Race on Montana's World War II Home Front* (University of Chicago Press, 2013) and *Men at Work: Rediscovering Depression-Era Stories from the Federal Writers' Project* (University of Utah Press, 2012).

Katherine Benton-Cohen is associate professor of history at Georgetown University. She is the author of *Borderline Americans: Racial Division and Labor War in the Arizona Borderlands* (Harvard University Press, 2009), and is completing a book about the Dillingham Commission of 1907–1911.

Michelle A. Charest is a lecturer in the Department of History of Art and Visual Culture and in the Department of Architecture at the Rhode Island School of Design, Providence. She is a historical archaeologist with research interests in the cultural world of nineteenth-century immigration to North America, as well as in the social role of drinking establishments in historic communities.

Brian Q. Cannon is professor of history and director of the Charles Redd Center for Western Studies at Brigham Young University.

Mark I. Choate is a history professor at Brigham Young University, specializing in migration and colonialism. He has published articles in *International Migration Review*, *French Colonial History*, *Modern Italy*, and *Italian Culture*. His book *Emigrant Nation: The Making of Italy Abroad* (Harvard University Press, 2008) won the Council for European Studies Book Award and the Marraro Prize.

Ryan Dearinger is associate professor of history at Eastern Oregon University, where he is chair of the history department. He is the author of *The Filth of Progress: Immigrants, Americans, and the Building of Canals and Railroads in the U.S. West* (University of California Press, forthcoming 2015).

Jessie L. Embry is the associate director of the Charles Redd Center for Western Studies and an associate research professor in the history department at Brigham Young University. She has written three books and over twenty articles on ethnic Mormons. Much of her work is based on Redd Center oral histories.

D. Seth Horton is a PhD candidate at the University of Maryland. His work has appeared in over a dozen publications, and his fifth anthology, *Road to Nowhere and Other New Stories from the Southwest,* was published by the University of New Mexico Press in 2013.

Anne M. Martínez is in the Department of American Studies at the University of Groningen in The Netherlands. She is the author of *Catholic Borderlands: Mapping Catholicism onto American Empire, 1905–1935* (University of Nebraska Press, 2014). Martínez's research interests include race, religion, and nation in the early twentieth-century United States.

Brett Garcia Myhren is assistant professor of English at Saddleback College. His scholarship explores the literature, history, and culture of early California. He recently coedited, with Seth Horton, *Road to Nowhere and Other New Stories from the Southwest* (University of New Mexico Press, 2013).

Andrew Offenburger earned his PhD in history from Yale University and is currently the David J. Weber Postdoctoral Fellow at Southern Methodist University's Clements Center for Southwest Studies.

Meisha Slight is a Spanish teacher in Herriman, Utah, and works to advocate for Latinos through education and community service.

J. Matthew Shumway is a professor of geography at Brigham Young University where he has been teaching for the past twenty-three years. His research focuses on migration as a mechanism of demographic and socioeconomic change with a particular focus on the Mountain West region.

Mindi Sitterud-McCluskey is a PhD candidate in history at the University of Arizona and an adjunct instructor at Northwest Vista College in San Antonio. She received her B.A. from Southern Utah University and her M.A. from Boston College.

Eileen V. Wallis is an associate professor of history at California State Polytechnic University, Pomona. She is the author of *Earning Power: Women and Work in Los Angeles, 1880–1930* (University of Nevada Press, 2010) and several articles on the history of Southern California and the urban West.

Karen S. Wilson is the Sady and Ludwig Kahn Postdoctoral Research Fellow with the UCLA Center for Jewish Studies. She curated the Autry National Center's exhibition "Jews in the Los Angeles Mosaic" (2013) and edited a companion volume of the same name published by the University of California Press.

Permissions and Credits

Chapter 7, "Locally Made: Immigrant Whiteness in Montana's Copper Communities" is adapted from Matthew Basso, *Meet Joe Copper: Masculinity and Race on Montana's World War II Home Front,* © 2013 by the University of Chicago. All rights reserved.

Most of the photographs on the front cover appear in the book. Please see individual captions for credit information. The following cover photographs are from the Library of Congress, Prints and Photographs Division, Washington, D.C., repository http://hdl.loc.gov/loc.pnp/pp.print.

A Case of "Economic Need" by Lewis Wickes Hine. National Child Labor Committee Collection. Reproduction number LC-DIG-nclc-00363 (color digital file from b&w original print)

Topeka, Kansas by Jack Delano. FSA/OWI Collection. Reproduction number LC-USW3-019309-D (b&w film neg.)

Chinese Immigrants at the San Francisco Custom-house by P. Frenzeny. Miscellaneous Items in High Demand Collection. Reproduction number LC-USZ62-93673 (b&w film copy neg.)

A Chinese Family, Detroit Photographic Co. Photochrom Collection. Reproduction number LC-DIG-ppmsca-17886 (digital file from original item)

William Dimotakis on His Farm in Manteca, California. FSA/OWI Collection. Reproduction number LC-DIG-fsa-8b32766 (b&w film nitrate neg.)

Index